THE TEN KATE COLLECTION 1882–1888

EUROPEAN REVIEW OF NATIVE AMERICAN STUDIES
MONOGRAPHS 4

SERIES EDITOR: CHRISTIAN F. FEEST

AMERICAN INDIAN MATERIAL CULTURE

THE TEN KATE COLLECTION 1882–1888

Pieter Hovens

with contributions by

Duane Anderson
Ted Brasser
Laura van Broekhoven
Alan Ferg
Ruth B. Phillips
Marian E. Rodee
David R. Wilcox

National Museum of Ethnology
Leiden, The Netherlands

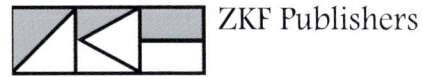 ZKF Publishers

The Ten Kate Collection 1882–1886. American Indian
Material Culture. / Pieter Hovens, with contributions by
Duane Anderson, Ted Brasser, Laura van Broekhoven,
Alan Ferg, Ruth B. Phillips, Marian E. Rodee, and David
R. Wilcox. Altenstadt 2010: ZKF Publishers
     Includes bibliographic references.
     ISBN 978-3-9811620-1-1 (paper)

Bibliographical Information
Die Deutsche Bibliothek lists this publication in the
German National Bibliography; detailed bibliographical
data are available in the internet at http://dnb.ddb.de

ERNAS MONOGRAPHS 4
European Review of Native American Studies
Fasanenweg 4a, D-63674 Altenstadt, Germany

Copy Editing and Layout: Sylvia S. Kasprycki
Cover and Graphic Design: Christian F. Feest

Cover illustrations
     front: Badger fetish, Zuni, ca. 1880 (RMV 674-11)
     back: War shield, Pima, ca. 1870–1880 (RMV 362-46)

Printed and bound in Austria (European Union)
by Holzhausen Druck GmbH, Vienna

Table of Contents

Preface

The anthropologist Herman Frederik Carel ten Kate (1858-1931) spent his whole professional life studying North American Indians. For these Native peoples of the northern hemisphere of the New World he developed a deep empathy in his youth, which in early adulthood turned into academic studies, scientific research, and political advocacy which he pursued throughout his lifetime. He was able to spend almost a year of fieldwork on Indian reservations in the American West from the fall of 1882 to the fall of 1883. During that time he conducted extensive anthropological researches among Native tribes in New York State, northwestern Mexico, California, Arizona, New Mexico, Colorado, and Oklahoma. In 1887-88 he was again in the field for about a year, this time as a staff member of the Hemenway Southwestern Archaeological Expedition, led by Frank H. Cushing. During that time he carried out excavations at Hohokam sites in the Sonora Desert of southern Arizona and at the site of Halonawan in Zuni Pueblo. In addition, he conducted anthropological fieldwork among the Pima and Zuni. Both research trips allowed Ten Kate to collect prehistoric, historic, and contemporary Indian artifacts. Being one of the first professionally trained anthropologists in the field and working for extended periods among many different North American tribes, he was able to bring together a unique collection of Indian art and material culture, exemplifying prehistoric cultures, traditional ways of life, and contemporary realities. As such, his collection of 476 objects is one of the earliest and largest in Europe from Native North America amassed by an individual scientific researcher during fieldwork. This unique collection is mainly curated at the Rijksmuseum voor Volkenkunde (National Museum of Ethnology) in Leiden, the Netherlands.

This catalogue is intended to make the Ten Kate collection available for a wide audience: Native American communities whose cultural heritage was fortunately preserved for posterity, the academic community to facilitate research into the collection, and a wider public to appreciate the technological, artistic, and ideological legacy of the Native peoples of North America, which is still resilient and relevant to our lives today.

The entries focus on the cultural and historical context of the artifacts. Much of this context is derived from the ethnographic studies of the early generation of American anthropologists who did fieldwork on Indian reservations between 1890 and 1930. Credit must be given to the many tribal elders and other informants willing to share their knowledge with these researchers. The initial plan to include information in the entries on the historical development and present situation as regards the artifact types in the Ten Kate collection was abandoned. It proved too ambitious, but, more importantly, the National Museum of the American Indian launched an impressive series of exhibitions, catalogues, and publications that address the current manufacture, use and meaning of historically rooted material culture and art for Native American communities, who build their lives on rich traditions and revitalize their societies in the face of contemporary challenges. As such, the treasures from the past and the present complement each other and tell a contemporary multiethnic audience an encouraging story of cultural survival, development, and pride.

Herman ten Kate himself deserves our gratitude for the scientific and cultural legacy he left us, especially in the field of North American Indian studies (see chapter 1, "Collecting Native America"). Making his work in this field known to Native peoples he visited, to the scientific community, and to a wider public began with a partial biography focusing on his work in the United States, continued with a catalogue of his major historic photograph collection, the annotated translation of his Hemenway Southwestern Archaeological Expedition diaries and fieldwork itinerary, and several topical studies, and is concluded for the time being with this catalogue. To complete accessibility of his work in North American Indian studies, a volume with annotated translations of a selection of his articles published in Dutch, German, and French is planned for the distant future.

Research for this catalogue was greatly facilitated by two institutions offering the curator a position as research associate, thereby making available all their resources. A special debt of gratitude is owed to the Laboratory of Anthropology of the Museum of Indian Art and Culture in Santa Fe, New Mexico, and the Harold S. Colton Research Center at the Museum of Northern Arizona in Flagstaff, Arizona. The following institutions and their staff were helpful with practical support and services of various kinds during the research for this catalogue: the Arizona State Museum and Arizona State Historical Society (Tucson, AZ), the Special Collections of the Cline Library of Northern Arizona University (Flagstaff, AZ), the Heard Museum (Phoenix, AZ), the Center of Southwest Research of the University of New Mexico (Albuquerque, NM), the Fray Angelico Chavez History Library and Photo Archives of the Museum of New Mexico (Santa Fe, NM), the New Mexico State Library (Santa Fe, NM), the Wheelwright Museum (Santa Fe, NM), the Maxwell Museum of Anthropology (Albuquerque, NM), the Oklahoma Historical Society (Oklahoma City, OK), the Western History Collections at the University of Oklahoma, the State Historical Society of North Dakota (Bismarck, ND), the Library of Congress and the National Anthropological Archives (Washington, DC), and the Koninklijke Bibliotheek (Royal Library, The Hague). The Ten Kate research project was partially funded by the Netherlands Research Council (NWO). Additional material support was received from the National Museum of Ethnology (Leiden), the Foundation of Art and Science (The Hague), the New Mexico Historical Society (Santa Fe, NM), the American Embassy (The Hague), and United Airlines (Amsterdam). The institutional and corporate material support for the project is gratefully acknowledged.

I want to thank the following individuals for their generous support, advice, and assistance during various stages of the research: Duane Anderson, Fred van Assen, Donald M. Bahr, Jonathan Batkin, Bruce Bernstein, Ted Brasser, Richard Conn, Mary Davis, Steven Engelsman, Christian F. Feest, Alan Ferg, Willem Fermont, Matthi Forrer, Barbara Gauger, Anine de Grood, Anneke Groeneveld, Tilly de Groot, Barbara Hail, Jiska Herlaar, Lou Hieb, Kit Hinsley, Eline Kevenaar, Tom Kolaz, O. Roland McCook, Sid and Rose Margolis, Milford Nahohai, Arthur Olivas, Ruth B. Phillips, Earl Ray, Marian Rodee, Richard Rudisill, Anine Singh-De Grood, Shelby Tisdale, Leo Triebels, Albert Trouwborst, Ed Wade, Alan Hunter Whiteford, Barton Wright, and David Wilcox. My wife Jeanne Hovens-Wijnhoven deserves more than honorable mention because of her continual support and assistance over many years.

At the National Museum in Leiden the Collections Department was most helpful in inventorying the whole collection, taking measurements, determining materials, carrying out preservation and small-scale restoration, handling the temporary loan of Ten Kate materials from the World Museum in Rotterdam, organizing a temporary exhibition, and assisting with photography: Conn Barrett, Karin Booij, Ester de Bruin, Farideh Fekrasanati, Monique Koek, Marijke Kunst, Birgit Maas, Margrit Reuss, Sybrand de Rooij, Graeme Scott. At the World Museum in Rotterdam effective assistance was given by Eline Kevenaar and Sietske Kentie of the Collections Department and photo archivist Anneke Groeneveld. Gillian Vogelsang-Eastwood, director of the Textile Research Center in Leiden, provided the technical details on most of the Zuni textiles. National Museum of Ethnology librarians David Stuart-Fox and Anneke van Beveren assisted with the acquisition of relevant published sources, and Paul van Dongen solved software and hardware problems. Anne-Marie Woerlee of the museum's Communications Department coordinated the Ten Kate exhibition of 2007–08. Interns Mette van der Hooft, Niels Rouwen, and Koen Maas and volunteer Josette van der Koogh also provided occasional assistance during the project. Ben Grishaaver of Leiden University's Audio-Visual Center was responsible for virtually all the photography. Museum director Steven Engelsman and Matthi Forrer, head of the research department, made funds available for travel, photography, and printing costs.

Work on the manuscript was completed in February 2008.

Collecting Native America:

Herman ten Kate, Anthropology, and Fieldwork in the American West

Although Herman Frederik Carel ten Kate, Jr., was born in Amsterdam on 7 February 1858, he spent his childhood and adolescence in The Hague. Not far from the Houses of Parliament his father had purchased a large house with a studio, working as an artist specializing in genre scenes. As a painter he was quite popular and even received royal patronage. Artistic talent was prevalent in the extended Ten Kate family, who counted many artists and writers among their members. Initially it seemed that the young Ten Kate would follow in the footsteps of his father when he registered as a student at the Art Academy in 1875. He spent the winter of 1876–77 in Corsica to paint, accompanying his father's illustrious friend Charles William Meredith Van der Velde, who had gained an international reputation as a painter, cartographer, and humanitarian. Having journeyed through the Indonesian archipelago, South Africa, and the Middle East, Van der Velde impressed young Ten Kate with his stories of foreign lands and peoples, touching upon an existing interest of Ten Kate, especially the Native peoples of the Americas. The young man was an avid reader of the novels by James Fenimore Cooper, Gustave Aimard, Gabriel Ferry, Mayne Reid, and other writers of Western adventure. When he returned to The Hague, Ten Kate surprised everyone with the announcement that he wished to enter university to become a scholar of non-Western peoples and cultures. His father agreed on the condition that he would simultaneously qualify himself in the fields of medicine and foreign languages, to assure future employment and an income.

In 1877 Ten Kate registered at the University of Leiden, where he studied medicine, geography, non-Western languages, and Indonesian ethnology with Professor P. J. Veth. At the National Museum of Ethnology he befriended director Lindor Serrurier. In 1879 he continued his medical, anthropological, and linguistic studies at the renowned École d'Anthropologie in Paris, where he attended the

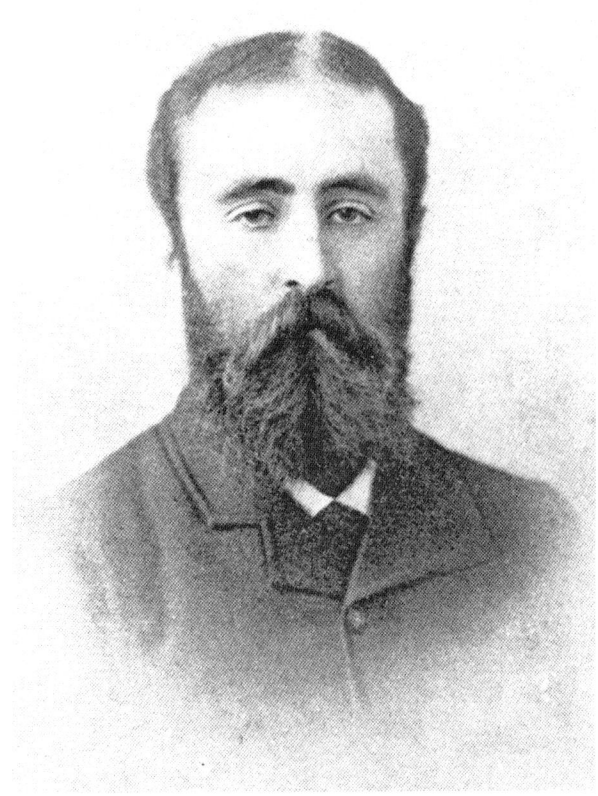

Fig. 1   Herman F. C. ten Kate; ca. 1880–81 (P. Hovens coll.).

courses of Paul Broca, Paul Topinard, and Etienne-Théodore Hamy, and at the Muséum d'Histoire Naturelle, where Armand Quatrefages taught. After the 1879–80 academic year Ten Kate spent a semester at the University of Berlin, where he attended lectures by Adolf Bastian and used the facilities at the Berliner Gesellschaft für Anthropologie, Ethnologie und Urgeschichte, arranged by Rudolph Virchow. He completed his studies in medicine, natural history, and anthropology at the universities of Göttingen and Heidelberg, obtaining a Ph.D. on the basis of his comparative research on the skulls of Mongoloid peoples (Hovens 1989: 15–45).

Ten Kate was educated in the staunchly empirical positivist tradition that characterized the academic disciplines he engaged in at European universities in the 1880s. Human evolution was only regarded as an interesting hypothesis. He learned that diversity of races and cultures should be regarded as non-qualitative and that all peoples were bonded by a common psychological unity. Despite Social Darwinist remarks in his publications, Ten Kate regarded races and peoples as different but equal and what separated them as essentially inconsequential and surmountable. This view was strongly underpinned by the humanist tradition of his family and teachers in Leiden. He underwent training in an interdisciplinary anthropology, uniting physical anthropology, ethnolinguistics, archaeology, and ethnology. His humanism led to a frequent emphasis in his work on the incorporation of ethnopsychology, the development of applied anthropology, and anthropological advocacy in support of the human rights of Native peoples. Thus Ten Kate combined a positivist science, a multidisciplinary orientation, and an explicit idealism, making him an exceptional representative of his time and discipline (Hovens 1989: 15-44, 197-200, 210-220; 1991b; Hovens and Hieb 2004: 22-27).

During his academic training Ten Kate undertook North American Indian studies on his own account. He studied the available scientific publications and ethnographic museum collections in the Netherlands, France, and Germany. In addition he kept abreast of current Indian affairs in the United States by reading American newspapers. It was his aim to complete his academic studies and subsequently embark on a year-long exploratory journey to the Indian tribes of the American West. The goal of this enterprise was to get a first impression of tribal lifeways and traditions and the fate of Indians under White domination. In addition, he wished to contribute to the study of the origin of the Indians and the interrelationship between tribes, based on comparative somatological, archaeological, ethnolinguistic, and ethnographic studies.

The fieldwork journey Ten Kate undertook was almost fully funded by his father. The only sponsorship he received was from the Royal Netherlands Geographical Society, who put 500 guilders at his disposal, in return for writing travel and research reports for their scientific journal. The anthropologist crossed the Atlantic and arrived in New York on 21 November 1882. He began his American journey by visiting scientific and governmental institutions in the east, to prepare for his fieldwork in the trans-Mississippi West. In Washington, DC, he was welcomed at the Bureau of [American] Ethnology and became acquainted with its director, Major John Wesley Powell, archaeologist Charles Rau, and ethnologist James Mooney. It was on request of the Bureau that the Dutch anthropologist would collect vocabularies of Indian languages for the planned encyclopedic Handbook of American Indians (Hodge 1907-1910). In return Ten Kate received a letter of recommendation from the Bureau, acknowledging the importance of his research and requesting support for it. Subsequently, at the War and Interior Departments he received letters of recommendation signed by secretaries William T. Sherman and Hiram T. Price, requesting commanders of military forts and superintendents of Indian reservations to assist Ten Kate in his work whenever possible by making travel arrangements, providing transportation, and offering the services of guides and interpreters. At the offices of the Geographical Survey Captain George M. Wheeler provided the traveler with the most recent maps of the regions he intended to explore (Hovens 1989: 49-54).

In December Ten Kate's year-long exploratory fieldwork journey began with a visit to Iroquois reservations in upstate New York (Hovens 1984). On Christmas Day he arrived in El Paso and visited the Tigua of Ysleta del Sur. In early January 1883 he was in the Tucson area and spent several days with the Papago at San Xavier del Bac. Subsequently he spent several months in northwestern Mexico, excavating in Baja California and visiting Yaqui settlements (Hovens 1991a). By mid-April he arrived back in the United States and did fieldwork among the Quechan, Mohave, Chemehuevi, and Las Vegas Paiute along the Colorado River on the Arizona-California border (Hovens and Herlaar 2004) and the Walapai near Kingman. In the Phoenix area he pursued his interest in archaeology and did a short archaeological survey and an exploratory dig at Casa Grande ruins. He continued fieldwork among the Pima and Papago and spent two weeks among the Apache in southern Arizona, facilitated by General Crook. By the end of June he was in the Rio Grande Valley of New Mexico, where he made the acquaintance of Frank H. Cushing and visited various pueblos. With army physician and self-trained ethnologist Dr. Washington Matthews he undertook research trips on the Navajo Indian reservation. He joined trader Thomas V. Keam on a visit to the Hopi and witnessed the Snake Dance (McIntire and Gordon 1968). Facilitated by Dr. Jeremiah Sullivan, he conducted fieldwork on First and Second Mesas. At Keam's Canyon he studied Alexander M. Stephen's collection of Anasazi and

Hopi pottery. During subsequent fieldwork among the Navajo he made the acquaintance of Colonel James Stevenson and Matilda Cox Stevenson. The high point of his journey was a one-week stay and fieldwork among the Zuni. During this time Ten Kate and Cushing established a lifelong friendship. The Dutchman continued his research among the Southern Ute in Colorado (Hovens and Herlaar 2004) and the Comanche, Kiowa, Cheyenne, Wichita, and Caddo in Indian Territory, now Oklahoma. The end of his journey neared and was concluded with visits to the Cherokee, Choctaw, and Creek. On 16 December 1883 the anthropologist was back in the Netherlands. His travel narrative was published in Dutch in 1885 and has only recently become available in English (Ten Kate 1885, 2004, Hovens 1989).

In the spring of 1886 Ten Kate visited the estate of Mary Hemenway at Manchester-by-the-Sea near Boston. Here Cushing was working on publications with several Zunis and on plans for an interdisciplinary archaeological expedition, to be funded by his wealthy patron. From November 1887 to August 1888 the Dutchman joined the Hemenway Southwestern Archaeological Expedition. He supervised excavations at several Hohokam sites in the Phoenix Basin, studied skeletal material, did an anthropological survey on the Pima Reservation, and finished fieldwork with excavations at the site of Halonawan in Zuni pueblo and research on Zuni ethnomedical knowledge and practice. Before returning to Europe, he paid a short visit to Central Mexico to gather relevant ethnohistorical materials for the expedition (Ten Kate 1925, Hovens 1995).

Collecting Native America and Ethnographic Salvage

Before 1880 most collecting of Native North American artifacts in the nineteenth century was an individual undertaking pursued on the basis of private interest in the curiosities made by "savage" races. The surge of academic interest in natural history during the latter quarter of that century stimulated the creation of collections of natural specimens and artifacts from tribal peoples. The aggregation of the latter was deemed scientifically important as tribal peoples were regarded to represent various stages in the evolution of man and culture. For the purpose of research into the development of mankind and civilization a large-scale effort was required, especially as tribal cultures were on the verge of disappearance and the Indian race either becoming extinct or being completely assimilated through intermarriage.

The Smithsonian Institution led the large-scale and systematic collection of Indian material culture. When Powell was enabled by the government to create the Bureau of (American) Ethnology (BAE) in 1879 to compile data on the Native peoples of the United States, he included the aggregation of extensive collections of material culture as an aim, as artifacts were expressions of man's mental and cultural development and thus valuable sources of data that would be available long after the Indians had changed their way of life to conform to Western standards or had become extinct. The construction of the United States National Museum and opening of the exhibitions was planned for 1881. Between 1879 and 1881 Colonel James Stevenson led three collecting expeditions for the BAE to the Southwest. During the first he left the young BAE ethnologist Frank H. Cushing behind at Zuni to begin an extended stint of fieldwork, pioneering participant observation being the principal method of ethnographic fieldwork. The BAE expeditions concentrated their collecting activities among the Zuni, Hopi, and Rio Grande Pueblos. The scale of collecting was immense and totaled tens of thousands of artifacts, with Pueblo pottery by far the largest category. Because the collections contained numerous doubles, many specimens were subsequently deselected and exchanged with other museums, including the National Museum of Ethnology in Leiden. From 1882 on, the BAE continued collecting in the Southwest on a smaller scale, supporting individual researchers from their own institution such as James Mooney and Frank Russell and making use of other collectors who lived in the field, including Washington Matthews, Thomas V. Keam, and Alexander Stephen. Only after the mid-1890s were collecting activities of individual fieldworkers directed at the non-Puebloan peoples of the Southwest, almost fifteen years after Ten Kate had gathered his collection. This early date of the non-Puebloan part of the Ten Kate collection from the Southwest lends it its special significance (Hinsley 1981; Parezo 1986; Kaemlein 1967: 132).

Two other Europeans linked to museums had collected in the Southwest at this early date. Alphonse Pinart (1852–1911) did ethnolinguistic fieldwork in Arizona and New Mexico in 1879 and purchased a ninety-six-specimen collection of mostly Rio Grande Pueblo pottery for the Musée d'Ethnographie in Paris (Parmenter 1966; Kaemlein 1967: 78–79). In 1883 the Norwegian Captain Johan Adrian Jacobsen (1853–1947) returned from a collecting trip to Alaska and British Columbia for the Ethnological

Museum Berlin, Bastian's main initiative directed at North America. Traveling eastward on the Southern Pacific railway, he made several stops in Arizona and New Mexico, using the opportunity to acquire sixty-seven artifacts from the Yuma, Pima, and Papago and a small Pueblo pottery collection (Bastian 1883; Woldt 1884; Kaemlein 1967: 93-94). With the exception of Berlin, European museums spent little effort on acquiring collections from Native North America in the latter decades of the nineteenth century. Because Native North American artifacts had to be acquired in a Western market, prices for specimens were relatively high and rapidly increased when American and Canadian museums began to compete for traditional objects (Cole 1985).

The evolutionist paradigm dominated Western society and anthropology in the latter decades of the nineteenth century, when Ten Kate pursued his academic studies and carried out his first fieldwork. Cultures were hypothesized to develop through a number of stages from primitive to civilized, with Euro-American society regarded as the pinnacle of human achievement. This evolutionary process was thought to be embedded in the artifacts different peoples and societies produced. As artifacts were evidence of stages of cultural development, awareness arose within the scientific community of the importance of salvaging data on traditional tribal lifeways (Hovens 1989: 23-24, 30-33, 215-219; Hovens and Hieb 2004: 22-24).

With the pace of colonialism and international trade accelerating in the second half of the nineteenth century, it became increasingly obvious to scientists that tribal lifeways were rapidly disappearing. Traditional rituals and customs were discontinued, either by coercion or choice. Authentic material culture and arts were increasingly corrupted or replaced by Western trade goods, while traditional arts and crafts production gradually ceased. It was believed that non-Western societies would inevitably either perish or gradually transform into a likeness of Euro-American society. The former fate was that of most tribal societies, while non-Western feudal and peasant societies had a change for transformation.

While attending courses in Berlin, Ten Kate heard Adolph Bastian's plea for salvaging anthropological data. On his travels around the world, the German scientist had witnessed the disastrous effect of European colonization on Native societies and advocated immediate action, pointing out the irony that the discipline of anthropology was emerging just at a time when many non-Western tribal societies were on the verge of disappearance (Koepping

1983: 107; Hovens 1989: 36). The awareness of cultural destruction outside Europe was also emerging in the Netherlands, and Lindor Serrurier, director of the National Museum of Ethnology in Leiden, became the most vocal advocate of anthropological salvage (Serrurier 1893; also cf. Steinmetz 1892: 329).

The awareness of the disappearance of tribal lifeways was also keenly felt in scientific circles in the United States of America. During his western journey in the 1850s, Lewis Henry Morgan graphically recorded the negative effects of White colonization (Morgan 1993, Eggan 1965). Joseph Henry, director of the Smithsonian Institution (founded in 1846), emphasized the tragic cultural consequences of American colonization of the West. He stressed the necessity for anthropological salvage and in 1879 supported the creation of the Bureau of (American) Ethnology. Its first director, Major John Wesley Powell, was able to gain political and financial support for the new institute by stressing that Indian cultures were disappearing at an alarming rate, without Americans having had an opportunity record the lifeways and traditions of the country's Native peoples. Scientists came to the conclusion that they had a last chance to rescue cultural data from oblivion (Hinsley 1981: 22-23, 34-42, 191-192, 207-208; Parezo 1985; 1986: 18-23; cf. Clifford 1986: 112-113).

Museums were among the first to undertake efforts to salvage the art and material culture of societies threatened with destruction. Because they were focused on objects, they began to collect artifacts in an increasingly determined way. American and European museums competed on the Northwest Coast of America in a scramble for tribal artifacts, and the Southwest was expected to be the next arena of frenzied competition (Cole 1985; Parezo 1985; 1986: 29). In the American Southwest the Smithsonian Institution razed the villages of the Rio Grande Pueblos, the Hopi, and the Zuni between 1879 and 1885, taking virtually anything they encountered. As late as 1906 Franz Boas warned his colleagues in an address to the International Congress of Americanists in Quebec: "Day by day Indians and their cultures are disappearing more and more before the encroachment of modern civilization, and fifty years hence nothing will remain to be learned in regard to this interesting and important subject" (Boas 1906: 152).

Ten Kate aggregated his collection during that same time. Although the salvage paradigm required collecting any vestige of tribal material culture, the dominant theoretical paradigm of cultural evolution required the collection of even the simplest artifacts, as they could document the evolution of the man-made material world as an expression of the cultural evolution of man generally, and specific groups specifically. It is therefore not surprising that the early collections took a comprehensive approach and included not only elaborately treated and visually stunning ceremonial and status objects, but also scores of utilitarian artifacts used in daily life such as tools, basketry, pottery, and undecorated dress.

Although many anthropologists stressed the need to record disappearing cultural data, some of them also showed a concern for the fate of Native peoples. Although all accepted that the demise of tribal cultures was inevitable from an evolutionary point of view (Stocking 1987: 283), some were not prepared to ignore the human costs involved and took a humanitarian stand, advocating an ethical policy toward colonized peoples. Among them were Frank H. Cushing, James Mooney, and Herman ten Kate, and their brand of salvage anthropology has aptly been characterized by Curtis Hinsley (1981: 23) as a unique combination of scientific interest, nostalgia, and guilt.

The salvage approach became one of the driving forces behind collecting data on tribal societies as soon as Western expansion began to erode Native societies in the course of the nineteenth century at an ever increasing pace. It is intimately associated with the emergence of anthropology as an academic discipline during the last quarter of that century. However, this paradigm has proven to be rather resilient as the process of Western expansion continued and is currently manifesting itself as globalization.

As a student of ethnology, medicine, and non-Western languages at the University in Leiden, Ten Kate was introduced to the National Museum of Ethnology. In the course of the nineteenth century Leiden had become the seat of most national museums. The city hosted one of the oldest universities in Europe, which since its foundation in 1574 had attracted an international student body from across Europe and even from Asia because of its high scientific standing. Oriental studies became a focal field of specialization at Leiden University. Collections in the fields of medicine, natural history, antiquities, ethnology, numismatics, etc. had been aggregated by scientists connected with this venerable institution and resulted in the foundation of a series of national museums during the "museum age" (Otterspeer 1989).

Although its roots were older, the National Museum of Ethnology officially started out in 1837 with a largely Japanese collection, although a few Northwest Coast artifacts were included. The collection steadily increased, especially

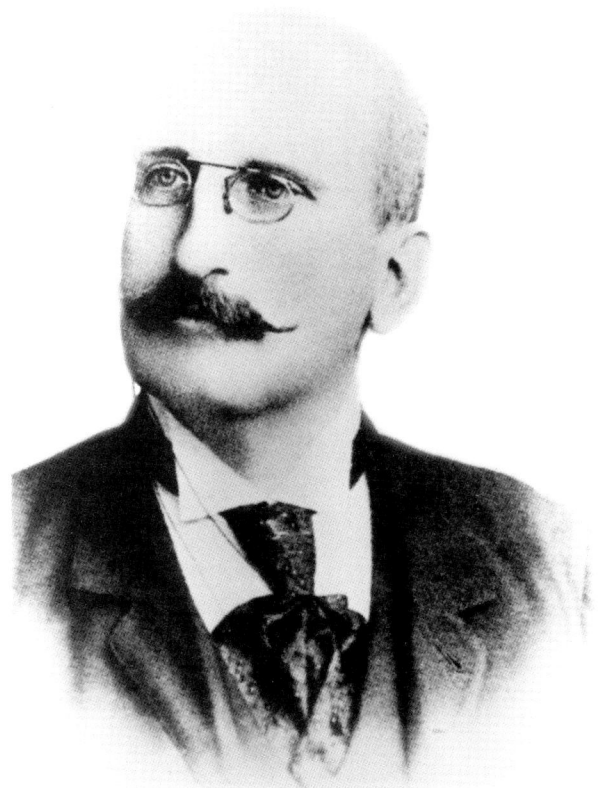

Fig. 2   Lindor Serrurier, director of the National Museum of Ethnology, Leiden; ca. 1880 (P. Hovens coll.).

with materials from Dutch overseas colonies: Indonesia, New Guinea, Surinam, and several Caribbean islands. Artifacts from Africa, Asia, and Latin America soon became of interest to the museum and were added to the national collection. Early North American Indian ethnographic objects were acquired mostly through purchase until 1882. By that time the transfer to Leiden of ethnographic artifacts from the Royal Cabinet of Rarities was under discussion, but this would only mean the addition of a few specimens from Native North America (Hovens in press).

When director Lindor Serrurier of the National Museum of Ethnology learned about Ten Kate's plan to undertake a year-long journey of fieldwork through the American West, he immediately contacted his compatriot, who was making preparations for the trip in Paris. Ten Kate was pleasantly surprised that the museum was keen on acquiring any archaeological and ethnographic artifacts from Native North America that he might collect. However, although Ten Kate appreciated the importance of the national ethnographic collection, he questioned whether Leiden would be the best repository of such materials. He suggested that Berlin or Paris provided a much better

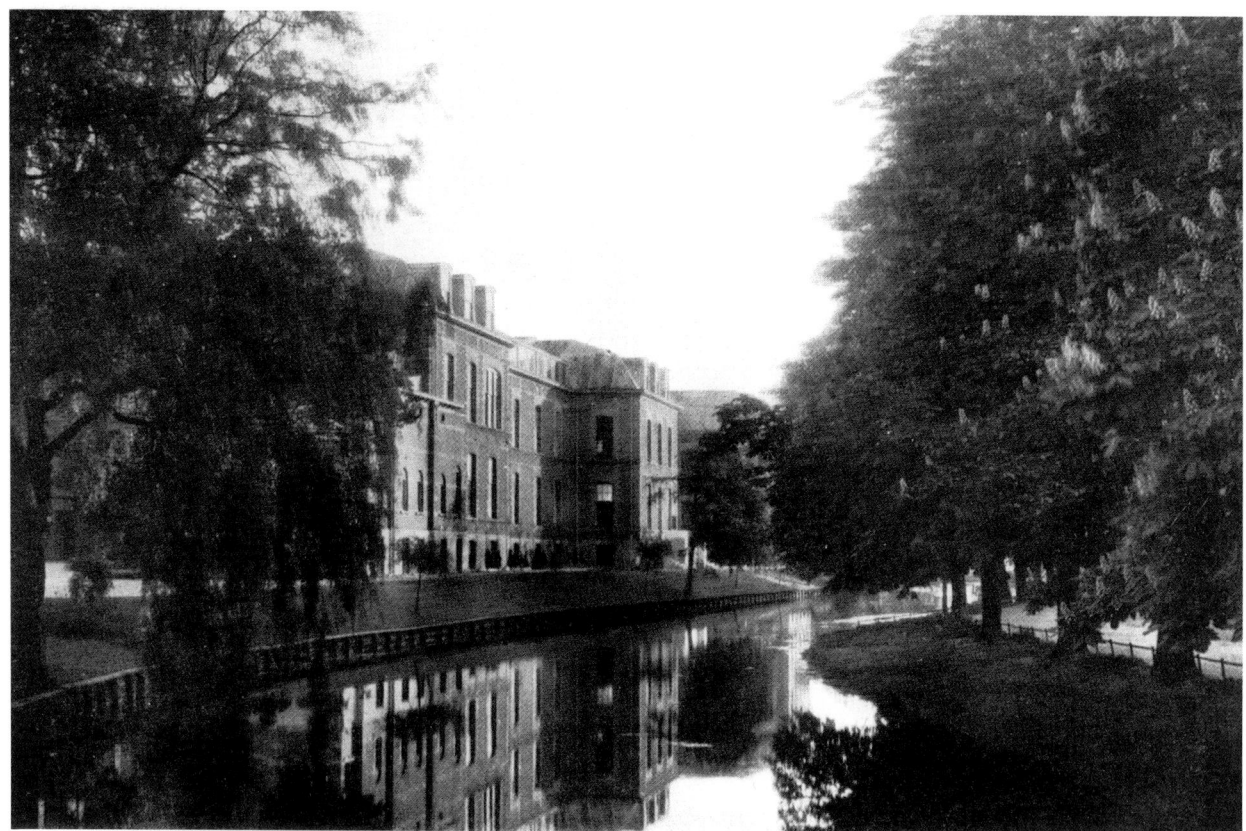

Fig. 3   The National Museum of Ethnology, Leiden (RMV coll.).

environment as Americanist studies were firmly established at the academic centers of these European capitals and assured future comparative studies of the North American Indian collections. He emphasized that his studies and collecting were meant as a contribution to science, not to a nation. However, Ten Kate suggested that the Royal Netherlands Geographical Society might make available a travel and research grant to him and that the museum might support such a request. In that case he would feel obliged to destine at least part of the collections he was going to assemble to the Leiden museum. Moreover, he promised to at least donate doubles and copies of photographs of physical types, scenes of Indian life, and landscapes he intended to make (Ten Kate to Serrurier, Paris, 9 June 1882; ARMV no. 80; cf. also Hovens and Groeneveld 1992).

Serrurier was not one to let a chance for the extension of the museum collections, especially the highly underrepresented region of North America, slip away. He and his assistant J. D. E. Schmeltz undertook a concerted effort through correspondence to convince Ten Kate of the importance of laying the groundwork for a North American collection in Leiden as a basis for developing Americanist

studies. Such an argument Ten Kate could not neglect, and it is quite possible that he speculated that this course of action might also lay the foundation for a position for him at the university or museum after his return. He informed Serrurier that his arguments were convincing and that Leiden would be given the preference as a repository of the intended North American collections, except for the skeletal material for which he was already under obligation to the Société d'Anthropologie in Paris (Ten Kate to Serrurier, Paris, 20 June 1882; ARMV no. 87). After completing preparations for his North American journey in Paris and a short trip to London to see collections in the British capital and seek advice at the Royal Geographical Society, Ten Kate returned to the Netherlands in the late summer of 1882 and had several meetings with Serrurier at the museum before committing himself definitely to channel most of his collections to that institution. Serrurier was successful in drawing the attention of the Holland Society of Sciences (Hollandsche Maatschappij van Wetenschappen) to the impending journey of Ten Kate to the Far West. A grant of 500 guilders was made available for the purchase of North American Indian artifacts for the Leiden museum.

In the 1880s the National Museum of Ethnology resorted under the Department of the Interior. Its funding was permanently precarious and director Serrurier had a hard time making ends meet. He used a series of imaginative tactics to draw attention to the problem, but these were not always appreciated by those in power. New conservation, collecting and research initiatives had little chance of being funded. However, the director enlisted the support of the Royal Netherlands Geographical Society in requesting a subsidy for the acquisition of North American Indian artifacts during Ten Kate's impending journey. His main argument was that this important region of the world was hardly represented in the national collection. However, the wheels of government ground slowly, and when Ten Kate embarked on his trans-Atlantic journey, a decision had not yet been reached in the corridors of power in The Hague.

In Niagara Falls Ten Kate bought a small collection of Indian artifacts from a reliable dealer and from Hodenosaunee (Iroquois) craftspeople. With the intention of attracting the interest of the people in charge of funding the Leiden museum and those controlling government expenditures, he took care to include a variety of artifacts from different Indian tribes and to present these as attractive as possible. Thus he included a Tuscarora baby cradle with a papier-mâché doll. The latter was not part of the original purchase but was added by Ten Kate's sister Madelon at the request of her brother to enhance its visual impact. With this strategy he tried to promote material support by the Netherlands' government for his collecting activities. The letter Ten Kate subsequently sent to director Lindor Serrurier stated that colleagues at the Smithsonian Institution in the capital had pointed out that the acquisition of traditional artifacts of good quality required substantial funds (Ten Kate to Serrurier, 16 December 1882; ARMV no. 273). Although it is not known whether this strategy influenced the outcome, Ten Kate was eventually informed that the government made 1,000 guilders available for purchases of ethnographic specimens. The letter reached him while carrying out archaeological surveys in Baja California (Ten Kate to Serrurier, 31 March 1883; ARMV).

In the opening paragraph of his 1882–83 itinerary, Ten Kate clearly stated the paradigm that guided his first endeavor into anthropological fieldwork: "If we consider the various peoples in different regions of the earth who still live wholly or partially in a state of nature and ponder: which of these races is destined to vanish within a rela-

tively short time span, our attention then promptly turns to those people whose territories, due to their natural condition, attract a steady influx of civilization. Primarily on that section of the western hemisphere extending northward from the Tropic of Cancer to form an immense continent do we encounter those peoples whose demise is imminent. Perhaps nowhere is scientific investigation more urgent than among the aboriginal inhabitants of North America" (Ten Kate 2004: 55).

While Ten Kate was forwarding the first shipments of artifacts he had collected to the museum in Leiden, director Serrurier was already developing a strategy to increase the collections from Native North America. He wrote to Ten Kate that he should concentrate on acquiring ethnographic materials that would be virtually impossible to obtain through exchange with the Smithsonian Institution, for which he intended to approach Spencer F. Baird. More explicitly, at one point he persuaded his compatriot not to purchase any more pottery or basketry. Serrurier hoped to arrange an exchange with the venerable institution in the American capitol, in which he would supply specimens from the vast collections from Indonesia and New Guinea in return for items from American Indian tribes. When Ten Kate was completing his fieldwork among the Civilized Tribes of Indian Territory, Serrurier sent him an official letter, written in English, requesting him to act on behalf of the Leiden museum in establishing such an exchange when he returned to New York by way of Washington, DC (Ten Kate to Serrurier, 2 June 1883; Serrurier to Ten Kate, 16 November 1883; ARMV no. 470). It is not known whether Ten Kate was able to do as asked, but the deal did not materialize. Only during the late 1890s several exchanges took place between the museums in Leiden and Washington, through which Hopi and Zuni materials, notably pottery, were obtained (Kaemlein 1967: 140–141).

After almost every visit to an Indian reservation Ten Kate carefully packed the artifacts he had collected and sent these through the available organized transportation channels to the Netherlands. The Southwest had just been opened by transcontinental railway links to the east, and most of the wooden boxes and crates traveled to New York by train, before being shipped across the Atlantic. In addition, he mailed short notes to Serrurier, usually no more than an inventory. Only in a few instances artifacts got lost or damaged during transportation (cf. Parezo 1986: 16–17). The collections Ten Kate aggregated during his initial year-long journey of fieldwork in 1882–83 and during his employment with the Hemenway Southwestern Archaeological Expedition in 1887–88 ended almost in their entirety at the National Museum of Ethnology in Leiden. Poor storage conditions in Leiden resulted in the material deterioration of all ethnographic collections, and Ten Kate's artifacts are no exception. Eventually this resulted in the resignation of director Serrurier and the donation by Ten Kate of his remaining private collection of Native American artifacts and most of his historic photographs to the Museum of Ethnology (now: the World Museum) in Rotterdam. Ten Kate donated a few archaeological artifacts he collected in northwestern Mexico and at Zuni to the Musée d'Ethnographie in Paris, and these were recently transferred to the Musée du quai Branly in the French capital. This enables us to focus our analysis of the collections primarily on the intentions of its collector and the institution that acquired it (cf. Appadurai 1986: 26–27).

Fieldwork: Observations and Experiences

Ten Kate's 1882–83 itinerary contains numerous observations and notes on material culture and its context. Especially dwellings, household goods and tools, weapons, dress, and jewelry received his attention. These were the most visible material expressions of the traditional way of life. Basketry was encountered among tribes for whom the gathering of wild foods was a traditional means of subsistence, such as the Pima, Papago, Chemehuevi, and Apache, although the horticultural Hopi also were proficient basket weavers, using their woven containers not only in the household but also in a variety of rituals. Pottery was especially prevalent among settled peoples, the Hopi, Zuni, and other Pueblos. A variety of weapons, bows and arrows, spears, and rabbit sticks were the means of hunters to provide their families with meat and of warriors to defend their people or undertake raids, during which they also wielded clubs and protected themselves with shields. The introduction of horses was associated with a certain degree of Western horse technology, although adapted to the new environment, and included saddles, stirrups, horseshoes, halters, quirts, lassos, and accessories such as saddle blankets, saddle bags, martingales, and cruppers. Dress varied greatly and included garments and blankets of plant fibers and animal furs, textiles woven from native-grown cotton, and clothing cut and sewn from tanned animal skins, mostly from buffalo, pronghorn antelope, and deer. These were made into

shirts, leggings, breechclouts, dresses, aprons, moccasins, and boots. Most of the time Indians wore everyday outfits, practical dress in which daily work and tasks could be performed without too much concern for appearance. However, even in daily dress people expressed differences in wealth and status as people do everywhere, by the quality of the fiber, fabric, or skin, the quality of manufacture, and accessories such as vestiges of decoration. However, most Indians also owned festive dress, worn on special occasions and distinguished by the quality of material and manufacture and the elaboration of decoration and accessories. Decoration included feathers and furs, surface decoration by painting and application of different materials, and woven materials with designs. Major accessories were a variety of headgear, capes and blankets, belts and sashes, decorated bags and pouches. Jewelry of many kinds, tattoos, and body paint completed personal presentation. A number of artifacts beyond the household were specifically associated with women, such as belts, awl and needle cases, cradles, etc. Men's items included pipes and tobacco bags. During recreational pursuits Indians played with balls, hoops and poles, gaming sticks, cards, etc. Drums, rasping sticks, and rattles provided the basic instruments for dances, and flutes played an important role in courtship. In the communal religious domain masks were donned during many rituals, altars constructed, and images of spiritual beings carved. On the personal level, medicine bundles and amulets provided supernatural protection. Shamans used different tools for preventive and curative care. These material and most visible expressions of traditional Indian life conveyed valuable information on subsistence, social relations, and worldview, and Ten Kate included most types of artifacts in his collection.

Ten Kate also pointed out intertribal similarities in material culture as expressions of exchange, such as between the horticultural Pueblos on the northern Rio Grande and the buffalo hunters of the southern Plains. Aware of the history of Indian-White relations, Ten Kate realized that changes in tribal material culture had often preceded direct Indian-White contacts. Horses, guns, and Western trade goods had reached tribes in interior regions through a network of intertribal trade relations, and these new introductions were accompanied by stories about a light-skinned people in possession of and producing large quantities of such desirable goods.

The establishment of trading posts near or on reservations had resulted in an unprecedented supply of Western materials, goods, and tools whose quality and durability

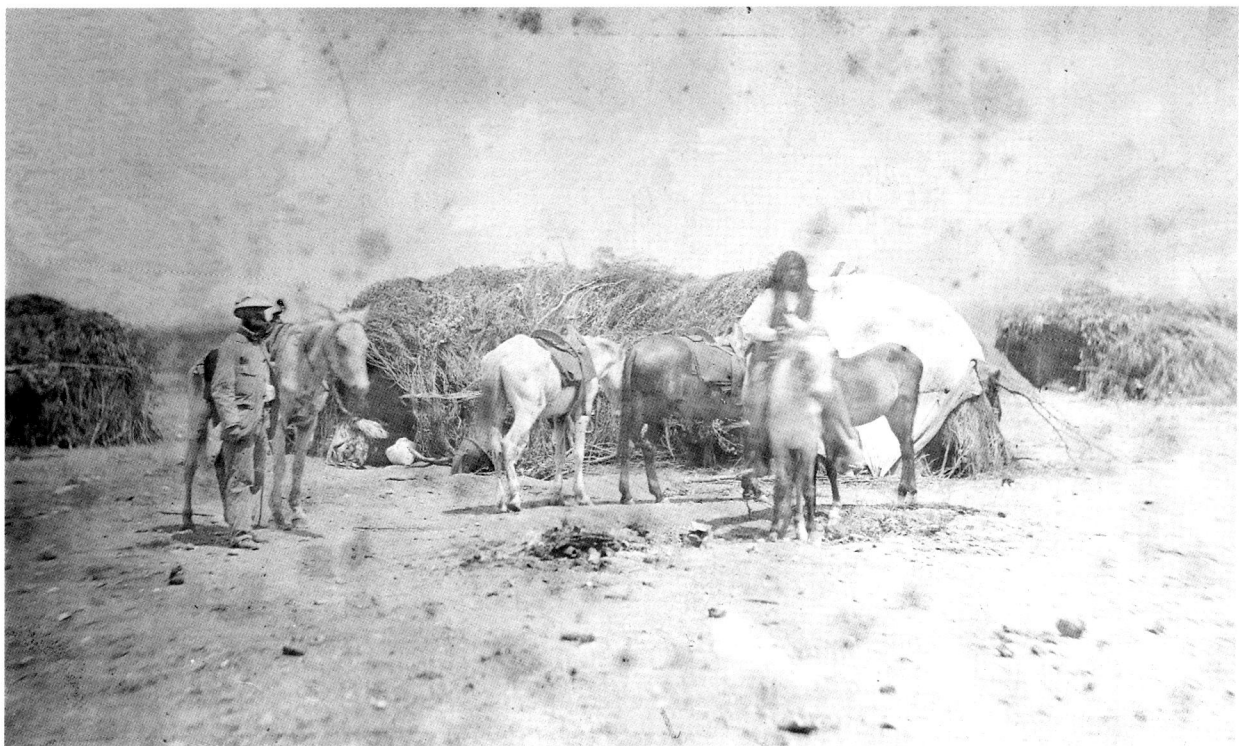

Fig. 4   Herman ten Kate in Apache camp; Arizona Territory, August 1883. Photograph by Constant Duhem (Ten Kate coll., RMV 414Kd2).

exceeded that of Native manufacture. Ten Kate noted that Indians at an early dated began to replace their stone arrowheads with points made from metal or glass, obtained through trade. Bows and arrows were not immediately and wholly replaced by the earliest industrially manufactured guns that were introduced. However, when these cumbersome weapons were replaced by Springfield and Winchester rifles, the traditional weapons were soon discarded. Somewhat later, metal containers replaced pottery, and guns and rifles replaced bows, arrows, clubs and spears. The diminishing supply of original raw materials also played a role. As wildlife was depleted, notably the buffalo and antelope herds, Indians had to rely increasingly on industrially manufactured Western textiles and clothing. Shirts, trousers, plain cotton, and printed calico were in ready supply, and soon most of them were wearing citizen's dress, notably the Iroquois and Five Civilized Tribes, who had experienced several centuries of contact with White traders and colonists. For a time, canvas replaced buffalo-hide tipi covers, some of them being decorated with painted designs, as among the Ute, Southern Cheyenne, Arapaho, Comanche, and Kiowa. Soon after, the Plains Indians began moving into log cabins and frame houses. In contrast, the Hopi, Zuni, and other Pueblo peoples still lived in their terraced adobe house complexes and many wore traditional dress in 1883.

Colonization and the loss of traditional means of subsistence compelled the Indians to look for other means of securing a livelihood. In addition, the availability of Western foodstuffs, raw materials, and goods instigated a demand for these. In a cash economy this necessity and demand could only be satisfied when cash income could be secured. One of the opportunities quickly grasped was the manufacture of traditional artifacts for which there seemed a demand among Whites. Soon Indian artists and craftspeople where adapting these traditional manufactures to Western needs and tastes to maximize sales and earnings. Ten Kate witnessed the emergence of tourism in the Southwest as the result of the completion of the transcontinental railroad and noted Indian women offering pottery and beadwork on the platforms of railway stations. At Las Vegas Hot Springs, New Mexico, hotels and shops sold Pueblo pottery to soldiers staying there to regain their health, and in the Niagara Falls area Ten Kate saw Indians actively involved in the arts and crafts trade, providing visitors with a plenitude of souvenirs with an Indian connotation.

Ten Kate's itinerary and collection are important because they present an instantaneous image of the manufacture and use of traditional artifacts in the early 1880s and the process of acceptance and use of Western material culture. It records a fixed moment in time in a process of continual cultural change, during which traditional material culture was increasingly replaced by Western trade goods.

The realization that traditional material culture and arts were being lost at a rapid pace motivated Ten Kate to spend much time and energy in the collection of such vestiges of aboriginal ways of life. Ten Kate had hoped to be able to acquire traditional artifacts in exchange for inexpensive trade goods or for small amounts of cash, an experience so many civil servants, missionaries, scientists, and travelers had shared with him while studying in Leiden, Paris, and Berlin. He apparently was not aware of the fact that conditions in the European colonies in Asia, Africa, and the Pacific were quite different from those in North America. Trade goods were in relative short supply in the colonies compared to the United States, where they could be had at reasonable prices. Moreover, the Indians had learned the value of money, and as they became increasingly involved in the cash economy demanded substantial prices for property in which White men seemed interested. The Navajo proved to be keen negotiators, fully aware of the interest of collectors and the value of their possessions, demanding substantial amounts of cash for their goods and crafts. Moreover, artifacts that had special significance for their owners, whether emotional or religious, were rarely on offer, but if so they demanded substantial prices (cf. Parezo 1986: 14).

The chances of collecting specimens of traditional material culture depended on the degree of cultural change that had taken place since the arrival of White colonists in different regions and the degree of separation maintained by both societies toward each other. Several centuries of intimate interethnic contact experienced by the Iroquois of New York State and the Tigua of Ysleta del Sur Pueblo near El Paso, Texas, had resulted in the loss of traditional architecture, dress, household wares, tools, etc. Only during festive occasions cherished items of traditional dress were worn, and in the rituals that were still being performed traditional sacred objects still played an important role. However, Ten Kate hardly had access to such objects because of his short stay among most tribes. Moreover, in many cases the owners, priests, and ritual specialists were probably not willing to part with such valued items of spiritual significance. On reservations Ten Kate noted that those Indians living close to Indian agencies, trading posts, and missions had been materially assimilated: They lived in log, frame, or adobe and brick houses, wore citizen's dress, and had furnished their homes with industrially produced Western goods. Among the Papago of San Xavier del Bac Ten Kate noticed no expressions of traditional material culture, while during a short trip into the remote Papaguería desert he was able to acquire pottery, baskets, sandals, and a bullroarer.

The best opportunities to add to his collection were when visiting reservations where Indians still lived somewhat isolated, geographically and socially, from White settlers. Also, when he stayed a longer time and visited Indian homes and camps on horseback over a large area, chances improved to obtain traditional items. This was the case when he joined Dr. Washington Matthews on a trip across part of the Navajo Reservation and another physician on tipi calls among the Southern Ute of the Los Piños Agency in Colorado. When he was among the Yuma and told them that he was interested in acquiring traditional items, Indians came from all corners to offer him their property. However, monetary constraints prohibited his purchasing everything that was offered to him.

Ten Kate also faced other complications in his collecting activities. Cherished personal memories could be associated with artifacts, making it difficult for the owners to part with them, such as in the case of the war captain of Isleta del Sur, who later regretted selling his war bonnet. It took all of Ten Kate's powers of persuasion and a substantial amount of money to acquire a painted shield from a Pima, as it had protected him during many battles and raids. Comanche Chief Tabenanneke even refused to sell his painted shield as it possessed supernatural powers that had sustained him during many years of warfare against enemies and only allowed Ten Kate to look at it. A similar impediment came into play when he expressed an interest in the hair ornament of an Apache girl, worn during the puberty ceremony. He was told that such a purchase was out of the question as it was the prerogative of the girl's prospective husband to remove the ornament during the wedding night. Instead, Ten Kate made a drawing of it in his sketchbook that was unfortunately lost.

Ten Kate noted that Indians had a distinct regard for property rights. He pointed out that on several occasions he had been unable to acquire an artifact because its owner was absent and nobody was entitled to enter negotiations on behalf of the proprietor. Several times a parent told him that they could not give away their children's belongings without their consent. Such attitudes stood in stark contrast to the often heard stories of thieving Indians.

Instead, Ten Kate pointed out that generally he encountered mutual respect for personal property within bands and tribes. Indians could leave their dwellings and belongings for days at a time without anyone to guard them, without fear of intrusion or theft. In this respect too he regarded Indian tribes as more civilized than Western nations.

Objects of religious significance were sometimes difficult to obtain. Custodians of communally used ritual artifacts almost always refused to part with such items, although occasionally a ritually significant artifact was sold when the price offered was sufficiently enticing. Apparently Ten Kate was not specifically focused on such materials. Whether because of ethical considerations or the constraints of time and funds cannot be determined. It took Matilda Coxe Stevenson until 1896 to obtain a Zuni kachina mask (Parezo 1986: 15).

Ten Kate acquired several masks among the Yaqui, Pima, and Pueblos, but these were not regarded as communal property. Artifacts of religious significance that were individually owned, including fetishes and personal medicine bags, could more readily be obtained.

It was easiest to acquire artifacts that were no longer functional or worn and had to be replaced soon. Some tobacco was usually sufficient for their Native owners to part with such items. Tools and utensils of daily use were a different matter. Only in cases of a surplus of such specimens was acquisition easy, depending on the price. However, in other cases the sale of a certain item would require immediate replacement and be more costly. Ten Kate usually acquired Indian artifacts by paying for them in cash, as the Indians began learning the value of money to buy Western goods from trading posts and stores. However, in other cases he supplied tobacco or in one case raw turquoise. The anthropologist was collecting in the Southwest at a time when barter gradually gave way to cash transactions, and by the turn of the century this transformation was virtually complete as Matilda Coxe Stevenson complained (Parezo 1986: 14).

Ten Kate's funds were far from sufficient to purchase everything that was of scientific and cultural interest. Thus he had to decline the offerings by the Navajo of shell and turquoise jewelry because of the high price demanded. The Yuma too asked steep prices for their arts and crafts, and when Ten Kate complained to Miguel, his Indian interpreter, he answered: "Don't you like the Yumas?" Among the Ute of southern Colorado he tried to acquire a calumet and tobacco bag, but its owner asked a prohibi-

tive price equaling that of a horse. While staying at Fort Defiance, the expedition of the Bureau of American Ethnology under the command of Colonel James Stevenson arrived and set up camp. With his modest private funds and small government grant for ethnographic purchases, Ten Kate's activities stand out bleakly against such large-scale and well-funded competition.

Ten Kate's itinerary of 1882–83 contains relatively few references to his feelings about purchasing artifacts from Indians. At that time there was little awareness of the ethics of collecting, and the salvage philosophy condoned almost any practice as long as Indians were not overtly coerced into parting with their property. Collectors were convinced that the specimens they obtained and hoarded were no longer functional in the new times, at least not those that were part of daily life. When it came to items of religious significance they reasoned that traditional rituals were eroding too and that collection of sacred paraphernalia was urgent as their disappearance was imminent. So, few qualms arose, and institutional and private collectors crisscrossed the American West like vacuum-cleaners, sucking up anything they could legitimately lay their hands on.

Every time Ten Kate spent one or a few days in a town between visits to Indian reservations, he prepared the collections he had made for shipment to the Netherlands. He packed all artifacts carefully to prevent damage during the long journey across country and across the Atlantic. In several cases he used an intermediary to expedite the materials, such as De Fremery, the Dutch consul in San Francisco, and Mr. H. Cazaux, the agent for the NASM, the Netherlands-American Steamship Company, based in Rotterdam and New York. The reliability of freighting companies, even when it came to intercontinental transportation, was quite remarkable at the time. Only once was a shipment lost, a small parcel with Papago materials that failed to arrive in New York, and in all other cases the collections arrived in Leiden without any damage (Ten Kate to Serrurier, 31 March 1883; 2 June 1883; 12 September 1883).

During his fieldwork in North America Ten Kate made notes on material culture and published most of these in a travel account (1885, 2004). In addition, he supplied occasional data in several articles and published letters. He only published one article specifically dealing with Native American material culture, on Zuni fetishes (1890). Some additional information can be gleaned from letters to Serrurier, the provisional inventory of acquisitions, data cards with a few notes, and remaining labels. Unfortunately, he never got around to further documenting his ethnographic collection because his income situation and restless nature forced him from one temporary appointment to the other, from one stint of fieldwork to another, eventually working and doing research on all continents (Hovens 1989: 197-232).

Ten Kate never saw his collection exhibited, except a few choice items that were individually displayed out of cultural context in the permanent collections in Leiden and Rotterdam. After World War II the National Museum of Ethnology in Leiden reestablished its permanent galleries and included a presentation on Native North America, with many artifacts from the Southwest and Plains collected by Ten Kate. The Columbus Quincentennial in 1992 was the occasion for a temporary exhibition on the Dutch anthropologist and his fieldwork and collecting in the American West. In 1998 a major temporary exhibition on Native North America at the Leiden museum included a number of artifacts collected by Ten Kate and drew a record number of visitors. Soon after, a complete renovation of the museum necessitated the closure and dissolution of all galleries. The museum reopened in 2001. North American and Arctic cultures are presented in a large hall, and artifacts from the Ten Kate collection are again on prominent display. In the winter of 2007-08 a small exhibition on Ten Kate was presented to the public. This catalogue is the culmination of the exhibition of the Ten Kate collection to a wide public.

The Ten Kate Collection: Context and Content

Questions

Ethnographic collections and their textual and photographic documentation in European and North American museums are cultural documents. On the one hand they document the lifeways of peoples across the globe at various points in time. On the other they exemplify the history of the struggle of Western society to come to economic, political, and intellectual terms with non-Western peoples, societies, and cultures. As such, ethnographic museum collections consist not only of artifacts from the cultures that created them, but at the same time these museum collections are artifacts of our own culture and should also be understood from that perspective (cf. Clifford 1985; 1988: 215-251; Feest 1993). Most ethnographic museum collec-

tions were assembled in colonial situations, and the Ten Kate collection is no exception. Recently Gosden and Knowles (2001) have stressed the need to analyze the intimate relation between collections and their colonial context and provided exemplary comparative examples from New Guinea (cf. Jones 1993: 214-215).

Museum collections are never random samples. To understand the Ten Kate collection in its totality as well as in its constituent parts, one needs to understand why and how the collection came into being. We already noted that the awareness that tribal cultures were disintegrating and disappearing at a rapid pace instilled a sense of urgency in the academic community to salvage as much cultural data as possible for future use, especially scientific study. This had special significance for collecting material culture. Fane (1992: 63-64) has stressed the importance of reexamining the salvage paradigm by asking hitherto ignored questions such as: Whose labor was collected? How and why was it made? What were the canons of selection? To what totality do the terms *representative* and *comprehensive* refer? Who were the makers, owners, and vendors, and what part did they play in the formation of the collection? What shifts in values and meaning occurred when the objects changed hands?

Colonialism

Ten Kate's fieldwork and collecting took place at a critical moment in time. The exchanges between individual Indians and the Dutch anthropologist during his collecting activities in the American West took place in a situation in which Native peoples had been forced to acknowledge the supreme power of the federal government, sometimes after military defeat by the U.S. army. The last tribes, notably the Apache and those on the Northern Plains, were being rendered politically powerless and forcibly settled on reservations. With their traditional means of livelihood virtually destroyed and loss of political independence, Indians faced the challenge to develop modes of accommodation in order to survive, not only physically, but also socially and psychologically. All tribes were faced with the need to develop new strategies for survival in a Western capitalist cash economy. Collecting artifacts from other peoples and cultures was intricately intertwined with late nineteenth-century Euro-American ideology. It expressed political supremacy, economic power and intellectual appropriation. The collection was regarded as a representation of the other, a way of life, a culture, despite its often fragmentary and unbalanced composition. Salvage ethnology and collecting was an integral part of the ultimate phase in the process of scientific colonization (Hovens 1989: 45-49; Hovens and Hieb 2004: 24-25).

Ten Kate was not directly associated with the American government, and at best he could obtain some logistical support from military and civil authorities. Officially he stood outside the unequal power relationship between political authority and conquered Native peoples and generally could not command any might to facilitate his collection activities. However, as a White man who made use of government facilities such as transportation, lodgings, and interpreters, the Indians must certainly have perceived him as part of the new power that had overwhelmed them—albeit an untypical one, as he visited their camps and households, was not adverse to eat their food, and showed a genuine interest in their way of life and traditions. However, although Ten Kate was extremely critical of government policy and had great sympathy for the plight of the Indians, occasionally he showed few qualms about using colonial interethnic relations to advance his research. Several times he pointed out that the Great White Father in Washington supported his research, trying to overcome opposition or reluctance among Indians, especially when taking somatological measurements. Because the funds at his disposal were rather modest, the anthropologist was generally in no position to offer enticing high prices for material possessions. Individuals determined their own prices, frequently resulting in the termination of exchange negotiations. However, precarious economic conditions and the attraction of Western goods and cash made them vulnerable in economic transactions. In conclusion, the Ten Kate collection is not only a reflection, although an incomplete and unbalanced one, of the tribal cultures he encountered in the Southwest, in Oklahoma, and New York State, it is also a reflection of contemporary colonial interethnic relations (cf. Gosden and Knowles 2001).

Content: General

For Ten Kate, collecting vestiges of traditional material culture fitted into the paradigm of the vanishing Indian. This vision was expressed in his petition for funds for fieldwork and the acquisition of artifacts, as well as in his private and professional correspondence and publications. However, it also appears that Ten Kate soon appreciated the advantages of collecting for the National Museum of

Ethnology: the recognition by the Dutch scientific community of Native North American studies as an academic field of research and collecting, the consequences of this recognition for his own position as the foremost expert in this area, and the improved access to Native communities that collecting artifacts provided.

Perhaps at no other time in the history of the academic anthropology was the aggregation of material culture collections regarded as of equal importance to the gathering of data on non-material aspects of life (cf. Feest 1993: 90; Parezo 1986: 4). The scientific naturalism of the nineteenth century led to gregarious collecting, and all ethnographic artifacts were incorporated into a taxonomic system in which each object was assigned to a systematic cultural category: subsistence, dress, architecture, household furnishings, weapons, transportation, games, religion, etc. This appetite for collecting the world was further intensified by the realization that tribal cultures across the globe, notably their material manifestations, were changing or even disappearing fast, resulting in a scramble for non-Western artifacts that gripped all North American and European museums with an interest in foreign lands and peoples (e.g., Cole 1985).

The paucity of North American Indian material in the collections of the Leiden museum did not require any selectivity in making acquisitions from this region. As is the case with much (but certainly not all) salvage anthropology, Ten Kate's collecting was not guided by one or more specific predefined selective criteria. Essentially, any artifact was regarded as of scientific value. Whatever was available was considered for acquisition; only price was a consideration. This pragmatic approach to collecting was further reinforced by the fact that this was his first fieldwork journey, only meant as a journey of recognizance, to be followed up as soon as possible with further research and collecting, possibly of a more strategic kind.

Ten Kate never regarded his ethnographic collection as representative of the indigenous cultures of the Southwest and Plains. He was only too aware of the limitations of his collecting activities, the constraints of time and funds, of access and availability of certain kinds of objects. However, he aimed at spreading his funds in such a manner that small collections from all the tribes he visited could be gathered. Only as such, the collection can be regarded as systematic (cf. Parezo 1986: 6). The importance and strength of Ten Kate's North American Indian collection is the available documentation as to when and where, and sometimes from whom, items were collected. As such, all of the objects he collected are invaluable in helping identify and place in time similar specimens in other collections that lack collection histories. In addition, he collected information about the context of the manufacture and use of artifacts, thus gathering important early ethnographic data. Ten Kate collected among non-Puebloan peoples in the Southwest at a time when these tribes were bypassed by the early collecting expeditions of the Smithsonian Institution and hardly the focus of individual researchers (Kaemlein 1967: 132). As such, his collection contains a number of artifacts that are the oldest of their category or type to have survived in museum collections.

Content: Specific

Many North American and European museums acquired much of their late nineteenth-century ethnographic collections from Native North America through a network of contacts with traders and professional people such as missionaries, civil servants, and teachers on reservations. White traders became middlemen in the flow of goods between Indian tribes and American society, and museums availed themselves of their services. In a few cases Ten Kate purchased small collections from traders, such as his important Yanktonai collection and a number of Mescalero and Jicarilla specimens. However, by far the majority of the artifacts in his collection were acquired in the field. The anthropologist personally visited almost all the tribes in the Southwest and acquired the artifacts directly from the Indians in a generally random way. However, when his presence on a reservation and inclination to purchase artifacts for cash became known or was explicitly announced through an interpreter, Indians visited the Dutchman and offered some of their belongings for sale, partially predetermining the selection.

The situation *in situ* predominantly structured and defined the collection. Not only was it relatively easy to acquire items of everyday life because these were still available in quantity, they were also either still being made or being disposed of as traditional lifestyles of nomadic hunting, fishing, and gathering were rapidly losing their relevance due to forced confinement on reservations and depletion of wildlife, while Western trade goods took their place. Thus pottery, basketry, weavings, moccasins, hide dress, toy, and games feature prominently in the collection. In addition, artifacts related to warfare were becoming increasingly obsolete and were disposed off, such as weapons like clubs, bows and arrows, bow cases and quivers, and shields. These are also well represented. Jewelry was still being made for personal adornment, sometimes combining old and new materials, but several types from traditional to modern could easily be acquired and became part of the collection. The male sphere of life is represented by artifacts related to hunting and warfare. Household goods represent the female domestic sphere. Cradleboards and toys relate to the lives of children. While most artifacts are utilitarian, a number relate to social status and religion, such as headgear, shields, and kachina dolls and masks, and they are also included in the Ten Kate collection.

Ten Kate regarded his collection of artifacts from the American West as documents of tribal ways of life, as material culture. However, he not only considered the artifacts from a utilitarian point of view. Because of his social and educational background he appreciated art and was sensitive to aesthetic expression in non-Western cultures. During his fieldwork in 1882–83 he repeatedly commented on the artistic qualities of certain categories of artifacts, notably Navajo jewelry and weavings, Hopi basketry, and Zuni pottery.

As a witness to the realities of Indian life in the 1880s Ten Kate was very much aware of the processes of cultural change taking place. On a number of occasions he pointed to processes of cultural change that emerged in earlier decades. Because of his interest in the origin of the Indians and the relationships between different peoples in North America this awareness went far beyond current and recent conditions, as Ten Kate repeatedly mentions processes of cultural change in tribal societies before White contact. The four-field approach to anthropology guaranteed a holistic approach to studying lifeways, considering synchronic as well as diachronic aspects of cultures (cf. Fontana 1978; Clifford 1988: 202, 230–232). This attitude prevented the anthropologist from exclusively collecting "authentic" artifacts, untainted by Western influence. Many artifacts he collected contain materials produced at factories in the eastern states that found a receptive market among Indian peoples in the American West. However, at that transitional point in time, these Western materials might receive an artisan's or artistic treatment inspired by tradition that would wane with time. Both Ten Kate (1885: 176) and Serrurier (1893: 11–21) regarded the collection of such artifacts of Native manufacture as exemplifying the process of Native-White relations worldwide and as seminal in the documentation and study of the process of cultural change (cf. Quimby 1966).

Scholars working in the Northeast began collecting in the Museum Age when tourism was emerging, and Native arts and crafts gained increasing economic significance for Indian communities. Phillips (1998: 50) has pointed out that these specialists generally avoided collecting Indian-made artifacts that displayed obvious Native accommodation to Western influences in order to maintain the imagery of Indians as a premodern people in their museum presentations. Likewise, they did not address such outcomes of contemporary interethnic relations in their writings. This colonial approach served both the romantic primitivists reacting against industrial modernity and the developers keen on acquiring Indian territory and displacing Native peoples from their homeland. It is a testimony to Ten Kate's modernity that he did not exclude the products of Native manufactures for the emerging tourist trade in his collecting activities nor avoided discussing the emergence of this interethnic market and its relevance to the survival of Indian communities. For Ten Kate, collecting became not an end in itself but a means to study tribal cultures in a diachronic perspective, providing clues to the past, present, and even future.

The Ten Kate collection from North America at the National Museum in Leiden is a legacy of the diversity of Native peoples, the richness of their cultures and traditions, the history of their encounter with Hispanic and Anglo-American societies, and of the emergence of anthropology as the academic discipline focused on the comparative study of man and his cultural diversity. The objects encapsulate the experience, knowledge, and beliefs of Native peoples, developed over millennia into valued lifeways. As such they provide the source for scholars to analyze the development of these cultures, for the public to be educated about their fellow man, and for Native peoples to access their past and address their present and future.

The Catalogue

Ten Kate's collection of North American Indian artifacts, funded by the Holland Society of Sciences, was officially acquired by the National Museum of Ethnology in Leiden in the fall of 1883 after Ten Kate's return home. It was registered as series 361 and consisted of sixty-five artifacts, mainly from the Apache and Navajo. With the subsidy from the Netherlands government Ten Kate was able to acquire 208 artifacts, mostly ethnographical but some archaeological. On his return to Holland this became series

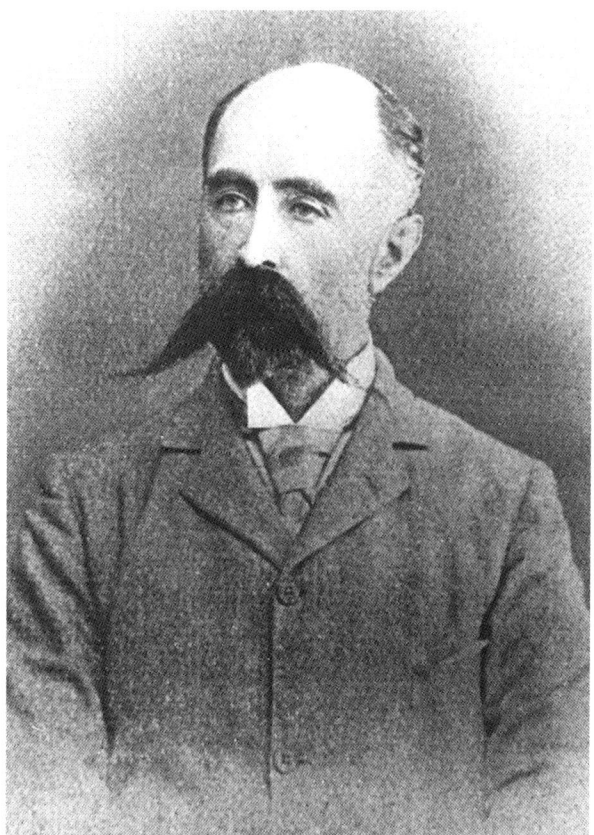

Fig. 5   Herman ten Kate, ca. 1900 (P. Hovens coll.).

362, which was officially added to the national ethnographic collection in Leiden in late 1883. It included materials from the Yaqui, Pima and Papago, Quechan, Mohave, Walapai, Hopi, Zuni, and Pueblos in the Southwest, Chemehuevi, Southern Paiute, and Southern Ute in the Great Basin, and a number of tribes from the southern Plains and Southeast who lived on reservations in Indian Territory, now Oklahoma (Kaemlein 1967: 134-138). His first small collection, originally acquired with private funds from Native craftspeople and a White trader in Niagara Falls, also became part of this series.

From November 1887 until October 1888 Ten Kate was back in the Southwest, this time on the staff of the Hemenway Southwestern Archaeological Expedition, directed by Frank H. Cushing. Most of this time was spent on excavating prehistoric Hohokam sites in south-central Arizona, but from July 1888 on the expedition worked at Zuni, where they concentrated on the site of Halonawan. Back in the Netherlands in late 1888 the Leiden museum purchased sixty-four artifacts from Ten Kate and added these as series 674 to the national collection. It cannot be established with certainty whether Ten Kate acquired these objects during his first (1882-83) or second (1887-88)

American journey. We are inclined to accept the earlier collection date as several artifacts are clearly documented as such, while others from that series were less likely to have been acquired during the Hemenway Expedition.

Ten Kate had also purchased Indian artifacts with his own funds in 1882–83, notably an outstanding northern Plains collection acquired from a trader in Niagara Falls. Additional choice specimens acquired during fieldwork made up his private collection, which he probably intended to use for furnishing his future home, including his study, to create an inspiring ambience. However, because of his roving way of life as a scientific nomad, he never stayed anywhere long enough to settle and grow roots. This resulted in his private collection being in storage much of the time. In 1889 he offered his prized northern Plains collection for sale, and again the National Museum of Ethnology in Leiden acquired the twenty-eight specimens which constitute series 710.

In 1914 the museum received a miscellaneous series of artifacts from a third person, including five arrows (series 1942). Although it has been assumed that these arrows came from the Papago and were collected by Ten Kate, the only documentation available suggests that they came from South America. In 1921 financial constraints forced Ten Kate to offer what remained of his private ethnographic collection for sale. Again the National Museum of Ethnology acted promptly and added sixteen North American objects as series 2012 to its collections, including Zuni pottery, Northeastern tourist arts, and Navajo textiles.

Apart from the acquisition of the collections made in the field or purchased from traders by Ten Kate during his two years of anthropological fieldwork in North America, the National Museum of Ethnology in Leiden obtained several other small collections which pertain directly or indirectly to Ten Kate's research and are therefore included in this catalogue. In 1888, when Ten Kate terminated his work with the Hemenway Expedition, director Frank Cushing donated several prehistoric artifacts from Halonawan, the prehistoric center of Zuni population, as well as a Zuni war club to the Leiden museum (series 675). In 1912 the museum obtained eight Hohokam artifacts formerly part of the Thomas V. Keam collection, which was obtained by Jesse Walter Fewkes in the 1890s on behalf of Mrs. Hemenway, Cushing's and Ten Kate's patron (series 1830). Finally, the Leiden museum purchased a Hopi kachina doll from the Amsterdam dealer Lemaire in 1956, formerly probably acquired by Ten Kate (RMV 3364-5).

These ancillary collections comprise fourteen artifacts and are included in this catalogue.

A small number of artifacts collected in North America by Ten Kate were donated to or purchased by other museums. The Musée d'Ethnographie in Paris, which became the Musée de l'Homme, obtained the archaeological finds from northwestern Mexico in 1883. These forty-six specimens were recently transferred to the new Musée du quai Branly. The Wereldmuseum (World Museum) in Rotterdam (formerly: Museum of Ethnology) acquired a series of ethnographic artifacts from Ten Kate on several occasions when the anthropologist was forced to sell anything of value to make ends meet. This included twenty-six specimens collected in the 1880s in North America, including Iroquois beadwork and Southwestern textiles. These small collections are also included in this catalogue, which contains 476 entry numbers.

In this catalogue Ten Kate's collection is grouped in thirteen chapters, each presenting the artifacts from a culture area, a linguistic group, or a tribe, the exception being the archaeological artifacts from the Greater Southwest, which are aggregated in a separate chapter. The narrative text of each chapter follows Ten Kate's travel book (1885, 2004) and mainly consists of paraphrased extracts and compilations of his fieldwork account, focusing primarily on material culture. This provides the context for the entries, which are organized topically and focus on single or small groups of similar artifacts, either with or without an introduction to the artifact type under consideration. Of each numbered museum specimen all available data from Ten Kate's writings, unpublished notes, and the museum archives are provided. Most artifacts are subsequently discussed as to their cultural and historical context.

All technical data are given in the captions to the illustrations, beginning with the specific identification of tribal origin (if relevant within the context of the chapter) and artifact type. Frequently this is followed by tribal names for the artifact, often based on Ten Kate's notes, but also using additional sources. Materials are identified as detailed as possible and measurements in centimeters are provided. The captions are concluded by the approximate date of manufacture of the artifact(s). In most cases Ten Kate accumulated his ethnographic collection on the Indian reservations during his fieldwork there in 1882 and 1883. However, exceptions are noted in the text preceding a group of entries or in individual entries.

Virtually all artifacts Ten Kate collected are illustrated in this catalogue and were photographed by Ben Grishaaver.

An exception is the small number of archaeological artifacts Ten Kate collected in Baja California, Sonora, and New Mexico, which are curated at the Musée du quai Branly in Paris. These can be consulted in the digital collection database available through that museum's website (see chapter 14, "Archaeology").

Contributions

Support from North American experts has been crucial in the production of this catalogue. Alan Ferg of the Arizona State Museum (Tucson, AZ) wrote the entries as well as critical text for the Apache chapter. Ruth B. Phillips of Carleton University (Ottawa, ON) provided most of the entries for the Northeast chapter. Pieter Hovens collaborated with Ted Brasser (curator emeritus, Canadian Museum of Civilization, Ottawa, ON) on the Plains materials, with Marian E. Rodee (curator emeritus, Maxwell Museum of Anthropology, Albuquerque, NM) on the entries for the Navajo and Zuni textiles, and with David R. Wilcox of the Museum of Northern Arizona (Flagstaff, AZ) on the prehistoric artifacts from Arizona for the Archaeology chapter. Duane Anderson (director emeritus, Museum of Indian Arts and Culture, Santa Fe, NM) authored the pottery entries for the Pueblo chapter. Laura van Broekhoven, Hovens' colleague at the Leiden museum and curator of the Latin American Department, provided the critical text and entries for the Central Mexico section of the Mexico chapter. Other American colleagues provided their expertise on the tribal and temporal identification of specific artifacts, as well as details regarding their cultural context, as noted in the appropriate entries. Wilma R. Kaemlein of the Arizona State Museum inventoried Southwestern American Indian collections in European museums in the 1960s (Kaemlein 1967). Alan Ferg made her original documentation for the artifacts from the Ten Kate collection available.

A Legacy with a Future

As outlined above, anthropology and ethnology museums are part of the colonial legacy. The discipline and its institutions have incurred a debt toward the Native peoples who became their focus of interest, scientific study, and sometimes human compassion and solidarity, as in the case of Ten Kate. Anthropologists and museums have collected and preserved much of the knowledge of Native peoples, shared and transferred by elders and common people, now embedded in books, on records and tapes, in fieldnotes, and in museum collections. These resources are part of the postcolonial world. It is our responsibility to open up and make accessible what has been preserved, to return knowledge to the people of the source communities so that they can reexamine and reevaluate their past, and where possible strengthen their tradition, proud of the legacy their forefathers, to value and cherish by generations to come. Ten Kate could not have been happier with such an outcome.

References

Appadurai, Arjun
  1986 (ed.) *The Social Life of Things: Commodities in Cultural Perspective*. Cambridge: Cambridge University Press.
ARMV
  1882-1883 Letterbooks. Archives, Rijksmuseum voor Volkenkunde/National Museum of Ethnology, Leiden.
Bastian, Adolf
  1883 *Amerika's Nordwest-Küste: Neueste Ergebnisse ethnologischer Reisen: aus den Sammlungen der Königlichen Museen zu Berlin*. Berlin: A. Asher.
Boas, Franz
  1906 Ethnological Problems in Canada. *Proceedings of the Fifteenth International Congress of Americanists*, 149-155.
Clifford, James
  1985 Objects and Selves: An Afterword. In: George W. Stocking (ed.), *Objects and Others: Essays on Museums and Material Culture* (Madison, WI: University of Wisconsin Press), 236-246.
  1986 On Ethnographic Allegory. In: James Clifford and George F. Marcus (eds.), *Writing Culture: The Poetics and Politics of Ethnography* (Berkeley, CA–London: University of California Press), 98-121.
  1988 *The Predicament of Culture: Twentieth Century Ethnography, Literature, and Art*. Cambridge: Harvard University Press.
Cole, Douglas
  1985 *Captured Heritage: The Scramble for Northwest Coast Artifacts*. Seattle, WA: University of Washington Press.
Eggan, Fred W.
  1965 Lewis Henry Morgan and the Future of the American Indian. *Proceedings of the American Philosophical Society* 109: 272-276.
Fane, Diana
  1992 New Questions for Old Things: The Brooklyn Museum's Zuni Collection. In: Janet C. Berlo (ed.), *The Early Years of Native American Art History* (Seattle, WA: University of Washington Press), 62-87.
Feest, Christian F.
  1993 Needs and Opportunities for Research in Ethnographic Museums. *Zeitschrift für Ethnologie* 118: 87-95.

Fontana, Bernard L.

1978 Artifacts of the Indians of the Southwest. In: Ian M. G. Quimby (ed.), *Material Culture and the Study of American Life* (New York, NY: Winterthur Museum–Norton & Co.), 75-108.

Gosden, Chris and Chantal Knowles

2001 *Collecting Colonialism: Material Culture and Colonial Change.* Oxford–New York, NY: Berg.

Hinsley, Curtis M.

1981 *Savages and Scientists: The Smithsonian Institution and the Development of American Anthropology, 1846-1910.* Washington, DC: Smithsonian Institution Press.

Hodge, Frederick Webb

1907-1910 *Handbook of American Indians North of Mexico.* 2 vols. Bureau of American Ethnology, Bulletin 30. Washington, DC.

Hovens, Pieter

1984 Between Survival and Assimilation: The Visit of the Dutch Anthropologist Herman ten Kate to the Iroquois in 1882. In: P. Hovens (ed.), *North American Indian Studies 2: European Contributions to Science, Society and Art* (Aachen–Göttingen: Alano Verlag–Edition Herodot), 36-42.

1989 *Herman F. C. ten Kate (1858-1931) en de antropologie der Noord Amerikaanse Indianen* (Herman F. C. ten Kate and the Anthropology of the North American Indians). Meppel: Krips. [Ph.D. thesis, University of Nijmegen.]

1991a The Origins of Anthropology in Baja California: The Fieldwork and Excavations of Herman F. C. ten Kate in 1883. *Pacific Coast Archaeological Society Quarterly* 27(4): 15-22.

1991b Veth, Pieter Johannes (1814-1895). In: C. Winters (ed.), *International Dictionary of Anthropologists* (New York, NY: Garland), 727-728.

1995 Ten Kate's Hemenway Expedition Diary, 1887-1888. *Journal of the Southwest* 37(4): 635-700.

i.p. *North American Indian Art: Masterpieces and Museum Collections from The Netherlands* (in preparation).

Hovens, Pieter and Anneke Groeneveld

1992 *Odagot: Photographs of American Indians, 1860-1920.* Amsterdam: Fragment Uitgeverij.

Hovens, Pieter and Jiska Herlaar

2004 Early Anthropology on the Southwest-Great Basin Frontier: The 1883 Fieldwork of Herman ten Kate. *Journal of the Southwest* 46(3): 529-558.

Hovens, Pieter and Louis A. Hieb

2004 The Science of the Indians: Herman Ten Kate, Anthropology, and Native American Studies. In: P. Hovens, L. A. Hieb, and W. J. Orr (eds.), *Herman Ten Kate: Travels and Researches in Native North America, 1882-1883* (Albuquerque, NM: University of New Mexico Press), 15-54.

Jones, Anna Laura

1993 Exploding Canons: The Anthroplogy of Museums. *Annual Review of Anthropology* 22: 201-220.

Kaemlein, Wilma

1967 *An Inventory of Southwestern American Indian Specimens in European Museums.* Tucson, AZ: Arizona State Museum.

Koepping, Klaus-Peter

1983 *Adolf Bastian and the Psychic Unity of Mankind.* St. Lucia: University of Queensland Press.

McIntire, E. G. and S. R. Gordon

1968 Ten Kate's Account of the Walpi Snake Dance. *Plateau* 41: 27-33.

Morgan, Lewis Henry

1993 *The Indian Journals.* New York, NY: Dover Publications.

Otterspeer, Willem

1989 (ed.) *Leiden Oriental Connections, 1850-1940.* Leiden: E. J. Brill–Universitaire Pers Leiden.

Parezo, Nancy J.

1985 Cushing as Part of a Team: The Collecting Activities of the Smithsonian Institution. *American Ethnologist* 12(4): 763-774.

1986 The Formation of Ethnographic Collections: The Smithsonian Institution in the Southwest. *Advances in Archaeological Method and Theory* 10: 1-47.

Parmenter, Ross

1966 *Explorer, Linguist and Ethnologist: Bibliography of Alphonse Pinart.* Los Angeles, CA: Southwest Museum.

Phillips, Ruth B.

1998 *Trading Identities: The Souvenir in Native North American Art from the Northeast, 1700-1900.* Seattle, WA: University of Washington Press.

Quimby, George I.

1966 *Indian Culture and European Trade Goods.* Madison, WI: University of Wisconsin Press.

Serrurier, Lindor

1893 *Museum of Pakhuis?* Leiden: De Breuk en Smits.

Steinmetz, Sebald R.

1892 Antropologie als Universiteitsvak. *De Nederlandsche Spectator:* 328-310.

Stocking, George W.

1987 *Victorian Anthropology.* New York, NY: Free Press.

Ten Kate, Herman F. C.

1885 *Reizen en Onderzoekingen in Noord Amerika.* Leiden: E. J. Brill.

1890 Zuni Fetishes. *Internationales Archiv für Ethnographie* 3: 118-119.

1925 *Over Land en Zee; Schetsen en Stemmingen van een Wereldreiziger.* Zutphen: W. J. Thieme.

2004 *Travels and Researches in Native North America, 1882-1883.* P. Hovens, L. A. Hieb, and W. J. Orr eds. Albuquerque, NM: University of New Mexico Press. [Translation of Ten Kate 1885.]

Woldt, A.

1884 (ed.) *Capitän Jacobsen's Reise an der Nordwestküste Amerikas, 1881-1883 zum Zwecke ethnologischer Sammlungen und Erkundungen.* Leipzig: Max Spohr.

2

The Northeast:
Indians of the Great Lakes and Woodlands

Well prepared for his journey of fieldwork across North America, Ten Kate boarded a steamship in Rotterdam in the fall of 1882 and crossed the stormy Atlantic Ocean, disembarking in New York harbor on 5 November. His first meeting was with Ely S. Parker, at that time police chief in the city. Parker was an educated Seneca leader who had worked with Lewis Henry Morgan when the latter was researching his classic book *League of the Ho-de-no-sau-nee, or Iroquois*, published in 1851. Subsequently Parker became a personal aide to General Ulysses S. Grant and served with him during the Civil War. When Grant became President of the United States, Parker was appointed Commissioner of Indian Affairs, serving in that capacity from 1869 to 1871. The prominent Seneca elder and government official impressed Ten Kate with his erudition and demeanor. Because of the genuine interest in indigenous North American peoples the Dutchman showed, Parker wrote letters of introduction and support for him, addressed to the Secretaries of the War and Interior Departments, several of his friends in the West, and his sister Caroline Parker, who lived on the Tuscarora Reservation near Niagara Falls.

It was Ten Kate's intention to familiarize himself with the physical type of the Hodenosaunee (Iroquois) and to establish the extent to which they had retained their traditions in the face of White colonization and government policy. He was aware that he could learn little new about the customs of the Iroquois that would add to the authoritative works of Cadwallader Colden and Lewis Henry Morgan. However, he regarded this as an outstanding opportunity for a first-hand acquaintance with the aboriginal inhabitants of the New World before traveling on to the Far West.

Ten Kate immediately set out for upstate New York and was pleasantly surprised by the clear and sunny skies and wonderful display of colors of the northeastern woods. It was a splendid Indian Summer that year. However, soon temperatures plummeted and it began to snow, making travel increasingly difficult. The abundant snowfall allowed him to visit only the Tuscarora Reservation at Lewiston near Niagara Falls and the Seneca Reservation on the Cattaraugus River, traveling mostly by horse-drawn sleigh.

During his trips across the Tuscarora and Cattaraugus Reservations Ten Kate noted that the Hodenosaunee had to a great extent adopted a Western lifestyle. Many lived in modern single-story clapboard houses, painted white, while other dwellings were constructed of roughly hewn planks or logs. The houses were spread across the reservation, each standing on its own farm lot. Only occasionally a small number of houses stood clustered. Fields were usually fenced, and many Iroquois had cattle and planted a variety of crops as a means of subsistence.

Ten Kate, like many of his contemporaries, was interested in the results of intermarriage and the physical description of aboriginal peoples. He noted that a significant degree of intermarriage between Iroquois and Whites had taken place, resulting in mixed-blood offspring, and in each generation children with decreasing amounts of Indian blood were born. The Dutch anthropologist was struck by the attractive build and fine facial features of these mixed bloods, especially among the women and girls. Despite intermarriage, most Iroquois had thick black hair. Those of the older generation still spoke their Native language and Ten Kate found their tone of voice heavy, deep, guttural, and nasal at the same time, but observed that they never spoke loudly. The younger generation who attended schools understood Hodenosaunee languages, although many were unable to speak them.

His hosts, Tuscarora Chief John Mount Pleasant and his wife, were representatives of the mixed-blood Iroquois. Like her brother Arthur, Caroline Parker—Mrs. Mount Pleasant—had had a Western education. In her bookcase Ten Kate noted modern scientific works on physical anthropology, ethnology, and geology. Named Ga-hah-no at

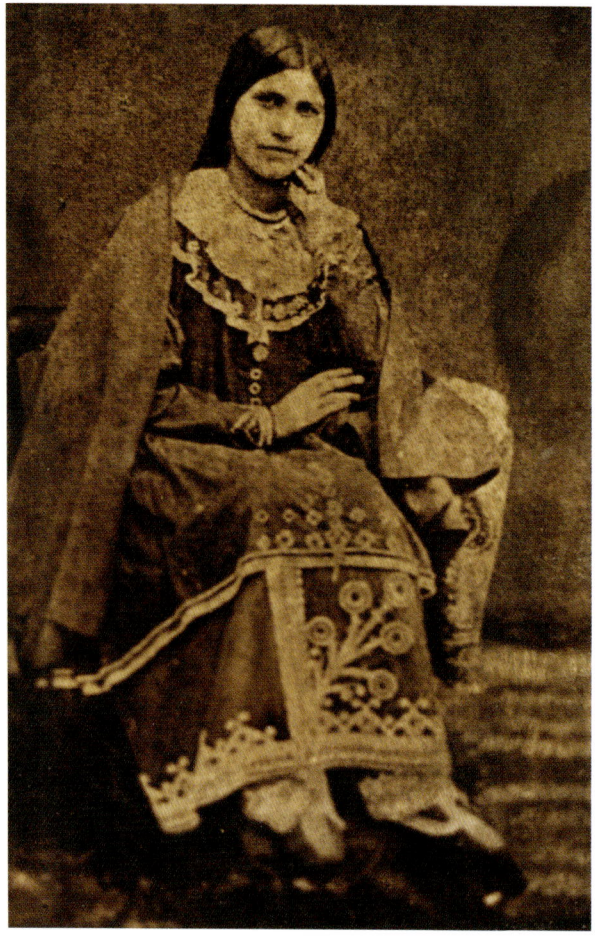

Fig. 6   Caroline G. Parker, Seneca; Tonawanda Indian Reservation, New York State, ca. 1860. Photographer unknown (Ten Kate coll., WMR 427754).

birth, Caroline Parker had pursued studies at Brockport and Cayuga Academies in New York and later at Albany State Normal School. Like her brother, she had assisted Lewis Henry Morgan during his ethnographic research, and she is pictured in Morgan's *League of the Ho-de-no-sau-nee, or Iroquois* (1851) wearing articles of clothing he collected for the state of New York. She gained the honorary title of *Ge-Keats-Sau-Sa* or 'Queen.' When Ten Kate explained the purpose of his visit and research, she graciously offered her assistance as informant, interpreter, and guide. With her the anthropologist visited Tuscarora homes and witnessed family life during several trips across the Tuscarora Reservation. Through her he also gained access to the council, the church, and the school.

While doing fieldwork, Ten Kate expressed his interest in traditional dances and songs. His Seneca hosts conferred among themselves, and soon one of them donned traditional dress, including a long buckskin shirt, decorated leggings and moccasins, and a feather headdress. His

face was painted black. Mrs. Mount Pleasant told Ten Kate that he was about to be adopted into the Wolf clan of the Seneca tribe and would thus become her brother. Seneca and Tuscarora men then sat down in a circle, after which Odagot (Clear Light), the man who had put on traditional dress and whose name Ten Kate would receive, began reciting an ode to the Seneca, stressing their courage as fierce warriors. This completed, he sat down and asked Ten Kate to sit next to him, handing him the calumet. Holding the anthropologist's hand, Odagot sang a song, shaking his turtle-shell rattle, while the other Senecas joined in. After finishing, Ten Kate received a small necklace of wampum from Mrs. Mount Pleasant as a token of his adoption.

After saying goodbye to his gracious hosts, Ten Kate traveled to the Cattaraugus Reservation of the Seneca in Erie County, where he visited the sachem Nicholson Parker and the Thomas Orphan Asylum. The latter institution educated Iroquois children from all tribes of the confederacy, especially orphans and children from poor families. He noted that the pupils were very bright, quickly became fluent in English, and showed an inclination for fine writing, drawing, and needlework.

Ten Kate noted that the traditional Senecas lived at Newtown, where they still engaged in ancient tribal ceremonies such as the White Dog Sacrifice in midwinter to carry the prayers of the people to the spirits, and the Green Corn Ceremony, a thanksgiving ritual celebrated when the corn began to ripen. At Gowanda, where the Christian Senecas lived, Ten Kate saw virtually no signs of traditional dress, except the occasional moccasins. He tried to collect traditional artifacts which, however, proved rather difficult because of the degree of culture change that had taken place after many centuries of indigenous-White relations. The Seneca made birchbark and beaded souvenirs, and these manufactures were sold to shops in Niagara Falls for cash. However, his prize acquisition was a traditional Tuscarora cradleboard.

After a visit to the Smithsonian Institution in Washington, DC, where he made the acquaintances of American colleagues, including Spencer Baird, John Wesley Powell, and James Mooney, Ten Kate left the eastern United States and turned south and west on 19 December 1882. By train he traveled to Little Rock, glad to distance himself from the snow and the cold. In the capital of Arkansas he bade farewell to his father and sister, who intended to spend some time with relatives and friends who had settled in the United States. Ten Kate journeyed on to St. Louis, where he visited the remains of Cahokia, the largest precontact Indian town north of Mexico. From there he embarked on his journey of fieldwork to the American Southwest, northwestern Mexico, and the southern Plains.

Ten Kate remained only a few days among the Aboriginal peoples of the Northeast, during which time he visited reservations belonging to two of the six nations of the Hodenosaunee (Iroquois) confederacy. These were the Tuscarora community at Lewiston near Niagara Falls and the Seneca community at Cattaraugus, south of Buffalo on Lake Erie. Since the 1830s tourism had made Niagara Falls the great center for trade in Native souvenir arts from northeastern North America and provided a market for Indian arts and crafts from the Northeast culture area (Phillips 1998). Thus, although Ten Kate's ethnographic collection from the region is rather modest and consists of only twenty-seven items, it represents peoples from across the region.

In addition to the traditional cradleboard he acquired at Tuscarora, Ten Kate collected examples of the souvenir arts made by the Mi'kmaq (Micmac) of Nova Scotia, the Wendat (Huron) living near Quebec City, and the Anishinaabe (Chippewa-Ojibwe, Potawatomi, and Odawa) of the central Great Lakes. He almost certainly purchased these items from shops run by non-Natives at the Falls. It is very likely that he also purchased some of his Iroquois beadwork there, either from shops or from the Tuscarora vendors who sold directly to tourists at Luna Island, and some of it from vendors on the reservations he visited.

Wendat (Huron) Moosehair-embroidered Ware

Northern Woodlands and Subarctic peoples have used the long hairs that grow under the neck of the moose to decorate clothing, accessories, and other items since before European contact (Turner 1976). During the early eighteenth century Ursuline and other French nuns at Quebec, who had learned how to use moosehair from Aboriginal women, invented new kinds of fancy wares of birchbark (*Betula papyrifera*) embroidered in dyed moosehair to give as gifts to their patrons in France and North America (Barbeau 1943). They ornamented boxes, fans, pincushions, and other items with floral motifs and idealized scenes of the forest life of the "noble savage." After the British conquest of Canada, these wares became extremely popular curiosities with the many officials and army officers who were stationed in Canada through the periods of the Revolutionary War and the War of 1812 (Phillips 1998: 103-109; cf. Thompson 1977: 134-139, 143; Coe 2003: 134-137; Cook 2005: 230-233).

By the 1830s Wendat (Huron) women had largely taken over the production of fancy bark works, and they further developed the iconographic and stylistic traditions the nuns had established during the eighteenth century. Wendat women also used moosehair embroidery to ornament hide moccasins, cloth seat covers for chairs, tablecloths, and other items that appealed to the tastes of Victorian buyers. They actively marketed their work not only at their village of Lorette (Morissonneau 1978), but also at popular tourist spots and in cities throughout the Northeast. In 1861, for example, when the German traveler Johann Georg Kohl (1861, 1: 180) visited the Wendat village of Lorette, outside of Quebec City, he saw "great tons and chests full of moccasins embroidered with flowers, cigar-cases, purses, &c., all made by the women in the village, and which were, I believe, destined to be sent to Montreal, and thence probably to Niagara and New York."

During the 1880s, when Ten Kate visited Niagara Falls, the quality of moosehair embroidery had begun to decline due to changes in consumer taste, shifts in the tourist market, and the advent of new forms of mass production at Lorette. By the end of the century, well organized cottage industries for the production of moccasins, snowshoes, and canoes had been developed. In 1898, for example, 140,000 pairs of moccasins were made there, the bulk destined for dealers in the Great Lakes region and major cities and resorts in the eastern Canadian provinces and northeastern American states, where the moccasins were sold to consumers who often used them as slippers. During his fieldwork in 1908-09 Frank Speck was unable to identify the natural dyes with which the Huron had originally used to color the moosehair, as they had been using commercial aniline dyes for such a long time (Gérin 1901: 553; Speck 1911a, 1911b; Brasser 1976: 43, 158-159; 1998: 49; Canada House 1985: 14-15, 20-22; Phillips 1990: 29-31; 1998: 125-126, 142, 162).

Travelers to North America liked to purchase domestic ornaments decorated with images of the indigenous peoples. Both this imagery and exotic indigenous materials such as birchbark, moosehair, and porcupine quills symbolized the uniqueness of the continent and served as mementos of their visits. The center of the lid on a box collected by Ten Kate (Fig. 7) shows two Indians paddling in a canoe, framed by a wreath of leaves and flowers. The

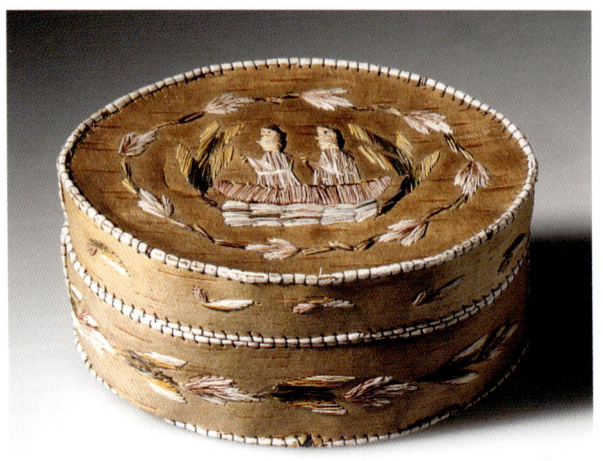

Fig. 7   Wendat (Huron) lidded box with embroidered decoration; birchbark, moosehair, pigment; l. 14.7 cm, w. 10.4 cm, h. 6 cm; ca. 1880 (RMV 362-5).

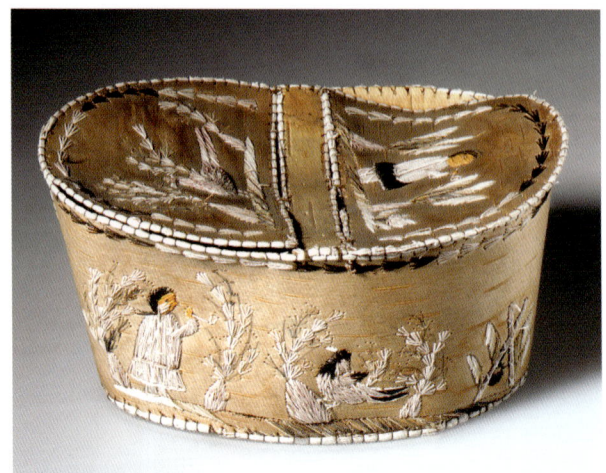

Fig. 8   Wendat (Huron) or Wendat-Mohawk lidded box with embroidered decoration; birchbark, moosehair, pigment; l. 14.6 cm, w. 10 cm, h. 7.5 cm; ca. 1880 (RMV 2012-11).

pictorial vignette is a direct descendant of an emblematic motif invented by the Ursuline nuns during the eighteenth century. The side of this birchbark box is embroidered in a floral motif, while the central scene on the lid is surrounded by a garland of flowers. Speck (1911a: 9) noted that, with the exception of the leaves and stems, the Huron generally did not imitate the natural coloring of the plants they represented in moosehair embroidery.

Another box (Fig. 8) with its hinged lid takes the form of a miniature workbasket or handbag. It is ornamented with imagined scenes of the hunting and gathering life of the forest. A woman smoking is seen on the lid, and another walks through rich vegetation toward a tripod from which hangs a trade kettle. For buyers, the disproportionate scale of the humans, plants, and animals in these scenes probably added a naive charm to the scene. Al-

though Ten Kate recorded that this box came from the St. Regis Reservation (today Akwesasne), a Mohawk community that straddles the U.S.-Canadian border in northern New York State, Ontario, and Quebec, it is typical of Wendat work (Ten Kate letter, St. Louis, 16 December 1882; ARMV no. 273; Fenton and Tooker 1978: 471). It could have been traded into Akwesasne from Lorette, or it might have been made there by a Wendat woman married into a Mohawk family.

During the nineteenth century women at the Wendat community of Lorette made moccasins in the puckered-toe style common among northeastern peoples such as the Abenaki, Penobscot, and Malecite. Wendat women were known for the richly colored moosehair embroidery with which they embellished their moccasins (Speck 1911b: 211–214; Hatt 1916: 168–169).

Fig. 9   Two pairs of Wendat (Huron) embroidered moccasins; cowhide, cloth, moosehair, pigment; l. 23 cm (both); ca. 1880 (RMV 2012-8, -9).

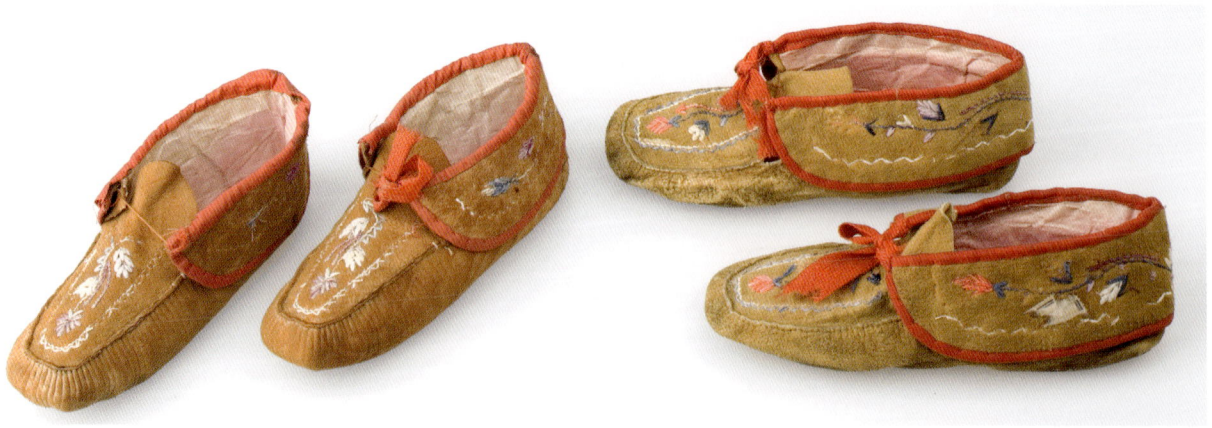

The two pairs in the Ten Kate collection (Fig. 9) are examples of the mass production of moccasins developed for the tourist market by Wendat entrepreneurs toward the end of the nineteenth century. By this period the loss of hunting lands and native-tanned hides had caused the Wendat and Hodenosaunee to use commercially processed hide, although they turned the untanned surface to the outside in order to more closely imitate the appearance of native-tanned hide. The hide of the moccasins numbered RMV 2012-9 is dyed. The moosehair-embroidered floral designs on the vamps and cuffs of Ten Kate's moccasins are much simplified from those used at Lorette fifty years earlier. The U-shaped embroidered curve of simple and zigzag blue and white lines remains characteristic of Huron work (Speck 1911b: 9–10). This tourist-style Indian footwear was sold for practical purposes, to be used as slippers, and also as a collectable souvenir (Conn 1979a: 54, 61; Phillips 1990: 31–32; 1998: 250–254; cf. Thompson 1977: 139, 142).

The question of whether floral imagery was used by Aboriginal people before the arrival of Europeans has been the subject of much debate among anthropologists, but most scholars have concluded that naturalistic floral representation was introduced by Europeans (Speck 1911b, 1925, Barbeau 1928, Conn 1979b, Brasser 1987, Penney 1991, Phillips 1998). The stylized floral motifs on Wendat moccasins from the early historic period are derived from skin painting traditions of the eastern Subarctic, while the floral imagery displayed by moosehair embroidery made from the 1830s on is more naturalistic (Phillips 1990: 30). When Speck conducted research on the topic at Lorette in 1911, an even more literal realism had developed and embroiderers identified their designs as representing particular local species. He also noted that "as to the flower designs, about the origin of which at present very little in general is known, it seems that with the Huron at least three are native" (i.e., of pre-European origin): balsam fir, cat's paw, and star (Speck 1911a: 8–9, 13). RMV 2012-8 exhibits cat's paw designs, executed in red, pink, and white on the vamp and cuff; white flox is depicted on the vamp of RMV 2012-9.

Iroquois Artifacts for the Tourist Trade

Because of the location of Niagara Falls within their territory, the Hodenosaunee (Iroquois) were the major suppliers of the souvenir arts sold there. Their main production was beadwork, applied in a number of distinctive styles

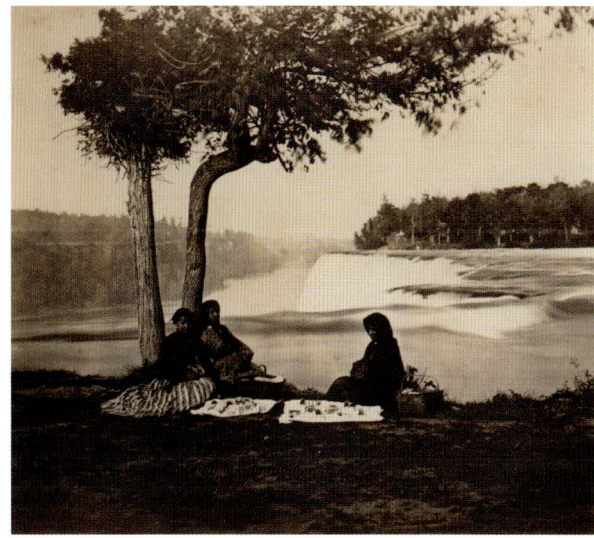

Fig. 10   Indian souvenir sellers at Niagara Falls. Photograph by J. G. Parks, ca. 1886 (WMR 904994).

and techniques to purses, moccasins, pincushions, and domestic ornaments that have been called "whimsies," a term used for imaginative novelties by non-Native needleworkers during the Victorian era. Hodenosaunee people prefer to use the categorical term "beadwork." Although Lewis Henry Morgan acknowledged the "mixed character" of these items, he also wrote that they "furnish no slight indication of the artisan capacity" (Tooker 1994: 73).

Women's beadwork increasingly provided Hodenosaunee families with much needed cash income, and Hodenosaunee people consulted by Beverly Gordon, who has made the most extensive study of their beadwork, emphasized that many Indian families would not have been able to survive without manufacturing for the tourist market (Gordon 1984: 65; Rickard 1992). Although production fell off during the twentieth century when other kinds of work became available, Hodenosaunee women have continued to make fine beadwork down to the present, both to ornament clothing worn by followers of the Longhouse religion and for sale. Contemporary Hodenosaunee regard beadwork as an important traditional art form (Hill 1994), and it is currently experiencing a revival.

On the Tuscarora Reservation or at Niagara Falls Ten Kate purchased a number of Tuscarora "whimsies," domestic ornaments of Euro-American derivation embellished with beadwork and moosehair embroidery (cf. Gordon 1984; 1986; Harding 1994; Bol 1998: 82–86, 88; Phillips 1998: 228–240). All the beadwork items Ten Kate donated to the World Museum in Rotterdam have a cardboard base, covered with cloth of various colors, with red clearly

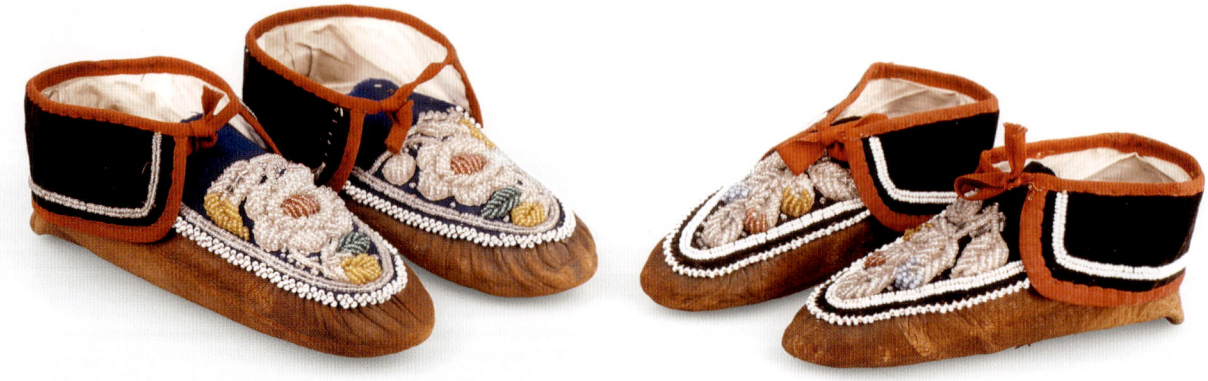

Fig. 11 Iroquois moccasins; *ahtáhkwa'o:weh* (Tooker 1994: 94, 155); cowhide, cotton, glass; RMV 710-15: l. 27.5 cm, w. 13.5 cm; RMV 362-1: l. 23.5 cm, w. 12 cm; both ca. 1880.

preferred. The bright and dark hued red and blue cloth set off the floral and zoomorphic designs (birds, butterflies), preferentially executed in white opaque raised beadwork.

Traditionally, Hodenausaunee women decorated tanned deerskin moccasins by embroidering the vamps, seams, and cuffs with porcupine quills dyed black, white, yellow, and red. They used both fine quills to embroider curvilinear designs and folded and sewed flattened quills to hide to form rows of complex geometric patterns. After contact, moccasins, bags, and other hide items were further enriched by borders of small white glass beads and silk ribbon trim, often sewn onto hide smoked to a dark brown or blackish color which set off the decorative elements (cf. Morgan 1850: 68–69; 1852: 94; FIA 1975: xxxv, 41–42; Thompson 1977: 124–125, 144; Lyford 1982: 28–29; Phillips 1984: 44–45; Tooker 1994: 115–116; Brasser 1976: 116, 118, 153; 1998: 49; Hall 2001; Coe 2003: 216–218).

By the middle of the nineteenth century Hodenosaunee women were making moccasins with multicolored floral patterns of raised or "embossed" beadwork sewn to velvet cloth backed with stiff paper or cardboard and then applied to the vamps. The cuffs could be treated the same way or covered with dark colored velvet and edged with ribbon or cotton tape. The sculptural, low-relief effect of the beadwork was achieved by stringing an excessive number of beads on the thread. The textured effect of the beadwork was often enhanced by the use of different sizes of beads and by the addition of cylindrical and faceted beads (Orchard 1929: 153–157; Brasser 1976: 43; Gordon

1984; Phillips 1990; 1998: 225). Although probably produced in many of the Hodenausaunee communities, raised beadwork was particularly typical of Tuscarora and Mohawk work. Moccasins made in this style were not only sold to tourists, but also acquired by aboriginal people from different nations and worn as part of formal dress (Fig. 11).

After the Civil War the federal governments of Canada and the United States embarked on a policy of directed assimilation, using Christianization and education as a two-pronged strategy designed to eliminate the vestiges of indigenous culture. Floral imagery in Native North American beadwork was understood by non-Natives to exemplify a rejection of traditional "pagan" images and beliefs and acceptance of a peaceful, civilized, and Christian way of life. During the second half of the nineteenth-century floral designs also carried positive associations with ideals of womanhood and domesticity, explaining why the floral beadwork used by Native women to ornament dress and household accessories was so popular with Victorian consumers (Phillips 1990: 32–33; 1998: 182–195).

Purplish-red glazed cotton and green glazed cotton line the outside and inside of the exquisite little lady's purse in the Leiden collection (Fig. 12), decorated with flat and raised beadwork with flower, foliage, and bird designs. This small bag is typical of a genre made for commercial sale and is a type of purse often purchased for children. An almost identical one can be seen being offered for sale at Niagara Falls in an 1889 photograph by J. G. Parks of Montreal (World Museum, Rotterdam no. F 4995/78; see also Hovens and Groeneveld 1992: 57, 101, 107).

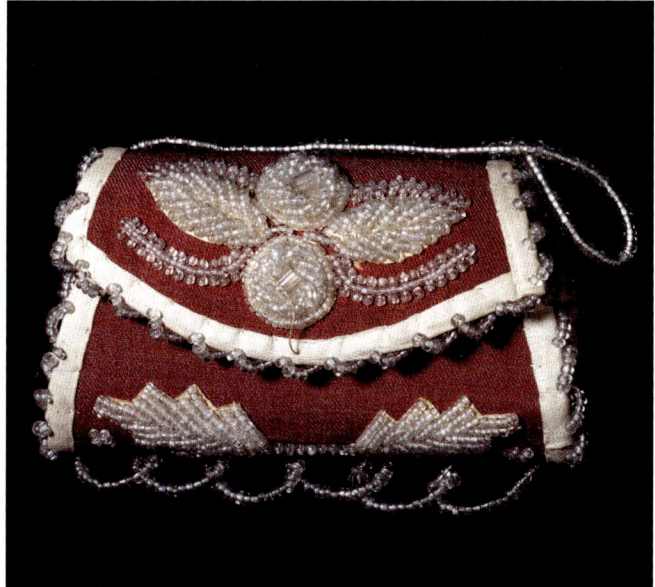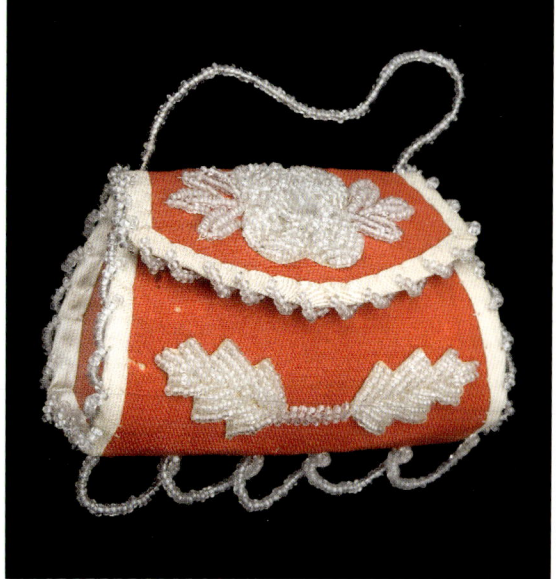

Figs. 12, 13   Tuscarora purses; RMV 362-6: cardboard, glazed cotton, glass; l. 9–13 cm, h. 7–8.5 cm, w. 4 cm; WMR 17989: cardboard, cloth, glass; l. 13 cm, h. 8 cm; both ca. 1880.

The Rotterdam specimen is simpler in execution (Fig. 13). The white-on-red beadwork on both purses is typical of the work of Tuscarora women during the second half of the nineteenth century. Both specimens have similar beaded designs, with a bird taking center stage. Large predatory birds are a typical motif in early Great Lakes Indian art and represent the Thunderer spirits of the upper world. Eagle motifs appear in tourist art at an early date, sometimes in combination with the American flag, and were intended to appeal to the nationalist sensibilities of the buyers. There is no indication that the little beaded birds on these purses and other Great Lakes souvenir arts of the period are derived from representations of the great supernatural beings of the upper world, although the persistent importance of bird motifs suggests continuity with earlier spiritual beliefs and imagistic traditions (cf. Phillips 1998: 139–140).

Iroquois Pincushions

During the late nineteenth-century pincushions assumed many fanciful forms that appealed to the Victorian taste for "novelties." When Niagara Falls became a market for Native-made souvenirs, pincushions—sometimes embroidered with dates, place names, and mottos—emerged as a popular type of curio to buy and take home for display and practical use. As well, Northeastern souvenir producers also made other sewing accessories such as scissors and needle cases of cloth ornamented with beads or birchbark

embroidered with porcupine quills. These could be purchased separately or with birchbark sewing baskets of various sizes and shapes.

Hodenosaunee souvenir producers invented pincushions that gave three-dimensional form to the bird and berry motif favored in their other embroidery. They also reinterpreted in cloth and beads the shape of a lady's shoe or boot that was popular in metal match safes and other industrially produced Victorian novelties. Their inventiveness participated in a longer tradition. Pincushions were first recorded in fifteenth-century England. Precious metal pins were formerly kept in ivory or silver receptacles, which became gradually replaced by stuffed "pin pillows" covered with silk and linen, often ornamented with embroidery, lace, tassels, and bead decoration. Over time, materials, shapes, and decoration took on immense variation, and in the eighteenth century pincushions emerged as a popular souvenir genre whose exotic materials, shapes, and decoration referred to the peoples and places visited. During the eighteenth and nineteenth centuries pincushions and other needlework accessories became icons of femininity and domesticity, womanhood and motherhood. In upper class circles they were sometimes incorporated into a woman's dress, attached to or hanging from a waist belt.

Ten Kate purchased an example of this kind of object at Niagara Falls, New York. It is a star-shaped pincushion, ornamented with a beaded floral design and a looped

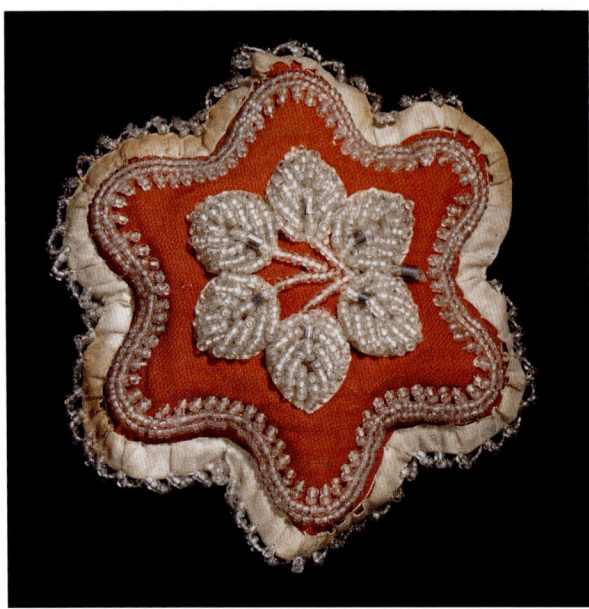

Fig. 14 Hodenosaunee (possibly Seneca) pincushion; *ye:wéotahkwa* (Tooker 1994: 101; also cf. 277); cloth, glass; d. 15 cm, h. 5 cm; ca. 1880 (RMV 362-23).

fringe (Fig. 14). He was told by the seller—an unidentified individual whom he deemed reliable—that it was made by a Kickapoo girl or woman and came from Kansas or Indian Territory (Ten Kate, letter from St. Louis, 16 December 1882; ARMV no. 273). However, it seems unlikely that this attribution was correct. The Algonquian-speaking Kickapoo, probably originally a branch of the Shawnee, had left their original homeland in southeastern Michigan in the early eighteenth century, just before the arrival of Europeans, and were living in Kansas by the time that this beadwork style was invented. The colors, materials, and white-on-red beadwork style of the pincushion are un-mistakably Hodenosaunee, most likely Seneca or Tuscarora. A very similar pincushion, possibly made by a member of the family of Ten Kate's host at Tuscarora, Caroline Parker Mount Pleasant, was illustrated by Lewis Henry Morgan in his classic 1852 publication (Morgan 1852: fig 19; Phillips 1998: 56).

It is possible that the Kickapoo attribution was recounted to Ten Kate to satisfy an interest in the western tribes he was about to visit which he had made obvious—for sellers everywhere do their best to please their customers. It is also true, however, that by the 1880s Hodenosaunee entertainers and beadwork sellers were traveling by rail to western Canada and the United States; a well-known photograph shows the St. Regis Indian Show Company (a Mohawk group from Akwesasne) wearing beaded clothing while visiting Lawrence, Kansas, in 1894 (Phillips 1998: 15). It is therefore not impossible that the pincushion was made by a Kickapoo woman married to a Hodenosaunee man.

The shoe or boot was a popular shape for manufactured Victorian novelties such as metal match safes and pincushions, but Hodenosaunee women made it peculiarly their own by rendering it in cloth, cardboard, and beadwork and it became one of their most popular souvenir wares (Fig. 15). Hanging ornaments in the shapes of birds holding beaded berries in their mouths also became popular toward the end of the nineteenth century and offer further evidence of the continuing importance of bird imagery in Hodenosaunee communities (Fig. 16). They have been in continuous production through to the present and are today sometimes used as Christmas tree ornaments (cf. Faulkner et al. 1998).

Figs. 15, 16 Effigy pincushions; WMR 17990: Hodenosaunee shoe effigy; cardboard, cloth, glass; l. 15 cm, w. 8 cm; WMR 17991: Tuscarora bird effigy: cardboard, cloth, glass; l. 22 cm, w. 15 cm; both ca. 1880.

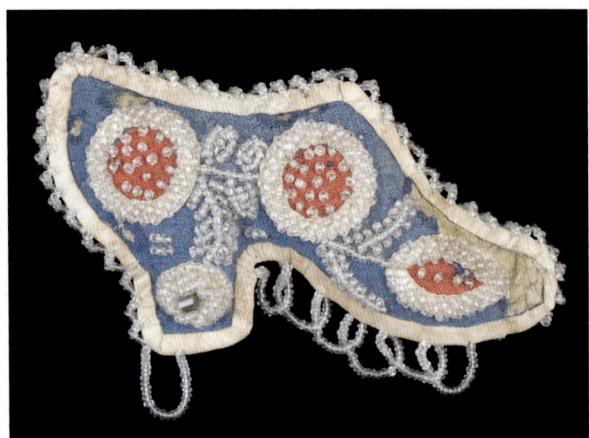

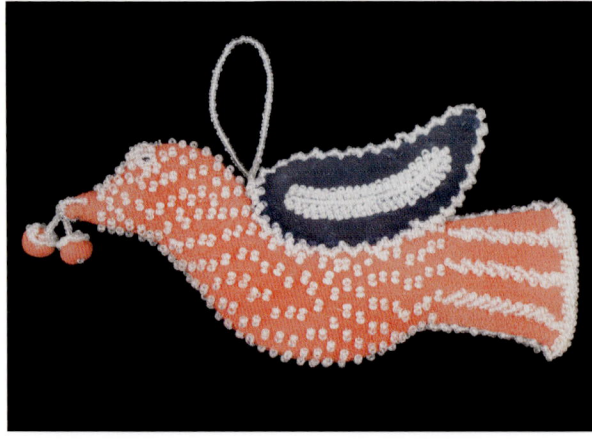

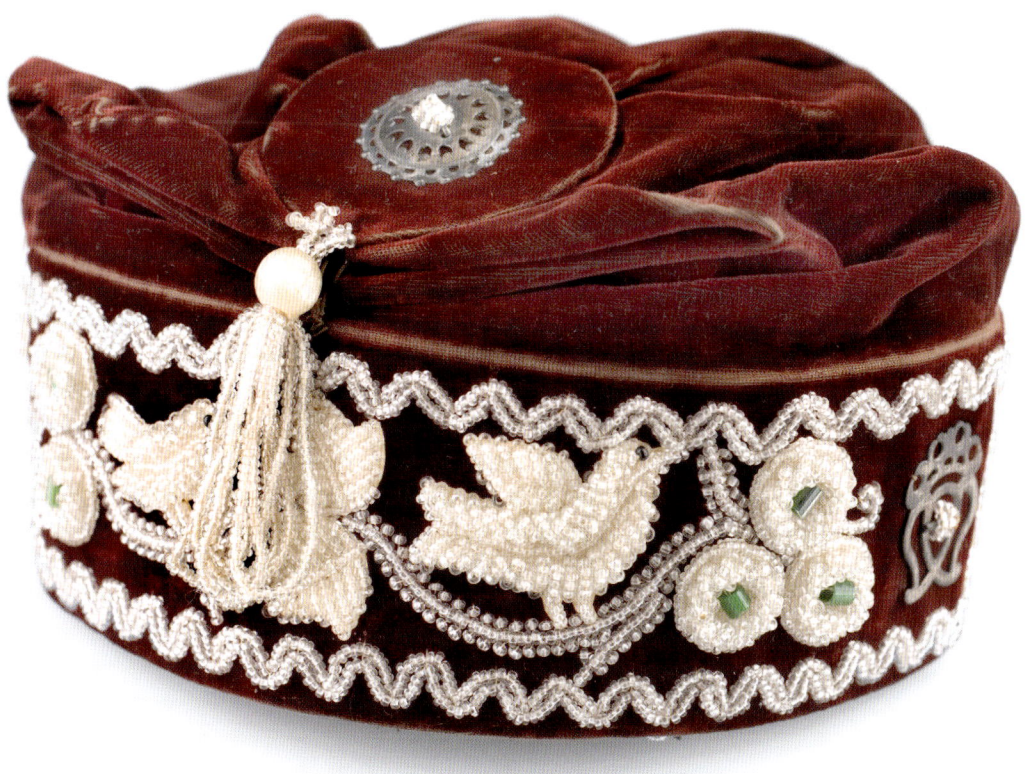

Fig. 17   Tuscarora smoking hat; velvet, cardboard, silver, glass; h. 11.5 cm, d. 19.5 cm; ca. 1880 (WMR 17977).

The traditional Iroquois chief's headdress was the *gustoweh*. Traditionally it consisted of a feathered hide cap, a sewn-on quilled headband with a prominent frontal decoration, often representing the sun, the major *manitou* of Woodland peoples. It underwent a series of changes due to interethnic contact and by the mid-nineteenth century was made of trade cloth with a cloth or silver headband and one or more rotating feathers on the top of the crown. Further alterations to the style of Hodenosaunee men's headgear took place when the headbands became scalloped, pierced, and decorated with raised floral beadwork.

Ten Kate's hat (Fig. 17) is of a very different kind, intended for use by the settlers and tourists who bought beaded headgear in a number of different styles to wear as traveling and smoking caps. This example is inspired by the orientalizing vogue for men's smoking caps. Its typical Tuscarora designs of birds, berries, and leaves are further energized and enlivened by bold double borders of zigzag lines and by the addition of a trade-silver brooch pinned to the top. Although such brooches commonly adopt sun-like rayed forms found also on the traditional *gustoweh*, silver brooches and other ornaments had first been introduced during the early contact period as diplomatic gifts made by Europeans to Aboriginal people as well as through the fur trade, but by the nineteenth century were also being made by Hodenosaunee silversmiths (Morgan 1851: 386–389; Canada House 1985: 7–9, 13; Lyford 1982: 67–70; Phillips 1990: 28–30; 1998: 240–247; Biron 2006: 27–29).

While staying on the Tuscarora Reservation near Niagara Falls, Ten Kate was hosted by the family of Caroline Parker, Mrs. Mount Pleasant. During this encounter a rapport seemed to be immediately established between the two intellectuals and they subsequently exchanged several letters. In one of these she commented on the disappearance of Indian tribes and wrote: "Among the names, the echo of which still resounds, is that of the once mighty Iroquois Confederacy. ... Oh, what are the poor Iroquois now! ... Their land no longer lies 'in the shadows.' One by one oblivion snatches away their finest children. Swiftly their wise sachems follow each other to the grave; swiftly, very swiftly not one shall remain unless Providence intervenes. In vain

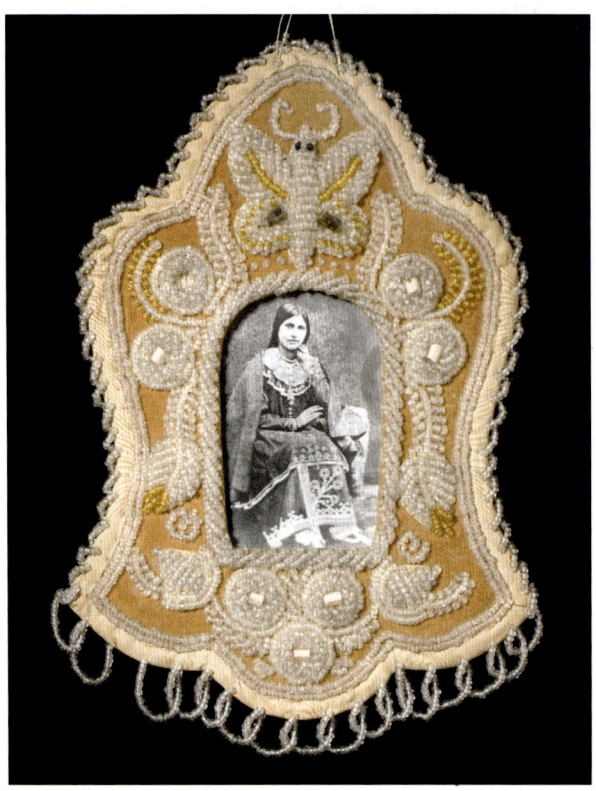

Fig. 18 Tuscarora picture frame with photograph of Caroline Parker, Seneca; cardboard, cloth, glass; h. 22 cm, w. 16 cm; ca. 1880 (WMR 17979).

does my spirit wander across mountains, lakes, and rushing streams to find anyone who is familiar with the old oral traditions of the Iroquois, but all have departed. Their council fires have died out and turned to cold ash and will never blaze again. Oh, worthy brother, forgive me for dwelling on a subject that always saddens me. It makes me sad to know that my people are vanishing, like the summer passes into the stormy winter."

From Caroline Parker Ten Kate received a picture frame with her photograph (Fig. 18). The frame exhibits an unusual motif of a beaded butterfly at the top. Its curving antennae create a focal point, beautifully set off by the late Victorian neo-gothic contours of the frame and rhythmically echoed by the tendrils that curve around the floral motifs on its sides and bottom. The floral beadwork is also mirrored in the ornamentation of the dress worn by Caroline Parker in the photograph—the same dress also seen on the engraving/lithograph in Morgan's *League of the Hodenosaunee* (1851: opp. p. 148) and in a contemporary daguerreotype in the Southwest Museum (Tooker 1994: 30–31; Phillips 1998: 224). The picture given to Ten Kate was probably taken around the same time. The beadwork on the picture frame is typical of 1880s Tuscarora

Figs. 19, 20 Tuscarora watch pockets; cardboard, cloth, glass beads; WMR 17992: l. 19.5 cm, w. 11.5 cm; WMR 25212: h. 19.2 cm. w. 9.5 cm, both ca. 1880.

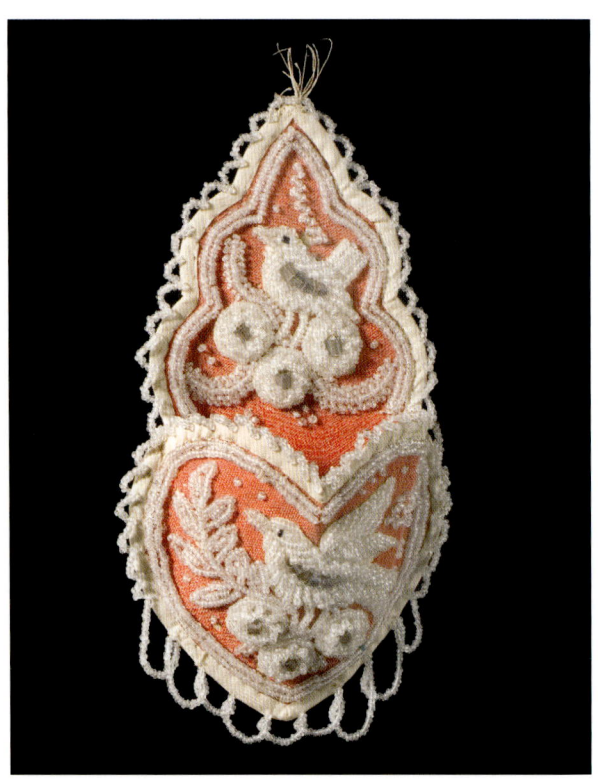

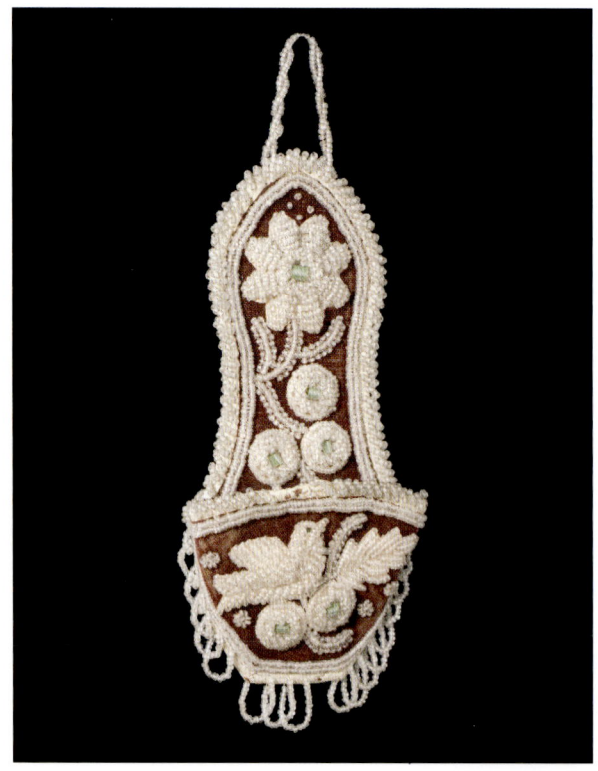

beadwork, but most probably not made by Caroline Parker herself, as she was known for her delicate style, expressed in the use of small beads and highly naturalistic designs.

Beaded wall pockets designed to hold matches, grooming accessories, letters and stamps, photographs, brooms, and other items became popular souvenir items. They functioned both as ornaments for the home and as devices for ordering and containing the plenitude of newly affordable manufactured objects that threatened to clutter the Victorian house (Phillips 1998: 219, 234–237). Birds and flowers are the motifs most frequently encountered on Iroquois beaded wall pockets of the period.

The two wall pockets collected by Ten Kate (Figs. 19, 20) were meant to be hung next to the owner's bed so that he could keep his silver or gold pocket watch safe and handy while he slept. Both display typical motifs of birds, flowers, and berries made of the translucent glass beads sewn onto red velvet or cotton cloth that were typical of Tuscarora souvenir crafts of the period. Contemporary Tuscarora beadworkers explain the positive associations of the motifs with fertility and spiritual communication (cf. Phillips 1998: 219).

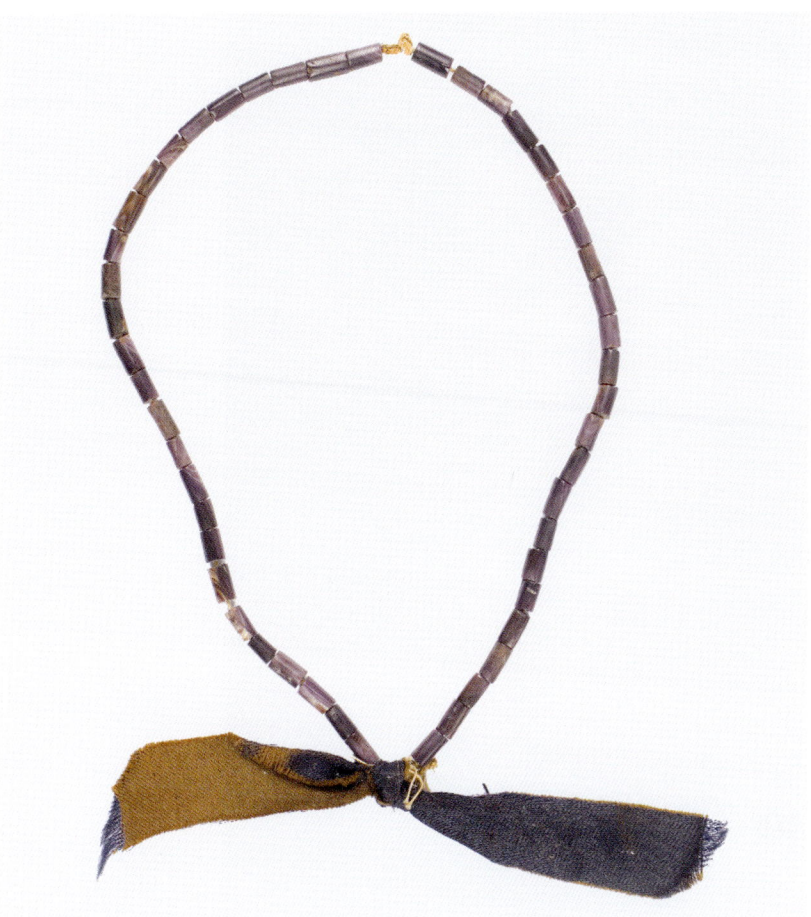

Fig. 21   String of wampum, Seneca; shell (*wampum*), cotton, silk; l. 26 cm; ca. 1880 (WMR 17978).

String of Wampum

Ten Kate received a string of wampum from Caroline S. Parker, Mrs. Mount Pleasant, after his Seneca adoption ceremony (Fig. 21). He cherished this token of status throughout the decades of fieldwork, research, and life on all continents. In 1910 he finally donated it, together with some other artifacts, to the Museum of Anthropology (now: World Museum) in Rotterdam.

In pre-Columbian times, shell was often used as material for beads. Frequently small shells were used whole on strings and large shells as pendants. Shell was also worked in various ways to produce a great variety of beads. The oceans as well as freshwater lakes, rivers, and streams pro-

vided a rich source of this raw material. In other cases shell was traded extensively with tribes in whose territory this material was not available, or small parties from inland people traveled far and wide to exploit coastal resources.

Wampum is a cylindrical white or purple shell bead, predominantly made from the quahog or hard-clam (*Venus mercenaria*). The introduction of iron tools by Europeans led to an explosion in the production of the tubular bead. This was done by cutting and polishing. The Iroquoian and Algonquian tribes of eastern North America used it as currency, as jewelry, to convey messages (by certain arrangements of colors), and woven into belts with purple figures against a white background as documents of major historical events such as treaties. When early White settlers became aware of their importance, some also became engaged in their manufacture, with the Dutch of New Netherlands (1606–1664) as the most active and productive in this craft (Orchard 1929: 19, 71–87; Gilman 1982: 99).

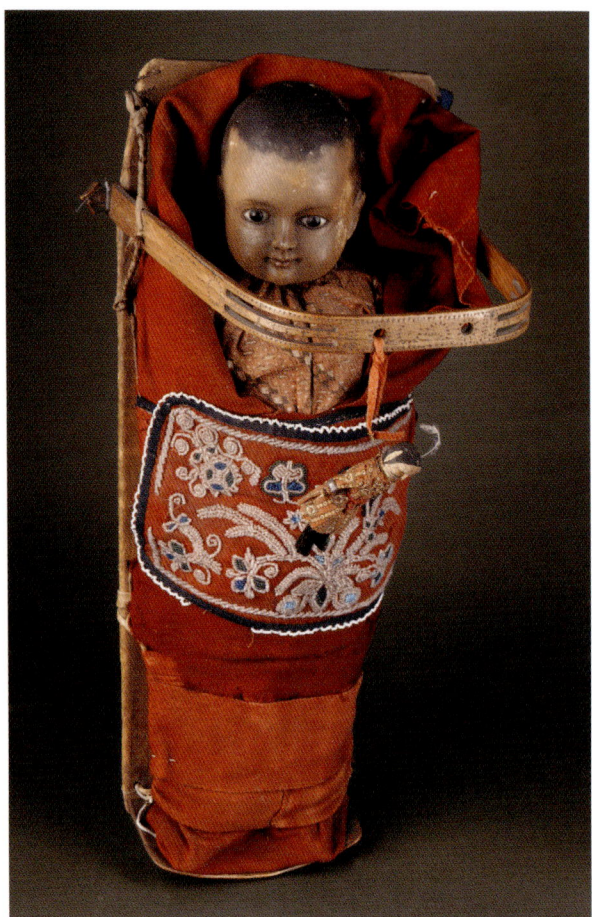

Fig. 22 Tuscarora cradle; *ga-on-seh* (Morgan 1850: 205, pl. 16; 1852: 76-77); wood, cloth, glass, papier mâché; h. 60 cm, w. 27-29 cm; 1870-1880 (RMV 362-7).

Fig. 23 Seneca model cradle; wood, silk, glass; l. 24 cm, w. 6.8-9.3 cm; ca. 1880 (RMV 710-26).

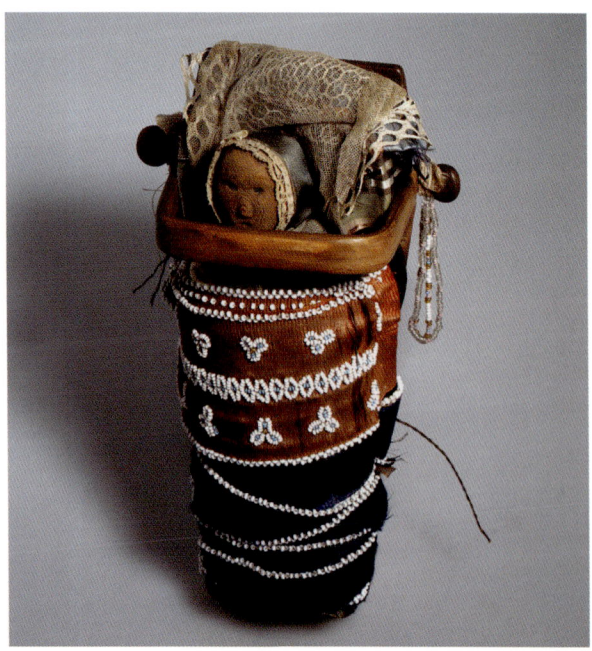

Northeastern Native cradleboards provided babies with comfort and security and were at once practical, beautiful, and uniquely North American. Borne by the mother on her back and supported by a burdenstrap tied across her forehead, they were easy to carry while traveling and could be secured to a tree while she was working. Hodenosaunee mothers tied shiny ornaments and charms to the hoop to entertain the child and protect it from harm, and they lavished some of their finest artistry and needlework on the embroidered outer coverings. The panel on this cradleboard cover in the Ten Kate collection (Fig. 22) displays floral designs and a butterfly executed in beadwork. Men carved intricate chipwork designs on the hoop, sun and moon designs in this case, and sometimes painted or carved birds, flowers, and the Great Tree of Peace on the back or foot board (cf. Brasser 1976: 154, 157; Conn 1979: 53; 1979a; Lyford 1982: 56, 58).

Ten Kate purchased this full-sized cradleboard on the Tuscarora Reservation, a few miles northeast of Niagara Falls, where members of the tribe had settled since the late eighteenth century, supporting themselves through farming, wage labor, and the production of souvenirs for the tourist trade (Landy 1978: 521–522; Hovens 1984: 38). The doll was not part of the original purchase, and Ten Kate asked his sister Madelon to add it before shipping the cradleboard to Europe to make it more eye-catching for museum and government officials in the Netherlands. Such a strategy would have been necessary to obtain financial support for his collecting project. Ten Kate reported to director Lindor Serrurier, for example, that colleagues at the Smithsonian Institution in Washington had stressed to him that the acquisition of traditional artifacts of good quality required substantial funds (Ten Kate to Serrurier, 16 December 1882; ARMV no. 273).

Cradleboards attracted the interest of visitors to North America from the earliest days of contact, and miniature cradleboards appear in a number of eighteenth-century European collections. Miniatures were made as educational toys for Aboriginal girls by many tribes. However, small cradles were also produced for the emerging souvenir trade, and it is difficult to know if the example collected by Ten Kate (Fig. 23) was intended to be a Native toy, a tourist souvenir, or made on commission for a specific customer (Hovens and Krosenbrink 1994: 56; Phillips 1998: 81–92; cf. FIA 1973: 100, fig. 469).

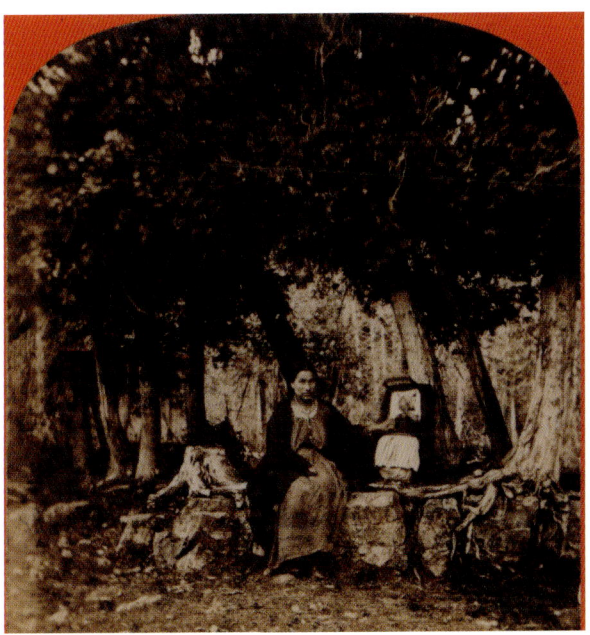

Fig. 24   Tuscarora woman with baby in cradle. Photograph (left side shown) by Saul Davis, ca. 1870–1880 (Ten Kate coll.; WMR 902281).

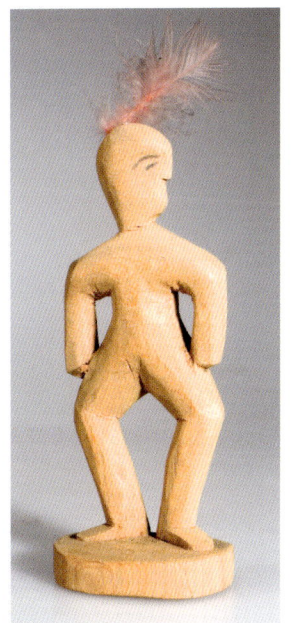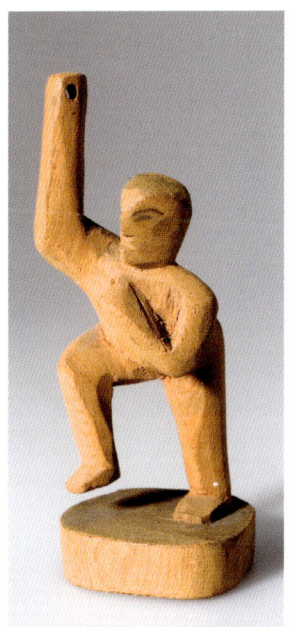

Figs. 25, 26   Tuscarora miniature human figures; RMV 2012-10: wood, feather; h. 10.5 cm; WMR 17994: wood; h. 10 cm; both ca. 1880.

Tuscarora Miniature Human Figures

Unlike the other pieces in Ten Kate's Northeastern collection, these figures are not representative of the contemporary souvenir genre. Rather, they appear to exemplify both the artistic innovation and the playing to stereotype that was stimulated by the tourist trade. The simply carved representation of an Indian warrior (Fig. 25) was probably created as a unique example or as one of a small number of similar items to satisfy the desire for cheap, quickly produced souvenirs. Though formally minimalist, the figure is linked to a long tradition of woodcarving and sculpture in northeastern North America that is characterized by a refined, simplified naturalism. The style can be seen in the beautifully carved anthropomorphic heads and figures incorporated into finely made war clubs, bowls, spoons, pipe bowls, masks, and lacrosse sticks, as well as on a few large-scale effigies. Most of these traditional types of sculpture ceased to be made or were removed from public view during the nineteenth and twentieth centuries as warfare ceased and Christian missionaries and government officials suppressed traditional forms of spirituality and ritual. Hodenosaunee anthropomorphic and zoomorphic flat wood carvings were also made for use in the traditional bowl game and were usually destroyed immediately after. These game pieces also might have served as a source of inspiration for this small sculpture (Blau et al. 1978: 497; Phillips 1987: 86–87; Maurer 1989). WMR

17994 (Fig. 26) is a well-carved three-dimensional "action-doll" and exhibits the qualities of the Tuscarora woodcarver, probably the same person who made the Leiden specimen. Similar three-dimensional carvings, including figures with False Face masks, are encountered in some museum collections, but are of a much later date.

Mi'kmaq Quilled Boxes

The Mi'kmaq originated the technique of porcupine quill appliqué onto the bark of the white birch (*Betula papyrifera*) to decorate birchbark boxes and other items. The earliest documents mentioning these objects date from the mid-seventeenth century, and during the first half of the eighteenth century the Mi'kmaq began making such decorative artifacts for the curio trade. Round and oval lidded boxes, the latter shape probably adapted from European wooden boxes used for packing and storage, became the most popular genre and account for seventy percent of Mi'kmaq quillwork in museum collections. They were often made in nested sets of graduated sizes. Birchbark sections were sewn together with the roots from black spruce (*Picea mariana*) and, in the case of boxes, attached to wooden bottoms. Over time, the Mi'kmaq quillwork repertoire came to include jewelry boxes, hat cases, flower pots and saucers, lampshades, wastepaper baskets, tea cozies, fans, cases for cigars, spectacles, watches, needles, and calling cards, and seat and back panels for European wood-framed chairs.

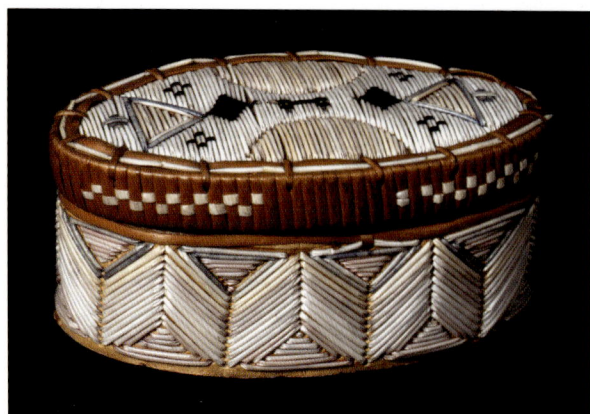

Fig. 27 Mi'kmaq oval lidded box; birchbark, spruce root, porcupine quills, wood, pigments; l. 11.7 cm, w. 6.5 cm, h. 5 cm; 1870-1880 (RMV 362-8).

quills were taken from porcupines (*Erithizon dorsatum*), the finer ones picked from young animals. Dyes came from vegetal sources, bloodroot (*Sanguinaria canadensis*) producing a glowing red-brown and red bedstraw (*Galium tinctorium*) a bright red, goldthread (*Coptis trifolia*) providing pale yellow, and logwood staining quills blue. Green dye was probably—obtained from the yew (*Taxus Canadensis*), and over time commercial indigo became increasingly popular. After 1860 aniline dyes came into use (Wallis and Wallis 1955: 87-92; Whitehead 1980; 1982; 1987: 35, 40-41; 1990: 31, 37-43; also cf. Conn 1979a: 67; Canada House 1985: 16-19; McBride 1990: 327; Spooner 2001: 54; Coe 2003: 124-128; Cook 2005: 228-230, 234-235).

Inventories of Mi'kmaq materials in European collections have been published by Ruth Holmes Whitehead (1988, 1989). Of the quilled birchbark box in the Ten Kate collection (Fig. 27), she observed: "Oval lidded box has wooden base, treen-pegged to exterior of a single large band of birchbark, quilled in the chevron pattern; with a border of spruce root at the top, oversewn with spruce root. Birchbark lining projects above box side; lid fits over lining. Lid side a ring of bark wrapped with spruce root; porcupine quills interwoven through the root wrapping in checker patterns, quills an undyed white. Lid top an oval of bark with a quillwork mosaic. Geometric patterns, with dye-colors undeterminable; border of one length of spruce

In the earliest boxes only the tops were covered with a colorful quill mosaic whose intricate geometries were often designed with the aid of a compass. During the nineteenth century Mi'kmaq women began to quill the sides of boxes as well. Although the geometric motifs appear to be decorative rather than symbolic, the semicircular design has been identified as an earth symbol, and Mi'kmaq artists also sometimes quilled representational images of animals or flowers. Although quilled barkwork developed specifically as a souvenir production, the Mi'kmaq had long used dyed porcupine quills to ornament clothing, pipestems, tobacco pouches, rattles, and snowshoes. The

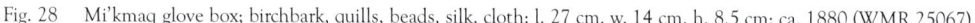

Fig. 28 Mi'kmaq glove box; birchbark, quills, beads, silk, cloth; l. 27 cm, w. 14 cm, h. 8.5 cm; ca. 1880 (WMR 25067).

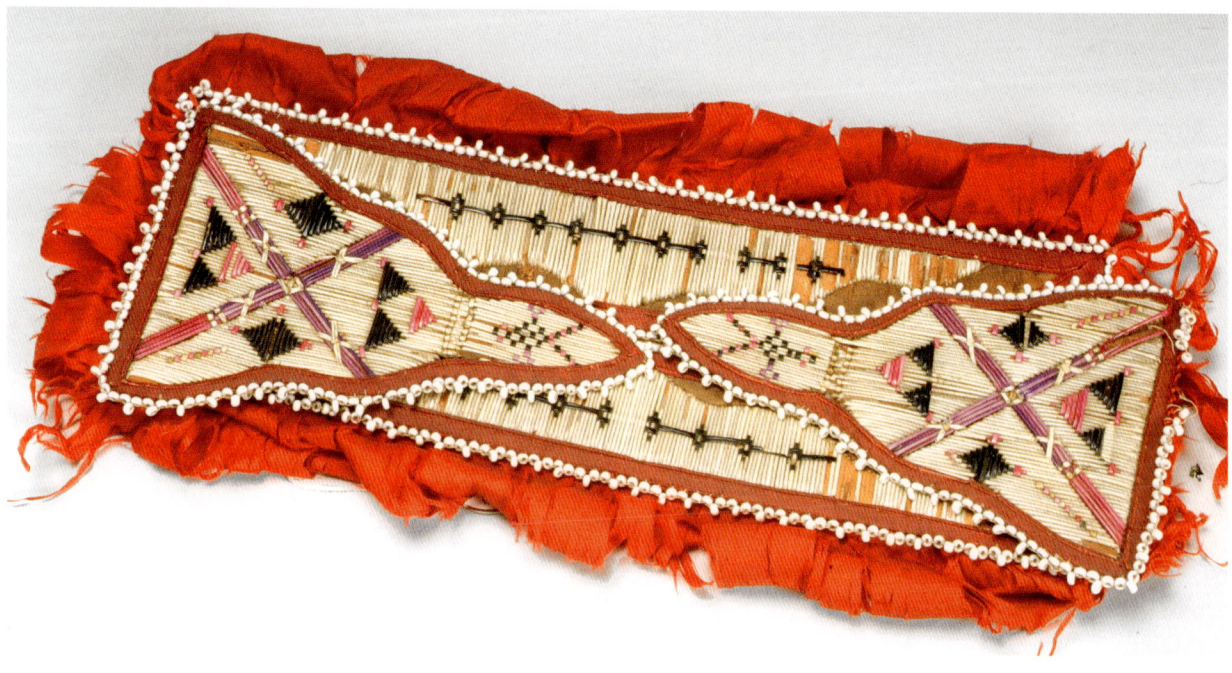

root and single lengths of telescoped quills. Lid sewn together with root. This root is still tan rather than faded brown, indicating it was never dyed and is relative late." The chevron pattern may be a stylized representation of a fir tree (Whitehead 1980: 43; 1989: 66, 68).

Glove boxes (Fig. 28) were popular with late nineteenth-century souvenir buyers and used to organize a lady's accessories and to ornament her dressing table or bureau. Such boxes were made by a number of different souvenir producers, such as the Huron-Wendat near Quebec City and the peoples of the Canada's Maritimes provinces, for sale at tourist resorts throughout the northeast. The German traveler Kohl (1861, 1: 180), for example, described seeing such wares being packed for transport to Niagara Falls when he visited the Huron-Wendat village of Lorette in the 1850s. This box can be attributed to the Mi'kmaq, who inserted porcupine quills into birchbark panels to form intricate geometric patterns. On this example red silk ribbon borders enrich the quillwork designs. The box is lined with muslin and a panel of bright red silk is inserted to form the sides. Ten Kate would have purchased the box at one of the souvenir shops at Niagara Falls.

Anishinaabe Quilled Boxes

The birchbark souvenir arts of the Anishinaabe include a wide range of boxes, wall pockets, mats, handbags, glove and handkerchief boxes, and other objects. These wares evolved rapidly during the middle decades of the nineteenth century, undoubtedly stimulated by the new markets that developed in the central Great Lakes and by the examples offered by the earlier Mi'kmaq and convent productions of birchbark fancy work. The Anishinaabe wares developed out of two precontact forms, a shallow bowl and a high-sided container. Both were made out of folded birchbark sewn with spruce root. The bowls were sometimes ornamented with colored porcupine quills wrapped around the rims and the containers with geometric designs scraped to reveal the lighter inner layer of bark. In contrast, the innovative floral and geometric motifs introduced around 1820 were formed by inserting dyed porcupine quills into the bark surfaces. Unlike Mi'kmaq quillwork, however, the designs were usually set off against the plain bark surface rather than covering it completely (cf. Strukelj 1979: 661–663).

Specific iconographic meanings have not been associated with these designs. Rather, they often suggest the fundamental concepts that structure the Anishinaabe cosmos. The scalloped circle formed by the decorative border on the lid of RMV 362-9 (Fig. 30), for example, resembles motifs found in other media that represent the sun, the supreme power of the cosmos, while the equal-armed cross combined with a square found on the lid of RMV 362-3 (Fig. 29 right) suggests the four cardinal directions of the universe. The design on RMV 362-4 (Fig. 29 left) can be interpreted as floral, while RMV 362-9 exhibits a six-pointed star motif (cf. Coleman 1947: 7–11). Two of the boxes collected by Ten Kate display the lavish use of aromatic sweetgrass (*Hieroclöe odorata*), which became popular during the latter decades of the nineteenth century.

Many of the vegetal dyes used by the Anishinaabe to color their porcupine quills are fugitive, as exemplified in

Figs. 29, 30   Anishinaabe quilled and embroidered souvenir birchbark boxes; RMV 362-4; birchbark, sweetgrass, porcupine quills, pigment; d. 11.5 cm, h. 6 cm; RMV 362-3: birchbark, sweetgrass, porcupine quills, pigment; d. 10.5 cm, h. 5.5 cm; RMV 362-9: birchbark, porcupine quills, pigment; d. 11.8 cm, h. 6.5 cm; all ca. 1880.

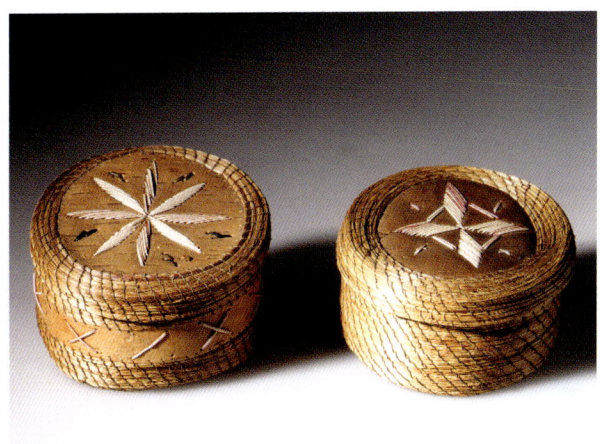

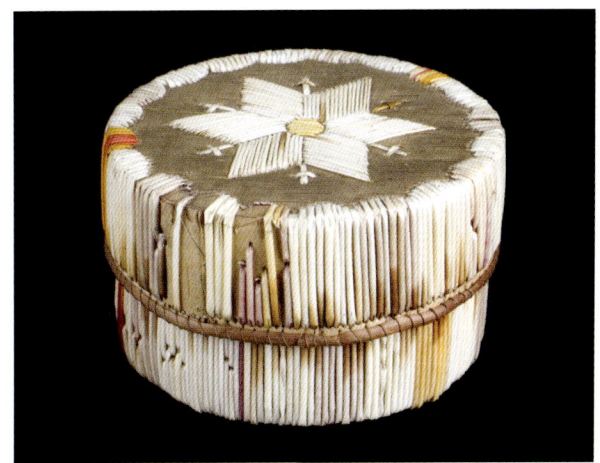

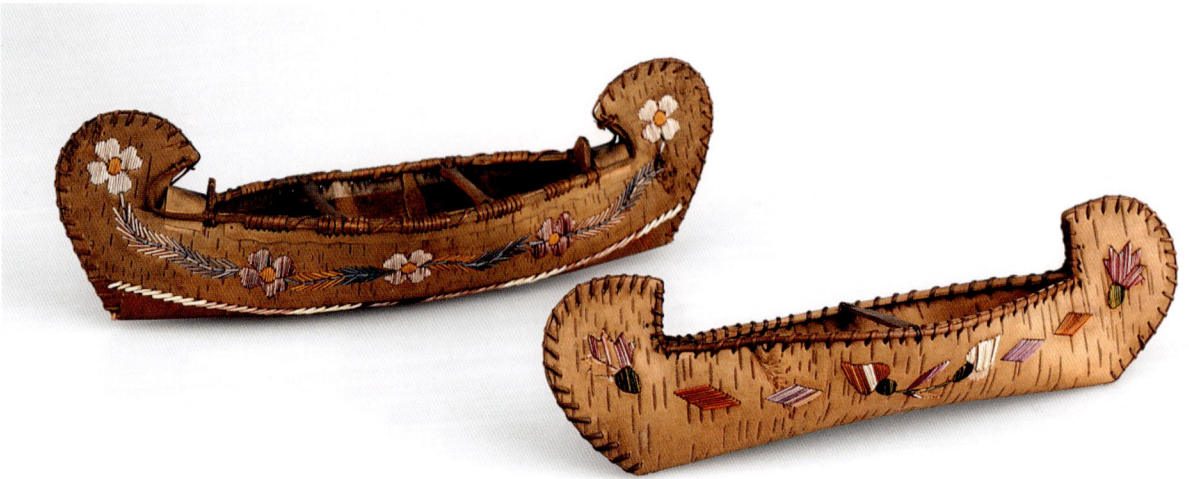

Fig. 31   Anishinaabe quilled miniature birchbark canoes; RMV 362-2: birchbark, porcupine quills, wood, pigment; l. 39.5 cm, w. 12.5 cm, h. 7 cm; RMV 2012-12: birchbark, porcupine quills, pigment; l. 39 cm, w. 9.5 cm; both ca. 1880.

these three boxes. Red came from blood root (*Sanguinaria*), as well as dogwood (*Cornus florida*), eastern hemlock (*Tsuga canadensis*), puccoon (*Lithospermum carolinense*), and wild plum (*Prunus americana*). Yellow was derived from gold thread (*Coptis*), lichens (*Usnea barbata*), and sumac (*Rhus glabra*). A second boiling strengthened colors, while mud with an iron content acted as mordant (Lyford 1942: 152–154).

Birchbark Canoes

Like cradleboards, birchbark canoes (Fig. 31) were widely admired as a quintessential invention of the Aboriginal peoples of northeastern North America. The finest were made by the Algonkian-speaking peoples of the northern woodlands and Great Lakes. Models of these canoes from Atlantic Canada are found in European collections that date to the seventeenth century, while many of the examples that date from the nineteenth century can be attributed to the souvenir production of the Anishinaabe (Ojibwe, Chippewa, Potawatomi, and Odawa) peoples of the central Great Lakes. As on Anishinaabe boxes and other birchbark wares, women formed floral, geometric, and figural motifs by inserting dyed and moistened porcupine quills into the surface of the bark through holes formed by awls. The expansion of the quills when dry and the shrinking of the bark around the inserted quill holds the design elements firmly in place (cf. FIA 1975: 99; Brasser 1976: 134; Thompson 1977: 146; McGregor 1983; Coe 2003: 182–185).

Anishinaabe, like other northeastern peoples, traditionally believed that many aspects of the non-human world, including canoes, are animated by spiritual powers (Hallowell 1976). One of the Ten Kate canoes (RMV 362-2) includes "man-boards" at the two ends that represent its spiritual powers (Ritzenthaler 1950: 20). The quilled, four-petaled flowers are representations of wild roses (Coleman 1947: 7–8, 11).

References

Barbeau, Marius C.
  1928   The Origin of Floral and other Designs among the Canadian and Neighbouring Indians. *Proceedings of the 23rd International Congress of Americanists*, 512.
  1943   *Saintes Artisanes I: Les Brodeuses*. Montreal, QC: Cahiers d'Art Arca.
Biron, Gerry
  2006   *Made of Thunder, Made of Glass: American Indian Beadwork of the Northeast*. Saxtons River, VT: Gerry Biron.
Blau, Harold, Jack Campisi, and Elisabeth Tooker
  1978   Onondaga. In: Bruce G. Trigger (ed.), *Northeast* (Handbook of North American Indians 15. W. C. Sturtevant, gen. ed.; Washington, DC: Smithsonian Institution), 491–499.
Bol, Marsha C.
  1998   *American Indians and the Natural World*. Pittsburgh, PA: Carnegie Museum of Natural History.
Brasser, Ted
  1976   *Bo'jou, Neejee! Profiles of Canadian Indian Art*. Ottawa, ON: National Museum of Man.
  1987   Flowers in Native American Art: A Review. Paper presented to the Native American Art Studies Association, Denver, CO.

1998 Blessed with Beauty: Quillwork and Beadwork of the Plains and Woodland Indians. In: Allen Wardwell (ed.), *Native Paths: American Indian Art from the Collection of Charles and Valerie Diker* (New York, NY: Metropolitan Museum of Art), 25-72.

Canada House

1985 *Mohawk, Micmac, Maliseet and Other Indian Souvenir Art from Victorian Canada.* London: Canada House.

Coe, Ralph T.

2003 *The Responsive Eye: Ralph T. Coe and the Collecting of American Indian Art.* New York, NY: Metropolitan Museum of Art.

Coleman, Sister Bernard

1947 *Decorative Designs of the Ojibwa of Minnesota.* Washington, DC: Catholic University of North America Press.

Conn, Richard

1979a *Native American Art in the Denver Art Museum.* Denver, CO: Denver Art Museum.

1979b Floral Design in Native North America. In: *Native American Art from the Permanent Collection* (Claremont, CA: Claremont Pomona College).

Cook, Stephen W.

2005 Baskets of the Northeastern Woodlands. In: Jill R. Chancey (ed.), *By Native Hands: Woven Treasures from the Lauren Rogers Museum of Art* (Laurel, MS: Lauren Rogers Museum of Art), 218-237.

Faulkner, G. F., N. T. Prince, and J. S. Neptune

1998 Beautifully Beaded: Northeastern Native American Beadwork. *American Indian Art Magazine* 24(1): 32-41.

Fenton, William N. and Elisabeth Tooker

1978 Mohawk. In: Bruce G. Trigger (ed.), *Northeast* (Handbook of North American Indians 15. W. C. Sturtevant, gen. ed.; Washington, DC: Smithsonian Institution), 466-480.

FIA

1975 *Art of the Great Lakes Indians.* Flint, MI: Flint Institute of Arts.

Gérin, Léon

1901 *The Hurons of Lorette.* Report on the Ethnological Survey of Canada; British Association for the Advancement of Science, Appendix 111. London.

Gilman, Carolyn

1982 *Where Two Worlds Meet: The Great Lakes Fur Trade.* St. Paul, MN: Minnesota Historical Society.

Gordon, Beverly

1984 The Niagara Falls Whimsy: The Object as Symbol or Cultural Interface. Ph.D. thesis, University of Wisconsin, Madison, WI.

1986 The Souvenirs of Niagara Falls: The Significance of Indian Whimsies. *New York History* 67: 389-409.

Hall, Judy

2001 To Make Them Beautiful: Porcupine Quill Decorated Moccasins from the St. Lawrence-Great Lakes. In: Judy Thompson et al. (eds.), *Fascinating Challenges: Studying Material Culture with Dorothy Burnham* (Canadian Ethnology Service Paper 136. Hull, QC: Canadian Museum of Civilization), 236-262.

Hallowell, A. Irving

1976 Ojibwa Ontology, Behavior and World View. In: Stanley Diamond (ed.), *A. Irving Hallowell: Contributions to Anthropology* (Chicago, IL: University of Chicago Press), 357-390.

Harding, Deborah G.

1994 Bagging the Tourist Market: A Descriptive and Statistical Study of Nineteenth Century Iroquois Beaded Bags. M.A. thesis, University of Pittsburgh.

Hatt, Gudmund

1916 *Moccasins and Their Relation to Arctic Footwear.* Memoirs of the American Anthropological Association 3. Menasha, WI.

Hill, Tom

1994 Visual Prayers. In: Tom Hill and Richard W. Hill (eds.), *Creation's Journey: Native American Identity and Belief* (Washington, DC: Smithsonian Institution Press), 14-19.

Hovens, Pieter

1984 Between Survival and Assimilation: The Visit of the Dutch Anthropologist Herman ten Kate to the Iroquois in 1882. In: P. Hovens (ed.), *North American Indian Studies: European Contributions to Science, Society and Art 2* (Aachen–Göttingen: Alano Verlag–Edition Herodot), 36-42.

Hovens, Pieter and Anneke Groeneveld

1992 *Odagot: Photographs of American Indians, 1860-1920.* Amsterdam: Fragment Uitgeverij.

Hovens, Pieter and Lilianne Krosenbrink-Gelissen

1994 Managing Papooses: The Anthropology of Cradling and Swaddling in Native North America. *Yumtzilob* 5(4): 283-314.

Kohl, Johannes Georg

1861 *Travels in Canada, and Through the States of New York and Pennsylvania.* London: George Manwaring.

Landy, David

1978 Tuscarora among the Iroquois. In: Bruce G. Trigger (ed.), *Northeast* (Handbook of North American Indians 15. W. C. Sturtevant, gen. ed.; Washington, DC: Smithsonian Institution), 518-524.

Lyford, Carrie A.

1942 *The Crafts of the Ojibwa.* Washington, DC: Department of Indian Affairs.

1982 Iroquois Crafts. Stevens Point, WI: Schneider. [Orig. ed.: Washington, DC: Department of the Interior; Bureau of Indian Affairs.]

McBride, Bunny

1990 *Our Lives in Our Hands: Micmac Indian Basketmakers.* Gardiner, ME: Tilbury House.

McGregor, Arthur

1983 The Tradescants as Collectors of Rarities. In: A. McGregor (ed.), *Tradescant's Rarities: Essays on the Foundation of the Ashmolean Museum, 1683* (Oxford: Clarendon Press), 17-23.

Maurer, Evan M.

1989 Representational and Symbolic Forms in Great Lakes-Area Woodland Sculpture. In: David W. Penney (ed.), *Great Lakes Indian Art* (Detroit, MI: Wayne State University Press), 22-39.

Morgan, Lewis Henry

  1850 Report to the Regents of the University upon the Articles Furnished to the Indian Collection. *Third Annual Report of the Regents of the University* (for 1849): 65–97.

  1851 *League of the Ho-de-no-sau-nee, or Iroquois.* Rochester, NY: Sage and Brother.

  1852 Report on the Fabrics, Inventions, Implements and Utensils of the Iroquois. *Fifth Annual Report of the Regents of the University* (for 1851): 67–177.

Morissonneau, Christian

  1978 Huron of Lorette. In: Bruce G. Trigger (ed.), *Northeast* (Handbook of North American Indians 15. W. C. Sturtevant, gen. ed.; Washington, DC: Smithsonian Institution), 389–393.

Orchard, William C.

  1929 *Beads and Beadwork of the American Indians.* Contributions from the Museum of the American Indian 11. New York, NY.

Penney, David W.

  1991 Floral Decoration and Culture Change: An Historical Interpretation of Motivation. *American Indian Culture and Research Journal* 15(1): 53–77.

Phillips, Ruth

  1984 *Patterns of Power: The Jasper Grant Collection and Great Lakes Indian Art of the Early Nineteenth Century.* Kleinburg, ON: McMichael Canadian Collection.

  1987 Northern Woodlands Artistic Traditions. In: Julia Harrison et al. (eds.), *The Spirit Sings: Artistic Traditions of Canada's First Peoples* (Toronto, ON–Calgary, AB: McClelland & Stewart–Glenbow Alberta Institute), 51–92.

  1990 Moccasins into Slippers: Woodlands Indian Hats, Bags, and Shoes in Tradition and Transformation. *Northeast Indian Quarterly* 7(4): 26–36.

  1998 *Trading Identities: The Souvenir in Native North American Art from the Northeast, 1700–1900.* Seattle, WA: University of Washington Press.

Rickard, Jolene

  1992 Cew Ete Haw I Tih: The Bird that Carries Language Back to Another. In: Lucy R. Lippard (ed.), *Partial Recall: Photographs of Native North Americans* (New York, NY: The New Press), 105–111.

Ritzenthaler, Robert E.

  1950 The Building of a Chippewa Indian Birchbark Canoe. *Milwaukee Public Museum Bulletin* 19(2): 53–99.

Speck, Frank G.

  1911a Huron Moosehair Embroidery. *American Anthropologist* n.s. 13(1): 1–14.

  1911b Notes on the Material Culture of the Huron. *American Anthropologist* n.s. 13(2): 208–228.

  1925 Dream Symbolism and the Desire Motif in Floral Designs of the Northeast. *The Guardian* 1: 124–127.

Spooner, Peter et al.

  2001 *Shared Passion: The Richard E. and Dorothy Rawlings Nelson Collection of American Indian Art.* Duluth, MN: Tweed Museum of Art.

Strukelj, Pavla

  1979 Applied Art of the Ojibwa Indians, 1830–1880. In:

Justine M. Cordell (ed.), *The Visual Arts: Plastic and Graphic* (The Hague: Mouton), 655–665.

Thompson, Judy

  1977 *The North American Indian Collection: A Catalogue.* Berne: Berne Historical Museum.

Tooker, Elisabeth

  1994 *Lewis H. Morgan on Iroquois Material Culture.* Tucson, AZ: University of Arizona Press.

Turner, Geoffrey

  1976 *Hair Embroidery in Siberia and North America.* Occasional Papers on Technology 7. Oxford.

Wallis, Wilson D. and Ruth S. Wallis

  1955 *The Micmac Indians of Eastern Canada.* Minneapolis, MN: University of Minnesota Press.

Whitehead, Ruth

  1980 *Elitekey: Micmac Material Culture from 1600 A.D. to the Present.* Halifax, NS: The Nova Scotia Museum.

  1982 *Micmac Quillwork: Micmac Indian Techniques of Porcupine Quill Decoration, 1600–1950.* Halifax, NS: The Nova Scotia Museum.

  1987 I Have Lived Here Since the World Began: Atlantic Coast Artistic Traditions. In: Julia Harrison et al. (eds.), *The Spirit Sings: Artistic Traditions of Canada's First Peoples* (Toronto, ON–Calgary, AB: McClelland & Stewart–Glenbow Alberta Institute), 17–50.

  1988 *Micmac, Maliseet and Beothuk Collections in Great Britain.* Nova Scotia Museum, Curatorial Report 62. Halifax, NS.

  1989 *Micmac, Maliseet and Beothuk Collections in Europe and the Pacific.* Nova Scotia Museum, Curatorial Report 66. Halifax, NS.

  1990 Micmac Porcupine Quillwork in the Derby Collection. In: David Wooley (ed.), *Eye of the Angel: Selections from the Derby Collection* (Northampton, MA: White Star Press), 21–24.

3

Western Arizona:
The River and Upland Yumans

Ten Kate arrived by train in Yuma on 17 April 1883. He spent four days in the town on the Arizona side of the Colorado River, packing and mailing his collections, writing letters to family, friends, and colleagues in the Netherlands, France, Germany, and the United States, and preparing for his research trip along the Colorado River. He intended to visit several of the Yuman-speaking tribes of western Arizona, traveling northward along the Colorado River where the Quechan and Mohave had their reservations, after which he would return south along an inland route, taking him to the Walapai, one of the Upland Yuman tribes.

The Yuma

Yuma was a city of contrasts. The town sat in the middle of the desert, which consisted of low hills without vegetation. The railroad hotel, a rather civilized place, provided accommodation and meals for well-dressed transcontinental travelers from eastern and western cities, enjoying good food in well-furnished surroundings and sleeping in comfortable beds. They were businesspeople, government officials, leisure travelers, well-educated, well-dressed, and well-to-do. A stone's throw away, the Mexican quarter of shabby adobe and straw huts spread out. Across the river a collection of simple brush and mud huts provided shelter for the Indians. The territorial prison stood east of town, where the Gila River united with the Colorado. Fort Yuma, situated on a hill on the Californian side of the Colorado River, and with shady cottonwoods, looked almost attractive with its white and light-green houses. Parts of the river plain were irrigated and greening. However, the hot and dry climate made it most unpleasant for people who had to stay for extended periods.

Fort Yuma was established to protect settlers moving west to California. For a few years the Quechan resisted encroachment into their territory, but soon they recog-

nized the inevitability of the White man's dominance, submitting to their new position of wards of the government. Because of armed conflicts and subsequent epidemics, the tribal population had declined from 3,000 to about 1,200 at the time of Ten Kate's visit.

Ten Kate spent four days of fieldwork among the Yuma, who called themselves Quechan, visiting several settlements in various parts of the reservation. The commander of Fort Yuma acted as his first guide, and Scared Eagle, called Miguel and destined to become the next chief, accompanied the anthropologist as interpreter. He visited the Chief Pascual and other Yuma homes. When asked about the purpose of his visit to the Quechan, the anthropologist explained that the White people across the ocean wanted to learn about the traditional way of life and customs of the Indians and about their arts and crafts, and that all this knowledge would be preserved in writing for a long time, even after the Quechan had become civilized. Proud of their Native ways and faced with rapid cultural change, the Indians appreciated such an explanation. The Quechans Ten Kate met during his visits to their camps were astonished about all the questions the strange White man asked, but were delighted when he accepted their traditionally prepared food and expressed his enjoyment of the dish. They were readily prepared to assist this White stranger who came into their huts, sat down, and ate with them.

Ten Kate aimed at putting together a small collection of the main types of artifacts of Native manufacture among the Quechan and wrote about his experience: "Everyone very quickly realized that I wanted to see all possible objects of Indian fabrication, and various people now came by with different items for sale. Things are different now, though, than in the days of Columbus when one could barter an old knife and a couple of beads for the finest things the Indians had. The Quechans wanted cash, and no bits or quarters but whole dollars, and not just a few of them. If I pointed out to Miguel that the prices were much too high, then he would ask: *No le gustan los Yumas?* (You don't like the Yumas?)" (Ten Kate 2004: 147). Because of his limited budget he had to be satisfied with a modest collection.

Dwellings, Households, and Pottery

Ten Kate found that the Quechan and Mohave had retained much of their traditional way of life. The Quechan lived in small settlements called *rancherias*, all located on the west bank of the Colorado River. The foundation of the huts consisted of a low framework of tree trunks and bundles of branches, rectangular, oblong, or round in contour and with flat roofs, the whole covered with a layer of earth for insulation against the cold and heat. The earth came from digging out the floors a couple of inches. The entryways faced east, according to Ten Kate as protection against the prevailing westerly winds that swept up severe sandstorms from time to time.

While visiting households, Ten Kate observed various kinds of pottery vessels in use, including ollas, cups, scoops, and ladles. Many items were decorated with black and reddish-brown designs. Basketry was also prevalent and came in a variety of shapes for different specialized uses, much of it obtained by barter from neighboring tribes such as the Papago to the east and Chemehuevi to the north.

The Colorado River Yumans (Quechan, Mohave, Cocopa) regarded the art and craft of pottery making as a gift of Mastamho, one of their major ancestral spirits who also created the Colorado River, bestowed language and rituals on the Yuman peoples, and assigned animals their

way of life. Pottery making was a women's art, practiced in seclusion to avoid disturbance and bad luck that could destroy their work during the firing process. Crushed potsherds or ground granite tempered the sedimentary clay from the river valley. The women built up their vessels with clay coils, smoothing the sides with a stone (Quechan, Mohave) or pottery anvil (Cocopa) on the inside and a straight cottonwood paddle on the outside. When fired for the first time, designs were applied with a bark brush or pointed stick, dipped in yellow ochre that first turned black and later red in the second firing. Mixed with the ochre was mesquite gum, which acted as a fixative for the paint on the pottery's surface. Sometimes vessels were left plain. Firing took place in a pit, with mesquite or dried cow dung used as fuel.

Geometric designs predominated on Yuman pottery and different motifs had specific names. Lines, dots, rectangles, triangles, herringbones, and several repeating and interlocking motifs predominated. Similar patterns appeared in facial painting. Among the less frequent naturalistic designs Ten Kate saw animal tracks, turtles, and spiders. Cooking wares were never decorated as the designs would soon become invisible from fire and smoke. Canteens, ollas, and ladles virtually always exhibited decoration.

Traditional pottery shapes included large water jars and stew pots, cooking pots and serving bowls, oval food platters, stirrers and scoops or ladles, parching trays, and effigy seed storage jars, shaped like a foot or a duck. Yuman ceramics are not technically sophisticated, as material possessions were valued little. Most personal property was destroyed when somebody died. However, not infrequently pottery exhibits the artistic inclination and talent of their makers in details of shapes and painted decoration. Yuman pottery and similar pottery of Native tribes from southern California and southern Arizona has been labeled "Southern Desert ware" and is probably rooted in the prehistoric Patayan-Hakataya tradition. After the arrival of the army and trading posts, traditional ceramics soon became replaced by metal substitutes (Forde 1931: 123-124; Rogers 1936; Kroeber 1925: 737-739; 1902-1904; Gifford 1928: 361-365; Douglas 1953; Kroeber and Harner 1955; Smith 1977: 25-29, 31-34, 93; Euler 1982; Waters 1982; Trippel 1984: 179, 179-180; Furst 2001: 21-25, 77-79; Spier 1933: 104-110; 1936: 17).

A ladle or scoop was oval or teardrop-shaped and often decorated on both sides, frequently with different patterns on the front and back. Some had hollow handles

Fig. 32   Quechan ladles; pottery, pigment; RMV 362-84a: l. 29.7 cm, w. 20.3 cm, h. 6.3 cm; RMV 362-84b: l. 15.2 cm, w. 10.5 cm, h. 6.3 cm; both ca. 1880.

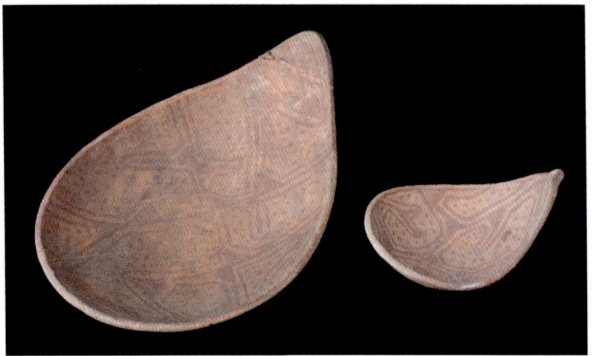

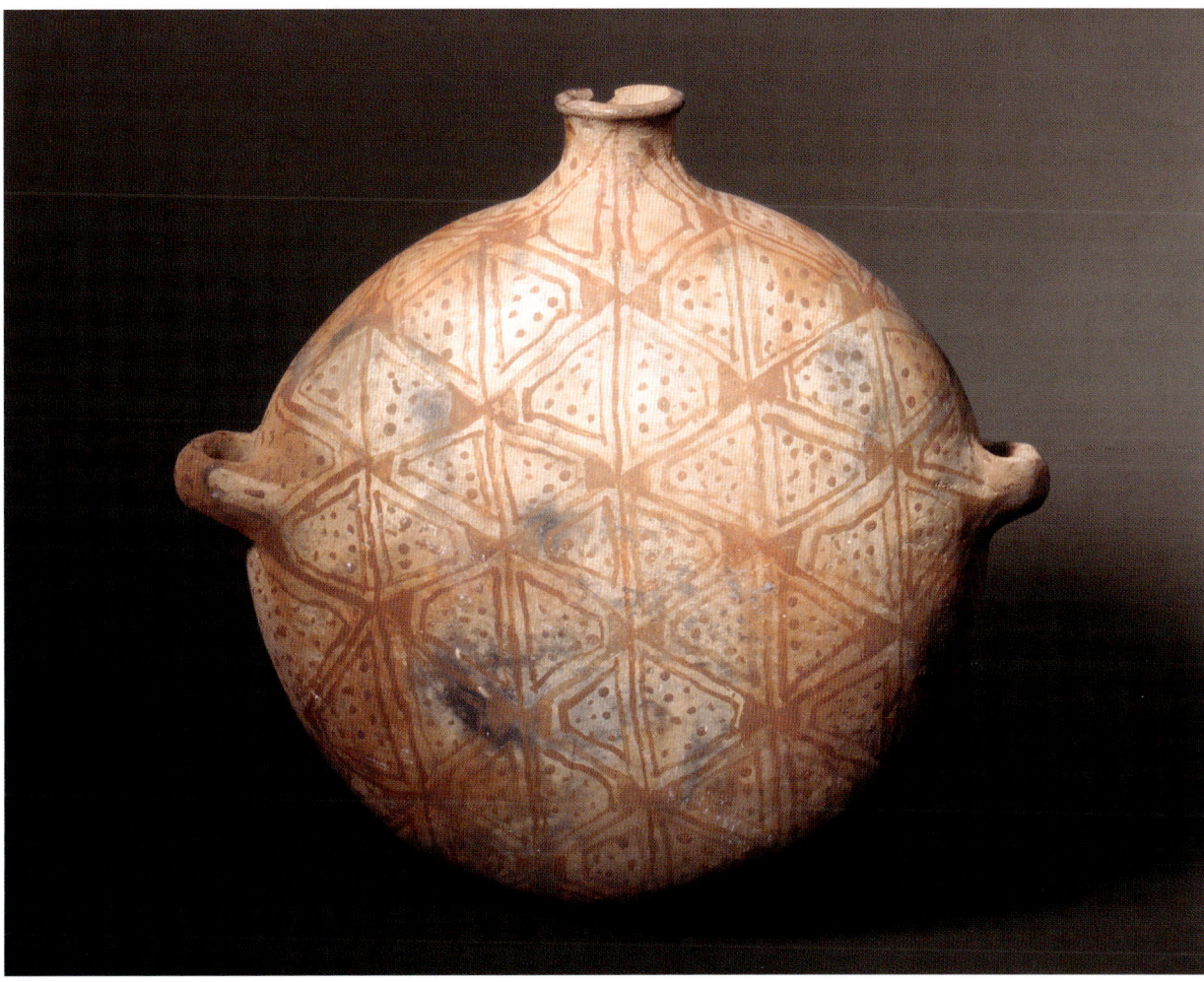

Fig. 33 Quechan canteen; pottery, pigment; h. 27.5 cm, w. 26 cm (with handles), depth 13 cm; ca. 1880 (RMV 362-87).

that rattled, sometimes shaped like effigies of people or animals. The ladles and scoops were used to serve and eat food and were called *kamotu*, which compares to the Mohave term of *kahmootah*, noted by Ten Kate and Kroeber and Harner (1955: 5). The design on the inside of both ladles collected by Ten Kate (Fig. 32) shows interlocking dark triangles with the spaces between them filled with dots; it is called "belly of yellowhammer," as it was inspired by the markings on the red-shafted flicker. The exterior of the large ladle has vertical lines, the alternating bands left open or decorated with a repeating V-pattern. The back of the small ladle is painted with horizontal and vertical lines, resulting in a block pattern, and mica flecks are visible in the clay. Both ladles show signs of use (cf. Forde 1931: 123; Furst 2001: 166–169).

Pottery canteens were not part of the traditional ceramic inventory in Quechan households. Water used to be stored in pitch-covered basketry bottles or gourd containers. Ceramic canteens probably were an innovation,

adopted when the Quechan saw White travelers and soldiers carrying and using such items. From then on these pottery water containers were made for their own use as well as for trade with outsiders. Hide rope fitted through the loops to secure the canteen during transportation. The decoration on this specimen with a flaring spout (Fig. 33) is different, back and front. The pattern on the front is not identified by a specific name and is among several "angled-and-forked continuous patterns" found on Quechan pottery. The back exhibits the "belly of yellowhammer" design (see RMV 362-84a, b, Fig. 32). The filled-in angles, as well as several other elements of pottery decoration, are sometimes labeled the same as elements in face painting (Kroeber and Harner 1955: 9–10, 23). The large size is exceptional, as is the quality of shape and design, and this specimen stands out as one of the finest surviving pieces of nineteenth-century Yuman pottery. Small-sized specimens were made for the tourist trade (cf. Furst 2001: 174–175).

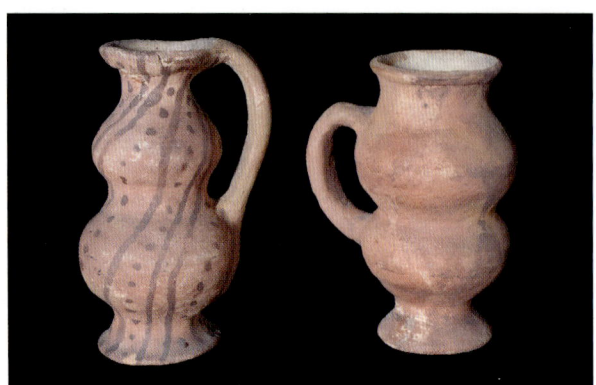

Fig. 34 Yuma red-brown double-bellied pitchers; pottery, pigment; RMV 362-88: h. 11 cm, d. 6.3 cm; RMV 362-89: h. 10.7 cm, d. 6.2 cm; both 1883.

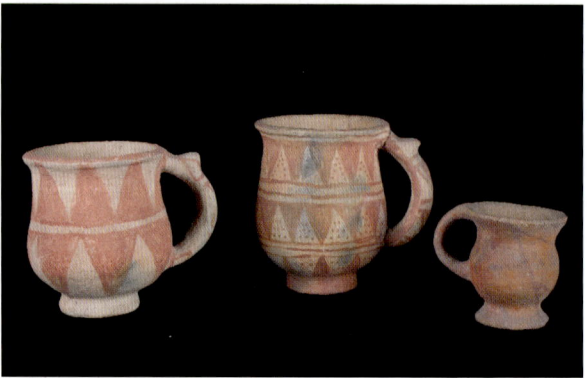

Fig. 35 Yuma red-brown cups or mugs; pottery, pigment; RMV 362-90: h. 10 cm, d. 8.5 cm; RMV 362-91: h. 9.3 cm, d. 8.2 cm; RMV 362-92: h. 6 cm, d. 5.6 cm; all 1883.

The Quechan and Mohave lived on main east-west routes of overland travel and trade. Ten Kate noted that Bartlett and Whipple had traversed their territory around 1850 and that Fort Yuma had been established at that time to protect gold seekers and settlers pouring into southern California. The Indians soon recognized this as an opportunity to sell items of Native manufacture to American travelers. The arrival of the railroad brought travelers to Colorado River towns, people on business staying in the area for a short while, other people traveling through and staying for a meal or a good night's sleep in a hotel. The Atlantic and Pacific Railroad (later Atcheson, Topeka & Santa Fe Railway) reached the Needles in 1883, where Ten Kate witnessed the construction of the bridge across the Colorado River. The Southern Pacific Railway likewise reached Yuma in 1883. These transcontinental lines were virtually completed that same year when they reached their terminus in San Francisco and Los Angeles, respectively. The Quechan and Mohave soon recognized this as an opportunity to market their pottery and beadwork, and they peddled their craftwork on railroad platforms, around the depots, and in the front of the restaurants and hotels that catered to the needs of travelers. Being almost naked and covered in body paint, they provided an exotic spectacle to passengers and visitors, who were startled, amused, and intrigued by what they witnessed. Kroeber noted that the Quechan were the first to realize the potential of the new market and that the Mohave followed their example. However, he only collected traditional material culture and later regretted that he had shunned purchasing tourist-style pottery (Stewart 1983: 59; Kroeber and Harner 1955: 2, 13).

Although at first the Quechan and Mohave traded their traditional wares, which were made with some care to ensure durability, they soon adapted their goods to produce them in a less time-consuming way to cater to the tastes of their White clientele and to satisfy the demands of a growing number of travelers. Pottery became increasingly crude in shape and painted decoration and was only fired for a short time, rendering it rather fragile. Pottery dolls, both unclad and clad in calico dress, seemed to attract much interest and command good prices and were therefore produced in growing numbers.

In hotels, restaurants, railroad dining cars and shops, and in Victorian homes Native women did the laundry and Native men worked on construction and delivered firewood. Here the Yumans witnessed china and glass tableware and soon began to make reproductions in pottery, albeit decorated with traditional designs. These included plates, cream pitchers, sugar bowls, cups, goblets, milk jugs, candy dishes, ashtrays, and vases in a variety of shapes and sizes. These became popular mementos for travelers to take home and a valued source of cash income for the Indians. Rogers (1936: 36) remarks that the Colorado River Yumans lowered their production of tourist style pottery after 1900 and concentrated more on beadwork as this brought higher returns because of a higher demand and consequently higher prices tourists were willing to pay. However, by the late 1930s Yuman potters were still producing ceramic vessels for the tourist market as well as domestic use, and shapes varied from traditional to innovative, such as coffee mugs (Douglas 1953).

Two small pitchers collected by Ten Kate (Fig. 34) exhibit quite different designs, dots and slightly meandering vertical lines on one and patterned triangles on the other. Such double-bellied pitchers are not represented in the extensive Dillingham collection of Mohave pottery at the School of American Research in Santa Fe (Furst 2001).

Two of the mugs in Ten Kate's collection (Fig. 35) exhibit a pear-shaped body and have a handle with what appears to be a thumb rest on top. The third is more globular in shape. The rows of triangles on RMV 362-90 and -91 are referred to by the Quechan as the "coyote teeth" design. The design on the other cup has faded to the extent that it could not be determined with certainty. Kroeber and Harner (1955: 7) point out that handles on pottery might not be aboriginal but an innovation inspired by seeing and copying Western tableware.

Although the design of oppositional and interlocking but separated triangles on the goblet (Fig. 36) falls within the spectrum of Quechan pottery motifs, it is rare, as is the shape of the vessel.

Non-traditional containers like ceramic "baskets" (Figs. 37, 38 right) were probably inspired by Victorian glass or contemporary china candy dishes. Indians saw these in parlors of affluent Whites who employed Native women as domestic workers or at the hotels and restaurants near the railway depot.

As with the previous items, the non-traditional shape of the Yuma pitcher (Fig. 38 left) was probably inspired by cream pitchers commonly used in White households and restaurants.

Anthropomorphic pottery figures have a long tradition in the Southwest and their production reaches far back into prehistory. In the Quechan origin story, Kwikumat created the land and made the Indians from clay. The Quechan used small pottery or wooden human figures of unknown manufacture in the *keruk*, the mourning ceremony, and the Mohave probably had a similar custom. Some had at least indications of facial tattoos or painting. The women went around the mourners, touching them with the figures as a reminder and solace that the places of the departed would be taken by newborns (Trippel 1984:

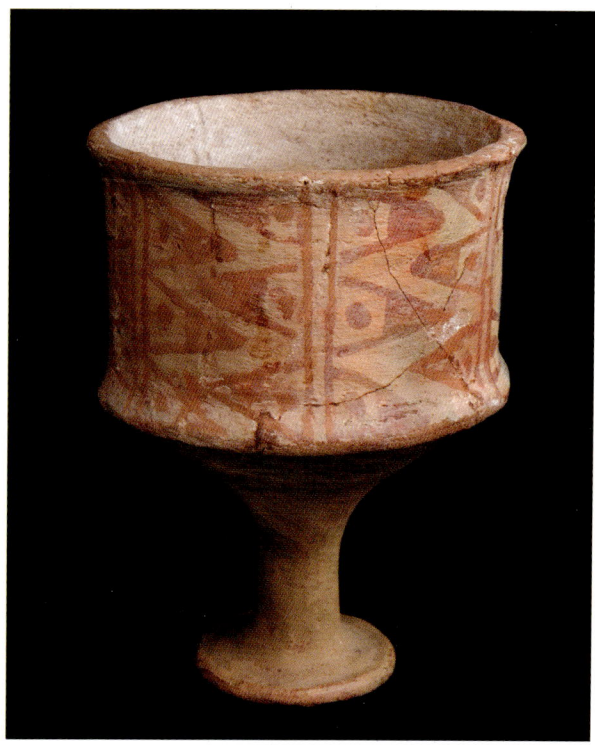

Fig. 36 Yuma red-brown goblet; pottery, pigment; h. 11.5 cm, d. 8.8 cm; 1883 (RMV 362-93).

173; Kaemlein 1954: 2, 6–8; Cleland 1980; also cf. Furst 2001: 17, 79–80).

In the 1870s the pottery dolls made by the Quechan were elaborated upon by dressing them up in fiber and calico clothes and adding features such as jewelry. Their bodies were partially painted, indicating facial tattoos and body painting. Tufts of hair, usually from horses, but sometimes from humans, were implanted to produce a long hairdo. Males, females, and children were all represented. Sometimes the female dolls carried babies or pottery vessels. It is assumed that the elaborate pottery dolls developed from simpler earlier types, in response to an

Fig. 37 Yuma red-brown ceramic "baskets"; pottery, pigment; RMV 362-94: h. 10.5 cm, d. 9 cm; RMV 362-96: h. 10.2 cm, d. 8.8 cm; RMV 362-95: h. 12 cm, d. 8 cm; 1883.

Fig. 38 Yuma red-brown pitcher; pottery, pigment; h. 5 cm, l. 6.5 cm; 1883 (RMV 362-98). Yuma red-brown ceramic "basket"; pottery, pigment; h. 11 cm, d. 8.2 cm; 1883 (RMV 362-97).

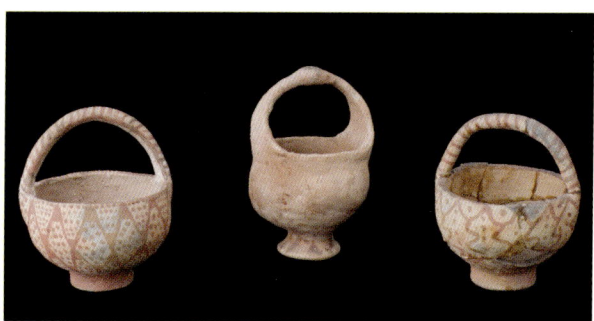

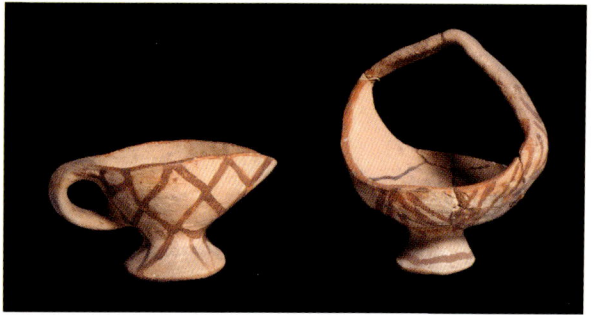

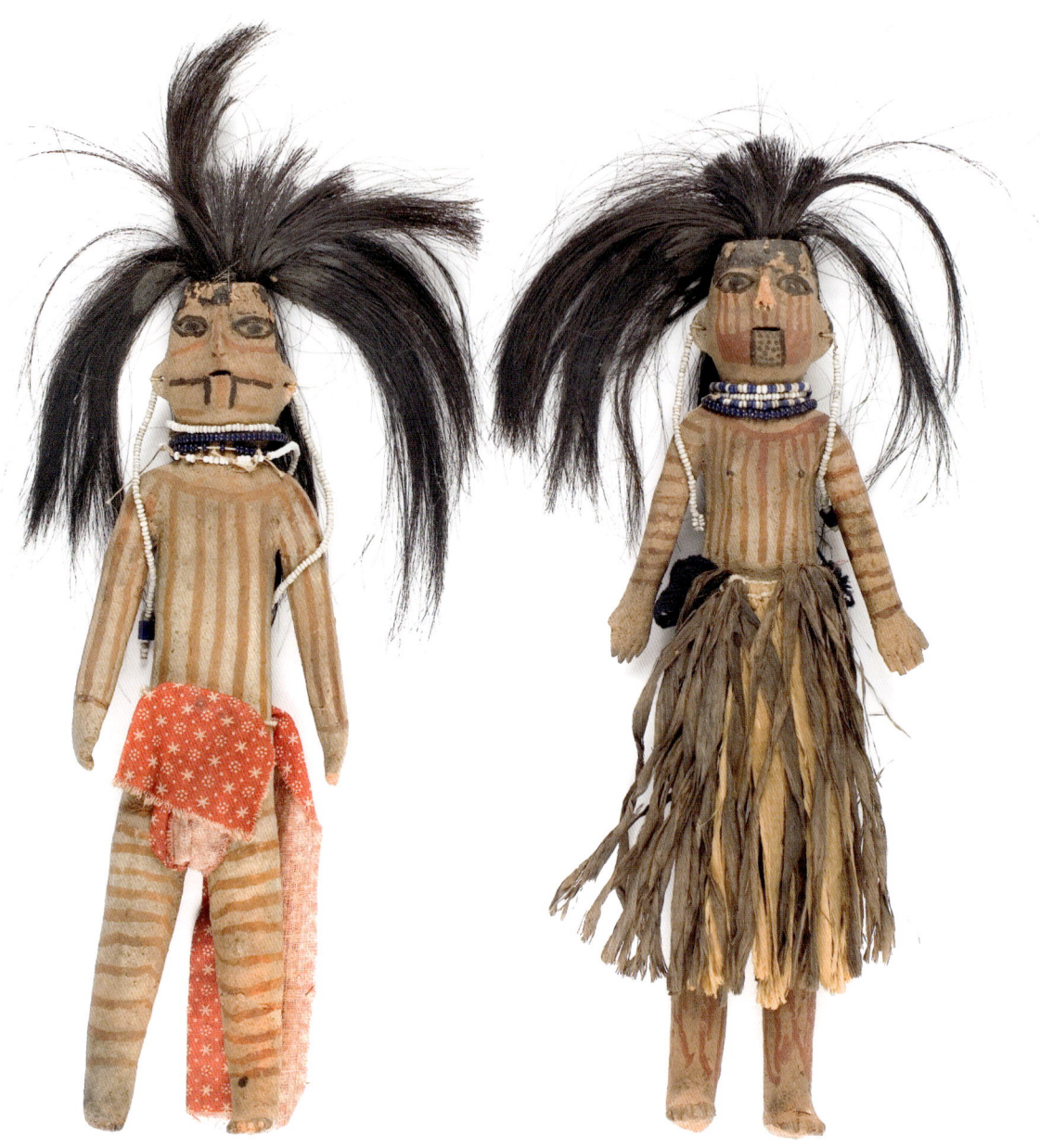

Fig. 39   Pair of Yuma male and female figures; pottery, pigment, cotton, bark, wool, glass, horsehair; h. 20–21 cm (without hair); ca. 1883 (RMV 362-99, -100).

emerging tourist market. The early female dolls show bare breasts, but later examples are covered with a cloth shawl, a concession to a more puritan taste among the White clientele. The pottery dolls of the Mohave are so similar to those of their southern neighbors to make distinction between them virtually impossible (cf. Trippel 1984: 179; Kaemlein 1954: 3–8; Kroeber and Harner 1955: 2; Cleland 1980; Bee 1983: 90; Stewart 1983: 63; Furst 2001: 80–137).

The male doll in the Leiden collection (Fig. 39) wears a calico breechcloth and back apron. Paint is used to indicate facial features, including facial tattoos, as well as body

painting (cf. Taylor and Wallace 1947). The scalp consists of horsehair. It has sculpted genitals, and the end of the penis is broken and missing. The female doll of the Leiden pair is similarly executed and shows the typical facial tattoo of vertical stripes and dots on her chin. Her breasts are bare, the genitals indicated, and she wears a bark fiber skirt and woolen belt. Both are outfitted with multi-stranded bead necklaces. Both figures have pierced ears. The two pottery Quechan dolls Ten Kate acquired in 1883 are among the earliest of their kind that are preserved with documentation.

Greening bushes of mesquites surrounded the houses, and when ripe the sweet fruits were picked, roasted, ground fine with a *mano* on a *metate*, kneaded into dough with water, and finally baked into cakes. This staple of what the Americans called "screw beans" because of their peculiar shape was a major part of their diet. Seeds of a certain species of grass bountiful on the alkaline soils of the region were harvested and treated in a similar manner. However, the Quechan, who traditionally had not only been gatherers but also horticulturists, also grew corn, wheat, and watermelons. In addition, they hunted rabbits, wood rats, and partridges and they fished. Hunting small game was often a communal affair, and Miguel demonstrated how effective it was when he set some bushes on fire. Soon the concealed rabbits, partridges, and doves scattered, becoming easy prey for adept hunters. Many Quechans owned handsomely painted bows and arrows with long iron points and used these with great accuracy. The Indians also had short wooden clubs with a thick cylindrical head which they used in close combat, one of which was acquired by Ten Kate.

The war club (Fig. 40), made from ironwood (*Olneya tesota*), is of the mallet or "potato-masher" type and decorated with painted designs, notably representing people and hands. The black dots are applied with black manganese dioxide; the red hematite hands are possibly a protective motif. The design on the flat top consists of five arms with hands in a whirlwind pattern, probably indicating manual dexterity of warriors fighting with these clubs.

These weapons for close combat were often carved from a single piece of hard wood, either ironwood or mesquite. Those of ironwood, such as the Leiden specimen, were somewhat smaller than those of mesquite because of their heavier weight. The head is cylindrical and has sharp edges to deliver cutting blows to an enemy in hand-to-hand combat. The end of the handle was sharpened to function as a dagger. Sometimes a separate sharp butt was carved or glued to the club, such as in this case. A leather thong through the handle provided easy carrying and prevented loss of the weapon in the heat of battle. The necessary accompaniment to the war club was the stiff leather circular shield with which the warriors fended off blows from their opponents.

In the worldview of the Quechan, warfare was a requirement for insuring and spiritual well-being and mater-

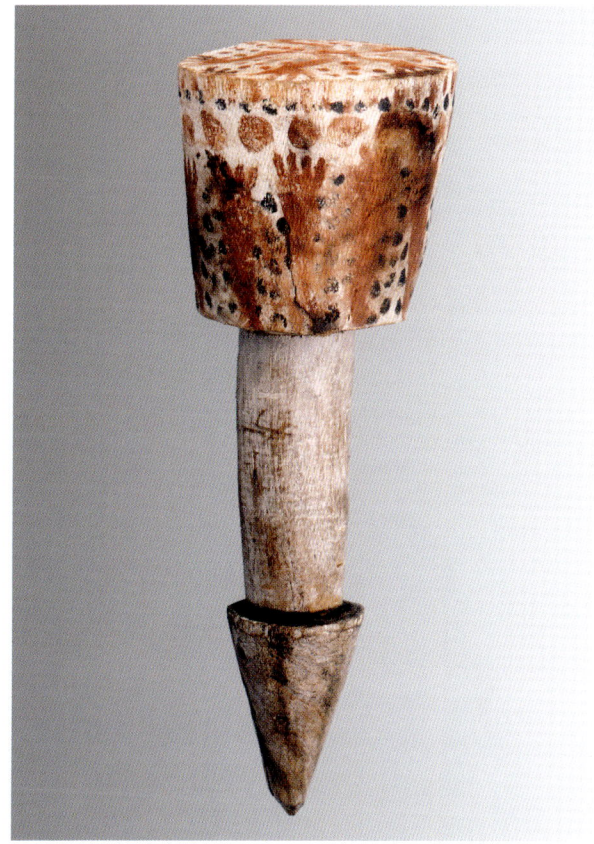

Fig. 40   Yuma war club; *keeleeahgwai* (TK); *ke'lyaxwai* (Spier 1931: 170); Mohave: *kalya'hwai* (Spier 1955: 10); Cocopa: *shyawhai* (Gifford 1933: 274); ironwood, pigments; l. 27.4 cm, w. at top end 9.5 cm; ca. 1870–1880 (RMV 362-78).

ial blessing and thus had a strong mystical connotation. However, a war complex never developed and their war chiefs (*kwanami*, 'brave men') generally led short, intermittent, and small-scale raids and attacks. Arranged pitched battles took place with traditional enemies such as the Maricopa and were accompanied by rituals, demonstrations of courage by warriors carrying feathered staves, and the taking of scalps. Between 1690 and 1848 slave raiding took place to some extent, Indian captives being sold to Spanish households in Sonora (cf. Forde 1931: 134–139, 160–170; Spier 1933: 131–137; 1936: 18; 1955: 9–10, fig. 2c; Gifford 1933: 274; Forbes 1965: 70–82, 251–256, 286–293; Bee 1983: 93; Trippel 1984: 180–181, fig. 4; Bolz and Sanner 1999: 106, fig. 85; see also Piman clubs and shield: RMV 362-36, -45, -46, 764-61).

In the Leiden museum's documentation this club was also at some time listed as Diegueño, but the source of this attribution is a mystery. However, Spier (1923: 354) noted that the Diegueño only used curved and hooked war clubs, although they knew about the potato-masher war clubs of the neighboring Yuma and Cocopa.

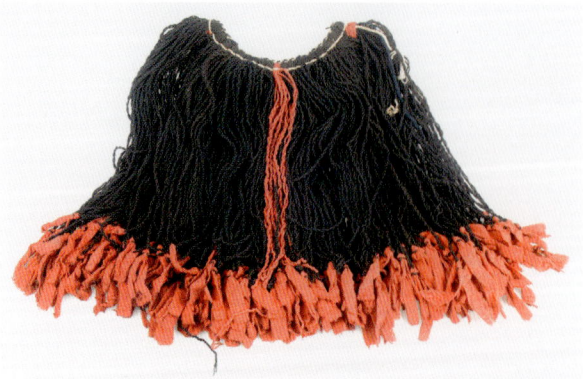

Fig. 41 Quechan woman's skirt, front panel; *altahwahdeek* (TK); willow, wool; w. 30 cm (at top), l. 50-57 cm; ca. 1870-1880 (RMV 362-64).

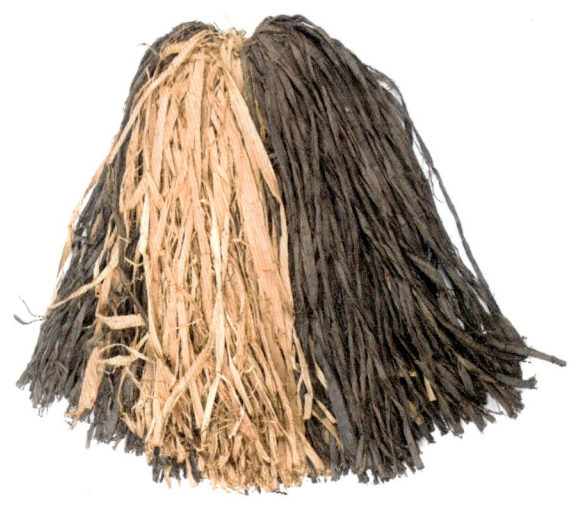

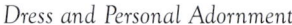

Fig. 42 Quechan woman's skirt, back panel; *njawayguy* (TK); willow, yucca; w. 22 cm (at top), l. ca. 77 cm; ca. 1870-1880 (RMV 362-65).

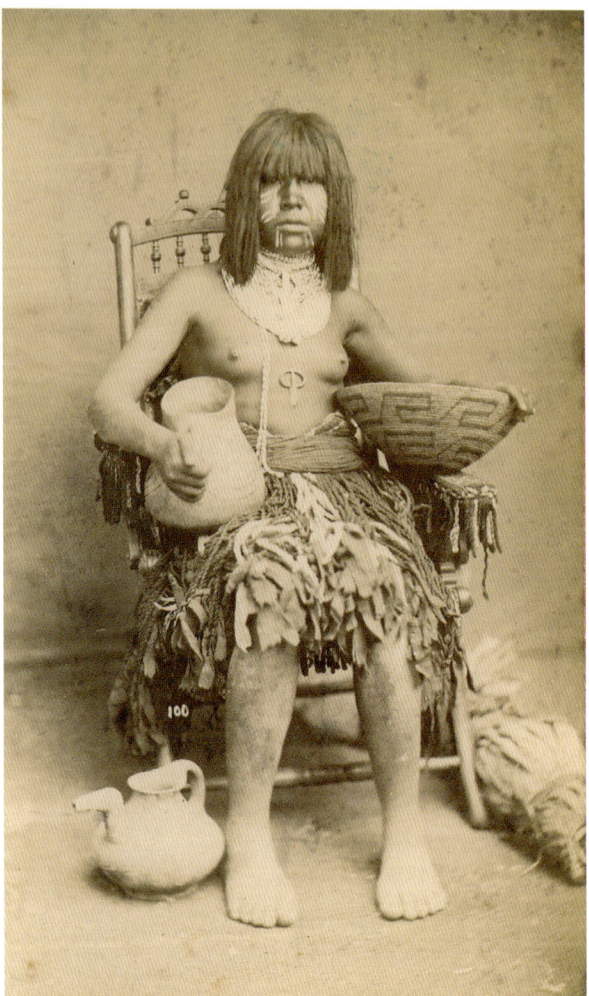

Fig. 43 Quechan woman with willow bustle skirt and necklace; Arizona Territory, ca. 1880. Photograph by Henry Buehman & Co., Tucson (Ten Kate coll.; RMV 414Cb14a).

Dress and Personal Adornment

Men went almost naked, except for a g-string, its end dangling at the back. Women were also scantily dressed, with bare torsos and short skirts of colorful calico, often covered with a short apron of black or red wool in twisted fringes, reaching to their knees, or a longer apron reaching to their ankles. No footwear was worn except in the summer, when the sand got too hot and leather sandals provided protection. The women adorned themselves with wide and narrow collars, necklaces, and bracelets of white and blue beads in tasteful designs, the collars often consisting of netted beadwork. To Ten Kate it seemed that blue was the favorite color, as exemplified in their facial tattoos, body painting, beadwork, and calico skirts. The Quechan had a light complexion and wore their hair long, the women in disheveled fashion and clipped in a straight

line right above the eyebrows. The men wore a large number of braids on their backs, with the tips wrapped with small red ribbons. The young men painted their faces, either partially or completely, in blue, red and yellow colors and smeared their bare legs with the same pigments. The women decorated themselves with blue facial tattoos, notably on the chin, using designs of four to eight vertical single or double stripes and dots in between. Mothers painted their babies in a variety of colors and adorned them with shell and bead jewelry. Ten Kate noticed that the older generation cut their hair short and refrained from body paint. He obtained several samples of body paint.

Women's skirts usually consisted of separate front and back panels, the former being shorter and thinner than the latter. They could be made from strands of bark, plant fibers, woolen strips, and twisted yarn and cloth, but the

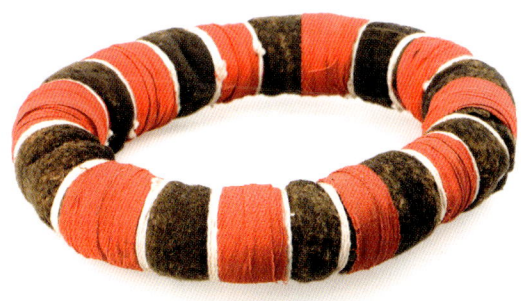

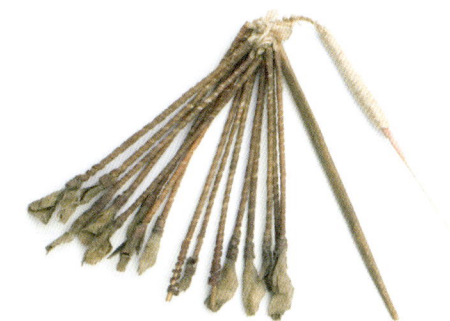

Fig. 44   Quechan cloth head ring; *koorajkahapíg* (TK), wool, cotton, felt; d. 27 cm; ca. 1870–1880 (RMV 362-67).

Fig. 45   Quechan hair ornament; wood, feathers, wool, cotton; l. 6 cm; ca. 1880 (RMV 362-68).

inner bark of swamp willow seemed to be preferred. The strands of material were secured in a twisted cord that acted like a waist belt (Spier 1955: 6; also cf. Spier 1933: 95–96, pl. IV; 1936: 16; 1955: 6; Gifford 1933: 275; Trippel 1984: 176).

This front panel of a woman's skirt (Fig. 41) consists of braided two-ply strands of black or dark brown wool, to which red flannel strips are attached as extensions and furnish a colorful fringe. The waist belt is made from heavy cotton two-ply yarn. This type of skirt became prevalent by the late 1860s, when they replaced simple willow bark bustle skirts and calico cloth was added to cover the upper part of the body (Trippel 1984: 176; Tsosie 1992: 38). The back panel of the skirt (Fig. 42) consists of strips of dried light and dark willow bark, doubled over and attached by twining to a three-strand yucca cord.

In earlier times the Yuma wove strands of willow bark and cotton into fabrics on looms borrowed from the Pima. Small blankets, belts, and cradle bands were the most frequent manufactures. The Gila River Yumans (Maricopa, Halchidoma, Kaveltchadom), who were intermediaries between the Quechan and the Pima, continued weaving into historical times, the craft being executed by men working on horizontal looms (Forde 1931: 126; Spier 1933: 110–122; 1936: 16).

The foundation of this head ring (Fig. 44) consists of black wool. It is wrapped with bands of colored cotton and felt, tied by native cotton string. Traditionally the core of such head rings consisted of willow bark or sometimes a bundle of thin twigs, wrapped with bark of other soft fiber. These head rings were worn by women for carrying water jars and other burdens, including cradles, as well as for softening the impact of the head strap used to carry loads on their back (cf. Spier 1955: 7–8). A note by Ten Kate indicates that he saw these rings being worn by old people.

The ornament collected by Ten Kate (Fig. 45) consists of a short pointed wooden stick as hairpin, with eighteen sticks attached, individually wrapped in red wool, ending in attached black, brown, and white feathers and two long red cotton ribbons. Most of the feathers and cloth have deteriorated and were lost, but originally it must have been a stunning hair ornament. Trippel (1984: 176) noted that in the late 1880s Yuma men were rather fond of hair ornaments fashioned from waterfowl feathers.

The vertically netted weave-beaded collar (Fig. 46) is showing signs of wear. These beaded collars covered the shoulder and upper arms and breast. A multiple stranded necklace of blue and white beads worn tight around the neck as a choker often completed the outfit (see Fig. 47). Such beaded collars began to be made around 1880 by the Quechan and Mohave, and women wore these over their calico shirts or blankets. Mostly a combination of white and blue seed beads were used, with a string of pony or crow beads as extra decoration on rims. The beads were strung on strands of cotton thread and woven vertically into a netted mesh, with beads forming knots in the weave. As looms Quechan women used U-shaped wooden

Fig. 46   Quechan beaded collar; glass, cotton; w. 59 cm, l. 15 cm (with fringe 19 cm); ca. 1880 (RMV 362-69).

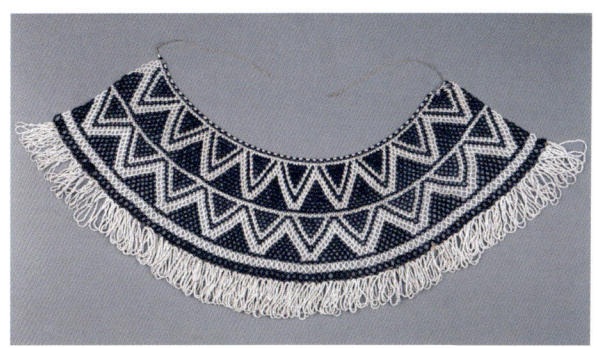

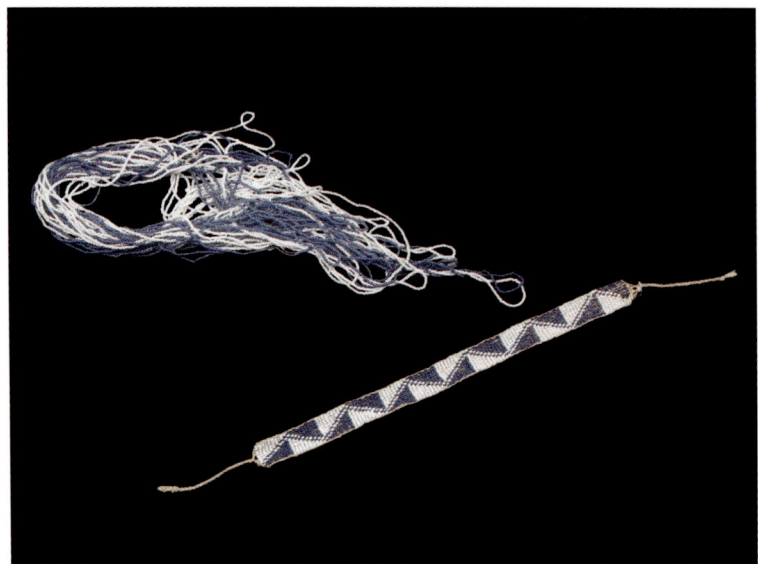
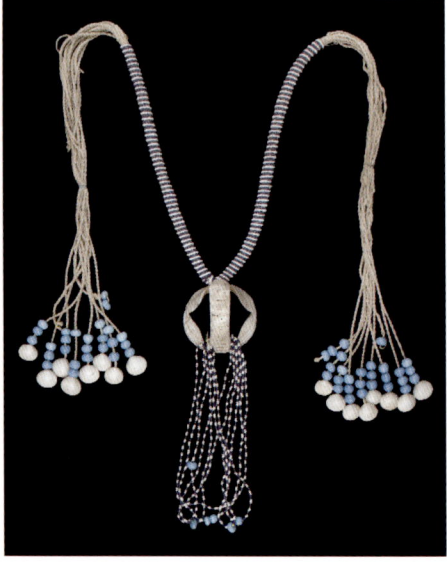

Figs. 47, 48 Quechan necklaces; RMV 362-70: glass, plant fiber, cotton; l. 32 cm; RMV 362-71: glass, vegetal fiber; l. 27 cm (without ties), w. 2 cm; both ca. 1880. Quechan woman's necklace; vegetal fiber, glass, shell, cotton, padre beads; l. 72 cm; ca. 1880 (RMV 362-72).

frames or pottery ollas. Short loose strands or loops of beads could be applied to the underside of the collar as an extra fringe decoration, as in this specimen. Designs were always geometrical, either consisting of triangles, sometimes designated as "coyote teeth," or rectangular linear motifs, some probably derived from Piman basketry designs. The Mohave called such beaded collars by the generic name for necklaces, *hulap*, or more specifically *vethamam*, meaning 'the lengthy one,' or 'where it ends, fits.' It is not known whether the Yuman netted weave-beaded collars originated among the Quechan or Mohave. The earliest Yuman collars of this type are mentioned in the literature in 1883 and appear in studio photographs since 1884. The collar Ten Kate collected among the Quechan is probably the oldest extant specimen. It can not be determined with certainty whether it was made by a Quechan or Mohave bead worker. A few contemporary Yuman bead workers still make netted-weave collars, and Indian women have adopted these items of apparel as part of the traditional tribal dress to be worn on special occasions (Orchard 1929: 139, 145–146; Smith 1977: 95; Conn 1979: 234; Stewart 1983: 68; Trippel 1984: 176; Tsosie 1992; Furst 2001: 53, 114, 116–117, 227–228).

The multi-stranded necklace of blue and white seed beads on vegetal fiber (Fig. 47 left) totals almost fifteen meters in length if measured by individual strand. Beaded necklaces had a longer history among the Yumans than the collars and were worn by both women and men. Reporting on his fieldwork among the Mohave, Kroeber

(1925: 739–740) remarked: "They took to imported glass beads more eagerly than most Californians ... Men as well as women coiled strands of blue and white venetian beads in thick masses around their necks; women wound them around their wrists; and donned showy shoulder capes of a network of beads. A definite style seems to have evolved early, which made use almost wholly of the two colors mentioned." The other neck ornament (Fig. 47 right) consists of opaque white and translucent dark blue seed beads applied in triangular designs on a woven fiber background.

Traditionally the Yumans valued jewelry, and the accounts of early explorers testify to the propensity of especially men to wear multi-stringed necklaces and nose and ear pendants of any kind of shell and coral procured in trade from the Gulf of California and even as far away as the Pacific coast. Shells were used in their whole or were shaped into beads of various shapes and sizes. However, women also wore a variety of jewelry made from aquatic raw materials (Spier 1933: 103; Forbes 1965: 52–53, 109–110; Ford 1983: 713, 719).

The multi-stranded woman's necklace Ten Kate acquired for his collection (Fig. 48) has a twined cord base, probably of native vegetal fiber, that has been partially wrapped and sewn into two thick coils by white and blue cotton string. At one end eighteen individually twined strands have their ends decorated with large opaque blue beads, also called padre beads, and small shells. The main ornament consists of a large shell carved as a *jacla*, with an appendage of six blue and white beaded strings. Very

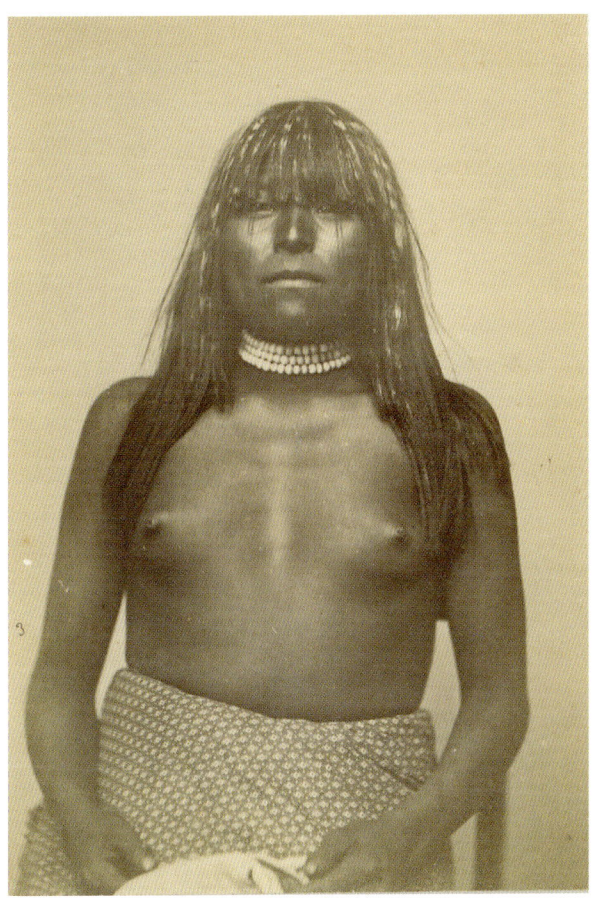

Fig. 49 Quechan woman with necklace. Photograph by Buehman & Co., Tucson, Arizona Territory, ca. 1880 (Ten Kate coll.; RMV 414Cb14b).

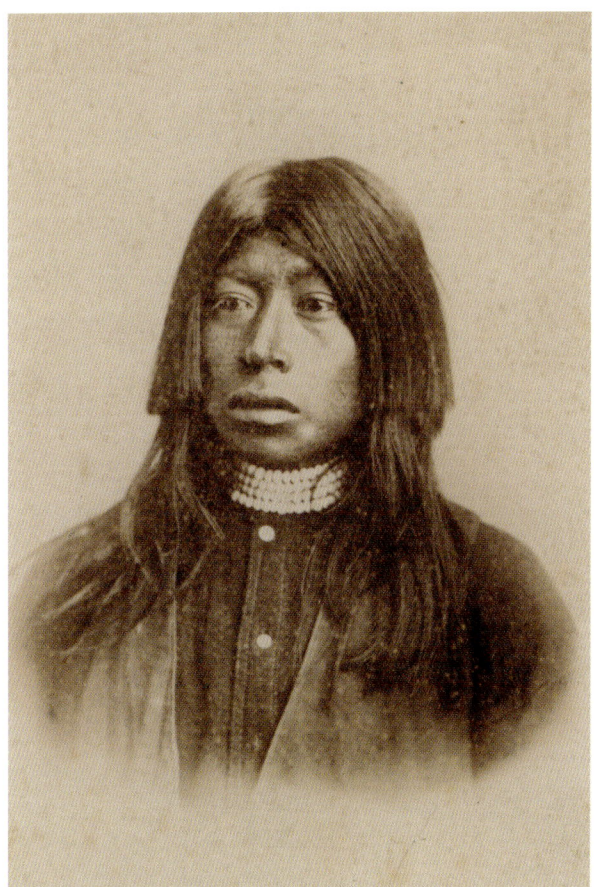

Fig. 50 Quechan man wearing shell choker. Photograph by Ben Wittick, ca. 1880 (Ten Kate coll.; WMR 900581).

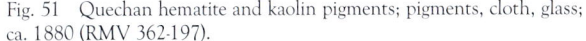

Fig. 51 Quechan hematite and kaolin pigments; pigments, cloth, glass; ca. 1880 (RMV 362-197).

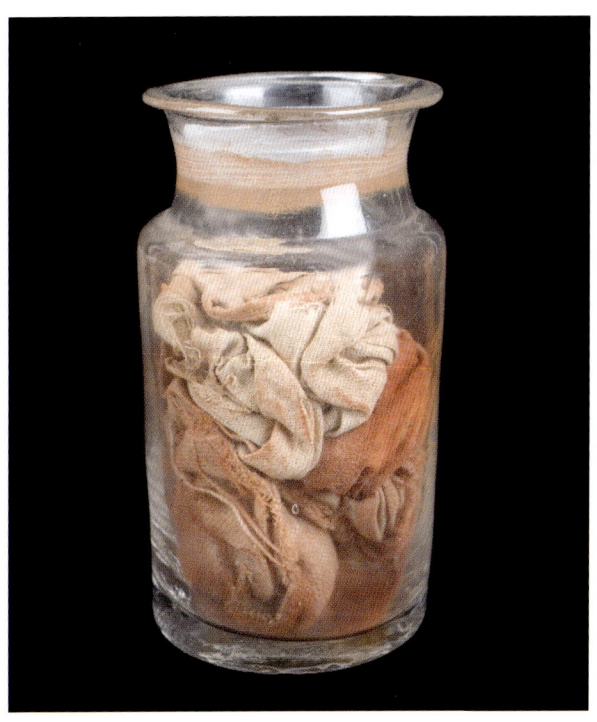

similar necklaces and pendants were collected by Johan Adrian Jacobsen for the Museum of Anthropology in Berlin among the Colorado River Yumans in 1883 (Bolz and Sanner 1999: 114, fig. 93) and by W. J. McGee among the Cocopa in 1900 (Williams 1983: 108).

Body painting was practiced for cosmetic reasons as well as ritual purposes. Colors could be obtained from a variety of natural pigments. The popular palette included black (hematite oxide), white (kaolin), and red (hematite). Deer grease was used as a base for mixing the pigments before application on the skin as well as the hair. Quechan men were known for the latter practice, using different colors to paint strands of their hair. Red hematite of good quality could sometimes be acquired in trade from the Walapai. In addition to painting, the Quechan adorned their bodies with tattoos, mostly confined to the face (Forde 1931: 155, 231; Spier 1933: 101; 1936: 16; cf. Gifford 1933: 277-279; Trippel 1984: 176). The two lumps of pigment Ten Kate collected among the Quechan are wrapped in cotton cloth and are preserved in glass flasks (Fig. 51).

The base of this cradle (Fig. 53) consists of a thick U-shaped twig and thinner twig crosspieces, covered with a padding of shredded bark strands. From the hood of the cradle dangle fluffy feathers, three brass bells, and a small pocket watch of French origin with the text "H. H. Breveté SGDG Paris," the latter attracting the child's attention by its glint as well as ticking sound. Such attachments were quite common and could also include shiny coins, beads, colored stones, metal bells, and the like. Thus the Leiden cradle has two brass bells on a string. The cradleboard for boys was wider at the top than the bottom, as in the Leiden specimen, for girls the other way round. Babies were traditionally swaddled and bound to the cradleboard on a mattress of shredded bark by animal hide blankets and later by pieces of cotton trade cloth, secured by two woven bands. In this case a native-woven cotton band is

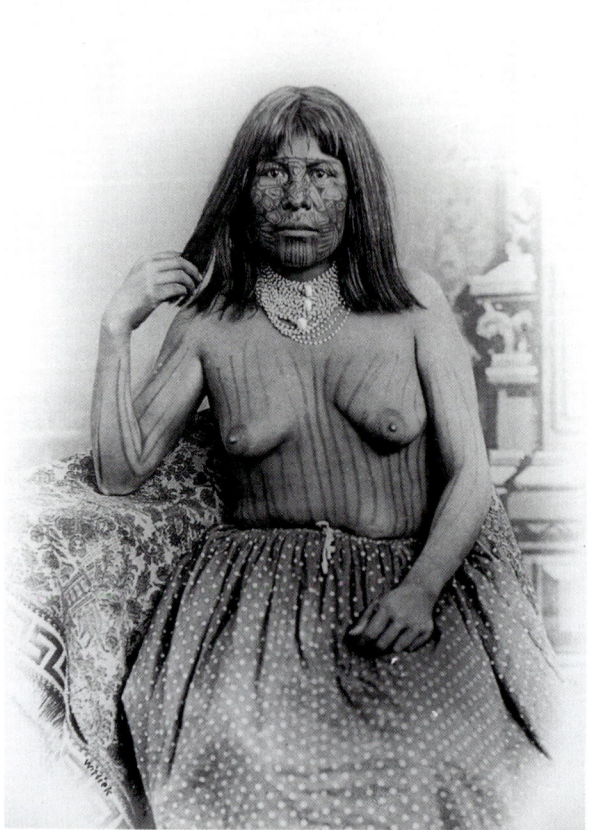

Fig. 52 Quechan woman with facial tattoos and body paint, wearing bead and shell necklace; Arizona Territory, ca. 1880. Photograph by Ben Wittick (RMV 414Ke).

Cradles

Women carried older babies on their lower backs, the upper part of their little bodies swaddled on cradleboards, their little legs dangling loose at the bottom and often clutching the hips of their mothers. By crossing their arms on their backs, the women supported the precious living bundles. Very young babies were completely swaddled and carried in a horizontal manner on their mothers' heads.

Cradleboards were made of reeds, woven into an arched wooden frame, often of mesquite, strengthened by wood splint crosspieces, often of arrow weed (*Pluchea sericea*), and supplied with an added basketry hood or awning, woven of willow bark and in later times covered with cotton cloth. Man usually constructed the base, as this required physical strength. Women wove the broad basketry hoods that protected the child against direct sunlight, animals, and insects and in case the board was dropped. Attached to and suspended from the hood were protective amulets and playthings to keep the baby amused, including small rattles.

Fig. 53 Quechan cradle; *gomáhra-deekwáh* (TK); wood, bark, cotton, felt, feathers, metal; l. 85 cm (with fringe 98 cm), w. 15–18 cm, h. of hood 37 cm, w. of hood 41 cm; ca. 1870–1880 (RMV 362-66).

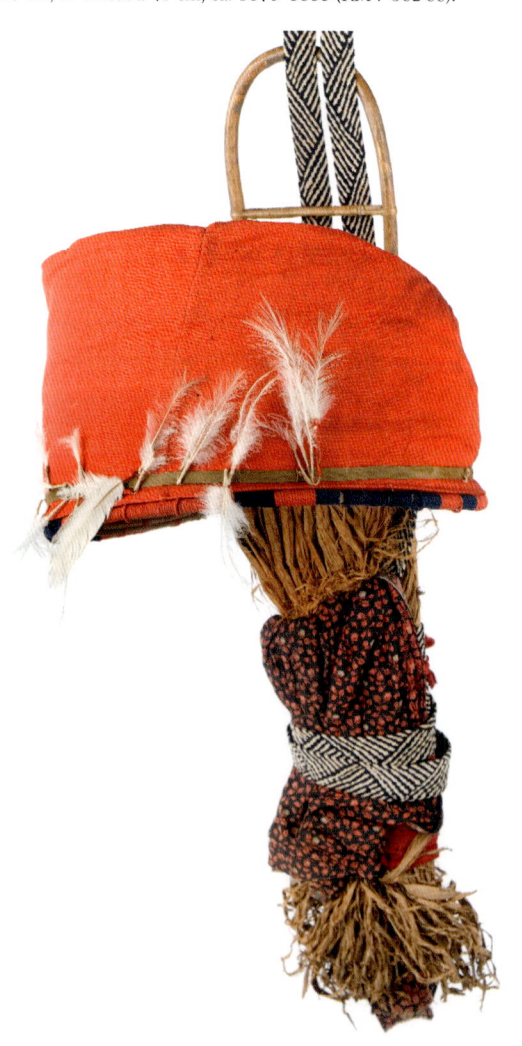

used. Cradles for boys and girls also differed in size, the design of the woven tying bands, and the design of the hood. The cradles were not carried on the back, but on the head, supported by a cloth head ring (see Fig. 44) or under the arm, supported by the hip. Babies stayed swaddled for about a year, after which the board was only used to sleep in (Trippel 1984: 162; Mason 1887: 183–184; Forde 1931: 160; Spier 1933: 314–320; 1936: 17; Furst 2001: 132–135; cf. Smith and Simpson 1964: 38).

Games and Music

During his fieldwork on the Yuma Reservation, Ten Kate came upon an excited crowd playing some kind of sport or game on the bank of the river. Nude, except for g-strings and body paint, two men ran next to each other, each armed with a long wooden stick, which they held in front of themselves. They chased after a rapidly rolling wooden ring that was tossed ahead by one of them. Suddenly they raised their sticks and hurled them at the tumbling and bouncing ring, stopping it in its course. Ten Kate realized that the contestants must earn points by either stopping the ring or getting a stick through it. Questioning spectators, the anthropologist learned that the Quechans were playing the *ohtoorbook* game and that the ring was called *kahptzór*. However, he got no clear statement on the point system involved in this hoop and pole game, so popular in many Native societies of North America. Among the Quechan the game had probably held some ceremonial significance in earlier days, and Ten Kate noted that Balduin Möllhausen, who was on the Whipple Expedition as an artist in 1854, was threatened by the Indian men to stay away or they would bash in his skull. However, no visible opposition occurred in 1883, and Ten Kate even found the Quechan of mild and carefree disposition. The Indians were even gay and prone to banter. They not only frequently engaged with much gusto in a variety of games and sports, but song and dance also played an important part in their everyday lives. Ten Kate observed a dice game played by women called *otóchuh-ee*, in which they manipulated four sticks of wood of approximately twenty centimeters long, on which black figures were painted. As for musical instruments, he saw gourd rattles and reed flutes with painted carvings, and the anthropologist purchased several of these specimens.

The Native term for flute is said to be derived from the sound of a small bird. Yuma flutes typically have four holes in the middle section and are played transversely.

The incised designs on the flute collected by Ten Kate (Fig. 54) are applied in three equally divided segments and filled in with reddish-brown pigment. The joints of the cane flute are decorated with a red painted band. In addition to these long flutes, the Yuma crafted shorter flageolets with three holes and a plugged end, to be played vertically. These instruments were used in courting rather than for accompanying songs. According to Yuma legend, the two sons of a yellow-breasted bird were the first to carve a flute and used it to make girls fall in love (Herzog 1928: 189; Forde 1931: 131; Densmore 1932: 25–27, 49, pls. 25–26; Spier 1933: 131; 1936: 18; Kaemlein 1954: 8–10; Trippel 1984: 174, fig. 2).

The sound compartment of the Yuma gourd rattle acquired by Ten Kate (see Fig. 70 below) consists of a hollowed-out dried squash; with arrow weed or mesquite resin this is attached to a wooden handle that has a cotton wrist string at the end. Many rattles were pierced with rows of little holes to strengthen the sound emitted. However, it seems that those used by shamans in curing rituals had circular or other patterns of holes, such as this one. In addition to four lateral double lines, several panels of holes are pierced around the circumference, and the top exhibits a circular pattern. Some rattles are painted, the upper part black, the lower section red or red with black stripes. This specimen is painted black and the designs are made by scraping through the paint. Some very early rattles were made of clay (Herzog 1928: 189; Forde 1931: 130–131; Densmore 1932: 25, pls. 23–24; Spier 1933: 235, pl. XII; Trippel 1984: 174, fig. 2; cf. Spier 1955: 8–9, fig. 2e).

Ethnomusicologist George Herzog (1928) found Yuman music unique because of its stylistic integration and

Fig. 54   Quechan cane flute; *ahloowheel* (TK) *wilwil* (Spier 1931: 131); cane, pigments; l. 47.5 cm, w. 2 cm; ca. 1880 (RMV 362-74).

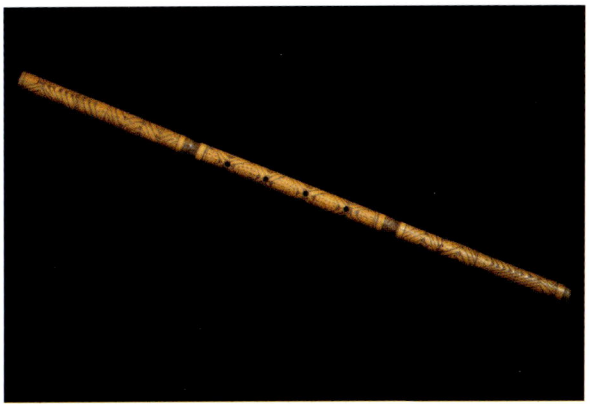

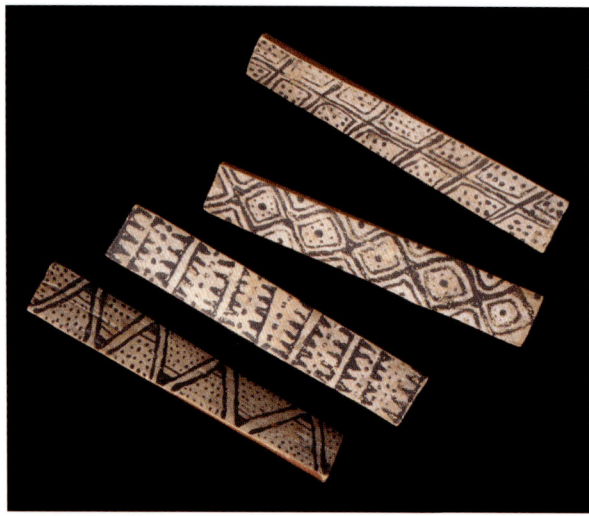

Fig. 55 Four Quechan Yuma gaming sticks; mesquite root, pigment; l. 19.2 cm, w. 3.5 cm; ca. 1880 (RMV 362-76).

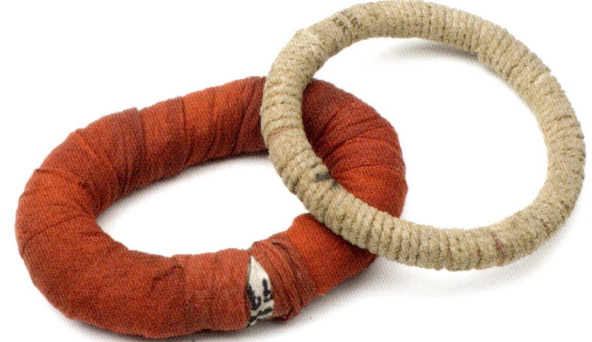

Fig. 56 Two Quechan gaming rings; *kahptzór* (TK); cloth, cotton; d. 18 cm; ca. 1880 (RMV 362-77a, b).

certain specific features that set it apart from other tribal ethnic or regional styles in Native North America. The latter includes the use of conventionalized movements of the hand in rattling, a feature that he compares to the symbolic movements and gestures in the ceremonialism of other Southwestern peoples.

According to Ten Kate, the sticks of mesquite root (*Prosopis*) were used for the *oohtochee-ee* game (Fig. 55), but this term means 'dice' and is probably the generic name of all dice games, several of which are played by the Quechan, using different types of dice, some made from the thin leg bones of cranes. This specific set of sticks was used for the game referred to by the Spanish term of *quince* ('fifteen'; see chapter 5, "The O'odam", Figs. 101, 110). The gaming sticks Ten Kate collected are painted with four different designs on a white painted background, indicating part of the range of designs. The rounded backs of the sticks are stained red. The game was played by two men sitting opposite each other, each casting the dice by hand or with a stone. Depending on the number of and what dice faced up, points were scored (Densmore 1932: 195; Spier 1933: 342–343, pl. XIII; cf. Culin 1907: 209–210).

The two rings in Ten Kate's collection (Fig. 56) were used for the most popular hoop and pole game of *ohtoor-book* (TK; *ortö'v*, Spier 1933: 132; *otu'r*, Densmore 1932: 194; *oh-toor*, Trippel 1984: 175). It was played by two boys or men, one of whom threw the hoop (*kep-a-choor*), after which both threw their six feet-long game poles along the ground to hit it. Depending on the position of the ring to the pole, one or two points were scored. Penetration of the ring did not count. A score entitled the player to the next

throw of the ring. The number of points required for a win was agreed before each game (Forde 1931: 132; Densmore 1932: 194–195; Spier 1933: 336; 1936: 18; Trippel 1984: 175; cf. Culin 1907: 526).

The foundation of the two hoops consists of a bundle of cloth, which in one case is tightly wrapped with a thick cord, probably of native cotton, in the other case wrapped in several pieces of colored cloth, in both cases sturdily sewn.

In May 1985 Travis Hudson of the Santa Barbara Museum of Natural History visited Leiden during a prolonged journey through Europe and Australia to compile an inventory of overseas collections of California Indian material culture. He was surprised to discover the artifacts Ten Kate collected in 1883 along the Colorado River and characterized them as "important" because of their early date (Blackburn and Hudson 1990: 141–143).

The Mohave

From Fort Yuma Ten Kate traveled north to the Mohave Reservation with a storekeeper's freight wagon. On 21 April 1883 the heavily loaded wagon crossed the Gila River, which had swollen because of spring rains, and became almost stuck in the middle of the streambed. However, the driver and Ten Kate eventually managed to get out of the mud by demanding the ultimate of the six-horse team, but this little adventure resulted in severe damage to his baggage. At Castle Dome he encountered a group of "Apache-Yumas," which he correctly considered to be Upland Yumans, as they were Yavapais.

The wagon continued its journey north along the Chocolate Mountains and the Colorado River. Ten Kate was pleasantly surprised to find that his companion had been traveling across Mexico with John Lloyd Stephens around 1840, when he was making his discoveries of the remains of Mayan cities in the jungles of the Yucatan peninsula and Chiapas. After a sandstorm and an exhausting ride through the desert they reached Ehrenberg, where Ten Kate slept in the gutter for lack of accommodation in the small frontier town. He made the acquaintance of several Mohaves who lived in a camp on the outskirts. On 29 April he reached Parker, the seat of the Colorado River Indian Agency, where the Indian Agent received him courteously, despite his disheveled look after a week's journey through the desert. After cleaning and resting up, he spent nine days on the reservation for fieldwork.

During that time Ten Kate also had the opportunity to make a trip upriver by steamboat to visit the approximately 700 Mohaves who had refused to settle on the reservation and preferred to stay further north at Fort Mohave. In the Parker area he was accompanied by his interpreter Joolevéekah (Two Ropes), a young handsome and pleasant Mohave. However, during his visit to the bands in the north near Fort Mohave, Masehàyewee, called "Lying Jim" by the soldiers but whose Mohave name translated as 'woman's buttocks,' was his guide and interpreter. He constantly begged for food and gifts, but despite this nuisance was rather helpful during the fieldwork.

Among the Mohave Ten Kate was quick to establish a rapport with the Indians, mainly due to his personality and genuine interest in the people and their traditional way of life. Soon he was on the best of terms with Chief Hookerau (Fast Boat), a robust man, 1.86 meters tall and weighing 220 pounds. At Fort Mohave he became acquainted with Chief Ampotumquittatshitsjùh (Hide Behind the Dust), called Potetshitsjùh in abbreviated fashion, the son of the great chief Iritéba, who had succeeded his father after his death in 1874. Ten Kate was much impressed by the man who was loved by his followers. Seldom had he seen a nobler type: small and slender in figure, with a pale complexion, deep, reflective eyes, and finely cut face. The anthropologist deemed his profile as handsome as a Greek image which nevertheless aroused sympathy and instilled confidence in people.

Ten Kate regarded the Mohave girls and young women as rather attractive: "With their black locks and brown tint, their dark gleaming eyes filled with mischief and love of life, their red lips on which a childlike laughter so often plays, and the delicately curved lines of their slender bodies, they provide in their natural simplicity a fitting image

of the 'peerless dark-eyed Indian girl' so eloquently intoned by Joaquin Miller" (Ten Kate 2004: 153-154).

Subsistence and Households

Ten Kate noted that all Native settlements on the Colorado River Reservation were situated in the bottomlands of the river, where periodic inundation left a fertile layer of silt and where crops could be planted. Their homes and villages were indistinguishable from those of the Quechan. As among the latter, Ten Kate noticed the effective storage system for the mesquite beans, a major wild food crop that was harvested. This consisted of a series of large round willow baskets, mounted on poles several feet above the ground. Such storage guaranteed a constant flow of air through the stock, preservation by dehydration, and protection against rodents. Mohave informants told him that they also had a "seed man" who was charged with collecting and preserving in a hidden place part of the harvest of corn and wheat in case of crop failure, food shortage, and starvation.

Hunting did not provide a substantial part of the subsistence needs of the Mohave, a circumstance caused by the extreme aridity of their territory according to Ten Kate. The sparse vegetation could not sustain big game such as pronghorn antelope and mountain sheep. This also prevented the tribe from developing herds of cows and horses, and nowhere was the tribal livestock so small. By keeping chickens, the Indians tried to compensate the shortage of meat in their diet. In addition, they hunted packrats and kangaroo mice and they fished, partly from dugout canoes. Moreover, White encroachment onto their lands had forced them to cede most of their territories in exchange for small reservations in the least fertile part of the Colorado River Valley, and thus the Indians had become to a great extent dependent on the weekly distribution by the government of flour, beef, and salt in the fall, winter, and spring. Mule meat was considered a rare delicacy, and Ten Kate witnessed an excited group of Mohaves getting hold of a dying mule, disemboweling it in a hurry and eating the fresh meat raw.

During his visits to Mohave camps and dwellings Ten Kate noted grinding stones (*ahgpáy* and *hamoostséé*), with which they finely ground corn and wheat. In the *achmó*, a wooden mortar, mesquite beans were pulverized. A variety of painted ceramic vessels was used for the storage of water and food. Pottery scoops (*kahmootah*) for food preparation and eating abounded. Some baskets, probably obtained in

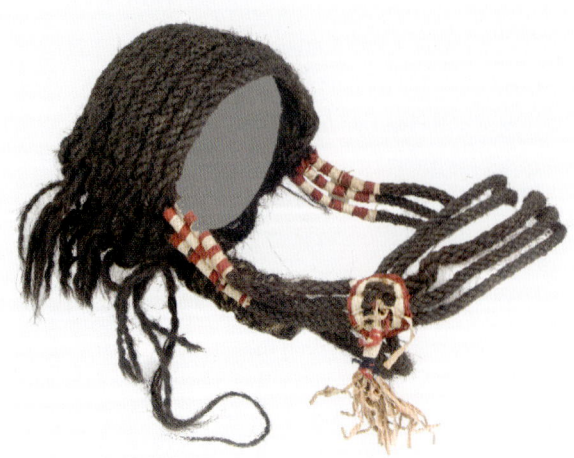

Fig. 57   Mohave horse halter; horsehair, cotton, wool; l. 53 cm, w. 14 cm; ca. 1870–1880 (RMV 362-105).

trade with the neighboring Chemehuevi and Yavapai, completed the household inventory. Besides the preparation of several of these kinds of food, the anthropologist saw the Mohave boiling willow leaves, resulting in a sweet beverage.

The Mohave seemed to be fond of animals. Pets not only abounded but were treated with affection, especially by the women. Dogs and even chickens looked well fed and were pampered, and canines were even dressed up with beaded and fringed ornaments.

A horse halter in Ten Kate's collection is made of very tightly braided strands of horsehair, with two rosettes of white cotton and red yarn on each side. Part of the horsehair rope is decoratively wrapped with alternating bands of red white flannel string and white cotton (Fig. 57).

Mohave bows, like those of all Yumans and Pimans, were generally shallow with a long and almost straight shaft and curved tips. The preferred wood came from screw bean mesquite (*Prosopis pubescens*), but most were made from willow. Tips were shaped by wrapping them with wet willow bark, thrusting them in hot ashes, and subsequently forcing them in the required form. The ideal size of the bow depended on the height of its user, and the standard was the measure from the ground to the chin. Stewart (1947b: 262) states that hunting bows were generally shorter and measured between three and a half to four feet, although Spier (1955: 8) doubts the validity of this dichotomy as this is not in keeping with findings among other Yuman peoples. Some bows were painted, often red in the middle, except at the grip, and black at the tips, and Stewart limits this practice to war bows. All had deer sinew string. Arrow shafts preferably came from the appropriately named arrow weed (*Pluchea sericea*), or sometimes cane, and were about three feet long. Three trimmed feathers provided stability in flight, and this part of the shaft was sometimes painted fully or decorated with painted dots, mostly in red and black. Arrows were held in quivers made from the hide of foxes, coyotes, wild cats, and deer. Wrist guards of bark and deer hide protected bowmen against injury. With round rawhide shields the Mohave tried to deflect arrows from their torsos (Stewart 1947b: 262–265; Spier 1955: 8–10, figs. 2a, b).

This bow (Fig. 58) has its outside convex surface still covered with bark, while the concave inside surface exhibits a pattern of incised and connecting crosses, painted reddish brown. This decoration does not necessarily identify it as a weapon of war rather than hunting. Hunters formed a special class among the Mohave, called *akwak konik* ('hunts deer'), and derived their hunting success from spiritual dreams in which they received the required

Fig. 58   Mohave bow and two arrows; bow: *otisa* (Stewart 1947: 262), *u'tic* (Spier 1955: 8); wood, feathers, sinew, pigment; l. of bow: 140 cm, w. 4 cm; l. of arrows: 97 cm; ca. 1870–1880 (RMV 362-106).

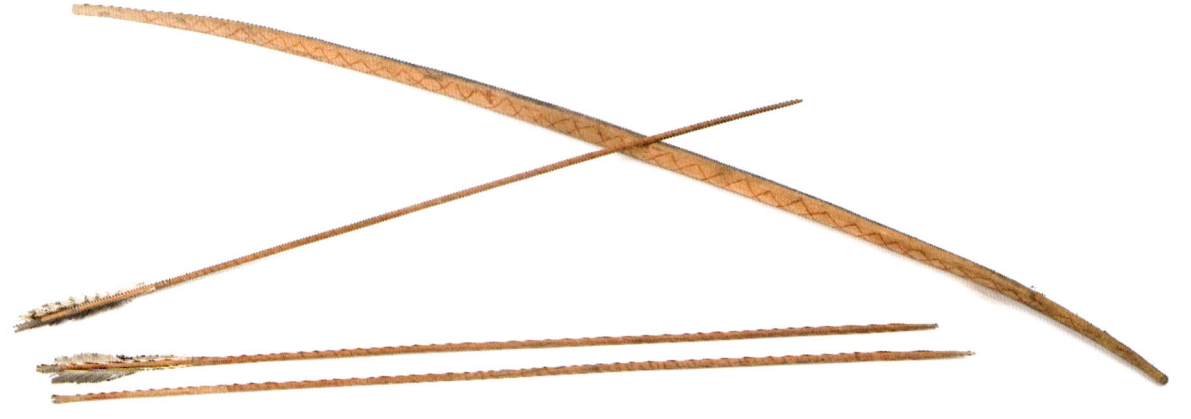

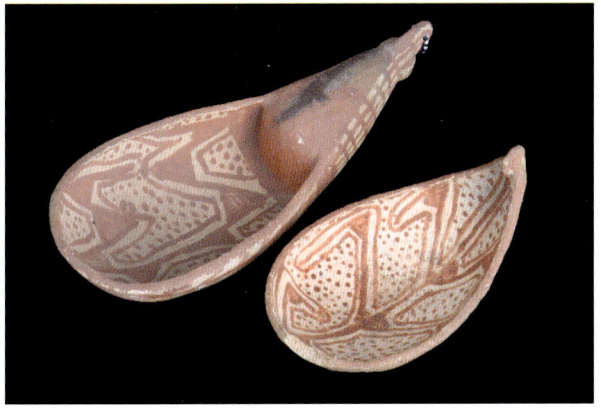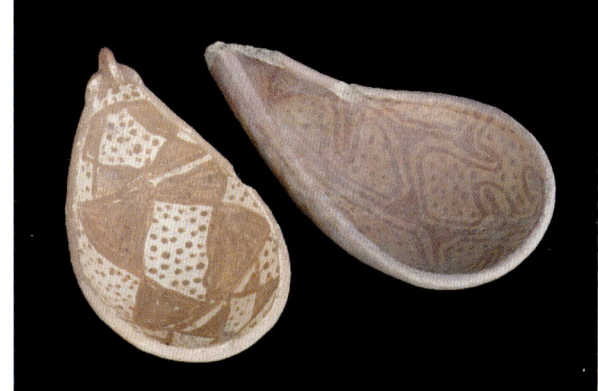

Figs. 59, 60 Mohave pottery ladles; *kahmootah* (TK); pottery, pigment; RMV 362-109: l. 22 cm, w. 9 cm, h. 5 cm; RMV 362-110: l. 13.5 cm, w. 9 cm. h. 3.8 cm; RMV 362-111: l. 14.8 cm, w. 8.3 cm, h. 3.8 cm; RMV 362-112: l. 12 cm, w. 7.8 cm, h. 3.7 cm; all ca. 1880–1883.

skills. This group of men also played a role in warfare as sharpshooters, but this function was not regarded as specifically supernaturally sanctioned. The carving and painting of symbolic designs on hunting bows is consistent with this ideology. The fact that the bow is rather short suggests that it was made for a young boy. Around the age of ten they began to practice under the guidance of male relatives and soon after participated in hunts (Stewart 1947a; Fathauer 1954: 99).

The arrows are notched and self-pointed and their shafts are decorated with red and blue spiral lines, a common design on such projectiles. They are fletched with feathers secured with sinew (cf. Mason 1894: pl. xli). In a note added to the bow Ten Kate pointed out that the weapon was in good condition when acquired, but later sustained damage when handled by an "ethnographico-phile Yankee."

Mohave pottery ladles (Figs. 59, 60) were molded over an appropriately shaped rock and could be oval or teardrop-shaped. The finishing of the handle varies from sharp V-shapes to knobs (RMV 362-112), sometimes containing a rattle (RMV 362-109) and effigy handles (Furst

Fig. 61 Mohave blackware bowls; RMV 362-113: h. 4 cm, d. 9 cm; RMV 362-114: h. 3.4 cm, d. 10 cm; both ca. 1880.

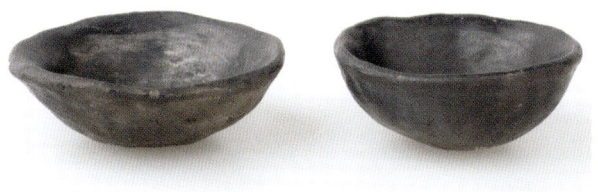

2001: 78, 166–169). RMV 362-109 has a perforated handle with a short string of white and blue seed beads. The Leiden ladles are decorated on the interior with different designs: "belly of yellowhammer" (362-110, -111) and cottonwood leaves (362-109, -112). The exteriors are undecorated (362-110, -112) or exhibit a repeating V-pattern in several opposing longitudinal rows (362-109, -111). Two of the four ladles are apparently new, while two others show signs of wear. Flecks of mica are visible in the clay of several ladles.

Black polished pottery is atypical of Mohave ceramics and is not mentioned by either Rogers (1936) or Kroeber and Harner (1955). The production of these bowls was probably a short-lived experiment, executed by a Mohave potter who must have been glad to find a customer willing to pay for her exceptional but not especially pleasing ware. Silvery flecks of mica show through the polished surfaces of both vessels collected by Ten Kate (Fig. 61).

Dress and Personal Adornment

The dress of the Mohave was virtually the same as among the Quechan. Body painting was rather popular, and especially the young men covered their face, torso, and extremities with colored clays and pigments. Ten Kate observed that the women used a blue dye to paint their eyelids and was told that this enabled them to ward off the glare of the sun and see farther. The Mohave and Quechan were in the habit of cleansing their hair with mud. After loosening their hair, they covered it completely with a layer of mud from the river. They left this coating to dry for several days, after which it was crumbled and the hair was brushed. Thus they not only got glistening black hair, but also got rid of lice.

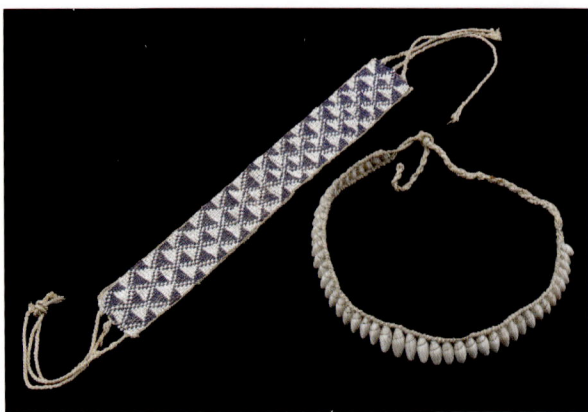

Fig. 62 Mohave bead and shell necklaces; RMV 362-102: cotton, plant fiber, glass; l. 25 cm (without ties), w. 3.8 cm; ca. 1880; RMV 362-103: *oliva* shell, cotton; l. 21 cm (without ties), w. 1.6 cm, d. 15 cm; ca. 1880.

A pair of Mohave women's earrings collected by Ten Kate (RMV 362-101), which is now lost, was made of strands of blue and white glass beads, combined with several large beads of white shell and blue glass.

The pretty band of woven beadwork in a repeating beaded pattern of oppositional white and blue triangles (Fig. 62 left) could equally have been used as a bracelet, choker, or garter and shows signs of considerable wear. On a base of commercial cotton a band of woven beadwork has been applied. The opaque white and clear blue beads are strung on plant fiber. The second necklace consists of a twisted cotton string that is threaded through the natural opening of the shells at the base and the manually perforated top, holding them securely in place in a tight row (Fig. 62 right).

The oldest known Mohave sandals were braided and stitched from willow bark, to be replaced by sandals made

Fig. 63 Mohave sandals; *hahmnjoe* (TK); *ha'myo* (Spier 1955: 7); buckskin, cotton; l. 25 cm; w. 7/12.5 cm (back/front); ca. 1880 (RMV 362-104).

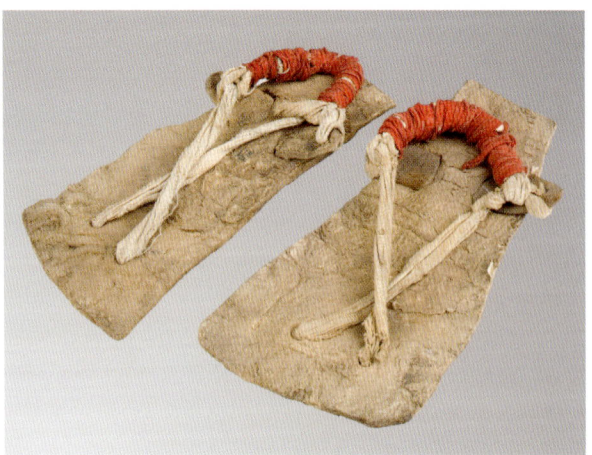

from badger skin and later horsehide. The soles were usually larger than the sole of the foot, and heel and toe straps of willow, leather, or cloth were added. The thick soles of rawhide sandals were often trapezoidal in shape, with an incline towards the left and right (Spier 1933: 97, pl. VIV; 1955: 7; cf. Gifford 1933: 276). The Leiden pair (Fig. 63) is probably made from antelope or deer rawhide. The ties are made from cotton cloth, which appears to be stained white and reinforced with red cotton cloth. In addition, there are two short leather ties at the back of the sole.

Games and Sports

While doing fieldwork among the Mohave, Ten Kate had several opportunities to observe games and sports being played, notably by boys and young men. A favorite pastime was the game of *ookáhnuh* or *ookáhnk*, named after the curved pole male adolescents used as a bat to hit a leather ball (*milekjái*) along. Almost every evening the boys crouched in a row near a fire and played *toowuhdooljk*, in which a small bundle of sticks was passed behind their backs, and the player in front of them had to guess who held the sticks. All the while they chanted and vigorously swayed their torsos to and fro to the rhythm, adding to the excitement and amusement. During evenings girls joined the boys in the game of *chejayresoowárwk*, in which the sexes faced each other, standing in two rows two paces apart. By the cadence of their communal chant, the rows walked slowly forward and backward in alternate turns.

Balls like those collected by Ten Kate (Fig. 64) were used for the *oohkáhnk* (TK) game. Sports and physically active games were very popular among the Mohave. In promoting fitness and stamina they prepared boys and men to become strong warriors. The Mohave played a number of different ball games. Kickball consisted of a race during which runners kicked a small ball forward for miles, competing against each other for speed and stamina. For ball-slinging they used flexible willow poles with which balls of clay were slung at opponents, an equivalent of a mock battle. When the White newcomers introduced soccer, the game was readily accepted by the Mohave and many other Indian tribes. However, shinny (*oohkáhnk*) as witnessed by Ten Kate was traditionally the most popular sport and was played by both sexes. The Mohave, Quechan, and Walapai used curved sticks, the Cocopa straight sticks to play the game (Culin 1907: 644-646; Devereux 1950; Gifford 1933: 281-282).

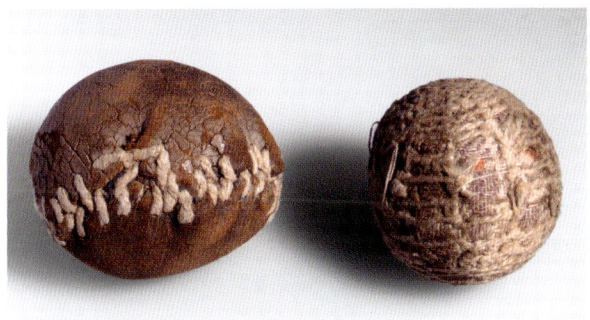

Fig. 64 Mohave buckskin game balls; RMV 362-107: hide, wool, cotton; d. 4.5–5.5 cm; RMV 362-108: cotton; d. 4 cm; ca. 1880.

RMV 362-107 is a rather worn and slightly egg-shaped ball, stuffed with blue wool cloth. The hide cover is stitched with heavy cotton thread. RMV 362-108 is round, filled with cotton cloth, covered with a sewn and woven mesh of braided cotton thread. It seems that four lateral segments are deliberately stained as decoration.

Religion

Ten Kate had a difficult time learning about the religious beliefs of the Mohave, as they were unwilling to divulge information on this subject to outsiders, and his notes were therefore rather fragmentary. The Indians regarded The Needles, a group of mountains on the west bank of the Colorado River, as the abode where their spirits dwelled. They called these mountains *Hohkeeampáypáy*. The Mohave referred to themselves as *Hahmookháhváy*, meaning 'Three Mountains,' but Ten Kate was not sure whether this term was related to The Needles. The Indians believed that after death they would be reborn in these mountains and enjoy eternal youth amidst plenty, especially an abundance of juicy watermelons, the epitome of blessing. They undertook small expeditions to these mountains to bring watermelons as offerings. Ten Kate also came away with the impression that the Indians regarded the beaver with reverence, since they never killed the animal and even tried to prevent trappers catching them.

Just as the Quechan, the Mohave believed in the power of an "evil eye," in black magic or witchcraft. In the past Indians were sometimes killed if they were suspected of casting an evil spell or making threatening predictions, as they believed this caused sickness and enemy attacks. Women and children were not exempt. Healing was the profession of medicine men who treated their patients in a semi-subterranean dirt-covered lodge. Heated stones were piled up in the center and the entrance was closed.

Water poured on the glowing stones created hot steam and made the sick person break out in a cathartic and healing sweat. In other cases medicine men massaged the body parts of their patients they thought were infected with evil in order to drive it out. Ten Kate probably witnessed such a treatment and regarded it as an artificial operation, as the healer apparently extracted foreign intrusions from the body of the patient, thereby removing the cause of the illness.

The Mohave cremated their dead, as did the Quechan. A cremation took place on the day Ten Kate had to leave, and he requested the agency physician Dr. C. C. Webb to attend the ceremonial event and record his observations. The doctor graciously complied and sent Ten Kate a letter with the following account:

"The first thing that caught my attention, when I arrived at the spot, was the lamentation of a group of Indians, which could be heard nearly a mile away. My arrival had caused some commotion among the Mohaves, and before long a circle formed around me until one of the chiefs spoke. When the interpreter I had with me translated his speech, I realized that they regarded me as an intruder and wanted me to leave. But when I promised them that I would not tell 'Washington' anything I saw, they hesitantly agreed, after considerable discussion among themselves, that I could stay. The body lay in the sand in front of a hut and was completely enveloped in a blanket so that nothing of its face or limbs was visible. It was surrounded by approximately three hundred Indians of both sexes and every age, roughly a third of whom served as mourners. Some of these mourners lay flat on the ground. Others were kneeling and jerking their bodies back and forth. Still others stood with their arms stretched above their heads, producing a monotonous hand clapping which could be heard without interruption. There was one man there who delivered a loud, long address with wild gesticulations."

"The section of the Indians present not taking part in the lamentations stood grouped in two rows between the spot where the body lay and the funeral pyre, so that there was space left between them. Roughly an hour passed, when six Mohaves, three on each side, lifted up the body and slowly carried it to the funeral pyre, followed by a throng of mourners who, with violent gestures and wringing of hands, filled the air with their sad cries. After the bearers had reached the funeral pyre, they lifted the body up three times and then laid it flat on its back on a hollow area of the funeral pyre formed by the bundles. The hollow was then filled with wood so that the body was completely and fully covered. The mourners and both ranks, which the retinue had passed between, now formed a double circle around the funeral pyre and walked around it three times. Then the fire was lit; and when the pyre was fully ablaze, the dead man's belongings—articles of clothing, blankets, jewelry, baskets, etc.—were tossed into the flames. Then the horse of the deceased was brought forward and three times was led as closely as possible around the fire, to then have its neck arteries slit open not far away. After the horse had bled to death, it too was laid on a woodpile and cremated. All during this time the heart-rending lamentation of the spectators continued, and at the same time they bent their upper bodies now backward, now forward" (Ten Kate 2004: 156-157).

Despite the physical hardships Ten Kate immensely enjoyed his stay among the River Yumans because the Indians were well disposed to him and of pleasant character. At the end of his stay he organized a dance event to ascertain himself of the predominant physical types among the Yumans and as an opportunity to observe some of their dances. The dance turned out to be more of a pleasant diversion for Ten Kate than expected, and he related the affair as follows:

"My proposal that I would treat the Mohaves to coffee with sugar and white bread if they later would agree to perform some dances was greeted with satisfaction; and when I was ready to leave, Jim told me that the Mohaves still found me 'a pretty good doctor,' and that I wasn't as bad as I at first seemed to be! ... During the evening, a throng of roughly 170 Indians—men, women, and children—came to the fort. I had arranged for nearly 500 small loaves to be baked and at the same time twenty-five gallons of warm coffee with sugar to be added, and this was distributed to the Indians at the door of the canteen. Then they headed to the two huge fires which the commandant at my request had ordered to start in a large space near the hospital. When they had made themselves at home and I had then passed around a quantity of tobacco, the dancing began."

"One of their dances consisted of a row of men and women facing each other and positioned close together moving slowly up and down to the monotonous sound of a chant and a rattle. The space where they were constantly moving backwards and forward in alternation took up just a few meters. The row of women was always in a crouching position, that of the men only toward the end of the dance when everybody stuck their heads together,

uttered a kind of growling noise, and then chanting and dancing both came abruptly to an end. Another dance consisted of the rapid rotation of several chanting bucks and squaws, gathered hand in hand around Indians, also chanting, who were in the middle of the circle. The finest dance consisted of a number of men, arrayed in two rows facing each other, up and down poised sideways in rhythm with a sorrowful chant. Then they grabbed the hands of the person standing next to them and leaned against each other with the underarm, then abruptly bent over forward, and, in time to the chant, shifted the left leg in turns forward and backwards while the right leg remained in place. This was also part of the ceremony somewhat vaguely described by Dr. Webb which takes place during the cremation ceremony."

"The half moon hovered high above the silent banks of the stream and until deep in the night the chanting of the Indians reverberated around the flickering fires. If ever people have approached Rousseau's ideal state of felicity, the Mohaves must be the ones. Children of the moment, content in the present and unconcerned about the future, their life passes by like a carefree dream. Now and then sickness and sorrow make their rounds among them. Both inflict wounds, but these quickly heal; and the child-like cheerfulness promptly returns like the sun of their homeland after a sandstorm or downpour. But this dream-like existence will not endure much longer. 'Civilization,' which has already taken root at several points along the silent stream, will spread. With the railway will come throngs of fortune-hunters, unprincipled and avaricious, who will settle on their best lands and burrow through their mountains for gold. ... There will be more sickness and sorrow. Death will cut a more rapid swathe than before. Discord, falsehood, greed, treachery will prevail among that people, who will scatter and in the course of time dissolve into the turbid stream of 'civilization'" (Ten Kate 2004: 159-160).

Rattles were made of hollowed-out and dried gourds, into which pebbles were put to produce sound. Heated and molten gum from greasewood (Sarcobatus) and arrow weed (Pluchea sericea) secured the wooden handle at one end, not protruding at the upper end (Spier 1955: 8). Some rattles were made from pottery, but probably only for external trade. As rhythm instruments rattles were used to keep time during singing, music, and dancing at both social and ceremonial occasions.

The gourd sounding body of this rattle is painted red, over which several broad white lines are applied

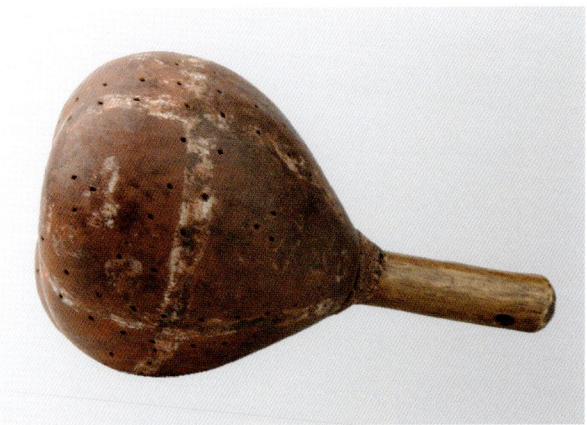

Fig. 65   Mohave gourd rattle; *agnáhljah* (TK), *axnalya* (Spier 1955: 8); gourd, wood, pigment; l. 25 cm, d. 14 cm; ca. 1880 (RMV 362-194).

longitudinally and one transversely across (Fig. 65). In addition, a design is applied in small perforations, partially following the outline of the white cross-bands, enabling the sound to emanate more strongly from the rattle (cf. Spier 1955: 9, fig. 2e). It consists of four double vertical lines of pricked holes, transected by one double horizontal line. In all of the eight subsections a triangle of three pricked holes is applied. The loop attached to the handle when Ten Kate collected it was lost in storage.

The Walapai

From Fort Mohave Ten Kate traveled by military ambulance to The Needles, a railway depot of the Atlantic and Pacific Railroad under construction. After spending a night on a blanket in a linen tent, housing the "French restaurant" which served bad whiskey and even worse food, he hitched a ride for a few miles with a railroad crew. The construction train took him twelve miles further east from where the passengers train took people on to Albuquerque. Ten Kate deboarded in Kingman, not more than a camp of linen tents, sheds, and a few buildings. Near the town was a camp occupied by Walapais who lived in a sad symbiosis with the frontier settlement as beggars, drunks, and prostitutes. Demoralization was rampant, as exemplified by the prevalence of alcoholism and venereal disease.

Ten Kate spent the night in a room above the store operated by Colonel S. and the next day rode south into the mountains with two Native guides to visit another camp. Because of the elevation, the scenery was verdant and the climate invigorating, a refreshing change after his stay in the hot Colorado River Valley. After a trek of ten miles, Ten Kate and his companions arrived in the camp

of Chief Leve-Leve, the peace chief of the Walapai. The headman's home consisted of a shelter of paloverde branches standing in a half-circle, over which pieces of old canvas and several Navajo blankets were spread. The chief was out hunting with the other men, and only the headman's son-in-law and women and children were present. Ten Kate approached the chief's in-law, who spoke some English, and found him willing to act as his informant.

The Dutch anthropologist learned that Walapai or Hualapai meant 'Forest People' and that their number was about 700. They lived throughout northwestern Arizona and had camps in such locations as Mineral Park, Hackberry, Peach Springs, and Kingman. Although they had recently been assigned a reservation, no one knew where it was located, not even the Indian Inspector from Washington. The Walapai war chief Serum (Cherum) had bravely led the opposition of the Walapai against the American army and White settlement of the area in 1867–69, but had been forced to surrender when the intruders depleted the game on which the Indians relied for their livelihood and settlers occupied their best lands by means of force. During the winter of 1879–80 the Indians were forced to ask for government rations to survive the cold season.

In 1883 the Walapai subsisted on mescal roots, yucca fruits, and grass seeds. The seeds were collected by the women. With a seed beater woven from young twigs they struck against the grass stalks and caught the seeds in a small basket tray that was repeatedly emptied in a large carrying basket. Ten Kate was offered cooked mescal and enjoyed its sweetish taste, much to the delight of the Indians, who appreciated that a White man accepted and valued their traditional cuisine. The Walapai carried their water in water jugs, *sowáh-ah*, often holding several liters, and consisting of tightly woven twigs covered with a thick layer of red resin. Handles were made of horsehair.

From rabbit skins and rodent skins the Walapai also made fine blankets or cloaks, which they exchanged with the Mohave and other tribes. Their footwear closely resembled that of the Southern Paiute. Most Walapai wore citizen's dress at the time of Ten Kate's visit, but kept their hair long and hanging loose, except for some men who bound it together with a purple head band.

Ten Kate only spent half a day among the Walapai and returned to Kingman that same evening to prepare for his journey to the Pima of south-central Arizona.

Rabbits were hunted individually and collectively. Their skins to be used for blankets were buried in damp soil before use to make them supple. They were worn during

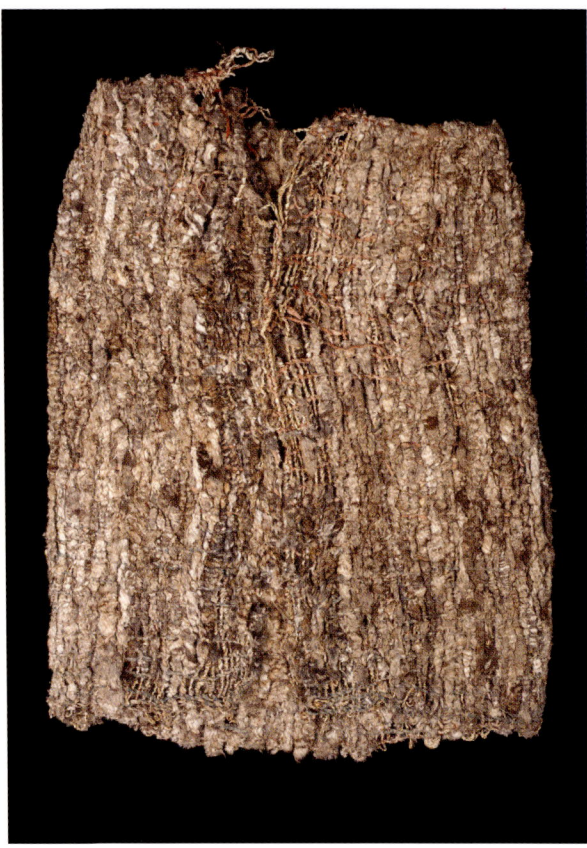

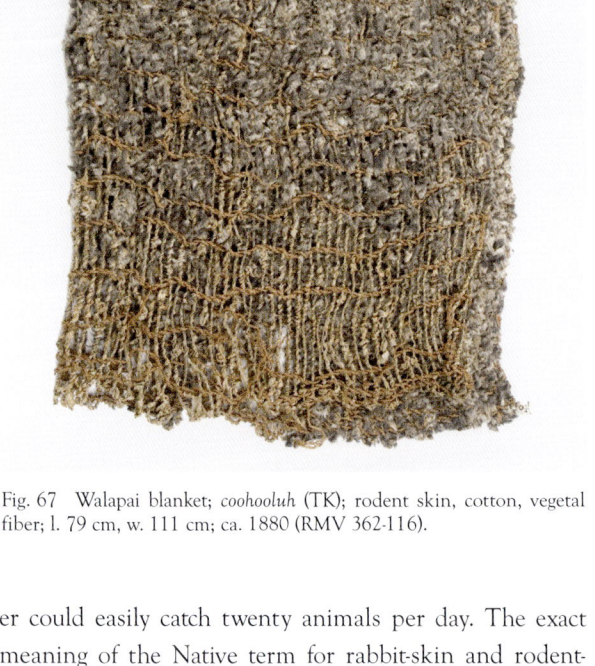

Fig. 66   Walapai blanket; *coohooluh* (TK); rabbit skin, cotton; l. 103 cm, w. 132 cm; ca. 1880 (RMV 362-115).

Fig. 67   Walapai blanket; *coohooluh* (TK); rodent skin, cotton, vegetal fiber; l. 79 cm, w. 111 cm; ca. 1880 (RMV 362-116).

the cold season (Fig. 66). Women had two such blankets sewn together at the shoulder and drew them close to the body with a yucca braided belt around the waist (Kroeber et al. 1935: 67, 91, 106; Ewing 1960: 65). This specimen has wefts consisting of strings of red and blue calico cloth.

A variety of rodents was hunted for their meat as well as skins, including kangaroo rats and prairie dogs. This was mostly an individual undertaking, but an adept hunt-er could easily catch twenty animals per day. The exact meaning of the Native term for rabbit-skin and rodent-skin blankets which Ten Kate recorded, *coohooluh*, is not known but is derived from *uhu'l*, the Walapai term for 'mice' (Kroeber et al. 1935: 67–68, 74–75). This specimen has wefts of tightly twisted two-ply reddish-brown vegetal fiber, possibly cedar bark. Double rows of wefts strength-en the top and bottom edge (Fig. 67).

Fig. 68   Walapai seed beater; *áhvayjay* (TK); willow; l. 38 cm, w. 11.2 cm; ca. 1880 (RMV 362-117).

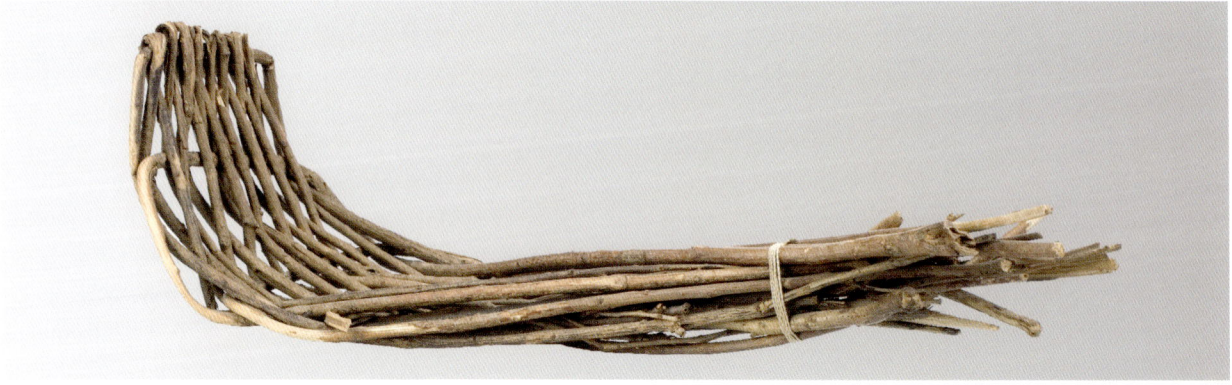

Virtually all Walapai basketry was made by twining, predominantly diagonally, and it was manufactured in a variety of utilitarian types: conical seed gathering baskets, large but light burden or firewood baskets, winnowing and parching trays, mush trays and bowls, globular water bottles with a cover of pitch, hats, etc. The material used for rods and splints was mostly squaw bush (*Condalia spathulata*), and before weaving began, the twigs were dried to prevent warping of the basket. Black willow (*Salix nigra*) and sumac (*Rhus*) were also used to a certain extent. Seed beaters (Fig. 68) were not made in a twining but a wicker technique. Ten Kate recorded the Native name of this artifact as *áhvajjay*, meaning 'beater,' but the full name was recorded by Robert McKennan of Kroeber's research team as *sele' a'via* ('seed beater'). The Walapai harvested a variety of wild seeds. These were gathered by beating the grasses and stems of plants with the beaters and catching the seeds and kernels in conical seed baskets or sometimes in basketry bowls. The major seed plant was called *sele'* and ripened in June/July. It was first boiled and roasted or immediately roasted with charcoal on a basketry parching tray, ground into flour, and baked into chunks or boiled in a mush. After drying and parching, the seeds could also be stored for later use (Mason 1904: 518; Kroeber et al. 1935: 48, 55, 79–81; Ewing 1960: 68–69; Whiteford 1988: 101–104; Bernstein et al. 2003: 73; Herold 2005: 80–81).

The Yavapai

Ten Kate did not visit the Yavapai in the Verde River Valley. However, on his way from Hermosillo to Yuma he encountered a group of Indian scouts in Calabasas who were employed by the American federal army to assist in the pursuit and capture of renegade Apaches. Two of them turned out to be Yavapais, and from one of them Ten Kate purchased a flute. Despite the anthropologist's pleas, the Indian refused to play it for him. When Ten Kate did fieldwork among the Apache at San Carlos, he encountered several Yavapais among them and acquired a feather hair ornament and a quiver with arrows from them.

Ten Kate (2004: 216) noted: "A head ornament of the Apaches-Yumas present at the same place [San Carlos, AZ] consists of feathers of the wild turkey and *A. chrysaëtos*." Ten Kate was fully aware that the term "Apache-Yuma" was a nineteenth-century misnomer for Yavapai groups. In addition to referring to the "Apache-Yumas," he states that they call themselves *Yavepé-Kutchán*, 'Yavapai-Yumas' (Ten

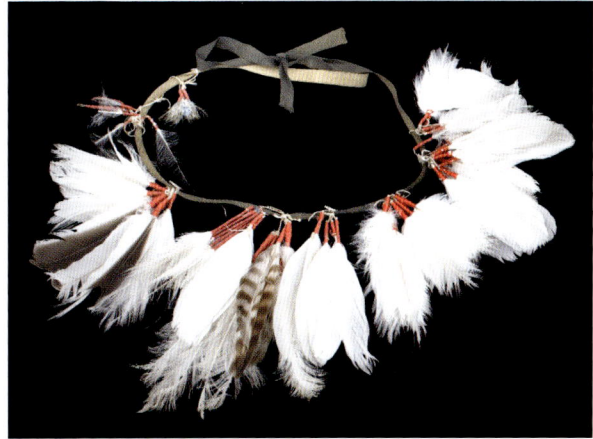

Fig. 69 Yavapai hair ornament; feathers, cotton, hide; l. (double) 56 cm; feathers: l. 8–16 cm; ca. 1880 (RMV 361-19).

Kate 2004: 208). There are several references of Yavapai boys or men wearing one or two feathers in their hair for ornamentation (Drucker 1941: 116; Gifford 1932: 228; 1936: 278), but Ten Kate's specimen, consisting of turkey (*Meleagris*) and two Golden Eagle (*Aquila chrysaetos*) feathers, looks more elaborate than that, nevertheless it is of exceedingly simple construction. He collected it at San Carlos, presumably from a Yavapai living among them (Fig. 69).

The four-holed flute, used in courting, has no carved mouthpiece or inner bridge (Fig. 70). The incised designs of dots and diagonal stripes, applied in four segments separated by painted blue bands, are colored with blue and red pigments.

Ten Kate collected a quiver with arrows at San Carlos, Arizona, in June/July 1883. The arrows are simple, solid wood shafts fletched with three vanes each. Two were notched for points which are now missing, and the other

Fig. 70 Yavapai flute; cane, pigments; l. 46 cm; ca. 1880 (RMV 362-73). Yuma gourd rattle; *gnagl* or *gnahl* (TK), *ekna'tl* (Forde 1931: 130), *axma'* (Densmore 1932: 25); wood, squash, paint, cotton, resin; l. 31 cm, w. 13 cm; ca. 1880 (RMV 362-75).

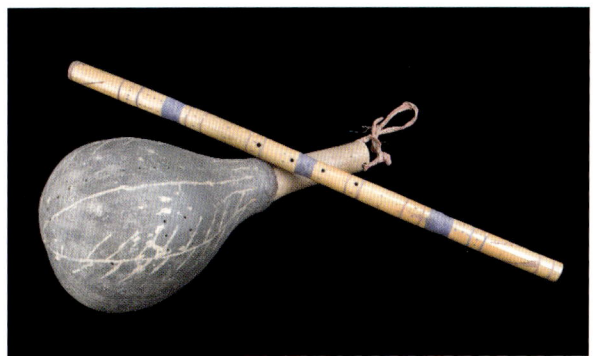

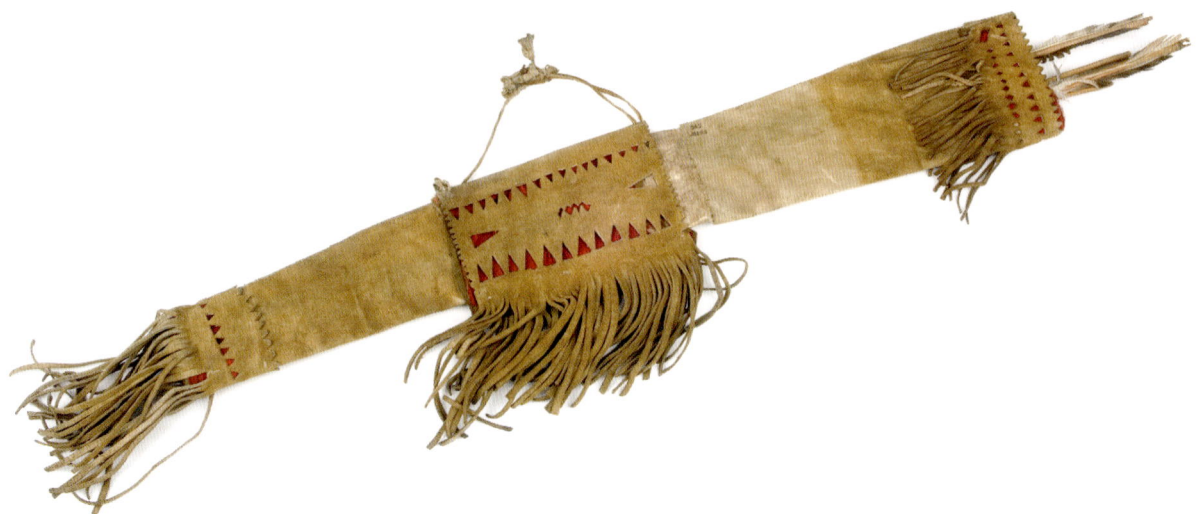

Fig. 71   Quiver with six arrows; buckskin, rawhide, red flannel, sinew, wood, feathers; quiver: l. 88 cm, w. 14 cm; arrows: average l. 90 cm; ca. 1880 (RMV 362-195).

four were simply sharpened to a dull point. The quiver is made of buckskin (Fig. 71). At the mouth and foot fringed cuffs of buckskin with decorative cut-outs were added, which allow red flannel underneath to show through. Around the body of the quiver is a short sleeve of thin rawhide, over which is sewn another piece of fringed buckskin with cut-outs atop red flannel. This type of decoration is commonly found on Chiricahua, Mescalero, and Western Apache saddlebags (see chapter 6, "The Apache," Figs. 139–142). The arrangement of three decorative zones at the mouth, sleeve, and base, each with fringe, appears to be a standardized arrangement on a number of Chiricahua quivers (Opler 1941: pl. XIIIa). How common it may be on Western Apache quivers is unknown. However, what makes this quiver collected by Ten Kate of more than ordinary interest is that it was catalogued as "Apache-Mohave"—a nineteenth-century misnomer for Yavapai groups. This is something that Ten Kate was well aware of (2004: 208–209), and he clearly identified the "Apache-Mohave" as the Yavepe subtribe of the Yavapai (see Khera and Mariella 1983: 38–39). Unfortunately, we cannot be certain whether this indicates that Ten Kate knew this quiver to have been *made* by a Yavapai, or whether it means it was *purchased* from a Yavapai whom Ten Kate encountered at San Carlos. Descriptions of Yavapai quivers are not detailed enough to shed light on this matter (Gifford 1932: 224; 1936: 286–287). Yavapai and Western Apache material culture are notoriously similar, and it would not be surprising if this quiver was indeed made by a Yavapai, but there is no way to be completely certain at

this time (cf. Mason 1894: pls. lxxvii, lxxviii; Ferg 1987: 50–52).

The Maricopa

During his 1882–83 journey of fieldwork Ten Kate also bypassed the Maricopa. However, while in Arizona in 1888

Fig. 72   Tobacco bag; hide, pigment; l. 114 cm, w. 22 cm; ca. 1870–1880 (WMR 17976).

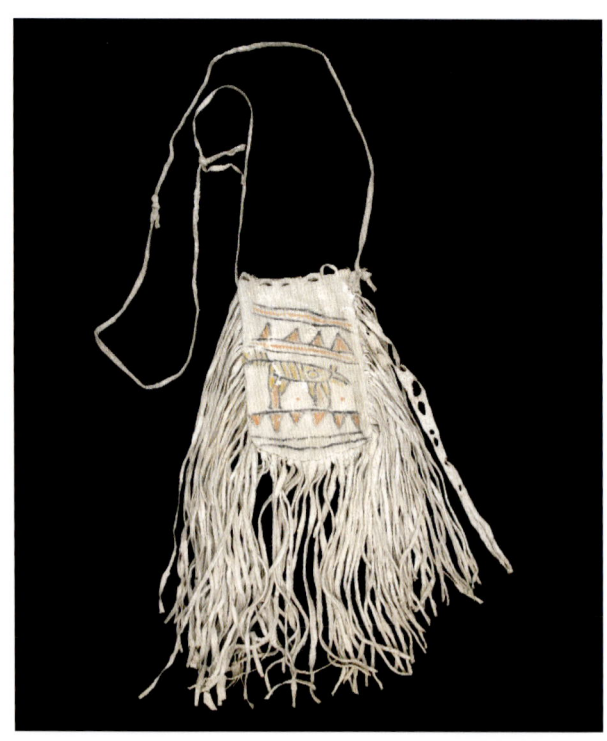

as a member of the Hemenway Southwestern Archaeological Expedition, he paid a visit to several Maricopa settlements on the Salt River near the Mormon town of Lehi. The Indian camps consisted of dwellings made of branches and reeds. Their occupants still wore the traditional scanty dress, although cotton shirts and women's dresses bought from traders were coming in vogue among the Indians who had converted to Mormonism (Ten Kate 1925: 118-119; Hovens 1995: 681-682).

Both men and women indulged in smoking tobacco in cane pipes or cornhusk wrappers for social purposes. Shamans smoked tobacco during curing ceremonies (cf. Gifford 1933: 269-270). This shoulder-strapped bag with leather fringe and painted triangular and leaf designs is a rare specimen (Fig. 72). One side has a painted geometric design, while the other exhibits an animal, a coyote according to Ten Kate, who collected this specimen in 1888 while working for the Hemenway Southwestern Archaeological Expedition (see chapter 14, "Archaeology").

References

Bee, Robert L.
1983   Quechan. In: Alfonso Ortiz (ed.), *Southwest* (Handbook of North American Indians 10. W. C. Sturtevant, gen. ed.; Washington, DC: Smithsonian Institution), 86–98.

Bernstein, Bruce et al.
2003   *The Language of Native American Baskets: From the Weavers' View*. Washington, DC: National Museum of the American Indian.

Blackburn, Thomas C. and Travis Hudson
1990   *Time's Flotsam: Overseas Collections of California Indian Material Culture*. Menlo Park, CA: Ballena Press.

Bolz, Peter and Hans-Ulrich Sanner
1999   *Native American Art: The Collections of the Ethnological Museum Berlin*. Berlin: G+H Verlag.

Cleland, Charles F.
1980   Yuma Dolls. *American Indian Art Magazine* 5(3): 36–41, 71.

Conn, Richard
1979   *Native American Art in the Denver Art Museum*. Denver, CO: Denver Art Museum.

Culin, Stewart
1907   *Games of the North American Indians*. Annual Report of the Bureau of American Ethnology 24. Washington, DC.

Densmore, Frances
1932   *Yuman and Yaqui Music*. Bulletin of the Bureau of American Ethnology 110. Washington, DC.

Devereux, George
1950   Amusements and Sports of Mohave Children. *Masterkey* 24: 143-152.

Douglas, Frederic H.
1953   *Ten Yuma Pots*. Material Culture Notes 19. Denver, CO.

Drucker, Philip
1941   *Culture Element Distributions: XVII Yuman-Piman*. University of California Anthropological Records 6(3). Berkeley, CA: University of California Press.

Euler, Robert C.
1982   Ceramic Patterns of the Hakataya Tradition. *Arizona Archaeologist* 15: 53-70.

Ewing, Henry P.
1960   The Pai Tribes. *Ethnohistory* 7(1): 61-80.

Fathauer, George H.
1954   The Structure and Causation of Mohave Warfare. *Southwestern Journal of Anthropology* 10(1): 97-118.

Ferg, Alan
1987   (ed.) *Western Apache Material Culture: The Goodwin and Guenther Collections*. Tucson, AZ: University of Arizona Press.

Forbes, Jack D.
1965   *Warriors of the Colorado: The Yumans of the Quechan Nation and Their Neighbors*. Norman, OK: University of Oklahoma Press.

Ford, Richard I.
1983   Inter-Indian Exchange in the Southwest. In: Alfonso Ortiz (ed.), *Southwest* (Handbook of North American Indians 10. W. C. Sturtevant, gen. ed.; Washington, DC: Smithsonian Institution), 711-722.

Forde, Cecil Darryl
1931   Ethnography of the Yuma Indians. *University of California Publications in American Archaeology and Ethnology* 28(4): 83-278.

Furst, Jill Leslie
2001   *Mojave Pottery, Mojave People: The Dillingham Collection of Mojave Ceramics*. Santa Fe, NM: School of American Research Press.

Gifford, Edward W.
1928   Pottery-Making in the Southwest. *University of California Publications in American Archaeology and Ethnology* 23(8): 352-373.
1932   *The Southeastern Yavapai. University of California Publications in American Archaeology and Ethnology* 29(3): 177-252.
1933   The Cocopa. *University of California Publications in American Archaeology and Ethnology* 31(5): 257-334.
1936   Northeastern and Western Yavapai. *University of California Publications in American Archaeology and Ethnology* 34(4): 247-354.

Herold, Joyce
2005   Baskets of the Southwest and Great Basin. In: Jill R. Chancey (ed.), *By Native Hands: Woven Treasures from the Lauren Rogers Museum of Art* (Laurel, MS: Lauren Rogers Museum of Art), 76-107.

Herzog, George
1928   The Yuman Musical Style. *Journal of American Folklore* 41: 183-231.

Hovens, Pieter

1995   Ten Kate's Hemenway Expedition Diary, 1887-1888. *Journal of the Southwest* 37(4): 635-700.

Kaemlein, Wilma R.

1954   Yuma Dolls and Yuma Flutes in the Arizona State Museum. *The Kiva* 20(2-3): 1-10.

Khera, Sigrid and Patricia S. Mariella

1983   Yavapai. In: Alfonso Ortiz (ed.), *Southwest* (Handbook of North American Indians 10. W. C. Sturtevant, gen. ed.; Washington, DC: Smithsonian Institution), 38-54.

Kroeber, Alfred L.

1925   *Handbook of the Indians of California.* Bulletin of the Bureau of American Ethnology 78. Washington, DC.

Kroeber, Alfred L. and Michael Harner

1955   Mohave Pottery. *University of California Anthropological Records* 16(1): 1-30.

Kroeber, Alfred L. et al.

1935   *Walapai Ethnography.* Memoirs of the American Anthropological Association 42. Menasha, WI.

Mason, Otis T.

1887   Cradles of the American Aborigines. *Annual Report of the Smithsonian Institution for 1886*: 161-212.

1894   North American Bows, Arrows, and Quivers. *Annual Report of the Smithsonian Institution for 1893*: 631-679.

1904   Aboriginal American Basketry: Studies in a Textile Art without Machinery. *Annual Report of the U.S. National Museum for 1902*: 171-548.

Opler, Morris E.

1941   *An Apache Life-Way: The Economic, Social and Religious Institutions of the Chiricahua Indians.* Chicago, IL: University of Chicago Press.

Orchard, William C.

1929   *Beads and Beadwork of the American Indians.* Contributions from the Museum of the American Indian 11. New York, NY.

Rogers, M. J.

1936   Yuman Pottery Making. *San Diego Museum Papers* 2: 1-44. [Reprinted 1973.]

Smith, Gerald A.

1977   *The Mojave Indians.* San Bernardino, CA: San Bernardino County Museum Association.

Smith, Gerald A. and Ruth D. Simpson

1964   *Basketmakers of San Bernardino County.* Bloomington, CA: San Bernardino County Museum Association.

Spier, Leslie

1923   Southern Diegueno Customs. *University of California Publications in American Archaeology and Ethnology* 20: 297-358.

1933   *Yuman Tribes of the Gila River.* Chicago, IL: University of Chicago Press.

1936   *Cultural Relations of the Gila River and Lower Colorado Tribes.* Yale University Publications in Anthropology 3. New Haven, CT.

1955   *Mohave Culture Items.* Museum of Northern Arizona Bulletin 28. Flagstaff, AZ.

Stewart, Kenneth M.

1947a   Mohave Hunting. *Masterkey* 21(3): 80-84.

1947b   Mohave Warfare. *Southwestern Journal of Anthropology* 3(3): 257-278.

1983   Mohave. In: Alfonso Ortiz (ed.), *Southwest* (Handbook of North American Indians 10. W. C. Sturtevant, gen. ed.; Washington, DC: Smithsonian Institution), 55-70.

Taylor, Edith S. and William W. Wallace

1947   Mohave Tattooing and Face-Painting. *Masterkey* 21(6): 183-195.

Ten Kate, Herman F. C.

1885   *Reizen en Onderzoekingen in Noord Amerika.* Leiden: E. J. Brill.

1925   *Over Land en Zee; Schetsen en Stemmingen van een Wereldreiziger.* Zutphen: W. J. Thieme.

2004   *Travels and Researches in Native North America, 1882-1883.* P. Hovens, L. A. Hieb, and W. J. Orr eds. Albuquerque, NM: University of New Mexico Press. [Translation of Ten Kate 1885.]

Trippel, Eugene J.

1984   The Yuma Indians. *Journal of California and Great Basin Anthropology* 6(2): 154-183. [Orig. ed.: *Overland Monthly* 13: 561-584; 14: 1-11; 1889.]

Tsosie, Michael Philip

1992   Historic Mohave Bead Collars. *American Indian Art Magazine* 18(1): 36-49.

Waters, Michael R.

1982   The Lowland Patayan Ceramic Tradition. In: Randall H. McGuire and Michael B. Schiffer (eds.), *Hohokam and Patayan* (New York, NY: Academic Press), 275-298.

Whiteford, Andrew Hunter

1988   *Southwestern Indian Baskets: Their History and Their Makers.* Santa Fe, NM: School of American Research Press.

Williams, Anita Alvarez de

1983   Cocopa. In: Alfonso Ortiz (ed.), *Southwest* (Handbook of North American Indians 10. W. C. Sturtevant, gen. ed.; Washington, DC: Smithsonian Institution), 99-112.

4

The Southern Great Basin

The Chemehuevi

While on the Fort Mohave Reservation on the Colorado River, Ten Kate learned that in addition to the 800 Mohaves, 200 Chemehuevis were living there. The latter had chosen an area in the northwestern corner of the reservation, across the river, on the Californian side. When the fort commander loaned him his own horse, the anthropologist immediately set out for their camps and visited Chief Thomas, whom he encountered with his face covered in red paint, playing cards in a sweat lodge. The Chemehuevi dwellings were similar to those of the Quechan and Mohave. Their earth lodges or winter houses stood in shallow excavated pits, surrounded by beams and poles, with a flat roof and covered with earth and mud. Shapes varied from round to oblong and rectangular. They also constructed separate sweat lodges.

Ten Kate found the Chemehuevi completely different from the Mohave in physique, character, and language. He

Fig. 73 Chemehuevi boots; *pagáp* (TK); hide; h. 34 cm, l. 27 cm; ca. 1870–1880 (RMV 362-120).

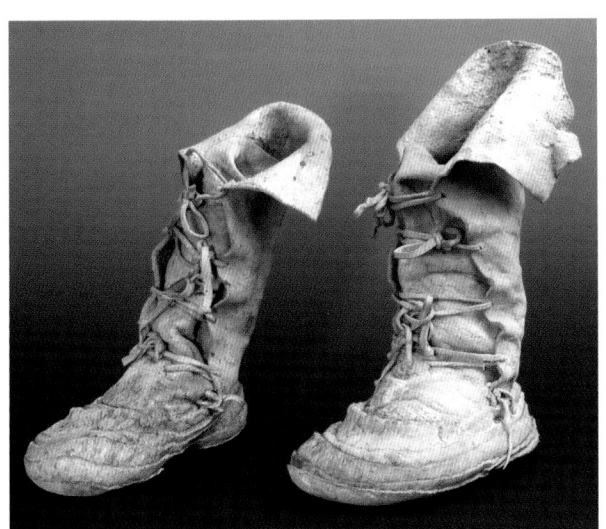

explained this by the different origin of the Chemehuevi, who were the most southern representatives of the larger group of Paiute speakers, who dominated the Great Basin. The Chemehuevi were of relatively small stature and had less rounded long skulls than the Mohave. Chemehuevi men wore thin moustaches, often clipped above the lip so that only the side parts remained. Women applied blue dye around their eyes to counter the glare of the sun. Much miscegenation had taken place with Whites, and Chemehuevi wives seemed popular among frontier men. Their languages sounded much harsher to Ten Kate than the melodious Yuman.

Dress

Ten Kate noted that the Chemehuevi cut their hair short and wore citizen's dress, including Western-style hats. He was unable to obtain items of their traditional dress, except a pair of buckskin boots and a pair of moccasins.

Clothing woven of a variety of plant fibers and rabbit skin blankets were traditionally worn by the Southern Paiute, including fiber sandals and basketry caps. Early Spanish sources mention the Chemehuevi wearing moccasins, antelope skin shirts, and feathered white headdresses (Euler 1966: 114; Stewart 1968: 12–13). When horses and firearms were acquired by the Southern Paiute after 1860, buckskin became readily available and changed clothing styles (Stewart 1968: 17, 22; Fowler and Matley 1979: 28–30).

The sturdy pair of boots collected by Ten Kate (Fig. 73) has exceptional three-layered soles of rawhide, overlapping each other slightly, with the front puckered to shape. One can speculate whether this construction is original to provide strength and warmth or the result of consecutive repairs. The hide parts of the soles and uppers are sewn with sinew, and the boots can be securely fastened with leather thongs.

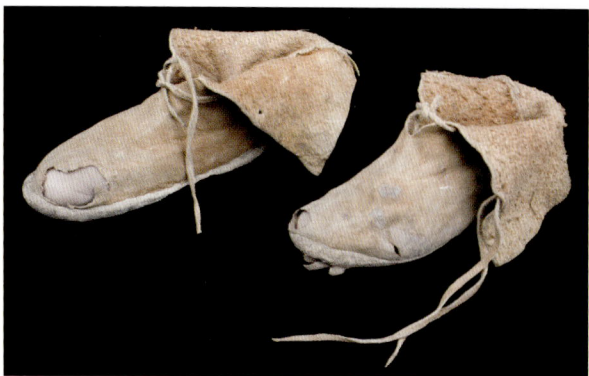

Fig. 74 Chemehuevi children's moccasins; *pagáp* (TK; Lowie 1924: 217–218), *paahts* (Van Valkenburgh 1976: 12); buckskin; l. 17 cm, w. 7 cm, h. 12.5 cm; ca. 1870–1880 (RMV 362-121).

The pair of rather worn children's moccasins (Fig. 74) have thin rawhide soles and soft buckskin uppers colored a reddish-brown. The uppers are stitched to the soles with sinew, and leather thongs are laced through holes from back to front (cf. Fowler and Matley 1979: 31–32).

Fig. 75 Chemehuevi basket maker; postcard (RMV 5910-44).

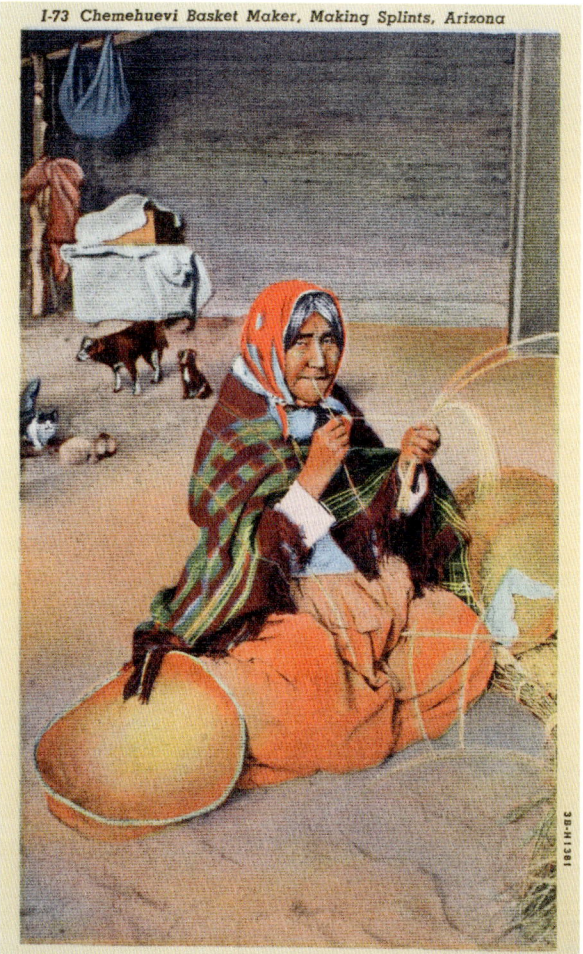

I-73 Chemehuevi Basket Maker, Making Splints, Arizona

Basketry

Comparing the material culture of the desert tribes of western Arizona, Ten Kate remarked that the pottery of the Chemehuevi was similar to that of the Mohave and Yuma, but that their finely woven and attractively decorated basketry more closely resembled that of the Papago. Notable were the waterproof quality of the most tightly woven specimens and the funnel-shaped burden baskets. Ten Kate saw similar baskets among the Yuma and Mohave and assumed that the Chemehuevi traded their crafts with those tribes.

Early documented collections of Chemehuevi basketry are preserved at the Natural History Museum of Los Angeles County (the Ammann collection from 1898–1913; Kania 2007), the National Museum of Natural History in Washington, DC (acquired from the Fred Harvey Company in 1903; Mason 1904: 518–519, pl. 232), the Carnegie Museum of Natural History in Pittsburgh, Pennsylvania (the George Wharton James collection, acquired in 1902), the Hearst Museum of Anthropology in Berkeley, California (collected by Kroeber between 1904 and 1908), and the Field Museum in Chicago, Illinois (acquired by George Dorsey in 1904; Kania 2006: 70). Thus the specimens Ten Kate collected on the Fort Mohave Reservation in 1883 are probably the earliest documented Chemehuevi baskets.

The study of Chemehuevi basketry has been neglected by anthropologists. Various observations on the craft are scattered throughout the literature, but do not provide a clear or coherent, let alone a complete picture (cf. Smith and Simpson 1964: 15–32). Clara Lee Tanner (1983: 216–225) offered the best initial study, based on an analysis of the large Birdie Brown collection at the Colorado River Indian Tribes Museum in Parker, Arizona, as well as many items from other museums and private collections. Santa Fe gallery owner John J. Kania (2006, 2007) must be credited with several subsequent studies of various collections.

The four Chemehuevi baskets collected by Ten Kate fit the characterization of the tribal craft by Tanner. All are coiled clockwise, using a three-rod foundation, and have decorative designs. These were considered as the personal property of weavers and one did not infringe thereon. Although some authors have stated that the Chemehuevi only made coiled baskets, others have qualified that statement (Smith and Simpson 1964: 16; Dalrymple 2000: 57–67). Ten Kate witnessed twined conical burden baskets and winnowing trays still being produced in 1883, types

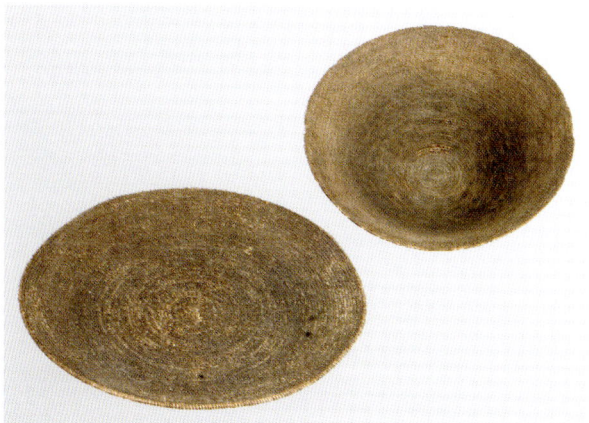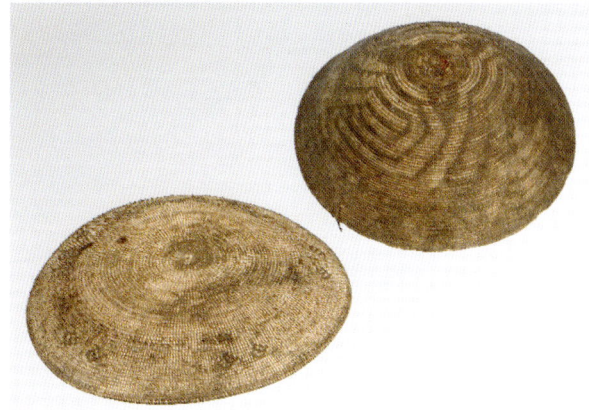

Figs. 76, 77 Chemehuevi basketry tray and bowl (left: top view; right: bottom view); RMV 362-118: *kjots* or *saghu* (Van Valkenburgh 1976: 15); willow, devil's claw; h. 5 cm, d. 43 cm; ca. 1880; RMV 362-119: *sa-puht* (Van Valkenburgh 1976: 15); willow, devil's claw; h. 15 cm, d. 43 cm; ca. 1870–1880.

typical of traditional Numic basketry from the Great Basin. He was correct in assuming that the Chemehuevi traded their fine basketry with other Colorado River tribes. When the transcontinental railroad was completed in 1883, Chemehuevi basket makers also produced wares for sale to travelers and tourists.

Ten Kate witnessed such coiled trays in use while preparing flat corn bread. Many were also used as parching trays to dry seeds and beans, including *opimpi,* mesquite beans. The harvest was put in the tray, mixed with hot charcoal, and shaken and stirred to speed up the process and prevent the food and tray from burning. This treatment not only aided preservation of the food but also improved the taste.

The preparation of the materials for making trays was carefully done, and the stripping of the bark from the willow took much time and effort. The weaving was executed precisely, the stitching tight, resulting in an even and uniform surface. The coils for the tray acquired by Ten Kate (RMV 362-118; Figs. 76, 77) have a three-rod foundation and the coiling is done clockwise. The basket shows several signs of use, including a few scorched areas, and the blackened remains of organic material between the stitched coils. Applied just below the rim, on the outside of this basket, a number of open diamonds are arranged in pairs, but have become damaged and rather faded.

Although the Great Basin Numic peoples preferred leftward coiling, clockwise coiling was typical for the Chemehuevi. However, some exceptions have been noted by Kania, who points out that the technique of rightward coiling was probably adopted from Californian neighbors. Although designs were almost exclusively executed in dark brown from yucca roots to black devil's claw (*Martynia*

proboscidea; Chemehuevi: *oah-oon-oop*), occasional use was made of the root of the Joshua tree (*Yucca brevifolia*), resulting in red designs. Designs were also applied in paint on baskets (Mason 1904: 518–519, pl. 232; Kroeber 1925: 597; Robinson 1954: 144; Miller and Miller 1967: 12; Van Valkenburgh 1976: 16; Kania 2006: 69–70).

The basketry bowl collected by Ten Kate (RMV 362-119; Figs. 76, 77) is coiled clockwise, using a three-rod foundation. It exhibits a decorative brown pattern on the outside, consisting of a solid center with diagonal meanders and triangles, faded to the extent that is has become almost invisible. The basket is blackened throughout by use and age.

A seed jar in the collection (Fig. 78) is round and bulbous in shape, but has a flat base. It is coiled clockwise, a peculiar characteristic of Chemehuevi basketry, as are the three willow rods that constitute the foundation of the coils, which are wrapped with light colored willow (*Salix*). The Chemehuevi distinguished two species of willow which they probably both used for their basketry and which they called *sagah* and *kanavi* (Laird 1976: 106). The design, applied in three horizontal bands around the jar at the top, in the middle, and on the bottom, is executed in black devil's claw (*Proboscidea altheaefolia*). Each band shows a different pattern: triangles at the top; a white zigzag pattern is the result of two interlocking bands of black triangles around the middle; and a stepped block band surrounds the lower part of the jar. The top pattern is separated from the rim coil, and the final coil is finished in black, another characteristic of Chemehuevi basketry. The application of three instead of two decorative bands is exceptional for such an early basket, but this practice became more common around the turn of the century. Two narrow buckskin loops are fastened to the rim, to

67

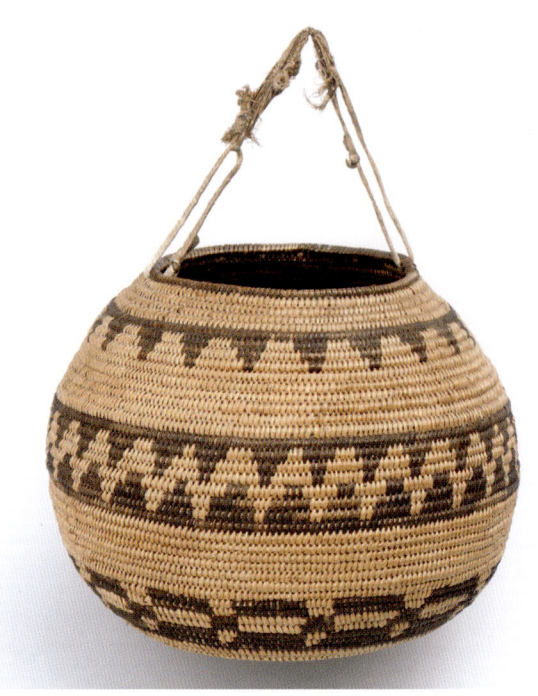

Fig. 78 Chemehuevi basketry jar; willow, devil's claw, buckskin, cotton; h. 16.5 cm, w. 19.5 cm; ca. 1880 (RMV 362-191).

which is attached a carrying handle made of cloth (Hovens and Herlaar 2004: 548; cf. Robinson 1954: 142–147; Smith and Simpson 1964: 16, 26, 29–32; Conn 1979: 239; Kania 2006).

Another basket (Fig. 79) is coiled clockwise, using a three-rod foundation, and the outer half of the tray shows

Fig. 79 Chemehuevi basketry bowl; willow, devil's claw; h. 17 cm, w. 54.5 cm; ca. 1880 (RMV 362-192).

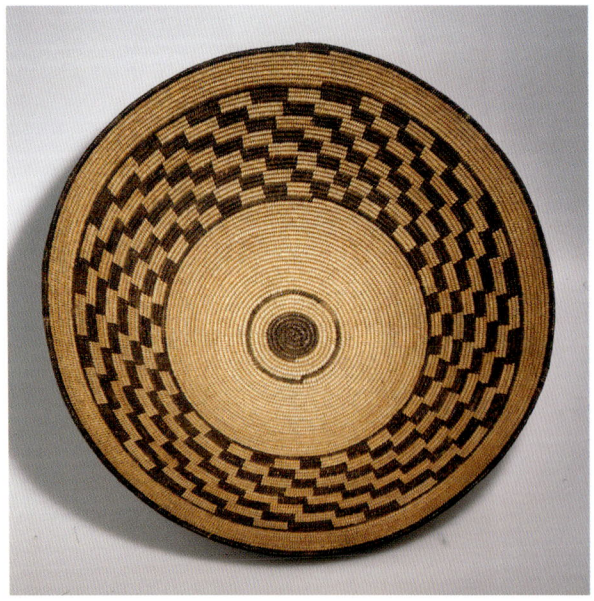

a design executed in dark devil's claw. The design consists of bands of stepped rectangles, suggesting motion by its whirling effect.

Although willow was used in most baskets, the Chemehuevi preferred to harvest another plant for basketry material if available. They called it *soo-hoo-vimp*, basket weed (Van Valkenburgh 1976: 15). However, it was rare and its botanical identity could not be established.

In addition to the baskets, Ten Kate was able to acquire a flute and a war club among the Chemehuevi for his collection.

The flute (Fig. 80) has delicately carved knobs on one end and incised crosses, accentuated by pigment, as decoration. It is probably made of elderberry, the preferred wood for carving flutes (cf. Steward 1933: 277).

Many Chemehuevis long resisted placement on a reservation, and small bands roamed the tristate region of Arizona, California, and Nevada. In 1880 engineer Oliver P. Calloway was killed by a group of Indians and they threatened war against all Whites. However, by a combination of military threat and diplomacy, the Chemehuevi were pacified, and the last bands settled on the Colorado River reservation (Stewart 1968: 24–25; Roth 1977).

The war club (Fig. 81) consists of a short stick with an enlarged cylindrical head, made from hardwood, and because of this shape is referred to as "potato masher" type. It was the principal weapon of war of the Chemehuevi and similar to Mohave war clubs (Stewart 1967: 19; cf. Euler 1966: 114–116; Fowler and Matley 1979: 68). The side of the head of the Leiden club is painted yellow, on which a zigzag pattern is applied in red, with red points in the middle of the resultant triangles. The top is stained black and a brass disk is inserted in the middle.

Ten Kate was aware of the fact that the federal government had forcefully removed the band from their fertile Chemehuevi Valley to the arid desert reservation, an "unselfish" act as he noted cynically, clearly showing where his sympathies lay. A number of Chemehuevi children visited the agency day school established in 1881. From one of the pupils Ten Kate acquired four pottery effigies. He also noted the similarity of pottery among the Yuma, Mohave, and Chemehuevi.

The similarity of pottery among these tribes as observed by Ten Kate was as well the result of the Mohave trading their wares with neighboring groups, as the Chemehuevi producing their own pottery and being substantially influenced by the craft of their neighbors (cf. Rogers 1936: 38; Baldwin 1950: 52). It was the women

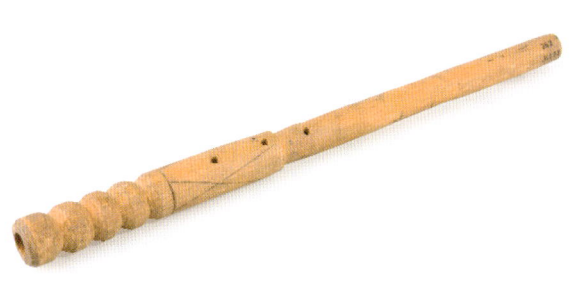

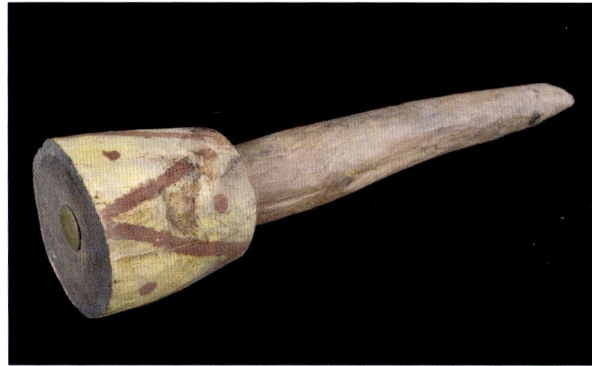

Fig. 80 Chemehuevi flute; wood, pigment; l. 37 cm; ca. 1880 (RMV 362-122).

Fig. 81 Chemehuevi war club; wood, pigment, brass; l. 39 cm, w. (at top) 11 cm; ca. 1860–1870 (RMV 362-193).

who made the pottery. The Chemehuevi dug the preferred clay with a spade made from mesquite and mixed it with crushed white rock for temper. Vessels were constructed with clay coils, smoothed inside and out by the paddle-and-anvil method, using a smooth stone on the inside and a cottonwood bark paddle on the outside surface. Cottonwood bark and wood were also used for firing. Sometimes red and black designs were applied with natural pigments (Van Valkenburgh 1976: 10–11, 23). The Southern Paiute, including the Chemehuevi, had their own pottery tradition that was less developed because of their semino-madism. Moreover, pottery making declined substantially soon after the arrival of White settlers and the introduction of Western trade goods among most bands (Lowie 1924: 225–226; Rogers 1936: 38; Baldwin 1950; Stewart 1967: 16).

Topilla, a Chemehuevi pupil at the government Indian day school in Parker, showed artistic talent by creating naturalistic clay effigies of humans and animals and making accomplished pencil drawings. Ten Kate purchased four

small human effigy busts from her (Fig. 82). It is not known whether the pottery classes during which these were made were part of the conventional art training in the regular curriculum at the school, or whether these classes were organized because of the strong pottery tradition among the Mohave that was later adopted by the Chemehuevi. In the base of one effigy (RMV 362-207) the name of Topilla is carved. This was probably encouraged by her teacher, but possibly suggested by Ten Kate. Small pottery effigies had been made for a long time among the Paiute and were used as children's toys (Fowler and Matley 1979: 84).

The women teachers told Ten Kate that the Chemehuevi youngsters generally were more intelligent than their Mohave counterparts. They had observed the same for boys compared to girls. Intertribal personality differences were also noted, the Chemehuevi being headstrong and unforgiving, while the Mohave were impulsive but light-hearted and humorous according to the notes of the Dutch anthropologist.

Fig. 82 Chemehuevi ceramic busts; pottery; h. 8.8–10.5 cm; 1883 (RMV 362-205, -206, -207, -208).

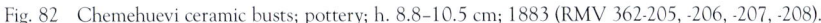

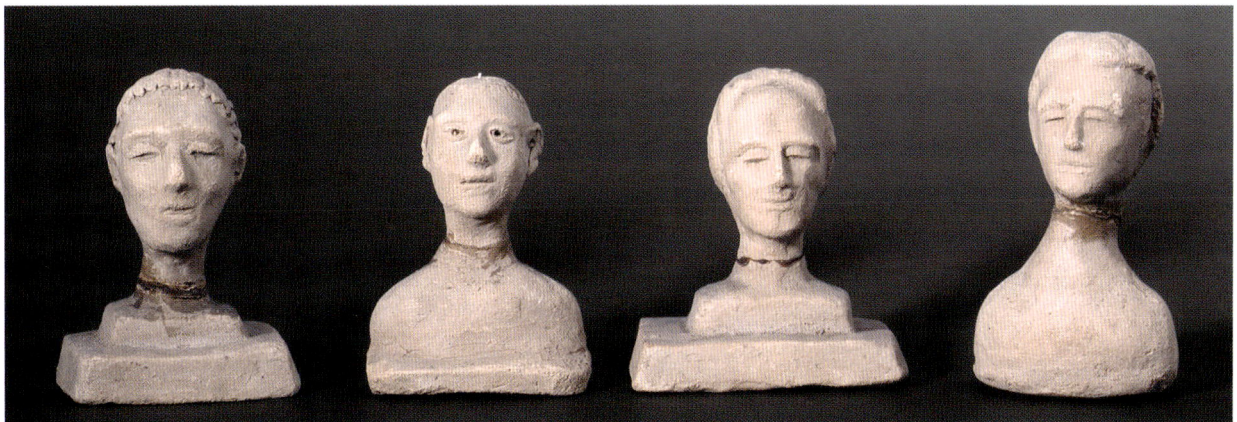

The Southern Paiute

On 14 May 1883 Ten Kate and General Charles H. Howard, the Indian Inspector from Washington, DC, boarded the steamer "Mohave" for a journey upriver to visit the Southern Paiute. That same day they reached Cottonwood Island, occupied by Paiutes who earned a livelihood by keeping steamboats supplied with firewood. The Indians had almost stripped the island of its cottonwood and mesquite trees. Most wore an approximation of citizen's dress. One carried a fine bow, decorated on the inside with numerous plumed scalps from quails. On the Nevada shore Mount Newberry rose. The Indians considered this the place where their former paradise was situated. According to tribal oral tradition as told to Ten Kate, when they had killed a good headman, the Great Spirit punished them by expulsion of the band to the hot river valley. However, the Indians stayed away from many of the mountains along the Colorado River, especially Mount Newberry, because the dreaded the evil spirits dwelling there.

At El Dorado Canyon a mining camp was operating, and General Howard called for a meeting of the local Paiutes. During the palaver the Indians stated that they wished to stay in their motherland and refused to be placed on a reservation far removed from their beloved country. Ten Kate was impressed with the tough looking people, hardened by their way of life in a barren and forbidding country, but satisfied with the meager rewards their environment provided.

The Paiute wore the same kind of partial mustaches as the Chemehuevi. At El Dorado Canyon a few still let their hair grow long, wore a headcloth and buckskin moccasins, in addition to Western-style shirts and pants. Here too miscegenation had resulted in numerous mixed-blood offspring. One man was willing to act as informant, and from him Ten Kate obtained a short vocabulary and other information. He learned that the Paiute called themselves *Nu*, meaning 'the people.' They still hunted mountain sheep (*Ovis montana*), and grass seeds and mesquite beans were still their main wild food resources. They participated in the Western cash economy by selling firewood to boat captains and the ore smelters.

The Southern Paiute lived in very simple dwellings that consisted of bundles of branches. The only craftwork they were still engaged in was basketry. Jimsonweed (*Datura stramonium*) was chewed, and the narcotic contained in the plant produced a valued state of delirium. Excessive alcohol consumption was a serious problem, but also produced a sought-after altered state of consciousness. Ten Kate criticized the abuse of this situation by unscrupulous American traders. The Paiute still cremated their dead. Formerly they were frequently at war with the Mohave, taking scalps from their enemies. However, the last battle had taken place more than ten years ago.

Ten Kate's stay among the Southern Paiute band, now referred to as Las Vegas Paiute, was of short duration, and on 18 May the anthropologist departed, traveling downriver to continue his fieldwork among the Pima, Apache, Pueblos, Navajo, Hopi, and Zuni, before paying a visit to another tribe living on the Southwest-Great Basin margin, the Southern Ute.

The tribes of the semiarid desert of the Great Basin lived to a substantial degree on a diet of wild plant foods. These were gathered in a seasonal round, determined by the annual harvest times of tubers, bulbs, roots, greens, fruits, seeds, and nuts. A variety of specialized baskets developed over time to gather, transport, store, prepare, and serve these foodstuffs.

Twining is one of the oldest techniques with which plant fibers are woven into a variety of shapes, degrees of rigidity, and products, from flexible mats and bags to sturdy baskets and sandals. In this technique the Southern Paiute wove winnowing trays, burden baskets, water jugs, cradles, seed beaters, and hats. In addition, they produced coiled basketry: parching trays, cooking and eating baskets, and water jugs. Twined baskets were stronger and lighter than coiled burden baskets (Fowler and Dawson 1986: 724-726; Whiteford 1988: 15-24; Tisdale 2001: 86).

Conical burden baskets, mostly in diagonal twine weave, came in all sizes, from small ones used by little girls to imitate and assist their mothers in gathering a wide variety of edible plant foods, to large ones measuring eighteen inches in height and sixteen inches across, also used to carry firewood and household goods while moving camp. On their seasonal round through their territory, Paiute bands collected lily bulbs, mescal roots and crowns, yucca and cactus fruits, berries, seeds, acorns, piñon nuts, and many other vegetal foodstuffs.

To protect burden baskets against wear and tear, their outer base was often covered with a protective piece of rawhide, later harness leather, as in the specimen collected by Ten Kate (Fig. 83 left). The carrying strap is made of cotton, as are the loops with which it is affixed to the basket, secured on the inside with wooden pegs to protect the inside from tearing. The rims are reinforced by incorporating warp

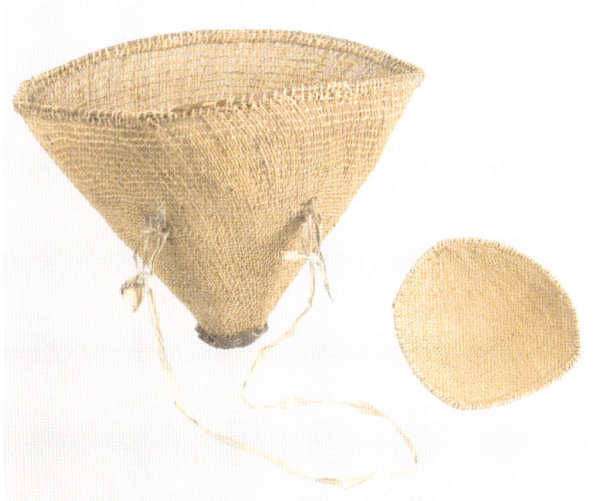

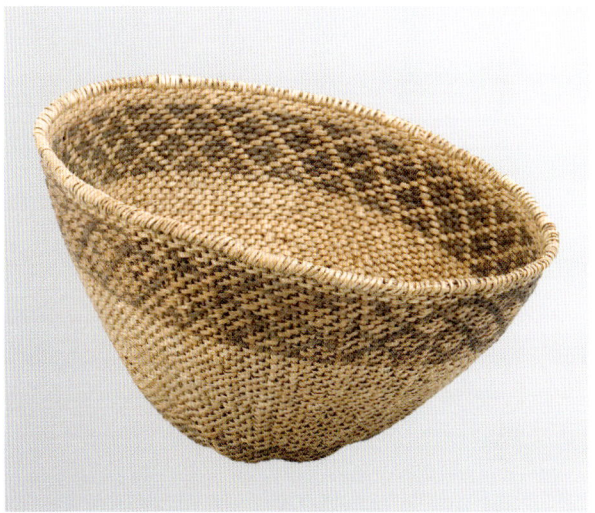

Fig. 83   Las Vegas Paiute burden basket and winnowing tray; RMV 362-123: willow, sinew, hide, cotton; h. 35.5 cm, w. 38 cm; RMV 362.124: willow; l. 20 cm, w. 19 cm, h. 6 cm; both ca. 1880.

Fig. 84   Southern Paiute woman's hat or seed basket; sumac, pigment; h. 12.5 cm, w. 21 cm; ca. 1880 (RMV 362-125).

rods and an extra rod into a bundle around the rim, sewn tightly together. The burden baskets were secured on a woman's back by a tumpline across the forehead or the upper breast. Early Southern Paiute baskets are rarely decorated as their utilitarian function was of primary importance (Mason 1904: 493-494; Steward 1933: 272-273; Fowler and Dawson 1986: 725; McGreevy and Whiteford 1985: 15-27; Whiteford 1988: 14, 17-19; Fulkerson and Curtis 1995: 38-39).

The winnowing tray (Fig. 83 right) was used to separate chaff and shells from seeds and nuts that were collected during the harvest season. The loosening of the chaff from seeds and the opening of pine nuts was accomplished by mixing hot charcoal with the seeds and nuts on roasting trays and rhythmically tossing the contents into the air, for the wind to dispose of the chaff and shells or to open the pine nuts. This required dexterity and attentiveness on the part of the women, as the trays should not be burned. With winnowing trays the vegetal foods were thrown up in the air or cascaded on the ground in the wind to separate the inedible parts from the food parts. The slightly trianguloid shape of this fine diagonally twined winnowing tray is characteristic of the Southern Paiute (Mason 1904: 489, 493-495; Whiteford 1988: 18-19; Fulkerson and Curtis 1995: 32-35; Bernstein et al. 2003: 55).

Protection against the sun was essential in the Great Basin desert, and Native women wore diagonally twined basketry hats that often doubled as seed baskets and vice versa. The hats also protected the forehead against the pressure of the tumpline while carrying heavy loads. A design band near the base is typical of such hats, in this case (Fig. 84) showing the same geometric design mirrored on the outside and inside in positive and negative form. This effect is sometimes the result of using splints from which the bark has been removed on one side. In other cases splints were dyed or designs were applied on a basket's surface with paint. Other hats have two or even three design bands of varying width (Mason 1904: 490-491; Whiteford 1988: 17-18, 21; Fowler and Matley 1979: 11, 14, 18-19, 22-23, 114, 122-123; Finger 2003).

The Southern Ute

When in Santa Fe in the late summer of 1883, Ten Kate read news reports about an uprising among the Ute in Colorado, whom he intended to visit. Instead of changing his plans, he seemed even more determined to do fieldwork among the Ute bands in the southwestern part of the state. In mid-September of 1883 the anthropologist left Santa Fe and journeyed northward, reaching Española, the terminus of the Denver and Rio Grande Railway, by mail coach in five and a half hours. The train took through the mountains via Cumbress Pass to Antonito in southern Colorado and then west to Ignacio, the agency of the Southern Ute. He enjoyed the autumnal colors displayed along the route by oak, aspen, and willows interspersed among the conifers, the blooming high meadows, and the peaks rising to increasingly greater heights. Although he slightly suffered from the altitude, the pure mountain air had a bracing effect on him.

Contrary to the newspaper reports he had read, Ten Kate found the situation at the Rio de Los Piños Agency quiet and peaceful. He surveyed the area around Ignacio and made several trips across the reservation, accompanied by the agency physician Dr. J. J. White and the interpreter John Taylor, a Black man who was adopted by the tribe after his marriage to a Ute woman. He recalled his first impressions:

"Along the rim of the high meadow, which rises above the bottomland of the river, stand a couple of Indian tents. They have the familiar pointed shape, which one sees in all illustrations regarding Indians: a number of poles standing in a circle with the top ends resting against each other and fastened together, serving as a frame for the material the tent consists of. These were the first Indian dwellings I encountered with this shape because one does not find these tents southwest of the Rocky Mountains. In the past couple of years the tents (*kani*) of bison hide have completely vanished because the Utes have had to terminate their bison hunts since settling on the reservation. Their tents now consist of white or yellowish canvas, which is supplied by the government. But some of their *kani* are painted in the old manner with hunting and war scenes and other figures, which are difficult to explain to the uninitiated. As a rule, several tents are situated close by each other, and such a small group of graceful tipis, from whose open tip a blue column of smoke rises upward, is ensconced among the dense vegetation along a babbling brook. It is an image so lovely and distinctive that one would not grow weary observing it, while it serves as a vivid reminder of the tableaux so vividly sketched in pencil by the Indian painter Catlin."

"Three long sticks always stand a short distance from the tents, set crosswise against each other on top, so that they form a kind of trestle. On it usually rest the best pieces of clothing and equipment because in the tent itself they would probably get soiled or damaged. In the tents there is a chaotic Babel of blankets, deer hides, clothes, weapons, household implements, and food which takes up practically all the surrounding space from the one side of the entrance to the other, while the center is occupied by the fireplace. Among the distinctive household items, which one could perhaps call field gear, long, flat, approximately one meter-long valises of handsomely prepared tough white leather painted in bright colors take pride of place. Their primary function is keeping dried meat. In addition, there is another kind of leather valise in the shape of a large quiver with a flap which holds various small items. The Utes make crude basketry and water jugs woven from twigs, resembling those of the Apaches. Small children are fastened to a large carrying plank rounded off at the top by means of a sturdy leather cover, which covers the plank at the same time. A large part of the widely protruding plank sticks far above the papoose's head so that it is well protected when it is being transported. These carrying planks, though quite distinctive, lack the ornamental features of the other tribes, and there is obviously something heavy and cumbersome about them, just like the Utes themselves."

"If I stepped or rather crawled inside a tent, then I found the inhabitants, both men as well as women, often playing cards, of which they are great devotees. Then again I saw young warriors who amused themselves in small groups by dancing to the sound of a leather drum. One, then the other, took turns; and the figures which were performed consisted chiefly of turning and twisting the trunk of the body with hands on their hips while the shuffling feet barely moved from their spot. Not infrequently I also found women at work. Some of them were mending clothes, others were ornamenting moccasins with beads, and still others were preparing meals."

"Outside the tents there were even more things to catch the eye. Here a band of young warriors, a short distance from the tent, were shooting with their Sharp rifles at a target, the trunk of a cottonwood; and every time that the sharp bang was repeated through the mountains, large chunks of bark and wood chips flew up into the air, followed by the mumbling approbation of the marksmen. Elsewhere some hunters were getting ready to ascend the mountains and go deer hunting to return several days, perhaps weeks later, amply laden with a supply of meat and fine hides. Everywhere I encountered a carefree attitude and good cheer, but I missed the childlike, kindly features that characterized the Yumas and Mohaves. The Utes, in contrast, must struggle more against man and nature. In the winter there is snow and icy cold, which reigns in the mountains, with which he must contend. The rest of the year it is game that he must pursue with difficulty, if he is to find food. Formerly his most dreaded enemies were the Comanches and Kiowas, who disputed with him the right to hunt bison on the plains; later he had to struggle with the whites ..."

"The men wear their hair with a part on the top or on the side of the head, and carefully divided in back into two long, heavy braids hanging down over the chest. The braids are mostly wrapped with precious otter hides or decorated with red ribbons, while the part is frequently colored red or yellow. The women wear their hair hanging completely loose, though not as long as the men. In their case, too, the part is, as a rule, in the middle, while the long luxuriant tresses rest on the back and the shoulders as well as upon the chest."

"The men still wear almost exclusively leather leggings of Indian make and moccasins, while the upper body, on the other hand, is usually covered by an ordinary shirt and a vest. The leggings of the Utes, and of the Indians generally, differ from our trousers, in that they cover just the legs but not the abdomen nor the posteriors. They are fastened by means of garters, which are tied onto a belt around the middle, as is the gee-string running between the legs. These leggings are, as a rule, very handsomely ornamented with colored beads and are bordered with fluttering side flaps on the seam. The moccasins too are almost completely covered with porcelain beads. Blue and white beads are used almost exclusively. If the Utes wear American shirts, they wear them hanging out with the vest on top, so that the dandies thus attired cut a rather ludicrous figure in our eyes. The women wear a kind of long dress which hangs half-way down to the lower leg. Leather dresses are already rare because now they are made of cotton and cloth. The women also wear leather leggings and moccasins, but, as a rule, the latter are not ornamented."

"The Utes' ornaments consist primarily of strings of beads, a type of plastrons from seashells, and, in addition, earrings, rings, and bracelets of silver and Berlin silver. They buy the beads and seashells, as they do the Berlin silver items, in the trader's store. The seashells ... are white in color and prepared especially for the Indians in the eastern states and sent to various stores out West. They are quite precious. ... The Utes acquire silverwork from the Navajos, their southwestern neighbors. Frequently they give them dollar coins to have them made into ornaments conforming to their own taste and instructions. And their harnesses and saddles are not uncommonly ornamented with Navajo silverwork. In addition, Navajo blankets are very much in vogue among the Utes. Many Ute men smear their faces from top to bottom with a yellow and red dye, a custom which is in vogue among the younger Indians especially. In addition, they pluck out eyebrows and eyelashes, giving their painted faces a glaring, rather bizarre expression. This dye is kept in an oblong bag of coarse leather, which has the same shape as their purses and is ornamented with beads. As amulets, some men

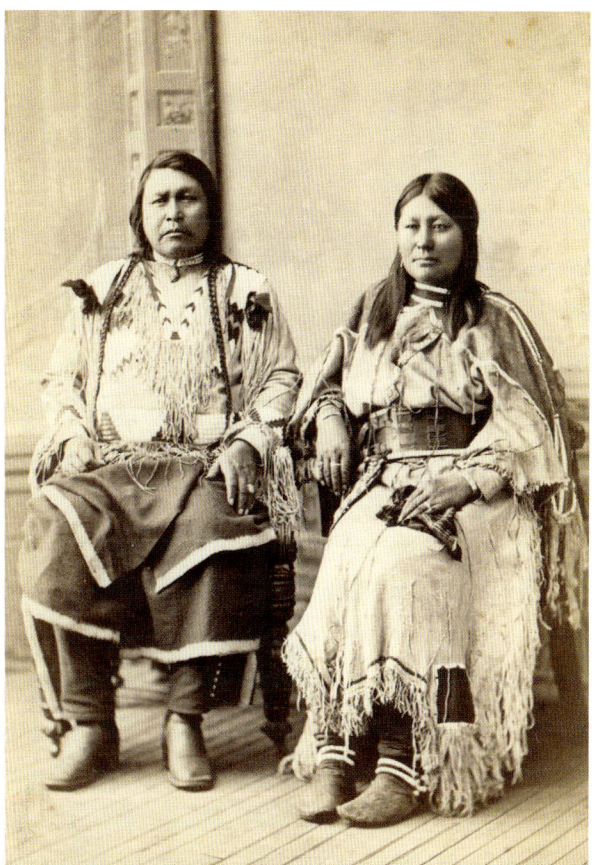

Fig. 85   Southern Ute chief Ouray and his wife Chipeta in traditional dress; Washington, DC, ca. 1880. Photographer unknown (Ten Kate coll.; RMV 414Cb46).

wear so-called 'medicine bags' on their clothing fastened to their chests, not far from the armpits."

"Much more precious than their livestock, though, are their horses—about 2,200 in number which in quality and vigor are perhaps on a par with those of the Navajos and generally of the same variety. The saddles—used by the women especially, who sit on their horses like men, just as all tribes do—consist of a wooden frame which is covered with rawhide. A very high pommel, adorned with long fringes of white chamois leather, sticks out in front and back. Some of the warriors sat silently on the ground, speaking softly now and then, while smoking their peace pipes, which made the rounds from mouth to mouth. Others stood alone or in groups, smoking cigarettes, while behind them their fine horses stood huddled together in colorful little herds. ... With a background of mountains blanketed with vegetation vanishing into a blue horizon, with a fixed cloudless sky on high and a blazing sun shining on everything, the colorful throng provided a spectacle so picturesque and distinctive that one would have wished one had the talent of a Bodmer or of a Catlin to put this on canvas and indelibly preserve it from oblivion."

"Although the Utes have the peace pipe or 'calumet,' they do not manufacture it themselves but obtain the pipe heads by barter with the Comanches. As is known, all the tribes who are in possession of the peace pipe use a single variety of rock, a variety of reddish-brown soapstone (so-called catlinite) coming from a quarry located on the Coteau des Prairies on the boundaries of present-day Minnesota and Dakota. According to Catlin, associated with the quarry (Red Pipestone Quarry) is the legend that the Great Spirit, weary of his red children's wars, summoned them all together to this spot and from the red stone of the cliff shaped a pipe that would be a symbol of peace for them. Earlier, in the vicinity of the Cimarron River in New Mexico, the Utes found a stone which has much in common with the one from up north and was, in fact, used for the same purpose as well. These pipes are very precious. A Ute, whose pipe I wanted to buy, along with the leather sheath and lovely tobacco bag ornament-

Fig. 86   Southern Ute paint bag; buckskin, glass, brass; l. 22 cm, w. 8.3 cm; ca. 1870–1880 (RMV 362-21). Southern Ute awl or needle case; *panákorokonoï* (TK); harness leather, glass beads; l. 10 cm, w. 5.8 cm; ca. 1880 (RMV 362-19).

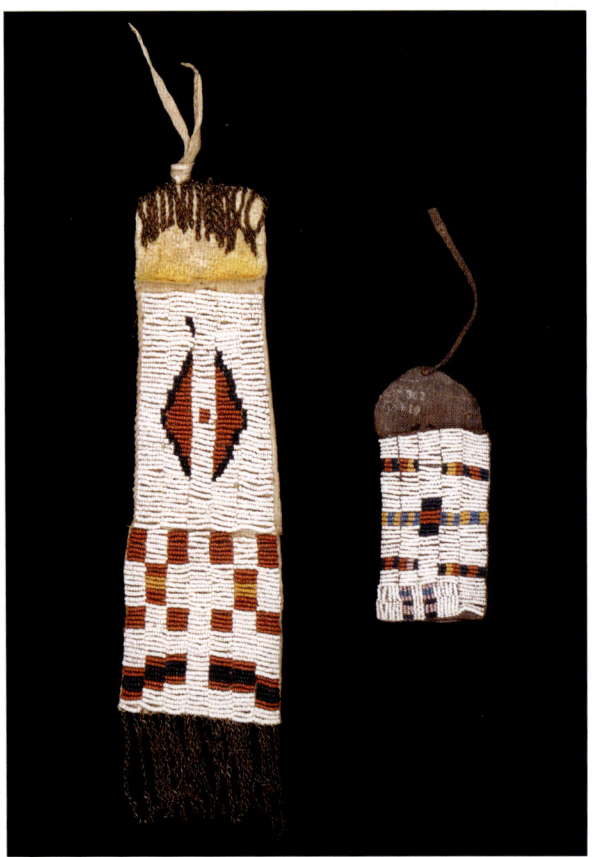

ed with colored beads, wanted nothing more or less than a horse in exchange for it. As much as I would also have liked to have enriched our Ethnographic Museum with a peace pipe, I had to let the warrior keep his treasure."

"At the present time the Utes are supplied almost exclusively with firearms and, indeed, with the finest Sharp, Winchester, and Ballard rifles. Bow and arrows are no longer much used. They have never possessed lances and tomahawks or battle axes, so it seems, differing in that respect from most Plains tribes. On the other hand, just like them, they practice the custom of scalping their enemies" (Ten Kate 2004: 302–308).

Among the Southern Ute the Dutch anthropologist collected five hide artifacts. All were decorated with either beadwork or paint, and the specimens exemplify the strong Plains influence on the material culture of the Southern Ute. The Utes closest to the Spanish settlements in the northern Rio Grande Valley had begun to acquire horses before the mid-seventeenth century and used these initially as beasts of burden. After the Pueblo Revolt of 1680 the number of Ute horses increased as the result of trade. In the course of the next century the most easterly Ute groups became equestrian nomads, lived in tipis, hunted buffalo on the Plains, raided for horses, and raced horses as a favorite pastime. However, after 1830 they were pushed back to the west by Plains tribes but in their way of life continued the Plains pattern of equestrian nomadism as much as possible, increasingly hunted elk and deer, kept up a reputation as fierce warriors, and retained the Plains-type of material culture. After the Southern Ute were placed on their reservation, their Indian Agents differed in their attitude towards Native beadwork produced by the women for an outside market, varying from support in recognition of the income-generating possibilities of the craft to outright condemnation of it as a vestige of an uncivilized way of life (Callaway et al. 1986: 338–350; Shimkin 1986; Osborn 1998: 52–54; Wroth 2000a: 62–63, 66; Bates 2000).

One of the five artifacts is a small case made of harness leather (Fig. 86 right), the front panel of which is covered in lazy-stitched white beads, with the small rectangular designs executed in black and red, always in opposition to each other, and in yellow, blue, and pink. Ten Kate's original handwritten label of the Native name has survived, and he calls it a "purse." O. Roland McCook, Sr., a Northern Ute representative on the Smithsonian's Native American Repatriation Review Committee, told Hovens that the correct Native term would be *panákorokonoiv* and that

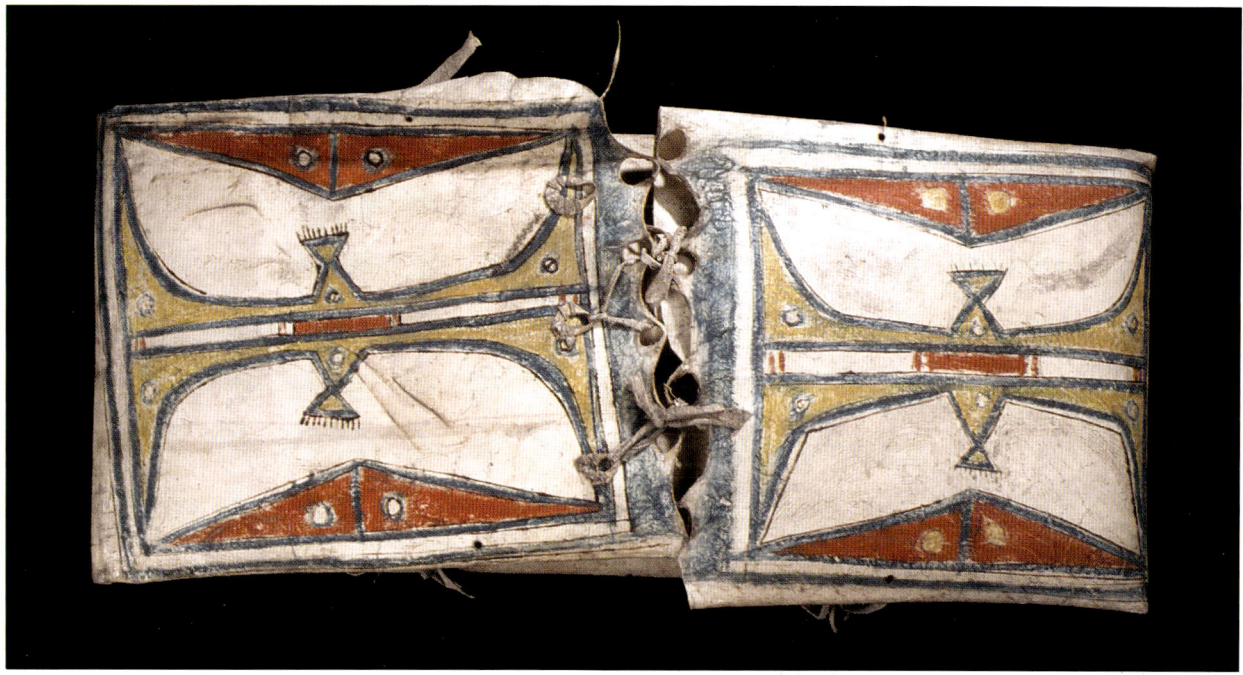

Fig. 87   Southern Ute parfleche; hide, pigments; w. 95 cm, h. 40 cm; ca. 1870–1880 (RMV 362-202).

Ten Kate's translation was generally correct, as the Ute term meant 'purse for metal.' However, as this specimen is much too small and tight to hold coins, I hazard the suggestion that this artifact might have been an awl or needle case, containing this sewing hardware that Indian women obtained through White traders.

Another such specimen (RMV 362-20) was stolen in 1964 during an exhibition on the Plains Indians at the Leiden museum. This awl case was beaded in white, yellow, blue, green, and red, and a snake design ran down both sides, executed in red and black beads, respectively, oppositional colors in Ute color symbolism. Red is associated with protection, represented in animal life by the weasel, while black stands for the negative power of the rattlesnake and symbolizes the underworld (Goss 2000: 47–49).

The paint bag in the Ten Kate collection (Fig. 86 left) still contains the remains of yellow ochre. The beadwork is done in lazy stitch, the background in white, and the rectangular and triangular designs in red and blue. Tassels of tiny brass chains decorate the top and bottom.

The parfleche acquired by Ten Kate (Fig. 87) was originally listed as Jicarilla, as it was part of a small collection a Santa Fe trader had bought from a band of Jicarilla Apaches passing through on their way south to internment at Fort Stanton. The trader told Ten Kate that the Native owner of the rawhide case had told him that he had acquired it in trade from the Southern Ute (Ten Kate,

undated note). The anthropologist labeled the parfleche as "hide travel bag." It is painted with geometric designs in green, red, and black. Apart from ties securing the frontal flaps, the Leiden parfleche has holes for ties to secure the side flaps. The three attachment rings for the frontal fastening thongs are reinforced.

Spier (1931: 297–298) described a parfleche as follows: "an envelope, made by folding in the longitudinal sides of a long rectangular piece of rawhide so that they meet. The short sides of this folded hide are again folded towards each other so that they meet. This provides two flaps, each of which is nearly square, and, when these are lifted, two side flaps are revealed. Each of the front flaps is decorated, the designs being almost identical. The side flaps are less frequently decorated. Sometimes the rear of the parfleche is bounded by a rectangle which connects the decoration of the two front flaps and the two side flaps. The whole design is laid out on the rawhide before it is folded."

Rawhide was animal hide that was only treated by drying, stretching, cleaning, and shaving, without being tanned. This left the hide smooth and stiff, but flexible enough to be folded as it retained sufficient elasticity when bent at any angle. Thick hides were preferred for rawhide articles, with buffalo skins most prevalent, followed by elk kin and thick deerskin (Douglas 1936: 107; Morrow 1975; Torrence 1994: 39–58).

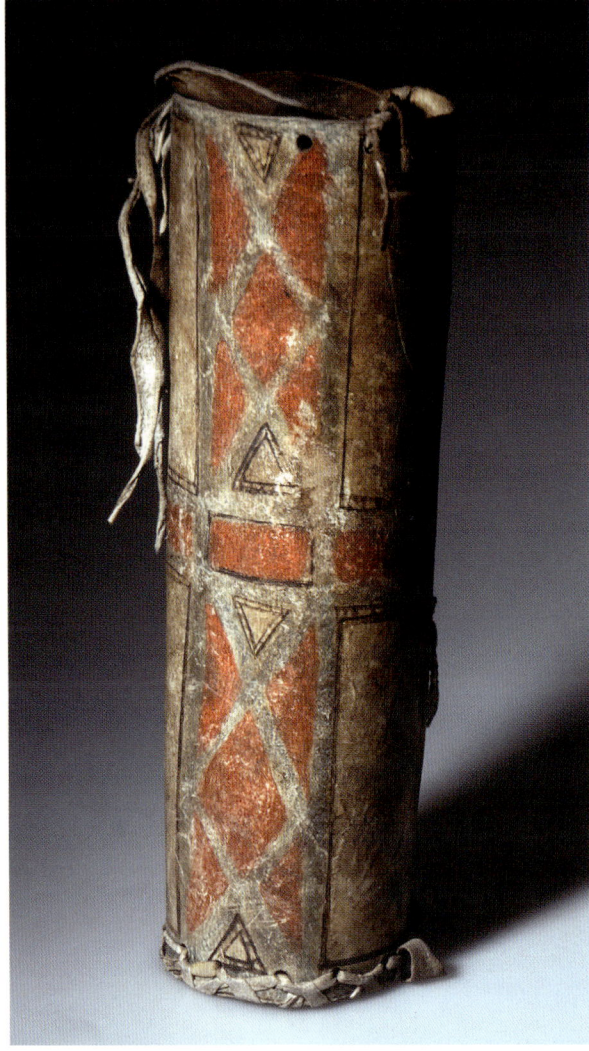

Fig. 88   Southern Ute tubular case; rawhide, pigments; l. 38 cm, d. 12.5 cm; ca. 1870–1880 (RMV 362-203).

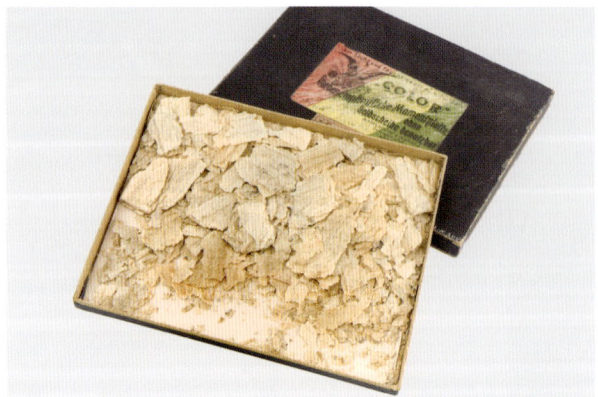

Fig. 89   Southern Ute wheat bread; 1883 (RMV 362-204).

Parfleches derive their name from the French "pare une flèche" ('stops or deflects an arrow'). Because of their versatility as containers for food and also personal possessions, they are encountered throughout the Plains area and beyond the Rocky Mountains. Most are envelope-shaped like this specimen, although the Plains tribes made trunk-shaped parfleches. While most of these containers are painted, some show incised designs, notably those from the Crow. Often the envelope-shaped parfleches were made in matching pairs. When used up, parfleches were cut up and used as rawhide soles for moccasins (cf. Douglas 1936; Morrow 1975; Conn 1979: 130–132, 134; Torrence 1994: passim; Coe 2003: 212–213).

Spier (1925) noted that designs on Southern Ute parfleches tended to be executed in two equal panels, separated by a double central stripe and bounded by a double stripe on all other sides. The panels tended to be symmetrically divided into smaller units, often by using triangular designs to break up the central spaces, creating horizontal as well as vertical symmetry. Lines were generally carefully aligned, and a black line is usually painted along the sides on the back of the container. Torrence (1994: 157–158) characterized the style of Ute parfleche painting as direct and austere, open and simple.

The tubular hide container (Fig. 88) was earlier also erroneously listed as Jicarilla Apache. Ten Kate applied the same label to this specimen as to the parfleche, noting its cylindrical shape. It is made from thin rawhide, and thus has strength as well as flexibility and was probably used to store a feather headdress, possibly also ceremonial items (cf. Douglas 1936: 110; Torrence 1994: 69–70; Wroth 2000b: 118–119). The designs on the Leiden specimen are outlined in black. The top and bottom covers are attached with hide thongs.

At the Los Piños Agency Ten Kate collected a loaf of wheat bread which the Ute baked, something they had learned from White colonists. When searching the Leiden collection, a shallow rectangular box was located, less than half an inch in height, with the correct label RMV 362-204 (Fig. 89). In it were the sorry remains of what had once been satisfying nourishment, but which time had turned into a jumble of dehydrated flakes and crumbs. After more than a century of "conservation," it is currently scheduled for deaccession.

On the morning of 1 October 1883 Ten Kate boarded the train to Cucharas and traveled by way of Trinidad in southeastern Colorado and through Kansas to the Indian Territory, now known as Oklahoma, to continue his fieldwork among the tribes of the Southern Plains and the Indians forcibly relocated from the Southeast.

References

Baldwin, Gordon C.
  1950   The pottery of the Southern Paiute. *American Antiquity* 16: 50–56.
Bates, Craig D.
  2000   An Artistic Style Uniquely Their Own: Basketry, Parfleches and Beaded Clothing of the Ute People. In: Wroth 2000b: 143–178.
Bernstein, Bruce et al.
  2003   *The Language of Native American Baskets: From the Weavers' View*. Washington, DC: National Museum of the American Indian.
Callaway, Donald G., Joel C. Janetski, and Omer C. Stewart
  1986   Ute. In: Warren L. d'Azevedo (ed.), *Great Basin* (Handbook of North American Indians 11. W. C. Sturtevant, gen. ed.; Washington, DC: Smithsonian Institution), 336–367.
Coe, Ralph T.
  2003   *The Responsive Eye: Ralph T. Coe and the Collecting of American Indian Art*. New York, NY: Metropolitan Museum of Art.
Conn, Richard
  1979   *Native American Art in the Denver Art Museum*. Denver, CO: Denver Art Museum.
Dalrymple, Larry
  2000   *Indian Basketmakers of California and the Great Basin*. Santa Fe, NM: Museum of New Mexico Press.
Douglas, Frederic H.
  1936   *Parfleches and Other Rawhide Articles*. Denver Art Museum Leaflets 77–78. Denver, CO.
Euler, Robert C.
  1966   *Southern Paiute Ethnohistory*. University of Utah Anthropological Papers 78. Salt Lake City, UT.
Finger, Judith
  2003   Twined Basketry Caps of Eastern California and the Great Basin. *American Indian Art Magazine* 28(2): 64–73.
Fowler, Catherine S. and Lawrence E. Dawson
  1986   Ethnographic Basketry. In: Warren L. d'Azevedo (ed.), *Great Basin* (Handbook of North American Indians 11. W. C. Sturtevant, gen. ed.; Washington, DC: Smithsonian Institution), 705–737.
Fowler, Don D. and John F. Matley
  1979   *Material Culture of the Numa: The John Wesley Powell Collection, 1867–1880*. Smithsonian Contributions to Anthropology 26. Washington, DC.
Fulkerson, Mary Lee and Kathleen Curtis
  1995   *Weavers of Tradition and Beauty: Basketmakers of the Great Basin*. Reno, NV: University of Nevada Press.
Goss, James A.
  2000   Traditional Cosmology, Ecology and Language of the Ute Indians. In: Wroth 2000b: 27–52.
Hovens, Pieter and Jiska Herlaar
  2004   Early Anthropology on the Southwest-Great Basin Frontier: The 1883 Fieldwork of Herman ten Kate. *Journal of the Southwest* 46(3): 529–558.

Kania, John J.
  2006   Chemehuevi Coiled Baskets: Origins and Stylistic Trends. *American Indian Art Magazine* 31(2): 66–73, 98.
  2007   Bread for Baskets: The Ammann Collection of Chemehuevi Baskets. *American Indian Art Magazine* 33(1): 42–51.
Kroeber, Alfred L.
  1925   *Handbook of the Indians of California*. Bureau of American Ethnology Bulletin 78. Washington, DC.
Laird, Carobeth
  1976   *The Chemehuevis*. Banning, CA: Malki Museum Press.
Lowie, Robert H.
  1924   Notes on Shoshonean Ethnography. *Anthropological Papers of the American Museum of Natural History* 20(3): 185–324.
McGreevy, Susan Brown and Andrew Hunter Whiteford
  1985   *Translating Tradition: Basketry Arts of the San Juan Paiutes*. Santa Fe, NM: Wheelwright Museum of the American Indian.
Mason, Otis T.
  1904   Aboriginal American Basketry: Studies in a Textile Art without Machinery. *Annual Report of the U.S. National Museum for 1902*: 171–548.
Miller, Ronald D. and Peggy J. Miller
  1967   *The Chemehuevi Indians of Southern California*. Banning, CA: Malki Museum Press.
Morrow, Mabel
  1975   *Indian Rawhide: An American Folk Art*. Norman, OK: University of Oklahoma Press.
Osborn, Katherine M. B.
  1998   *Southern Ute Women: Autonomy and Assimilation on the Reservation, 1887–1934*. Albuquerque, NM: University of New Mexico Press.
Robinson, Bert E.
  1954   *The Basketweavers of Arizona*. Albuquerque, NM: University of New Mexico Press.
Rogers, Malcolm J.
  1936   *Yuman Pottery Making*. San Diego Museum of Man, Museum Papers 2. San Diego, CA.
Roth, George
  1977   The Calloway Affair of 1880: Chemehuevi Adaptation and Chemehuevi-Mohave Relations. *Journal of California and Great Basin Anthropology* 4(2): 273–286.
Shimkin, Demitri B.
  1986   Introduction of the Horse. In: Warren L. d'Azevedo (ed.), *Great Basin* (Handbook of North American Indians 11. W. C. Sturtevant, gen. ed.; Washington, DC: Smithsonian Institution), 517–524.
Smith, Gerald A. and Ruth D. Simpson
  1964   *Basketmakers of San Bernardino County*. Bloomington, CA: San Bernardino County Museum Association.
Spier, Leslie
  1925   *An Analysis of Plains Parfleche Decoration*. University of Washington Publications in Anthropology 1(3). Seattle, WA.
  1931   *Plains Indian Parfleche Designs*. University of Washington Publications in Anthropology 4(3). Seattle, WA.
Steward, Julian H.
  1933   Ethnography of the Owens Valley Paiute. *University of*

California Publications in American Archaeology and Ethnology 33: 233–350.

Stewart, Kenneth M.

    1967   Chemehuevi Culture Changes. *Plateau* 40(1): 14–21.

    1968   A Brief History of the Chemehuevi Indians. *The Kiva* 34(1): 9–27.

Tanner, Clara Lee

    1983   *Indian Baskets of the Southwest.* Tucson, AZ: University of Arizona Press.

Ten Kate, Herman F. C.

    1885   *Reizen en Onderzoekingen in Noord Amerika.* Leiden: E. J. Brill.

    2004   *Travels and Researches in Native North America, 1882–1883.* P. Hovens, L. A. Hieb, and W. J. Orr eds. Albuquerque, NM: University of New Mexico Press. [Translation of Ten Kate 1885.]

Tisdale, Shelby J.

    2001   Intermontane West. In: Lydia L. Wyckoff (ed.), *Woven Worlds: Basketry from the Clark Field Collection* (Tulsa, OK: The Philbrook Museum of Art), 79–106.

Torrence, Gaylord

    1994   *The American Indian Parfleche: A Tradition of Abstract Painting.* Seattle, WA: University of Washington Press.

Van Valkenburgh, Richard F.

    1976   Chemehuevi Notes. In: D. A. Horr (ed.), *American Indian Ethnohistory: California and Basin-Plateau Indians; Paiute Indians* (New York: Garland), 2: 225–253.

Whiteford, Andrew Hunter

    1988   *Southwestern Indian Baskets: Their History and Their Makers.* Santa Fe, NM: School of American Research Press.

Wroth, William

    2000a   Ute Civilization in Prehistory and the Spanish Colonial Period. In: Wroth 2000b: 53–72.

    2000b   *Ute Indian Arts and Culture: From Prehistory to the New Millennium.* Colorado Springs, CO: Taylor Museum of Anthropology.

The O'odam: Papago and Pima

In late December 1882 Ten Kate traveled by train on the Southern Pacific Railroad line across southern New Mexico and Arizona. On New Year's day the passengers had lunch at Bowie and that late afternoon crossed plateaus and hills clad in saguaro cactus. In the early evening the Santa Catalina Mountains emerged in the distance, and shortly thereafter the train arrived in Tucson, where the tired Dutch traveler checked in at the Palace Hotel, a rather humble establishment, despite its name. In 1882 Tucson was a city of 7,000 inhabitants, mostly Mexicans, with sprinklings of Whites, Chinese, and Indians.

The Papago

The Papago, who lived on a small reservation at the San Xavier del Bac mission south of town, were frequent visitors to the city, where they sold firewood, basketry, and pottery. They wore Mexican-type dress, but could easily be distinguished from Mexicans because of their peculiarity to walk behind each other instead of next to each other. On the day after his arrival Ten Kate rode to Camp Lowell, where he received instructions for visiting the reservation from commanding officer General Eugene Asa Carr. On 3 January he hired a buggy, loaded up his luggage and hunting rifle, and proceeded to San Xavier. The impressive church was situated at the foot of a hill, and the dwellings of the Indians were spread in the wide vicinity. The church provided a romantic spectacle: a baroque European building, much of it in ruins, situated squat in the southern Arizona desert. Inside, traces of old frescos remained, and Ten Kate recorded that upon entering he saw a wealth of shades and play of beautiful colors that in his view could well be compared to St. Mark's in Venice. The anthropologist stayed at the ranch of John Berger, called Don Juan by the Indians, the only White man on the reservation.

Dress

The Papago at San Xavier del Bac seemed to have given up much of their traditional way of life, probably because of the work of the Franciscans among them. The Indians cut their hair short and dressed like the general Mexican population. The men wore hats and the women a head cloth, the only peculiarity in their style of dress.

Sandals were required to travel through the rough desert terrain. Their soles were cut from stiff rawhide, and leather thongs, two passing between the toes and the others around the heel, were tied around the leg (cf. Russell 1908: 122). The pair collected by Ten Kate (Fig. 90) has a two-layered sole, with the bottom layer thicker than the upper, probably made from recycled harness leather since both show a tooled pattern. One piece has a series of non-functional perforations and an incised pattern, probably derived from earlier use. The leather thongs go through two holes at the ankles and a hole between the toes, providing a secure lashing.

Fig. 90 Pair of Papago sandals; hide; l. 25.5 cm, w. 10 cm; ca. 1880 (RMV 362-39).

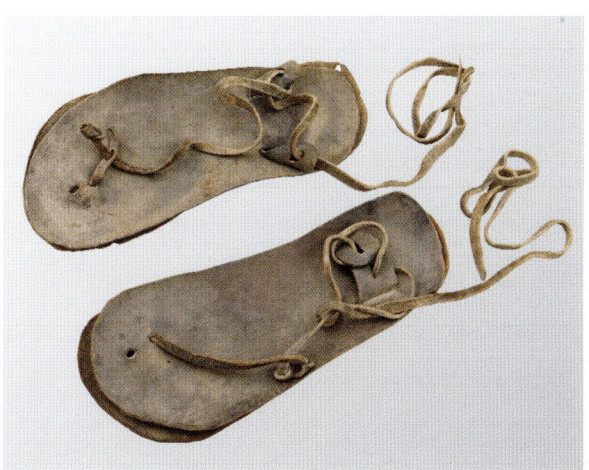

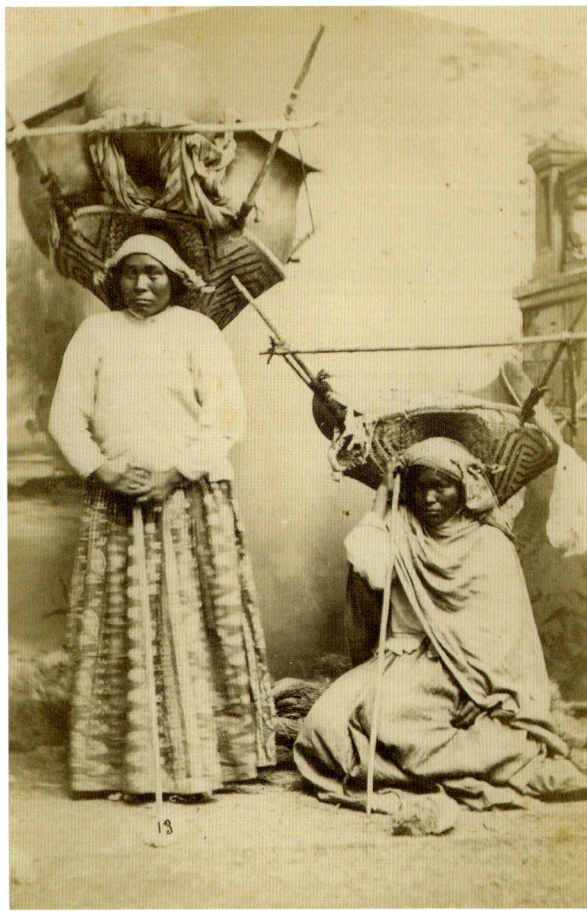

Fig. 91 Papago women with *quijo*; Arizona Territory, circa 1880. Photograph by Henry Bueman & Co., Tucson (Ten Kate coll.; RMV 414Kf).

Subsistence, Dwellings, and Households

The federal government had assigned the driest land in the area to the Papago and showed little interest in their fate. They received no rations or annuity payments, but tried as best as they could to till the best parcels of land, on which they planted wheat, barley, oats, corn, and water melons. In good years their harvest yielded a surplus that was sold on the market in Tucson. The region around San Xavier had abundant small game, including hares, rabbits, doves, and partridges, and Ten Kate thus provided meat for his meals, wielding his rifle expertly. However, he noted that the Papago had almost abandoned hunting as a way to sustain themselves.

About half of the Indians at San Xavier del Bac still lived in traditional dome-shaped circular dwellings. These consisted of a wooden frame over which branches and twigs were attached along the sides and on top. Sand was heaped up on the sides for stabilization. A low bow-shaped opening provided entry, and a woven mat served

as a door. On average the houses measured 2.30 meters in height, 4.70 meters in width, and 4.80 meters in depth.

Inside these homes Ten Kate noted many baskets and pottery vessels in various shapes and sizes, as well as grinding stones in the shape of rectangular flat bases called *metates* and round *manos* or *manitas*, used for milling corn, wheat, and seeds. However, Western-style tables, beds, and trunks were likewise encountered. The pottery was reddish-brown. Water was stored in large pots, and the Papago traded their ollas with their neighbors, both Native and White. About the basketry the anthropologist observed: "The Papagos' basketry is primarily of two kinds: The first kind is prettier than the other and is very tightly woven together from willow sprigs and ornamented with tasteful dark meandering lines. The shape is best compared to a very deep, round dish without pedestal. The measurements greatly vary, just like those of the second variety, which is less ingenious and consists of square little baskets of rectangular or square shape, which are with or without lid, depending on their function. Baskets play a major role in the domestic life of the Papagos because they hold all kinds of items for household use, in addition to provisions and sometimes even water" (Ten Kate 2004: 78).

Ten Kate provided a good description of the large carrying nets which Papago women used to haul large and heavy loads: "One of the most characteristic items still generally found among the Papagos is the carrying basket or *quijo* (Papago, *kjéoh*), which one repeatedly encounters with the women. The *quijo* is a trap-shaped net prepared from plant fibers, which is spread out between four long sticks that are tied together at the bottom and extend outward toward the top. Although the *quijo*, upon which sometimes heavy burdens such as firewood are borne, is balanced on one's back, the hauling strap rests against the forehead. Support while walking is provided by a fork-shaped stick (*sahrkuh*), which is used also to prop up the basket when it is loaded or the carrier puts down her load for a moment. The younger and more coquettish the woman or girl is, the lovelier the red-dyed *sahrkuh* is ornamented with leather fringe or colorful pieces of cloth" (Ten Kate 2004: 78). Later, among the Pima, the anthropologist was able to collect a helping stick (see Fig. 123, p. 96).

Piman pottery is technologically unsophisticated compared to Pueblo ceramics but can be aesthetically attractive. Vessels were built up from wet clay coils that were shaped and smoothed over with a wooden paddle and a stone anvil. When almost dried, the outside was sanded with a stone, after which a clay slip was applied and finally finely sanded with a stone before being fired about twenty minutes in a shallow pit. Decoration was applied on the still warm vessels with gum from mesquite trees (*Prosopis*), using a sharpened stick. A short additional firing rendered the decoration on the Pima creamware and Papago redware a deep black. Some designs were inspired by motifs from potsherds found in prehistoric Hohokam ruins in the area. Pottery making was a women's craft and considered a menial art, with little or no associated taboos.

The Papago were the better potters and they traded their wares, often filled with cactus syrup, with the Pima, receiving grain in return. The Kohatk Papago were the main intermediaries, and Russell has surmised that the best Pima potters were of Kohatk descent or learned the craft during extended visits. Underhill has stressed that the craft of pottery, as well as skin dressing and weaving, was only learned after women reached their middle age (Russell 1908: 124-131; Underhill 1939: 91; Fontana et al. 1962: 9; Hayden 1959: 10). The technical aspects of Piman pottery are addressed by Russell (1908: 124-128), Beals (1934: 28-31); Boggs (1936: 102-110), Hill (1942: 531-533) and Hayden (1959; also cf. Douglas 1953).

On some early Papago pots a green (copper) or white (lead) pigmented glaze was used to apply shiny decorative lines in addition to non-glazed red lines on the surface of vessels. The Native name for the green glaze was *wáchuk*, possibly the original name for the Huachuca Mountains in Papago territory, where blue-green rocks were found containing copper ores. The production of glazed ware, always a small part of total tribal pottery production, was concentrated between 1790 and 1850 and ceased by 1860. An association has been noted between Papago glazed ware and Spanish mission sites. By Ten Kate's time the manufacture of glazed ware had probably completely ceased, and Papago informants commented on their rarity in the 1890s. Thus the bowl he collected might be an old specimen, manufactured twenty or more years earlier (Fig. 92).

Glazed ware was regarded as a luxury and primarily used for food serving bowls. The few surviving specimens show an exterior design of concentric scroll patterns of red paint, alternating with green glaze, and a running parallel wavy line around the interior. The bowl collected by Ten Kate fits this pattern exactly. Later, commercial glaze was purchased at traders' stores, a white powdered compound

that was mixed with water and then applied in a thin coat on the exterior surface of the vessel (Fontana et al. 1962: 45-48, 78, 99, 103-104, 106, 114, 127, 130, 144).

Papago pottery making declined to a certain extent with the increasing proliferation of more durable industrially manufactured Western trade goods during the second half of the nineteenth century. However, because of the lack of cash income, household wares remained in production to some degree, especially in the more remote areas of Papagueria. As water vessels in a desert environment, ollas remained functional in any household, whether Native, Mexican, Hispanic, or Anglo, and were traded as a household ware, remaining in use well into the twentieth century (Underhill 1940: 24-25).

After the transcontinental Southern Pacific Railway was completed in 1880, a new market emerged for Papago, Pima, and Maricopa pottery. Travelers and tourists wanting to take home souvenirs as mementoes of a visit to the Arizona desert were offered such objects at railroad depots and trader stores. These wares were of appropriate small size to fit into luggage and included tableware such as cups, small bowls, pitchers, etc. This new source of income caused the Papago to develop black-on-red ware already known to the Pima and the polishing of such pottery to comply with the tastes of their White clientele. While the Pima and Maricopa often sold their wares at train depots, Papago souvenir pottery was distributed through trading posts (Fontana et al. 1962: 8-13, 108-109).

Fig. 92   Papago glazed redware bowl with greenish black decoration; pottery, pigments, glaze; d. 13.8 cm, h. 9.5 cm; ca. 1850-1860 (RMV 362-33).

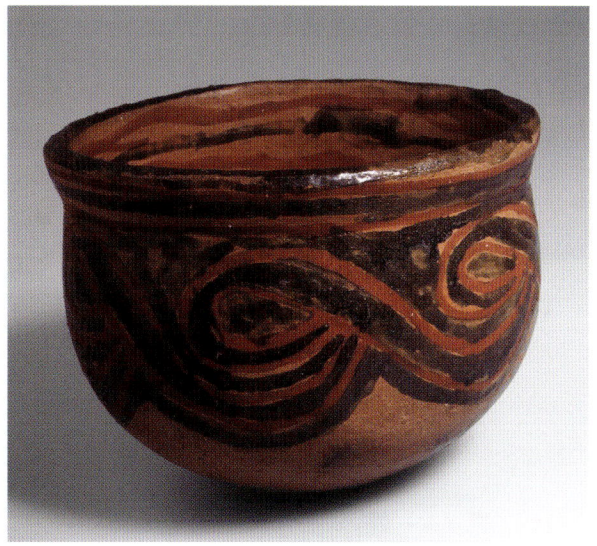

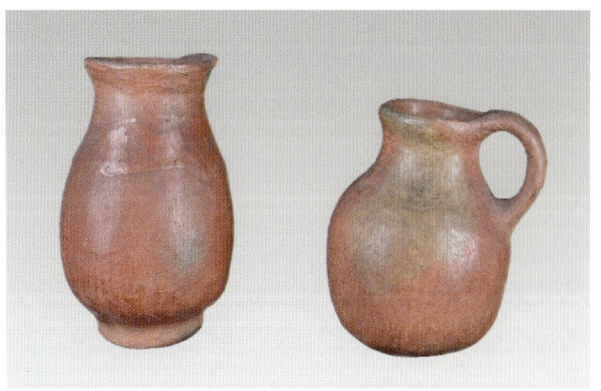

Fig. 93 Papago redware pitchers; pottery; RMV 362-34: d. 8.5 cm, h. 12 cm; RMV 362-35: d. 8 cm, h. 13.7 cm; ca. 1880.

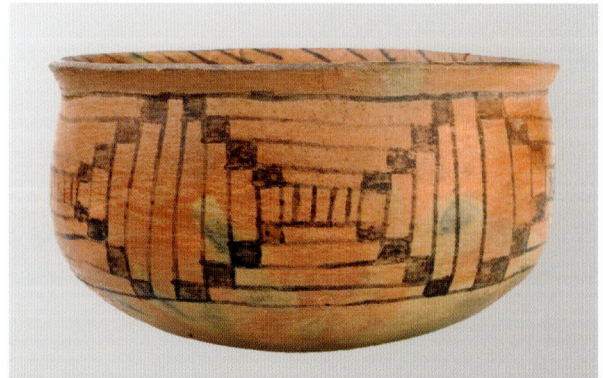

Fig. 94 Papago/Pima/Maricopa bowl; pottery, pigment; d. 27 cm, h. 15 cm; ca. 1880 (RMV 362-82).

Both Leiden pitchers (Fig. 93) have a globular body and a constructed neck. Their exterior surface is slipped and slightly polished, as are the rims. The loop handle on RMV 362-35 is broken off and missing. Both exhibit slight fireclouds.

A large vessel (Fig. 94), as well as four smaller bowls (Figs. 95–98), were purchased by Ten Kate in the town of Yuma, and he listed them as made by the Yuma. However, in style they are clearly Piman. The most probable explanation is that Piman potters availed themselves of the opportunity to sell their wares at the Yuma railway depot to visitors and passing travelers on the Southern Pacific Railroad, as they did at other stations between Tucson and Yuma.

Paddle-and-anvil marks are visible on the interior and exterior surface of the large bowl, and the exterior and inside of the flaring rim are decorated with painted designs. The motifs on the outer surface are very similar to those on Papago baskets used to gather saguaro fruits collected

by Carl Lumholtz (1912: 56). This vessel was probably used for the fermentation and storage of saguaro wine.

The four Piman redware bowls are of various sizes, slipped and polished, and are treated differently as to embellishment. Two vessels exhibit decoration on the interior and exterior (Figs. 95, 96), and two others only have painted designs on the exterior (Figs. 97, 98). The bowls show paddle-and-anvil marks, fire clouds, and mica flecks. Fontana et al. (1962: 107–109) noted that this type of redware was primarily produced by Papago, Pima, and Maricopa potters living along the tracks of the Southern Pacific Railroad. This redware united the expertise of the Papago in polishing pottery with Pima traditions of using black mesquite paint for decorative purposes. The paint was derived from boiling down shredded sap-soaked mesquite bark with mesquite gum. After applying the decoration on the surfaces of the vessels, they were fired or heated a second time, resulting in the blackening and fixing of the paint (Fontana et al. 1962: 77–78).

Figs. 95, 96 Piman redware bowls; pottery, pigment; RMV 362-83: d. 24.8 cm, h. 10 cm; RMV 362-84: d. 19.2 cm, h. 6.6 cm; both ca. 1880.

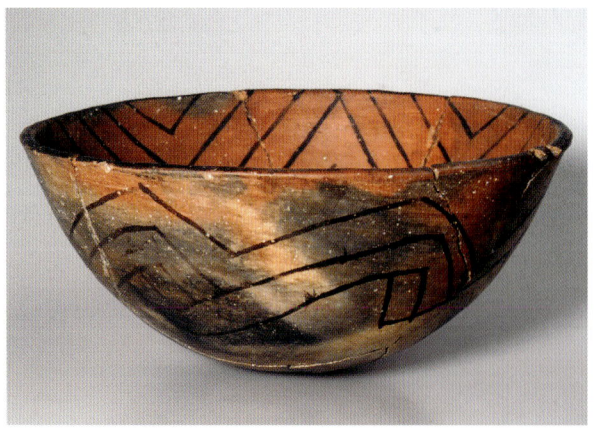

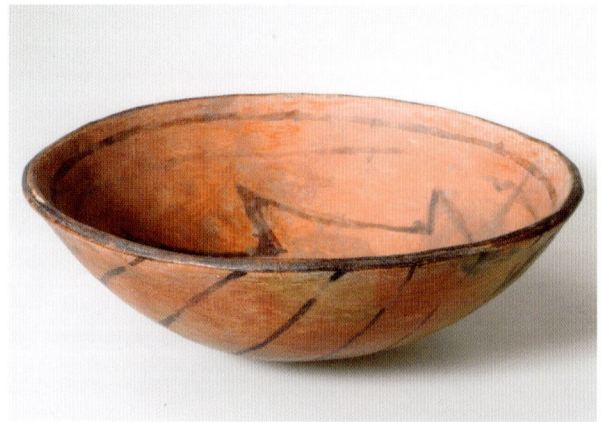

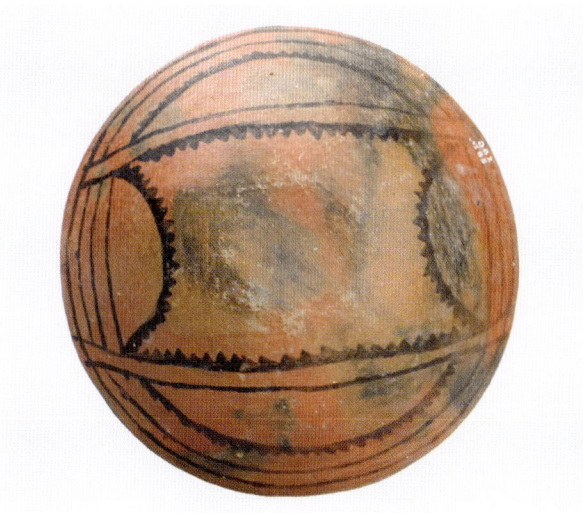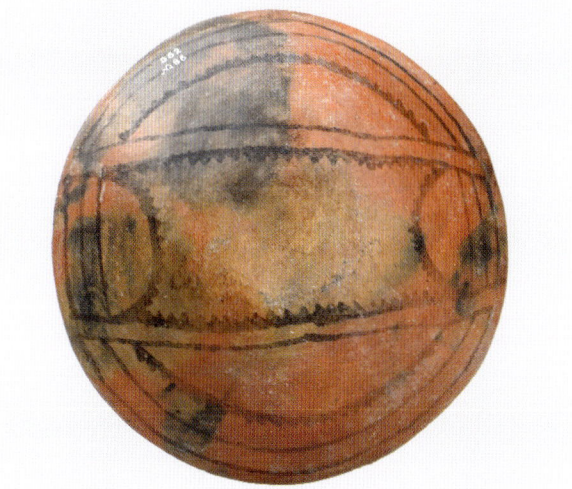

Figs. 97, 98   Piman redware bowls; pottery, pigment; RMV 362-85: d. 17.3 cm, h. 5.5 cm; RMV 362-86: d. 17.4 cm, h. 4.8 cm; both ca. 1880.

Weapons

Traditional weapons were not in use anymore during Ten Kate's visit at San Xavier del Bac, but after a long search the anthropologist found a wooden club and a bow with arrows, the points of which consisted of cut glass.

According to Ten Kate, the Papago called the Apache *Ohp*, which compares with the Pima *Aw-op* (Whittemore 1893: 68), and Underhill (1939: 129) states that this term translated as 'enemy.' The Apache were the major enemies of the Pimans, and both had repeatedly assisted the Mexican and American army during their expeditions against that tribe. Slightly more than a decade before Ten Kate's visit, the Apache had penetrated into the Santa Rita Mountains near San Xavier del Bac. However, the Papago resisted this movement by using fortifications of the prehistoric Hohokam inhabitants of the area, now called *trincheras*, from which they defended their territory and homes, as the anthropologist observed during an excursion through that area. Direct contact with the enemy was considered not only physically dangerous but also leading to contamination. In his fieldnotes Ten Kate recorded that both Papagos and Pimas who killed an Apache enemy had to undergo a purification ceremony, during which warriors were kept in isolation from their communities for four days and were fed by friends bringing food to them.

The Papago club collected by Ten Kate (RMV 362-36, Fig. 99 far left) is painted black on the side and red on the top, the colors of war. The long handle shows remains of red pigment. This club used to have a cotton strap. Raw-

hide shields, often with painted designs, served the Papago to ward off arrows and blows by clubs (cf. Russell 1908: 96; Lumholtz 1912: 110; Fontana 1983: 142).

Fig. 99   Papago warclub; *sontjik* (TK); wood, pigments, cotton; l. 39.5 cm, w. at top 6 cm; ca. 1870 (RMV 362-36). Pima warclubs; *sónjik* or *són-tjik* (TK), *shonchki* (Saxton et al. 1983); RMV 674-61: wood, pigment; l. 40.5 cm, w. 6.5 cm; RMV 362-45: wood; l. 42.5 cm, w. 8.3 cm; both ca. 1870–1880.

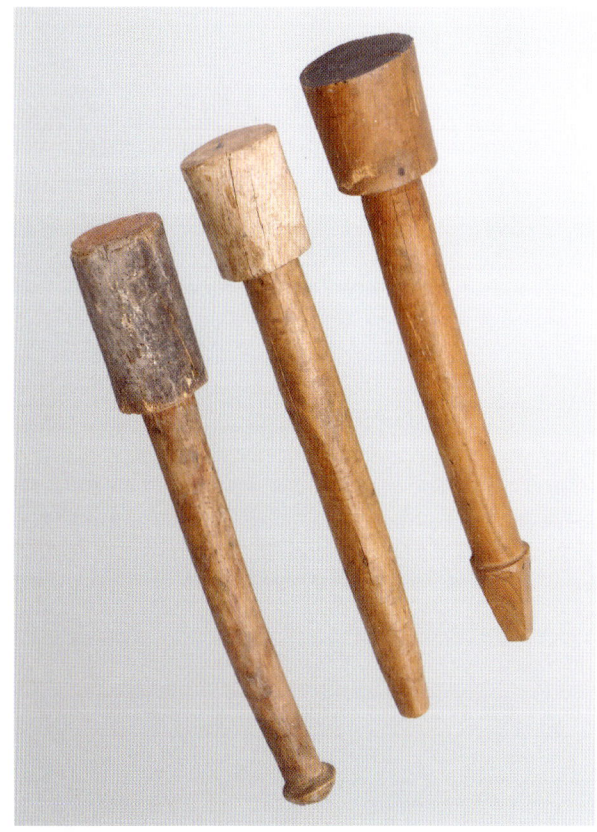

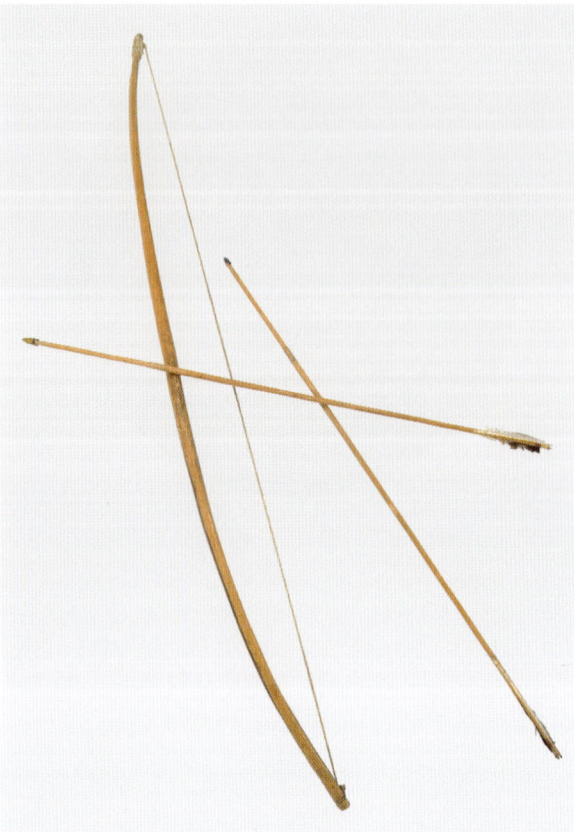

Fig. 100 Papago bow and arrows; wood, sinew, feathers, obsidian; bow: l. 113 cm, w. 2.5 cm; arrows: average l. 86 cm; ca. 1870-1880 (RMV 362-37).

Weapons were required for hunting as well as warfare, both defensive and offensive. Generally little effort was invested in making weapons for utilitarian hunting, while much more time and effort was spent on the manufacture of weapons of war, as this required maximum effectiveness and ritual observances during the production process. Both the Papago and Pima preferred mulberry for their

Fig. 101 Papago gaming sticks; wood, pigments; average l. 18.3 cm, w. 1.2 cm, d. 0.6 cm; ca. 1880 (RMV 674-59).

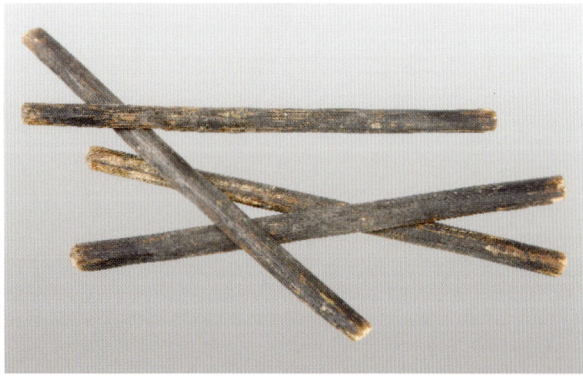

war bows and gathered the wood in the Pinal and Super-stition Mountains. Osage Orange and even willow was used for hunting bows (Russell 1903: 95–96, pls. 7b, 13a).

Ten Kate noted that the bow he obtained (Fig. 100) is of a crude type and that the arrowheads were made from obsidian, i.e., volcanic glass. The bow is ovoid in cross-section and strung by twisted two-strand sinew. Both extremities of the bow exhibit remains of red paint. The arrows have notched and fletched ends and foreshafts to which the points of volcanic glass are attached by sinew. Ten Kate acquired this set at San Xavier del Bac.

Except for baskets and some pottery, these arrows and the wooden war club were the few manifestations of traditional material culture Ten Kate was able to salvage at San Xavier del Bac.

Games

Ten Kate witnessed one of the games played by the Papago at San Xavier del Bac: "a kind of ball game with a ball of hard rubber being continuously kicked about by two men trotting across a large stretch of land. A crowd of spectators on horseback and on foot follows the two players at the same pace. ... Still vivid in my memory is the shouting band of bronzed chaps running across the sun-drenched plain" (Ten Kate 2004: 80).

He noted that the set of four gaming sticks he collected (Fig. 101) was used for the *quince* (Spanish: 'fifteen') game, played by women, and recorded the Native name for the game as *pahahi* or *pakaki*. Underhill (1939: 144–145) records the Papago name for the game as *kinyskut*, a derivation of the Spanish name, but states that the game was played by men, never by women and children. The slightly rounded backs of the sticks are painted black, the flat fronts have been stained red, but lack incised and painted designs, which would indicate their numerical value. Because of its good material condition, this set was probably still unfinished when Ten Kate purchased it. Quince was played by many Indian tribes in the Greater Southwest, including the Pima and Tarahumara (cf. Culin 1907: 148; Russell 1908: 175–176; Smith 1945; Fontana 1979: 67; see chapter 3, "Western Arizona," Fig. 55).

Religion

South of the Papago village at San Xavier del Bac lay a traditional burial ground where the non-Christian Papagos were buried. Their graves consisted of coffins of chunks of lava, piled up around the body, positioned in a sitting or crouching position. The deceased were clad in good clothes and provided with personal possessions before being laid to rest. On the stones of the top layer of some graves Ten Kate noted incised designs, mostly spirals.

About the bull roarer (Fig. 102) Ten Kate noted: "This contraption is swung around at a quick pace and creates a strong humming. It is used to treat the sick to induce the spirits to provide healing" (RMV file card) The piece was carved in such a way that it produced a strong sound when it was swung around on a cord. The distal end was carved round and all sides are thinned to increase vibration. The board is covered with a foundation of white pigment, on which a series of connecting triangles in red are painted on the upper side, and a repeating meandering pattern on the underside. The cord attaching the board to the stick handle is made of twisted native cotton. According to Lumholtz (1912: 88, 95-96; cf. Fontana 1983: 139), who did fieldwork among the Arizona Papago in 1909-10, the painted triangular patterns symbolize clouds, the connecting lines lightning, and the dots corn, the sound and imagery of the bull roarer geared to attract rain for crops. In addition, the sound of the instrument announces both beginning and end of feasts and ceremonies. Although bull roarers play an important part in ceremonies of many Southwestern tribes, they are remarkably rare in archaeological contexts (Brown 1967: 78-79).

The Pima

In late May of 1883 Ten Kate concluded his fieldwork among the Yuman tribes of western Arizona, left Kingman, and proceeded south by mail coach to Phoenix, reaching that town on the 26th. Arrival there was a relief from travel through the hot desert wilderness. Lanes with shady green cottonwoods connected blocks of houses, constructed from wood or adobe. There was a choice of hotels to stay and restaurants to eat, and Ten Kate used the opportunity for a thorough cleanup and a good rest. Physically and mentally invigorated, he departed two days later and by way of Casa Grande and Sacaton traveled to the Pima Reservation by horse and wagon, reaching it on 1 June. The temperature was a stifling 110 degrees Fahrenheit in the shade.

The agency consisted of a few modest government buildings on the south bank of the Gila River and a Pima village, including the home of the aged Chief Antonio. On the other side of the river the Indians had their fields,

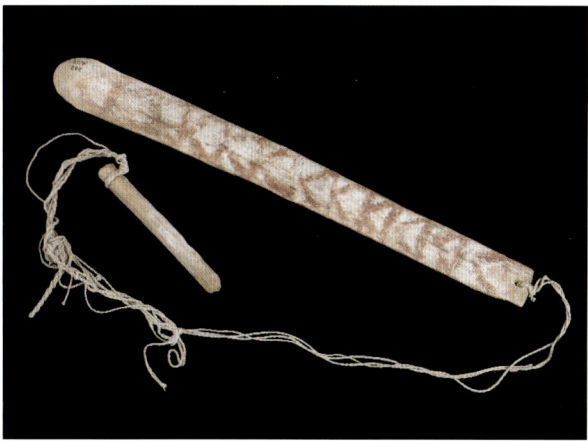

Fig. 102 Papago bull roarer; *weehoowikkaytuhkuh* (TK); saguaro wood, pigments, cotton; l. of board 46.4 cm, w. 4.4 cm, th. 1.4 cm; ca. 1880 (RMV 362-38).

where they cultivated several varieties of grains. Indian Agent Dr. A. H. Jackson was most accommodating, introduced Ten Kate to potential informants, and provided two interpreters. One of them was Antonito, whose Native name was Hotontóahim, Evening Thunder, and he became one of the most effective interpreters to assist the Dutch researcher during his year of fieldwork in the American West. Ten Kate spent eight days among the Pima.

Subsistence, Dwellings, and Households

Pima homes resembled those of the Papago Ten Kate had earlier seen at San Xavier del Bac, but their entrance always faced east. He speculated that this was because the land of *Siárree-táhkjoh*, 'the Rising Sun,' regarded as the Garden of Eden, is located in that direction. Almost all the Indians had loaded up their horses and burros, left their winter dwellings, and had moved into summer houses of simple construction, not more than roofs of branches, supported by two or four vertical posts. These were situated near their fields, where they tended their crops and harvested in the late summer and early fall. Ten Kate saw that the Pima still used the traditional fire stick to ignite a fire (see Fig. 104 below).

The Spanish had introduced horses to the Pima in the seventeenth century. The Indians soon learned how to ride them, but the supply of animals was lagging far behind demand until the last quarter of the nineteenth century. The mounts also had difficulty finding sufficient fodder in the desert and lived on saltbush in wintertime. In the spring the sprouting mesquite provided nourishment, followed a little later by mesquite beans. Summer rains

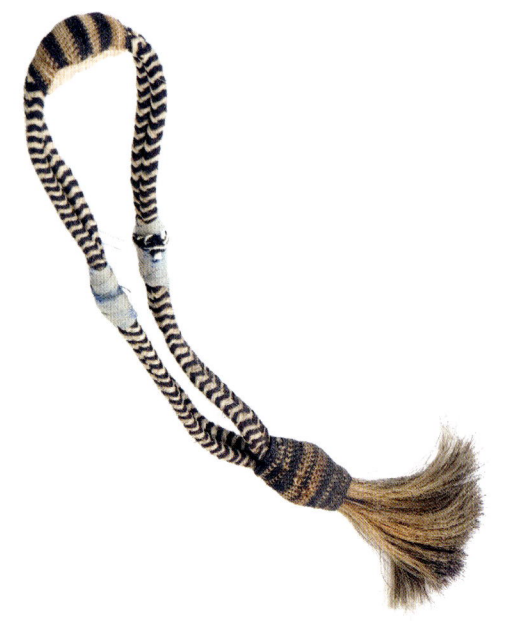

Fig. 103 Pima braided horse halter; *saachki* (TK), *sha:kim* (Saxton et al. 1983); horsehair, cloth; l. 38 cm; ca. 1880 (RMV 362-48).

As many other North American peoples, the Pima made fire with a two-piece fire-drill (Fig. 104). A stick of soft wood, in this case a dry saguaro (*Cereus giganteus*) rib, was pinned down by sitting upon it with the knees spread and is referred to as "hearth" by anthropologists. A stick of hardwood was put on it vertically and set into a rapid motion between the moving palms of the hands. The friction thus engendered in the socket first produced heat and subsequently a red hot glow which set the wood dust on fire. This in turn kindled dry fibers and twigs, thus enabling to build a fire for cooking and warmth. The kitchen hearth was situated in a brush enclosure and usually consisted of three stones, on which earthen pots were placed for cooking. In Pima villages fire was often preserved in an old tree stump, kept smoldering and ready to use. The Pima considered the sun as the source of fire, but according to tribal tradition they had learned the art of fire making from Blue Fly (Russell 1908: 69, 102, 216; Beals 1934: 18).

Dress

Only a few Pima men wore citizens' dress, as most maintained traditional attire, consisting of little more than g-strings. Full cotton colored shirts were coming into fashion. The women wore short skirts of dyed cotton that fitted tightly around their legs and a short white jacket with pouf sleeves.

The men usually had their hair in long, abundant braids hanging down at the back. Some older men sometimes took the hair up and wound it together with a colored piece of cloth, creating a turban-shaped head cover. Although commercial cloth was used in Ten Kate's time, they traditionally used a beautifully woven *kaywoot* or head cloth made from dyed cotton fibers. The Pima also used to weave fine blankets. Their original leather moccasins had been replaced by sandals, partly of Western manufacture.

The women wore their hair hanging down over their foreheads, cut right above the eyebrows and otherwise hanging loosely down at a length of thirty centimeters. Men and women enhanced the luster of their hair by smearing it with a mixture of mesquite gum and black alkaline mud. Most Pimas had facial tattoos, notably around the eyes.

On the origins of the craft of weaving among the Pima, little is known with certainty. In ancient times the Pima spun an unidentified grass species into thread that was used for weaving purposes. They used arrow weed

nurtured a variety of grasses. In times of famine horses were eaten. Horsehair was used for making rope, tumplines, cinches, and hair extensions, the latter a practice of the men. Different colors of horsehair were used for aesthetic effect (Russell 1908: 28, 81, 84-85, 106, 113, 115, 143, 158).

The horse halter collected by Ten Kate (Fig. 103) consists of a two-strand loop of braided black and white horsehair and is partially reinforced with a netted cover in the center and two wrappings at the sides. The loop is held together by a netted knob, and the ends of the horsehair are left loose. A Pima informant of Hovens stated that such halters were also specifically used to whip people suspected of witchcraft and drive the evil out of them.

Fig. 104 Pima fire-making equipment; *áywaytahkoot* (TK); saguaro wood; l. 37 cm; ca. 1870-1880 (RMV 362-55).

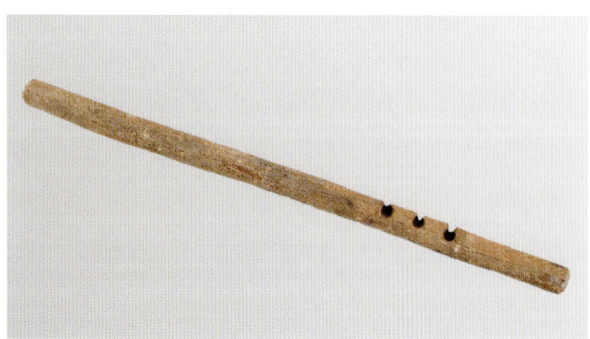

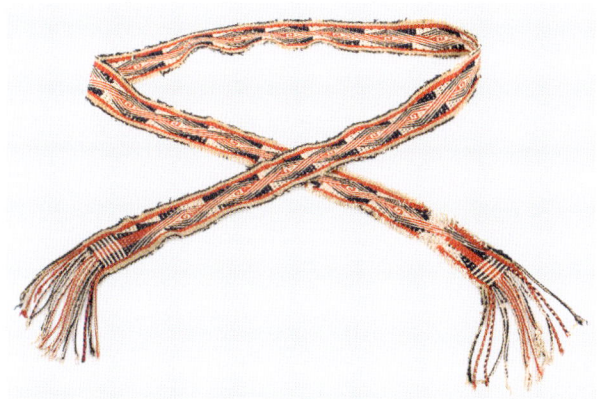

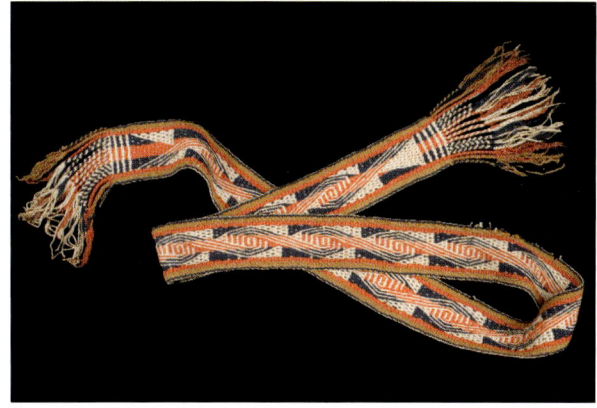

Fig. 105 Pima woven belt; *káywoot* (TK), *giwud* (Saxton et al. 1983); cotton, pigments; l. 207 cm (incl. fringe 233 cm); w. 6.7 cm; ca. 1870–1880 (RMV 362-49).

Fig. 106 Pima woven belt; *káywoot* (TK), *giwud* (Saxton et al. 1983); wool; l. 219 cm, w. 7.7 cm; ca. 1870–1880 (WMR 17987).

(*Pluchea sericea*) spindles with stone, ceramic, and wooden whorls. Since at least the seventeenth century the Pima also raised cotton that was spun into thread and then woven into fabric on a horizontal loom, spread between four stakes in the ground. Women did the spinning, but weaving seemed to be a craft in which older men specialized. They produced generally white square or rectangular cloths in plain weave, which were used as robes and blankets. Waist belts and headbands were two other items woven with some frequency, reaching a length of two meters and a width of six to seven centimeters. Some of these were double weaves. The Pima used mineral pigments to dye their thread, including an ochre with a high iron oxide content bartered with the Papago. They later raveled Mexican trade cloth to obtain red and blue thread for weaving into their fabrics. The Pima traded their textiles with the Yumans on the Colorado River and with Mexican Indians (Whittemore 1893: 52; Russell 1908: 148–153, 157; Beals 1934: 27–28; Di Peso 1956: 385–408; Irving 1981; Ezell 1983: 152, 158).

About the type of woven belt represented in his collection (Fig. 105) Ten Kate wrote: "The *káywoot* is worn not only around the head but is used as a sash at the same time. Also small children are tightly fastened to the carrying board with the *káywoot*; and in former times, when the Yumas still wore white blankets, the *giwud* served as a belt. In the Pima village Komertkewóótsje, by the Sierra de Estrella along Gila Crossing, I managed to see one of these ancient blankets. This was very coarse, woven from cotton, and white in color" (Ten Kate 1925: 101; Hovens 1995: 652). The warp and the weft of the Leiden specimen are made of native cotton, mostly two-ply, dyed in various colors. The central patterned area stands in low relief on both faces of the belt. The design is a series of diamonds with a scroll inside.

In 1887–88 Ten Kate took part in the excavations carried out by the Hemenway Southwestern Archaeological Expedition in southern Arizona. While working at Casa Grande, the expedition camp was frequented by Pimas who lived nearby. Ten Kate noted in his diary: "From one of the men I bought a *káywoot*, a woven wool band more than two meters long, with a beautiful pattern of four double interlocking hooks of warm light brown, red, blue and white. The *káywoot* serves several different purposes: to hold the long black hair of the men together, with which it forms a turban; to attach a baby to a carrier of willow branches; and as a belt. These belts are becoming increasingly rare as the Pimas are neglecting and forgetting their old industries, including weaving" (Ten Kate 1925: 110; Hovens 1995: 652). Ten Kate subsequently donated the belt to the Museum of Anthropology (now: World Museum) in Rotterdam (Fig. 106).

Religion

Ten Kate noted that the Pima still retained the beliefs of their fathers, despite the sustained missionary work of Reverend Cook. They acknowledged a Supreme Being whom they called Tsjerwúrte-mahke (Earth Prophet), but they worshipped his son Seuh-heu (Suhu, Sugh-ha), who, according to oral tradition, survived a great deluge and repopulated the earth after the waters had subsided. Seuh-heu killed the evil spirit who caused the flood, after which he had to fast sixteen days to cleanse himself from the impure contact. The Pima believed that he went on to live in the land of the rising sun, the destination of all good

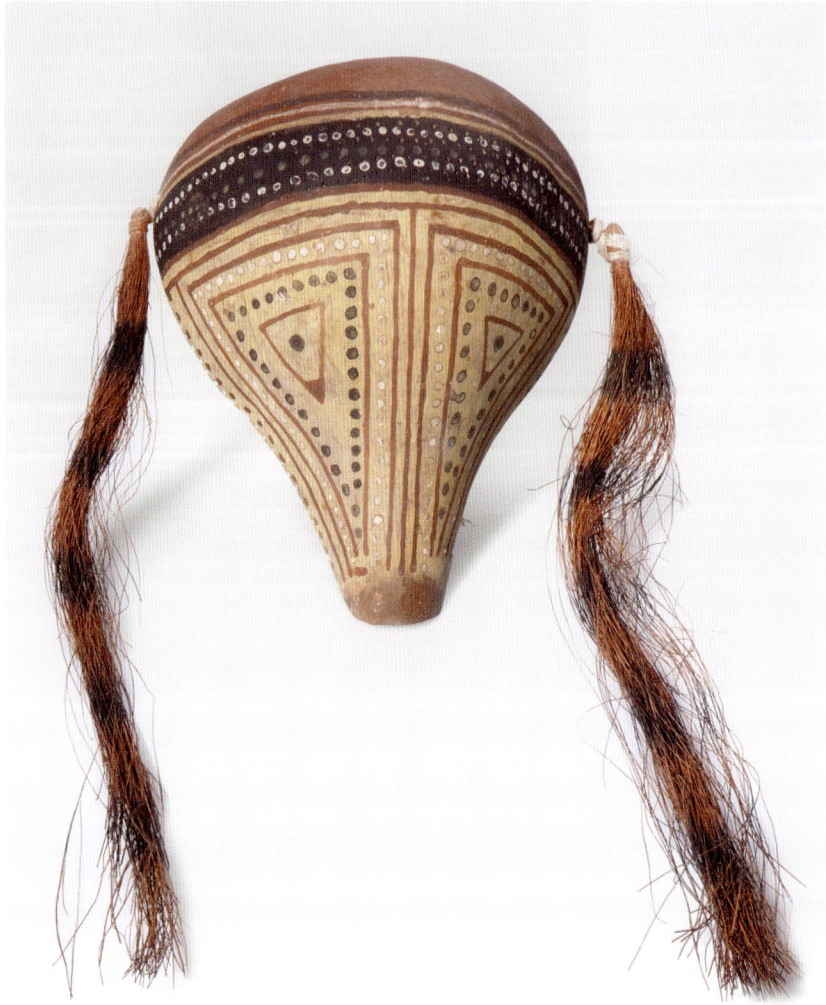

Fig. 107 Pima mask; *wipenjùh mhawayhosa* (TK); squash, horsehair, pigments, cotton; l. 21/39 cm, w. 8.5 cm; ca. 1880 (RMV 362-50).

ed Ten Kate to one of these caves high on a mountainside. Not far from the entrance he discovered an oblong lidded basket, in which there were a bundle of feathers, bracelets, bead necklaces, short arrows, bands or rings of sinew, and some textile fragments. At the back of the cave a bundle of arrows stood against the wall, most without tips. Evening Thunder protested when Ten Kate took away the basket and arrows, but acquiesced when the anthropologist assured him that everything would be returned if requested. Two days later an old Pima approached him and the items were handed back, about which the man was much pleased. He allowed Ten Kate to take one of the items from the basket and keep the bundle of old arrows, after which he returned the basket to the cave.

Comparatively little is known about Pima religion, and they have few eye-catching ceremonies. Men possessing magical powers over the weather performed a rain ritual in times of continued drought, and shamans, male and female, practiced several curing ceremonies. In ceremonies they rarely used masks, as few examples are known, and it has been suggested that those made from wood were obtained from the Yaqui (cf. Russell 1908: 108, fig. 26). Already in 1883 Ten Kate noted that there were a small number of Yaquis living among the Pima and that Yaqui women were held in regard because of their skills as midwives.

In the *Navitco* ceremony two masked medicinemen usually treat several patients at a time for afflictions of the eyes and joints. One represents *Navitco*, the evil spirit derived from the Papago, who caused the sickness. His counterpart is *Kâkspakam* and both perform healing acts, during which each patient touches the latter's mask and his diseased body parts. In addition to this curing ritual performed whenever required, every four or eight years, depending on the plenitude of the crops, a larger ceremony

Pimas after death. Siwanno, the descendant of Seuh-heu, led the Pima to power and greatness, but intratribal strife and powerful enemies eroded their position over time.

The belief in witchcraft was quite common, and shortly before Ten Kate's arrival a person accused of practicing sorcery had been killed. Owls were also feared, as they were believed to carry the souls of the dead to the afterworld.

In the mountains on the reservation and in their former tribal territory, the Pima (and the Papago too) had many sacrificial caves. On stones near their entrance petroglyphs or rock paintings were often encountered, frequently man and animal shapes and spirals, clear indication of the ritual significance of these sites. Some probably dated back to prehistoric times, but even these could still be in use. Evening Thunder, his Pima interpreter, guid-

took place in which *Navitco* played a central role (Russell 1908: 91, 107–108, 250–266, 326; Beals 1934: 37). This latter ceremony is unquestionably the Pima counterpart of the Papago *Vikita* ceremony and referred to as *Wi:gita* (Donald M. Bahr, personal communication 2007; cf. Bahr n.d.: 65–71). This periodic fertility or harvest festival involving whole communities is rather elusive, as only few outsiders have witnessed these rare communal affairs and published their experiences. No reliable accounts of the Pima equivalent are known (Fontana 1987).

Carl Lumholtz (1912: 92–98) provides a short early description based on informants' testimony on the Papago *Vikita*, but Julian D. Hayden wrote two ethnographic accounts of *Vikitas* he witnessed among the Papago in 1936 and 1945 and is the main source on this ceremony. Masked clowns and masked singers take central stage in the *Vikita*. The *Navitcos* wore elaborate turkey feather headdresses, sack-like masks of deerskin, later replaced by canvas, decorated with painted chevron designs, reaching onto the shoulders, and ending in a fringe. At the back of these masks a panel of colored cloth was attached, decorated with hide or tin templates of geometric figures, ending in feather fringe. Most of these masks had long bunches of human or horsehair attached to the sides, decorated with brightly colored, often red, downy feathers. Their bodies were clad in white garments, including shirts, tunics, and aprons. The members of the chorus wore gourd masks, variously decorated with painted abstract motifs resembling designs on pottery, distributed in different panels created by colored horizontal and vertical bands. The latter contained pricked holes to allow vision. Hayden (1987: 277–279, pls. 1–5, 11) also provided colored drawings of the participants in the ceremony and the ritual paraphernalia they used.

In 1909–10 Carl Lumholtz (1912: 93, 96) collected four gourd masks among the Arizona Papago, which are of the same type as the Ten Kate specimen (Fig. 107), although they lack the tails of hair and are rather crudely shaped and painted compared to the Leiden example. He also noted that local communities had their own characteristic pattern of decoration. Informants told him that zigzag lines symbolized clouds and lighting, while dots stood for corn. He also provides a photograph of a *Vikita* clown. Although the Leiden Pima mask exhibits characteristics of both types of masks worn during the *Vikita* ceremony, it much more closely resembles the masks worn by the singers in the chorus. These singers are called *wipiñy-im*, while the second part of the Native term for the mask

recorded by Ten Kate refers to face covering or mask (Donald M. Bahr, pers. com. 2007). More than fifty years separate the Leiden Pima mask and the Papago rituals as described by Hayden, and it is well possible that the tails of variously ornamented hair characteristic of the *Navitco* mask were originally also a part of the masks of the singers but that this element was subsequently lost. Therefore it is safe to assume that the mask Ten Kate collected was part of the Pima's *Wi:gita* ceremonial that was the equivalent of the Papago's *Vikita*. A written note from Ten Kate regarding this mask has survived and states that it was used in a ceremony "to conjure up high spirits" rather than healing spirits, affirming this interpretation.

The black band across the head is pricked through with tiny holes for vision and breathing. The gourd shell is geared for wear with a native cotton string. This Pima mask is not only the oldest known to exist in museum collections, but also aesthetically the finest example of its kind.

Traditionally, Pima musical instruments were limited to the rattle and scraping stick or rasp, made from bone or antler. In addition, they had trumpets made from *strombus* shells and bullroarers, probably used in ceremonies. They later adopted the basket drum and the three-holed cane flute from the neighboring Maricopa. Rattles made from gourds came in many shapes and sizes. After hollowing out a gourd and drying the remaining rind, a stick was fitted through it after putting small stones in it to produce sound. Many rattles were perforated "to let the sound out," the holes sometimes forming geometric patterns. In the case of a rattle acquired by Ten Kate (Fig. 108), the gourd surface is perforated with tiny holes in a scroll pattern. Rattles were used as a rhythmic instrument in virtually all ceremonies and during celebrations on social occasions (Russell 1908: 166–170; Spier 1936: 18; Underhill 1940: 28; Di Peso 1956: 421–424).

Fig. 108 Pima rattle; *sáhwegkoot* (TK), *shawikud* (Saxton et al. 1983); gourd, wood; l. 24.5 cm, d. 8 cm; ca. 1880 (RMV 362-51).

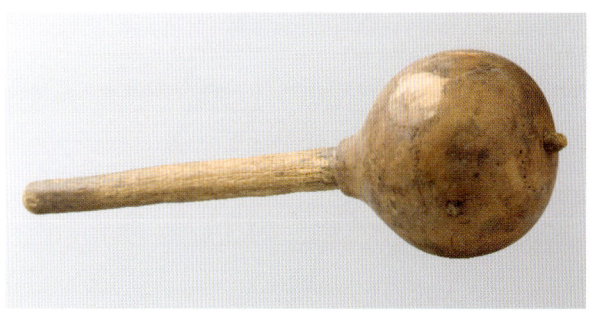

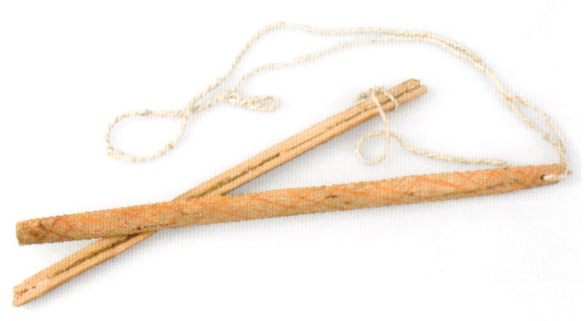

Fig. 109 Pima bullroarer; *weehayweekùhtáykùh* (TK), *wiwkud* (Saxton et al. 1983); wood, pigments, cotton; l. of board 39 cm, w. 2.7 cm, th. 1 cm; ca. 1880 (RMV 362-54).

The Piman bullroarer usually consisted of two pieces of saguaro wood, tied together with a leather thong or cotton rope (Fig. 109; cf. Fig. 102, p. 85). The smaller of the two pieces served as handle, and the larger produced the typical whirring sound when it was swirled around through the air (Beals 1934: 37). The whirring board of this specimen is decorated on both sides with a diamond design with central dots, applied in red paint. Russell (1908) does not mention this artifact in his Pima ethnography.

Games

Ten Kate witnessed the Pima playing a game they called *keensùh*, which resembled the *otóchùh-ee* and *ootahá* games of the Yuma and Mohave. They also played a game like soccer with balls (*sónjikjo*) made from the gum of grease-wood and sand.

Gambling with gaming sticks was mainly a men's game. Such games were played by two to eight men, sitting down and in turn throwing a flat stone on the sticks. These jumped up in the air, and when fallen down, the marks showing on the sticks were counted. Scores were kept with little sticks and the stakes could be high. Games lasting a whole day could end in losing or winning a horse (Whittemore 1893: 65). Ten Kate recorded the name for this game as *keensùh*, a term he later identified as *quince*, a Spanish name signifying 'fifteen.' In a note added to the gaming set (Fig. 110) Ten Kate noted that one stick of the set was lost in the luggage room of his hotel, but that he would try to get a complete set through an intermediary (cf. Culin 1907: 150-151; Russell 1908: 174–181).

Physical fitness was a necessity for survival in the desert and in the vicinity of enemies who frequently engaged the Pima in battle. Footraces were popular, often using a ball being kicked along cross-country or along a specific track. Pimas competed against Papagos individually or in relay teams, and the former were most often victorious. During preparations and training songs about blue-bird and hummingbird, both associated with speed, were sung and dancing took place. Women played a kind of shinny with willow sticks and a pair of balls, tied with a six-inch leather thong.

These game balls were made of mesquite or paloverde (*Parkinsonia*) wood or stone and covered in a layer of black creosote (*Larrea tridentata*) gum (Fig. 111). The stone cores measured three and a half to six centimeters in diameter, but the wooden balls were the size of a croquet ball. While the wooden balls were manufactured by the Pima and Papago themselves, the stone balls were found at prehistoric sites of the Hohokam, the ancient occupants of the area. These were believed to possess magical powers and giving the runners physical strength (Whittemore 1893: 64–67; Russell 1908: 171–174, 284; Bahr 1983a: 191).

Figs. 110, 111 Pima gaming sticks (three of a set of four); wood, pigment; l. 18.5 cm, w. 1.8 cm, th. 0.8 cm; ca. 1880 (RMV 362-52). Pima game ball; stone; d. 5.5 cm; n.d. (RMV 362-53).

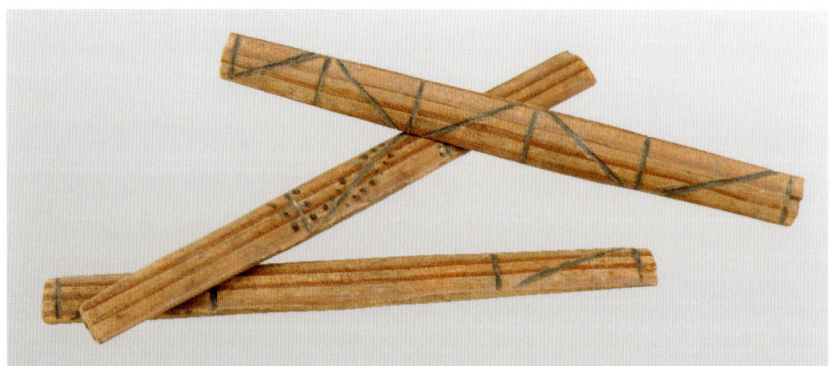

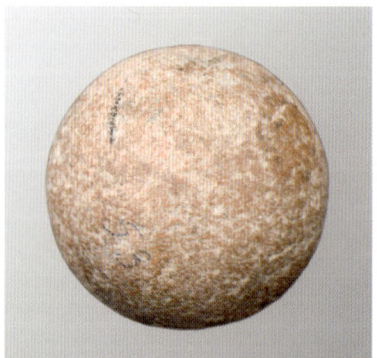

The Pima had a reputation of being peaceful and friendly to Whites, who had not infrequently found refuge with them during raids by the Apache, their arch enemies. In 1872 General O. O. Howard established peace between these tribes. Traditional weapons included bows and arrows and clubs, the latter made from hard mesquite wood. A rawhide shield with painted designs in different colors served for defense. After a long search, followed by protracted negotiations, Ten Kate managed to buy one from an old Pima. Vivid and cherished memories were attached to the shield, and the anthropologist had to pay four dollars to obtain it.

The Pimans had to fight off encroaching and raiding Apaches to the east almost continually, and they allied with the Maricopa to fight the neighboring Lower Colorado River Yumans and Yavapai in the west and north. Pimans guarded their camps with sentries. Their warriors were outfitted with shield and war clubs and fought on foot, while warriors fighting with bows and arrows became more prevalent after they acquired more horses. Scalps were prized war trophies. Boys trained and warriors kept in shape by staging sham battles (Whittemore 1893: 68–72; Beals 1934: 30–31; Underhill 1939: 135–36).

Clubs were usually made of the heaviest wood available, mesquite or ironwood (*Olneya tesota*). Although carved in one piece, they consisted of two parts, a short thick, and slightly tapering handle and a wider cylindrical head. Because of their shape these war clubs have been labeled "potato masher" type or have been compared to mallets. Sometimes the end of the handle was slightly carved in a way to increase the grip of the hand. The handles sometimes have a hole through which a leather thong is drawn, which could be tied around the wrist to prevent loss in battle. In many cases the handles tapered in such a way that their end was almost pointed, and in reverse fashion the club could thus serve as a dagger in close combat. Such clubs vary in length from about thirty-eight to forty-six centimeters. One club collected by Ten Kate (RMV 362-45, see Fig. 99, p. 83) is painted black on the top end, and the surface of the handle is polished or waxed. This club is among the oldest Pima clubs extant in a museum collection (Russell 1908: 96; Di Peso 1956: 488–490). Another war club of the potato masher type, made from ironwood (*Olneya tesota*), was acquired by Ten Kate at the Pima village of Lower Stótovick, Arizona, in March 1888 during the Hemenway Expedition (RMV 674-61, see Fig. 99, p. 83).

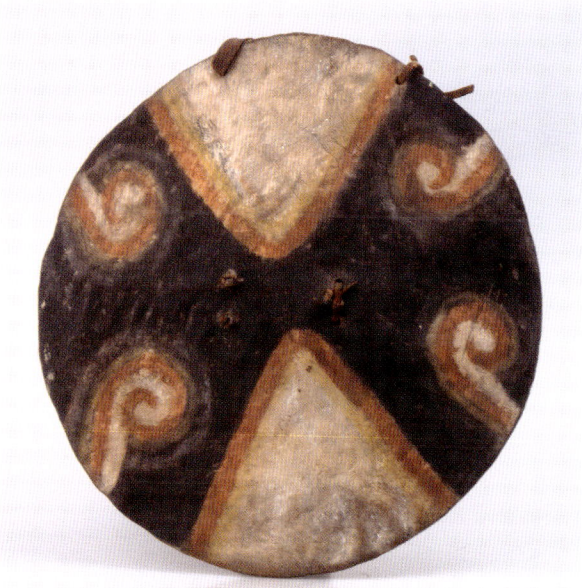

Fig. 112   Pima war shield; *káwats* (TK), *kawad* (Saxton et al. 1983); buckskin, wood, pigment; d. 44–46 cm; ca. 1870–1880 (RMV 362-46).

When the Pima prepared for war, they evoked the spirits to grant them magical powers that would render the enemy's magical powers impotent and make the Pima victorious. It was believed that magical powers that could be obtained by either party were the decisive factor in the outcome of a battle. Pima warriors were divided in two classes of specialists: archers armed with bow and arrows and battlemen with a war club in the right hand and their protective shield in the left. The latter often fought crouching to the ground, so that the shield protected their whole body. Jumping from left to right in this squatting position was a strategy to confuse and elude the enemy. Moreover, the battlemen had painted their shields with magical symbols in strong colors, and by their jumping and partially rotating it from the wrist or forearm in a rapid manner, they tried to confuse the enemy with their dazzling act until a decisive blow could be struck to the opponent.

Shields (Fig. 112) were made from thick rawhide, cut in a circular shape, and had handles of carved wood, fastened to the back of the shield by means of deer sinew or leather thongs, the attachments strengthened on the inside by a square piece of hide. The painted designs on the front in black, red, yellow, and white include triangles and swastikas or whirlwinds, radiating suns representing the God of War. Their shapes and vibrant colors certainly must have confused enemies when they were waved and whirled before their eyes in hand-to-hand combat (Russell 1908: 120–122, 149, 200–202; Shaw 1974: 35–46, 58–63).

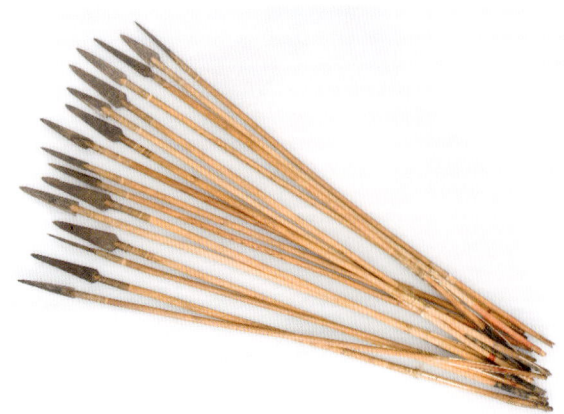

Fig. 113 Bundle of sixteen Pima arrows, placed as offering in a cave; wood, feathers, sinew, iron; average l. 79 cm; ca. 1880 (RMV 362-47).

Surveying Pima territory during the Hemenway Expedition in 1887-88, Ten Kate noted: "Certain signs or symbols which I found among ancient petrographs at different places on the Pima reservation are equally found in Pima body paint and tattooing, on old fashioned war shields (*káwats*) and among the decorations on Pima pottery. I refer here more particularly to different forms of crosses, fylfotlike figures and various forms of coils" (Hovens 1995: 666). The shield collected by Ten Kate and the one obtained in 1883 by Johan Adrian Jacobsen for the Museum of Anthropology in Berlin (Bolz and Sanner 1999: 115, fig. 94) are probably the oldest Pima shields in existence.

The Pima had a reputation of being fierce warriors, keeping fit by staging sham battles, defeating the Yuma to the west repeatedly, and standing up to the Apache in the east. The Sobaipuri, who intermarried with the Pima, were regarded as having the fiercest warriors, a matter of necessity because they were the most immediate neighbors of the Apache (Russell 1908: 23, 165, 186-187, 200-202, 353-356; Shaw 1974: 10-13, 37-42, 58-62).

Sinew-stringed bows made from osage orange (*Maclura pomifera*) wood or willow, of simple manufacture and undecorated, were the weapons for daily use in hunting. For warfare special bows were made of mulberry (*Morinda*), which grew in the Superstition and Pinal Mountains. Arrows were made from the appropriately named arrow weed bush (*Plucea sericea*), providing straight twigs. Hunting arrows generally have two long split feathers, while war arrows have three short feathers (cf. Mason 1894: pl. xli). The Pima and Papago collected stone arrowheads made by the prehistoric Hohokam to tip their war arrows. However, a few men were specialist stoneworkers and manufactured projectile points from flint, obsidian, and shale.

Bows and arrows are often painted red, the color associated with blood. For this purpose the Pima used jackrabbit blood or cochineal insects living on prickly pear cacti (*Opuntia*). Quivers were made from the skin of mountain lions. In 1864 the Pima obtained firearms from the federal government and partially under the leadership of Owl Ear assisted the American army in controlling the Apache (Russell 1908: 51, 95-95, 111; Beals 1934: 30-31).

Ten Kate collected a set of arrows from a sacrificial cave (Fig. 113), their material condition suggesting that they had been placed there only recently.

Basketry

All authors who studied Piman basketry have stressed that it is often difficult to distinguish between Pima and Papago baskets (Kissell 1916; Tanner 1983: 120-174; Whiteford 1988: 117-142). Although tribal identifications of early baskets have been and still are based on raw materials used, basket shapes, and decorative treatment, these and other authors also point to the trade in raw materials for basketry between the Pima and Papago, the exchange of baskets in trade, and intermarriage in the nineteenth century (e.g., Underhill 1939: 103). The degree of intervention of these factors on tribal typology of basketry styles is difficult to determine, but at any rate renders tribal attribution of basketry a somewhat tenuous endeavor. For this chapter of the Ten Kate catalogue a cautious approach is employed. In every case it is indicated among which group Ten Kate collected the individual baskets. Tribal identifications are suggested on the basis of diagnostic traits, following the lead of American experts in the field.

The Pima were the most productive weavers of containers, as the raw materials required for their manufacture were relatively abundant in their territory, which was dissected by watercourses such as the Gila, San Pedro, Santa Cruz, and Aravaipa. In the more arid Papaguería these were much harder to find. Thus the Pima traded raw materials, as well as many of their own baskets, with their southern neighbors. In their coils they used bundles of cattail (*Thypha agustifolia*) and sometimes cottonwood (*Populus fremontii*) as a substitute, resulting in a thinner, more pliable, but less durable container. Papago baskets are thicker, stiffer, and sturdier because of the use of bundles of beargrass (*Nolina microcarpa*) for the foundation, and sometimes Spanish bayonet (*Yucca baccata*) as a substitute. For the binding the Pima used light-colored willow (*Salix nigra* or *Salix gooddingii*) and cottonwood extensively, while

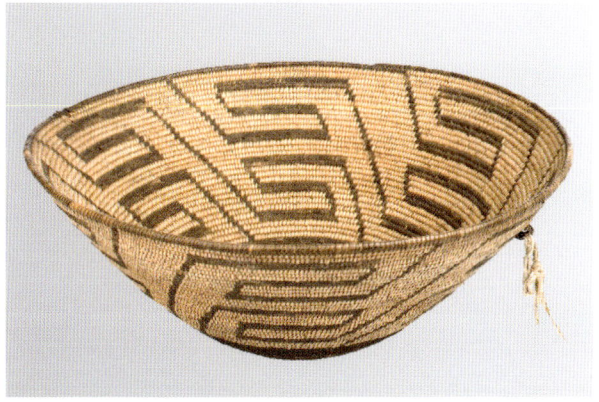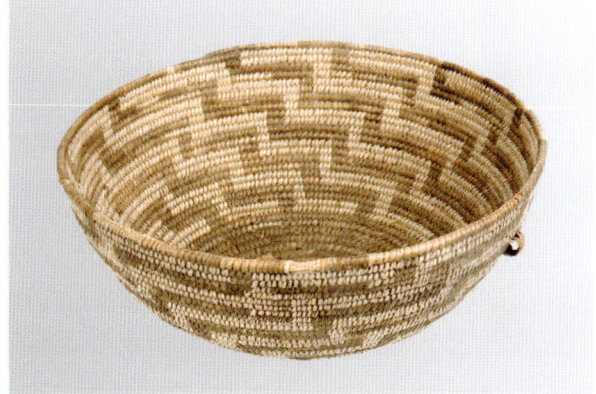

Figs. 114, 115 Papago basketry bowls; RMV 362-28: willow, devil's claw (*Martynia*), native cotton; d. 40 cm, h. 16.2 cm; RMV 362-29: willow; d. 21.5 cm, h. 9.7 cm; both ca. 1880.

dark-colored devil's claw (*Martynia fragrans*) was used only sparingly and that almost exclusively limited to designs. In contrast, the Papago overwhelmingly wove with devil's claw, only sometimes with sotol leaves (*Dasylirium wheeleri*, also popularly referred to as spoon cactus) and used willow for the design. Only when they wove with willow, the designs were applied in a heavy pattern of devil's claw. Thus in Papago baskets dark tends to dominate light, while in Pima basketry light tends to dominate dark. Tray and bowl shapes tend to differ slightly between the tribes, although the differences are more marked among the latter. The Papago weave bowls of more globular form, while the Pima bowls tend to be bell-shaped. Papago trays tend to be a bit deeper and have a flatter base. Both groups flattened the coiled surfaces of their baskets by pounding them between stones when they were still moist. This created a flatter surface than usual in coiled basketry.

Diagonal twilled plaiting is the second technique of basketry weaving the Papago and Pima used frequently. Manufactures in this technique included mats for a variety of utilitarian purposes in the household and to protect a woman's back while carrying heavy loads, headbands for tumplines and headrings for carrying pots, cylindrical storage baskets with a square base, and rectangular medicine baskets. The Papago and Mexican Pima used the thorny leaves of the sotol plant for plaiting. These were first stripped of their sharp spines and subsequently split lengthwise and dried. Before use they are moistened and left over-night in damp earth to make them flexible and easy to weave with. The Pima used river cane (*Phragmites communis*) for plaiting baskets. Plaited baskets were almost always left undecorated. The square-bottomed baskets were used to store food, household utensils, tools, and a variety of personal possessions. The Papago also strained their

saguaro wine through such baskets. The Northern Papago were most adept at making coiled basketry, while the Southern Papago excelled in plaiting baskets and matting (Mason 1904: 519–525, pls. 50, 58–61, 63, 233–235; Russell 1908: 145–148; Kissell 1916: 150–165; Beals 1934: 21–24; Spier 1936: 17; Shreve 1943; Douglas 1939; Di Peso 1956: 408–415; Cain 1962: 28–30; Whiteford 1988: 120, 132; Bernstein et al. 2003: 35, 70–71).

The O'odam used baskets for a great variety of utilitarian purposes, notably the gathering, preparation, serving, and storage of food and the keep of personal belongings. Beyond that daily sphere, baskets were made by girls during their menstrual seclusion period and used in gift exchanges within extended families (Underhill 1939), were used as drums, and held ceremonial items of healers.

Many Piman baskets have a black center from which a variety of patterns radiate outwards. George Wharton James (1901: 214–215) has interpreted this center as being a lake and the radiating designs as water courses. However, his approach was hardly based on empirical research and fitted the romantic mood of the time when it came to folk art (Cohodas 1992: 91, 127). Present-day weavers sometimes interpret the centrifugal design as representing a dust devil, so frequently encountered in the Sonora desert (e.g., Bernstein et al. 2003: 30–31, 70). Tightly woven deep basketry bowls, turned upside down, doubled as resonators for rasps during dances. The two Leiden specimens collected at San Xavier del Bac (Figs. 114, 115) have a small loop of native cotton (RMV 362-28) or *Martynia* (RMV 362-29) on the rim, probably for suspension. The design on RMV 362-28 possible represents devil's claw (cf. Lumholtz 1912: 354). The flaring sides of the bowls are more typical for the Pima, as Papago bowls of the period are generally more globular and have a flatter base.

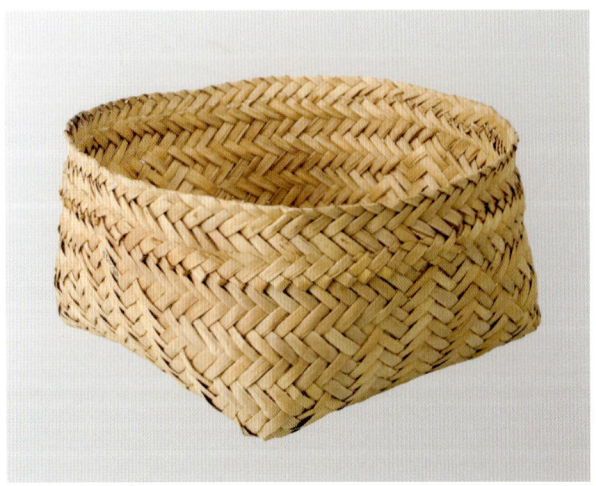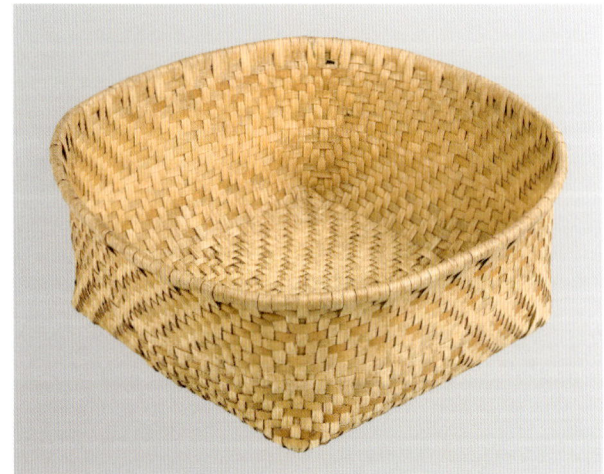

Figs. 116, 117   Papago plaited baskets; sotol; RMV 362-30: d. (at rim) 23.5 cm, w. 22 cm, h. 10.8 cm; RMV 362-31: d. (at rim) 29 cm, h. 11.7 cm; both ca. 1880.

At San Xavier del Bac Ten Kate also collected two Papago square-bottomed and round-rimmed baskets manufactured from sotol leaves (Figs. 116, 117), which were used for storing food, household utensils, tools, and personal belongings. The plaiting of baskets and mats was often done by elderly women who were too old to gather wild foods or do corn grinding. Rim treatment is usually simple, but in some cases "fancy," such as in the Leiden herringbone twill specimen (RMV 362-30), exhibiting an extra decorative woven pattern. The rim of the evenly plaited basket (RMV 362-31), which contains yucca strands, is very flexible. The interior of this container is slightly scorched, and it is showing some signs of wear on its base (Russell 1908: 145-148; Kissell 1916: 150-165; Underhill 1939: 103; Tanner 1983: 148-151; Whiteford 1988: 120, 132).

A diagonally plaited Papago medicine or "prayer" basket with cover, woven from sotol leaves in a herringbone pattern, was likewise collected at San Xavier del Bac (Fig. 118). Rectangular or oblong twill plaited baskets with overlapping covers were made for ceremonial purposes by the mothers or wives of medicinemen or by female shamans. They vary greatly in size, from thirteen to eighty-six centimeters in length, seven to fifteen centimeters in height, and four to twenty-one centimeters in depth, and the Leiden medicine basket sits on the small side of the scale. They could contain paints, medicines, amulets, feathers, shells, rattles, or scalps, and the like, all used in magical performances to heal the sick, drive away bad luck and evil, and attract good luck and prosperity (Russell 1908: 145; Kissell 1916: 165-172; Underhill 1940: 24; Cain 1962: 29-30; Kaemlein 1967: 134; Tanner 1983: 148-151; Bahr 1983b: 195; Whiteford 1988: 132).

A basketry bowl collected by Ten Kate among the Pima (Fig. 119) has a vegetal fiber coil foundation and willow

Fig. 118   Papago plaited medicine basket; sotol; 17.5 cm, w. 8 cm, h. 8.8 cm; ca. 1880 (RMV 362-32).

Fig. 119   Pima shallow basketry bowl or tray; vegetal fiber, willow, devil's claw; d. 17.3 cm, h. 4.3 cm; ca. 1880 (RMV 362-40).

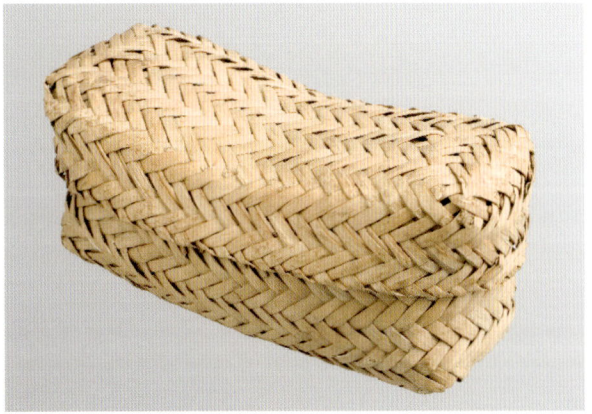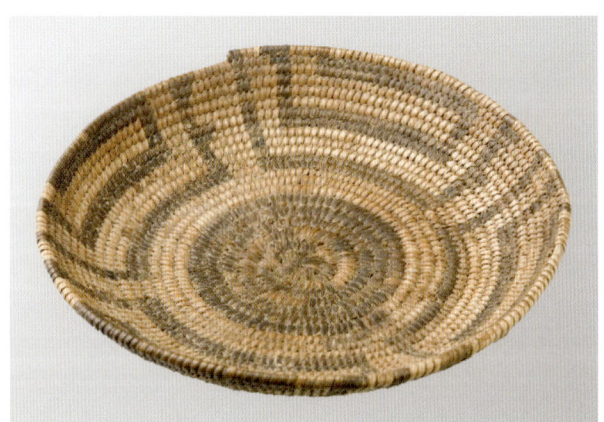

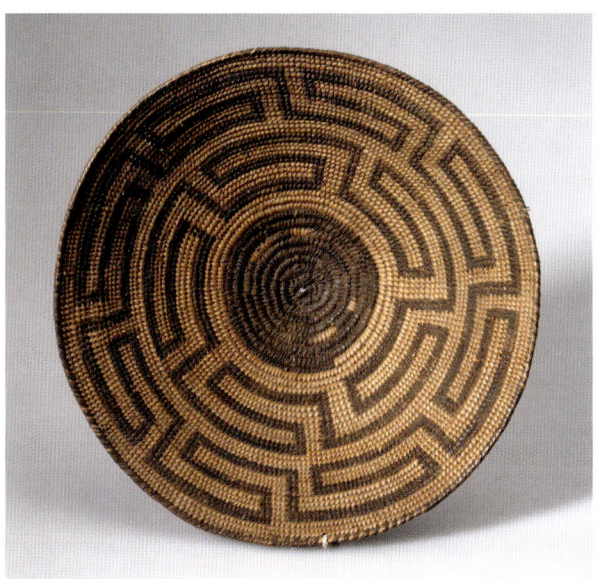

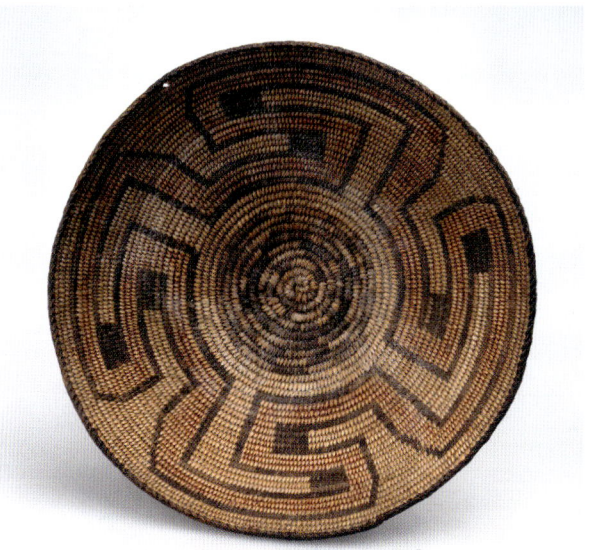

Fig. 120 Pima shallow basketry bowl or tray; vegetal fiber, willow, devil's claw; d. 27.4 cm, h. 9.8 cm; ca. 1880 (RMV 362-41).

Fig. 121 Pima basketry bowl; vegetal fiber, willow, devil's claw, red pigment; d. 33 cm, h. 9.4 cm; ca. 1880 (RMV 362-42).

and devil's claw binding. The design on this shallow bowl or tray seems to run over the rim, as if it was finished prematurely. The interior looks greasy and exhibits remains of what seems to be organic material, probably food.

Devil's claw is a plant that grows on good soil in places that keep moisture. In the Sonora Desert it can be found along intermittent water courses and near Indian fields. Its pods are harvested for the seeds that are part of the Pima diet, and their two upper extensions end in two ten to twelve inch-long fiber horns with sharp hooks, hence its name. The outer black skin of these horns is removed from the core, dried, and stored in coils. Before use the fiber is wetted for maximum flexibility (Brezeale 1923: 42–44).

Another such bowl, likewise acquired among the Pima (Fig. 120), has a round base and is rather deep, with flaring sides. In a few places the interior of the coils are visible, showing a bundle of vegetal fibers. The coils are finely stitched and the rim is unbraided. This type of bowl was versatile and used in Pima households for a great variety of purposes from food preparation and storage to containers for personal possessions. The centripetal design has frets radiating from a central black base. This is the most common design on Pima basketry bowls and is known in numerous variations, referred to as whirlwind, swastika, and vortex patterns. The designation "whirlwind pattern," however, was not a Native name but an invention of White traders. The basic fret design is called *jo-jer-a-vah* in Pima (Brezeale 1923: 52–83; Beals 1934: 24; Whiteford 1988: 125–127).

A further example in the Ten Kate collection (Fig. 121) shows a vegetal fiber coil foundation and willow and devil's claw binding. It has a rounded base, rounded out flared sides, and a braided black rim. The black interior center is mottled, and the meanders of the pattern radiating from the center are filled in with red paint, sometimes encountered on early baskets. The addition of black rectangular blocks to the frets emboldens the design even further. The Pima smoothed their finest baskets by beating the surfaces between two flat stones and final polishing with a cloth (Whiteford and McGreevy 1999: 132). This specimen was acquired by Ten Kate among the Pima.

The black rim of devil's claw is the only decoration on another bowl-shaped basket (Fig. 122). Its plant fiber coils are stitched with willow and it shows signs of wear. This basket was likewise among those collected from the Pima.

Fig. 122 Pima basketry bowl; plant fibers, willow, devils claw; d. 20.2 cm, h. 8.5 cm; ca. 1880 (RMV 362-43).

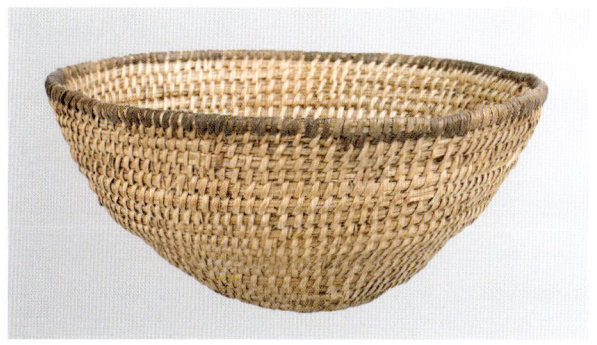

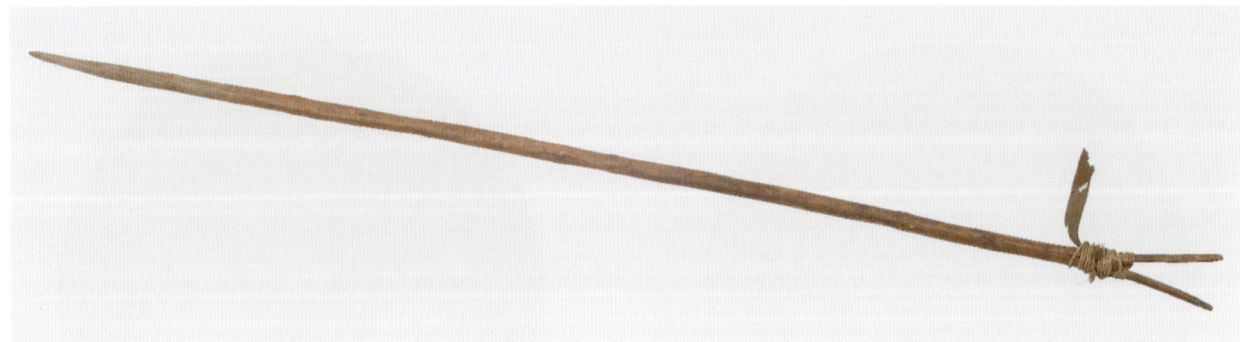

Fig. 123 Pima wooden stick; *sahrkuh* (TK) for carrying a *kéoh* (TK) or *kiaha*, alt. *giha*; wood, buckskin, yucca, pigment; l. 123 cm, d. 2 cm; wood; ca. 1880 (RMV 362-44).

Pima women carried heavy loads on their heads and backs in two ways. One was by means of a twilled fiber headring, on which bundles of firewood and large pottery ollas were transported. A tumpline for carrying loads on the back was also employed, the forehead protected by a twilled fiber headband. The most ingenious and versatile mode of transportation of heavy loads in this way was by *kiaha*, a carrying net. Fibers from the maguey (*Tasylirioni wheeleri*), an Agave species, were spun and twisted in a two-ply twine into cordage, before being woven into nets by a technique referred to as lace coiling. This fabric was attached to and suspended from a double willow hoop that was in turn attached by cords of human hair to the top of a four-pole frame of light ribs of the saguaro (*Cereus giganteus*), thus creating a large conical container in which anything might be transported: firewood, raw materials, harvested food such as mesquite beans and screw beans, pottery, even a baby. The large basketry net was furnished with a plaited head strap, woven from softened yucca fibers, to steady heavy loads. A long forked helping stick is used to set up the net for loading and for getting up with a heavy load, sometimes up to one hundred pounds. The back is protected by a plaited mat of agave or beargrass (*Nolina*) leaves, sometimes river cane.

Girls as young as eight or ten began using small *kiahas* and learn carrying loads and they mastered the net weaving technique soon after. Decorative geometric patterns result from the differences in coiling, varying from plain and twisted to elaborate, and from the application of blue and red mineral dye. The poles of the carrying frame of adolescent girls are painted with colored spots, and woven cords of hair are suspended from them. The helping stick has a long deerskin pendant at the forked end. When carrying a load, this stick extends from the load over the woman's head, with the skin dangling in above and in

front of her head. The Papago used the same carrying device as the Pima, but they used fibers from the century plant (*Agave heteracantha*) for weaving the nets that were shallower and wider than those of their neighbors (cf. Fig. 91 above). Moreover, the poles for suspending and carrying the net on the back extended beyond the net (Whittemore 1893: 54; Mason 1904: 294, 339, 520; Russell 1908: 140-143; Kissell 1916: 225-244; Shreve 1943: 15; Cain 1962: 25-26; Katzenberg 1977: 137, 142; Bahr 1983a: 188; Tanner 1983: 151-155, 172-173; Bernstein et al. 2003: 70; Herold 2005: 94-95).

In a note added to the carrying stick (Fig. 123), Ten Kate showed himself much impressed by the dexterity with which Indian women handled their carrying nets and supporting sticks and added that he doubted whether he would have been able to handle the large contraption, especially when loaded. The fork of the Leiden specimen is held apart by a piece of buckskin going through the split, securely fastened on the fork ends and stick by cordage of twisted yucca. The stick shows some remains of red pigment.

Three Pima baskets collected among the Yuma at Fort Yuma demonstrate intertribal trade. The design on RMV

Fig. 124 Pima coiled basket; vegetal fiber, willow, devil's claw; d. 39 cm, h. 11.2 cm; ca. 1880 (RMV 362-81).

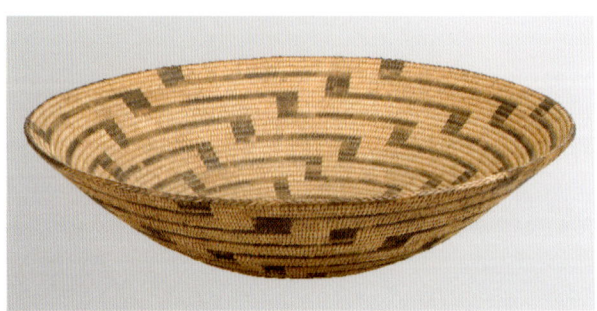

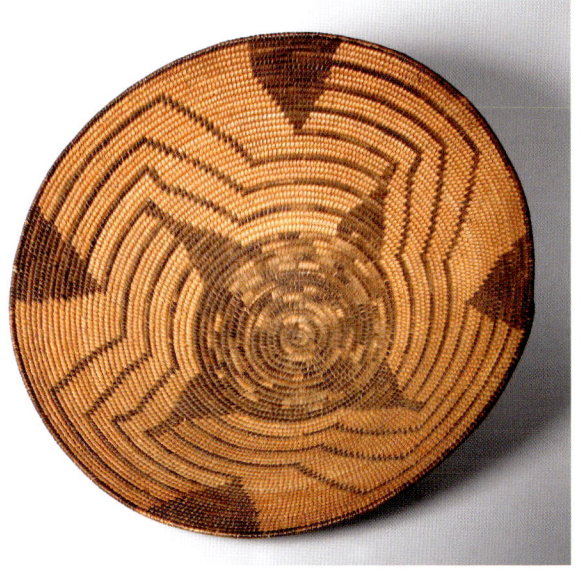 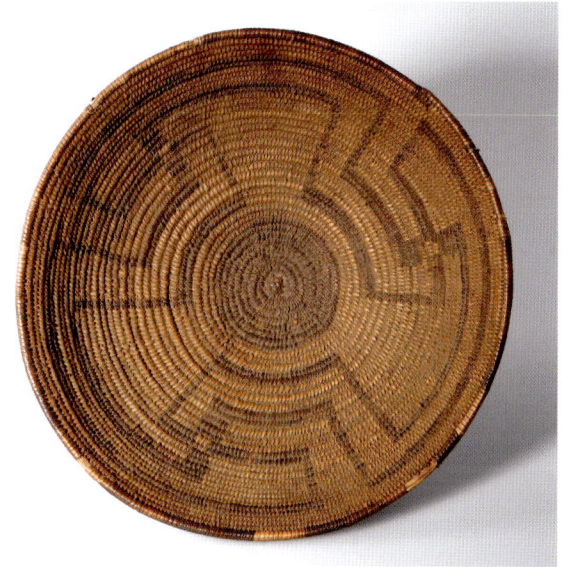

Figs. 125, 126   Two coiled Pima baskets; vegetal fiber, willow, devil's claw; RMV 362-79: d. 37.2 cm, h. 13.7 cm; RMV 362-80: 30 cm, h. 10 cm; both ca. 1880.

362-81 (Fig. 124) shows stepped meanders, uniting the black center and rim. The design on RMV 362-79 (Fig. 125) consists of triangles from which meandering lines emanate, circling the surface of the basket. On RMV 362-80 (Fig. 126) the design radiates inward from the rim, and the black center remains free-floating. They illustrate well the variations on a basic pattern, as pointed out by Brezeale (1923: 52–83; cf. also Fig. 120 above). All three baskets show signs of use, and there are residues of organic remains, probably flour.

References

Bahr, Donald M.
1983a   Pima and Papago Social Organization. In: Alfonso Ortiz (ed.), *Southwest* (Handbook of North American Indians 10. W. C. Sturtevant, gen. ed.; Washington, DC: Smithsonian Institution), 178–192.
1983b   Pima and Papago Medicine and Philosophy. In: Alfonso Ortiz (ed.), *Southwest* (Handbook of North American Indians 10. W. C. Sturtevant, gen. ed.; Washington, DC: Smithsonian Institution), 193–200.
n.d.   How Mockingbirds Are. Manuscript in author's possession.

Beals, Ralph L.
1934   *Material Culture of the Pima, Papago and Western Apache*. Berkeley, CA: U.S. Department of the Interior; National Park Service; Field Division of Education.

Bernstein, Bruce et al.
2003   *The Language of Native American Baskets: From the Weavers' View*. Washington, DC: National Museum of the American Indian.

Boggs, Stanley H.
1936   A Survey of the Papago People. M.A. thesis, University of Arizona, Tucson, AZ.

Bolz, Peter and Sanner, Hans-Ulrich
1999   *Native American Art: The Collections of the Ethnological Museum Berlin*. Berlin: G+H Verlag.

Brezeale, J. F.
1923   *The Pima and His Basket*. Tucson, AZ: Arizona Archaeological and Historical Society.

Brown, Donald N.
1967   The Distribution of Sound Instruments in the Prehistoric Southwestern United States. *Ethnomusicology* 11(1): 71–90.

Cain, H. Thomas
1962   *Pima Indian Basketry*. Phoenix, AZ: Heard Museum of Anthropology and Primitive Arts.

Cohodas, Marvin
1992   Louisa Keyser and the Cohns: Mythmaking and Basket Making in the American West. In: Janet C. Berlo (ed.), *The Early Years of Native American Art History: The Politics of Scholarship and Collecting* (Seattle, WA: University of Washington Press), 88–133.

Culin, Stewart
1907   *Games of the North American Indians*. Annual Report of the Bureau of American Ethnology 24. Washington, DC.

Di Peso, C. C.
1956   *The Upper Pima of San Cayetano del Tumacacori*. Publications of the Amerind Foundation 7. Dragoon, AZ.

Douglas, Frederic H.
1930   *Pima Indian Closed Coiled Basketry*. Denver Art Museum Leaflets 5. Denver, CO.
1939   *Types of Southwestern Coiled Basketry*. Denver Art Museum Leaflets 88. Denver, CO.
1953   Five Pima Pots. *Material Culture Notes* 11: 43–46.

Ezell, Paul H.

1983 History of the Pima. In: Alfonso Ortiz (ed.), *Southwest* (Handbook of North American Indians 10. W. C. Sturtevant, gen. ed.; Washington, DC: Smithsonian Institution), 149–160.

Fontana, Bernard L.

1979 *The Material World of the Tarahumara.* Tucson, AZ: Arizona State Museum.

1983 History of the Papago. In: A. Ortiz (ed.), *Southwest* (Handbook of North American Indians 10. W. C. Sturtevant, gen. ed.; Washington, DC: Smithsonian Institution), 137–148.

1987 The Vikita: A Biblio History. *Journal of the Southwest* 29(3): 259–272.

Fontana, Bernard L. et al.

1962 *Papago Indian Pottery.* Seattle, WA: University of Washington Press.

Hayden, Julian D.

1959 Notes on Pima Pottery Making. *The Kiva* 24(3): 10–16.

1987 The Vikita Ceremony of the Papago. *Journal of the Southwest* 29(3): 273–325.

Herold, Joyce

2005 Baskets of the Southwest and Great Basin. In: Jill R. Chancey (ed.), *By Native Hands: Woven Treasures from the Lauren Rogers Museum of Art* (Laurel, MS: Lauren Rogers Museum of Art), 76–107.

Hill, Gertrude

1942 Notes on Papago Pottery Manufacture at Santa Rosa, Arizona. *American Anthropologist* 44(3): 531–533.

Hovens, Pieter

1995 Ten Kate's Hemenway Diary, 1887–1888. *Journal of the Southwest* 37(4): 635–700.

Irving, W. D. S.

1981 Pima Weaving: The Demise of a Major Indigenous Textile Industry. M.A. thesis, University of Denver, Denver, CO.

James, George Wharton

1901 Basket Makers. *Sunset Magazine* 8(1): 2–14.

Katzenberg, Dena S.

1977 *And Eagles Sweep Across the Sky: Indian Textiles of the American West.* Baltimore, ML: Baltimore Museum of Art.

Kissell, M. L.

1916 Basketry of the Papago and Pima. *Anthropological Papers of the American Museum of Natural History* 17: 115–264.

Lumholtz, Carl

1912 *New Trails in Mexico.* London–New York, NY: T. Fisher Unwin–Charles Scribner's Sons.

Mason, Otis T.

1894 North American Bows, Arrows, and Quivers. *Annual Report of the Smithsonian Institution for 1893:* 631–679.

1904 Aboriginal American Basketry: Studies in a Textile Art without Machinery. *Annual Report of the U.S. National Museum for 1902:* 171–548.

Russell, Frank

1903 Pima Annals. *American Anthropologist* 5: 76–80.

1908 *The Pima Indians.* Bulletin of the Bureau of American Ethnology 26. Washington, DC.

Saxton, D., L. Saxton, and S. Enos

1983 *Dictionary: Papago and Pima to English, English to Papago and Pima.* Tucson, AZ: University of Arizona Press.

Shaw, Anna Moore

1974 *A Pima Past.* Tucson, AZ: University of Arizona Press.

Shreve, Margaret

1943 Modern Papago Basketry. *The Kiva* 8(2): 10–16.

Smith, William N.

1945 The Papago Game of Gince Goot. *Masterkey* 19: 194–197.

Spier, Leslie

1936 *Cultural Relations of the Gila River and Lower Colorado Tribes.* Yale University Publications in Anthropology 3. New Haven, CT.

Tanner, Clara Lee

1983 *Indian Baskets of the Southwest.* Tucson, AZ: University of Arizona Press.

Ten Kate, Herman F. C.

1885 *Reizen en Onderzoekingen in Noord Amerika.* Leiden: E. J. Brill.

1925 *Over Land en Zee; Schetsen en Stemmingen van een Wereldreiziger.* Zutphen: W. J. Thieme.

2004 *Travels and Researches in Native North America, 1882–1883.* P. Hovens, L. A. Hieb, and W. J. Orr eds. Albuquerque, NM: University of New Mexico Press. [Translation of Ten Kate 1885.]

Underhill, Ruth M.

1939 *Social Organization of the Papago Indians.* Columbia University Contributions to Anthropology 30. New York, NY.

1940 The Papago Indians of Arizona and Their Relatives the Pima. *Indian Life and Customs Pamphlets* 3: 1–68.

Whiteford, Andrew Hunter

1988 *Southwestern Indian Baskets: Their History and Their Makers.* Santa Fe, NM: School of American Research Press.

Whiteford, Andrew H. and Susan Brown McGreevy

1999 Baskets. In: D. Anderson (ed.), *Legacy: Southwest Indian Art at the School of American Research* (Santa Fe, NM: School of American Research Press), 125–150.

Whittemore, I. T.

1893 *Among the Pimas, or the Mission to the Pima and Maricopa Indians.* Albany, NY: Ladies Union Mission School Association.

The Apache

In June 1883 Ten Kate arrived in Tucson and found the city in a mood of excitement. General Crook had just returned from Mexico after a successful campaign against the Chiricahua Apache. The Indians were on their way back to be placed on reservations in southeastern Arizona, and the Dutch anthropologist who intended to carry out fieldwork among them was keenly aware of the unique historical moment. When Ten Kate met Crook and stated the purpose of his visit, permission was immediately granted to spend two weeks visiting at San Carlos on the San Carlos Reservation and at Camp Apache on the White Mountain Apache Reservation (now the Fort Apache Reservation). On this and a subsequent occasion Ten Kate was able to discuss Indian policy with the military leader, and the anthropologist found Crook to be quite knowledgeable about the character of the Indians and the causes of interethnic conflict which often arose from the actions of settlers, local officials, and even federal Indian policy.

On the San Carlos Reservation Ten Kate found Indian Agent P. P. Wilcox most unwelcoming, despite his letters of recommendation, but Army Captain Emmett Crawford was quite helpful. Ten Kate's sixteen days at the San Carlos Agency at the end of June/beginning of July were far from pleasant, with temperatures reaching 120 degrees Fahrenheit, brackish drinking water, and malaria widespread. He then went to the much higher, more pleasant environment of Camp Apache on the White Mountain Reservation and spent four days there, with the agreeable assistance of Captain William Dougherty and Indian scout commander Lieutenant Charles B. Gatewood.

Photography

Ten Kate was aware of the historical opportunity he had for doing fieldwork among the Apache, collecting artifacts, and documenting their way of life at this critical juncture.

Therefore he hired photographer Constant Duhem, a Frenchman working in Tucson at the time, to accompany him to the San Carlos Reservation. Duhem made sixty glass-plate photographs for Ten Kate, who sent them to the Leiden museum (Heyink 1983; Hovens and Groeneveld 1992: 100; Ten Kate 2004: 215n7).

Ten Kate was assisted by a most effective interpreter, the Mexican Antonio Díaz, who had been an Apache captive for twelve years before being employed by the government. It was Díaz who persuaded Chiricahua chiefs Loco and Nané to have their photographs taken. Duhem overcame any lingering reluctance by offering the Indians a small tin-type portrait of themselves, while Ten Kate distributed tobacco and a small amount of coins.

Collecting

Ten Kate was able to acquire a small but representative collection of Apache artifacts during his sojourn at San Carlos and Camp Apache, paying for items in cash or goods. One item he did try but failed to obtain was the flat, hourglass-shaped hair ornament of the type worn by young women from the time they began menstruating until they were married and had their first child. Ten Kate provided the following description: "An oblong piece of wood covered with leather, which is adorned with numerous brass tacks. In the middle, where the little board becomes narrower, it is wrapped with red cloth and fastened from behind to the hair at the back of the head, covering part of the neck." However, the anthropologist added wryly that the young women's "mothers steadfastly refused to allow their daughters to give them [the hair ornaments] up, the reason being that no one but the young spouse could remove the ornament from their hair on their wedding night. Because an Apache marriage did not fit in well with my prospective plans, I abandoned further efforts and contented myself with making a sketch of the item desired" (Ten Kate 2004: 196–197). Unfortunately, his sketchbook is lost, but examples of these ornaments can be seen in historical photographs and have made their way into various museum collections (cf. Basso 1983: 475; Ferg 1987: 96).

Ten Kate collected over thirty Western Apache items, some more specifically identified as Coyotero (White Mountain), San Carlos, or Tonto. Two items specifically identified as Chiricahua were collected, one at San Carlos, the other at an unknown location. Ten Kate did not actually visit the Jicarilla or Mescalero Apache: The Jicarilla had recently been removed to Fort Stanton in southern New Mexico, where he did not travel, and the group of Mescaleros who had attended the Tertio-Millennial Exposition in Santa Fe left just as he arrived in town. Ten Kate purchased the dozen Jicarilla and Mescalero items in his collection from "an American merchant" in Santa Fe, who had obtained them during the Exposition.

The importance and strength of Ten Kate's collection of Apache materials, and indeed all the Southwestern materials he collected during his travels, is the documentation as to when and where, and sometimes from whom, items were acquired. As such, all of the objects he collected are invaluable in helping to identify and place in time similar specimens in other collections which lack collection histories. Seven items are of particular note. Ten Kate collected four attractive, but seemingly mundane, saddlebags. Their value lies in having been collected simultaneously from four different groups, providing us with a rare, well-dated, comparative collection for this type of artifact. Two painted shirts and a shield, from two different groups, offer us a glimpse of high-status objects imbued with power to protect their owners.

The Apache did some "collecting" of their own. At San Carlos, despite the fact that Ten Kate and Duhem were staying in an open room which Apaches visited at will, none of their clothes, blankets, or other possessions were disturbed. But there was one item that the Apache men coveted: Ten Kate's hunting jacket had copper buttons embossed with animal heads which the men constantly wanted to touch, and by the time he left, the anthropologist had only one button left on this garment.

Subsistence

Ten Kate noted that the natural environment of the Apache in Arizona was quite diverse, ranging from the dry lowland Sonoran desert around San Carlos to high-

elevation Ponderosa Pine forests around Camp Apache. As a consequence, they had developed a variety of subsistence strategies to exploit the available resources. In pre-reservation days the Western Apache hunted, gathered wild plant foods, farmed on a small scale, and raided for both food and hard goods. Horsemeat was eaten without any qualms.

With confinement to reservations and infringement of those lands by surrounding ranchers, wildlife became scarcer and hunters were no longer allowed to range freely in pursuit of their prey. As a result, the Apache increasingly raided livestock, but those who had been living on the reservation the longest began to ranch and farm themselves. With a drier, more open range, groups around San Carlos emphasized cattle ranching, while the Coyotero near Camp Apache tilled the fertile soil along the White River and its tributaries. Corn was the main crop on both reservations, which Indian agents viewed as a mixed blessing, because corn was the basis for *tulpai*, a weakly fermented beer that was the source of much strife among the Apache and between the Apache and agents. Gathering wild plant foods by women was still practiced, and at San Carlos Ten Kate saw them collecting saguaro fruit *(Cereus giganteus)*, a crop unavailable at the higher elevations of the White Mountain reservation (Ten Kate 2004: 204). Not mentioned by him, but perhaps the most important of the gathered wild foods was agave, also known as century plant, maguey, mescal, and American aloe *(Agave sp.)*.

In addition, the Indians received weekly rations of beef and flour as compensation for the loss of their land and freedom, the depletion of wildlife, and to make them sedentary and pursue a Western lifestyle. It was Ten Kate's view that although the U.S. government's policies had trampled on the rights of the Indian groups it had subdued and had failed to protect them from the corruption of Indian Agents and the treacheries of private citizens, that the Apache had been "progressing along the path of civilization" in the twelve years since General Crook's initial campaigns against them.

Dwellings, Cradleboards, and Basketry

Around the San Carlos Agency the Apache lived in dwellings which consisted of a structure of branches, covered with bundles of beargrass, blankets, canvas tarps, or some combination of all three. Ten Kate referred to these as *khonge*. This is a term unfamiliar to us, and often these abodes have been referred to as *wickiups*, although the correct Western Apache term is *gowa*. Household goods were few, usually including a *metate* and *mano*, milling stones for grinding corn and acorns, scavenged wooden boxes, metal cans, and cloth sacks as containers, an ax for cutting wood, a coffee pot, big knives and spoons and enameled metal basins for cooking, a cradleboard for the youngest child, a few toys, blankets, horsegear, and baskets of course: pitch-coated jar baskets for holding water, bowl baskets for serving food, jar baskets for storage, and large conical or bucket-shaped carrying baskets, in which the women transported heavy burdens such as corn, agave heads, firewood, and camp equipment.

A typical Apache cradleboard in miniature (Fig. 128), made as a toy for a child, was collected by Ten Kate in June/July 1883 at San Carlos or Camp Apache, Arizona. It has a wooden frame covered with buckskin decorated with fringes and a simple red painted design. It is laced up the front to secure the doll, as in full-size cradleboards, to keep the blanket-wrapped child safe. This toy has twigs wrapped horizontally around the sunshade; vertical yucca slats are also common, and explanations of the significance of the two forms are many and varied, but are usually said to signify regional styles or preferences (Ferg 1987: 79–80, 160; cf. Mason 1887: 193–195 on full-sized Apache cradles).

The baskets made by the different Apache groups are quite distinct from one another and from Navajo baskets, suggesting that each learned basket making from a different source. Late nineteenth- and early twentieth-century Western Apache baskets, along with those made by Yavapai groups, are widely acknowledged as some of the finest, if not *the* finest baskets made during the historic era in the Southwest. Semi-nomadic groups often excel in basketry arts: Baskets are light-weight, strong, and do not break if dropped. The Apache used various types of baskets in most of the roles that pottery containers played for sedentary Puebloans.

For some reason Ten Kate collected only a few Apache baskets. In one sense this is unfortunate, in that it would have been wonderful to have some well-dated specimens available in his collection. On the other hand, he may have understood that baskets were relatively commonplace and concentrated therefore on acquiring lesser-known items of material culture. The baskets he collected are representative examples of their kind, although several have interesting attributes. The four Mescalero baskets deserve closer analysis in that they exhibit a range of foundation construction techniques. Whiteford (1988: 56–60) has

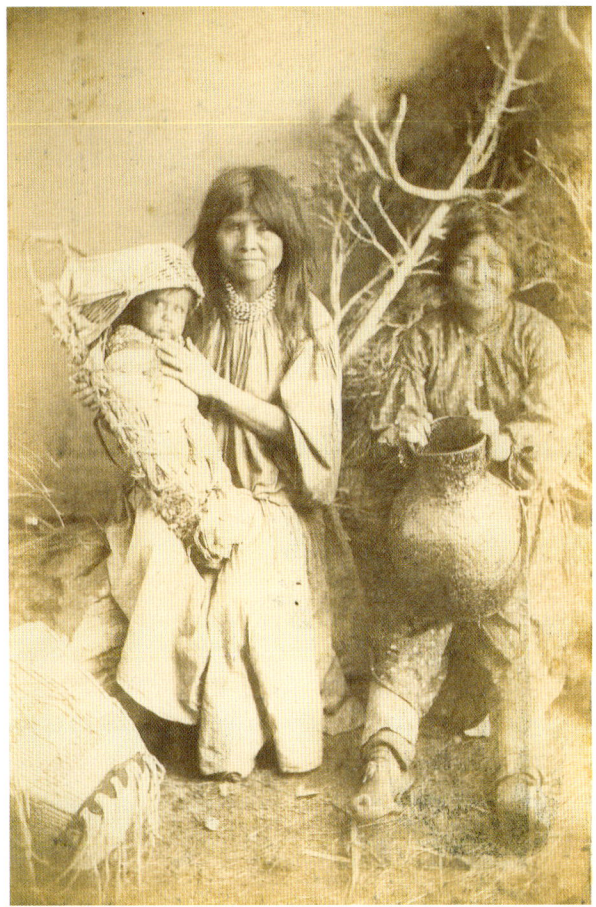

Fig. 127 Apache women with baby in cradle and baskets; Arizona Territory, June/July 1883. Photograph by Constant Duhem (Ten Kate coll.; RMV 414Cb).

Fig. 128 Tonto Apache cradleboard toy with doll; twigs, buckskin, calico cloth, hair, red paint; l. 37 cm, w. 16 cm, h. 16 cm; ca. 1880 (RMV 361-34).

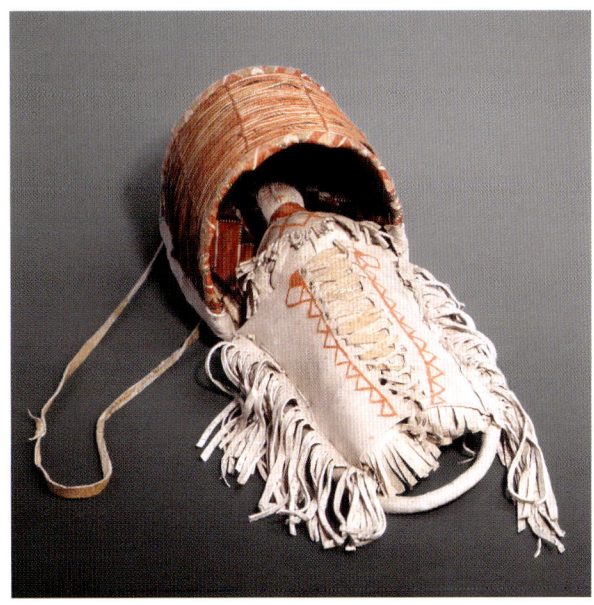

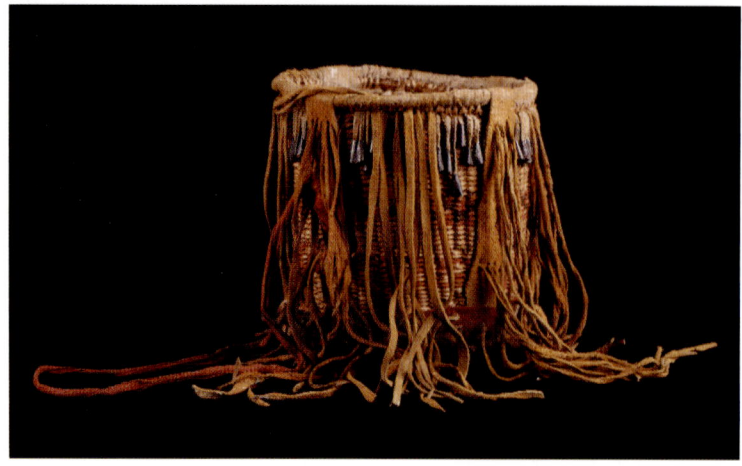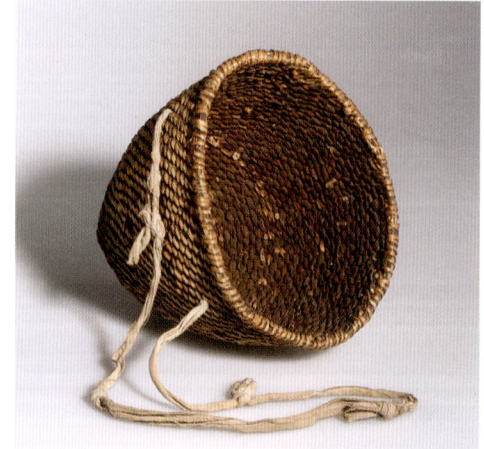

Figs. 129, 130   Tonto burden basket models; RMV 361-35: willow or sumac, buckskin, cotton cloth, red flannel, sheet metal, paint; h. 18 cm, d. 17 cm; RMV 361-37: willow or sumac, cotton cloth, paint; h. 16 cm, d. 14 cm; both ca. 1880.

discussed this aspect of Mescalero basket weaving and the questions surrounding its origins. Ten Kate's four baskets offer a nice "snapshot" of techniques which were obviously in use simultaneously in 1883.

The following basketry section is organized by form and function. Essentially four different Apache groups are represented: Tonto and San Carlos (both divisions of the Western Apache), Mescalero, and Jicarilla. Apache basketry has been documented and analyzed thoroughly, as several studies of construction techniques, design repertoires, and historical change exemplify (Roberts 1929, Tanner 1982, 1983, Whiteford 1988, Dittemore and Odegaard 1998, and Dittemore and Notarnicola 1999).

Two burden basket models (Figs. 129, 130) were collected at San Carlos or Camp Apache, Arizona, in June/July 1883. These twined baskets are too big to have been made as accouterments for dolls, but are certainly not full size. They may have been made for children to use as toys or to actually help adults in gathering or carrying tasks. Both have twisted cotton cloth carrying straps. Whether by accident or design, Ten Kate collected an example of each of the two main types of full-sized burden baskets as recognized by the Western Apache (Ferg 1987: 73–75).

RMV 361-35 (Fig. 129) has two sticks, crossed at the base, woven into the walls as structural supports and is decorated with buckskin fringes, metal tinklers, painted designs, and a base covered with red flannel and cotton cloth. This fancy style of burden basket was used for carrying personal possessions (cf. Tanner 1982: 83–89; Whiteford 1988: 86–88; Herold 2005: 87). RMV 361-37 (Fig. 130) has no additional supports, a more rounded bottom, and no decoration except traces of three horizontal

bands of red paint. This plainer type was used for gathering and transporting a host of plants foods (seeds, acorns, ears of corn, mescal heads), as well as firewood, rocks, and dirt (Ferg 2003). As Whiteford (1988: 65) has pointed out, baskets of Tonto Apache manufacture are rarely identified in museum collections. In this case we encounter a lucky exception.

Basketry water bottles were made by many tribes in the Southwest and Great Basin and bear a general resemblance to one another in being twined, usually without decoration, and then coated with pine pitch inside and out. "Classic" examples from different tribes can often be identified on the basis of typical shapes and minor decorative features, but poorly made specimens may be impossible to attribute to a specific group. Ten Kate collected two small water bottles, which are both difficult to identify as to group of origin because it was not recorded where they were collected: One is quite generic, and the other one, while quite distinctive, exhibits attributes that could point to different tribes.

Apache basketry water bottles are called *tus* and come in various shapes and sizes. The main shapes are round-bodied, shouldered, and double-lobed. The neck varies in height and width (Tanner 1982: 80–81).

A small water bottle (Fig. 131 right), collected in June or July 1883 in Arizona, is rather asymmetric, lacks decoration, and has a coating, inside and out, of what is probably piñon pine pitch. It could be a canteen or was perhaps made for a child. It is most probably Western Apache in origin, but other groups cannot be ruled out. The commercial leather thong looped through the twig handles was not noted by Arizona State Museum curator Wilma

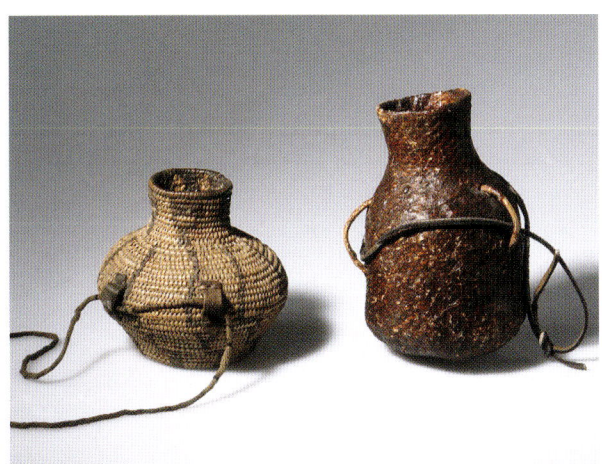

Fig. 131 Western (?) Apache water bottles; RMV 361-40: coiled; sumac or willow, devil's claw, pine pitch; h. 11 cm, d. 12 cm; RMV 361-39: twined; sumac or willow, pine pitch, commercial leather thong; h. 17 cm, d. 11 cm; both ca. 1880.

Kaemlein when she examined this piece in 1964, and it may have been added since then. While the San Carlos Apache used willow for most of their water bottles, the White Mountain Apache, living at a higher elevation, used sumac (*Rhus trilobata*), also referred to as squawberry (Whiteford 1988: 84–85).

Another specimen (Fig. 131 left) was collected in June/July 1883 at San Carlos or Camp Apache, Arizona. It is beautiful little jar, coiled not twined, with a woven-in black design that appears to be devil's claw *(Martynia proboscidea)*, two loop handles of harness leather, and a carrying strap of twisted cotton cordage that was wrapped with what appears to be black hair, but whether horse, human, or something else is unknown. The interior was made waterproof with a coating of pine pitch. Jars pitched only on the interior are a hallmark of Jicarilla water bottles and are unlike those of most other tribes (Herold 1999: fig. 10; Whiteford 1988: 53). However, Jicarilla bottles are generally larger, more globular, and if decorated at all, it is usually with a few vertical lines of overstitching (see Herold 1999: fig. 10; Tanner 1982: fig. 5.1b; 1983: fig. 5.12; Whiteford 1988: 53). This brings us to the black devil's claw decoration. No author could be found who mentions the use of this material by Jicarilla weavers, and Whiteford (1988: 52) flatly states that it was not used. Based only on an examination of a photograph, Arizona State Museum curator Diane Dittemore, very familiar with Western Apache basketry (Dittemore and Notarnicola 1999, Dittemore and Odegaard 1998), felt that the shape and decoration of this basket fall within the range of variation seen in Western Apache baskets. We are left

with the need to more fully identify the materials of which this basket is made, but tentatively identify it here as of Western Apache manufacture, largely because it seems more likely that Western Apache weavers might make this somewhat anomalous coiled bottle than it does that Jicarilla weavers would use devil's claw.

The Western Apache made wide, shallow bowls and ollas in the coiling technique. The Mescalero produced similar trays in great quantities. Shallow and deep bowls were used for serving and preparing food. Often these exhibited no decoration as they soiled from the start and had a limited life span. However, there are exceptions. In these cases two designs predominate: a fret/whirlwind/lightning pattern radiating outwards towards the rim from the black center or a floating star/petal/flower motif (Whiteford 1988: 57–58, 78–79).

One of the baskets in the collection (Fig. 132) is a remarkably simple specimen with only a black disk of devil's claw splints in the center, which Ten Kate collected in June/July 1883 at San Carlos, Arizona. The broken outer coil reveals a three-rod foundation. It is unclear whether this is an unfinished basket or one that has had its outer coils broken away. As Whiteford (1988: 80) noted, a black center disk and a black rim are nearly universal on Western Apache bowl baskets regardless of the nature of the design in between the two. In this case it appears that there may have been no further decoration.

Fig. 132 Western Apache bowl basket; coiled; willow, devil's claw; d. 18 cm, h. 3.5 cm; ca. 1880 (RMV 361-36).

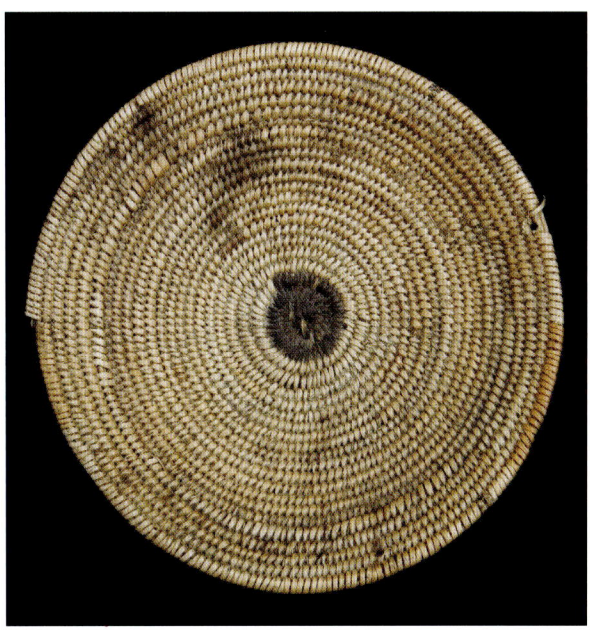

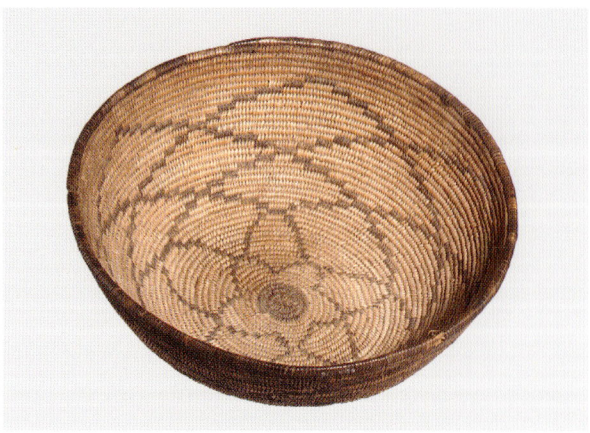

Fig. 133 Western Apache bowl basket; coiled; willow, devil's claw; d. 23.5 cm, h. 8.5 cm; ca. 1880 (RMV 361-38).

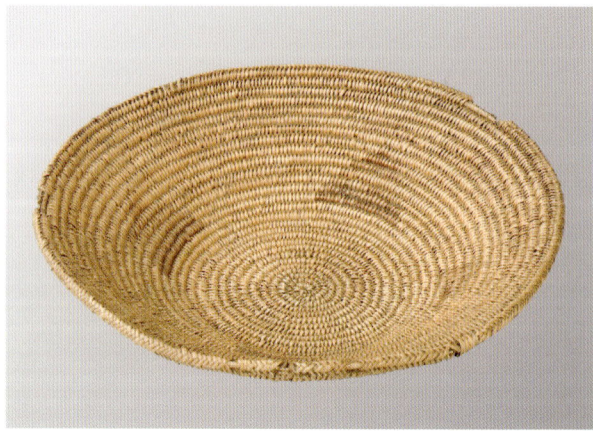

Fig. 134 Jicarilla Apache bowl basket; coiled; sumac or willow; dye; d. 41 cm, h. 10.5 cm; ca. 1880 (RMV 361-41).

Another basket (Fig. 133) has a simple, elegant design of the type often described as interlocked stars or petaled flowers, composed of curved lines of black devil's claw radiating from the center. It apparently had a varied use-life, with a worn exterior, scorched on one side, and with residues of meal or pollen between stitches on the interior. It was collected in June/July 1883 at San Carlos or Camp Apache, Arizona.

A third specimen (Fig. 134) was purchased in Santa Fe in July 1883 from a trader who had obtained it from Jicarillas who had been at the Tertio-Millennial Exposition. Considerable wear to this basket reveals what appears to be a three-rod foundation. The four triangles are

now a faded brown; their original, dyed color is uncertain. The base is flat and the rim is braided. Its extremely simple design recalls other baskets thought to be early Jicarilla (cf. Tanner 1983: fig. 5.7a).

Ten Kate also bought several Mescalero baskets from the same trader, likewise originally obtained from members of that tribe who had attended the Tertio-Millennial Exposition: RMV 361-42, -43, and -44 (Figs. 135, 138) and probably also RMV 2012-13 (Fig. 137). Mescalero coiled baskets are generally easily identified by their unusually flat, wide coils that are unique in the Southwest. They are constructed by stacking two, sometimes three, sumac rods one atop the other and then adding a thin bundle of yucca

Fig. 135 Mescalero Apache bowl baskets; RMV 361-43: coiled; sumac, yucca root; d. 21 cm, h. 7 cm; RMV 361-44: coiled; sumac, yucca, yucca root; d. 27.5 cm, h. 9 cm; both ca. 1880.

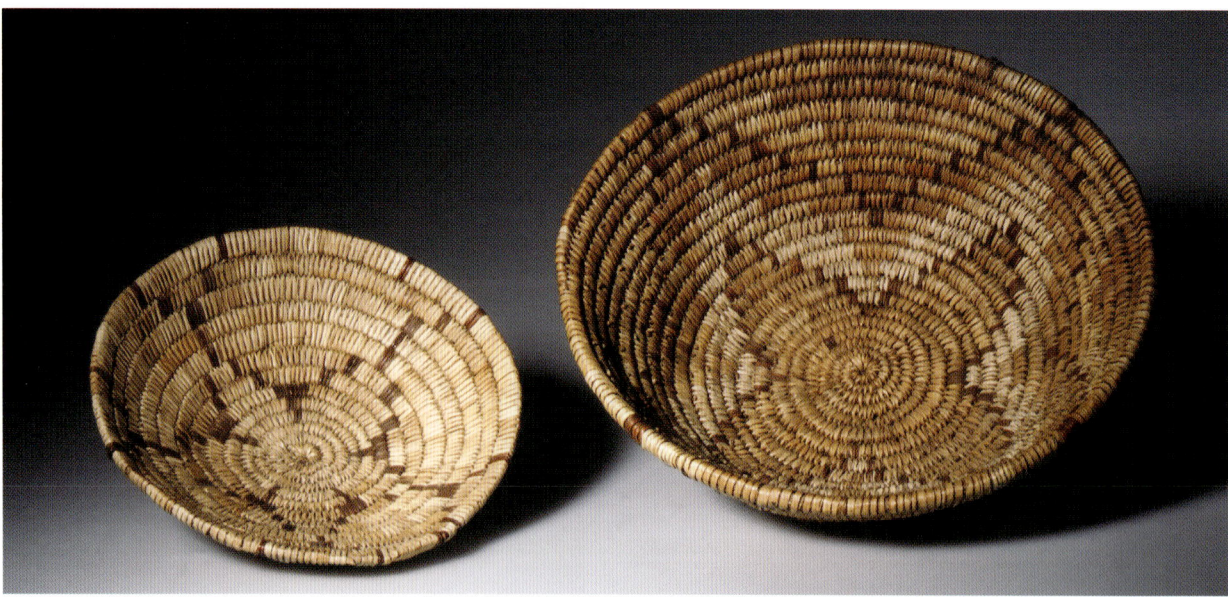

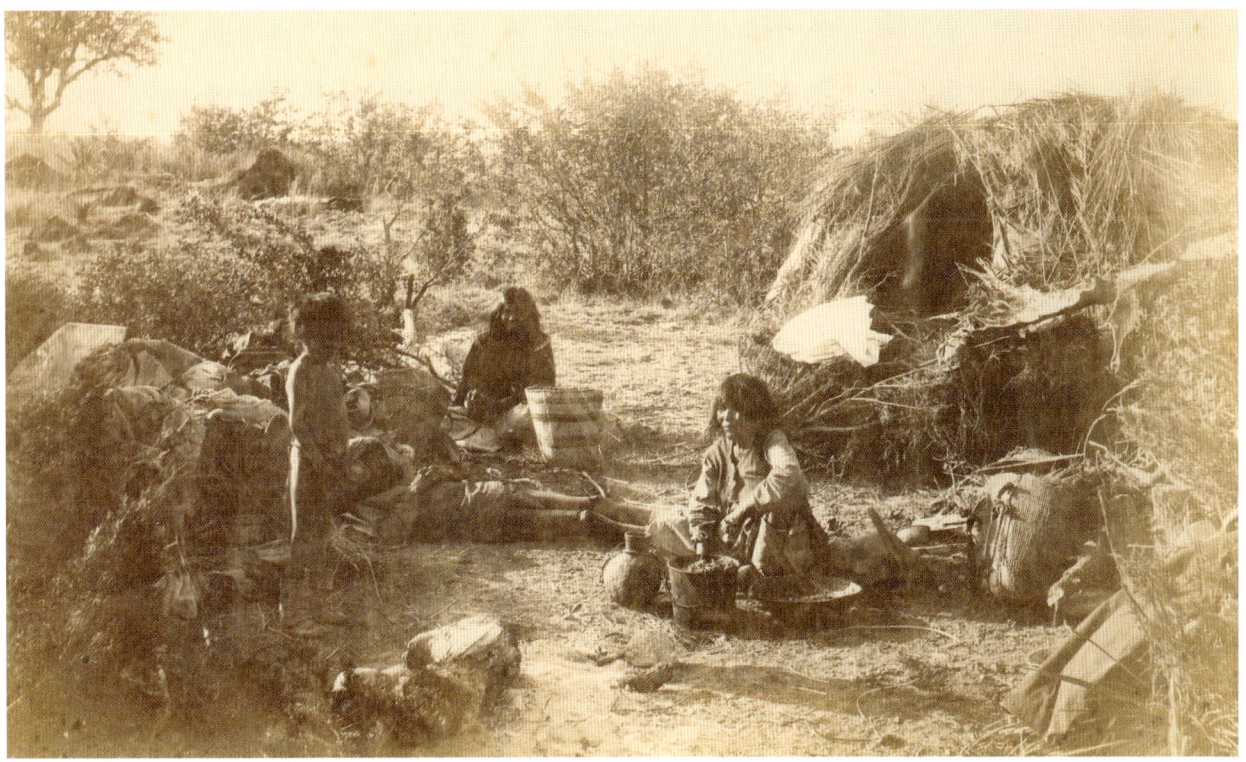

Fig. 136   Apache household with a variety of baskets. Photograph by Constant Duhem, Arizona Territory, June/July 1883 (Ten Kate coll.; RMV 414Kd3).

or beargrass (*Yucca glauca*) fiber. Yucca splints are sewn through the fiber bundle, holding the stacked coil together and binding it to the next. Sometimes a thin slat of wood is substituted for the stacked rods. The origin of this technique is unclear (Whiteford 1988: 59–60).

RMV 361-43 (Fig. 135 left) appears to have a two-rod foundation with the design executed in brown yucca root stitches. This basket has a five-pointed design that various authors have called "flowers" or "stars," but Farrer (1991: 77–78, 82) states that such designs are clearly identified by the Mescalero as stars and suggests that only baskets with four-pointed stars would have been used domestically or ceremonially by the Mescalero themselves. Baskets with stars with five or more points are more probably made to be sold to outsiders, although stars with six points (an even number) and eight points (a multiple of four) might be acceptable for Mescalero use (Farrer 1982 in Whiteford 1988: 57). While based on traditional Mescalero belief systems, it would nevertheless be interesting to compare these twentieth-century ideals with the use and wear patterns found on nineteenth-century baskets, in order to see how universally they might have been observed in earlier days.

RMV 361-44 (Fig. 135 right) has a four-pointed star design done in yellowish-brown splints and dark brown

yucca root. The coils of the body are nearly round in cross-section, but their foundation cannot be seen; the rim coil has a triangular cross-section, suggesting that three narrow rods were bundled together rather than stacked.

Another basketry bowl (Fig. 137), which the Leiden museum purchased from Ten Kate in 1921, displays a lopsided four-pointed star design done in bleached white yucca splints and brown yucca root against a background of unbleached yucca. The coils of this basket are likewise nearly round in cross-section and may be three rods and a fiber bundle, bundled all together.

Fig. 137   Mescalero Apache bowl basket; coiled; sumac, yucca, yucca root; d. 19 cm, h. 6.5 cm; ca. 1880 (RMV 2012-13).

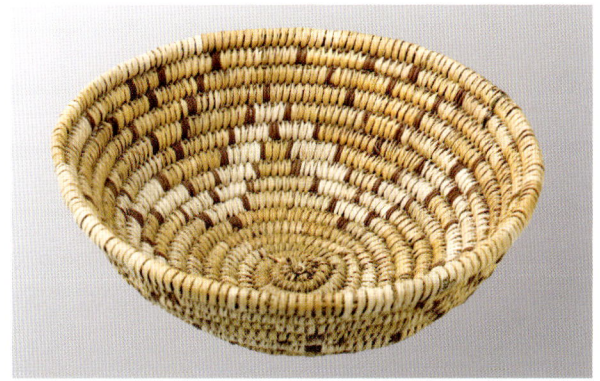

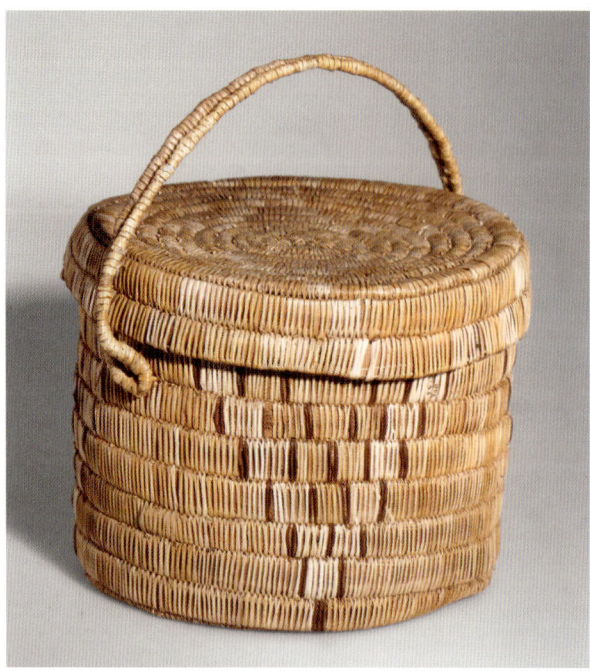

Fig. 138 Mescalero Apache lidded basket; coiled; gambel oak or willow, yucca, cordage; d. 28 cm, h. 19 cm (incl. handle 31 cm); ca. 1880 (RMV 361-42).

A lidded basket in the collection (Fig. 138) has been discussed by Whiteford (1988: 58–59) as being unique in the Southwest, both in its having completely vertical walls and a flat base and lid and having, in place of a stacked rod foundation, a thin slat split from gambel oak (*Quercus gambelli*) or willow (*Salix*). The design on the body consists of four triangles, point down, made of brown stitches (small unidentified twigs with bark on) and white (bleached yucca). Fading of the colors makes it difficult to be certain, but there may also have been triangles of bleached yucca stitches on the lid. The handle is not sturdy: A length of soft (commercial?) cordage was doubled over, wrapped with yucca strips, and secured to the basket wall with a few yucca stitches (also cf. Tanner 1982: 164–166).

Horses and Horsegear

Ten Kate scorned romantic novelists' notions of the Apache possessing splendid horses and was unimpressed by the animals he observed at San Carlos. They were of small but robust stature, bred for physical endurance, and appeared poorly cared for. Riders seemed to have little regard for their mounts and often rode them to death on raiding expeditions, when spare animals were also taken along, making them move swiftly over large distances. Ten Kate did not consider the Apache very good riders and

remarked that their wooden stirrups were short and that they thus rode with their knees drawn up. Ten Kate found the riding style of the Apache inelegant, with their trunks and heads in perpetual motion and their arms flapping up and down their bodies.

While in pre-reservation days lost horses could be replaced by stealing more, the animals were certainly considered valuable and all Apache groups cared for their horses, making a variety of horsegear, usually modeled on Spanish and Mexican equipment. Considerable effort could be lavished on saddles, wooden spurs, quirts, ropes, rawhide horseshoes, tack, and saddlebags, and Ten Kate collected several such artifacts: four saddlebags from different groups, rawhide horseshoes or boots at San Carlos, Mescalero stirrups, and a rawhide rope and two quirts (horse whips), which may be either Apache or Navajo, but are listed as Apache in the Leiden inventory, based on Ten Kate's notes. All of these articles, as well as simple rawhide hobbles, were undoubtedly made on similar patterns by several Southwestern groups, and it is often impossible to know if examples obtained from a group were made by them or exchanged in trade from another. The horseshoes are of a simple style known to have been made by several Apache groups, the Navajo, and various Puebloan tribes, all of whom almost certainly were copying those used by early Spanish explorers (Clark 1963: 246). The stirrups and rawhide rope are both known to have been made by various Southwestern groups, and Ten Kate (2004: 206, 244) specifically mentions stirrups for both the Apache and Navajo. And again, the braided leather and braided horsehair quirts are known to have been made by various groups, but their specific origin is uncertain. The importance of the two specimens collected by Ten Kate, regardless of which group made them, is that they document that both techniques were fully known and in use in 1883; braiding of horsehair hatbands and curios among the Western Apache may be a later introduction (Ferg 1987: 99, 102).

One of the strengths of Ten Kate's Apache collection are the four rawhide saddlebags he acquired, one each from the White Mountain Apache, Chiricahua, and Mescalero, and an Apache-made saddlebag from the Navajo in New Mexico. Saddlebags made by many groups consist of a flat, elongate "envelope" with fringes on the short edges, folded in half across the rump of a horse or over one's arm or shoulder. Saddlebags made by Plains groups generally have a slit opening along the fold of one of the long edges, while saddlebags made by the Western Apache and

Chiricahua have a longitudinal slit in the center of the top face of the "envelope" (Ferg 1987: figs. 5.48, 8.11). This distinctive construction appears to be peculiar to these two groups, at least in the Southwest, but Feest (2006: 78, 96-97) has pointed out their similarity to slit pouches used by various tribes in the eastern United States and suggested that both may be derived from European predecessors, with Spaniards, of course, being the most probable source to have introduced the form to the Apache. There are a few virtually identical bags in various collections attributed to the Mescalero and Jicarilla Apache, but research to date has not precluded the possibility that they were received in trade from the Chiricahua or Western Apache. The Mescalero and Jicarilla more typically made rawhide parfleches. The Navajo apparently did not make such saddlebags, although the construction of *jish* bags, made by medicine men to carry their paraphernalia, appears identical (Franciscan Fathers 1910: 382; Frisbie 1987: figs. 4, 7, 10, 13b; Kluckhohn et al. 1971: 333–336). The saddlebags collected by Ten Kate from the Mescalero and the Navajo in New Mexico possess no attributes that distinguish them from known Chiricahua and West-

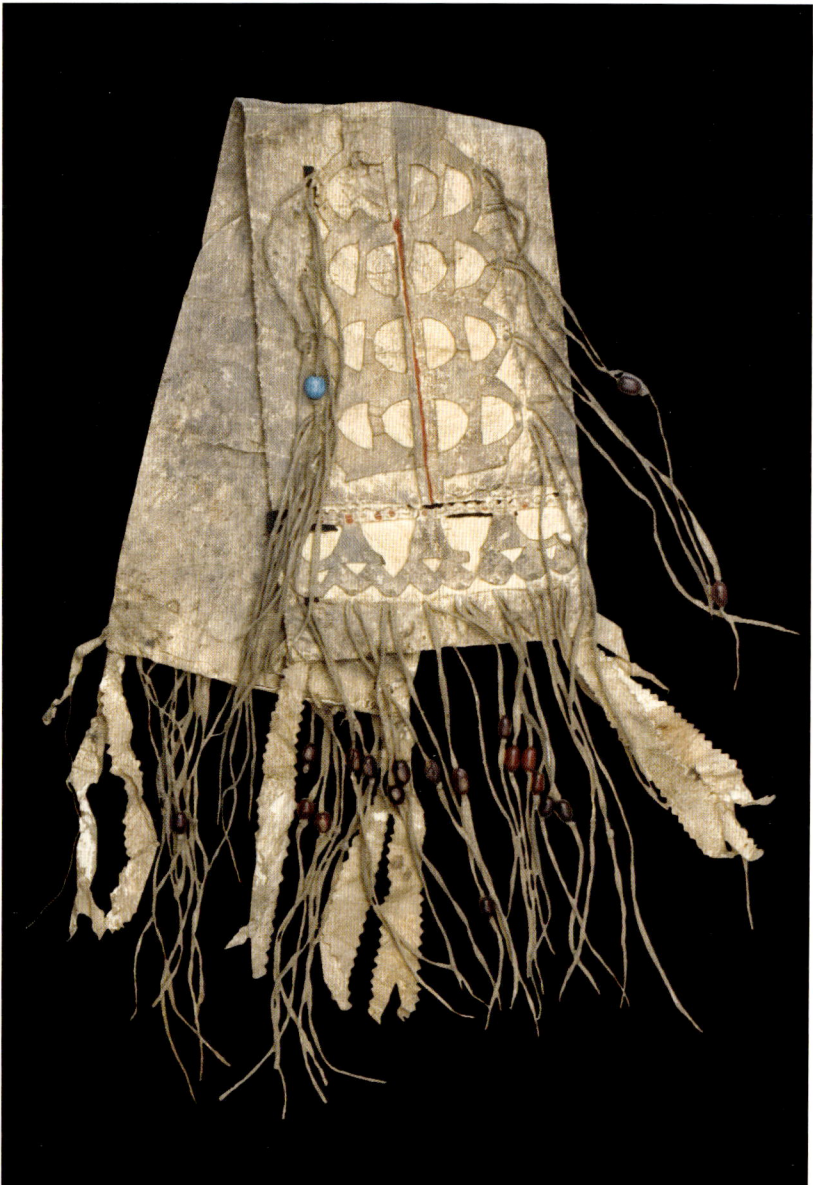

Fig. 139 Chiricahua Apache saddlebag; rawhide, cloth, seeds, turquoise; l. (unfolded, incl. fringes) 96 cm, w. 20 cm; ca. 1880 (RMV 361-48).

ern Apache saddlebags, and we suggest that those are probably the groups that actually made those bags. We know that various items made by the Apache in Arizona were traded long distances, including a beautiful Western Apache or Chiricahua rawhide saddlebag collected at the Sioux Agency in 1888 (Vincent et al. 2000: 246).

All four of Ten Kate's saddlebags are made of a folded piece of rawhide for the body, with panels of rawhide overlay with elaborate geometric designs cut out of them. There may be a piece of red, black, or blue cloth under the overlay to accentuate the cut-out designs. Rawhide corner tabs are serrated and sometimes perforated. Fringes are of

rawhide or buckskin. Assembly of nineteenth-century bags was usually done with sinew or buckskin thongs.

The Chiricahua bag (Fig. 139) was probably collected in June/July 1883 at San Carlos, Arizona, and displays red and black cloth under parts of the overlay. Many of the fringes have beads made from red seeds, probably either mescal beans *(Sophora secundiflora)* or coral beans *(Erythrina flabelliformis)*. One turquoise bead is also present. Merrill (1977: 72) notes a similar specimen, also identified as Chiricahua. The small size and relatively elaborate decoration are consistent with miniature saddlebags made as toys for children (Ferg 1987: 160–161).

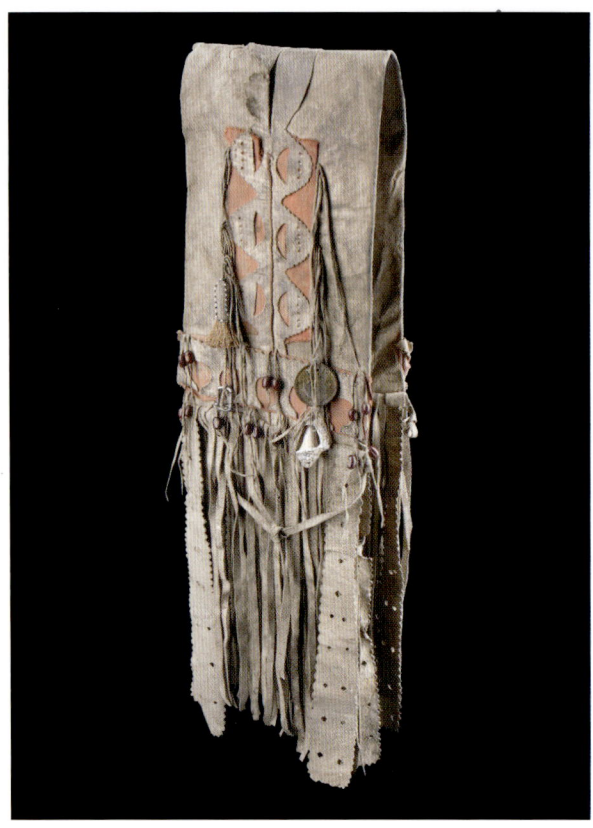

Fig. 140   Mescalero Apache saddlebag; rawhide, cloth, misc. attachments; l. (unfolded, incl. fringes) 155 cm, w. 26 cm; ca. 1880 (RMV 361-49).

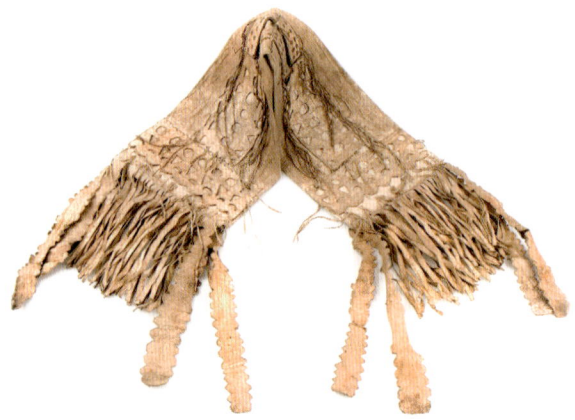

Fig. 142   White Mountain Apache saddlebag; rawhide, cloth, glass bead; l. (unfolded, incl. fringes) 200 cm, w. 35 cm.; ca. 1880 (RMV 674-2).

The Mescalero bag (Fig. 140) has ribbed red cloth under parts of the overlay. There are numerous attachments, including mescal bean or coral bean beads, a broken piece of perforated abalone *(Haliotis* sp.) shell, a gastropod shell with part of the back cut away to reveal the interior, three small white buttons, a metal buckle, a metal disc from the inside of a pocket watch, and a small grass brush with a beaded buckskin cover. Most of these attachments could be categorized as decorative, but the shells and brush suggest that some may have served double duty as protective charms. The intermediate size of the bag and its heavy use-wear suggest it was used on a burro or per-

haps carried by a person. It was among the several artifacts purchased by Ten Kate from a trader in Santa Fe in July 1883, which were originally obtained from Native attendants at the Tertio-Millennial Exposition.

A third Apache bag (Fig. 141) has red flannel cloth under parts of the overlay panels, which are further decorated with edgings of black and white glass seed beads and small metal tinklers on short buckskin thongs. The serrated corner tabs have daubs of red paint on them as well as more tinklers. A few fringes on the body have large, opaque, light blue glass "trade" or "padre" beads knotted into them. The intermediate size of the bag and its use-wear again suggest it was used on a burro or perhaps carried by a person. Construction and decoration are consistent with bags made by the Chiricahua and Western Apache. This specimen was collected at San Carlos or Camp Apache, Arizona, in the summer of 1883.

Shreds of fabric suggest that the cut-out panels on the body of the White Mountain Apache saddle bag (Fig. 142) were formerly backed with red flannel cloth. Decorative cut-out panels flanking the slit opening were backed with brown cloth. A single end fringe has one large, opaque, light blue

Fig. 141   Apache saddlebag; rawhide, cloth, metal tinklers, glass beads; l. (unfolded, incl. fringes) 190 cm, w. 30 cm; ca. 1880 (RMV 674-1)

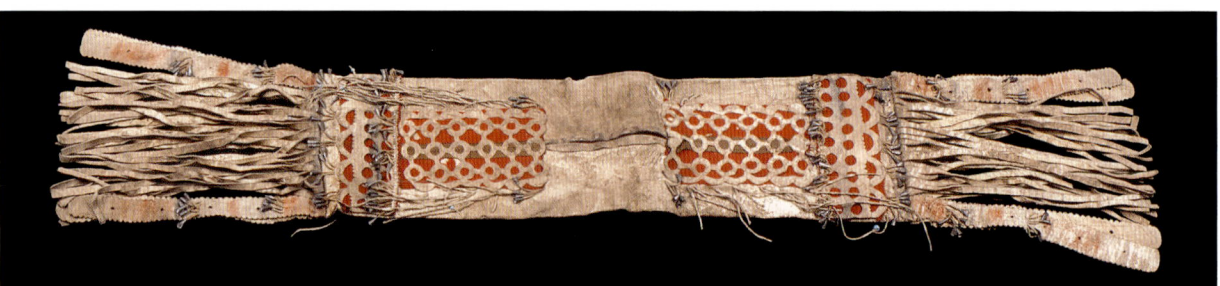

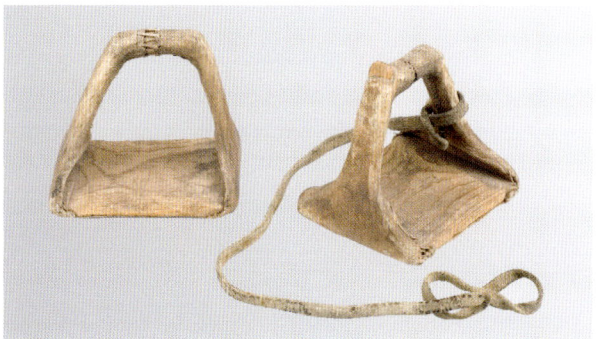

Fig. 143 Mescalero Apache stirrups; wood, rawhide; h. 13.5 cm, w. 15 cm; ca. 1880 (RMV 361-50).

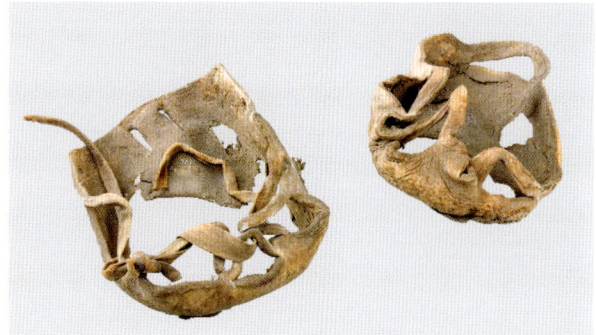

Fig. 145 Western Apache horseshoes; rawhide; l. 15.5 cm, w. 12 cm; ca. 1880 (RMV 361-54).

glass "trade" or "padre" bead knotted into it. The relatively large size of this bag and its use-wear suggest it was used on a horse. It was collected in the summer of 1883 in Arizona.

The Mescalero stirrups (Fig. 143) have a wood foundation encased in rawhide, which was stitched in place while wet and shrank as it dried, creating a strong, rigid sheath. The covering obscures the joints, and it is uncertain whether the foundation was assembled from separate pieces of wood or from a single piece, kerfed and bent to shape (cf. Wissler 1915: 14–17). One stirrup retains the strap with which it was tied to the saddle. They were purchased in Santa Fe in July 1883 from the same source as other material intially acquired on the occasion of the Tertio-Millennial Exposition. The museum catalog card includes a notation by Ten Kate that this type of stirrup was also used by the Navajo, Pueblo peoples, and Zuni.

The hidden foundation of a quirt in Ten Kate's collected (Fig. 144) may be the proximal ends of the two harness-leather lashes. It is covered in bundles of black and white horse tail hair, braided in bands of herringbone pattern alternating with open netting, with knots and tassels

Fig. 144 Apache quirt; horsehair, harness leather; flannel; l. 100 cm; ca. 1880 (RMV 361-51).

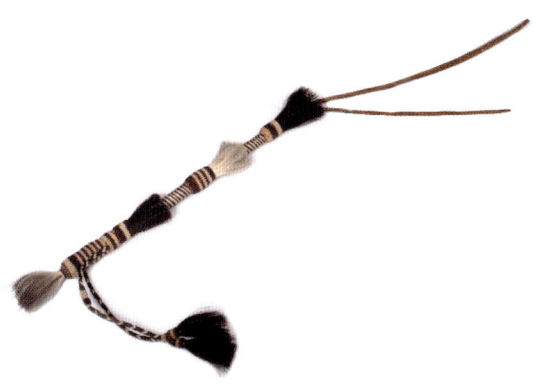

on the body and wrist-loop. The base of the handle has a piece of red flannel, which shows through the netting covering it. Braided horsehair quirts were made by both the Navajo and Apache (Ferg 1987: 82; Kluckhohn et al. 1971: 87), and Arizona State Museum curator Wilma Kaemlein, who examined the Leiden specimen in 1964, noted that it closely resembled known Yuman/Quechan examples. Wissler (1915: 27) noted that the horsehair quirts made by Southwestern Indians were obtained through trade by Indians across the trans-Mississippi West. The manufacture of horsehair objects became popular among military and civil prisoners in the course of the nineteenth century, as these could be exchanged for tobacco, food, and cash. A number of these "soumak" style Apache artifacts became part of the Goodwin and Guenther collections at the Arizona State Museum. In several cases these items were associated with an Apache prisoner (Ferg 1987: 82, 99, 102, 152, 180, 188). The Leiden example was collected in the summer of 1883 in the Southwest.

Ten Kate (2004: 206) recorded: "To protect the hooves of horses as much as possible from the rocky ground and the spines of the plants, the Apaches use coverings of thick, untanned leather with the hairy side facing outward, which are wrapped around when wet and, once dry, fit tightly around the hoof" (Fig. 145). Opler's (1941: 396) Chiricahua informants said such shoes were always of cowhide, but generally whatever was available was used (Clark 1963: 246–248). Although the shrinking of the rawhide is important, the shoes that Ten Kate collected, and all others known, also feature laces passed through slits in the edge of the shoes to help keep them on; such shoes might have holes cut in the bottom to let gravel out, and smaller shoes of this type were also made for burros (G. Baldwin 1965: 87; Ferg 1987: 81). The specimens Ten Kate collected in June/July 1883 at San Carlos, Arizona, look well-used.

Ten Kate was refreshingly frank in his remarks about what he was able to learn regarding Apache religion. And it is a fairly blunt indictment of expansive discussions of religion made by *Stubenethnologen* (armchair ethnologists) who never set foot in the field or met their subjects face to face: "There was nothing I could learn with any certainty regarding the Apaches' religious concepts. Years would have been needed for this, during which time I would have had to learn their language and gain their confidence ... Just ask a people who do not know you and mistrust you, and with whom you have stayed just a short time, what they believe and why they do this or that! It is impossible to get anything out of them that one can rely on. What passing travelers like me, in no matter what part of the globe, may serve up regarding the religion of a people whose language they do not know deserves very little credence—this I can state without hesitation. And yet how often have the *"Stubenethnologen"* forgotten this!" (Ten Kate 2004: 208).

While at San Carlos, Ten Kate observed three dances in the evenings. The first, on the evening of his arrival, consisted of men and women engaged in a social dance associated with a girl's puberty ceremony, sometimes called a girl's coming out dance, a sunrise dance, or, in Apache, *naihes*. This is the ceremony at which a young woman is formally acknowledged as an adult and possessing the necessary skills to get married. Although Ten Kate saw at this dance the woman for whom the ceremony was being given and noted her "fine leather costume" (a beaded buckskin poncho and skirt), he apparently did not see the daylight portions of the ceremony. He recounts: "To the monotonous drum beat and savage shouts of an equally monotonous, dull chant, a number of Indians, men and women, are dancing around a huge flickering fire, whose glimmering illuminates the bronze-colored dancers in the most fantastic manner. The men and women dancers are packed tightly together in small rows, mostly in groups of four with the upper arm against each other, while the forearms are stuck forward with the fists against each other and the elbow resting on the chest. They stand facing away from each other, with the understanding that in every row there two walk forward and two backward. The rows move up and down at a brisk, skipping pace. At intervals this movement momentarily comes to a halt. Then the men walk toward the circle of musicians, and the women also separate themselves for a moment only to ask their partners a moment later

for another round with a tap on the shoulder. The young squaw, as the principal personage of the festival, dances through the rows alone decked out in a fine leather costume, shuffling slowly, but buoyantly moving her feet forward" (Ten Kate 2004: 194).

On two other nights Ten Kate attended what he called (for unknown reasons) a "peace dance," which was a *gaan* or Mountain Spirit dance, also associated with a *naihes* ceremony: "Around a huge fire several hundred Indians, crouching or standing, formed a gigantic circle, illuminated by the ruddy glimmer of the flickering flames. In rapid gait two men and a boy of eight or ten years trotted behind one another around the fire. These three were the principal personages of the evening."

"The first Indian, a fellow of splendid stature, had drawn a chamois leather mask tightly over his entire face, and on his head he wore a large wooden contrivance, colored red and white, the principal contours of which recalled a trident. His muscular, toiling torso was painted completely white. From his shoulders hung long colored strips decorated with feathers. His hips and thighs were wrapped in a short animal skin skirt with long dangling fringes. Finally, his feet were covered with the usual high boots. In each hand he held a short crooked wooden sword. The second 'dancer' was attired in nearly the same way, but the upper part of his trunk was colored black, the lower part white, while instead of a leather skirt he wore one of transparent white cotton. The boy was completely unclad, except for his breechcloth, and painted from head to foot with white dye. He wore a mask, too, but wore no wooden contraptions on his head like the other two. In each hand he held a short slender stick."

"The trotting about in buoyant double time was at once transformed into leaping, stomping, and crossing of swords. Now their movements resembled those of an enraged bull, who glances haughtily about the arena and suddenly lunges upon his enemy, and then again those of a prancing horse who recalcitrantly shakes its mane and, sniffing and snorting, tramples the ground with its stomping hooves. From time to time they utter an abrupt, shrill cry. The largest of the three was always in the forefront, the boy in the rear. After they had trotted around for awhile, three other men joined in, two of whom were dressed more or less like the former, while one of them, entirely in white and likewise masked, played the role of clown. Running after the others, he mimicked their movements in the most ludicrous fashion. Sometimes he got in the way and danced out in front of them with provocative gestures. Sometimes all of them quickly ran away behind the row of spectators to catch their breath for a moment and then start anew in the same fashion. The music, which accompanied all this, was produced by a number of men hunkered down who were striking with long sticks on a hard cowhide lying on the ground and on small drums."

"The longer the spectacle lasted, the more excited the dancers and spectators became. The latter eventually gathered in a tightly closed circle. Men, women, and children moved about monotonously chanting, slowly bounding around the fire with the painted figures–always in motion, more and more flushed–forming a spectacle as savage as it was bizarre. The climax of exuberant savagery was reached when the first 'dancer' with a gigantic leap lifted himself above the flames and, uttering a fiendish cry, came down on the other side of the fire. It is a pleasure to view such a spectacle, but a savage, unfamiliar pleasure. Involuntarily one is carried along with the wild excitement. All that is savage and slumbers within oneself comes alive. Ones muscles tense up. One's feet itch to move about in the whirling rows of fantastically illumined figures" (Ten Kate 2004: 203-204).

Ten Kate's images of what the dancers wore are good and describe what is now referred to as a *gaan* mask (the wooden "crown" with attached buckskin hood), strips of cloth (usually red) tied around the dancers' biceps with eagle feathers attached, a buckskin kilt, moccasins with buckskin uppers and rawhide soles, and carrying wooden wands. Interestingly, the trident-shaped "crown" that he describes is, perhaps, the archetypal shape for *gaan* masks and could be found among all three groups that have Mountain Spirits, namely, the Chiricahua, Mescalero, and Western Apache. The popularity of this shape has waned among Western Apache groups, although it is still the standard among the Chiricahua and Mescalero (cf. McCoy 1985; Opler 1983b: 415). There are numerous accounts of *naihes* ceremonies, some scholarly, some popular, which the reader can consult for fuller descriptions of this ceremony and photographs of the dances, masks, paraphernalia, and girl's dress and accouterments (Annerino 1998; Basso 1966; 1970: 53-72; Ferg 1987: 109–125; Golston 1996; Opler 1983a: 374-376; Quintero 1980).

About the Coyotero Ten Kate remarked that they "had a very simple way of burying their dead. The body is brought to a place where a number of loose blocks of rocks are available–in a cleft, for example. A number of these blocks are removed until there is room enough to lay the body down. Then they are put back in place again, and at the same time some heavy branches are stuck between the chinks to prevent the coyotes from violating the grave. According to what I learned, the closest relatives mourn the deceased for thirty days, venting their grief in howls of anguish" (Ten Kate 2004: 212).

Dress: Protective and Secular

While hunting, or raiding, or on the warpath, the attire of Western Apache men was basic and functional. They wore only a breechcloth and hightop moccasins, to protect the feet and legs from thorns and brush. A cartridge belt was fastened around the hips, from which pouches, awl or knife cases, and small sacks of food were suspended. Buckskin caps were prevalent in earlier days, but Ten Kate said they were still occasionally worn in his time, and their use on special occasions actually has lasted to the present.

In camp nearly all men wore a cloth headband. Their dress showed an eclectic mix of Apache and European clothing items and styles, including blankets of Indian, Mexican, or American manufacture and sometimes shirts, pants, shoes, and cowboy hats. Women wore calico cloth "camp dresses" patterned after abundantly pleated Mexican and American dresses. It was obvious to Ten Kate that items of Western manufacture were replacing traditional costume, but he still saw fancy buckskin shirts worn by men, and both men and women continued to wear buckskin moccasins (*khé*) with rawhide soles and toe tabs, beaded buckskin pouches, and awl and knife cases. Although little jewelry was in evidence, he managed to collect a number of interesting necklaces.

"Leather war hats or caps *(sjach, tsjach)* decorated with eagle or wild turkey feathers, whose shape vaguely recalls Roman helmets, are still worn now and then," Ten Kate (2004: 197) observed. His generalization that these were "war" caps is too broad. In the 1930s the Western Apache described six different traditional types of caps, two primarily for secular use and the other four having subtly overlapping functions related to curing, warfare, and protection (Ferg 1987: 132). Both caps collected by Ten Kate are of a type covered with split owl flight feathers, and the presence of two painted triangular or trapezoidal tabs in the back is common. Statements about who wore owl caps and why vary, suggesting that they were only worn by San Carlos men or only by old men, but historic photographs show young men wearing them as well, including scouts in

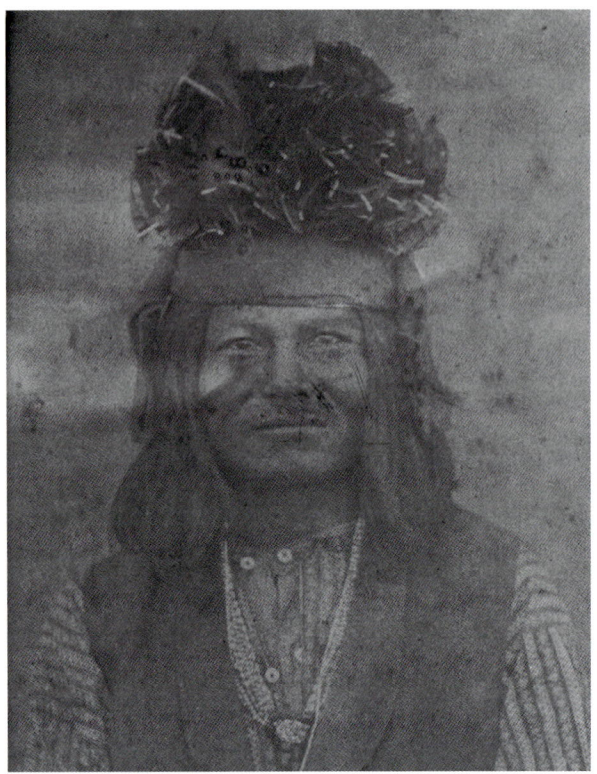

Fig. 146 Apache man with feather cap; Arizona Territory, June/July 1883. Photograph by Constant Duhem (Ten Kate coll.; WMR 900618).

the U.S. Army. The common thread among the descriptions seems to be that any man could wear an owl-feather cap and that it served to protect the wearer from harm in general and perhaps owls and ghosts in particular.

Fig. 147 Coyotero (Western) Apache owl-feather cap; *sjach, tsjàch* (TK); mountain lion skin, feathers, brass tacks, paint; h. 15 cm; ca. 1880 (RMV 361-17).

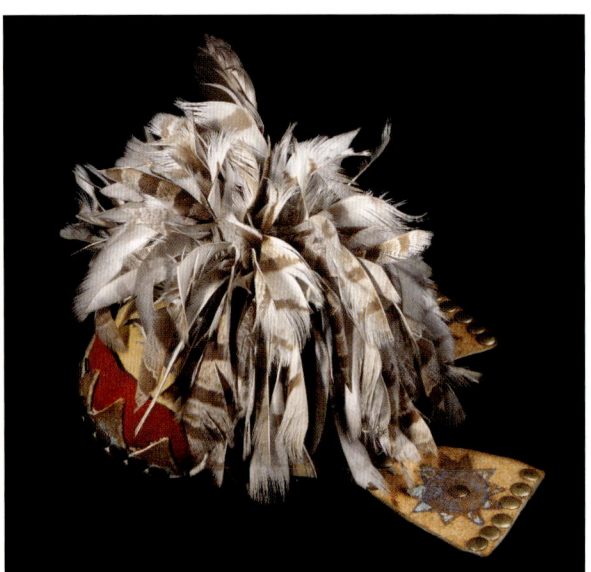

Ten Kate collected a typically elaborate, beautiful example of this type of cap with a full crown of split Great Horned Owl flight feathers atop a cap made of mountain lion skin (Fig. 147). Whether the use of mountain lion skin indicates that this was indeed a cap intended to be worn primarily on raids is uncertain; other men's items such as quivers and a type of pouch were made of mountain lion skin. Certainly there are war/mountain lion associations among Pueblo groups. In the 1800s the Navajo made a host of similarly elaborate caps using mountain lion and with equally mixed discussions of their functions (Kluckhohn et al. 1971: 272–278). Silhouetted against a strip of red flannel in the front is a row of upright buckskin triangles and brass buttons or tacks. Two trapezoidal tabs in the back are decorated with "sunburst" motifs painted in a turquoise blue paint and more brass buttons. This specimen was collected in June/July 1883 at either San Carlos or Camp Apache, Arizona.

At San Carlos Ten Kate acquired another cap (Fig. 148), of which he noted: "The leather war cap, which I sent to the Ethnographic Museum in Leiden, is decorated with split feathers of *Otus americanus, Bubo virginianus* [Great Horned Owl], a feather of *Aquila chrysaëtos*, juv. [juvenile Golden Eagle], and a specimen of *Sylvicola citreola*" (Ten Kate 2004: 216n17). *Otus americanus* is not a species name that could be found, but *Asio otus*, Long-eared Owl, is most likely what Ten Kate observed. Likewise, *Sylvicola citreola* could not be positively identified, but may be some species of woodpecker; flicker feathers are known to have been used as protective amulets on children's carrying jackets (Ferg 1987: 92). Ten Kate's cap is a simple buckskin example with a serrated edge, two

Fig. 148 Western Apache owl-feather cap; *sjach, tsjàch* (TK); buckskin, feathers, paint; h. 28 cm, d. 28 cm; ca. 1880 (RMV 361-18).

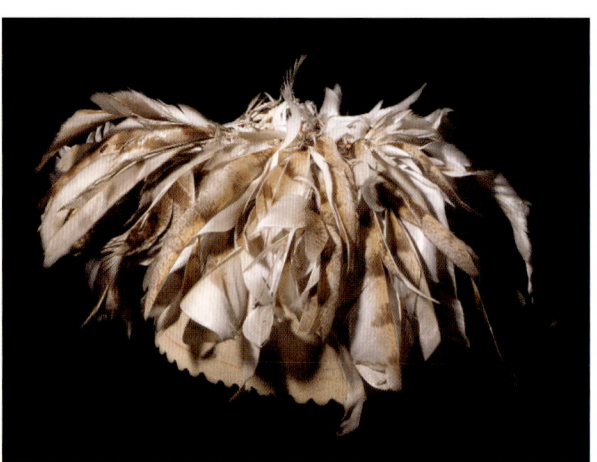

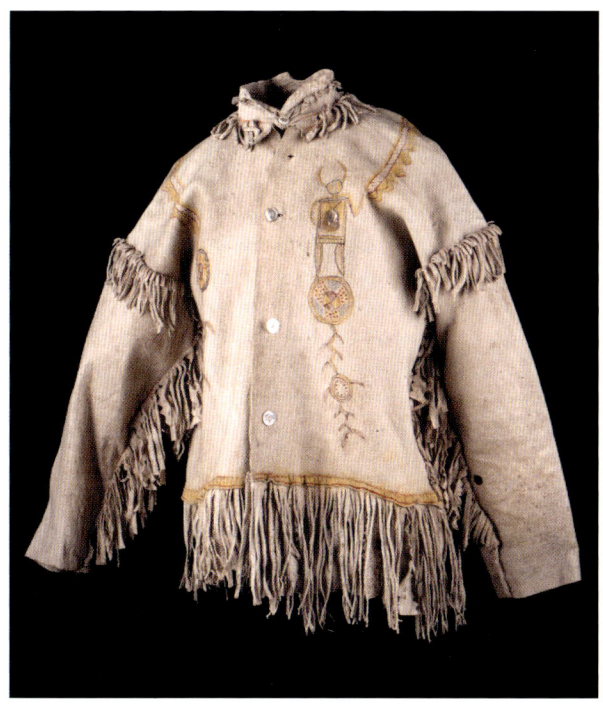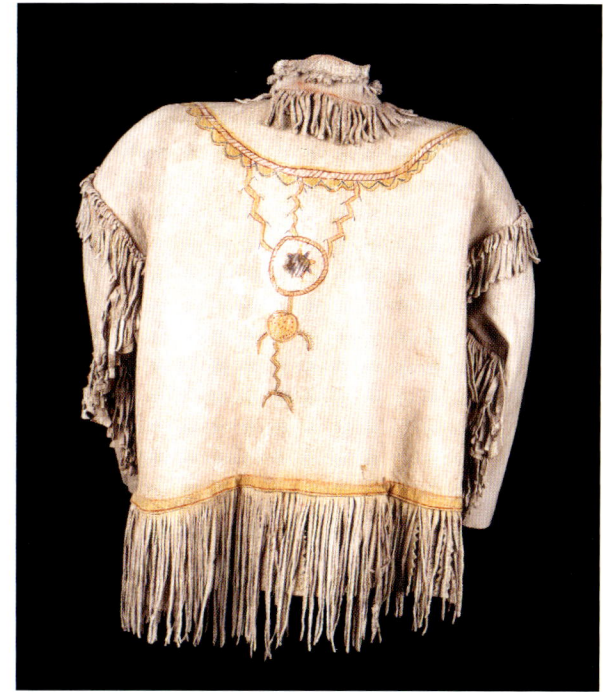

Figs. 149, 150   Western Apache man's shirt (front and back); buckskin, sinew, abalone shell, commercial buttons, paints; l. 73 cm, w. (at shoulders) 145 cm; ca. 1880 (RMV 361-4).

lines painted above the edge, and a bundle of split owl feathers at the crown.

Ten Kate (2004: 197) wrote: "I noted the handsome chamois leather shirts with painted figures and long fringes just a few times, and I bought one from a young warrior for ten dollars." The transaction took place in June/July 1883 at San Carlos, Arizona. This tailored buckskin shirt (Figs. 149, 150) is open at the front and closed with four large, flat, commercial mother-of-pearl buttons, with a fifth at the collar. The collar, sleeves, and fringes were added; all sewing is with sinew. The fringes on the outer sleeve edges and around the bottom include serrated tabs. The sleeve and body seams are highlighted with red paint, and just above the bottom fringe is a band of yellow paint. The most striking feature of this shirt is the elaborate painted design: It is the shape of a horseshoe encircling the neck with the arms coming over the top of the shoulders onto the front. Pendant from the arc on the back and from the end of each arm on the front panels are elaborate designs painted in black, blue, red, and yellow, with two abalone *(Haliotis sp.)* pendants sewn onto the designs.

If this shirt is not unique at the present time, it is certainly of an extremely rare variety: a tailored buckskin shirt with sleeves, of the type known to have been worn by Western Apache army scouts, but with elaborately painted imagery, of the type typically seen on buckskin caps and the painted hides and sleeveless ponchos used in curing ceremonies. Ganteaume (1993) has discussed Western Apache army scouts wearing tailored buckskin shirts that seem clearly modeled on U.S. Army officers' full-dress coats. For the army scouts, it seems to have been a simultaneous assertion of their identity as Apaches, as well as a visible statement of their alliance with the powerful forces of the U.S. military and the high status derived from that association. And while these shirts may be elaborately ornamented with fringe, beadwork, and silver buttons, they do not bear painted designs like the ones on the shirt acquired by Ten Kate.

Most Western Apache ceremonial objects were decorated with stylized symbols. Many supernatural beings, according to Apache beliefs, have powers that can be called upon to protect the petitioner or, with the assistance of a medicine man, to cure a patient of disease or injury. Each medicine man had his personal group of holy beings or powers on which to call. Painted medicine hides and very similar looking medicine "shirts" (which, at least physically, are essentially ponchos made by adding a head-slit to the center of a medicine hide) were employed to draw the attention and assistance of holy beings and *gaan* (e.g., see Bourke 1892: pls. VI, VII, VIII; Ferg 1987: color ill. 1, lower right; Opler 1983a: fig. 7). Specific and correct

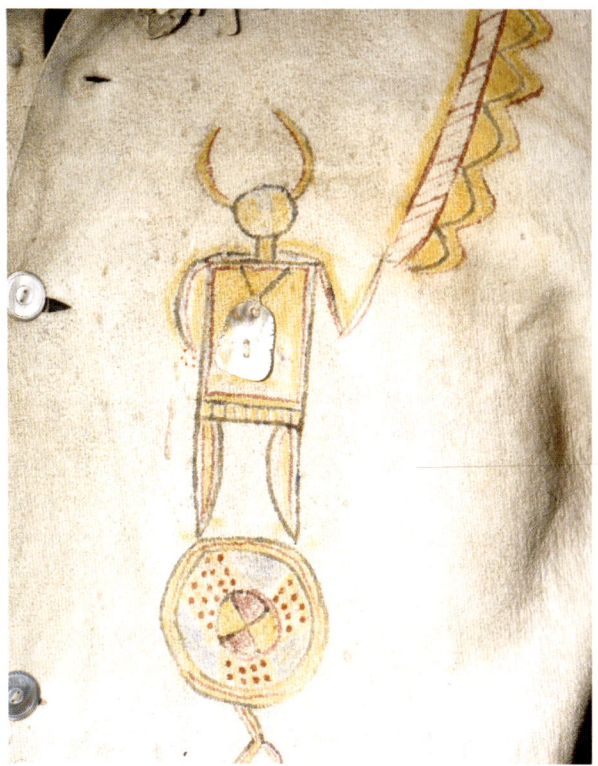

Fig. 151 Detail of imagery on Western Apache man's shirt (see Figs. 149, 150).

identification and interpretation of the images on these items (as Ganteaume 1993 has endeavored to do) is made difficult by the idiosyncratic ways in which Apache medicine men acquired their knowledge and painted their paraphernalia with designs that were often understood only by them.

Without the input of the medicine man who either painted or supervised the painting of the images on Ten Kate's shirt, interpreting the designs can be done in only the most general (and hypothetical) terms. The horseshoe/arc may be a rainbow. The zigzag lines pendant from it and the several circular elements may be lightning. The dot patterns may be rain. The anthropomorph with horns, on the left breast, is doubtless a Holy Being or *gaan* (Fig. 151). An abalone shell pendant with notched edges is sewn to this figure's chest, and the two painted lines above it make it appear as if the pendant was on a necklace around the figure's neck. The message seems clear that the abalone pendant worn by this Holy Being is analogous to the pendant on the back of the shirt, and both are giving protection to the wearer of the shirt. The palette of four colors used—black, blue, red, and yellow—may have been meant to invoke directional referents or to simply remind the viewer of the holy nature of the images.

We are, perhaps, on slightly firmer ground in proposing that the presence of such ritual imagery on what for all other purposes would have been identified as a shirt for an Apache army scout or an influential person suggests that the shirt is *not* a ritual object per se and not for use by a medicine man. The possible rain, rainbow, and lightning images hint at a connection to lightning power, which is among the strongest a medicine man can possess. That, combined with the general implication of protection implied by abalone pendants, leads us to hazard a guess that this shirt was indeed a functional item, but augmented with ceremonial designs intended to invoke supernatural protection. The most logical identification is therefore a shirt to be worn by a man going into a potentially (or known) dangerous situation, who will need protection. Ten Kate said the man was a warrior. Perhaps it was a man going on a raid or onto the warpath to kill an enemy. Such speculation is reasonable, but can probably never be absolutely confirmed by anyone now living.

Finally, the fact that it was sold to Ten Kate suggests that the shirt was no longer needed, that the owner felt it was worth selling, or that the shirt was no longer efficacious. Ten Kate's remark that the man was young probably excludes the last explanation: A power generally abandoned a person only when it was mistreated or when the person was old and too weak to use it effectively (Basso 1970: 40). No matter which, the owner almost certainly "decommissioned" the shirt with a prayer to his power, as occurred between 1901 and 1903 when Charles L. Owen collected two medicine shirts and Albert B. Reagan collected three medicine caps, a medicine shirt, and a shield (Owen 1903: 56, 174; Reagan 1930: 303–306).

Ten Kate purchased another shirt in Santa Fe in July 1883 from a merchant who had obtained it from Mescaleros attending the Tertio-Millennial Exposition (Fig. 152). This pullover buckskin shirt is painted dark blue all over, with a red stripe down the center front and back. The sleeves, triangular flaps at the neck, and all fringes were added; all sewing is with sinew. Fringes are painted yellow. There are narrow bands of white and dark blue beadwork at the cuffs, where the sleeves are attached to the body, and down the outside of the sleeve from shoulder to elbow. There are two open circles of blue and white beadwork on the top of each shoulder, with the interiors painted yellow on the near circles and red on the outer. On the front flap is a four-pointed star inside a crescent in white beads; the same motif is repeated on the back flap in light blue beads.

Although this shirt may strike modern viewers as exceptionally stunning and beautiful (which it is), it is apparently fairly typical of Mescalero shirts of the 1880s. Certainly not every man would have owned such a shirt, and a man wearing one would have been recognized as having some importance, and perhaps wealth. But thanks to photographs taken at the Tertio-Millennial Exposition, it is clear that quite a few of the Mescalero men there were wearing this same type of shirt (Broder 1990: figs. 31, 94, 95; Mails 1974: 337–338). Conceivably, the shirt Ten Kate obtained might actually be worn in one of these photographs, but thus far it has not been identified in any of the pictures examined. Although such shirts were once a relatively commonplace sight, Ten Kate's example has gained some cultural and artistic significance because today, over 120 years later, they have become very old and rare.

The star and crescent designs on the flaps of this shirt are of additional interest. Between 1903 and 1908 a religious movement took place among the Western Apache known as *daagodighá*, which has been variously translated as 'they will be raised up' or 'rising upward' or 'spiritual movement starts' (Ferg 1998a: 72). While the Western Apache, and probably all Apache groups, have used crosses (stars) and crescents (moons) singly and together as designs on many items, both sacred and secular, the medicine man who started this religion, Daslahdn, prescribed that followers should mark their belongings with a combined cross-and-crescent symbol, with the two elements sometimes fused into a single anchor-shaped design (Ferg 1998a). The movement came to an end after the death of Daslahdn and four other medicine men who were involved. Although *daagodighá* was short-lived, the extensive use of the cross-and-crescent motif on men's caps, pollen pouches, baskets, and saddlebags had a long-lasting impact on the decoration of Western Apache objects.

Daslahdn never specifically stated what the cross-and-crescent motif signified. In looking for what this design may have meant for the Western Apache, its use was examined among neighboring Apache groups earlier in time (Ferg 1998b). Its presence on this Mescalero shirt, which predates *daagodighá*, is of interest because it suggests connections with other, earlier religious beliefs. For many Native American groups cross and crescent motifs relate in various ways to the Morning Star (Venus) and the moon, and sometimes to the manner in which the two are positioned relative to one another and the roles these heavenly bodies play in traditional stories. In addition to this shirt, beaded cross-and-crescent motifs can be seen on

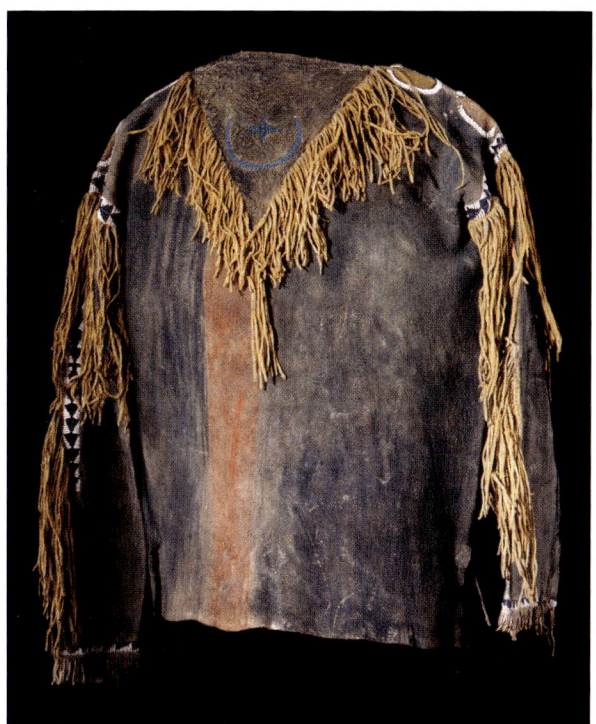

Fig. 152   Mescalero Apache man's shirt; buckskin, sinew, glass beads, paints; l. 57 cm, w. (at shoulders) 51 cm; ca. 1880 (RMV 361-5).

a Mescalero man's cap in a photograph believed to date around 1885 (Ferg 1998b: fig. 4) and a few other objects of uncertain age. At least three possible sources for the Mescalero use of cross-and-crescent motifs suggest themselves, but what the truth may be is difficult to assess given the nature and remoteness of the data. The Mescalero may have created this motif themselves, as part of their iconography for representing the cosmos (Farrer 1991: 60–100; Farrer and Second 1981). A second possibility is that the design is related to the Mescalero's participation in peyote ceremonies starting around 1870 or their familiarity with its use by groups in Mexico perhaps as early as 1770 (Opler 1936: 143n4; 1938: 271, 273; Stewart 1948: 34–35). Designs incorporating crosses and crescents are integral to the peyote symbolism of many groups (e.g., Ferg 1998b: fig. 6). A third possibility for the origin of the Mescalero use of cross-and-crescent motifs would be designs borrowed from Plains Ghost dance paraphernalia, probably clothing. But Ten Kate's shirt predates the 1890 Ghost dance movement, and it is unclear whether such motifs were used in the 1870 cult. What future understanding of these matters may be gained is unknown, but the importance of Ten Kate's shirt will remain, as one of the few pieces of solid, well-documented evidence of the use of cross-and-crescent motifs among the Mescalero in 1883.

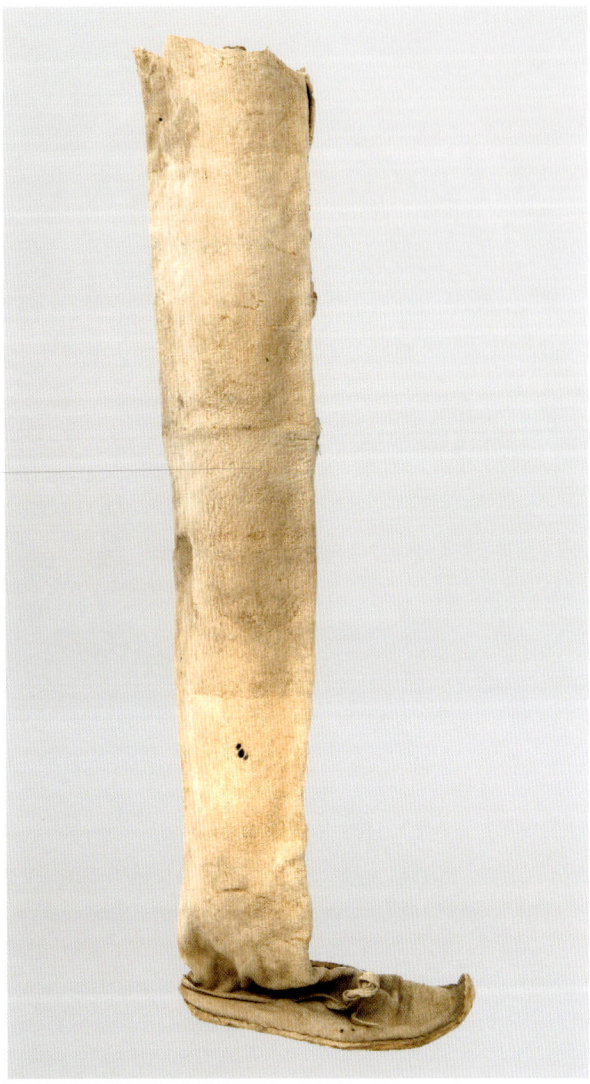

Fig. 153 (Western?) Apache moccasin; *k(h)é* (TK); buckskin, rawhide, sinew; h. 84 cm, l. (of sole) 28 cm, w. (of sole) 18 cm; ca. 1880 (RMV 361-11).

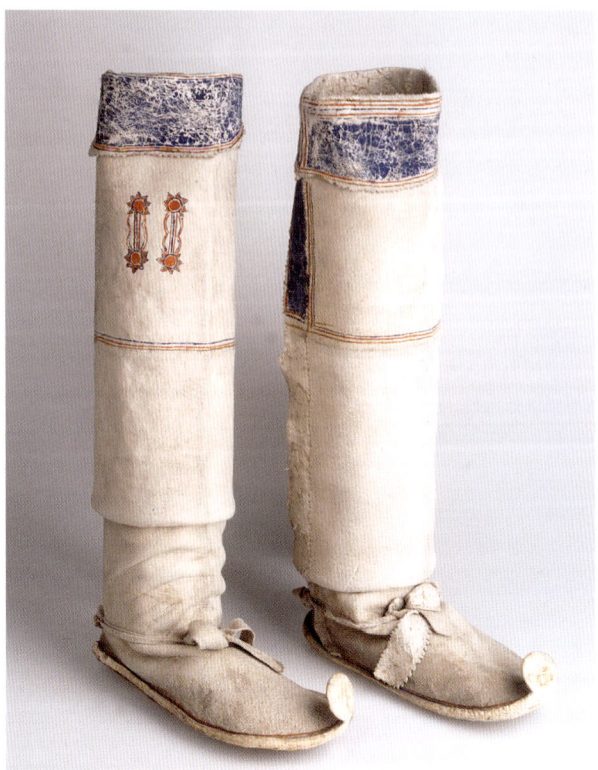

Fig. 154 (Western?) Apache woman's moccasins; *k(h)é* (TK); buckskin, rawhide, sinew, paints; h. (folded down) 52 cm, h. (unfolded) 124 cm, l. (of sole) 28 cm, w. (of sole) 11 cm; ca. 1880 (RMV 361-10).

The moccasin collected by Ten Kate (Fig. 153) is the most basic version of the classic thigh-high, hard-soled moccasin (or "boot") worn by Chiricahua and Western Apache men and women (cf. Hatt 1916: 198–200). The upper is buckskin stitched with sinew; there is a buckskin tie at the ankle. Ten Kate noted this was a woman's moccasin. Men and women used to pull the tall cuff up above the knee when going through rough brush, but around camp it was folded on itself several times, with a fold sometimes used as a pocket to carry small objects. The sole is rawhide, probably cowhide, with the hair typically left on, and it wears off as the moccasins are worn. The sole comes up in front and forms a circular "toe tab." These tabs are called "noses" by the Western Apache and were regarded in the 1930s as a purely decorative accesso-

ry that had nothing to do with protecting the toes from rocks and cactus as is endlessly repeated in popular descriptions of these "toe protectors" or "toe guards" (Ferg 1987: 94). Interestingly, Farrer (1991: 244n12) notes that the modern Mescalero and Chiricahua also say these are for toe protection. She is correct in noting this feature as distinctive of Chiricahua moccasins and absent on the Mescalero's, but is incorrect in stating that only the Chiricahua wear this type: The Western Apache acknowledged seeing this feature on Chiricahua moccasins during joint raids into Mexico in the nineteenth century and adopting it. The Western Apache did not invent toe tabs, but they have become a traditional feature of Western Apache moccasins since sometime back in the 1800s. Ten Kate acquired this item at San Carlos, Arizona, in June/July 1883.

Ten Kate also identified another pair as woman's moccasins (Fig. 154), and they are essentially of the same construction, with the addition of some painted designs. The carefully finished top of the cuff has a wide band of blue paint and thin lines of red, blue, and black; on the outer side are a pair of double red circular designs joined by straight and zigzag lines. Similar painted motifs can be found on both ceremonial and secular Western Apache

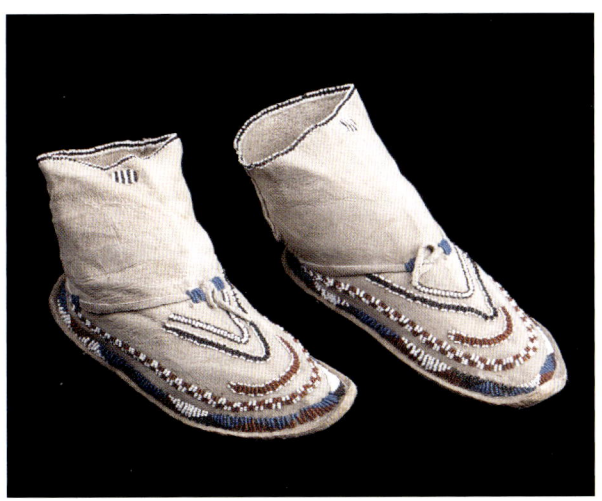

Fig. 155 (Western?) Apache moccasins; *k(h)é* (TK); buckskin, rawhide, sinew, glass beads; h. 13 cm, l. (of sole) 26.5 cm, w. (of sole) 9.5 cm; ca. 1880 (RMV 361-7).

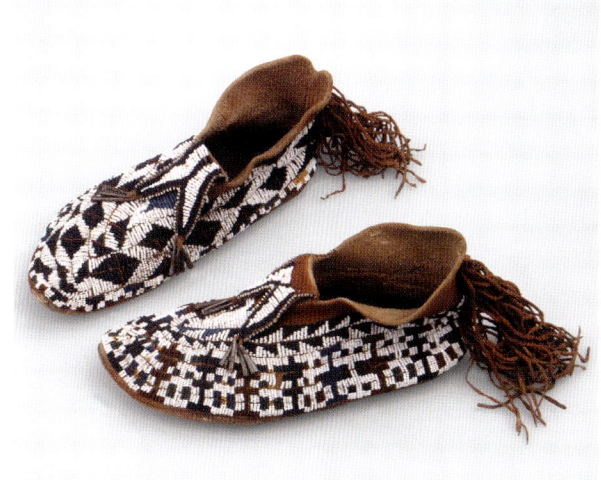

Fig. 156 Mescalero Apache moccasins; *k(h)é* (TK); buckskin, rawhide, glass beads, metal tinklers, paint; l. (of sole) 30 cm, w. (of sole) 10 cm, h. 12 cm; ca. 1880 (RMV 361-6).

objects, including painted hides for curing, amulets, rock art, fiddles, and playing cards (Wayland et al. 2006: fig. 8). It is not known whether this design is decorative or protective or whether that depends on the context. There is also a blue line painted around the seam where the upper meets the sole, and the inside of the "nose" is painted blue (cf. Hatt 1916: 198–200). This pair was obtained at San Carlos, Arizona, in June/July 1883.

In pre-reservation times Western Apache men reportedly wore three lengths of moccasins: knee-high, mid-calf, and ankle-high (Ferg 1987: 94). A pair of hard-soled, ankle-high moccasins (Fig. 155), collected at either San Carlos or Camp Apache, Arizona, in June/July 1883, is probably Western Apache, but a Chiricahua origin cannot be ruled out. They are beautifully decorated with white, red, blue, and black beadwork (cf. Hatt 1916: 192–194).

The Mescalero low-top moccasins (Fig. 156) have a rawhide sole and buckskin uppers which, except for the narrow cuff at top, are covered with an elaborate design of white and blue lazy-stitch beadwork. They have forked "tongues" on top with small metal tinklers at the tips. The cuff and long fringes at the heel are painted a brick red (cf. Hatt 1916: 181, 184). The pair was purchased in Santa Fe in July 1883 from a merchant who obtained it from Mescaleros attending the Tertio-Millennial Exposition.

A pair of beaded miniature high-top moccasins with toe tabs (Fig. 157) are so small that they were presumably made to go on a child's doll. The soles are also buckskin; the uppers and cuffs are decorated in white, black, and green beadwork. This set was acquired in June/July 1883 at either San Carlos or Camp Apache, Arizona.

Decorated buckskin pouches were used to carry, or sometimes store, any imaginable small personal items, including paint, pollen, playing cards, mirrors, amulets, and tobacco. Pouches collected from both the San Carlos and Fort Apache areas in the early 1900s appear to exhibit a dichotomy between rectangular pouches with metal tinklers and round pouches with very full buckskin fringes (Ferg 1987: 97). The significance, if any,

Fig. 157 (Western?) Apache moccasins for a doll; buckskin, sinew, glass beads; l. (of sole) 5 cm, h. 9 cm, w. 2.5 cm; ca. 1880 (RMV 361-64).

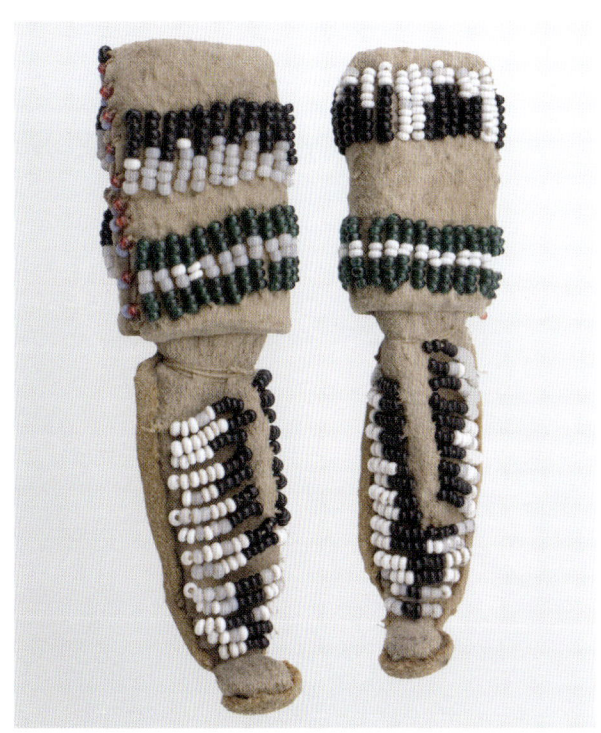

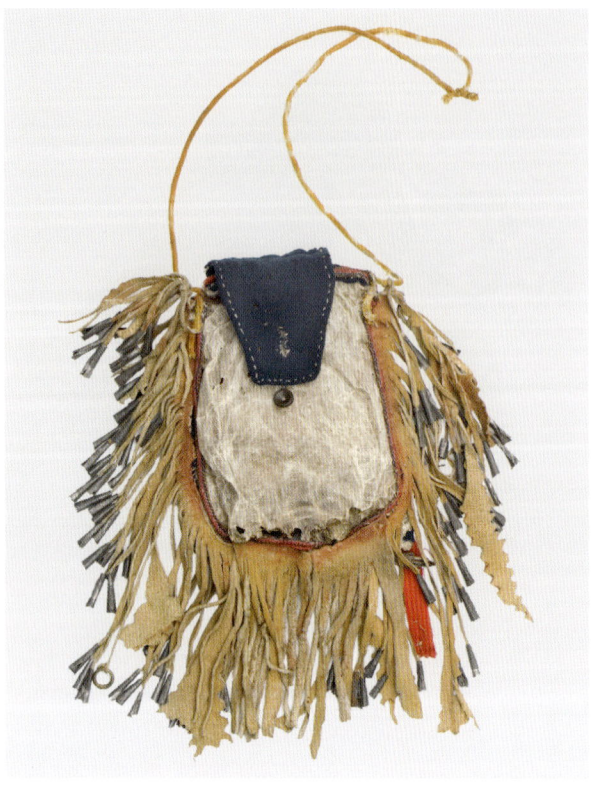

Fig. 158 (Western?) Apache pouch; tanned prairie dog skin, red and blue flannel, paints; l. (incl. fringe) 38 cm, w. (incl. fringe) 45 cm; ca. 1880 (RMV 361-1).

is unknown and does not appear to hold for Ten Kate's sample of three pouches, one of which has both a full

Fig. 159 Western Apache pouch; buckskin, pigments; l. (incl. fringe) 23.5 cm, w. 20 cm (with fringe 30 cm); ca. 1880 (RMV 361-2).

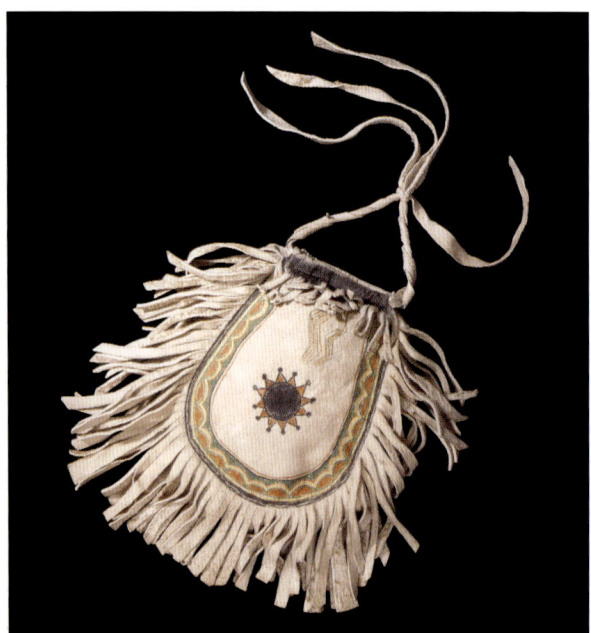

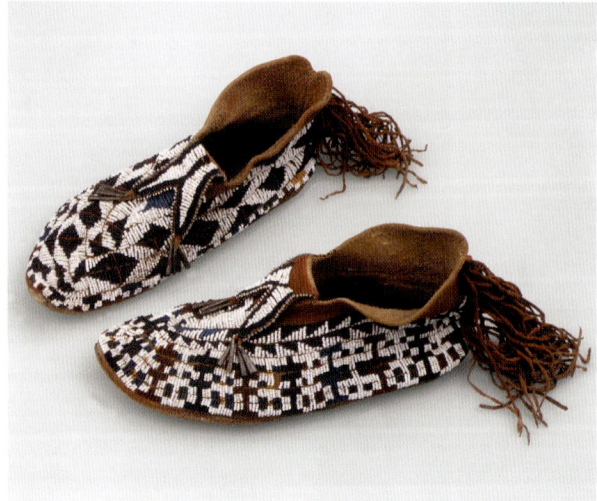

Fig. 160 Coyotero (Western) Apache pouch; buckskin, paints; l. (incl. fringe) 26 cm, w. (incl. fringe) 35 cm; ca. 1880 (RMV 361-3).

fringe and tinklers. It may be that the decoration of pouches (and awl cases?) follows only very general patterns and is far more open to individual expression and improvisation than has been recognized.

Collected at either San Carlos or Camp Apache, Arizona, in June/July 1883, one of the pouches was catalogued as a tobacco pouch of prairie dog skin (Fig. 158). It has a tangle of fringes around the edge, including some serrated tabs, some painted yellow or red; on the left side some of the fringes have individual metal tinklers attached, while on the right side there are fringes with two tinklers. The carrying strap is a piece of commercial cordage painted yellow. The flap is closed with a commercial button. The back of the pouch appears to have been covered with red flannel and the front with blue; that on the flap is intact, but most of the cloth on both sides has been eaten away, and the revealed hide beneath is now thin and parchment-like. This, and the presence on the back of the pouch of a small hide's tail and back feet, suggest that it was originally tanned with the hair on and that perhaps dermestid beetles ate the fur and clothes moths the flannel covers. In the 1930s the Western Apache talked about storing tobacco, after it was harvested, in pouches made from the whole skin of a young deer, a fox, or of two Abert's squirrel (*Sciurus aberti*) hides sewn together (Ferg 1987: 132). One can easily imagine that Ten Kate's pouch was being used as a man's personal tobacco pouch.

A second pouch of white buckskin (Fig. 159) has thick fringes, a buckskin drawstring closure, and painted designs in green, reddish brown, black, and yellow. The designs on front and back include a border around the edge (scallops on front, triangles on back) and a central circular motif edged with triangles. The front also has green zigzag lines descending from the mouth. The pouch was collected at San Carlos, Arizona, in June/July 1883.

The third specimen (Fig. 160), collected at San Carlos at the same time, is a beautiful pouch with heavy fringe, four wide tabs, a buckskin drawstring closure, and painted on the front in red and blue; the back is plain. The designs include very traditional Apache motifs like the alternating triangles around the edge and the circle motifs, but also some delicate floral motifs that are less commonly used.

Many men and women carried an awl of bone, antler, wood, or iron in buckskin cases ornamented with fringes, beadwork, painting, and sometimes metal tinklers. Men used awls for mending horsegear, and, while away from camp, moccasins and clothing. Women used awls in weaving baskets and in sewing and decorating buckskin clothing (Ten Kate 2004: 197).

Ten Kate collected a typical awl case, decorated with red, white, blue, and pink glass beads and numerous metal tinklers, at either San Carlos or Camp Apache, Arizona, in June/July 1883 (Fig. 161 left). Awl cases often simply have tapered or squared-off bottoms, with attached fringe. The circular form of the decorative flap at the bottom of this case is not common; whether it has any regional or temporal significance is unknown at this time. This, and its multiple rows of tinklers, are reminiscent of an awl case that may have belonged to the Chiricahua leader Juh (Opler 1983b: fig. 11).

A second specimen (Fig. 161 right) was either likewise collected in at San Carlos or Camp Apache at the same time or may have been among the material acquired from the Santa Fe trader in July 1883, who originally obtained it from Mescalero or Jicarilla attendants at the Tertio-Millennial Exposition. Rather plain at first glance, this awl case is actually rather elaborate in both construction and decoration. The simple sheath with a buckskin suspension loop was sewn with thread, but the bottom was then tightly braided. The bottom has eight flat fringes with a German silver band clipped onto the end of each. Finally, now nearly invisible, the body of the case was decorated front and back with parallel lines and chevrons tooled into the leather. What Apache group made this awl case is unknown at this time. A San Carlos example with no fringe or engraving is known, as is what is probably a Mescalero example, with no fringe, but with a fitted cap of the same harness leather.

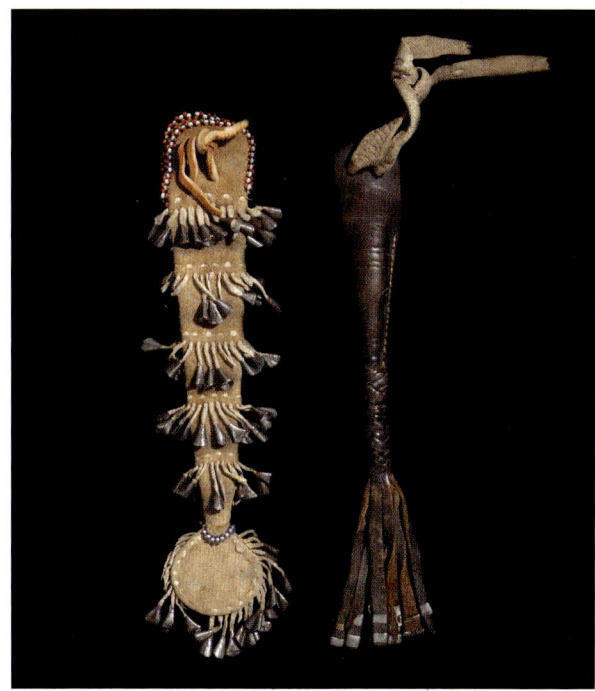

Fig. 161 Apache awl cases; RMV 361-32 (Chiricahua or Western Apache): buckskin, glass beads, metal tinklers; l. 28 cm, w. 5 cm; RMV 361-33: harness leather, buckskin, thread, German silver; l. (incl. fringe) 25.5 cm, w. 3.5 cm; both ca. 1880.

Ten Kate remarked that the Apache applied little or no body or face paint, although face painting is known to have been done by both men and women for various social occasions and by men returning from raids (Ferg 1987: fig. 3.6). Tattooing was rare, and he saw only a few individuals with small bluish figures on their faces. Jewelry was the primary form of personal adornment, including hair ornaments, earrings, necklaces, bracelets, and finger rings.

These items incorporate various beads and pendants, some of which the Western Apache could obtain themselves and others that had to be obtained by trade, raid, or purchase. Ten Kate wrote: "The Apaches have few ornaments, and these consist primarily of necklaces and bracelets of beads, red beans, and the bark of a certain plant called *yerba del manso* (*Anemopsis californica*) by the Mexicans. This bark, which has the color of cork, is characterized by a distinct, aromatic fragrance and astringent taste and is also chewed by the Indians because they maintain it is good for their gums" (Ten Kate 2004: 197).

Glass beads, of course, came from the outside world. In the 1800s large size "pony" and "trade" beads seem to predominate and were strung on necklaces and earrings, as we see among Ten Kate's specimens. As traders started carrying more small seed beads, these were strung in quantity as simple loops, flat woven beadwork items, and

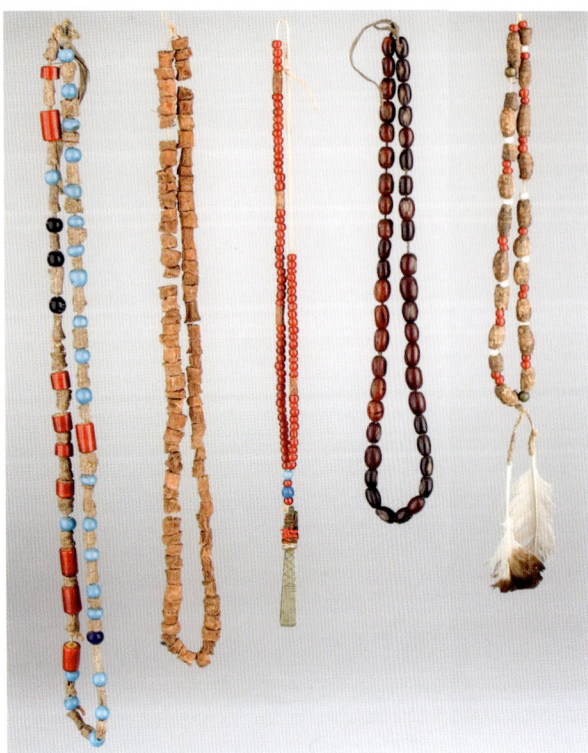

Fig. 162 Apache necklaces; RMV 361-22 (Tonto): cloth, glass and *yerba del manso* beads; l. (doubled over) 43 cm; RMV 361-20 (Tonto): cotton string, *yerba del manso* beads; l. (doubled over) 38 cm; RMV 361-24 (Western Apache?): cordage, glass and *yerba del manso* beads, brass; l. (necklace doubled over) 18 cm., l. (of tweezers) 7 cm; RMV 361-21 (Chiricahua): buckskin, "red bean" beads; l. (doubled over) 28 cm; RMV 361-23 (Coyotero [Western] Apache): *laga banishe* (TK); cotton thread, feathers, and glass, copper and *yerba del manso* beads; l. (doubled over) 17 cm; all ca. 1880.

sewn onto buckskin clothing and accessories. Early beads included red beads with a white center, known variously as *cornaline d'Aleppo*, Hudson Bay, or "white-heart" beads.

Ten Kate's "red beans" are beads made from red seeds, either coral beans *(Erythrina flabelliformis)* or mescal beans *(Sophora secundiflora)*. Both have shiny seeds, so hard that they are generally perforated for stringing by burning a hole through the seed coat with a hot wire or metal awl, rather than by trying to drill a hole. Coral beans grow in southeastern Arizona, southwestern New Mexico, and on south into Old Mexico. Mescal beans are found in extreme southeastern New Mexico, much of southern Texas, and on south into Old Mexico (Merrill 1977: fig. 3). As such, in the 1800s the Chiricahua and Western Apache generally used coral beans and the Mescalero used mescal beans.

Yerba del manso, also known as *Yerba mansa*, could also have been collected by the Western Apache themselves. It grows in *cienegas* and swampy places. Coral-colored stolons, or runners, grow outward and were cut into segments for use as beads that had a strong, pleasant fragrance. Ten

Kate's noted that the Apache chewed it to promote healthy gums, which was also a practice in Hispanic communities throughout the Southwest and northern Mexico (Ford 1975: 341–343) and continued into the 1900s (Rea 1997: 215).

RMV 361-20 (Fig. 162 center left) is a simple necklace of approximately seventy-five squat, vaguely cylindrical or disc-shaped beads of *yerba del manso*, probably just unmodified segments cut from the stems. These were then strung on a four-strand commercial cotton string. It was collected in June/July 1883 at San Carlos, Arizona.

Another simple necklace (RMV 361-21, Fig. 162 center right) consists of forty-four perforated coral bean beads *(Erythrina flabelliformis)*. The beads have darkened with age and absorption of oil from the skin of the wearer. Whether this necklace is purely decorative or was meant to have some protective value is unknown. The Western Apache are known to have used coral beans as amulets (Ferg 1987: 129). Such necklaces are still being made: A very similar Mescalero example, made of mescal beans and thought to have been made specifically for sale, was collected in 1956 or 1957 (Merrill 1977: 72). Ten Kate's specimen was collected at either San Carlos or Camp Apache.

RMV 361-22 (Fig. 162 far left), collected at San Carlos, is strung on a tightly twisted length of cloth. The only pattern is that a glass bead (of whatever color) alternates with a cylindrical *yerba del manso* bead. The glass beads include spherical light blue, three black and one dark blue, and large red white-heart beads of various lengths.

A further example (RMV 361-23, Fig. 162 far right) is made of white and red white-heart glass beads and two copper beads interspersed with beads made from segments of *yerba del manso*, roughly carved into ovoid shapes. All are strung on a piece of commercial tan thread. There are two small feathers tied to it with sinew. It too was collected at San Carlos, Arizona, in June/July 1883.

Ten Kate (2004: 197) remarked that "not infrequently they suspend a couple of small feathers or a tweezers of Berlin silver on the necklace, which they use for carefully plucking out their facial hair." In the 1800s the Apache considered facial hair unattractive and men would use these "Apache razors" to pluck the hairs. This continued into the 1900s, but by then necklaces with tweezers seem to have been worn only by older men, many of whom had been army scouts. Ten Kate's necklace (RMV 361-24, Fig. 162 center) is strung on a vegetal fiber cord with sections of eleven to fourteen red white-heart glass beads divided by one or two cylindrical beads of *yerba del manso*. The pendant has two large light blue glass beads alternating with

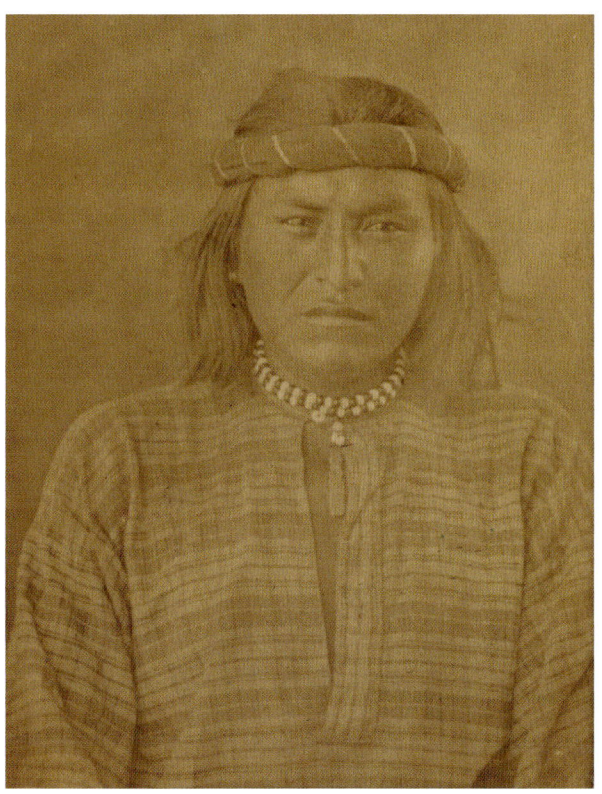

Fig. 163 Apache man with necklace and tweezer pendant; Arizona Territory, June/July 1883. Photograph by Constant Duhem (Ten Kate coll.; WMR 412719).

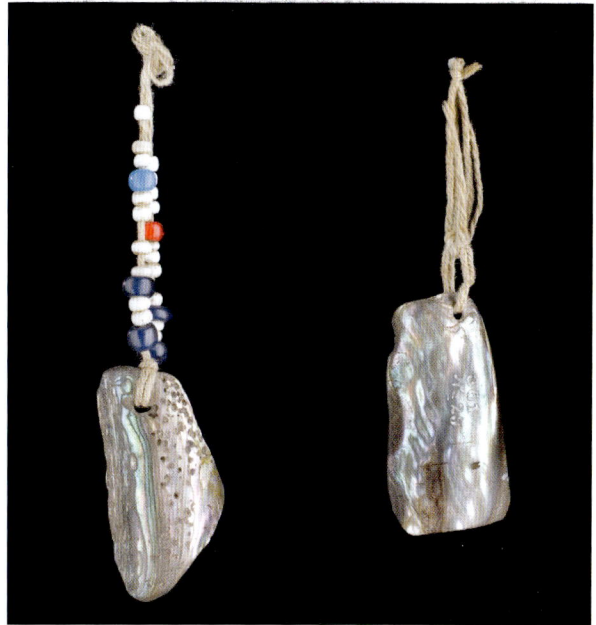

Fig. 164 Pair of Tonto Apache ear pendants; cotton string, abalone shell, glass beads; l. (whole specimen) 7 and 10 cm; ca. 1880 (RMV 361-25).

two more red white-heart beads, and tweezers of brass with incised decoration. Silver and brass tweezers on Apache necklaces often appear to be Navajo-made. This neck ornament was collected at San Carlos or Camp Apache, Arizona, in June/July 1883.

Both men and women might wear ear pendants, and Ten Kate recorded that the pair he collected (Fig. 164) were women's. One is longer than the other, but both are simply large white, blue, black, and red white-heart glass beads strung on commercial cotton thread, with an irregularly shaped pendant of abalone shell *(Haliotis* sp.). Abalone shells come from the California coast, and any owned by the Western Apache were obtained through trade with various middlemen, including the Zuni (Goodwin 1942: 81). As such, these ear pendants were probably highly valued, with abalone pendants being more commonly used in special contexts, for example as a girl's forehead pendant at her *naihes* ceremony or as an amulet on a medicine man's cap. This set was collected at San Carlos or Camp Apache, Arizona, in June/July 1883.

A bracelet (Fig. 165) was acquired from Ten Kate in 1929 by the Museum of Ethnology in Rotterdam, now renamed the World Museum. It has forty-three beads

carved from *yerba del manso* on a cotton string. The anthropologist collected it during his fieldwork at San Carlos, Arizona, in the summer of 1883.

Fig. 165 Apache bracelet; cotton string, *yerba del manso* beads; l. (whole specimen) 24 cm; ca. 1880 (WMR 17998).

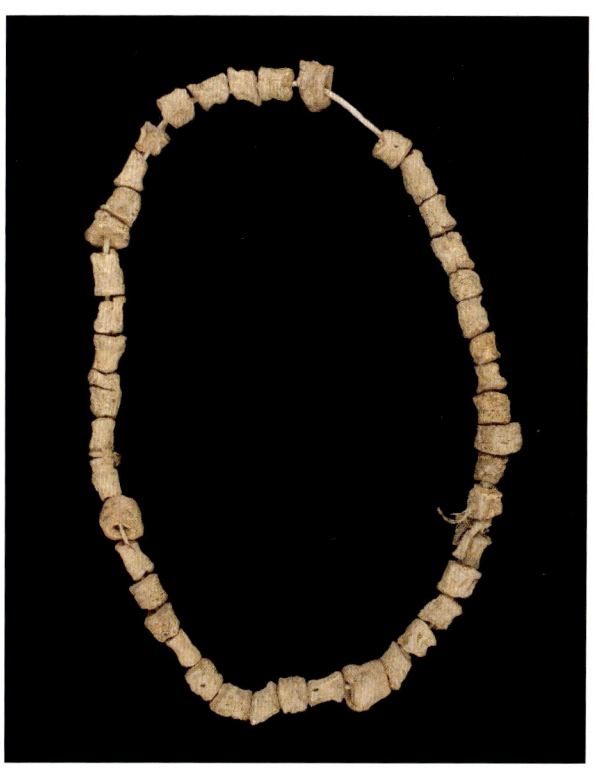

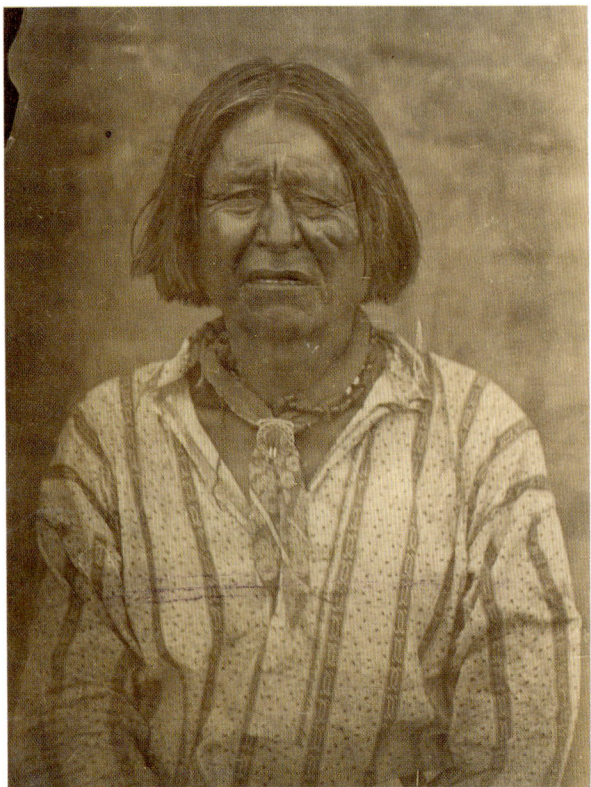

Fig. 166 Chiricahua Apache chief Loco, wearing bead and/or bean necklace; Arizona Territory, June/July 1883. Photograph by Constant Duhem (Ten Kate coll.; RMV 414Cb7a).

Warfare and Weapons

Ten Kate pointed out that the Western Apache were not communal horseback warriors like the Plains tribes, but practiced guerilla warfare, which was well adapted to the mountain environments of Arizona. The Apache operated in small groups who carried out hit-and-run attacks. A thorough knowledge of the landscape, physical endurance, determination, and courage qualified young men to become respected warriors. The Apache were a hardened people because of their environment and way of life. With a clinical tone (as befits a physical anthropologist), mixed with a touch of romanticism, Ten Kate noted the Apache's slender but muscular bodies, a gait which he compared to that of a tiger, and a piercing gaze. Many chiefs and warriors showed old scars and recent injuries. At San Carlos, Chief Loco (Fig. 166) discussed the cause of his five major wounds with the anthropologist, and Ten Kate noted that the left half of Loco's face bore the signs of heavy trauma and that he was blind in his left eye.

Chiefs, called *nahntáhn*, had reputations based on their success in leading raids. However, authority was quickly lost when physical prowess waned, enabling ambitious young warriors to prove themselves and ascend to positions of leadership. Old Nané and especially Loco were cases in point. Ten Kate also encountered Eskiminzin, who had fought with Geronimo but had since turned to a quiet life of farming.

In pre-reservation times bows and arrows were used for hunting and as weapons in raiding (to steal property) or warfare (to exact revenge by killing people). Lances and clubs were mainly offensive weapons used in war. In early times, arrows and lances were tipped with flaked stone points, replaced in later years with metal points on arrows and long metal blades on lances, the latter sometimes made from captured Spanish, Mexican, or American cavalry sabers. A distinctly Apache style of clubs for close combat, called *zendízj* (Ten Kate 2004: 197), was made of a spherical stone, the size of a billiard ball, sewn into a rawhide covering and attached by a flexible thong to a handle. In the late 1800s traditional weapons were almost completely replaced by rifles and handguns, with one, and often two, ammunition belts worn around the waist.

For protection, the Apache carried large, round rawhide shields. Also worn on raids or in warfare were buckskin caps decorated with eagle, hawk, or turkey feathers. Shields and caps were imbued with supernatural power to protect their owner, as were amulets and possibly painted buckskin shirts. By the time of Ten Kate's visit a number of men still owned shields, and caps were still worn for protection against supernatural dangers.

Ten Kate collected a set of bow, bowcase, arrows, and quiver at San Carlos or Camp Apache in June/July 1883 (Fig. 167). The gently recurved double-arc wood bow has a twisted sinew string and is reinforced with sinew wrapping at five points along its length, including the middle and ends. The bow ends are not notched. At the end of the bow, where the string was tied (the other end is a loop), is also tied a short buckskin thong; the Western Apache also do this to indicate the bottom end of the bow (Ferg 1987: 50). The solid wood arrows have triangular metal points and sinew wrapping to secure the points and fletching. Incised wavy or spiral lines run the length of the shafts. Sometimes called "blood grooves," the lines on these arrows appear more decorative than functional; one has red paint worked into it.

The quiver has an attached bowcase and a wide carrying strap; all are made of buckskin, which is now very dirty from much use, and all stitching is sinew. A polished dowel-like stick, decoratively wrapped with a strip of red flannel, serves as a rigid support between the quiver and

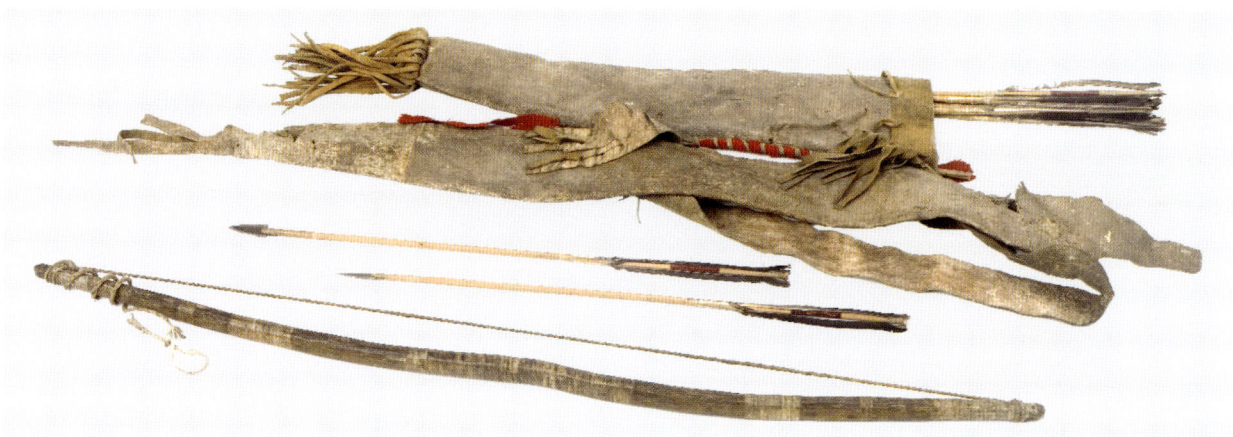

Fig. 167 Mescalero Apache bow, bowcase, nine arrows, and quiver; buckskin, rawhide, red flannel, sinew, wood, iron, paint, feathers; bow: l. 108 cm; bowcase: l. 79 cm; arrows: average l. 105 cm; quiver: l. 60 cm; ca. 1880 (RMV 361-55).

bowcase. The mouth of the case has been folded back on itself to form a reinforced cuff; the base is a double thickness of stiff rawhide, surrounded with buckskin fringes. This basic construction pattern is typical of many groups in the Southwest. The whole is undecorated except for what may have been light yellow ochre paint on the quiver cuff. Examples of similar construction, but with beaded decoration on the quiver, bowcase, and strap, and some with the hair left on the hide (mountain lion?), can be seen in various photographs taken of the Mescalero men who visited the Tertio-Millennial Exposition (see Broder 1990: figs. 95, 96; Ferg 1998b: 61; Opler 1983c: 429; cf. Mason 1894: pls. lxxvii, lxxviii); apparently they were willing to sell only the plainest on their way out of town. Had Ten Kate arrived a day earlier, he might have secured a far more elaborate example.

The bow Ten Kate purchased in Santa Fe in July 1883 and which had originally been sold by Mescalero attendants of the Tertio-Millennial Exposition is a sinew-backed, gently recurved, double-arc bow (Fig. 168). The ends of the bow are not notched or grooved to receive the

bow string, which is made of twisted sinew. The ends and grip are wrapped with sinew, and the entire back of the bow is reinforced with sinew. Sinew-backed bows were apparently not used by the Western Apache, but are recorded for all other Apachean groups in the Southwest, including the Navajo (Gifford 1940: 29), and it has been suggested that the Apache introduced this type of bow to the Pueblos in the fifteenth century (S. Baldwin 1997: 3–8).

Fig. 169 Apache boys with bows and arrows. Photographer unknown, ca. 1880 (Ten Kate coll.; RMV 414Ch6).

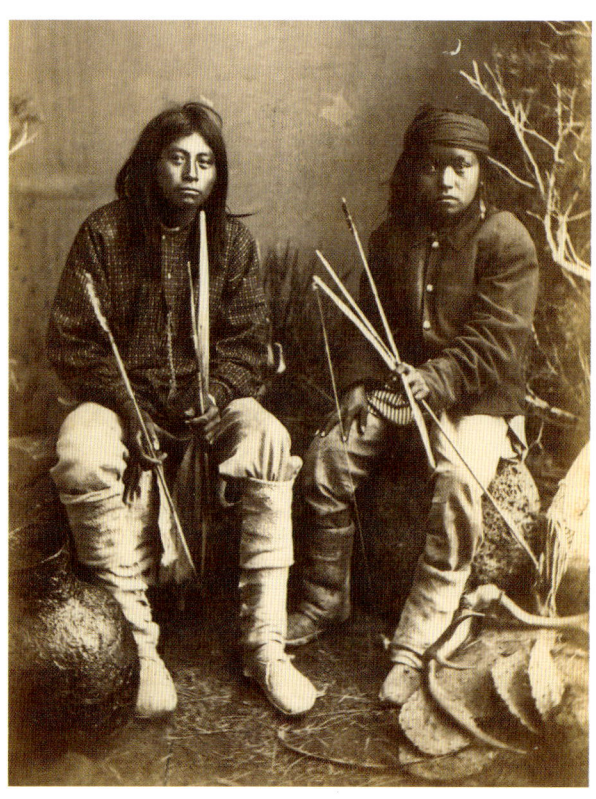

Fig. 168 Jicarilla Apache bow; wood, sinew; l. 110 cm, w. 5 cm; ca. 1880 (RMV 361-56).

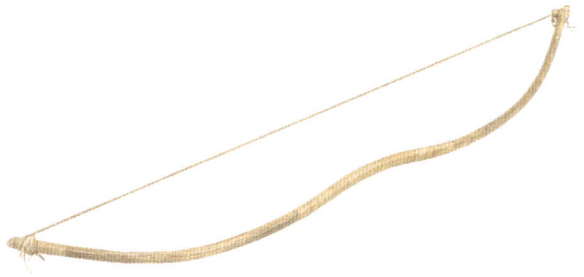

123

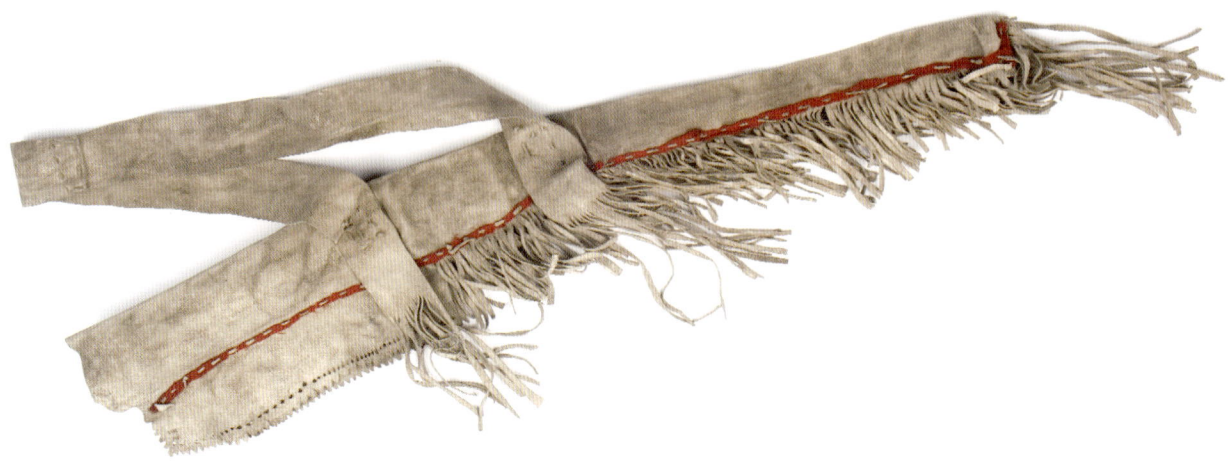

Fig. 170   Jicarilla Apache rifle scabbard; buckskin, red flannel; l. (without fringe) 103 cm; ca. 1880 (RMV 361-57).

Likewise acquired in Santa Fe in July 1883 was a quiver-like carrying case for a rifle, narrow at the bottom and wide enough for the rifle butt at the top, with a wide carrying strap (Fig. 170). The seam is stitched with a buckskin thong and edged with red flannel. The lower portion and bottom of the scabbard have buckskin fringes. A wide, decorative tab at the top has a serrated edge and cutouts to reveal the red flannel beneath.

Like arrow quivers, rifle scabbards undoubtedly could also be heavily decorated with beadwork. Ewing (1982: 170) illustrates an elaborately beaded and fringed 1880s example from the Southern Plains, identified as Apache, but not to tribe. Mails (1974: 280) illustrates a Western Apache example decorated with ribbons, but does not give its age.

A round rawhide shield in the collection (Fig. 171) has a slightly convex front decorated with painted designs and attached feathers and strips of cloth and ribbon. In the center is a black circle outlined in green. Although worn in spots, it appears originally to have had a painted band around the entire circumference: The shield edge was painted red, inside of which was a wide black band, inside of which was a narrow green line. At the bottom are remnants of a few painted feather motifs that extended inward from the green line. Around the upper portion of the shield, just inside the painted border, a red flannel strip was attached with copper tacks that go through the rawhide. Inside that is a black silk ribbon, similarly attached with a lesser number of tacks. Inside that is an arc of black feathers tied with sinew to buckskin thongs that can wave freely. The flannel strip extends, unattached,

beyond the edge of both sides of the shield and has attached feathers. When held upright, feathers cover most of the front, with the cloth and feather strips hanging down below each side.

The concave back is completely painted bright red in smeared-on paint. A roughly rectangular strip of harness leather is attached just above the center, with two tacks at the top and one at the bottom. Tied to the bottom tack are some broken strands of vegetal fiber string, suggesting that something may once have been attached there, perhaps small feathers or an amulet of some sort. The shield was collected in June/July 1883 at San Carlos, Arizona.

Ten Kate (2004: 197, 216n19) noted that the Apache used round leather shields that were "sometimes painted and adorned with feathers" and that the feathers on this shield are *Corvus americanus* (now *Corvus brachyrhynchos*, American Crow). Although the use of crow feathers on shields is known for the Western Apache, only two feathers were used along with a majority of eagle or hawk feathers (Basso 1971: 242); the feathers on Ten Kate's shield appear to be flight feathers from a Golden Eagle *(Aquila chrysaëtos)*.

This shield is one of the more important items collected by Ten Kate because shields were few in number and valuable, but also simply because we know when and where it was collected. Of the Apache shields in public and private collections, most have no useful collection history and their attribution is usually based on construction and the painted designs. It seems probable that Ten Kate obtained this shield at San Carlos, but even if acquired at Camp Apache, at least we know it was collected among the Western Apache. Even that does not completely preclude the shield actually having been made by some other group, but Ten Kate's shield fits well with what we know of other Western Apache shields. They were generally made of a single thickness of rawhide, taken from the neck, shoulder, or hips of a horse, cow, or bull. The Western Apache sometimes made buckskin shield covers, but more often did not. Shields were imbued with great protective and concealing powers and could only be safely made by men with knowledge of the appropriate supernatural power. Shields were not destroyed upon the death of the owner, but were passed on to a relative (Basso 1971: 241).

In decoration, Ten Kate's shield shares with four other Western Apache shields (G. Baldwin 1965: 105; Ferg 1987: 140–142; Hall 1926: 47) an emphasis on a centrally-positioned circle motif, three of them known to be done in either green or black paint. All have eagle feathers attached in some way to the circumference, including two with streamers and attached feathers like Ten Kate's. In short, Ten Kate's shield both compares nicely with the other known Western Apache shields, as well as increases our sample with good collection histories.

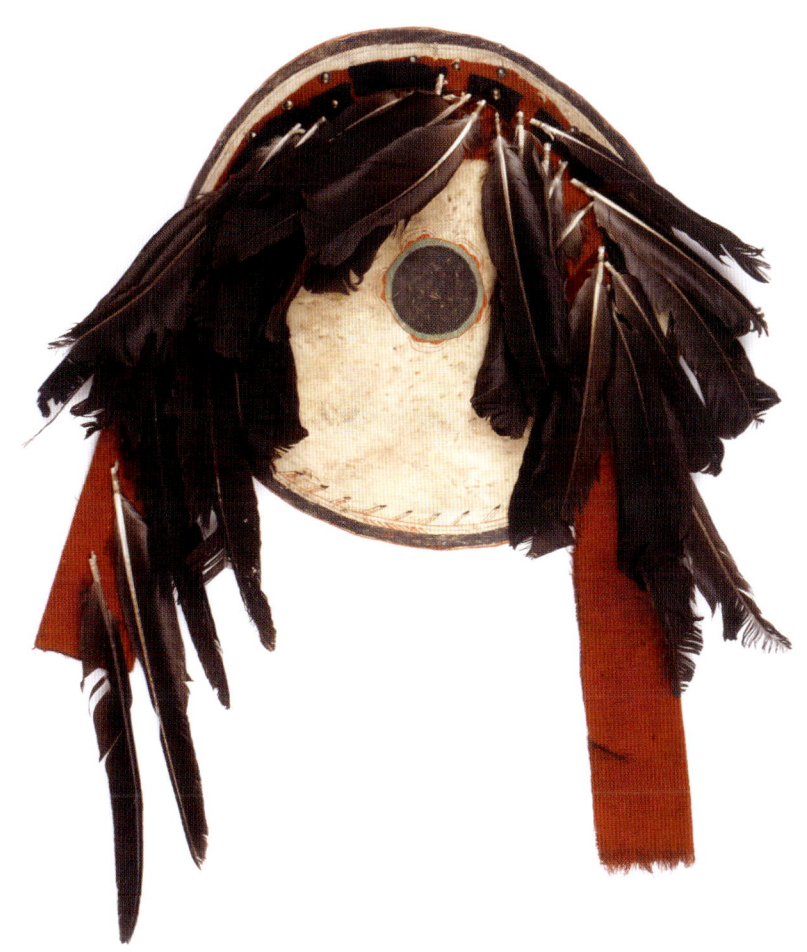

Fig. 171   Apache shield; rawhide, feathers, red flannel, black silk, copper, paints; d. 40 cm; ca. 1880 (RMV 361-58).

Games, Music, and Social Dances

Freed from subsistence activities because of the distribution of rations, the Apache spent much of their time on games and dancing, and every day they seemed to engage in games and sports, while in the evening ceremonial and social dances took place. Ten Kate observed one of their favorite games called *nazjozj* or *nazjoozj*, which was played for hours on end. He described it as follows: "… two men play at the same time, continually changing places. With big, slow steps, each one holding a long wooden pole in both hands, they go part way along a track across which rolls a ring tossed by one of them. This ring is evidently made of rope and is twisted together in such a way that the surface forms, so to speak, a number of joints. Suddenly the players extend their bodies forward and, with a forceful lunge, thrust the sticks next to each other across the sandy course after the ring, halting their running at the very moment the ring topples over. Now one of the players takes a blade of grass or a thin twig and counts the number of transverse joints of the ring with regard to the position of the poles, which have to fall over the ring. Depending on how the counting turns out, one of the players gets another turn or is replaced by another person. I usually saw them gambling with rifle cartridges, which lay in a small pile in the sand. There was always a large number of spectators present, both on foot as well as on horseback" (Ten Kate 2004: 203).

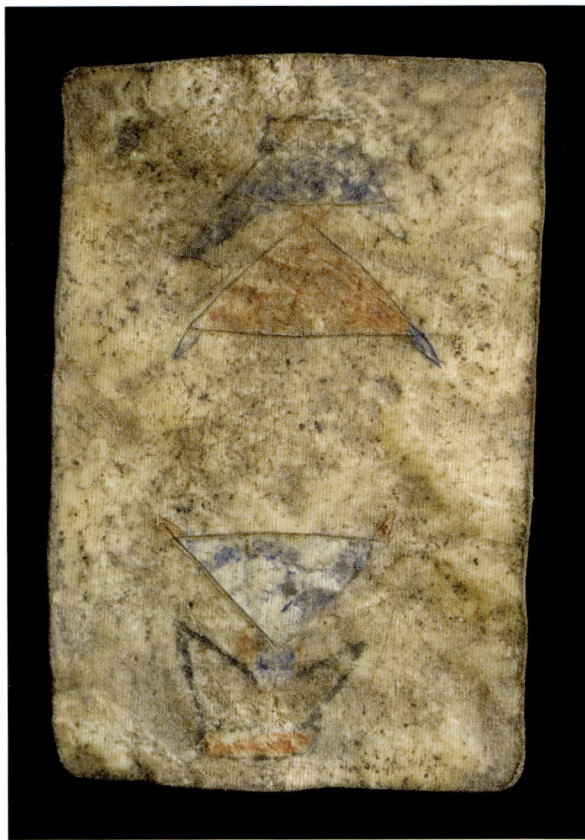

Fig. 172   Western Apache playing card "Two of Cups"; rawhide (probably horsehide), paints; l. 8.3 cm, w. 5.8 cm; ca. 1880 (RMV 361-60).

The Apache also indulged in playing cards, using cards of Mexican manufacture. However, in former days they made facsimiles of Western playing cards or inspired imitations on rawhide. Ten Kate managed to obtain one of these, but only with difficulty as these were no longer in use at the time.

During the dances Ten Kate observed the Indians drumming, shaking rattles, and playing flutes, but he was not very much impressed with their musical talents. However, he became interested in what he regarded as a curiosity, an Indian fiddle, played by men. It was made of a piece of agave stalk that was strung with horsehair and played with a bow. He acquired one for his collection and had Duhem take a photograph of an Apache man playing it (Fig. 174).

Card games were quite popular among the Apache, including, in Ten Kate's day, Monte and Con Quien, which were the most popular games played by Americans and Mexicans in the Southwest. Originally introduced to paper cards by Spanish explorers, the Apache readily adopted these foreign objects and the games played with them. In the early 1800s, when relations between Apache

groups and the newly independent Mexicans became increasingly hostile, paper cards apparently became more difficult to obtain, and the Chiricahua and Western Apache began to hand paint their own versions on dried rectangles of horsehide. Some of these decks of cards were careful imitations of the paper Mexican cards, while others replaced European dress and symbols with those traditionally found on other Apache painted objects. For an unknown reason Ten Kate was under the impression that such cards were rare at the time of his visit, though in fact they were still relatively common. But by the early 1900s Mexican paper cards were once again readily available and Apache-made rawhide cards were remembered only by the older generation (Wayland et al. 2006).

Italian, Spanish, and subsequently Mexican paper playing cards use the first suit symbols introduced to Europe: Coins, Cups, Clubs, and Swords. The Apache copied these forty-card packs, painting them with motifs that over time became increasingly Apache in design and could be difficult to recognize as the coins, goblets, clubs (cudgels), and swords that inspired them. The two Coin symbols on this card collected by Ten Kate are quite abstract (Fig. 172). They are also so similar in design and color combinations as to suggest that this card may be part of the same pack as eleven cards in the collections of the Beinecke Rare Book and Manuscript Library at Yale University, New Haven, Connecticut (Wayland et al. 2006: 48, 159, 200, 280). The grime that has worn off and obscured much of the paint indicates that this card was well used by the Apache. Ten Kate acquired it in June/July 1883 at San Carlos, Arizona.

The Apache fiddle or violin is unique in that it is the only stringed musical instrument in Native North America (McAllester 1961: 11). Apache fiddles or violins (also transcribed as *tsii edo átli*; McAllester 1956) were generally made of short segments of dry agave (mescal) flowerstalk and had one string, or sometimes two; considerably larger, two-string examples were made in the 1920s and 1930s primarily for sale to outsiders (Ferg 1981). Bourke (1886: opp. p. 49) illustrates a small fiddle with three strings, but no example like it is known. Fiddles were played by men for their own entertainment or for a group of friends, and melodies based on *tulpai* songs constitute the main repertory (McAllester 1961: 11). Hrdlicka's (1908: 52) allusion to a ceremonial use is, so far, unique. Ten Kate (2004: 203) wrote that when a fiddle is "being played, it is placed on the left near the chest at stomach level, and with the small bow-shaped fiddle stick a number

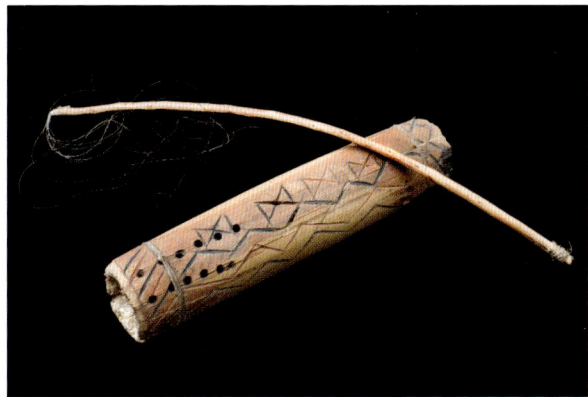

Fig. 173 Western Apache fiddle and bow; *tseenvealkskjùh* (TK); agave, resin (probably pine pitch), wood, horsehair, sinew, paints; fiddle: l. 23 cm, d. 5 cm; bow: l. 36.5 cm; ca. 1880 (RMV 361-59).

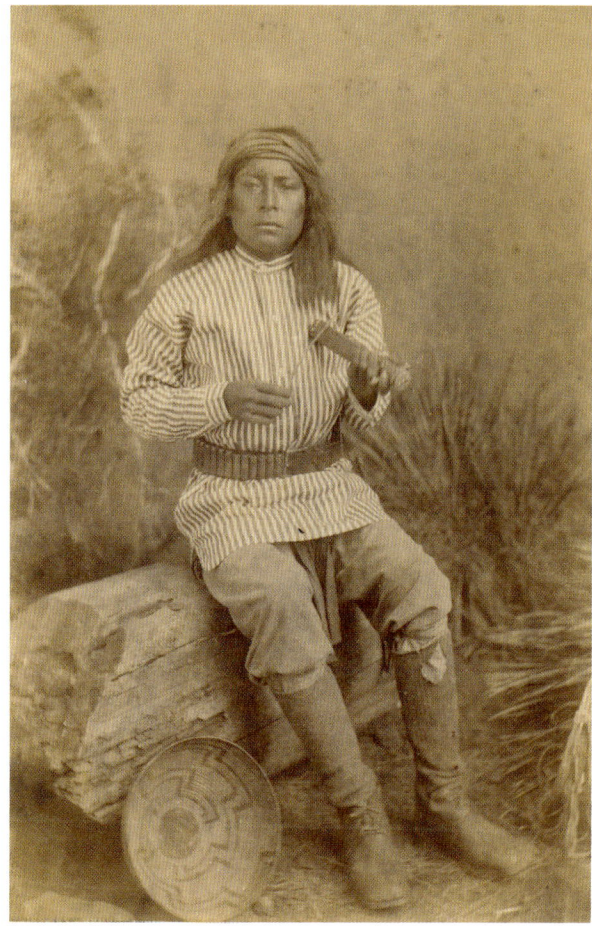

Fig. 174 White Mountain Apache man with violin; Arizona Territory, June/July 1883. Photograph by Constant Duhem (Ten Kate coll.; RMV 414Lc1).

of scratchy sounds are coaxed from it. It is possible that originally the fiddle was not a musical instrument of the Apaches but came from the Mexicans." Ten Kate's inference is presumably impossible to prove, but does appear probable based upon research on Apache and Seri fiddles by Dittemore (1978: 8), who suggests the mid-1800s as the most likely date of introduction.

The fiddle collected by Ten Kate (Fig. 173) was made by splitting the stalk segment, incompletely removing the soft pith, and securing the halves with sinew ties seated in grooves at each end. The string and wooden pegs that would have anchored it are missing. There are numerous small, round sound holes burned through, probably using a heated wire or awl. The decoration consists of incised lines filled with red and black paint. It is uncertain what the hourglass-shaped designs represent; they recall the shape of an unmarried girl's hair ornament among the Western and Chiricahua Apache. The bow is a bent twig, painted red, with long hair from the tail of a horse secured with sinew (cf. Densmore 1927: 98, pl. 45; Thompson 1977: 213–214; Ferg 1987: 162–163). Ten Kate acquired this specimen in June/July 1883 at San Carlos.

Flutes could be played by men for their own amusement, but are more strongly associated with young men playing them while courting young women; this association is described in traditional Apache stories, along with the butterfly designs that are sometimes carved on Apache flutes (Ferg 1987: 162; Goodwin 1939: 27–28; McAllester 1961: 11).

This flute (Fig. 175) is made from a segment of what is probably giant reed *(Arundo donax)*, which was usually collected during raids into Mexico. It has three drilled finger holes and a cut and burned sound hole centered over the

septum of a joint in the cane, covered with a strip of buckskin painted red. It was collected at San Carlos, Arizona, in June/July 1883.

Fig. 175 Western Apache flute; cane, buckskin, paint; l. 54 cm, d. 3 cm; ca. 1880 (RMV 362-59).

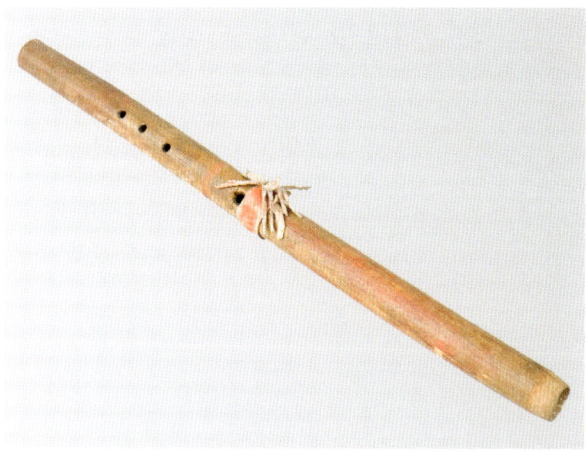

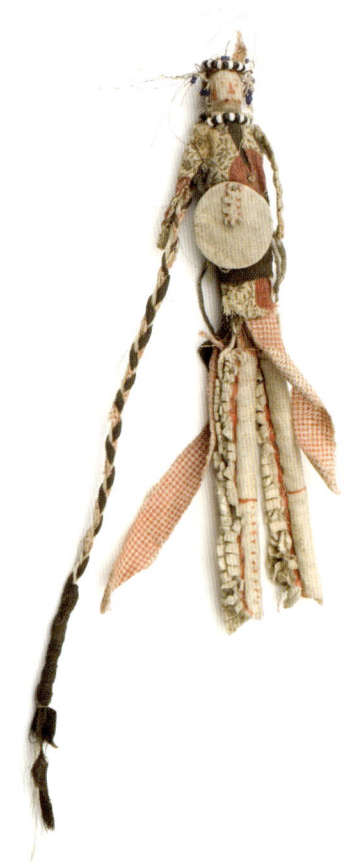

Fig. 176 Apache or Southern Plains doll; wood, buckskin, cloth, hair, sinew, glass beads, red paint; h. (excl. hair lock) 21 cm, w. 3 cm; ca. 1880 (RMV 361-65).

A doll featured in Ten Kate's collection (Fig. 176) was presumably collected in Santa Fe in July 1883. A twig forms the body and legs of this male doll, with the top wrapped in buckskin to form a head with painted features. It wears full-length buckskin leggings decorated with fringes and red painted designs, a long calico breechclout, and a printed cloth shirt that has sleeves (but no arms inside). Attached to a wide black cloth belt or sash is a plain buckskin shield decorated with a notched rectangular buckskin tab. There are earrings of blue beads, a choker of black and white beads, and a disproportionately long lock of hair braided with strips of black and calico cloth that is attached to a headband of black and white beads.

Although we know that this object was obtained from from the Apache, it is not exactly certain when and where and whether it depicts a man from an eastern Apache group or perhaps one from a Southern Plains tribe. If the exaggerated lock of hair is a depiction of a scalp lock, this, the clothing, and the doll's tall, skinny proportions would correspond with dolls known from various southern

Plains, non-Apache groups. But if the doll originally had two such hair braids, it could fit the clothes and hairstyles of the Jicarilla, Mescalero, Lipan, and Kiowa-Apache (Goodwin 1938), and alternating black-and-white beads are a most typical Apache color scheme (Lanford, pers. com., 29 January 2008; Stockel 2001). For the moment, cultural identification of this doll is a mystery.

On 18 July 1883 Ten Kate departed and from Camp Apache traveled to Holbrook by buckboard. The same day he took a train east to continue his fieldwork in New Mexico, Colorado, and Indian Territory.

References

Annerino, John
  1998 *Apache: The Sacred Path to Womanhood*. New York, NY: Marlowe & Company.
Baldwin, Gordon C.
  1965 *The Warrior Apaches: A Story of the Chiricahua and Western Apache*. Tucson, AZ: Dale Stuart King.
Baldwin, Stuart J.
  1997 *Apacheans Bearing Gifts: Prehispanic Influence on the Pueblo Indians*. The Arizona Archaeologist No. 29. Phoenix, AZ: Arizona Archaeological Society.
Basso, Keith H.
  1966 *The Gift of Changing Woman*. Anthropological Papers 76, Bulletin of the Bureau of American Ethnology 196. Washington, DC: Smithsonian Institution.
  1970 *The Cibecue Apache*. New York, NY: Holt, Rinehart and Winston.
  1971 (ed.) *Western Apache Raiding and Warfare: From the Notes of Grenville Goodwin*. Tucson, AZ: University of Arizona Press.
  1983 Western Apache. In: Alfonso Ortiz (ed.), *Southwest* (Handbook of North American Indians 10. W. C. Sturtevant, gen. ed.; Washington, DC: Smithsonian Institution), 462–488.
Bourke, John G.
  1886 *An Apache Campaign in the Sierra Madre; an Account of the Expedition in Pursuit of the Hostile Chiricahua Apaches in the Spring of 1883*. New York, NY: Charles Scribner's Sons.
  1892 The Medicine-men of the Apache. *Annual Report of the Bureau of American Ethnology* 9: 443–595.
Broder, Patricia Janis
  1990 *Shadows on Glass: The Indian World of Ben Wittick*. Savage, MD: Rowman & Littlefield Publishers, Inc.
Clark, LaVerne Harrell
  1963 Early Horse Trappings of the Navajo and Apache Indians. *Arizona and the West* 5(3): 233–248.
Densmore, Frances
  1927 *Handbook of the Collection of Musical Instruments in the U.S. National Museum*. Bulletin of the U.S. National Museum 136. Washington, DC.

Dittemore, Diane D.

　1978　A Comparison of Seri and Western Apache One-String Fiddles. Master's thesis, University of Denver, Denver, CO.

Dittemore, Diane D. and Cathy Notarnicola

　1999　Anonymous Was a Weaver: In Search of Turn-of-the-Century Western Apache/Yavapai Basketry Artists. *American Indian Art Magazine* 24(3): 54–65.

Dittemore, Diane D. and Nancy Odegaard

　1998　Eccentric Marks on Western Apache Coiled Basketry. *American Indian Art Magazine* 23(2): 34–43.

Ewing, Douglas C.

　1982　*Pleasing the Spirits: A Catalogue of a Collection of American Indian Art.* New York, NY: Ghylen Press.

Farrer, Claire R.

　1982　Signs of Self and Other in Mescalero Apache Basketry. Paper presented at the 3rd Native American Art Studies Association Conference, Ames, IA.

　1991　*Living Life's Circle: Mescalero Apache Cosmovision.* Albuquerque, NM: University of New Mexico Press.

Farrer, Claire R. and Bernard Second

　1981　Living the Sky: Aspects of Mescalero Apache Ethnoastronomy. In: Ray A. Williamson (ed.), *Archaeoastronomy in the Americas* (Anthropological Papers No. 22. Los Altos, CA–College Park, MD: Ballena Press–Center for Archaeoastronomy), 137–150.

Feest, Christian F.

　2006　Slit Pouches of Eastern North America. *American Indian Art Magazine* 31(3): 66–79, 96–97.

Ferg, Alan

　1981　Amos Gustina, Apache Fiddle Maker. *American Indian Art Magazine* 6(3): 28–35.

　1987　(ed.) *Western Apache Material Culture: The Goodwin and Guenther Collections.* Tucson, AZ: Arizona State Museum, University of Arizona, and University of Arizona Press.

　1998a　Cross-and-Crescent Motifs Among the Western Apache. Part 1: Daagodighá. *American Indian Art Magazine* 23(2): 70–83.

　1998b　Cross-and-Crescent Motifs Among the Western Apache. Part 2: Antecedents and Descendants. *American Indian Art Magazine* 23(3): 58–67.

　2003　Traditional Western Apache Mescal Gathering as Recorded by Historical Photographs and Museum Collections. *Desert Plants* 19(2). Superior, AZ: The University of Arizona for the Boyce Thompson Southwestern Arboretum.

Ferg, Alan, Virginia Wayland, and Harold Wayland

　2006　The Tonto Naipero: A Nineteenth-Century Apache Playing Card Artist. *American Indian Art Magazine* 31(4): 52–61.

Ford, Karen Cowan

　1975　*Las Yerbas de la Gente: A Study of Hispano-American Medicinal Plants.* Museum of Anthropology, Anthropological Papers 60. Ann Arbor, MI: University of Michigan.

Franciscan Fathers

　1910　*An Ethnologic Dictionary of the Navaho Language.* St. Michaels, AZ: St. Michael's Press.

Frisbie, Charlotte J.

　1987　*Navajo Medicine Bundles or Jish: Acquisition, Transmission, and Disposition in the Past and Present.* Albuquerque, NM: University of New Mexico Press.

Ganteaume, Cécile R.

　1993　Western Apache Ge'estcin: A Visual Signification System. Paper presented at the 8th Native American Art Studies Association, Santa Fe, NM.

Gifford, Edward W.

　1940　*Culture Element Distributions: XII Apache-Pueblo.* University of California Anthropological Records 4(1). Berkeley, CA: University of California Press.

Golston, Sydele E.

　1996　*Changing Woman of the Apache: Women's Lives in Past and Present.* Danbury, CT: Franklin Watts.

Goodwin, Grenville

　1938　White Mountain Apache Religion. *American Anthropologist* 40(1): 24–37.

　1939　*Myths and Tales of the White Mountain Apache.* Memoirs of the American Folk-Lore Society 33. New York, NY.

　1942　*The Social Organization of the Western Apache.* Chicago, IL: University of Chicago Press.

Hall, H. U.

　1926　Some Shields of the Plains and Southwest. *The Museum Journal* 17(1): 36–61.

Hatt, Gudmund E.

　1916　Moccasins and Their Relation to Arctic Footwear. *Memoirs of the American Anthropological Association* 3: 147–250.

Herold, Joyce

　1999　Showing the Sun: Mythological-Ceremonial Foundations of Jicarilla Apache Basketry. *American Indian Art Magazine* 24(3): 66–79.

　2005　Baskets of the Southwest and Great Basin. In: Jill R. Chancey (ed.) *By Native Hands: Woven Treasures from the Lauren Rogers Museum of Art* (Laurel, MS: Lauren Rogers Museum of Art), 76–107.

Heyink, J.

　1983　*Dr. Herman F. C. Ten Kate en de Apache Indianen.* Bennebroek: Kiva Reeks.

Hovens, Pieter and Anneke Groeneveld

　1992　*Odagot: Photographs of American Indians, 1860–1920.* Amsterdam: Fragment Uitgeverij.

Hrdlicka, Aleš

　1908　*Physiological and Medical Observations Among the Indians of Southwestern United States and Northern Mexico.* Bulletin of the Bureau of American Ethnology 34. Washington, DC.

Kluckhohn, Clyde, W. W. Hill, and Lucy Wales Kluckhohn

　1971　*Navaho Material Culture.* Cambridge, MA: Belknap Press of Harvard University Press.

Mails, Thomas E.

　1974　*The People Called Apache.* Englewood Cliffs, NJ: Prentice-Hall.

McAllester, David P.

　1956　An Apache Fiddle. *Ethnomusicology*, Newsletter 8: 1–5.

　1961　*Indian Music in the Southwest.* Colorado Springs, CO: The Taylor Museum.

McCoy, Ronald

1985   Gan: Mountain Spirit Masks of the Apache. *American Indian Art Magazine* 10(3): 52-58.

Mason, Otis T.

1887   Cradles of the American Aborigines. *Annual Report of the Smithsonian Institution for 1886*: 161-212.

1894   North American Bows, Arrows, and Quivers. *Annual Report of the Smithsonian Institution for 1893*: 631-679.

Merrill, William L.

1977   *An Investigation of Ethnographic and Archaeological Specimens of Mescalbeans (Sophora secundiflora) in American Museums.* Technical Reports 6. Ann Arbor, MI: Museum of Anthropology, University of Michigan.

Opler, Morris E.

1936   The Influence of Aboriginal Pattern and White Contact on a Recently Introduced Ceremony, The Mescalero Peyote Rite. *The Journal of American Folk-Lore* 49(191-192): 143-166.

1938   The Use of Peyote by the Carrizo and Lipan Apache Tribes. *American Anthropologist* 40(2): 271-285.

1941   *An Apache Life-Way: The Economic, Social and Religious Institutions of the Chiricahua Indians.* Chicago, IL: University of Chicago Press.

1983a   The Apachean Culture Pattern and Its Origins. In: Alfonso Ortiz (ed.), *Southwest* (Handbook of North American Indians 10. W. C. Sturtevant, gen. ed.; Washington, DC: Smithsonian Institution), 368-392.

1983b   Chiricahua Apache. In: Alfonso Ortiz (ed.), *Southwest* (Handbook of North American Indians 10. W. C. Sturtevant, gen. ed.; Washington, DC: Smithsonian Institution), 401-418.

1983c   Mescalero Apache. In: Alfonso Ortiz (ed.), *Southwest* (Handbook of North American Indians 10. W. C. Sturtevant, gen. ed.; Washington, DC: Smithsonian Institution), 419-439.

Owen, Charles L.

1903   Notes on the White Mountain Apache. Field Museum of Natural History, Anthropology Archives: Field Notebooks. Chicago, IL.

Quintero, Nita

1980   Coming of Age the Apache Way. *National Geographic* 157(2): 262-271.

Rea, Amadeo M.

1997   *At the Desert's Green Edge: An Ethnobotany of the Gila River Pima.* Tucson, AZ: University of Arizona Press.

Reagan, Albert B.

1930   *Notes on the Indians of the Fort Apache Region.* Anthropological Papers of the American Museum of Natural History 31(5). New York, NY: American Museum Press.

Roberts, Helen H.

1929   Basketry of the San Carlos Apache. *Anthropological Papers of the American Museum of Natural History* 31(2): 121-218.

Stewart, Omer C.

1948   Ute Peyotism: A Study of a Cultural Complex. *University of Colorado Studies, Series in Anthropology* 1: 1-41.

[Reprinted 1984: *University of Utah Anthropological Papers* 108: 3-46.]

Stockel, H. Henrietta

2001   Chiricahua Apache Women: A Photo Essay. *The Journal of Arizona History* 42(1): 81-108.

Tanner, Clara Lee

1982   *Apache Indian Baskets.* Tucson, AZ: University of Arizona Press.

1983   *Indian Baskets of the Southwest.* Tucson, AZ: University of Arizona Press.

Ten Kate, Herman

1885   *Reizen en Onderzoekingen in Noord Amerika.* Leiden: E. J. Brill.

2004   *Travels and Researches in Native North America, 1882-1883.* P. Hovens, L. A. Hieb, and W. J. Orr eds. Albuquerque, NM: University of New Mexico Press. [Translation of Ten Kate 1885.]

Thompson, Judy

1977   *The North American Indian Collection: A Catalogue.* Berne: Berne Historical Museum.

Vincent, Gilbert T., Sherry Brydon, and Ralph T. Coe

2000   (eds.) *Art of the North American Indians: The Thaw Collection.* Cooperstown, NY: Fenimore Art Museum—University of Washington Press.

Wayland, Virginia, Harold Wayland, and Alan Ferg

2006   *Playing Cards of the Apaches: A Study in Cultural Adaptation.* Tucson, AZ: Screenfold Press.

Whiteford, Andrew Hunter

1988   *Southwestern Indian Baskets: Their History and Their Makers.* Santa Fe, NM: School of American Research Press.

Wissler, Clark

1915   Riding Gear of the North American Indians. *Anthropological Papers of the American Museum of Natural History* 17(1): 1-38.

The Pueblo Peoples

Ten Kate's first visit to an Indian tribe west of the Mississippi took place between Christmas and New Year 1882. From Little Rock, Arkansas, he had continually traveled westward by train, crossing the border at Texarkana, then across central Texas with Dallas and Abilene the major stations and short stops further on at Colorado City and Big Spring. From his Southern Pacific railroad car Ten Kate saw that the prairie landscape gradually gave way to semiarid desert with drifting sands, prickly pear cactus, yucca, and colonies of prairie dogs. After crossing the Pecos River, the train stopped at Toyah for supper. The overnight journey took him to El Paso, where he arrived on Christmas morning.

When he stepped from the train, the Dutch traveler was immediately struck by the change in the man-made environment. Low houses with flat roofs, built of adobe, revealed the Mexican origin of the architecture. The roofed sidewalks along the main streets recalled American influence. El Paso was a major border town, and many people and large amounts of goods came through, rendering the place busy and humming with activity. The town had earned a reputation as a "hard place" because of its numerous bars, gambling places, and brothels, as well as frequent fights, shoot-outs, and murders.

The Dutchman stayed at the Central Hotel, an old Mexican-style building with a *zaguan*, a grand entryway, and a patio, an inner courtyard along which the rooms were located on several levels, provided with galleries. During Christmas afternoon he visited a market and attended a bullfight, where people clad in colorful serapes and wide-brimmed sombreros provided a pleasing spectacle.

Ysleta del Sur

The next day Ten Kate visited the commander at Fort Bliss for advice on his visit to the Tigua of Ysleta del Sur, a Native settlement eight miles south of El Paso. That small village had been established after 1680, when the Pueblo peoples of the upper Rio Grande Valley rebelled against the Spanish, who were forced to flee south to El Paso. They were joined by their Native allies, notably Tiwas from Isleta Pueblo, south of Albuquerque, and some Piros. In 1682 the Pueblo refugees established Corpus Christi Mission and the village of Ysleta del Sur, where indigenous traditions were maintained against Mexican and American influences (cf. Houser 1970, 1979, Bronitsky 1987). Ten Kate spent three days at the transplanted pueblo to carry out fieldwork and noted that full-bloods made up about half the population of the village, while the younger generation showed intermixture with Mexicans and Americans.

The massive church devoted to San Antonio looked like a fortress and with its robust slanting walls dominated the pueblo. The interior had a wooden ceiling with primitive carved and painted figures. Although the inhabitants were nominally Catholic, they retained many of their Native religious traditions. The forty-odd houses were of adobe and built separate from each other. Distinctive dress was rare, except for a few serapes and sombreros, as almost everybody wore citizen's dress. The only exception was the footwear, and many people still valued their traditional undecorated moccasins. Some old men wore their hair in the old style, rolled together in the back in a short, stiff tail wrapped with colored cloth. Ten Kate learned that the Indians called themselves Tiwa, just as the Indians of the Pueblos of Isleta, Sandia, Taos, and Picuris further north, and recognized that they were one branch of the Tano, the others being the Tewa of Hano, Nambe, Pojoaque, San Ildefonso, San Juan, Santa Clara, and Tesuque, and the Towa of Jemez Pueblo.

The Indians were spending the final days of the year between Christmas and New Year in a festive manner. Dancing took place every day between noon and midnight, and Ten Kate noted an interesting amalgamation of

131

traditional Pueblo performances with Christian elements. He observed: "From ten to fifteen men and boys, holding rattles made from gourds, hopped up and down alternately behind or next to each other in a tightly closed row, without, however, leaving their place and practically without lifting their feet. Now and then, in time to the rhythm from the monotonous chanting, the dancers bent their upper body strongly to the side and stretched the right arm with the rattle out to the ground. All this is accompanied by monotonous droning from a leather drum. The Indian beating the drum and a couple of the most prominent people from the tribe stood behind the row of dancers and did not budge. They were all bare-headed, and many had smeared part of their faces with red paint. They did not wear special attire, however. In various places in the village the same dance is repeatedly performed, always starting in front of the entryway to the church" (Ten Kate 2004: 70-71).

The anthropologist spent his three days at Ysleta del Sur going around the village, visiting people, and talking to those inhabitants who were interested in the strange visitor. The anthropologist was much interested in the *ace-quias*, the irrigation canals, by which the Indians irrigated their fields. The construction of the canals and high banks to divert water from the nearby Rio Grande was an impressive feat. Artificial irrigation enabled the Tigua to subsist for a considerable part on agriculture, as this system insured a good crop in most seasons. The surplus harvest was stored in granaries on scaffolds of tree trunks and sometimes on scaffolds built in cottonwoods, places safe against plunder from most rodents.

Ten Kate's main encounter was with the governor of the pueblo, José Maria Duran, an impressive looking man. He was tall, and although of a certain age his long hair was still raven black. The anthropologist received an invitation to the chief's home and in return for the hospitality offered, he took several photographs of the governor and his wife.

Although Ten Kate saw little traditional material culture, he made his wish known to acquire old artifacts. On the evening before his departure, the war captain Bernardo Holquin approached him and expressed his willingness to divest himself of a few traditional items. After protracted negotiations the men reached a deal, and Ten Kate acquired a war bonnet (*emóh*, TK) decorated with feathers (never acquired by the Leiden museum), a round leather shield, a large drum coated with red paint, and a drumstick. The following day the warrior expressed his

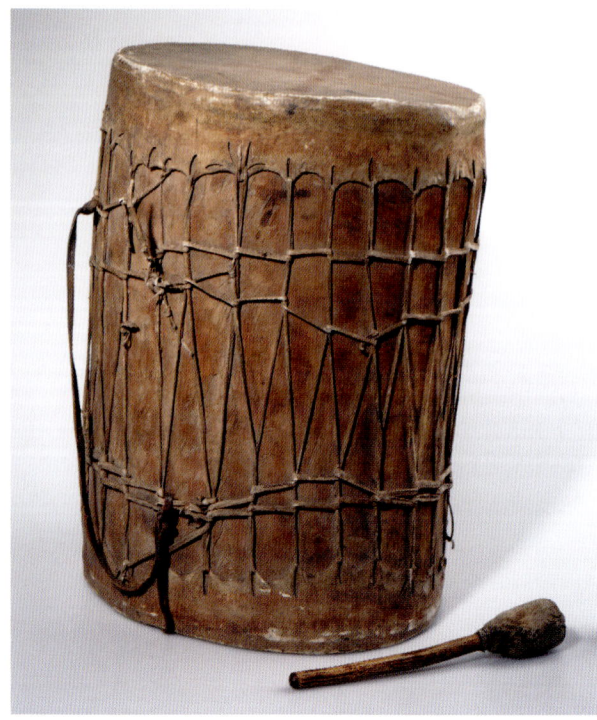

Fig. 177 Tigua double-headed drum and drumstick; *póhojèt* and *làh* (TK); cottonwood, hide, pigment; drum: h. 56.5 cm, w. 30-39.5 cm; ca. 1880 (RMV 362-135).

remorse over the sale of his war bonnet that held dear memories of campaigns against the Apache, but Ten Kate stood firm and took photographs of the man, his wife, and two daughters after Bernardo had painted his face red and yellow and donned an American army officer's coat for the occasion.

Late in the evening of 29 December 1882 Ten Kate returned to El Paso. The following day he packed his acquisitions and shipped them to the Netherlands. Unfortunately, the war bonnet was lost during transportation.

Pueblo double-headed drums were made from cottonwood (*Populus deltoides*). A piece of the stem the length of the desired height of the drum was hollowed out to a thickness of about two inches. The exterior often remained raw or was only superficially treated, with knotholes plugged. Only in the twentieth century Indians in some pueblos (e.g., Santo Domingo, Taos) began to paint drum exteriors. Two pieces of water-soaked hide cut in round sections and with perforated edges were fastened to both sides of the drum by hide thongs running along the sides of the drum and stretched to keep the surface taut. Elk hide was preferred because it produced a finer sound, but was later replaced by the more easily available cow and mule hides. The drumstick consists of a skin head, fixed to a wooden handle.

The Leiden specimen (Fig. 177) has remains of red pigment all over the wooden surface. It is double-headed and the covers show remains of painted designs. The top hide exhibits an outer and an inner circle, divided in four sections by a cross. Within each of the sections the remains of additional designs are visible, but they are too faded to be interpreted. The bottom hide is divided by a cross, and on the rim semicircles are added to each quarter section. Sun and moon motifs are most frequently encountered on Pueblo drums, and the decoration of drum surfaces has continued in Ysleta del Sur, as is shown in a 1968 photograph of the Tigua Pueblo war captain with his drum, showing a star on the upper hide. The wooden hull of the Leiden specimen is artificially perforated, and through this hole the drum is fed, a periodically repeated ritual performed for such drums (Densmore 1938: 40-45; 1957: 2; Hurt 1952: 113-114; Kurath and Garcia 1970: 290–291; Houser 1979: 337; Bill Wright 1993: 20-21; cf. Thompson 1977: 220; Eickhoff 1996: 104).

Gourd rattles are frequently encountered in archaeological contexts of the Anasazi ancestors of the Pueblos (Brown 1967: 75-76). The wooden stem of a Tigua gourd rattle collected by Ten Kate (Fig. 178 left) extends from the top. A wooden peg secures the sounding body, and the handle has a buckskin loop. The Tigua refer to these instruments as *guajes*, a Spanish term meaning 'gourds,' and they were used in virtually all ceremonies. Ysletans were involved in frequent dances, both ceremonial and secular, according to a calendrical cycle. A major event was the *Shiâfürd* or Rattle dance, taking place during the festival of the Ysletans' patron saint Nuestra Señora del Carmen. The first part is performed by two men and two women, and the second part by a large number of male dancers, all using rattles. The sequence of the dances takes the participants and spectators from the cemetery to the home of the majordomo and finally to the church (Fewkes 1902: 66; cf. Bill Wright 1993: 26, 119, 121, 125, 132–133; see also the section on Pueblo music below).

The unfinished rattle (Fig. 178 right) consists of a partially hollowed-out gourd. The hollowing is done by putting small sharp rocks into the body of the squash and having children shake it to remove as much of the internal fiber as possible to improve the sound. A Tewa informant added: "For ceremony, apply mud, for tourists paint in bright colors" (Kurath and Garcia 1970: 290). The Tigua and others regard the rattle as representing rain. It should be handled with care, as the rain must be earned by correctly performing rituals (cf. Bill Wright 1993: 132–133, 153).

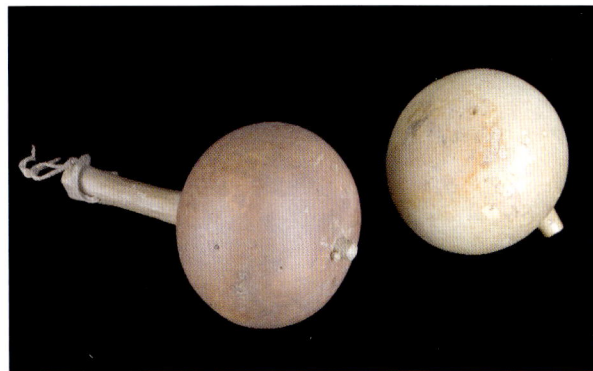

Fig. 178 Tigua rattle and unfinished rattle; RMV 362-138: gourd, wood, hide; l. 21 cm, d. 11 cm; ca. 1880; RMV 362-138a: gourd; d. 11 cm, h. 12 cm; 1882.

The Ysletans were in frequent conflict with the neighboring Apache, and many served as scouts for the U.S. army in campaigns to crush their resistance to Anglo-American domination and forced settlement on reservations. With their robust shields they protected themselves against Apache arrows or blows with clubs during close combat. In 1902 Jesse Walter Fewkes visited Ysleta and noted that former scouts like war captain Bernardo Holquin, from whom Ten Kate purchased a shield (Fig. 179), did not receive a pension or extra rations. Fewkes (1902: 61) described their inhabitants as "although poor, they are

Fig. 179 Tigua shield; *gweeyèr* (TK); wood, hide, cloth, feathers; d. 45 cm, h. 7 cm; ca. 1870–1880 (RMV 362-141).

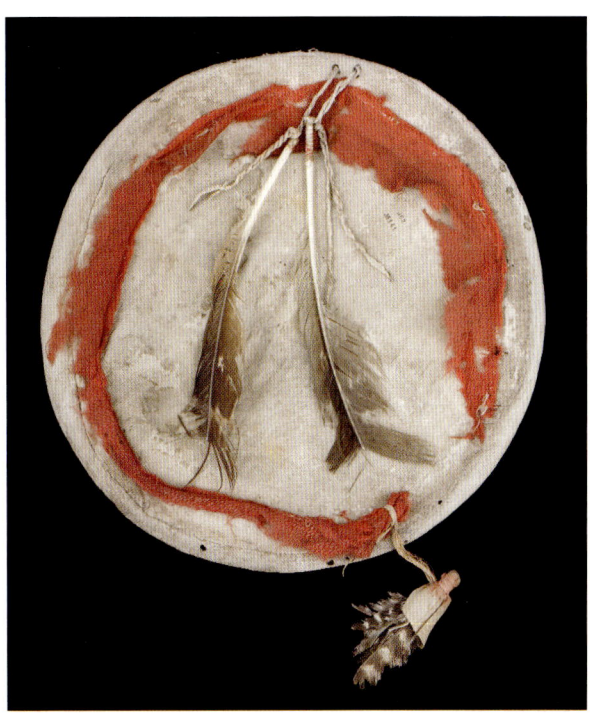

industrious, self-respecting, law-abiding citizens." The engagement of Pueblo peoples in staunch defense of their villages and fields and their willingness to undertake raids and to resist Indian and White enemies in a violent manner mitigates the popular image of an unassertive people (Dozier 1970: 78–82).

The circular shield is made from untanned buffalo skin, probably from the neck of the animal as this was preferred because of its thickness and strength. In pre-horse days the shields were larger to protect a large part of the body, but after the introduction of horses, shields generally became smaller among Southwestern and Plains tribes (Barton Wright 1976a: 8; Baldwin 1997: 11–14). As the cover of this shield has no painted designs, the rawhide surface of this specimen was originally probably completely covered with red cloth, of which only the frayed margins remain. However, Pueblo shields with painted designs on their surface had such cloth linings around the perimeter (e.g., Bolz and Sanner 1999: 111, fig. 90). Pendants on the shield's rim include (the remains) of several feathers and a hide cone, from which a bundle of small feathers emanate. This latter type of shield pendant is not recorded in Barton Wright's (1976a) study of Pueblo shields.

In the Southwest hide moccasins replaced prehistoric fiber sandals. The sole of this pair (Fig. 180) is of rawhide, while the upper consists of soft buckskin dyed a reddish brown, for which mountain mahogany was used. The upper consists of three pieces, including the separate cuff, and all parts are stitched together with sinew. While moccasins for everyday use showed little decoration, those worn at ceremonial occasions could be elaborately embell-

Fig. 180 Tigua moccasins; hide, sinew, dye; l. 25 cm, h. 10 cm; ca. 1880 (RMV 362-142).

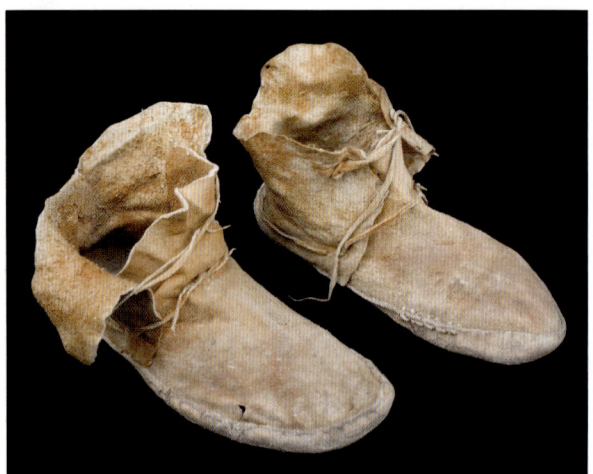

ished, the hide stained with pigments, strips of fur sewn on, or patches of beadwork applied (Jeancon and Douglas 1930: 15).

Laguna Pueblo

Laguna was conveniently situated on the railway line but lacked a station. However, the train driver accommodated his European passenger by stopping there anyway in the middle of the night to let him off. At the foot of a telegraph pole the anthropologist spread out his blanket and spent the night there until he was awakened by the morning sun. His first port of call was the house of the missionary who also was the acting Indian Agent, Presbyterian Reverend John Menaul, an Irishman. However, the minister showed him no hospitality on this Sunday morning, but soon Ten Kate was hosted in the pueblo by a friendly couple, he an American, she a Laguna lady, who provided an ample meal.

A visit to St. Joseph church, dating from Spanish colonial times (1699), enabled Ten Kate to get an impression of the language of the inhabitants of Laguna, who spoke a dialect of Keresan, also spoken at nearby Acoma and in the Rio Grande pueblos of Cochiti, San Felipe, Santa Ana, Santo Domingo, and Zia. Only a few Indians attended the service. After mass Reverend Menaul showed himself a little bit more forthcoming and told Ten Kate that his missionary work showed but little progress, even despite translating the bible into Keresan and printing it on the press he had hauled in. However, he was a man not to be deterred. Ten Kate asked him about the traditional beliefs of the people of Laguna, but the minister was not able to answer his questions, even showing contempt for ancient cosmology and rituals. The anthropologist noted that Menaul and many like him forgot that not every change they induced was for the better.

Laguna was situated on a hill overlooking the San José River, which emptied into the Rio Puerco to the east. To the northwest towered Mount Taylor, a dormant volcano and regarded by the people of Laguna and Acoma as the abode of the Rainmaker of the North. The inhabitants called themselves *Kawáikäme* and their pueblo *Kawáik* or *Kawáika*. The name Laguna was derived from a nearby lake created by a beaver dam, which suddenly vanished in the early nineteenth century by draining into the San José River. The pueblo was the largest in New Mexico and according to government reports housed nearly a thousand people. However, most inhabitants were absent, engaged in harvesting the fields in the surrounding area. The architecture of Laguna resembled that of Tesuque. As there was little more Ten Kate could learn, he boarded the next train at midnight and continued his journey to the Navajo.

The Rio Grande Pueblos

When Ten Kate arrived in Albuquerque on 21 July 1883, he made the acquaintance of Frank Hamilton Cushing, who was living at Zuni doing ethnological fieldwork. With him and a small group of Zunis he visited the Presbyterian Indian Boarding School, more popularly known as the Albuquerque Indian School. The institution had been established two years before and was supervised by R. W. D. Bryan. It primarily taught Pueblo children, boys and girls, and used military drill to establish an orderly and studious environment. Bryan and the teachers assured the visitors that this system of education yielded results, but Ten Kate had his doubts as to whether the Native students would benefit from Western education.

From Albuquerque Ten Kate continued his journey northward to Santa Fe, first by train. At Wallace the passengers had breakfast and were met on the platform by Indians from Santo Domingo Pueblo, who offered bluish-green turquoise jewelry and small cream-colored pottery with attractive black designs painted on their exterior surfaces. Ten Kate (2004: 227) wrote in his notebook: "One would have to be very unfeeling not to buy a small item from the dark Pueblo girls, with a blush on their cheeks as fresh as a peach while they ask me, bashfully and comically at the same time, for a real," the equivalent of one-eighth of a dollar, commonly referred to as "a bit."

At Lamy he transferred to the spur line running north to Santa Fe. The capital of New Mexico was situated at a higher elevation than Albuquerque and the climate was cool and bracing. Upon his arrival Ten Kate found Santa Fe predominantly consisting of the same squat adobe houses so common everywhere else in the Southwest. However, the town also had several churches, hotels and restaurants, and the Palace of the Governors, thus making it a place of some civilization in the desert. At the time of the Dutchman's visit the town was celebrating the "Tertio-Millenial" festival, the largest event staged in New Mexico up to that time. Taking 1550 as its date of founding, Santa Fe found reason to celebrate its one-third of a millennium. Ten Kate found it a typical example of American humbug, and in his eyes it did not amount to much more than a

large regional fair, showcasing agricultural produce, prepared foods, and arts and crafts. However, his spirits lifted when Indian dances were announced. A poster advertising the "Santa Fe Celebration," which has been preserved, listed Zuni War dances (accompanied by Frank H. Cushing), the Antelope dance of the Acomas, the Devil's dance of the Na-Pa-Johi-Tal, Camp Fires of the Apaches, and Apache Ceremonial (Ellis 1958: 128). A group of Mescalero Apaches had just left the town after their performance, but Ten Kate was able to witness traditional dances from several pueblos. The Indians were camped around town and received free meals and small amounts of money for the entertainment they offered. The anthropologist visited their camps every day and found the Pueblo people a friendly crowd, good natured, cheerful and quick to laugh, intelligent in their expression, and fond of the cigarettes he distributed. Soon Ten Kate detected traces of contact and ethnic intermixture of the northern Rio Grande Pueblos with their neighbors to the east and northwest. He noted linguistic similarities between Keresan and Kiowa, the residence of a number of Jicarilla Apaches at Picuris Pueblo, the popularity of a Ute dance in San Juan Pueblo, and the personal acquaintance of an Indian from Tesuque with Comanches, Cheyennes, and Pawnees. As to material culture he noticed the frequency of buffalo hides, traded with Plains neighbors for agricultural produce.

The Pueblo men wore skin leggings with long fringes along the seams, but their torsos were clad in cotton shirts of Western make. Their hair hung loosely down to the neck and over the forehead, cropped above the eyebrows or in other cases parted in the middle of the scalp and hanging in two long braids over the chest. Eagle feathers, sometimes wrapped in otter fur, were woven into the braids, a style probably adopted from Plains tribes. Pueblo women's attire was more traditional and consisted of closely woven black woolen mantas with embroidered or interwoven red designs along the fringes. They were fastened around the middle with a woven belt. Their footwear consisted of so-called "squaw boots," moccasins with long strips of white buckskin that were wrapped around the lower leg, giving the lower extremities a rather bulky appearance. Their style of hair was similar to that of the men, but they had no hair ornaments.

A major surprise to Ten Kate was the fact that after centuries of Spanish influence and having become nominally Catholics, the Pueblo people had retained so much of their traditional customs and beliefs. This went against the reasoning that tribal ways would disappear after a few generations of Western influence. The first dance Ten Kate witnessed was the Deer dance, performed by representatives from Picuris Pueblo. Ten almost naked men appeared, their bodies covered in paint and their heads crowned with elk antlers, imitating a herd of animals stalked by hunters. In their hands they carried short sticks on which they leaned forward, their backs reaching almost a horizontal position. They played their role convincingly, according to the Dutch observer, grazing peacefully one moment, then scurrying away as if frightened, closing ranks, with the antlers bent backwards toward the nape of the neck. Then four or five hunters, armed with bows and arrows, began stalking the animals, trying to remain undetected. On the margin of this scene two women in black mantas jumped up and down, holding green spruce branches in their hands. The whole affair was accompanied by the rhythmic sound of small round drums, beaten by a number of Indians standing nearby.

The groups from San Juan Pueblo performed an Eagle dance, covered in eagle feathers, again perfectly mimicking the natural behavior of the predatory bird: arranging the plumage with the beak, flying away with fluttering wings making a rustling sound. It proved the Native dancers to be experts in the observation of animal behavior and dramatic performance. The sound of a flat drum accompanied the slow dance, while the attending Indians softly shouted an unintelligible song or poem. Ten Kate saw the Matachina dance being performed twice by inhabitants of San Juan Pueblo, and this event surpassed the more traditional animal dances in liveliness and the number of different participants. It was clearly not a Native dance, as Montezuma and Malinche, two historical figures from Spanish colonial times, played major parts in the performance. Ten Kate therefore regarded the Matachina dance as a historical pantomime, expressing the lover's quarrel of Montezuma, the emperor of the Aztecs. Although historically Malinche (Malintsin), called Donna Marina by the Spanish, was the Native mistress of the conquistador Hernando Cortés, in the Matachina dance she played this role vis-a-vis Montezuma, an example of historical license. The name of the dance derived from Italian, a mattaccino being a 'charlatan,' 'jester,' or 'mimic,' and in this Pueblo dance referred to the participation of the clowns.

Ten Kate gave the following account of the dance: "All the dancers, roughly thirty in number, are masked, with the exception of Malinche, represented by the graceful Pueblo girl Requesita. She has heavy, dark, wavy hair hanging loosely over her shoulders. Her small graceful figure is enveloped in two fine white blankets which are sewn together, decorated with broad black borders, but in such a way that the left half of her fine bust and her bare left arm visible. On her foot she wears leather moccasins. Montezuma, wearing a black mask, is wrapped in colorful garb. The two ahuelos, half beast, half devil, have large leather masks completely covering their heads—one black, the other brown, with long ears. They are also attired like the other dancers who have loosely-fitting white clothes ornamented with beads, shells, and colorful ribbons on their bodies. On their heads they wear a black or red cap shaped liked a miter, which is covered with numerous silver ornaments, crosses, and tiny bars. They have tied a white cloth in front of their faces. In their left hands they hold a rattle made from a gourd shell covered with a cloth, in the right a colorful wooden trident."

"The dancers gather in three rows, standing a few paces apart from each other. Malinche has taken her place in the middle, between the rows. Montezuma stands on the same line, but outside the rows. The ahuelos and the toro (the bull), an Indian wrapped in bison hide whom they will eventually kill, flank the musicians and participate in the presentation only toward the end. Before long the violins can be heard, beginning with an allegro, fiery and catchy like a Spanish waltz, then reverting again to the sad, plaintive tones of an Indian chant. There is quivering and glimmering all through the colorful rows, which move forward twisting and twirling, to the stomping of feet in rhythm and the sound of little bells dangling from their knee joints, without their line-up undergoing any changes in the process. The shy Malinche dances gracefully along through the rows, slowly traipsing her eyes downward, while the tridents wave like ornaments. Now the dancers kneel down, and Malinche and Montezuma take turns pursuing each other, in a winding, twisting line or wheeling about in sudden turns. Then, in a skipping gait, the dancers change places again. Eventually, the monsters, the bull, and the ahuelos intervene in the struggle, but Montezuma triumphs over all of them. Triumphantly he emerges from the arena, taking Malinche with him as his prize" (Ten Kate 2004: 229–230).

During his visits to the Native encampments around town, Ten Kate successfully bargained with the Indians for the purchase of items of dress, musical instruments, a mask, other dance paraphernalia, and various other ethnographic artifacts.

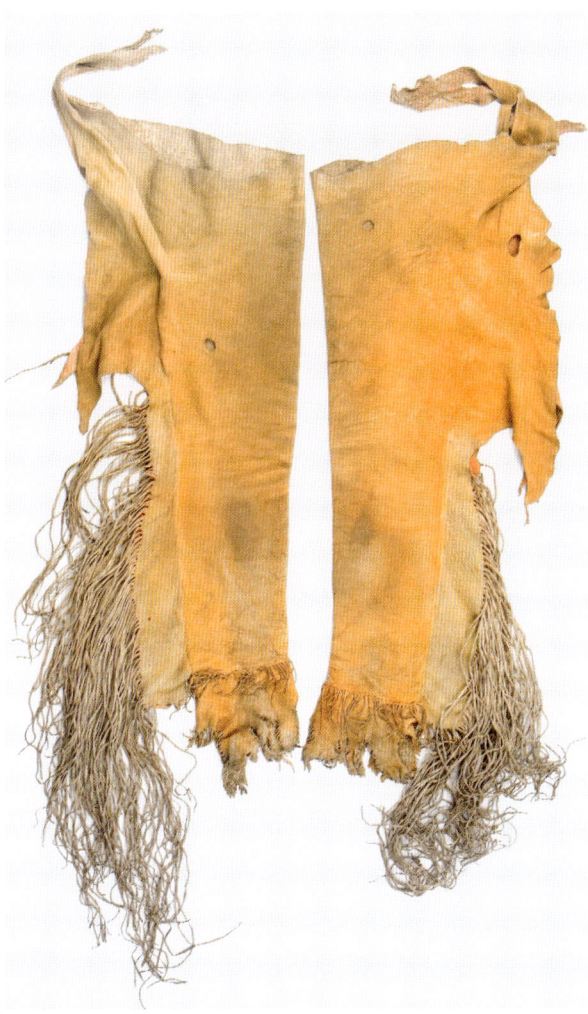

applied by embroidery and brocading. From the 1870s on the trade on the Santa Fe Trail began to furnish commercial cloth, and soon the Puebloan weaving tradition waned (Jeancon and Douglas 1930; Douglas 1939a, 1939b, 1940a, 1940b).

In prehistoric times Pueblo women went barefoot or wore fiber sandals that were later replaced by hide moccasins. Increasing trade with Plains tribes in the nineteenth century resulted in the rapid proliferation of hide clothing among the Rio Grande Pueblos, especially the northern villages. On special social and ceremonial occasions they wore moccasins with soft buckskin flaps attached to this footwear, stained white with kaolin clay, wrapped upwards around the lower leg, reaching the knees, and fastened by a buckskin thong or woven garter. Hip length buckskin leggings such as the Leiden pair (Fig. 181) were also traditionally worn by Pueblo men (Jeancon and Douglas 1930). This specimen has straight fringes and a serrated fringe at the bottom. It was stained and shows the remains of yellow and red pigment. Leggings in the shape of footless stockings were also crocheted or knitted from white cotton or dark wool from prehistoric until historic times (Fox 1978: 61–63; Kent 1983: 83–85, 87).

Ten Kate's collection contains a hide paint bag on a bracelet with stone beads and an abalone (*Haliotis*) shell tab, which contains pigment for body painting (Fig. 182).

Pueblo Indian religion finds expression in a great variety of restricted-access kiva ceremonies and performances of ritual drama in public spaces, often on the centrally located plaza. Song and dance are integral parts of belief and ritual. Emphasis is placed on the correct performance of ceremonies and dances as regards attire, choreography, music, and texts, all to insure fertility and well-being. Most

Fig. 181 Pair of leggings from San Juan Pueblo; hide, sinew, pigment; l. 84 cm, w. 15–40 cm; ca. 1880 (RMV 362-126).

After the Spanish introduced sheep to the Southwest, textiles of wool were woven by Puebloan men on traditional upright looms and to some extent replaced men's shirts of deerskin. Blankets and garments were also produced for Spanish settlers, partially as compulsory tribute, partially in interethnic trade. Embroidery was introduced, and prehistoric designs were thus applied to new textiles, especially along borders. Red commercial cloth was raveled for reuse, and from Mexico indigo became available. When the Americans took control of the Southwest in 1848, they encountered a strong Puebloan textile tradition that had incorporated Spanish elements. The Hopi were the most productive weavers and traded their textiles with the Zuni and the Rio Grande Pueblos. Typical woven Pueblo items of dress included *mantas* (shoulder and dress blankets), shawls, shirts, kilts, belts, sashes, breechcloths, leggings, garters, and headbands. Decorative designs were

Fig. 182 Bracelet with paint bag from Tesuque Pueblo; hide, turquoise and hematite beads, abalone, pigment; l. 7.5 cm; ca. 1880 (RMV 362-128).

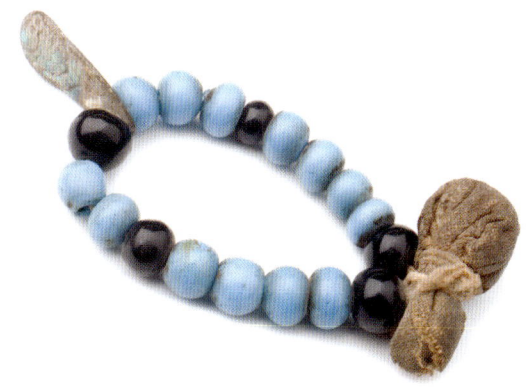

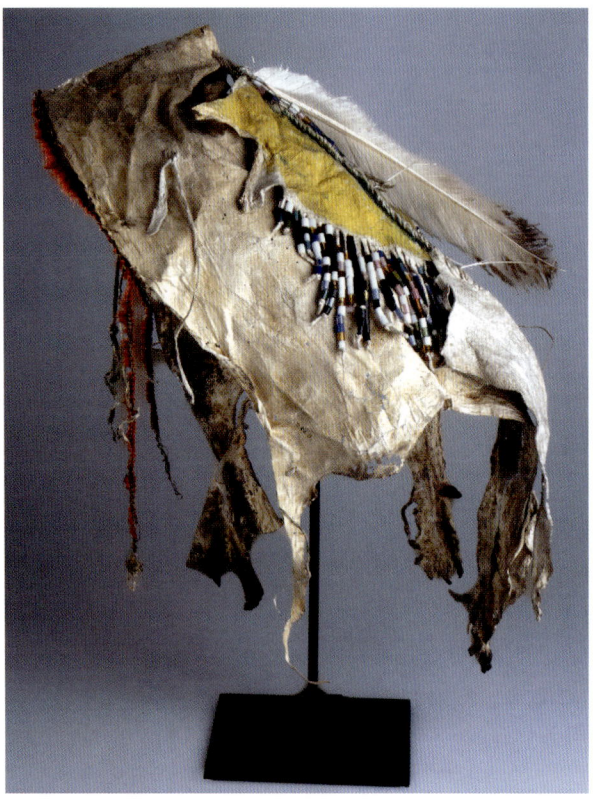

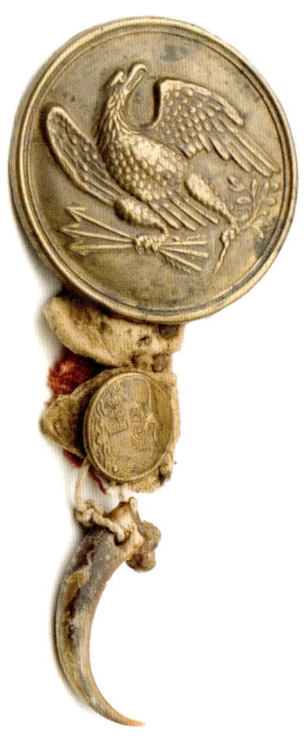

Fig. 183 Dance cap from Picuris Pueblo; *khendzèh* (TK); buckskin, eagle feathers, glass beads, wool, pigment; h/l. 42 cm; ca. 1880 (RMV 362-129).

Fig. 184 Pueblo dress ornament; hide, brass, eagle claw, flannel, cotton; d. 6.4 and 2.1 cm; l. 10 cm; ca. 1880 (RMV 362-130).

rituals, organized in a calendrical cycle, are oriented toward securing supernatural blessing for crops, wildlife, and health. Social or recreational dances are also a valued part of Pueblo life (Ortiz 1969, Dozier 1970, Roberts 1980).

The type of dance cap collected by Ten Kate (Fig. 183) was probably derived from war caps that were in turn fashioned after southern Plains models. The Pueblo war caps can be distinguished by their row of upright feathers. In other features the war and dance caps were similar, with their side streamers of feathers, painted surfaces, and leather and beaded fringes (Roediger 1941: 156). The Rio Grande Pueblos borrowed freely from their Plains neighbors, including songs and dances that were subsequently made over in a Pueblo mold (McAllester 1961: 6-7).

The large button on a dress ornament in the Ten Kate collection (Fig. 184) shows a Phoenix with three arrows in its claws, a banner, a fortress, sun symbol, and waves. The smaller button exhibits a bird with a ribbon, with the text "ESSAYONS" flying over a fortress with the sun setting over an expanse of water. An eagle claw completes the ornament. Both buttons are associated with the U.S. Army Corps of Engineers. This decorative set of machine-made

military buttons and eagle claw has a buckskin backing, stitched on a piece of red flannel. It is all that remains of a Pueblo war cap Ten Kate collected.

The Matachina dance is of Spanish origin and was introduced into the American Southwest by the Spaniards throughout Mexico. According to the people of San Juan, the dance was introduced to them by the early Franciscan missionaries from Spain. There is some debate as to the original narrative underlying the dance. Those favoring a completely European origin regard the dance as a depiction of the battle between Christians and Moors, who invaded the Iberian peninsula in the eighth century. Others do not dispute the Spanish origins of the music (Iberian Polka and Basque tunes), instruments (violin and guitar), and dance steps, but regard the historical episode of the Spanish conquest of Mexico and its Aztec ruler Montezuma as original impetus for the dance. However, a fusion of the two in the Meso-American melting pot of Native and Hispanic cultures cannot be ruled out, and Kurath and Garcia (1970: 265-268) have outlined the complexity of the origins discussion. In Tewa mythology the culture hero Poseyemu is credited with instituting the Matachina dance, and Parmentier (1979) has argued that

138

the figure of Montezuma was used in Pueblo ceremonial context to communicate between two religious traditions. Matachina dances are performed in Pueblo and Hispanic communities in the American Southwest, at Pascua by the Yaqui (see chapter 13, "Mexico") and in Mexican non-Native and Native (Yaqui, Tarahumara, Huichol, and other) villages (Champe 1983, Rodriguez 1996). In different societies the dance and its constituent parts and roles can have more or less divergent meanings as comparative studies have shown (e.g., Kurath 1957, Robb 1961, Lea 1964, Saldaña 1966, Champe 1983).

Interestingly, the people of Santo Domingo Pueblo believed that this dance was instituted by Montezuma so that the Indians could mock their conquerors (Dumarest 1919: 186). The Matachina dance, integrated into the calendrical cycle of Pueblo ceremonies (Ortiz 1969: 104, 143), is generally performed during wintertime, in San Juan usually on 24 and 25 December. There a series of eight performances are given: in front of the church, the priest's house, the homes of the principal characters, Monanca and Malinche, the homes of the Summer and Winter caciques, and on the north and south plaza (Parsons and Beals 1934: 498, 509–510; Parsons 1939: 852–855; Kurath 1958; Kurath and Garcia 1970: 38–45; Sweet 1985: 42, 89–90; Rodriguez 1996: 97–101).

The Abuelos, 'Grandfathers,' are clowns, but should not be confused with the traditional Pueblo clowns, whipper kachinas who are called *Tsaviyo* at San Juan. Abuelos act as masters of ceremonies or dance leaders and clowns. They sometimes mimic the dancers or join them, and they perform a closing act in which they tease the bull with their whips and theatrically kill and slaughter the animal, only to revive it as a climax. These characters are a syncretism of European and Native American traditions (Parsons and Beals 1934: 508–510; Champe 1983: 12–14; Rodriguez 1996: 40–42, 100).

The Abuelos' costume and masks are eclectic. Dress varies from loin cloth and tattered rags to skin leggings and Western pants. Masks are generally not complex and consist of cloth or cone-shaped skin hoods, but sometimes are more elaborate to approach kachina masks. Abuelo masks from San Juan and Cochiti are very similar. The Leiden mask (Fig. 185) is painted monochrome and has a separate nose and two ears affixed. This mask is made from thin rawhide with the hairs on the inside and is tied and decorated vertically along the back with painted fringe. The outside surface is painted black, on which red designs are applied at the eyes, the nose, the chin, and on

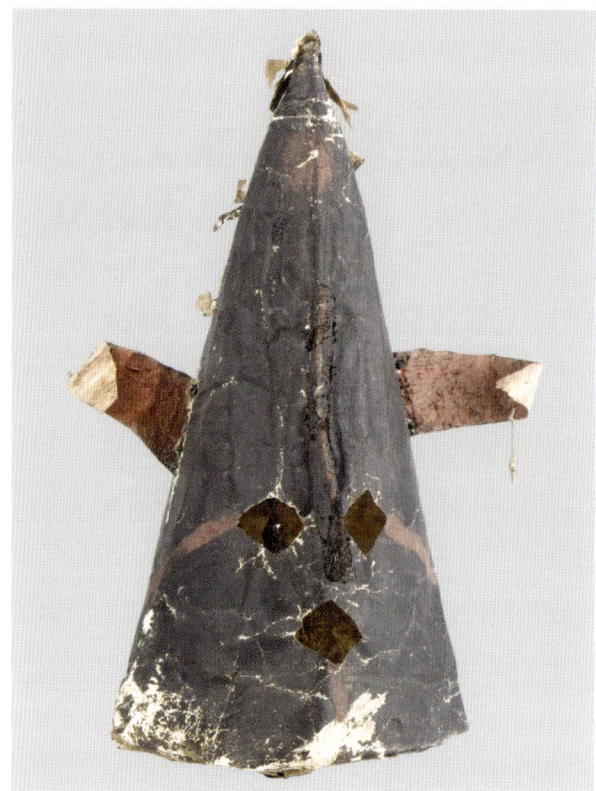

Fig. 185 Abuelo mask, San Juan Pueblo; rawhide, pigment; h. 45 cm, w. 27–37 cm; ca. 1880 (RMV 362-131).

the forehead. The nose and ears are separately attached (cf. Parmentier 1979: 613).

A variety of carved wooden serrated rods were used as rasping sticks during dances and singing. These were played with a second stick being pressed against and moved up and down the serrated rod in a rhythmic manner. To reinforce the sound, rasping sticks were pressed against a dried hollow squash or an upturned bowl-shaped basket, acting as an amplifier. Ten Kate noted that one of the rasping sticks he collected (Fig. 186) was used during

Fig. 186 Rasping stick, San Juan Pueblo; *mwo-áy* (TK); wood, pigments; l. 105.5 cm, w. 5.3 cm, th. 2 cm; ca. 1880 (RMV 362-132).

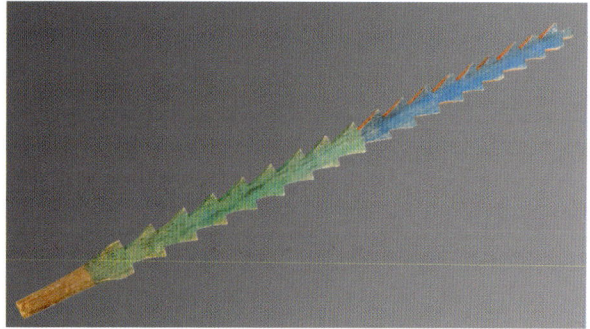

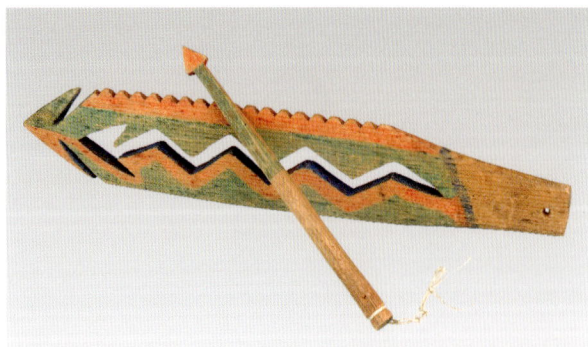

Fig. 187 Rasping stick, San Juan Pueblo; *muo-áy* (TK); wood, pigments; l. 34.5 cm, w. 6.5 cm, th. 1.2 cm; ca. 1880 (RMV 362-134).

site sex. They are referred to as *Pinin Kossa*, 'fake clowns' (Ortiz 1969: 169–170).

Carved and painted trident slat wands (Fig. 188), often additionally decorated with feathers and painted geometric designs, are held in the left hand by the Monanca alt. Monarca (derived from the name for king and personified in Aztec ruler Montezuma), the dance leader, and the nine other Matachinas, who wave it horizontally. In their right they hold a gourd rattle that is shaken vertically, contrary movements that require quite adept coordination. It has been suggested that that the trident or *palma* was derived from the Aztec feather fan (Champe 1983: 9–10).

The tambourine-type drum is constructed of a flat wooden ring, which overlaps slightly and is lashed with rawhide. The head of the drum consists of rawhide, stretched over one side and lashed at the back as well as stitched to the frame at the sides. The head and sides are painted in green, yellow, white, and reddish-brown (Fig. 189).

A gourd rattle obtained by Ten Kate is undecorated, but its dried surface has developed an aesthetically pleasing copper patina in different patterns on both sides. The gourd is filled with small pieces of rock, infused through a small hole in the underside, closed with a wooden peg, and further secured with cotton string (Fig. 190).

the performance of the Matachina dance. As he did not specify that it was used to make music, it could also have been used as a dance wand during the ceremony. Rasping sticks made from wood, bone, and antler have been excavated in prehistoric sites of the Pueblos' ancestors, the Anasazi (cf. Brown 1967: 77; Kurath and Garcia 1970: 290; Lange 1979b: 381).

Ten Kate recorded that specimen RMV 362-134 (Fig. 187) was played by women during the Xicara (Jicara) or Gourd dance, held at the time of the vernal equinox in February or March, in which men reverse roles, dress as women, and perform a parody of the behavior of the oppo-

Fig. 188 Matachina dance wand, San Juan Pueblo; wood, pigment, iron; h. 53 cm, w. 35 cm; ca. 1880 (RMV 362-133).

Fig. 189 Pueblo drum and drumstick; wood, hide, pigments; d. 28 cm, h. 8.7 cm; ca. 1880 (RMV 362-136).

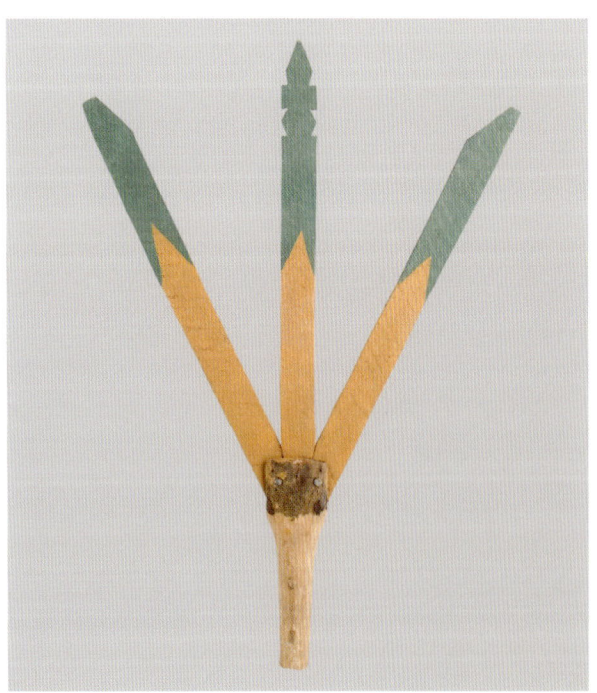

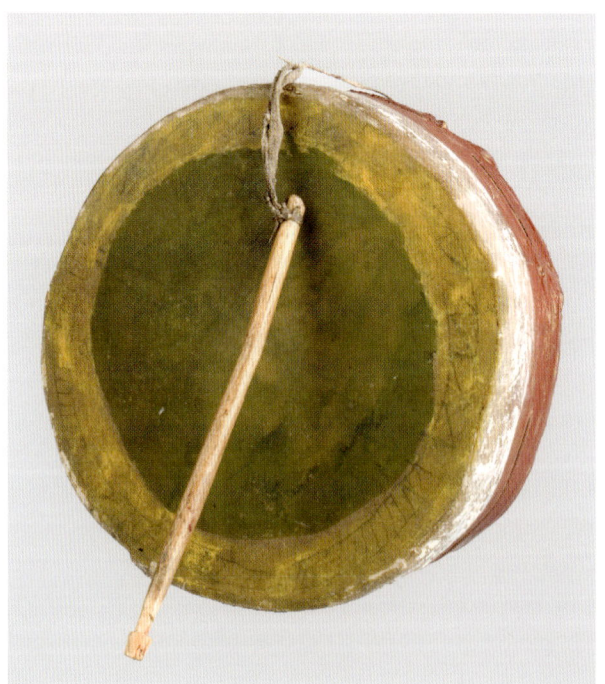

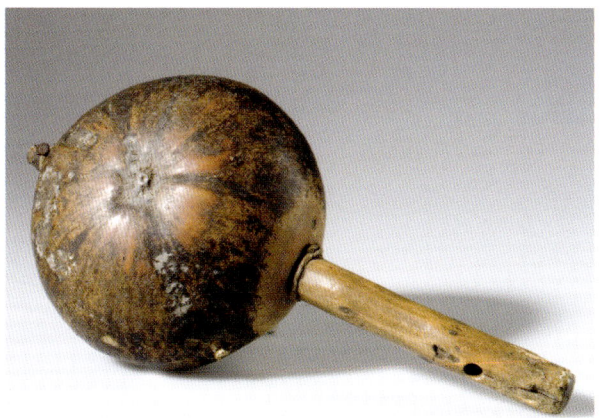

Fig. 190 Pueblo hand rattle; wood, gourd, cotton, stone, iron; l. 26 cm, w. 8–12 cm; ca. 1880 (RMV 362-137).

Gourds (*Lagenaria vulgaris*) of several varieties were not only a traditional staple food, their dried shells were also the raw material for several kinds of containers, such as canteens, bowls, and dippers. Very large gourds could be fashioned into kachina masks. Gourds also provided the raw material for rattles, of which a great variety of shapes and sizes were manufactured to be used at social and ceremonial occasions. After cleaning out the interior through a small hole, the shell was boiled and dried and subsequently filled with dried corn kernels, quartz crystals, turquoise, or other small stones believed to have magic properties, warding off sickness, and attracting rain. Handles of wood or dried corncob are fitted. Gourd rattles come in undecorated and in painted varieties, the latter including symbolic designs referring to fertility. The rhythm instruments are fitted with an eagle feather as a blessing before being used (Roediger 1961: 82–83, 145–146; see also Fig. 178 above). In addition to gourds, dried animal skin was sometimes used as a sounding body for rattles, including the dried animal scrotum, again signifying fertility.

The desert tortoise lives in riparian habitats like water holes or springs scattered throughout the semiarid Southwest. The animal exemplifies life and survival in the desert and is associated with the gods that provide life-sustaining rain. The Pueblo peoples believe that when the Rain Gods hear their leg rattles sounding, they will send rain for their crops. Tortoise-shell leg rattles with deerhoove pendants (Fig. 191) are worn just below the knee, tied with hide thongs such as this specimen, or are sometimes attached to the top of moccasins, as in the case of the San Juan clowns participating in the Raingod ceremony (Laski 1959: 142; Roediger 1961: 145–146; Fane 1991: 118).

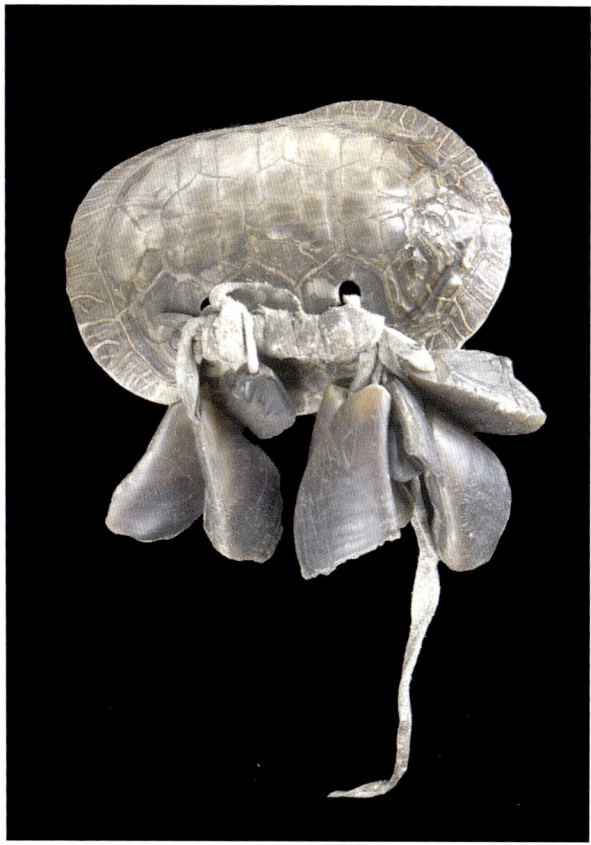

Fig. 191 Leg rattle from San Ildefonso Pueblo; tortoise shell, deerhooves, hide; l. 13 cm, h. 9 cm; ca. 1880 (RMV 362 139).

Tablitas are usually carved from a flat panel of cottonwood and fastened on the head by means of hide straps. The inverted stepped carving of the wooden panels symbolizes rain clouds, and the dances were aimed at producing rain to enhance fertility. This type of women's head ornament was especially manifest during Corn dances, also referred to as Tablita dances. Generally, the Rio Grande Pueblo tablitas where somewhat simpler and less elaborate than those of the Zuni, while those of the Hopi show the most elaborate construction, carving, painting, and decoration. However, according to Hopi tradition, the tablita headdress was introduced among them by people from the Rio Grande who settled among them. They taught them the Butterfly dance, in which such head ornaments figure prominently and have reached the highest level of decorative complexity. The common name for this ceremonial headdress, tablita alt. *tableta*, is derived from the Spanish and means 'small wooden panel.' However, the various Pueblo villages have different and complex names for these ritual accessories (Roediger 1941: 157–158; Lange 1957; 1979b: 384; Brown 1967: n.p.; Barton Wright 1976b; 1979: 38–39).

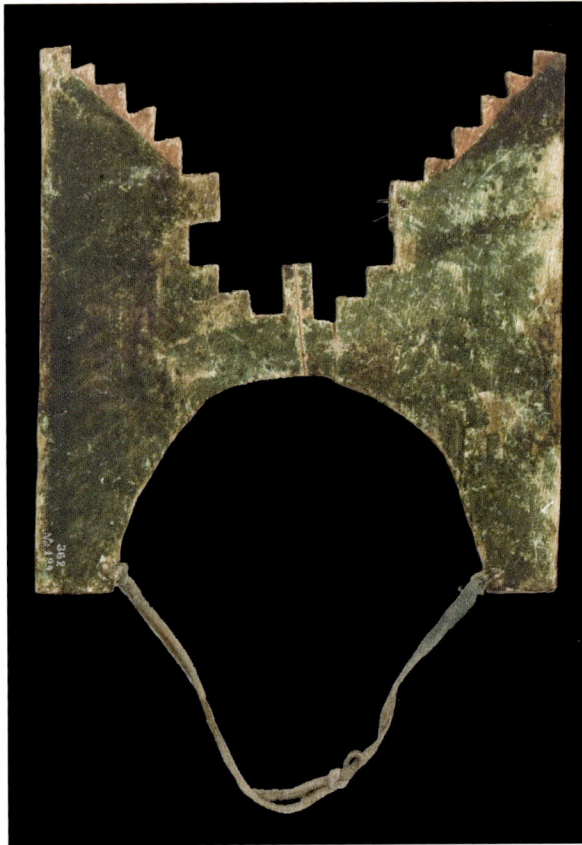

Fig. 192 San Juan Pueblo tablita headdress; cottonwood, hide, metal, pigment; h. 20 cm, w. 20 cm; ca. 1880 (RMV 362-199).

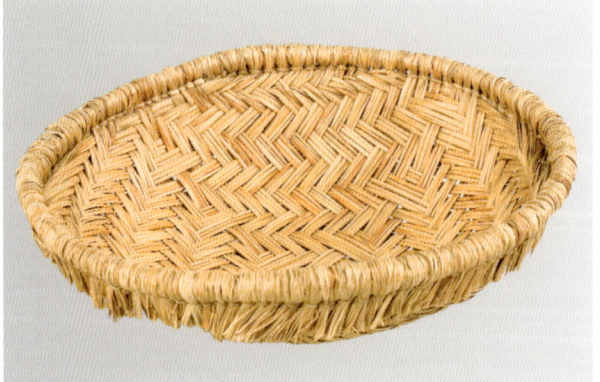

Fig. 193 Plaited ring basket from Cochiti Pueblo; sumac, yucca; d. 28 cm, h. 9 cm; ca. 1880 (RMV 362-140).

A tablita headdress collected by Ten Kate from the San Juan Pueblo dancers performing in Santa Fe (Fig. 192) is painted green on the front and back; the stepped cloud symbol is accentuated in red on both sides, while the inside is stained black. Some repairs have been made with metal wire. The straightforward design and execution, lacking decorative painting, is typical of the simple type of tablitas from the Rio Grande Pueblos. They are much rarer in museum collections, because they were not collected as intensively as the elaborate dance headgear of the Zuni and Hopi, but also because ceremonial life of the New Mexican Pueblos was more secretive than further west, thus limiting access to such ritual artifacts (Barton Wright 1976b). The Leiden specimen is one of three such objects collected by Ten Kate; two others (RMV 362-200, -201) have not survived.

In addition to the artifacts associated with various ritual dances, Ten Kate also acquired some miscellaneous objects, among them a type of basket that was made in different sizes at several Northern Rio Grande Pueblos (Fig. 193). Sumac (*Rhus*), also referred to as squaw bush, was used for the ring and yucca for the weaving. These baskets

were used to sift flour, to winnow seeds and grains, to serve food, and as containers for a variety of household utensils and personal items. In addition, wicker and coiled baskets were made in the Rio Grande Pueblos, but the craft never evolved as far as among the Hopi, because baskets were also purchased from other peoples such as the Apache, Ute, and Upland Yumans (Havasupai, Walapai). Jemez seems to have been a center for the production of plaited yucca ring baskets, but in the Rio Grande Pueblos women likewise produced these items. Typical of those made at Jemez is the rather long outward fringe below the rim (Williamson 1937a; 1937b: 11; Sando 1979: 427; Tanner 1983: 79–86; Whiteford 1988: 163–170; Bernstein et al. 2003: 66). There are two similar Hopi specimens in Ten Kate's collection (see Fig. 223, p. 166).

A model plow in the collection is carved from heavy, light-colored wood (Fig. 194). The blade thins and narrows almost into a sharp point to break the soil. It cannot be determined whether this plow was made for Ten Kate as a model or was collected as a child's toy.

During the second half of the nineteenth century anthropologists tried to classify ethnic groups on the basis of physical characteristics. Diagnostic traits included the form of skulls, skin color, shape and color of eyes, and stature. Hair could also be classified as to pigmentation, thickness, and degree of curliness. The French anthropologists Paul Broca and Paul Topinard, with whom Ten Kate studied in Paris, devised classificatory schemes for all these traits. Like his contemporary colleagues, Ten Kate took photographs en face and en profil, carried out somatological measurements, stole skulls from graves, and collected hair samples during fieldwork. He published the results of his physical anthropological research in North America in a series of articles. An endeavor by Ten Kate

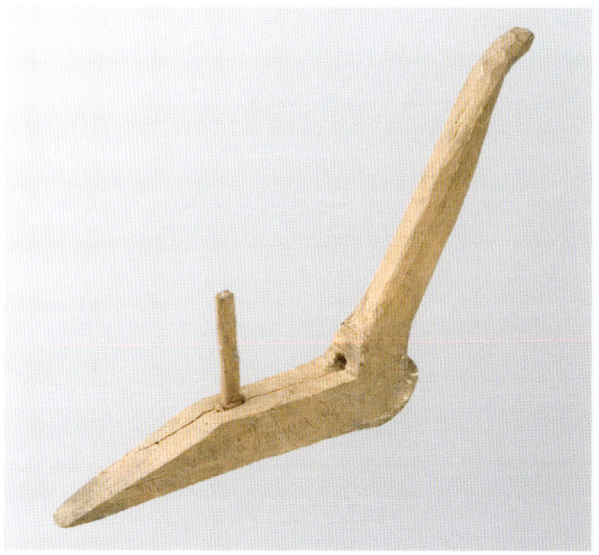

Fig. 194 Model of wooden plow, Pueblo; wood; l. 23 cm, h. 23.5 cm; ca. 1880 (RMV 362-143).

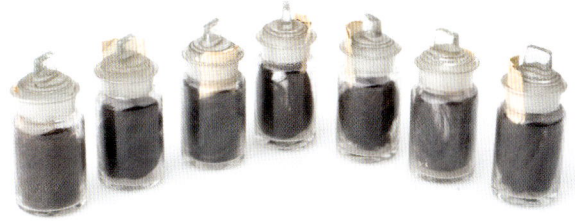

Fig. 195 Seven Indian hair samples, preserved in glass flasks; 1883 (RMV 362-210a–g).

and director Lindor Serrurier to establish a physical anthropological collection and to found an international scientific periodical entitled *Notices Anthropologiques du Musée Royal d'Ethnographie de Leyde* was short-lived because of lack of funding (e.g., Ten Kate 1917; Hovens 1989: 75–92). The record of who had provided hair samples for Ten Kate's collection (Fig. 195) has been preserved, and they were mostly Pueblo Indians from New Mexico: (a) "Hosteen Tso, Navajoe, Aged 25," (b) "Joe Navajoe, Aged 18," (c) "Pasqual Lucero, Pueblo of Sandia, Aged 7," (d) "Gonzalez H....?, Aged 8," (e) "Juandra Argin, Pueblo of Isleta, Aged 10," (f) "Francisco Abeyta, Pueblo of Isleta, 10 years," and (g) "Andres Sandoval, Pueblo de Santo Felipe, Aged 18." At Ysleta del Sur Ten Kate obtained a hair sample of Bernardo, an Indian who sold a number of artifacts to the anthropologist (Ten Kate 2004: 16, 72), but it is not known where this ended up.

Tesuque Pueblo

On 26 July 1883 Ten Kate made a trip north to Tesuque Pueblo, as he wished to gain a representative impression of a traditional Upper Rio Grande pueblo. He stayed there for two nights and in his travelogue recorded his observations: "Three rows of houses forming right angles to each other enclose a spacious plaza, which is open on the east side. These houses, built of adobe, form two terraces resting on top of each other, which are accessible by means of broad wooden ladders. The doors are small and the windows tiny. At various places on the roofs of the houses, one notices a number of ovens with the shape of large beehives. Next to them lies a pile of cakes of dry sheep dung, which serves as fuel. The houses' chimneys are of adobe but end in an *olla* from which the bottom has been tapped out. The rooms of these dwellings are, as a rule, small and low in height. In many there is a large chimney and four or five grinding stones (*metates*) in a row in wooden troughs. In addition, on the ceiling beams above the floor of the room are suspended a number of long sticks equal to a man's height, upon which articles of clothing, blankets, harnesses and weapons are suspended. A number of sheep skins and blankets lie on the ground—this is the sleeping area. Further, a number of pots of painted clay and a couple of baskets are the sum total of native domestic utensils. Red peppers and watermelons can be found in practically every dwelling. In many dwellings I found pictures of Catholic saints' and colorful, ugly prints with Biblical scenes, which the owners displayed with a certain pride" ´(Ten Kate 2004: 232).

The Tewa of Tesuque were agriculturists and tilled their fields of corn and watermelons situated around the pueblo with wooden plows, drawn by a team of oxen. Massive wooden oxcarts with large creaking and squeaking wheels served to haul harvests. The Indians constructed these themselves, using wooden pegs and untanned leather straps. In addition, they had flocks of sheep and goats that grazed beyond and were driven into corrals to spend the night.

After having become familiar with the pottery of the Zuni and Hopi, Tesuque pottery impressed Ten Kate little. The Tesuque ware was generally of a light gray or cream color and sometimes reddish-brown. Part of the pottery showed a glittering of mica, which was contained in some of the clay deposits in the area. Small items could also be glossy black. The traditional ollas, the water storage jars, showed some craftsmanship. The designs were applied in

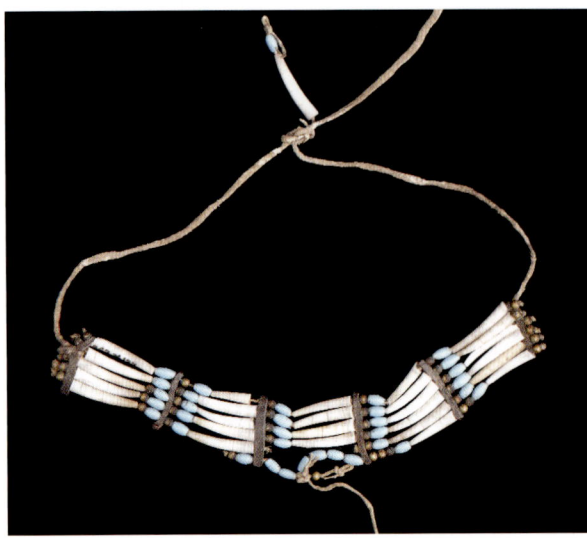

Fig. 196 Choker from Tesuque Pueblo; shells, brass and glass beads, leather; l. of shell panels 21 cm, w. 2.5 cm; ca. 1880 (RMV 362-127).

black and included a variety of wavy lines, meandering figures, and arabesques, set off clearly against the light background. The anthropologist found the animal effigy vessels, often representing birds, grotesque and even monstrous. Other figures were of dancers and clowns who figured prominently in their dances. At Picuris he purchased several pottery figurines.

On 1 August 1883 Ten Kate was back in Santa Fe, where he made the acquaintance of Professor Almon H. Thompson, a brother-in-law of Major John Wesley Powell. Thompson was heading a topographical survey in northeastern Arizona on the Navajo reservation and invited Ten Kate to pay the expedition a visit. The Dutchman gladly accepted and on 3 August he departed from Albuquerque on the Atcheson, Topeka & Santa Fe Railroad. However, before embarking on fieldwork on the extensive Navajo reservation, Ten Kate took the opportunity to visit Tesuque Pueblo again.

Chokers of hair pipe beads and shells with bead spacing were common among the Pueblo Indians (Fig. 196). Shell was especially valued as it was rare, a natural material obtained through trade from the Pacific or Gulf of California coast. This choker consists mainly of *Dentalium* shells. Hair pipes in Pueblo jewelry testify to Plains influence (Jeancon and Douglas 1931; Ford 1983: 713, 719).

The turquoise beads Ten Kate collected from San Juan Pueblo (RMV 362-147) are missing. They were worked and used to be part of a necklace.

Plain pottery vessels first appeared in the American Southwest around A.D. 200. By Pueblo I times (A.D. 700),

a variety of shapes and sizes were in use, reflecting an increasingly settled life based on the cultivation of corn, beans, and squash. Vessels were decorated with geometric designs using vegetal and mineral paints. Regional styles became widespread in the Classic Pueblo period (A.D. 1200), with distinctive traditions centered at Mesa Verde, Chaco Canyon, and Kayenta. Trade networks existed for both raw materials and finished products.

Immediately prior to the arrival of the Spanish in 1540, lead-based glaze paints were used in the Rio Grande region to decorate pots. When the Spanish took over the lead mines, the Indians returned to the use of matte-painted pottery during the long period of turmoil leading up to the Pueblo Revolt of 1680, when the Spanish were expelled. When they returned in 1692, they were more tolerant of Native customs and the Indians returned to their pueblos and soon developed distinctive village pottery styles that are recognized today.

With the opening of the Santa Fe Trail in 1821 and the arrival of the railroad in 1880, the Indians came under American influence. Pottery arts declined due to the availability of utility wares through the traders. Some villages stopped making pottery completely. By 1880 several groups were taking advantage of the tourist trade by producing figurines, miniature pots, and other wares for sale to outsiders. This continued into the late 1920s and 1930s, when the transcontinental highway, Route 66, passed through the Southwest connecting Chicago with Los Angeles.

At the same time the arts were deteriorating through the manufacture of items for the tourist trade, Edgar Lee Hewett and his associates operating out of the Museum of New Mexico and the School of American Research began discouraging what he considered to be inferior products and encouraging a renaissance of "traditional" arts. Hewett established the Indian Fair as an outlet for good work for sale to outsiders. This has led to a florescence of the arts as expressed in today's Santa Fe Indian Market.

Due in part to their proximity to Santa Fe, villagers from Tesuque Pueblo were active in the production of items for the tourist market beginning around 1870. In addition to traditional decorated black-on-cream pottery, they also produced a variety of figurines and animal effigies made of micaceous clay or slipped with a micaceous clay slip. Working in collaboration with Santa Fe traders, Tesuque potters also produced so-called clay idols that roughly paralleled the hollow figurine tradition that developed simultaneously at Santo Domingo Pueblo. The clay idols evolved into a series of smaller and more portable

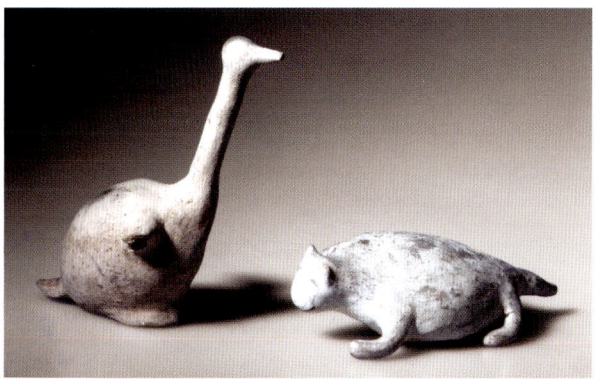

Fig. 197 Animal effigies, Tesuque Pueblo; RMV 362-144: pottery, cream slip; h. 12 cm, l. 10 cm, w. 9 cm; RMV 362-145: pottery, cream slip; l. 14 cm, h. 4 cm, w. 9 cm; both 1883.

"gods" that were sold in large quantities via the railroad and through mail order catalogs across the United States. There were gods of war, gods of pain, and gods of rain, among others. The rain gods eventually gained popularity over the others and formed a tradition of manufacture at the pueblo which continues to the present day. In the 1920s Tesuque artists began using bright colors of poster paint applied after firing. It was as popular with tourists as it was unpopular within the academic and museum communities, who favored "more traditional" art forms and condemned the brightly colored pots and rain gods as "tourist junk." Today pottery wares are still produced for the tourist market at Tesuque. Artists have shifted away from poster paints to the use of earlier plain micaceous and decorated cream-slipped forms (Anderson 2002, Fogelman Lange 2002, Batkin 1998, 1999a).

Of the two animal figures Ten Kate obtained at Tesuque, one is a goose effigy with long neck and out-stretched wings (Fig. 197 left). One wing tip and the front of the beak are damaged. The effigy stands on a footed base similar to that used on pottery vessels influenced by Spanish design. The object is but one of many examples of animal figurines made for the tourist trade from 1870 until about 1920.

The other figure is a horned toad effigy, probably the northern subspecies of *Phrynosoma platyrhinos*, the Desert Horned Toad (Fig. 197 right). Although horned toads were common to the Tesuque Pueblo region in the nineteenth and early twentieth centuries, they were seldom incorporated into Native art. "Animalitos" produced at the turn of the century include dogs, bears, and pigs. One leg extremity of this specimen is missing, while two others have been restored.

Effigies of people, animals, and gods have a long tradition in Pueblo ceramics since A.D. 300, probably as part of fertility rituals in societies struggling against all odds to survive in the semiarid desert by practicing horticulture. They are known from Casas Grandes, Chaco Canyon, and elsewhere in the Southwest. The Spanish were probably responsible for the repression of such expressions of religious beliefs, explaining their virtual absence from the archaeological record since 1500. However, by the fourth quarter of the nineteenth century figurative Pueblo ceramics once again appeared and were produced in ever increasing numbers due to demand from the emerging tourist market (Babcock 1987).

The exact identity of a male human figure in Ten Kate's collection (Fig. 198) remains in doubt. It could represent a warrior with the round shield on his back, the war cap, gun and spear, and leggings. However, equally possible is its interpretation as a circus figure, possibly a juggler, because of the pointed hat, flaring trousers, juggling paraphernalia, and gaudy orange-red color of dress and facial paint. Indians occasionally obtained rare glimpses of the

Fig. 198 Human figure, Tesuque Pueblo; micaceous pottery, pigment; h. 13.2 cm; 1883 (RMV 362-146).

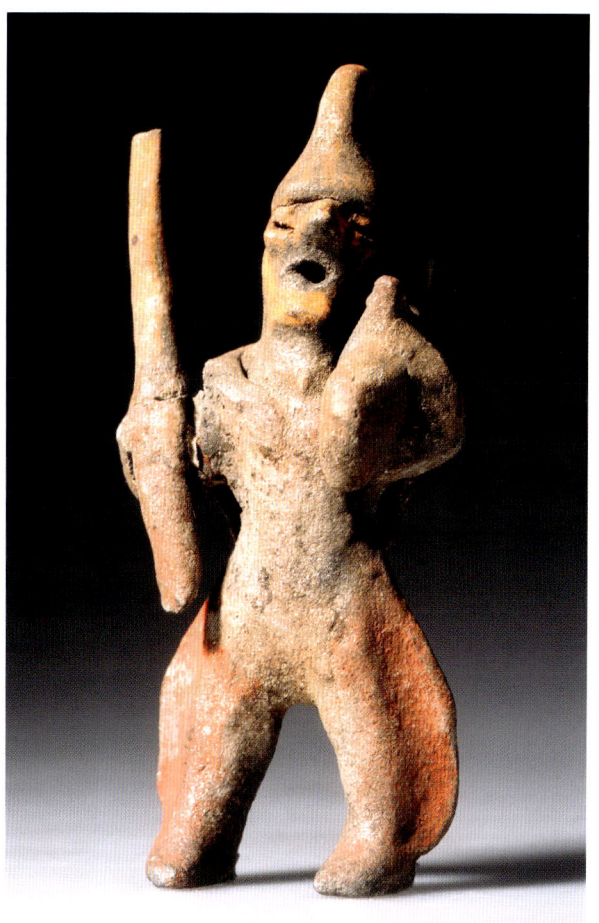

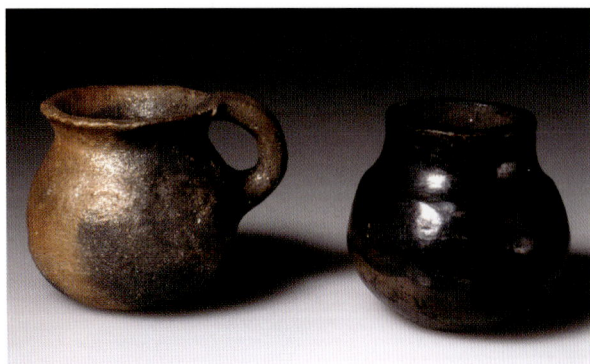

Fig. 199   Miniature jars; RMV 2012-5: from Picuris or Tesuque Pueblo; pottery; h. 5.6 cm, w. 6.2 cm (with handle); RMV 2012-7: from Tesuque or Santa Clara; micaceous pottery; d. 6.5 cm, h. 6 cm; both 1883.

outside world through circus acts that traveled through the region. However, Pueblo ceramic figures often manifest a combination of elements from their own society and the unfamiliar outside world. Figurines produced both at Tesuque and Santo Domingo pueblos interpreted outsiders including priests, cowboys, and merchants, in addition to figures like the one illustrated here. Outsiders often purchased early figurines believing they were religious objects, "clay idols," when in fact they were often parodies revealing the Native view of outsiders or figures suggested by White traders catering to popular ideas about and imagery of Indians in Anglo-American society (Batkin 1998, 1999a; Batkin 1999b; Falkenstein-Doyle 1999; Fogelman Lange 2002; Bernstein 2005: 38–39, 80, 95; cf. Fane 1991: 118).

Clay rich with mica was commonly used in northern New Mexico to make cooking pots because of its ability to withstand thermal shock from repeated use over open

fire. It was commonly used by all of the Northern Rio Grande pueblos beginning ca. 1300 and continued to be popular until ca. 1900, when its use was suspended in all but Taos and Picuris Pueblos. Today there has been a resurgence of interest in micaceous clay, and it is used by a variety of groups for utilitarian purposes as well as the production of figurines and art pottery (Anderson 1999). The clay used for RMV 2012-5 with loop handle contains much mica, and the surface exhibits fireclouds (Fig. 199).

Black wares (Tewa Polished Black) were common to all Northern Rio Grande pueblos after ca. 1300 (cf. Stevenson 1883a: figs. 656–659, 660–672; 1883b: 443–447; Batkin 1987: 36, 40, 66, 69, 75–76). In addition, villages had polychrome, black-on-white, micaceous, corrugated, and plain wares, all for different purposes including storage, cooking, serving, and ceremonial use. The manufacture of black pottery died out in most pueblos early in the twentieth century. However, black wares have received a good deal of revived attention at Santa Clara and San Ildefonso since the 1920s, when Maria and Julian Martinez (San Ildefonso) began making their famous black-on-black art pottery.

The unique tan, unpolished, and enigmatic animal whistle in the Ten Kate collection, possibly inspired by a camel as seen in a circus, appears to be made of Tesuque clay (Fig. 200). It illustrates the variety of objects and effigies made for the tourist trade. Such objects were probably inspired by Santa Fe traders, who were constantly looking for items of interest to railroad travelers (cf. Gratz 1976, Batkin 1998, 1999a).

Fig. 200   Plain ware animal effigy whistle, probably from Tesuque; pottery, pigment; l. 7.3 cm, h. 5 cm; ca. 1883 (RMV 2012-6).

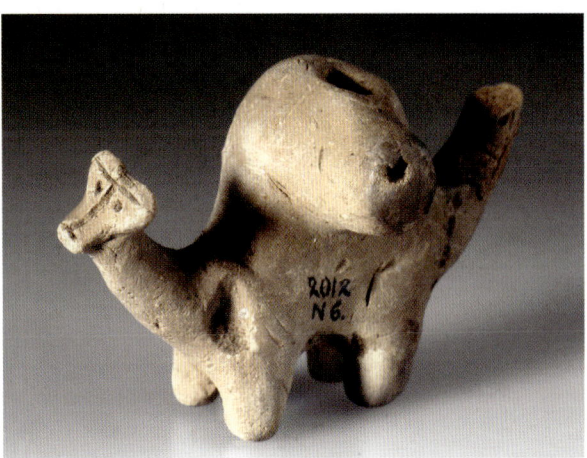

References

Anderson, Duane
1999   (ed.) *All that Glitters: The Emergence of Native American Micaceous Art Pottery in Northern New Mexico*. Santa Fe, NM: School of American Research Press.
2002   *When Rain Gods Reigned*. Santa Fe, NM: Museum of New Mexico Press.

Babcock, Barbara A.
1987   Those, They Called them Monos: Cochiti Figurative Ceramics, 1875–1905. *American Indian Art Magazine* 12(4): 50–57, 67.

Baldwin, Stuart J.
1997   *Apacheans Bearing Gifts: Prehispanic Influence on the Pueblo Indians*. The Arizona Archaeologist 29. Phoenix, AZ.

Batkin, Jonathan
1987   *Pottery of the Pueblos of New Mexico, 1700–1940*. Colorado Springs, CO: Taylor Museum of Anthropology.

1998   Some Early Curio Dealers of New Mexico. *American Indian Art Magazine* 23(3): 68–81.

1999a   Tourism is Overrated: Pueblo Pottery and the Early Curio Trade, 1880–1910. In: Ruth B. Phillips and Christopher B. Steiner (eds.), *Unpacking Culture: Art and Commodity in Colonial and Postcolonial Worlds* (Berkeley, CA: University of California Press), 282–300.

1999b   (ed.) *Clay People: Pueblo Indian Figurative Traditions.* Santa Fe, NM: Wheelwright Museum of the American Indian.

Bernstein, Bruce

2005   The Southwestern United States: Continuity and Change. In: Ramiro Matos et al., *Born of Clay: Ceramics from the National Museum of the American Indian* (Washington, DC: National Museum of the American Indian), 35–43.

Bernstein, Bruce et al.

2003   *The Language of Native American Baskets: From the Weavers' View.* Washington, DC: National Museum of the American Indian.

Bolz, Peter and Hans-Ulrich Sanner

1999   *Native American Art: The Collections of the Ethnological Museum Berlin.* Berlin: G+H Verlag.

Bronitsky, Gordon

1987   Indian Assimilation in the El Paso Area. *New Mexico Historical Review* 62(2): 151–168.

Brown, Donald N.

1967   The Distribution of Sound Instruments in the Prehistoric Southwestern United States. *Ethnomusicology* 11(1): 71–90.

Champe, Flavia Waters

1983   *The Matachinas Dance of the Upper Rio Grande.* Lincoln, NE: University of Nebraska Press.

Densmore, Frances

1938   *Music of Santo Domingo Pueblo, New Mexico.* Southwest Museum Papers 12. Los Angles, CA.

Douglas, Frederic H.

1939a   *Weaving in the Tewa Pueblos.* Denver Art Museum Leaflets 90. Denver, CO.

1939b   *Weaving of the Keres Pueblos, the Tiwa Pueblos and Jemez.* Denver Art Museum Leaflets 91. Denver, CO.

1940a   *Main Types of Pueblo Cotton Textiles.* Denver Art Museum Leaflets 92–93. Denver, CO.

1940b   *Main Types of Pueblo Woolen Textiles.* Denver Art Museum Leaflets 94–95. Denver, CO.

Dozier, Edward P.

1970   *The Pueblo Indians of North America.* New York, NY: Holt, Rinehart and Winston.

Dumarest, Father Noël

1919   *Notes on Cochiti.* Elsie C. Parsons ed. Memoirs of the American Anthropological Association 6(3). Lancaster, PA.

Eickhoff, Randy Lee

1996   *Exiled: The Tigua Indians of Ysleta del Sur.* Plano, TX: Republic of Texas Press.

Ellis, Bruce T.

1958   Santa Fe's Tertio-Millennial. *El Palacio* 65(4): 121–135.

Falkenstein-Doyle, Cheri

1999   Cochiti Ceramic Figures, 1880–1915: Possible Sources of Inspiration. *American Indian Art Magazine* 24(4): 38–47.

Fane, Diana

1991   (ed.) *Objects of Myth and Memory: American Indian Art at the Brooklyn Museum.* New York, NY: The Brooklyn Museum.

Fewkes, Jesse Walter

1902   The Pueblo Settlements near El Paso. *American Anthropologist* 4(1): 57–72.

Fogelman Lange, Patricia

2002   *Pueblo Pottery Figures: The Expression of Cultural Perceptions in Clay.* Albuquerque, NM: University of New Mexico Press.

Ford, Richard I.

1983   Inter-Indian Exchange in the Southwest. In: Alfonso Ortiz (ed.), *Southwest* (W. C. Sturtevant, gen. ed.; Handbook of North American Indians 10. Washington, DC: Smithsonian Institution), 711–722.

Fox, Nancy

1978   *Pueblo Weaving and Textile Arts.* Santa Fe, NM: Museum of New Mexico Press.

Gratz, Kathleen

1976   Origins of the Tesuque Rain God. *El Palacio* 82(3): 3–8.

Houser, Nicholas P.

1970   The Tigua Settlement of Ysleta del Sur. *The Kiva* 36(2): 23–39.

1979   Tigua Pueblo. In: Alfonso Ortiz (ed.), *Southwest* (W. C. Sturtevant, gen. ed.; Handbook of North American Indians 9. Washington, DC: Smithsonian Institution), 336–342.

Hovens, Pieter

1989   *Herman F. C. ten Kate (1858–1931) en de antropologie der Noord Amerikaanse Indianen* (Herman F. C. ten Kate and the Anthropology of the North American Indians). Meppel: Krips. [Ph.D. thesis, University of Nijmegen.]

Hurt, Wesley R.

1952   Tortugas: An Indian Village in Southern New Mexico. *El Palacio* 59: 104–122.

Jeancon, J. A. and F. H. Douglas

1930   *Pueblo Indian Clothing.* Denver Art Museum Leaflets 4. Denver, CO.

1931   *Pueblo Beads and Inlay.* Denver Art Museum Leaflets 30. Denver, CO.

Kent, Kate Peck

1983   *Pueblo Indian Textiles: A Living Tradition.* Santa Fe, NM: School of American Research Press.

Kurath, Gertrude P.

1957   Origin of the Pueblo Indian Matachinas. *El Palacio* 64(9–10): 259–263.

1958   Plaza Circuits of Tewa Indian Dancers. *El Palacio* 65(1): 16–26.

Kurath, Gertrude P. and Antonio Garcia

1970   *Music and Dance of the Tewa Pueblos.* Santa Fe, NM: Museum of New Mexico Press.

Lange, Charles H.
1957   Tablita or Corn Dance of the Rio Grande Pueblos. *Texas Journal of Science* 9(10): 39-74.

1979a   Cochiti Pueblo. In: Alfonso Ortiz (ed.), *Southwest* (W. C. Sturtevant, gen. ed.; Handbook of North American Indians 9. Washington, DC: Smithsonian Institution), 366-378.

1979b   Santo Domingo Pueblo. In: Alfonso Ortiz (ed.), *Southwest* (W. C. Sturtevant, gen. ed.; Handbook of North American Indians 9. Washington, DC: Smithsonian Institution), 379-389.

Laski, Vera
1959   *Seeking Life*. Memoirs of the American Folklore Society 50. Philadelphia, PA.

Lea, Aurora Lucero-White
1964   More about the Matachinas. *New Mexico Folklore Record* 11: 7-10.

McAllester, David P.
1961   *Indian Music in the Southwest*. Colorado Springs, CO: The Taylor Museum.

Ortiz, Alfonso
1969   *The Tewa World: Space, Time, Being, and Becoming in a Pueblo Society*. Chicago, IL: University of Chicago Press.

Parmentier, Richard J.
1979   The Mythological Triangle: Poseyemu, Montezuma, and Jesus in the Pueblos. In: Alfonso Ortiz (ed.), *Southwest* (W. C. Sturtevant, gen. ed.; Handbook of North American Indians 9. Washington, DC: Smithsonian Institution), 609-622.

Parsons, Elsie Clews
1939   *Pueblo Indian Religion*. 2 vols. Chicago, IL: University of Chicago Press.

Parsons, Elsie Clews and Ralph Beals
1934   The Sacred Clowns of the Pueblo and Mayo-Yaqui Indians. *American Anthropologist* 36(4): 491-514.

Robb, J. Donald
1961   The Matachines Dance: A Ritual Folk Dance. *Western Folklore* 20(2): 87-101.

Roberts, Don. L.
1980   A Calendar of Eastern Pueblo Indian Ritual Dramas. In: Charlotte J. Frisbie (ed.), *Southwestern Indian Ritual Drama* (Albuquerque, NM: University of New Mexico Press), 103-124.

Rodriguez, Sylvia
1996   *The Matachines Dance: Ritual Symbolism and Interethnic Relations in the Upper Rio Grande Valley*. Albuquerque, NM: University of New Mexico Press.

Roediger, Virginia Moore
1941   *Ceremonial Costumes of the Pueblo Indians: Their Evolution, Fabrication, and Significance in the Prayer Drama*. Berkeley, CA–Los Angeles, CA: University of California Press.

Saldaña, Nancy H.
1966   La Malinche: Her Representation in Dances of Mexico and the Unites States. *Ethnomusicology* 10(3): 298-309.

Sando, Joe S.
1979   Jemez Pueblo. In: Alfonso Ortiz (ed.), *Southwest* (W. C. Sturtevant, gen. ed.; Handbook of North American Indians 9. Washington, DC: Smithsonian Institution), 418-429.

Stevenson, James
1883a   Illustrated Catalogue of the Collections Obtained from the Indians of New Mexico and Arizona in 1879. *Annual Report of the Bureau of American Ethnology* 2: 311-428.

1883b   Illustrated Catalogue of the Collections Obtained from the Indians of New Mexico in 1880. *Annual Report of the Bureau of American Ethnology* 2: 429-465.

Sweet, Jill D.
1985   *Dances of the Tewa Pueblo Indians*. Santa Fe, NM: School of American Research Press.

Tanner, Clara Lee
1983   *Indian Baskets of the Southwest*. Tucson, AZ: University of Arizona Press.

Ten Kate, Herman
1917   Mélanges Anthropologiques: Indiens de l'Amérique du Nord. *L'Anthropologie* 28: 129-155, 369-401.

1885   *Reizen en Onderzoekingen in Noord Amerika*. Leiden: E. J. Brill.

2004   *Travels and Researches in Native North America, 1882-1883*. P. Hovens, L. A. Hieb, and W. J. Orr eds. Albuquerque, NM: University of New Mexico Press. [Translation of Ten Kate 1885.]

Thompson, Judy
1977   *The North American Indian Collection: A Catalogue*. Berne: Berne Historical Museum.

Whiteford, Andrew Hunter
1988   *Southwestern Indian Baskets: Their History and Their Makers*. Santa Fe, NM: School of American Research Press.

Williamson, Ten Broeck
1937a   The Jemez Yucca Ring-Basket. *Indians at Work* 5(2): 33-35.

1937b   Bread: A Story in Pictures of Wheat Culture at Jemez Pueblo. *Indians at Work* 5(4): 7-14.

Wright, Barton
1976a   *Pueblo Shields from the Fred Harvey Fine Arts Collection*. Flagstaff, AZ: Northland Press.

1976b   Tabletas: A Pueblo Art. *American Indian Art Magazine* 1(3): 56-65.

1979   *Hopi Material Culture: Artifacts Gathered by H. R. Voth in the Fred Harvey Collection*. Flagstaff, AZ–Phoenix, AZ: Northland Press–Heard Museum.

Wright, Bill
1993   *The Tiguas: Pueblo Indians of Texas*. El Paso, TX: Texas Western Press.

The Hopi:
People of the Mesas

8

Doing fieldwork on the Navajo Reservation in the summer of 1883, Ten Kate learned that the Hopi would perform their Snake dance on 13 August. To witness this major sacred Native ritual which was only performed every other year, the anthropologist set out to Black Mesa from Fort Defiance, accompanied by Professor A. H. Thompson, naval officer Marsh, and a Navajo guide. They spent a night at Keam's Canyon, where they were joined by the prominent Indian trader Thomas Varker Keam, who guided the small party to First Mesa.

Ten Kate graphically recounts his impressions of the Hopi villages: "Before long, high rocky walls rise up ahead of us in the distance, and only when we have nearly reached the foot of the steep rocks do we discern the terrace-shaped houses and ladders of a pueblo, while dark figures are moving about on the roofs and along the edge of the mesa. One moment we ride under the shade of a peach tree orchard, then we cautiously climb the narrow winding path hewn out of sandstone rocks, which eventually lands us in Tehua. Here we unsaddled our horses and took up quarters in the dwelling of an Indian friend of Mr. Keam. Before the snake dance began at 4 o'clock, we had some time to orient ourselves and take an excursion through the pueblo."

"We found ourselves on a sandstone mesa about 600 feet high, running roughly from north to south, which with its yellowish-white, bare walls rose perpendicularly above the plain. A lifeless, drab desert extended as far as the eye could see. In the Southwest along the distant horizon glistened the snow-covered peaks of the San Francisco Mountains. In between, though more to the south, at a distance of six or seven miles arise the high mesas, on which the villages Moshóngnavé, Shepálavé, and Shongápavé are perched like eagles' nests. In the sandflats between our vantage point and the aforementioned pueblos skimpy cornfields and small clusters of sunflowers extend outward. The Moqui Buttes, a group of cathedral- and pyramid-shaped sandstone colossi, broke up the endless

plain, which rolled toward the south. Moreover, this was a series of mesas—once the shores of a sea—which bounded the horizon to the East and the North. A blue, fixed sky vaulted over the landscape, the image of which remains indelibly imprinted on my mind."

"Three pueblos are located on the mesa where we were staying: Tehua, Setshómové, and Hualpé. The last-named is the southernmost and largest of the three and is situated somewhat apart from the other two. Setshómové is the middle one and the smallest, and is located in close proximity to Tehua. The terrace-shaped architecture and the tiny rooms of the houses, the low doors and narrow windows, the wooden ladders and the pale, ash-gray color pervading everything—all this recalls the other pueblos. The distinctive feature of the Moqui villages, though, is their lofty, secluded location. What may have motivated a people to settle on these barren rocky cliffs, where they must arduously fetch water and food from below, in a region which is one of the most arid in the Southwest? Probably it was the sense of security in the midst of hostile tribes, with whom their forefathers had to contend as well, just as they do today with the Navajos and Apaches. The residents of Tehua are proof of an exodus which occurred in historic times ..." (Ten Kate 2004: 247–249).

In Walpi Ten Kate encountered Dr. Jeremiah Sullivan, the son of the Hopi Indian Agent. A trained physician, Sullivan had settled among the Hopi at Sichomovi on First Mesa in 1881 and had become involved in studying their language and customs. The Indians called him *Oyiwisha*, 'He Who Plants Corn.' Because of their similar interest, the men soon bonded, and Sullivan became Ten Kate's guide and interpreter during his stay.

Religion: Kachinas and the Snake Dance

Ten Kate continued his narrative: "We make the round over the entire mesa and enter many dwellings, everywhere welcomed with hearty laughter. Repeatedly we bump our heads going in, and the tallest of us can barely stand upright in the rooms. Just like Tesuque and Laguna, here, too, we encounter the slanting row of grinding stones in wooden troughs, numerous baskets and basketry plaques, pottery, woolen blankets, sheepskins, and rabbit fur blankets. Not infrequently we encounter colorfully painted wooden dolls with grotesque faces and strange head coverings. Sometimes a row of these deformed images is suspended on a cord stretched above the chimney or elsewhere in the apartment. Sometimes some of them are also lying on the floor; and one of my comrades ventures the observation that the Moquis do not have a very reverent relationship with their household gods, treating them this way. Here he erred just like ... others. The so-called household gods are nothing more than models of persons from the corn dance—a child's toy. The Moqui name for these dolls is *dicha* ('ch' aspirated). The mere fact that a Moqui, with the greatest willingness, relinquishes one or more of these *dichas* to you in return for a quarter is enough to demonstrate the erroneousness of this opinion."

"In every room hangs a so-called 'breath-feather,' a downy little feather, which is regarded as a lucky charm. At the same time, like the feathers of the prayer sticks, it is some sort of emblem—more about this soon. Frequently we find carefully closed small bundles of leather hanging on the wall. These are dance paraphernalia—sacred items. Just touch them and ask them whether they would like to sell, then you will see at once whether they treat them like their 'household gods,' the *dichas*. An unwilling, pained expression suddenly comes to the owner's face, a gesture of refusal with the hand, at best a 'no quiero' (I don't want to), which he utters with a tone whose meaning is unequivocal—and you know exactly where you stand" (Ten Kate 2004: 249).

With Sullivan Ten Kate visited a kiva, a rectangular structure, partially built underground, and used as a workplace by the men and as a ceremonial chamber during ritual events. The men descended the ladder into the room and Ten Kate related the event as follows: "Having arrived below, I encountered a row of hideously painted Indians sitting along the wall in the small oblong, square room, busily putting the final touches to their dance toilette. Above their heads were suspended eagle feathers, fox hides, rattles, tortoise shells, and other necessities with which they, the priests of the Order of the Serpent, will initiate the dance later. In a corner lay a heap of live snakes, incessantly writhing about, which are kept under

control by an Indian waving a bundle of feathers. In the middle of the kiva stood a clay basin, filled with a pale brown liquid which had an astringent taste and with a large white seashell, serving as a drinking bowl, floating on top of it. This liquid was an antidote for snakebite, which the priests had been drinking for four days while fasting. The discontented expression appearing on the faces of some priests after my appearance in the kiva and the time already far-advanced, which meant that the dance should soon start, prompted us to leave the room and take our place on the flat roof of a house on the east side of Walpi, where we could have a good view of the dance" (Ten Kate 2004: 249-250).

From Thomas V. Keam Ten Kate learned the origin legend of the Snake dance, as related to the Indian trader by one of the Hopi chiefs: "A very long time ago there was a beloved chief of the Moquis who, returning from far distant journeys, had brought home his lovely bride from another tribe. The Moqui women, envious that an outsider had won the heart of the bravest and wisest of all Moqui warriors, were relentless in devising ways of hectoring and inflicting insults to make the poor woman's life miserable. Too proud to complain, she brought a brood of poisonous snakes into the world, immune to the arrows and clubs of the Moquis, who killed their children and women, forcing the survivors to flee to another land. Finally, a huge snake delivered them from their dreadful pursuers by slaying them and directed the Moquis to live in the land they now possess, at the same time admonishing them henceforth to live in peace with their natural companions, the snakes. In gratitude for their deliverance, the Moquis initiated the snake dance as a religious ceremony and since that time have never killed a snake" (Ten Kate 2004: 250). According to Ten Kate, the core meaning of the Snake dance was more existential, a communal prayer for rain, the life-giving force that made their corn, squashes, and peach trees grow and bear sustenance in their precarious desert environment.

Ten Kate gave the following account of the Snake dance he observed: "... the dance took place on the eastern side of Hualpé at the edge of the mesas, where a roughly twenty foot-high sandstone column, which had defied the gnawing ravages of water and time, rises up. Near this column a dense shelter of green cottonwood branches was erected. In the shelter more than a hundred snakes were sprawled out for the priests to keep an eye on. A dense throng of spectators from both sexes and every age had gathered in an extended circle along the mesa and along the roofs of the houses. Among the many who had thronged there from afar were a number of Navajos as well, and some shabby frontiersmen, prospectors, and cowboys."

"Before long we hear a rattling noise, and a row of more than twenty Indians, walking one after another, emerge from the kiva. All are unclad except for their breech clout and a fox hide hanging down from behind over their hips. On their feet they wear beautifully ornamented leather moccasins. A wreath of cottonwood leaves adorns their heads. Their faces are painted white and black, the trunk pink, the arms and legs dark-brown. In the right hand they hold a white rattle in the form of a 'T,' in the left a bundle of eagle feathers. A tortoise shell is fastened under the right knee, together with a number of deer and antelope hooves, which make a peculiar hollow rattling noise whenever they move around. There are eight boys in the row. Up front moves an Indian, who with his right hand whirls around a leather sling, humming, while in his left hand he holds a finely ornamented bow. Behind him moves a second medicine man firmly grasping a clay bowl with water, from which he sprinkles water on the ground now and then using a bunch of feathers. With nimble gait they all move around in a circle, while the medicine man with the water has positioned himself in the middle. Then they gather next to each other on both sides of the shelter."

"Immediately afterwards, a second row of serpent priests, roughly thirty in number, appears, attired almost like the previous ones, but without garlands of leaves and without rattles, while on their heads they wear feathers dyed red. They, too, move around in a circle repeated times and then gather next to each other, facing the first row. In plaintive tone they strike up a gentle chant, at the same time waving their feather bundles up and down and stomping rhythmically with their right feet."

"After this scene has gone on for awhile, the latest row arriving divides up into small groups of three, which halt by the shelter, one after the other. A moment later one of them, who is partly stooped over, emerges from there again with a writhing serpent, which he holds crosswise in his mouth. One of the dancers now places his right arm around the neck of the one holding the snake, while, using his left hand which is armed with a bundle of feathers, he continually fondles the snake's head and keeps it turned away from his companion's face. The last person from the group of three gathers behind these two dancers who, in a crouching position, stick their upper bodies outward, moving along in the circle, leaping and stomping. Before

long there are ten of these groups moving about, which over and over put fresh snakes in their mouths until the supply is exhausted and everyone is loaded up with several snakes in the mouth and hands. Every now and then a snake drops to the ground. Now they try to slither away and escape between the rows of spectators, thereby creating a commotion; but the Navajos have their thick blankets with them which, cleverly, they suddenly drop at the spot the snake is escaping to, thus heading them off. Then they rear up again—eyes glittering, the forked tongue darting with lightning speed, the tail rattling—ready to strike their death-dealing fangs into the flesh of their attackers. But the fluttering eagle feathers of the priests work wonders. They seem to cast a spell as they whiz right past the monster's head so that a moment later they can be taken up without warning in a nimble grip to be led around once more, impotently twisting and writhing inside the row of dancers."

"A number of women, grouped in two rows, are continually scattering sacred corn flour on the ground, which must charm the snakes, too. The medicine man has been standing in the middle all this time, sprinkling water and chanting slowly, assisted by the priests with leaf garlands, who alternately put their right foot forward and backwards, their bodies gently bobbing up and down."

"The longer the ceremony lasts, the more excited the dancers become. Their eyes radiate wild abandon. Their movements become more violent and savage. Their sweat mingles with the garish colors of their naked torsos and—shrieking, and yelling, and heaving—they jump around. One completely loses track of things. Breathless and tense, one gazes upon a scene, which in dismal savagery knows no equal. One could shout from savage delight, but suddenly the enchantment gives way. With the white flour the women delineate a large circle on the ground and divide it into four segments. Immediately thereafter the dancers toss all the snakes together in a heap inside the circle, while at the same moment all the spectators spit on the ground, 'so not to take the snake venom into their bodies and hence swell up'—as Oyiwisha informs me. Now a moment of indescribable confusion ensues. The snake dancers suddenly assault the heap of snakes slithering in hundreds of coils, take as many as they can carry in their hands, and run with their dangerous burden, as fast as their legs can carry them, down the mesa in all four directions to grant the snakes their liberty once more in the rocky plain. Long before sundown everything is over, as the rite indeed prescribes" (Ten Kate 2004: 250-252).

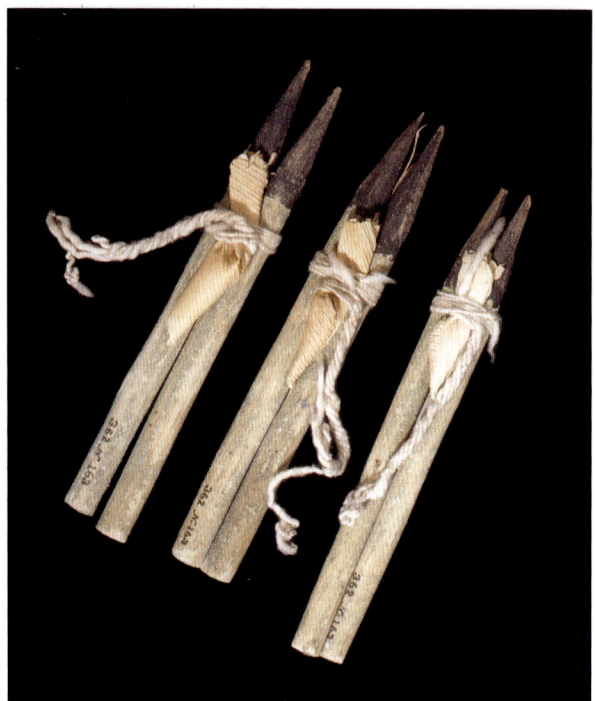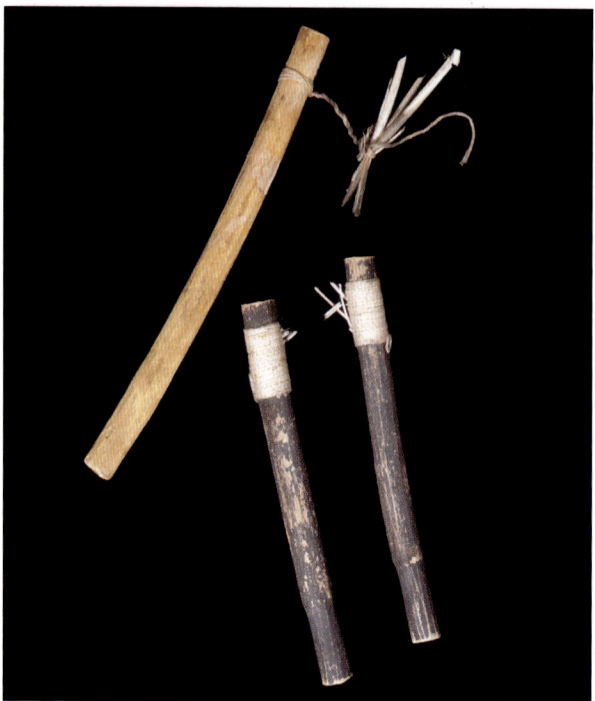

Figs. 201, 202 Hopi prayer sticks; *tci'tolakwe awa telhl, awan awa ne kwe, teli-ki-naatchi* (TK); RMV 362-163: willow, pigment, corn husk, cotton, feathers; l. 13.5 cm; RMV 682-6: wood, pigment, feathers, cotton; l. 12.5–16 cm; all 1883.

Prayer Sticks

Prayer sticks, called *paahos* by the Hopi, the generic term referring to 'praying for water,' come in a great variety of shapes and sizes, depending on their specific use and maker. The making of some types is restricted to members of specific societies; some types are only used in certain ceremonies or for special purposes. Each type is distinct in material, composition, color, design, and name, made according to prescribed rules set out by the chief kachinas. They are offerings to the kachinas, prayers requesting general or specific benefits for the people. Most prayer sticks have a turkey feather, but adding a bundle of turkey feathers makes them a prayer for game. Adding a duck feather turns the stick into a prayer for rain; an owl feather added means a prayer for warm weather to assure a good harvest of peaches. Grass stems added to a stick turn it into a prayer for abundant grass cover that attracts deer and antelope. If a youth wishes to pray for physical strength and endurance, he adds the feather of a hummingbird to the stick. The Sun sees the new prayer sticks every day and absorbs the essence of their prayers, carrying it to the underworld, where they are received by *Müiyiñwûüh*, who knows all types and distributes them to the appropriate chief kachinas. These kachinas take the feathers from the sticks and decorate their foreheads with them, while sending the wished-for blessings to the people (Stephen 1936: 1269–1270).

About these prayer sticks Ten Kate noted: "Heading across the surface of the mesa, which extends along the side of Moshóngavé, Oyiwísha directed my attention to a couple of small sticks dyed green, ornamented with downy feathers, which were planted in the ground. They were offerings of a priest from the Order of the Serpent and marked the spot where he had prayed for rain. Oyiwísha was later able to provide me a couple of these gems in the envelope of corn husks and sacred flour in which they were wrapped before making the offering. They closely resembled those I later obtained from the [Zuni] priests of the Order of the Bow" (Ten Kate 2004: 258; see chapter 10, "The Zuni"; cf. Voth 1901: pl. 41).

It was through Jeremiah Sullivan that Ten Kate obtained a bundle of willow (*Salix*; Hopi: *qaha'vi*) prayer sticks (Fig. 201). The three pairs of *sakwa-vaho* (blue-green prayer sticks) consist individually of a blue-green colored stick with a black tapering point to which small turkey feathers used to be attached at the top. A conical folded cornhusk, filled with cornmeal and a drop of honey, referred to as *mösi'at*, 'food for the spirits,' is attached to each pair of sticks with handspun cotton string. On two

152

sticks the remains of tiny twigs are tied, possibly the remnants of blossoms. The color green is symbolic for fertility and refers to vegetation. The lightness of the feathers refers to the ephemeral clouds and mist, and the mythological deities and chiefs whom these natural phenomena represent wear mantles made of feathers. *Sakwa-vaho* are associated with the sun.

Prayer sticks are made by the men, who concentrate their thinking on the prayer they want to offer, and care is taken to produce well finished and correctly made prayer sticks. The pointed shape is achieved by rubbing the sticks on a sanding stone and cannot be cut with a Spanish or Mexican knife, because this metal tool is associated with non-Hopi outsiders, who have not been initiated and whose influence on the Hopi is considered detrimental. However, American knives can be used because these people have powers that the Hopi also wish to possess. Ten Kate's specimens are typical of water prayer sticks, used to be placed anywhere, but often near fields, streams, and springs as a prayer for water. This set was made by a member of the Snake-Antelope society and is typical of *Pala'tk-wabi* (Red Land) prayer sticks, referring to the place of origin of the Patki clan and the home of Cloud and Water Serpent. In 1852 the Hopi offered a set of such prayer sticks to U.S. president Millard Fillmore to establish diplomatic relations (Hough 1902: 467; Dorsey and Voth 1902: 174, pls. 84, 114, 123; Voth 1903: 274-279, pl. 153; Stephen 1936: 32, 54-56, 529, 651, 848-849; Wright 1979: 85-86; Whiteley 2004).

Ten Kate also acquired another set of three prayer sticks with the remains of feathers, attached by native cotton string (Fig. 202). The long stick is unpainted and has a carved incision; the shorter ones are painted black. Ten Kate noted that the Hopi referred to these prayer sticks as "*tsjee*" and that this set came from a snake priest.

Kachina Dolls

The earliest kachina doll preserved in a museum collection was collected by army physician Peter Gerald Stuyvesant (P. G. S.) Ten Broeck (1822-1867). He came from a prominent Dutch-American family, who established themselves in New Netherland in the seventeenth century, when Wessel Ten Broeck crossed the Atlantic in search of better prospects in the New World. At least some of his descendants were successful, and P. G. S.'s father, a minister, was able to put his son through medical school (Walter Gilbert, Ten Broeck family genealogist, pers. com., 29 August

2001). In the 1850s P. G. S. served as a physician with the army in the Southwest.

Ten Kate recorded the Native term of *dicha* for these dolls, but the meaning of this could not be ascertained. However, it is possible that he only heard this term once and recorded it wrongly, as the Hopi call these dolls *ti'hü*, meaning 'doll' or 'effigy.'

In 1894 Jesse Walter Fewkes, in his capacity as successor to Frank H. Cushing as director of the Hemenway Southwestern Archaeological Expedition, published a long article on Hopi kachina dolls in the *Internationales Archiv für Ethnographie*, the ethnological journal published by the National Museum of Ethnology in Leiden since 1888 and focusing on studies of art and material culture. Among the periodical's international board of editors were Franz Boas and Edward B. Tylor. Ten Kate was a strong supporter of the scientific journal and of the inclusion of North American material. He published a series of short articles in it on his work for the Hemenway Expedition and on Zuni fetishes, as well as many reviews of books on Native American subjects by his American colleagues. It was probably Ten Kate who was instrumental in getting Fewkes to submit his manuscript, based on his colleagues' research and collection activities at Walpi in 1891-92 and the exhibition of many of the kachina dolls on the occasion of the Historico Americana Exposicion in Madrid in 1892, which commemorated the arrival of Christopher Columbus in the New World.

Kachinas are supernatural beings whose exact character is difficult to define. They are regarded as spirits who represent the forces of life and the quintessence of natural phenomena. They return to the Hopi villages on a regular basis to bestow their blessings, embodied by members of kachina societies during ceremonies between the winter solstice and July. Their spiritual essence is called *navala* and manifests itself by rainfall. The whole ceremonial complex of the desert-dwelling Hopi is oriented toward securing rainfall and fertility, dependent as they are for their survival on the annual yield of their crops (Hieb 1979: 577; 1994; Wright 1986: 9-17). Hopi boys are initiated into religious societies and in this way become intimately acquainted with the kachinas of Hopi cosmology. Girls learn about them when they receive wooden kachina dolls from the kachinas who appear in the Hopi villages for the different calendrical rituals. The dolls are suspended from the rafters of houses, and the elders tell the children about the role the kachinas play in the well-being of the people.

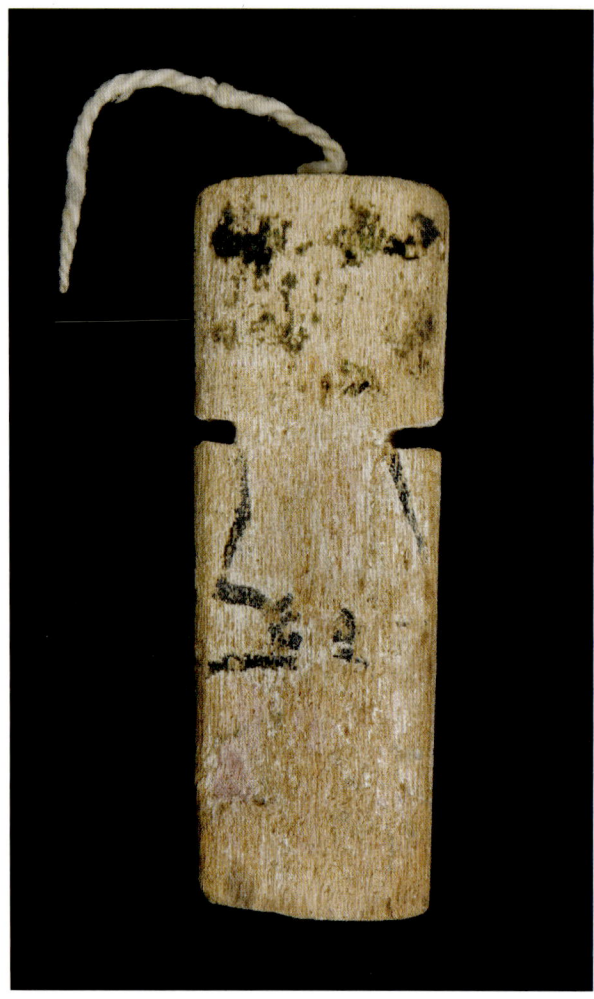

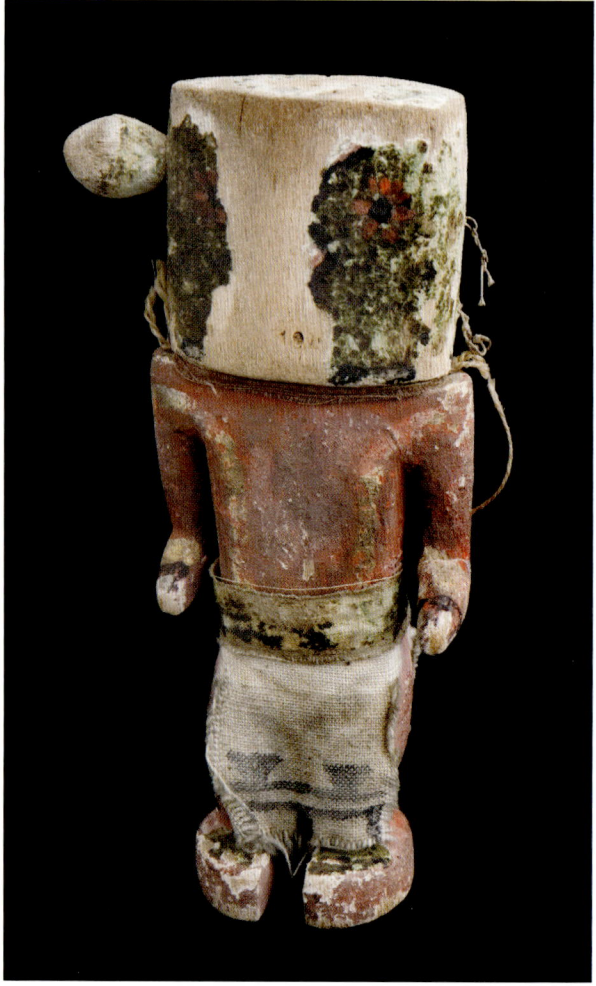

Fig. 203 Turkey kachina (*Koyona kachina*); cottonwood, pigment, cotton; h. 9 cm, w. 3.2 cm, th. 1 cm; ca. 1880 (RMV 362-164).

Fig. 204 Zuni Corn kachina; cottonwood; pigments, native cotton; h. 15.8 cm, w. 6.5 cm; ca. 1880 (RMV 362-165).

Kachina dolls are carved from cottonwood (*Populus monilifera*), which is soft and easy to carve, light in weight, and available in quantity along streambeds. The Hopi call cottonwood *pa she hurps be* (Hough 1919: 275). Mineral and vegetal pigments are used to paint the effigies, and accessories are added in the way of items of dress, headgear, and objects carried. Most kachina dolls from the Ten Kate collection suffered severely due to bad storage conditions and lost many of their attachments. However, Barton Wright generously lent his expertise in their identification.

Kachina dolls were made in all degrees of craftsmanship and complexity, varying from simple and small flat slabs of wood with little decoration, called *püchi tihu*, to elaborately carved, painted, and outfitted dolls with cloth and skin dress and separate single or double tabletas. Small flat kachina figures such as the one collected by Ten Kate (Fig. 203) were given to infants. The cotton string indicated that it was fastened to a cradle. The Leiden specimen

has lost most of its paint. However, the body was pink and white, the face shows traces of green, and the hair and outlines of hands are black. The eyes are pothook-shaped. While traces remain of a zigzag design under one eye, there is apparently no design on the forehead. Barton Wright identified this little doll as Turkey (*Koyona*) kachina, inducing the reproduction of the turkey flocks. Koyona, often appearing during the Powamu ceremony, has a long beak, red wattles made from cloth, and is covered in feathers (cf. Fewkes 1903: 80, pl. xviii).

Barton Wright identified another Hopi kachina in the collection as being of Zuni (*Sio*) derivation (Fig. 204). It comes in two varieties: the black-faced with an embroidered robe as a kilt and the blue-faced with a rain belt. This is an example of the former. It has a squash bud on its right ear and remains of feathers, set vertically, on the opposite side. The eyes are set in a flower design. The body is usually red, the shoulders yellow. The set of double yellow bars on both sides of the torso are still recognizable. The remains of pigment indicating the green moccasins are still visible. The ears of (speckled) corn or rasping stick they usually hold are lost. The Zuni Corn kachina (*Sio Avach-hoha*) appears frequently during the Powamu ceremonies on First Mesa, but also in Laguna and possibly Acoma as well. Its Zuni name is Lawisa (cf. Fewkes 1903: 64–65, pl. v; H. Colton 1959: 59; Wright 1977: 108; 1979: 120; Hartmann 1978: 203–204, photos 101–102; Secakuku 1995: 72, 74).

Another effigy (Fig. 205) belongs to a group of ancient (*Hisot*) kachinas. The doughnut-shaped eyes are usually found on kachinas regarded as threatening. The transverse red hourglass-design around the eyes is an old feature of unknown meaning, not encountered after 1900. The cotton garments imitate a yucca skirt. The *Hisot* kachinas represent the ancients of the different Hopi clans and notably appear during the Niman ceremony in the summer. At other ceremonies their presence is only occasional, but one finds them more often at initiation rites (Fewkes 1903: 16–17; Wright and Portago 2006: 137, 143, pls. 53, 54, 98).

Shalako Mana, a major mythical being of the Hopi, represents a virginal girl. She wears a *tablita* (alt. *tablita*, Sp.), a wooden head ornament called *nák-tci* by the Hopi, on which designs representing rain clouds are carved by means of the stepped sides and painted in the shape of half-domed circles. At the height of the ears she wears representations of squash blossoms, either attached to the head ornament or the hair. The black headband Shalako Mana wears shows white rectangles which represent ears of corn. Tufts of feathers and dark red fur are suspended from it at the ears, and an abalone (*Haliotis*) shell on the forehead. The designs of her facial paint are characteristic of Shalako Mana. The red crescent arching over her mouth represents the sky or the sun, and the colored stripes radiating downward from her lower lip across the chin symbolize the rainbow. The blue and yellow colors of her eyes refer to the spring and summer in Hopi color symbolism. Red triangles or dots are painted on the cheeks. The vertical red stripes across her body may refer to the blood associated with childbirth. During the dances Shalako Mana wears a dress of vertically arranged eagle feathers, a reference to rainclouds, and high white boots. No accessories are carried. She is the quintessential female fertility figure with power over rainfall, fertility, and crops, and thus over Hopi population numbers and material well-being. With her male counterpart Shalako Taka she appears during the Shalako ceremony, which is

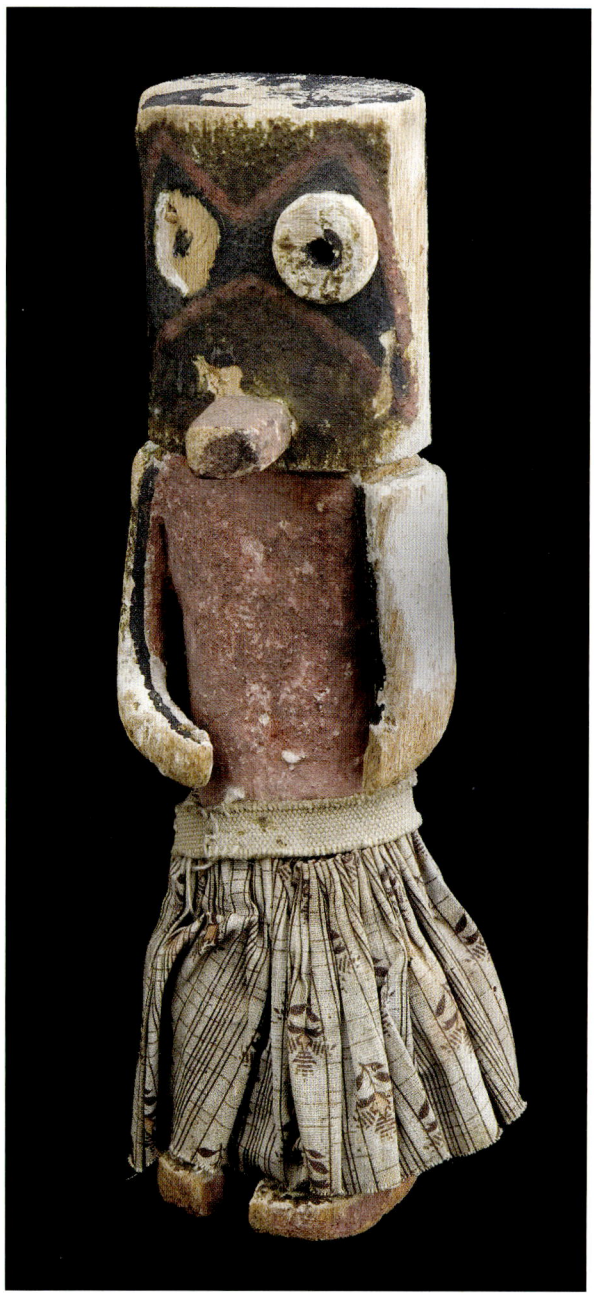

Fig. 205 Ancient kachina; cottonwood, pigments, cotton; h. 22 cm, w. 7.2 cm; ca. 1880 (RMV 362-166).

only an occasional event among the Hopi, but an annual event among the Zuni. However, she also appears at other occasions, such as the initiation of women into the Maraw society, when her dance is a reenactment of the creation of corn. Fewkes noted that Shalako Mana kachina dolls were the most prevalent to be encountered at Hopi (cf. Stevenson 1883: 395–396, figs. 566, 567, 569, 571; Fewkes 1894: 67–68, pls. VI/10, IX/28, X/31; Hartmann 1978: 180–185, figs. 65–74; Secakuku 1995: 53; Wright and Portago 2006: 132, 140, pls. 6, 76).

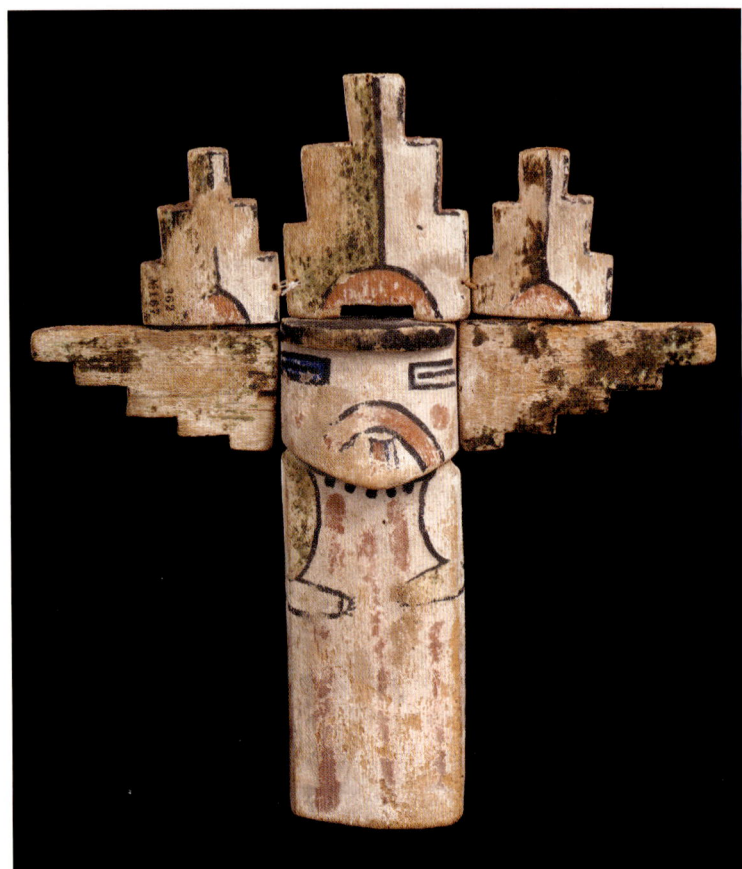 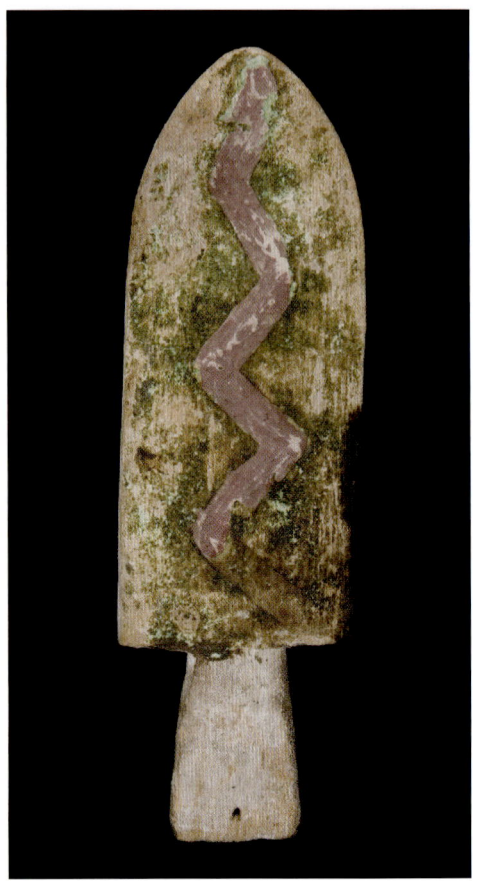

Figs. 206, 207   Shalako Mana kachina; cottonwood, pigments; h. 31.5 cm, w. 29 cm, th. 3.7 cm; ca. 1880 (RMV 362-167). Dance wand; cottonwood, pigment; l. 24.1 cm, w. 7.4 cm; ca. 1880 (RMV 362-168).

The face and body of the Shalako Mana kachina doll collected by Ten Kate (Fig. 206) are painted white, the body decorated with vertical red-pink stripes on front and back, the facial features, green arms, and neck pendant are outlined in black. A red circle appears on each cheek. The chin area below the arched red mouth is divided into vertical panels colored red, white, and blue. The large terraced tableta headdress with its cloud symbolism is painted white, red, and green (cf. Frigout 1979: 570, fig. 11; Secakuku 1995: 53, 125).

The collection also contains a children's dance wand, used during the Powamu ceremony (Fig. 207); its blade is painted green with a red zigzag pattern along it, symbolizing lightning, the short stem is painted white. Adults carried much larger dance wands, painted with fertility symbols, often corncobs and clouds, and representations of kachinas (cf. Stevenson 1883: 393, figs. 555, 556).

The blue face of another kachina doll (Fig. 208) displays two red triangles on the cheeks. A small rosette is carried in the hair. The ruff consists of alternating squares, painted blue, red, and white. The black torso and arms display

vertical yellow lines on both sides. The kachina wears a white kilt and an embroidered dance sash with a serrated edge. Barton Wright identified it as one of the Long Hair kachinas (*Palasowichmi Angak'chinakachina*). Their long hair and beard symbolize showers, and these kachinas bring long gentle rains that enable to crops in the desert to mature. They usually appear during the Niman ceremony on First Mesa. The Kokokshi is the Zuni equivalent of the Hopi Long Hair kachina (Wright 1977: 86; 1979: 103–104; Hartmann 1978: 237–238, photo 143; Secakuku 1995: 79).

This kachina doll was part of a 1956 museum purchase of a series of six artifacts from Lemaire in Amsterdam, a trader in ethnographic artifacts. A tag preserved with the figure bears the date 8 April 1918 and the text "Pacab Kachina Mana," indicating its clan origin rather than a more specific identification. In her catalogue of the Southwestern ethnographic collections in European museums, Wilma Kaemlein (1967: 144) notes that the doll was formerly owned by Herman ten Kate. The basis for this ascription is not known, but one might assume that she saw

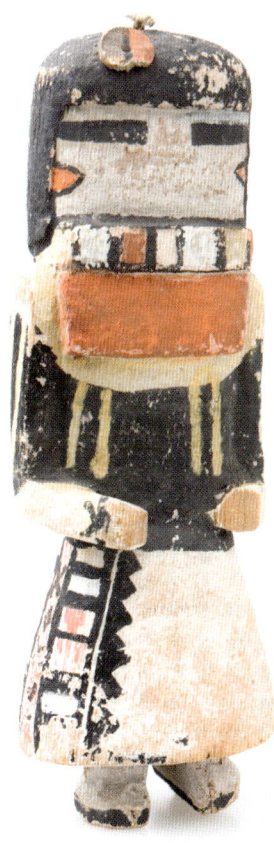

Fig. 208 Red Bearded Loose Hair or Long Hair kachina; cottonwood, pigments; h. 22.3 cm, w. 8.2 cm; ca. 1880 (RMV 3364-5).

some kind of documentary evidence of its provenance that has not been preserved since.

The day after the Snake dance took place at Walpi, Ten Kate's travel companions departed and the anthropologist remained behind, staying in the house of the war chief of Walpi, where a room was made available to him. In his notebook he wrote: "Unforgettable is the view I enjoy that evening sitting on the roof of one of the highest houses and sharing the evening meal with a kindly Indian family, while the sun, like a fiery orb, sets, its rays casting a glowing farewell greeting on the mesa. Everywhere there is peace and calm: in the smoke columns around the pueblo, which rise up in stately fashion toward the sky; in the evening wind, which cools your temples; in the silent desert, which veils itself in the pale tints of the night; in the minds of the many people who, in the simplicity of their hearts, have performed a sacred duty; finally in the stars replete with splendor, which radiate in the firmament" (Ten Kate 2004: 252).

Before going to bed that night, he made some final observations of the day: "Long-haired goat skins and sheepskins are spread out on the floor for me, and the other

residents, too, make preparations for the night by bringing their rabbit skin blankets up on the roofs and lying down. The priests from the Order of the Serpent—who have been fasting for four days and, now that the period of tension is over, are sitting down exhausted and emaciated—make a lunge for the piles of *píkị* [wafer bread], which the women bring to them. But they must spend the night together at the entrance of the sacred kiva. My sleep is disturbed by nothing other than the barking now and then of one of the numerous dogs, the everlasting bane of every Indian village. But here I am safe under the hospitable roof of these gallant people who would not touch a hair on my head" (Ten Kate 2004: 252). Over the next days Ten Kate visited all the villages on First Mesa and made a short trip to Second Mesa, where he saw another Snake dance at Mishongnovi, accompanied by Jeremiah Sullivan. He made observations on their physical type and took somatological measurements of twenty Indians, an affair facilitated by the esteem and trust in which Oyiwisha was held by the Hopi.

Dress

Ten Kate noted that most Hopi men wore citizen's dress, although their attire was often a mixture of Indian and Western elements, whether Hispanic or American. Moccasins, leggings, and breechclouts remained as part of traditional dress, although many leggings were made of dark-blue trade cloth. *Fajas*, woven sashes, and woven knee garters bridged the Indian and Western dress traditions and were much like those common among the Navajo. Calico shirts, obtained from Keam's Trading Post, were generally worn. Hairstyles remained largely traditional, with the men carrying it long and loose or bound at the back with a scarf. Women had retained most of their traditional attire, with black woolen dresses. Common were also small woolen blankets, either white or black, the former with wide black and narrow red borders. Women went barefoot around the mesa tops, but when going down to draw water, they donned high-top moccasins, with the legs wrapped in a thick layer of skin flaps. Married women braided their hair in two long strands, hanging on their chest. Unmarried girls had a peculiar hairstyle, with braided hair shaped into round whorls, fastened with a wooden hairpin at the side of the ears. Ten Kate noted that the Hopi, Zuni, and Navajo took good care of their hair, cleaning and combing it with brushes made of dried bundles of coarse grasses. They could even serve as "a model for the 'clean' Dutch," he wrote.

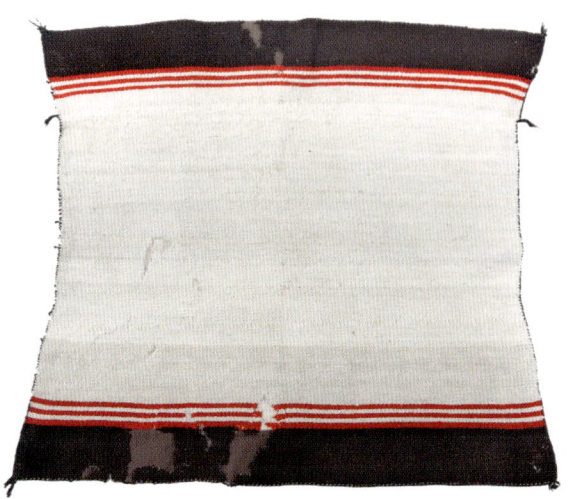

Fig. 209 Hopi women's blanket or manta; wool; 98 x 86 cm; ca. 1870-1880 (RMV 362-186).

During the Pueblo I period (900-1100), the Anasazi ancestors of the Hopi, Zuni, and Rio Grande Pueblos began cultivating a native species of cotton, *Gossypium hopi*, that was well adapted to the altitude and semiarid climate of the Colorado Plateau. It was used to weave garments, varying from breechcloths, shirts, and sashes to kilts, shawls, dresses, and belts, and especially the Hopi developed into accomplished cotton growers and weavers, trading their textiles with neighboring tribes (Kent 1957, 1983b, Teague 1998). After the Spanish introduced sheep to the Southwest in the early seventeenth century, textiles of wool were woven by Pueblo men and increasingly replaced clothing from animal skin. Typical woven dress items included *mantas* (shoulder and dress blankets), shirts, kilts, belts, sashes, breechcloths, leggings, garters, and headbands. Cotton garments became increasingly associated with ceremonial occasions, except for white cotton pants, which were commonly worn by the men. Hopi men did the spinning and worked the traditional upright looms in the kivas. The Hopi went to great lengths to assure the quality of their textiles. Thorough carding and spinning resulted in a strong yarn, which was twisted evenly with a spindle. The yarn was sometimes finished by smoothing it with a corncob. Different types of weaving and cording were mastered and could occur in the same textile (Stevenson 1884: pl. 44; Hough 1915: 84-86; M. Colton 1931: 4-5; Bartlett 1949; Kent 1983a: 9-13, 33-38).

Cotton and wool were initially dyed with a variety of natural pigments, derived from minerals and plants. To assure the effective connection between the fabric and dye and to render the yarns colorproof, a variety of mordants were used, including alum, limonite, rock salt, copper carbonate, tannic acid, human urine, sheep manure, and smoke (Hough 1919: 235, 252-255; M. Colton 1965; Kent 1983a: 31-34). The Spanish introduced indigo and lac dyes, as well as commercial cloth, the *bayeta* variety which was often raveled for the red yarn to be reused in Hopi textiles (Kent 1983a: 29-30).

In 1848 the United States wrested control of the Southwest from Mexico, and from 1875 on the amount of industrially produced textiles, commercial wool (Germantown) yarns, cotton string, and aniline dyes arriving by way of the Santa Fe Trail steadily increased. The arrival of the railroad accelerated the import of such Western trade goods, and traditional weaving among the Hopi, Zuni, and Rio Grande Pueblos declined as a result (Kent 1983a: 14-19).

Mantas were woven in various types by the Hopi: the white cotton wedding manta, the white cotton manta with embroidered borders, and the white manta with blue and red borders. These could be worn as shoulder blankets or dresses.

The type of manta with colored borders in Ten Kate's collection (Fig. 209) is often referred to as maiden's shawl, suggesting that it was worn only by unmarried women. However, such a manta was part of the wedding garments of Hopi women and could be worn over daily dress and on ceremonial occasions. Women wear this type of blanket or shawl on the occasion of the Maraw, Owaqol, and Lakon ceremonies, but male chiefs and kachina dancers can don these garments too on ceremonial occasions and also when representing male kachinas (Hough 1915: 84; 1919: 249-250; Bartlett 1949: 2; Fox 1978: 50-52; Wright 1979: 17; Kent 1983a: 61-62; Whitaker 2002: 370).

The Hopi call these mantas *atü'ü*, 'white blanket' (Stephen 1936: 272, 515, 1204). These are of two types: woven from white wool with a broad blue or red woolen border at the long sides, or woven from white cotton with a border of dark indigo blue or red wool at the long sides, often with two or three narrow red stripes adjacent on the white background. About the manta collected by Ten Kate, Marian Rodee (1992) noted: "Warps are of handspun white, and the wefts of handspun natural white and natural dark brown wool, the latter probably overdyed to enhance the color; three-ply aniline or perhaps cochineal yarn; edge cords are two two-ply Z-S spun dark brown handspun wool" (cf. Rodee 1977: 120).

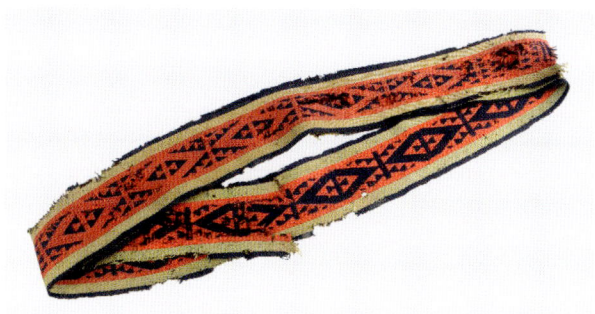

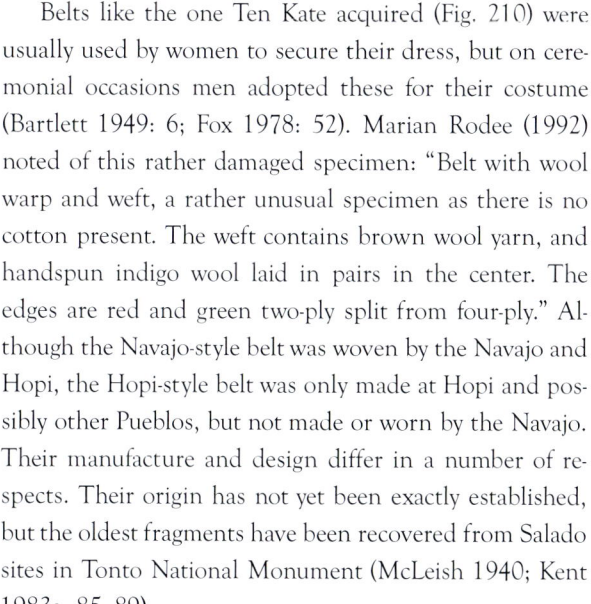

Fig. 210 Hopi woven belt; *faja* (TK); wool; l. 239 cm, w. 9 cm; ca. 1880 (RMV 362-187).

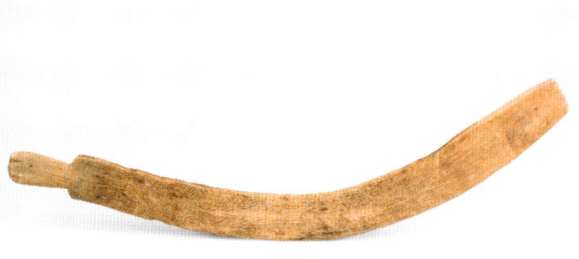

Fig. 211 Hopi rabbit hunting stick; wood; l. 61 cm, w. 5.3 cm; ca. 1880 (RMV 362-169).

Belts like the one Ten Kate acquired (Fig. 210) were usually used by women to secure their dress, but on ceremonial occasions men adopted these for their costume (Bartlett 1949: 6; Fox 1978: 52). Marian Rodee (1992) noted of this rather damaged specimen: "Belt with wool warp and weft, a rather unusual specimen as there is no cotton present. The weft contains brown wool yarn, and handspun indigo wool laid in pairs in the center. The edges are red and green two-ply split from four-ply." Although the Navajo-style belt was woven by the Navajo and Hopi, the Hopi-style belt was only made at Hopi and possibly other Pueblos, but not made or worn by the Navajo. Their manufacture and design differ in a number of respects. Their origin has not yet been exactly established, but the oldest fragments have been recovered from Salado sites in Tonto National Monument (McLeish 1940; Kent 1983a: 85–89).

The Ten Kate collection also includes a type of kachina dance sash predominantly woven by the Hopi, but also manufactured by other Puebloans in the same style, although in much lesser quantities. One rarely sees such a non-Hopi sash illustrated. Ten Kate collected this specimen at Zuni, and it is included in the Zuni chapter (RMV 674-3, -6, see Fig. 255, p. 190).

Economy

The Hopi were sedentary horticulturists who traditionally planted varieties of corn, beans, squashes, and sunflowers. The Spanish introduced apricots and peaches, which the Indians readily adopted. In favorable locations at the bottom of the mesas Ten Kate noticed the fields, which were irrigated by diverting water from small streams or ponds through *acequias*, artificially dug ditches. Because he had taken no food along on his trip to the Hopi country, Ten Kate had ample opportunity to sample Hopi cuisine. From

blue corn the Indians made *piki* bread and from brown corn *pigami*, a corn mush tasting like pancakes. Another porridge of cornmeal and red peppers was baked in corn husks. Ten Kate ate all the dishes offered to him by his hosts, but he thoroughly detested *paywilpiki*, large wet clumps of undercooked blue corn.

The Hopi also had sizeable herds of sheep and goats, which they grazed in canyons during the day and penned into corrals near their villages during the night. Horses, mules, and donkeys were left grazing almost permanently, guarded by herdsmen. *Nookwibi* was a mutton broth with green peas and corn, which apparently appealed to Ten Kate's taste. In addition to horticulture and cattle-raising, the Hopi occasionally engaged in hunting. Ten Kate saw flat wooden throwing sticks, slightly bent like boomerangs, with which the Hopi hunted rabbits. Most were plain, but a few were finely painted with geometric designs.

The rabbit hunting stick obtained by Ten Kate (Fig. 211) is rather thin compared to other examples and is undecorated. In their desert environment the Hopi hunted most small mammals as a source of food, for their skin, and as pest control to protect their harvest. These included prairie dogs, rabbits, hares, raccoons, badgers, porcupines, foxes, coyotes, and wolves. Communal hunts were partially a ritual affair, carried out during or in association with ceremonies, notably Maraw, Wuwuchim, and Niman. In such cases rabbit meat was secured to feed the eagles held captive for ceremonial purposes and for feeding the people participating in the ceremonies. On some of these hunts girls went along to collect the animals. Such affairs were an ideal opportunity for courtship. During rabbit hunts each man took four of five projectile sticks along (Palmer 1878: 311; Stevenson 1883: 392, figs. 548–549; Bourke 1890; Dorsey and Voth 1902: pls. 87, 88, 93, 94; Beaglehole 1936: 3–4, 11–14; Devereux 1941; Ritzenthaler 1967).

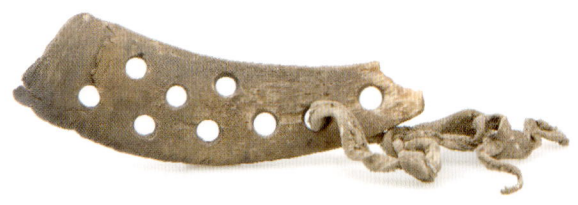

Fig. 212 Hopi arrow shaft straightener; antler, hide; *hoth-quen* (Stevenson 1883: 396), *al-teikwanpi* (Carnegie Museum 3165-243); l. 15 cm, w. 4.3 cm; ca. 1870–1880 (RMV 362-196).

The favorite and most effective weapon for killing small game was the curved throwing stick or club, either round or flat, and often erroneously referred to as boomerang (e.g., Parry 1871). However, the Hopi hunting stick does not return to the hunter. The Hopi called the flat type *putc kohu* ('broad stick'), rendered as *peushkway* by Ten Kate. Most were made of a naturally curved piece of scrub oak (*Quercus gambelli*; Hopi: *kwi:'ngvi*), but hickory, greasewood, and cedar were also used. The flat type needed the most workmanship, and these rabbit sticks had carved handles, a pointed end, and were polished and partially decorated with painted designs. The designs at both ends are called *ta'bo na'kabü*, meaning 'rabbit ears,' while the short double stripes along the edges are the 'rabbit eyes,' *bo'shiadta*. The rabbit stick was associated with Kih'sha, the hawk who hunted rabbits with it and carried the stick under its wings. The stick had the shape of the hawk's wing and was presented to the Hopi as a gift. By using a rabbit stick, an animal could be killed without tearing skin or shedding blood. The offering of such perfect and undamaged animals was required in certain ceremonies (Parry 1871; Hough 1919: 286–287, pl. 44; Stephen 1936: 99–100).

Similar round and flat curved sticks have been excavated at prehistoric sites in the Southwest, and it has been suggested that the type with longitudinal grooves was used as a defensive weapon against darts launched with an atlatl, and as a throwing weapon as well as in close combat. After the introduction of the bow and arrow, such war clubs changed their function and became hunting weapons with carved handles (Parsons 1918: 401; Stephen 1936: 99–100; Heizer 1942).

In addition to the flat and curved rabbit hunting stick, the Hopi also used a straight throwing club of greasewood, round in cross-section and about sixty centimeters long, called *makmorziko*, for the hunt (Devereux 1941: 66–67). Ritzenthaler (1967: 104) suggests that this is a more recent type and came in use because it was easier to manufacture.

Ten Kate also added an arrow shaft straightener or arrow wrench to his collection of Hopi artifacts (Fig. 212). The Hopi call it *tcikwanpi*, which means 'shaft straightener,' with the prefix *ahl* if made out of horn. Horns of mountain sheep and buffalo were traditionally used, later also horns from domesticated goats. Other arrow shaft straighteners were made from stone, bone, antler, or wood. This tool was also used for aligning spindles and fire drills. The holes, often of different sizes, were burned into the material. Arrow shafts made from willow, oak, or wild currant were then pushed, twisted, and drawn through these (progressively smaller) holes, thus straightening them by removing any unevenness and smoothing the surface, resulting in a straight and round arrow shaft required for exact shooting. The arrows were shot with short sturdy bows made from oak or shadblow (Stevenson 1883: 396, fig. 576; Hough 1919: 287–288, pl. 46; Whiting 1939: 23–24; Wright 1979: 50–51).

Pottery

While visiting their homes, Ten Kate had ample opportunity to make observations on the Hopi's pottery and basketry. He relates: "The Moquis are masters in pottery making and basket weaving. Not only in form, but in ornamentation as well, the pottery of the Moquis surpasses that of the Pueblo Indians—except for that of the Zuni—and corresponds more closely to the pottery of the cliff dwellers. The basic color of the Moqui ollas is white, the color for decoration black, brown, or red. These decorations are frequently related to the Moquis' mythology and at the same time are symbols and signs for various things. Thus, not infrequently one finds the image of Balilekóa, the most important water god, depicted on the urns. He has the shape of a bird with teeth that carries a big horn, the lightning, and the clouds. The symbol of growing force is a composite figure of wavy lines (meanders), triangles, and stair-shaped figures. Black is the symbol of heaven, brown or red the symbol of earth. The whirlwind is a spiral. Standing water is expressed by a number of lines crossing each other at a right angle, flowing water by a number of slanting parallel lines. Clouds are indicated by semi-circles with the chord facing downwards, the curve upwards. If one wishes to signify that it is raining, one has a number of parallel, perpendicular lines descend from the circle's chord."

"Among the Moquis the ollas serve rather varied purposes. Besides holding food and drink, they serve as a certain item of furniture [i.e., a chamber pot], which usually has a less conspicuous place in our bedrooms than among the Moquis. In their case the object in question is, for the most part, a very large black olla of crude fabrication outside the house, located not far from the door. Without diffidence both men and women make use of it (they urinate standing up), and would give rise to the assumption among foreigners that the Moquis, too, know the 'qui se gêne est gêné' and put the item in question to better use than we do."

"In addition the ollas are used for that section of the chimney protruding from the roof. One knocks the bottom out of a number of large pots and places them one on top of the other, provided that the bottommost part of one olla fits into the topmost part of the next one. Four or five of these pots already form a rather long chimney, which is fastened at the bottom with adobe to the flat roof or wherever it may emerge" (Ten Kate 2004: 255-256).

Ten Kate had the opportunity to examine the collection of Hopi and Anasazi pottery which Thomas Varker Keam and Alexander M. Stephen had stored at Keam's Canyon Trading Post, while the latter was busy cataloguing. Stephen (1846-1894) was a Scotsman who came to America, where he enlisted in the army and after the Civil War prospected in California and the Greater Southwest. From 1880 until his death he lived at Keam's establishment, continuing his prospecting, making archaeological and ethnographic collections, doing ethnographic research on Navajo culture, and since 1891 assisting Jesse Walter Fewkes in the research on Hopi ethnology for the Hemenway Expedition. Ten Kate noted that the Hopi expressed an understanding of the designs on the prehistoric Anasazi pottery and that the Indians regarded the cliff dwellers as their ancestors. Designs encountered on prehistoric wares were copied from shards picked up from the surface. In 1884 that collection was acquired by the U.S. National Museum, while a later collection was purchased by Mrs. Hemenway in 1892.

Pottery is made by the women. Early summer and the time after the harvest are the preferred seasons for pottery making, and calm windless days are perfect for firing. Clay for the vessels is dug from seams in the sandstone and sand is added as temper. Different sorts of clay are used for different types of vessels, cooking ware requiring different specifications than other wares. Vessels are built up from coils of clay that are flattened both inside and outside, first with the fingers, then by using a dried gourd rind. The dried outer surface is smoothly polished with a sanding stone, after which a white kaolin slip (*küchachka*) is applied with a rabbit fur cloth and again polished when

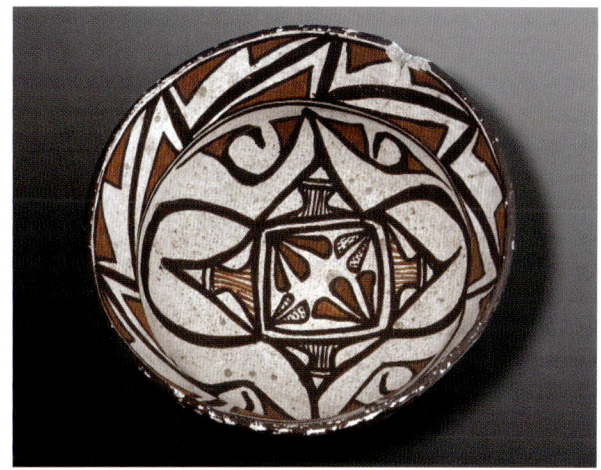

Fig. 213   Hopi pottery bowl; *chakápta* (Wright 1979: 72); clay, pigment; d. 21 cm, h. 8.5 cm; ca. 1880 (RMV 674-32).

dry. Decoration is applied with yucca splints, often splayed at the end into brushes. Pigments from yellow ochre turn red during firing; ironstone, mixed with seeds of the tansy mustard, turns dark brown to black. Dried corn cobs and dried sheep dung are the preferred fuel for firing. Sometimes bones of deer, cattle, or sheep are added to the fire pile, as their burning is believed to impart extra whiteness to the white slipped surface. Bones of horses and mules are not used for this purpose, as they have a darkening effect. Sacred cornmeal is spread on the fire. If the wind picks up during the firing process, a windbreak is hastily made, piling up a bank of sand and stone. A firing lasts between two and four hours (M. Colton 1931: 4-5).

In Ten Kate's time, First Mesa was the center of pottery production, and the women of Walpi were by far the best potters. At Sichomovi there were also potters active, and some Tewa women at Hano also made pottery, but were less adapt at the art and craft, excepting Nampeyo, who had been taught at Walpi and would become an innovator in the 1890s (Stephen 1939: 35, 130, 482–483, 1020-1092, 1187-1190; Allen 1984: 21-23).

The shape, designs, and colors of a vessel in the Ten Kate collection (Fig. 213) are clearly of Zuni derivation. Pottery making had declined significantly among the Hopi until the 1690s, when Tewa refugees from the Rio Grande, fleeing possible Spanish reprisals for the Pueblo Revolt of 1680, settled on First Mesa and built the village of Hano. The Tewa revived pottery making, and notably Hopi women from Walpi became actively involved. At Oraibi an older form of Hopi pottery survived to a limited extent, some of it imitating Zuni ware in shape and decoration, a tendency strengthened when the Hopi took

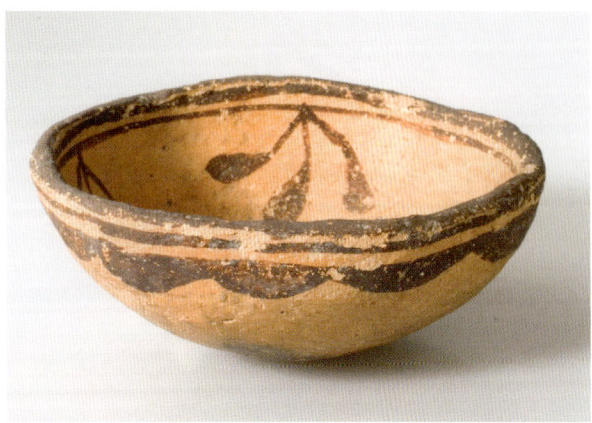

Fig. 214 Small Hopi pottery bowl; *chakap'hoya* (Wright 1979: 72); clay, pigment; d. 12.3 cm, h. 4.6 cm; ca. 1880 (RMV 2012-16).

temporary refuge with the Zuni in the 1860s because of prolonged drought and a smallpox epidemic (Hough 1919: 275; Dockstader 1979: 525; Wright 1979: 72; Allen 1984: 16, 18, 30-37). Ten Kate's bowl is a typical example of the latter style, in which designs became simpler and technical execution less precise. When Thomas V. Keam began trading in the area in 1875, he greatly impacted Hopi pottery by encouraging production of pottery for an outside market (Wade and McChesny 1981: 143-455).

Another bowl collected by Ten Kate (Fig. 214) has a scalloped band on the outer rim and a leaf or flower design along the inner rim, showing no line-break. The vessel has an orange-yellow slip. Its origin remains in doubt, and suggestions include identification as a prehistoric specimen, a traditional early 1880s Walpi bowl, or a 1880s souvenir made for the tourist trade. Ten Kate kept this bowl in his private collection until 1921, because he probably found it aesthetically pleasing.

Basketry

Ten Kate wrote: "The pottery and baskets are the most important item in the Moqui household, and a number of these items can be found on the floor in every room. The basketry, in particular consists of flat, round dishes, of varying dimensions from a large fish dish to a tea saucer. They have the shape of a spiral winding tightly inward and are frequently colored in the most tasteful fashion with red, black, and white; but the most common colors are black and yellow. The Moquis of Oraybe, the largest and most westerly pueblo, prepare baskets differing notably from the aforementioned ones both in style of weaving as well as design and color."

"Another type of basketry, no less lovely, samples of which one now and then finds in the Moqui houses, is derived from the Kochoníno or Havasúpai Indians, a small tribe, which lives far to the West in a deep canyon along Cataract Creek. Both tribes visit each other now and then and remain on the best footing" (Ten Kate 2004: 256).

The sedentary and horticultural Hopi produced a vast amount of basketry in different techniques, a tradition reaching back into prehistoric ancestral times labeled "Basketmaker I, II, and III" by archaeologists because of the prevalence of basketry artifacts at these sites. This era stretched the period from A.D. 1 until A.D. 700-50. Coiling, plaiting, and wickerwork were the main weaving techniques for baskets, with twining a minor technique used for mats to wrap wedding blankets. The Hopi obtained twined baskets from the Ute in trade, but also traded their own baskets with neighboring tribes (Hough 1919: 251; Morris and Burgh 1941; Adovasio and Andrews 1985).

The plant materials used in Hopi basketry show a variety of natural colors and shades. Yucca splints from outer leaves are olive-green. Bleaching in the sun turned the splints yellow, while fresh inner shoots gathered during the summer months are almost white, and freezing turned them even whiter. A variety of vegetal and mineral agents were used in boiling the splints to dye them in various colors: kaolin limestone (white); sunflower seeds, sumac, navy and kidney beans, soot, lignite coal (black); navy and kidney beans, sunflower shells, trade indigo from Meso-America (dark blue); larkspur (*Delphinium*) (light blue); greenthread or Hopi tea (*Thelesperma megapotanicum*; Hopi: *hohoisi*), Navajo tea (*Thelesperma subnudum*; Hopi: *siita*) (orange-red); *Thelesperma* grass, alderbark, sumac berries, cockscomb (*Rhinanthus minor*) flowers, iron ochre (red); pink corn, amaranth, cockscomb, pigweed (*Cycloloma atriplicifolium*) (pink); cockscomb, sunflower seeds (violet); rabbitbrush (*Chrysothamnus*; Hopi: *siváapi*) flowers, flowers of fetid marigold (*Pectis angustifolia*; Hopi: *tu'i'tsma*), ochre (yellow); rabbitbrush bark, copper carbonate (malachite and azurite) (green). Vegetal dyes tended to fade rapidly in sunlight. To assure the effective bonding between the fibers and dyes and to render the colored fibers more color-proof, a variety of mordants were used, including alum, limonite, rock salt, copper carbonate, tannic acid, human urine, sheep manure, and smoke (Hough 1902; 1919: 265; Whiting 1939: 26-28; M. Colton 1965; Teiwes 1996: 23-29, 42-49).

Designs on traditional Hopi basketry are primarily symbolic and only secondarily aesthetic. Most designs refer to religious ideas about fertility and include birds, feathers, clouds, rainbows, lightning, planets and stars, snakes, butterflies and flowers, and kachinas. These are represented in abstract and geometric form as well as more naturalistic ways, with a tendency toward the latter, especially in coiled basketry, where production for an external market is involved. This external market expanded rapidly with the completion of the transcontinental railroad in 1882 (Hough 1919: 268-270).

The Hopi used their basketry for a great variety of utilitarian, social, and ceremonial purposes. As domestic containers they held food stuffs such as corn, flour, bread, beans, fruits, nuts, and seeds. In their ceremonies basketry sometimes played a significant role. Marriage customs involve reciprocal gifts of coiled plaques, laden with food, between the families of the bride and groom. The women's Lakon society performed the Basket dance, carrying several varieties of baskets and distributing them at the end of the ceremony. At the occasion of the Powamu or Bean dance, baskets are given to girls, and baskets are also buried with eagles that are ceremonially killed. Part of marriage rites is the giving of basketry plaques, some with a specific marriage-design, by the bride's family to the family of the groom, in exchange for the wedding dress (Stephen 1936: 323, 837; Wright 1979: 64; Breunig 1982: 10; Tanner 1983: 49; Whiteford 1988: 150; Miller 1989).

Coiled Basketry

Much Hopi basketry is woven in a coiling technique, in which round bundles of twigs and plant fibers are wrapped with thin splints of yucca leaves into a thick strand, which is then coiled in a circle and sewn together with a bone, wooden, or metal awl. The first coil and last coil taper to facilitate the beginning of the basket at the bottom and finish it in a smooth manner at the rim. For the starting and ending of the coils, yucca is used as a filler because of the flexibility of the fibers, while for the remainder Galleta grass (*Pleuraphis*; Hopi: *sühü* or *takashu*) or rabbitbrush (*Chrysothamnus nauseosus*) is used. Because this type of coiled basketry is prevalent among the Hopi, Pima, and Papago, a Hohokam origin has been suggested for this technique, the prehistoric occupants of the Gila and Salt River areas in south-central Arizona.

In the coiling technique Hopi women created flat plaques, shallow trays, deep bowls, and a great variety of small and large baskets of various shapes. Sometimes lids and handles were added, often based on external models.

Patterns emerged by using colored strands of yucca for the wrapping of the coils.

The art and craft of coiled basketry survived especially on Second Mesa, which was also the traditional center of manufacture. Coiled basketry was increasingly produced for an external market after the completion of the transcontinental railroad through northern New Mexico and Arizona in 1883. However, an even earlier type of innovative coiled product made since about 1872 were sombreros. Old coiled basketry was recovered during excavations at Walpi (Mason 1904: 503-505, pls. 30, 93, 215-216; Hough 1915: 91-92; 1919: 266-267, pls. 38-41; M. Colton 1965; Mori 1972: 55-80; Adovasio and Andrews 1985: 37-54, 91-99; Wright 1979: 66-68; Tanner 1983: 50-63; Whiteford 1988: 144-149; Teiwes 1996: 10-29).

Small plaques or trays of yucca-wrapped bundles of vegetal fibers like the set in Ten Kate's collection (Fig. 215) have sometimes been regarded by outsiders as "basket bottoms," the beginnings of coiled baskets. However, they constitute a distinct category of basketry, which the Hopi call *wutak'-wwalu oi'pi*, meaning 'small ceremonial plaque.' The small plaques are not unfinished, and their last coil is usually tapering and tightly sewn to the body as in complete plaques. In some cases the final coil is cut at a right angle (RMV 362-174, -177). They are either plain or show a variety of decoration, some diffuse, others in patterns such as triangles (RMV 362-176) and "whirlwinds" (RMV 362-178). Many are used during the Wuwuchim ceremony in the kiva, when the boys who are undergoing initiation are fed with corn mush, which is served on these plaques (Wright 1979: 66-68).

Fig. 215 Small Hopi coiled plaques; plant fibers, yucca; RMV 362-170: d. 10.3 cm; 362-171: d. 11.2 cm; 362-172: d. 10 cm; RMV 362-173: d. 10.3 cm; 362-174: d. 9.5 cm; RMV 362-175: d. 12 cm; RMV 362-176: d. 15.5 cm; 362-177: d. 11.8 cm; 362-178: d. 16.8 cm; all ca. 1880.

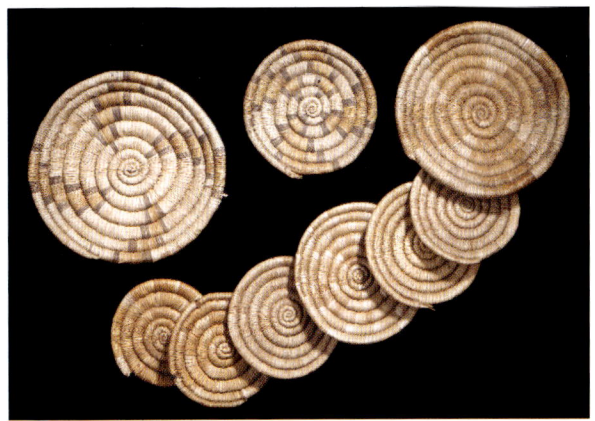

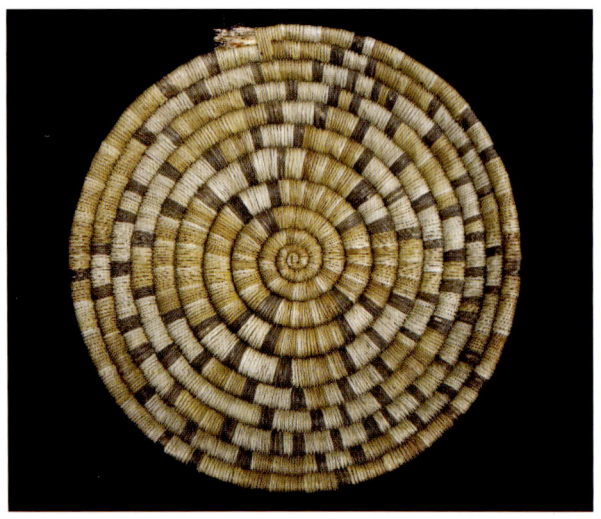

Fig. 216 Hopi coiled plaque; *poota* (sing.); plant fibers, yucca; d. 27 cm; ca. 1880 (RMV 362-179).

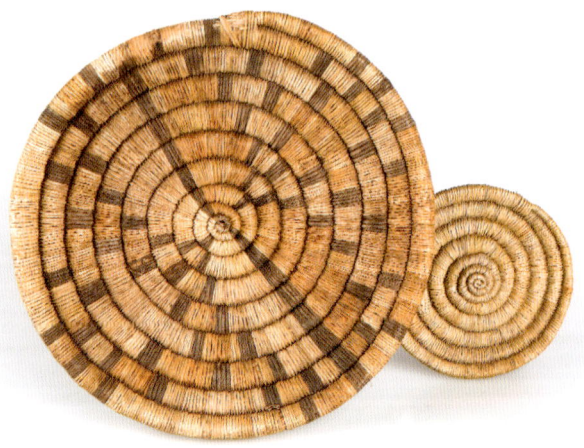

Fig. 218 Hopi coiled plaques; plant fibers, yucca; WMR 17985: d. 23 cm; WMR 17986: d. 11.5 cm; both ca. 1880.

Plaques represent a certain value and are used to pay for goods and services received and for work performed. Women of the Lakon and Owaqol societies often use these plaques in their Basket dances, after which they give them to relatives. The plaques made for these dances are of the best technical and artistic quality, as women take pains to produce a perfect basket.

The designs on coiled basketry can be geometric or flowing, abstract or naturalistic. They often represent concepts relating to fertility, such as kachinas, wind and clouds, rain and lightning, flowers and blossoms, or ears of corn. Until 1880 the designs were characterized by an indefinite geometry, but they soon became more focused and varying, including an increasing number of naturalistic designs in the late nineteenth century, when an outside market provided a valued emerging source of cash income

(Wright 1979: 68; Tanner 1983: 54; Teiwes 1996: 51–59; Nichols et al. 2000: 154–157, 224–225). The faded central design on 362-179 (Fig. 216) possibly represents a flower or a star. RMV 362-180 and -181 (Fig. 217) exhibit a design popularly referred to as "whirlwind", but which to the Hopi represents the moon. They refer to this type of plaque as *muy' yungyápu* or 'moon tray' (Wright 1979: 63). Of two other plaques collected by Ten Kate at Walpi (Fig. 218), the larger one has a radiating pattern of yucca in various shades of reddish-brown, while the smaller one is plain.

Early coiled jars, such as the one collected by Ten Kate in August 1883, probably on Second Mesa, are relatively rare (Fig. 219). Coiled jars gradually became more popular when transcontinental travelers visited the Four Corners area in increasing numbers after the completion of the railroad across northern New Mexico and Arizona.

Fig. 217 Hopi coiled plaques; *poota* (sing.); plant fibers, yucca; RMV 362-180: d. 32.2 cm; RMV 362-181: d. 32 cm; ca. 1880.

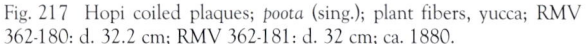

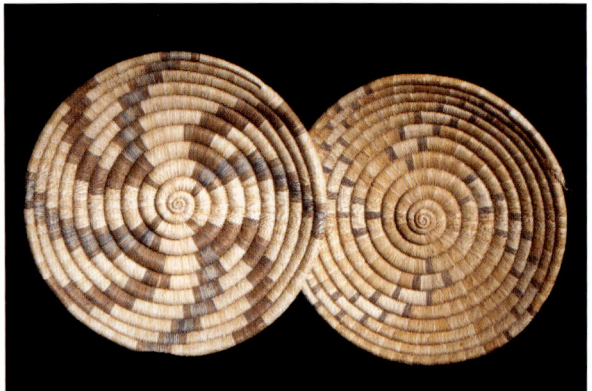

Fig. 219 Hopi coiled squat-shaped basketry jar; plant fibers, yucca; d. 13.5 cm, h. 8.5 cm; ca. 1883 (RMV 362-182).

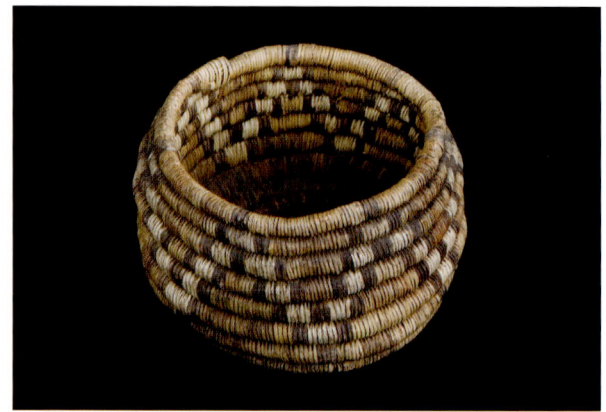

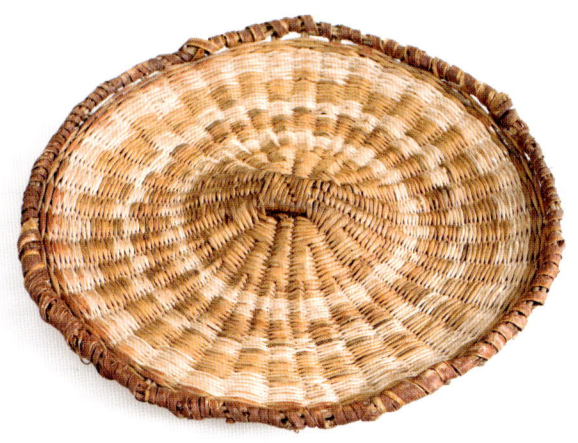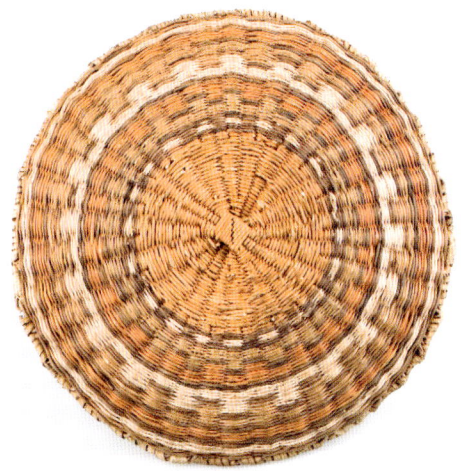

Figs. 220, 221   Hopi wicker plaques; sumac, rabbit brush, yucca; RMV 362-183: d. 17 cm; RMV 362-184: d. 26 cm; both ca. 1880.

New shapes developed, some with lids and handles, re-ferred to as the cornplanting type (Tanner 1983: 58-59). This specimen displays a light-and-dark colored triangular design.

Wicker Basketry

The wicker technique of basketry weaving is relatively rare in Native North America, but prevalent among the Hopi and Zuni. Other than for plaques, the wicker technique was employed in making bows for cradleboards, bowls, and peach baskets, the latter woven by men as an exception. A few kachina masks were also woven in wicker, in-cluding Aholi and Broadface. Among the Hopi, Third Mesa, and notably Oraibi, was the center of production of such baskets. Materials used were sumac (*Rhus trilobata*) for the foundation and rabbit brush (*Chrysothamnus grave-olens*) and golden crownbeard (*Verbesina encelioides*) for the weft. After gathering, peeling, and smoothing the stems, they were dyed in a variety of colors. Melon seeds were chewed and the mixture of seed oil and saliva, acting as a mordant, was mixed with a series of coloring agents.

Traditional shapes of wicker baskets include round plaques, either flat (*yungyapu*) or slightly curved upwards along the rim (*yungyapugölökpu*) for holding corn meal, fruit, and *piki*, the wafer-thin Hopi bread, rectangular or sometimes square trays for corn bread, shallow and deep bowls, and bucket-shaped burden baskets with rounded bottoms, often referred to as peach baskets. For an outside market, right-angled deep baskets were developed after 1880. Wicker plaques are very much in use in ceremonial

contexts for holding prayer sticks, prayer feathers, bean sprouts, or sacred corn meal. In the Owaqol and Lakon ceremonies, women dance in a semicircle, holding wicker plaques in front of their bodies, which they give away after the ritual. Kachinas also present wicker plaques to those attending their dances, notably to the girls during Powa-mu, the Bean dance, when they each receive a plaque and a small kachina doll. Plaques are part of the gift of the bride's family to the family of the groom.

Designs are manifold on wicker basketry and vary from purely geometric to naturalistic. Many such geomet-ric designs have their own names. Naturalistic designs in-clude depictions of kachinas and animals, notably birds and butterflies. This type of basket is still being made today for a tourist and collector's market (Mason 1904: 504–506, pls. 47, 85; Hough 1915: 92; 1919: 264–265, pls. 33–37; Stephen 1936: 162–163, 240; Douglas 1940: 198; Mori 1972: 32–54; Wright 1979: 61–66; Breunig 1982; Tanner 1983: 63–73; Whiteford 1988: 149–155; Teiwes 1996: 32–49; Dalrymple 2000: 119, 122–125; Nichols et al. 2000: 158–159, 226–227).

Of the two wicker plaques collected by Ten Kate (Figs. 220, 221), RMV 362-183 exhibits a design of radiating col-ored circles, the two prominent ones consisting of bands of shifting squares. This design is possibly *qöqön*, 'circles going round,' but it also could be a variation of *nan-gu'yungyapu*, 'holding together,' the marriage tray which symbolizes the union between two families, represented by the squares (Wright 1979: 65; Breunig 1982: 10, 12; cf. Teiwes 1996: 136 for a contemporary example). The rims of both plaques are stitched with yucca and stained red.

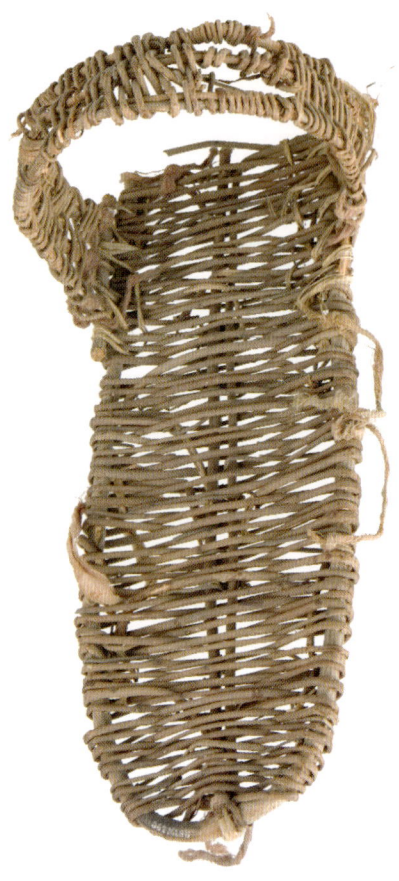

Fig. 222   Hopi model cradle; willow, yucca, pigments, cloth; l. 23.6 cm, w. 11.2 cm, h. 10 cm; ca. 1880 (RMV 362-185).

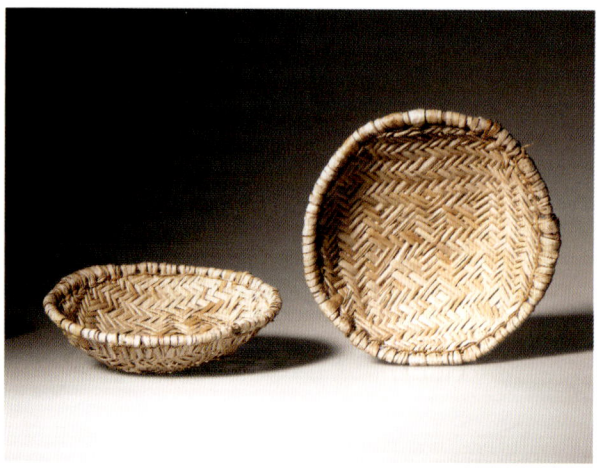

Fig. 223   Hopi twilled sifters, *tüchaïya*; wood, yucca; RMV 362-189: d. 18 cm, h. 5 cm; RMV 362-190: d. 19.5 cm, h. 6 cm; ca. 1880.

Plaited Basketry

Much Hopi basketry was made by weaving flat strips of yucca over and under each other in angles of ninety degrees and pushing this mat into a circular rod of sumac, sewing it to the rim. Thus they created mostly round but sometimes also oblong trays and bowls, often referred to as ring baskets or sifters (Fig. 223). Also typical are square-bottomed baskets with the inclined sides ending in a circular rim, also referred to as amole bowls (Fig. 224), or oval baskets, sometimes with lids, which were a late development, and rings for supporting bulbous pottery ollas (water vessels) when carried on the head or for placement on the floor. By using differently hued strands of yucca, a geometric design can be woven into the basket, including

Fig. 224   Hopi plaited twill basket; yucca, cotton; w. (at bottom) 19 cm, d. (at rim) 19 cm, h. 9 cm; ca. 1880 (RMV 362-188).

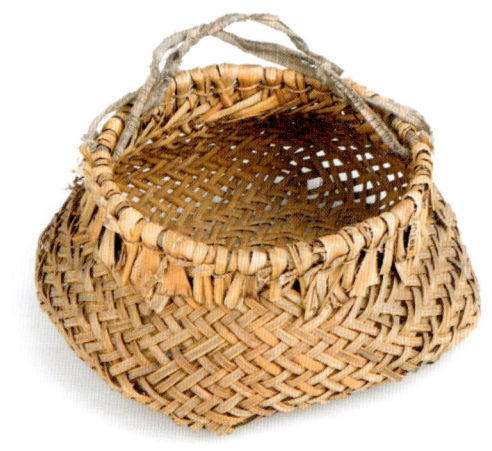

The most prevalent type of cradle (*tahpu*, Wright 1979: 47) among the Hopi of First and Third Mesas was made of wicker basketry. Between a U-shaped sapling of juniper, a strong but slightly flexible carrying tray was woven with sumac stems. A wicker bow was added to the upper part as head protector (*kokutspi*). Infants were swaddled in an animal skin or blanket, placed on the cradleboard on a layer of shredded bark of the cliff rose (*Cowania stanburiana*), and secured tightly with skin rope or woven bands. The cradleboard was carried by the mothers with a head strap. For Second Mesa, both wooden cradleboards with collapsible faceguards as well as wicker cradles have been reported. Model cradles were made for girls to play with. However, these miniatures also appealed to White travelers and visitors and since the early 1880s were made in large numbers for the tourist trade (Hough 1919: 241, pls. 25, 49; Whiting 1939: 25-26; Dennis and Dennis 1940: 108-110; Wright 1979: 47-48; Teiwes 1996: 74-81). The sunshade of this specimen (Fig. 222) is stitched to the frame with yucca and cloth strands.

squares, diamonds, crosses, differently shaped bands, etc. (Mason 1904: pls. 16, 217; Hough 1919: 264; Mori 1972: 15–31; Wright 1979: 59–60; Tanner 1983: 73–75; Whiteford 1988: 155–157; Teiwes 1996: 29–32).

Ten Kate recorded that the yucca basket with calico carrying string he collected was woven in Mishongnovi. Early twill plaited baskets were recovered from excavations at Walpi (Adovasio and Andrews 1985: 54–72, 100–103).

Sifters are the most versatile of all Hopi baskets and are used for an infinite variety of purposes. Their sifting function results from the relatively coarse strands that can be woven in different degrees of space between the strands, resulting in a sieve-like appearance in the more open-weave specimens. The name of these shallow trays is derived from their use in the sifting of sand to build the altars for ceremonies, but they are also used to sift seeds and grains. These baskets also serve as temporary containers for almost everything in the household. In food preparation the trays are used to wash and clean food (Stephen 1936: 1022; Wright 1979: 59–60; see Fig. 193 for a comparable Rio Grande Pueblo specimen).

References

Adovasio, J. M. and R. L. Andrews
  1985 *Basketry and Miscellaneous Perishable Artifacts from Walpi Pueblo, Arizona.* University of Pittsburgh, Ethnology Monographs 7. Pittsburgh, PA.
Allen, Paula Graves
  1984 *Contemporary Hopi Pottery.* Flagstaff, AZ: Museum of Northern Arizona.
Bartlett, Katharine
  1949 Hopi Indian Costume. *Plateau* 22: 1–10.
Beaglehole, Ernest
  1936 Hopi Hunting and Hunting Ritual. *Yale University Publications in Anthropology* 4: 1–26.
Bourke, John Gregory
  1890 Sacred Hunts of the American Indians. Proceedings of the 8th International Congress of Americanists (Paris), 357–368.
Breunig, Robert
  1982 Cultural Fiber: Function and Symbolism in Hopi Basketry. *Plateau* 53: 8–13.
Colton, Harold S.
  1959 *Hopi Kachina Dolls.* Albuquerque, NM: University of New Mexico Press.
Colton, Mary Russell Ferrel
  1931 Techniques of the Major Hopi Crafts. *Museum Notes* 3: 1–7.
  1965 *Hopi Dyes.* Flagstaff, AZ: Northern Arizona Society of Science and Art.

Dalrymple, Larry
  2000 *Indian Basketmakers of the Southwest.* Santa Fe, NM: Museum of New Mexico Press.
Dennis, Wayne and Marsena Galbreath Dennis
  1940 Cradles and Cradling Practices of the Pueblo Indians. *American Anthropologist* 42: 107–115.
Devereux, George
  1941 La Chasse Collective au Lapin chez les Hopi, Oraibi, Arizona. *Journal de la Société des Américanistes de Paris* 33: 63–90.
Dockstader. Frederick J.
  1979 Hopi History, 1850-1940. In: Alfonso Ortiz (ed.), *Southwest* (Handbook of North American Indians 9. W. C. Sturtevant, gen. ed.; Washington, DC), 524–532.
Dorsey, George A. and H. R. Voth
  1902 The Mishongnovi Ceremonies of the Snake and Antelope Fraternities. *Publications of the Field Museum, Anthropological Series* 3: 159–261.
Douglas, Frederic H.
  1940 *Southwestern Twined, Wicker and Plaited Basketry.* Denver Art Museum Leaflets 99–100. Denver, CO.
Fewkes, Jesse Walter
  1894 Dolls of the Tusayan Indians. *Internationales Archiv für Ethnographie* 7: 45–74.
  1897 Tusayan Kachinas. *Annual Report of the Bureau of American Ethnology* 15: 251–320.
  1903 *Hopi Kachinas.* Annual Report of the Bureau of American Ethnology 21. Washington, DC.
Fox, Nancy
  1978 *Pueblo Weaving and Textile Arts.* Santa Fe, NM: Museum of New Mexico Press.
Frigout, Arlette
  1979 Hopi Ceremonial Organization. In: Alfonso Ortiz (ed.), *Southwest* (Handbook of North American Indians 9. W. C. Sturtevant, gen. ed.; Washington, DC), 564–576.
Hartmann, Horst
  1978 *Kachina-Figuren der Hopi Indianer.* Berlin: Museum für Völkerkunde.
Heizer, Robert F.
  1942 Ancient Grooved Clubs and Modern Rabbit Sticks. *American Antiquity* 8(1): 41–56.
Hieb, Louis A.
  1979 Hopi World View. In: Alfonso Ortiz (ed.), *Southwest* (Handbook of North American Indians 9. W. C. Sturtevant, gen. ed.; Washington, DC), 577–580.
  1994 The Meaning of "Katsina": Toward a Cultural Definition of "Person" in Hopi Religion. In: Polly Schaafsma (ed.), *Kachinas in the Pueblo World* (Albuquerque, NM: University of New Mexico Press), 23–34.
Hough, Walter
  1902 A Collection of Hopi Ceremonial Pigments. *Annual Report of the U.S. National Museum for 1902*: 465–471.
  1915 *The Hopi Indians.* Cedar Rapids, IA: Torch Press.
  1919 The Hopi Indian Collection in the United States National Museum. *Proceedings of the U.S. National Museum* 54: 235–266.

Kaemlein, Wilma R.

1967 *An Inventory of Southwestern American Indian Specimens in European Museums*. Tucson, AZ: Arizona State Museum.

Kent, Kate Peck

1957 *The Cultivation and Weaving of Cotton in the Prehistoric Southwestern United States*. Transactions of the American Philosophical Society 47(3). Philadelphia, PA.

1983a *Pueblo Indian Textiles*. Santa Fe, NM: School of American Research Press.

1983b *Textiles of the Prehistoric Southwest*. Santa Fe, NM: School of American Research Press.

McLeish, Kenneth

1940 Notes on Hopi Belt-Weaving of Moenkopi. *American Anthropologist* 42(2): 291–310.

Mason, Otis T.

1904 Aboriginal American Basketry: Studies in a Textile Art without Machinery. *Annual Report of the U.S. National Museum for 1902*: 171–548.

Miller, Sheryl F.

1989 Hopi Basketry: Traditional Social Currency and Contemporary Source of Cash. *American Indian Art Magazine* 15(1): 62–71.

Mori, Jocelyn Ire

1972 Changes in Hopi Material Culture. Ph.D. thesis, University of Missouri, Department of Anthropology, Columbia, MO.

Morris, Earl H. and Robert Burgh

1941 *Anasazi Basketry: Basketmaker II to Pueblo III*. Carnegie Institution Publication 533. Washington, DC.

Nichols, Linda Foss et al.

2000 *Voice of Mother Earth: Art of the Puebloan Peoples of the American Southwest*. Nagoya: Nagoya–Boston Museum of Fine Arts.

Palmer, Edward

1878 Notes on Indian Manners and Customs. *American Naturalist* 12(5): 308–313.

Parry, C. C.

1871 On a Form of Boomerang in Use among the Moqui Pueblo Indians. *Proceedings of the American Association for the Advancement of Science* 20: 397–400.

Parsons, Elsie Clews

1918 War God Shrines of Laguna and Zuni. *American Anthropologist* 20: 381–405.

Ritzenthaler, Robert E.

1967 Hopi Rabbit Hunt. *Lore* 17(3): 100–104.

Rodee, Marian E.

1977 *Southwestern Weaving*. Albuquerque, NM: Museum of New Mexico Press.

1992 Southwestern Textiles Report. Manuscript, National Museum of Ethnology, Leiden.

Secakuku, Ralph

1995 *Following the Sun and Moon: Hopi Kachina Tradition*. Flagstaff, AZ: Northland Press.

Stephen, Alexander M.

1936 *Hopi Journal*. Elsie Clews Parsons ed. New York, NY: Columbia University Press.

Stevenson, James

1883 Illustrated Catalogue of the Collections Obtained from the Indians of New Mexico and Arizona in 1879. *Annual Report of the Bureau of American Ethnology* 2: 311–428.

1884 Illustrated Catalogue of the Collections Obtained from the Pueblos of New Mexico and Arizona in 1881. *Annual Report of the Bureau of American Ethnology* 3: 517–594.

Tanner, Clara Lee

1983 *Indian Baskets of the Southwest*. Tucson, AZ: University of Arizona Press.

Teague, Lynn S.

1998 *Textiles in Southwestern Prehistory*. Albuquerque, NM: University of New Mexico Press.

Teiwes, Helga

1996 *Hopi Basket Weaving: Artistry in Natural Fibers*. Tucson, AZ: University of Arizona Press.

Ten Kate, Herman F. C.

1885 *Reizen en Onderzoekingen in Noord Amerika*. Leiden: E. J. Brill.

2004 *Travels and Researches in Native North America, 1882–1883*. P. Hovens, L. A. Hieb, and W. J. Orr eds. Albuquerque, NM: University of New Mexico Press. [Translation of Ten Kate 1885.]

Voth, Henry R.

1901 The Oraibi Powamu Ceremony. *Field Museum of Natural History Publication 61, Anthropological Series* 3(2): 67–158.

1903 The Oraibi Summer Snake Ceremony. *Field Museum of Natural History Publication 83, Anthropological Series* 3(4): 262–358.

Wade, Edwin L. and Lea S. McChesny

1981 *Historic Hopi Ceramics: The Thomas V. Keam Collection of the Peabody Museum of Archaeology and Ethnology, Harvard University*. Cambridge, MA: Peabody Museum Press.

Whitaker, Kathleen

2002 *Southwest Textiles: Weavings of the Navajo and Pueblo*. Seattle, WA–Los Angeles, CA: University of Washington Press–Southwest Museum.

Whiteford, Andrew Hunter

1988 *Southwestern Indian Baskets: Their History and Their Makers*. Santa Fe, NM: School of American Research Press.

Whiteley, Peter M.

2004 Bartering Pahos with the President. *Ethnohistory* 51(2): 359–414.

Whiting, Alfred F.

1939 *Ethnobotany of the Hopi*. Northern Arizona Society of Science and Art, Bulletin 15. Flagstaff, AZ.

Wright, Barton

1976 Tabletas: A Pueblo Art. *American Indian Art Magazine* 1(3): 56–65.

1977 *Hopi Kachinas*. Flagstaff, AZ: Northland Press.

1979 *Hopi Material Culture: Artifacts Gathered by H. R. Voth in the Fred Harvey Collection*. Flagstaff, AZ–Phoenix, AZ: Northland Press–Heard Museum.

1986 *Pueblo Cultures*. Leiden: E. J. Brill.

Wright, Barton and Andrea Portago

2006 *Classic Hopi and Zuni Kachina Figures*. Flagstaff, AZ: Northland Press.

9

The Navajo:
Shepherds and Weavers of the Colorado Plateau

After Ten Kate paid a short visit to Laguna Pueblo, he boarded the westward-bound Atcheson, Topeka & Santa Fe Railway. After a short ride he stepped off at the Wingate train depot, from where a mail wagon took him to Fort Wingate, three miles south of the railroad tracks. There he met Prof. Almon H. Thompson, a brother-in-law of Major John Wesley Powell, and members of his topographical expedition, with whom he stayed for several days. He also made the acquaintance of the physician of the fort, Dr. Washington Matthews (1843-1905), who had previously worked in Dakota Territory carrying out linguistic and ethnographic investigations among the Hidatsa. Ten Kate was familiar with the publications of his American colleague, who now continued his anthropological fieldwork among the Navajo. Matthews was pleased to meet a European colleague with medical training and an explicit interest in the cultures of the Native peoples of North America, and he offered his services as guide and interpreter to Ten Kate, who gladly accepted. Together they made a number of trips on horseback from Fort Wingate and from Fort Defiance to visit Navajo camps both on and off the reservation. This enabled the Dutch anthropologist to make observations on the material culture and art of the Indians, as well as to assess their living conditions after a long ordeal that involved violent and cruel army campaigns led by Colonel Kit Carson, forced deportation and internment at Fort Sumner (1865-68), and finally their return to a reservation in the region of their former homeland. During one of his visits to Navajo camps Ten Kate encountered the prominent headman Ganado Mucho, the chief who had counseled his people during imprisonment and after, stressing the need for peace with the Americans to assure prosperity.

Economy

Ten Kate was surprised at the relative wealth of the Navajo, who lived in the semiarid desert of the Colorado Pla-

teau, an enormous expanse of rather barren sandstone and limestone plains, dissected by mountain ranges, canyons, arroyos, and mostly dry riverbeds. He noted that Navajo wealth mainly consisted of livestock, and the government report for 1882 listed 1.1 million sheep, 40,000 horses, 1,200 cows, and 500 mules. Although he saw the Indians cultivate corn, which they called *natáh*, wheat, watermelons, and peaches in several locations, he regarded the Navajo as a nomadic equestrian people, herding their extensive flocks of sheep on horseback and continually moving with the herds to fresh pastures over an immense area in the Four Corners region. Ten Kate pointed out that the Navajo were not only the most numerous Indian tribe, but in his estimation also the most prosperous.

The Navajo shaped small effigies of horses and sheep from stone. These were kept in little hide sacks, filled with pollen. Such fetishes were believed to protect the animals, contribute to their well-being, and insure their fertility. When animals became ill, the fetishes were used in curing ceremonies (Kluckhohn et al. 1971: 340-341). RMV 647-28 (Fig. 225) is a rather stylized representation of a quadruped, probably a sheep. Although Ten Kate collected this specimen while he was in the Zuni area, the museum's documentation contains a note that it was Navajo. Ten Kate

Fig. 225 Flock fetish; stone; l. 3 cm, h. 2 cm, w. 0.5 cm; ca. 1880 (RMV 674-28).

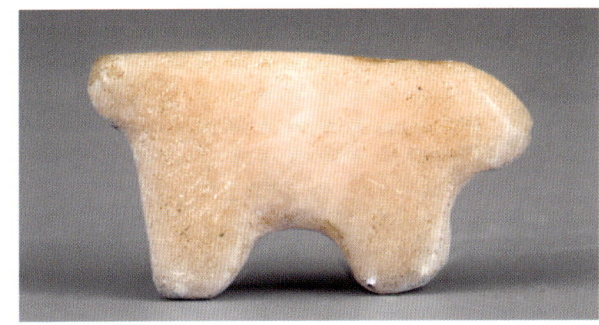

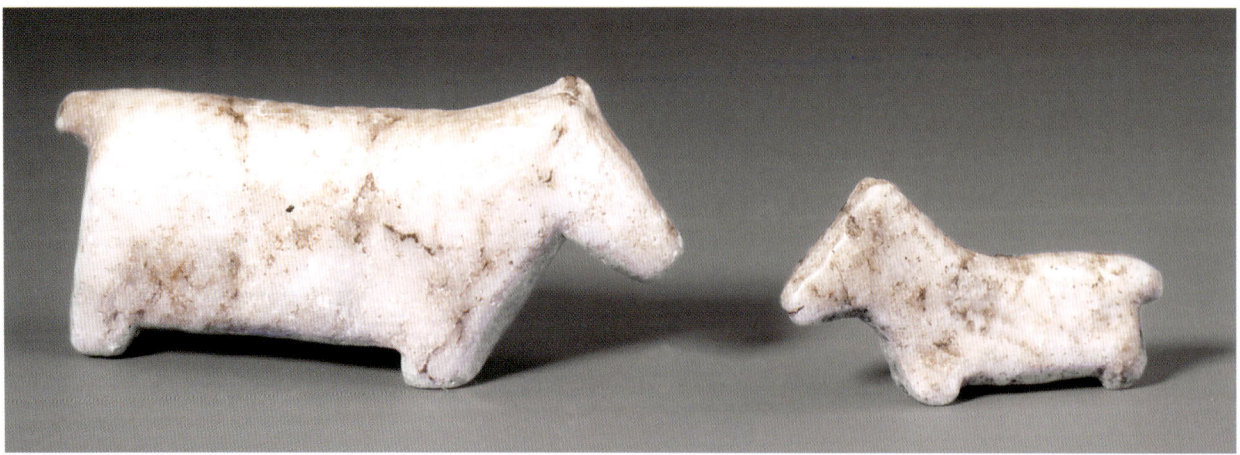

Fig. 226   Flock fetishes; stone; RMV 674-30: l. 5.5 cm, h. 2,5 cm, w. 1 cm; RMV 674-29: l. 3.6 cm, h. 2 cm; both ca. 1880.

(1890: 119) tended to interpret two other figures obtained by him as horse rather than sheep fetishes (Fig. 226).

Dwellings and Households

Accompanied by Washington Matthews, Ten Kate visited a number of families in their traditional *chogáns* (TK), houses consisting of a framework of sturdy beams covered with branches and a layer of soil. However, many lived in brush shelters during the summer, resembling those of the Apache. Inside their dwellings any number of sheepskins, goat hides, and blankets could be found, serving as bedding and as seats. He also saw baskets holding water, made possible by the application of a layer of resin to make them waterproof. The Navajo called these *tus* (TK). The anthropologist also noted a crude type of dark colored pottery of their own manufacture and small ceramic containers which they obtained in barter from their Hopi neighbors. As domestic animals the Indians kept dogs of various crossbreeds and even some tamed coyotes.

Dress

Ten Kate graphically described the dress of the Navajo: "In their attire, which has already been mentioned, they recall the Pueblo Indians in many respects, and particularly the Moquis and Zunis. In this regard many women can hardly be distinguished from their sisters in the aforementioned tribes. As a rule, the men wear a purple or red head cloth after the fashion of the Apaches, but differ in that a bundled-up lock of hair is suspended from the back of their heads. Except for the blankets, leg attire, and moccasins, their garb is a cheap, unsightly hodgepodge of cot-

ton prints and cloth; and darker colors, black and dark-blue, are particularly in vogue. The leg attire consists of large pieces of brown leather, which are tightly bound below the knee with a band (Sp. *faja*) woven from red wool and reaching down to the ankles. The moccasins envelop the feet like a stocking and consist of soft, smooth leather, with a sole, which is only a little harder and thicker than the leather covering the toes and the insteps. The sole ornamentation of their footwear consists of a pair of silver buttons, allowing it to close below the ankle. Sometimes the leggings, too, are ornamented on the outside with a row of silver buttons. Not uncommonly both leggings and moccasins are entirely black. Both sexes wear broad leather belts decorated with lovely silver plates. The men, in addition, often wear well-made bags of leather or puma (*Felis concolor*) over their shoulders. Painting or tattooing the face is apparently rare. Now and then one sees Navajos with broad-brim grey felt sombreros, with an eagle feather (from *Aquila chrysaetus*) attached to them, or, indeed, a leather cap decorated just like the Apache *tsjagg*" (Ten Kate 2004: 243–244).

Making footwear was regarded as a craft of Navajo men. The soles of moccasins and boots were traditionally made of several layers of thick deerskin or badger skin, taken from the neck of the animals. Later rawhide became more common, while buckskin was always used for the upper parts. After cutting the parts, they were sewn together with sinew thread through perforations made with an awl and then tightened by hand. The early awls were made of deer bone and were replaced by needles stuck in a wooden handle. The heel was finished last, after fitting the footwear for size and comfort. Leather thongs, threaded through holes in the upper, secured the footwear. In other cases, brass and silver buttons were sewn on one part of the upper and holes cut in the other part. Moccasins covered the ankle or about ten centimeters of the leg, and both these types were worn by men and women (Fig. 228). In addition, boots were made by sewing a large piece of buckskin to the moccasins and wrapping this around the lower leg, securing it with a leather thong or woven garter. These were usually worn by Navajo women on ceremonial occasions, and this type of footwear was probably adopted from Pueblo neighbors. Navajo moccasins are hardly decorated. Most moccasins were dyed red with mountain mahogany (*Cercocarpus montanus*), and some early ones have some bead- and quillwork, inspired by Ute examples. Metal buttons are sometimes applied for utilitarian of decorative purposes (Franciscan Fathers 1910: 305–311; Ostermann 1917: 7–9; Kluckhohn et al. 1971: 282–290; Conn 1974: 106–107).

The Navajo say that they began to make a Pueblo-influenced style of women's moccasins or boots such as the ones collected by Ten Kate (Fig. 229) after their release from Fort Sumner in 1868. Each moccasin consists of a rawhide sole, a reddish-brown buckskin upper, and, attached at the heel, a very long wrap of buckskin. Two slight variations in construction technique are known, but both involve splitting an entire buckskin from neck to tail, producing two long pieces, each with one straight edge and one irregular edge that may retain holes from where the hide was pegged out during tanning (as Ten Kate's moccasins do; Kluckhohn et al. 1971: 286–287). At the top of this wrap is sewn an equally long (142 centimeters) buckskin strap. When the moccasin is put on, the hide wrap is wound spirally up the leg and secured at the top with the strap. All stitching is with sinew.

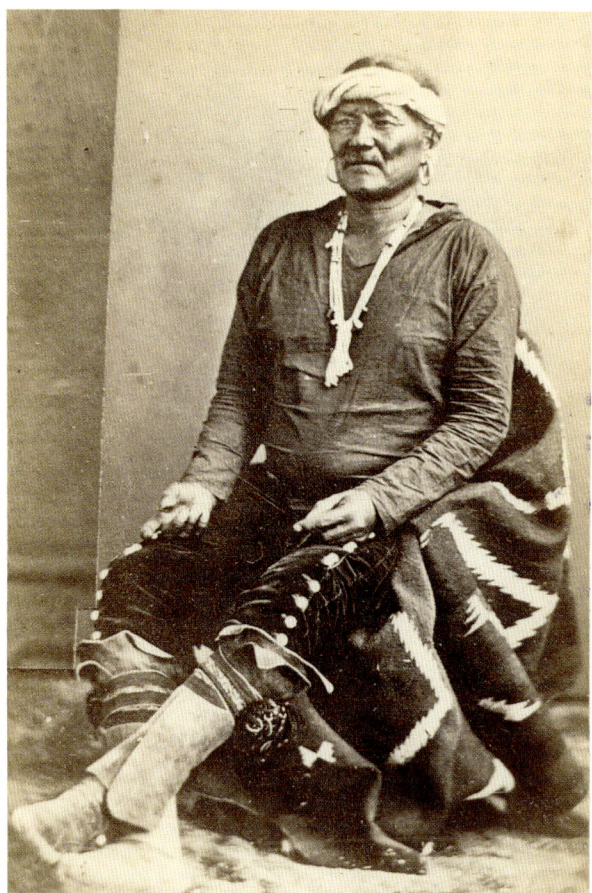

Fig. 227 Manuelito, Navajo headman. Photograph by Continent Stereograph Company, ca. 1880 (Ten Kate coll.; RMV 414Cb39).

Fig. 229 Women's boots; *ké* (TK); buckskin, rawhide, sinew; h. 137 cm, l. of sole 27 cm; ca. 1880 (RMV 361-9).

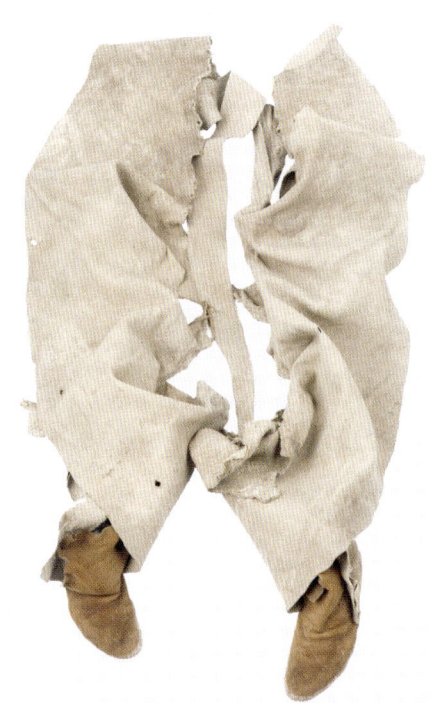

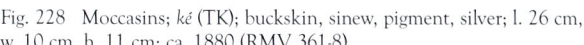

Fig. 228 Moccasins; *ké* (TK); buckskin, sinew, pigment, silver; l. 26 cm, w. 10 cm, h. 11 cm; ca. 1880 (RMV 361-8).

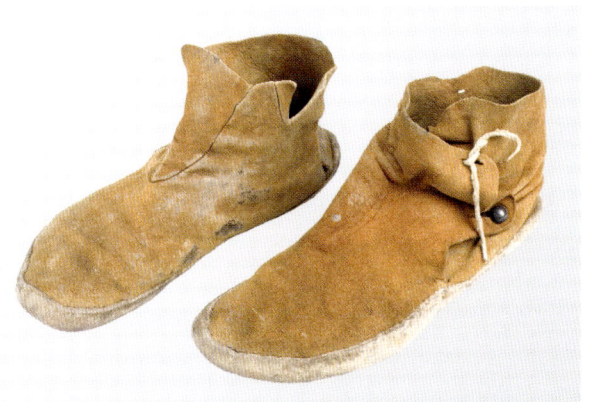

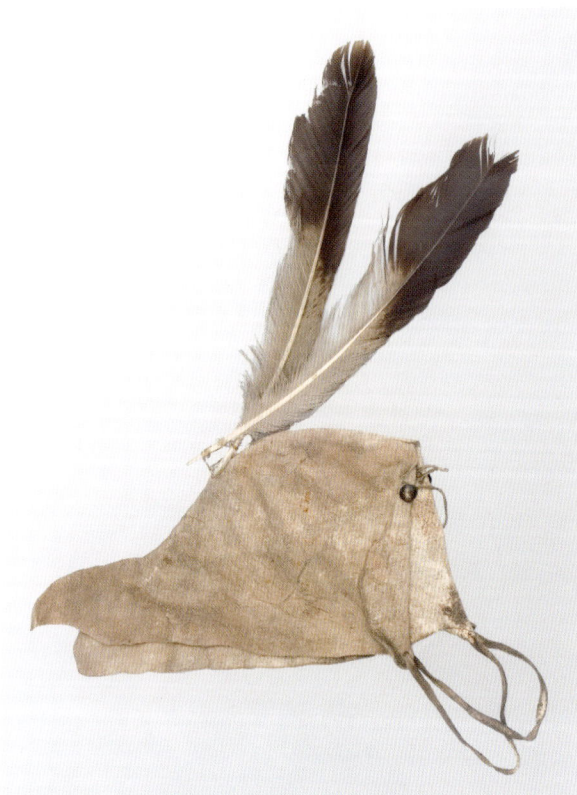

Fig. 230 Men's cap; *tshàch* (TK); hide, eagle feathers, silver; l. 35 cm, h. (only cap) 16 cm; 1870–1880 (RMV 361-16).

The Navajo donned leather caps when they embarked on long journeys or when men went on the warpath. In the latter case, specific feathers with protective magic were attached. Such caps were preferably made of skins of deer, mountain lion, or lynx. Shapes varied and could be domed or helmet-shaped, pointed, but also formed so as to resemble a predatory animal, with ears and horns. The cap Ten Kate collected (Fig. 230) is in the shape of a horn, arching backward, and has chin straps like most Navajo caps. War caps could be adorned with feathers of owls, eagles, crows, and turkeys, patterned bands of leather, fur trim, shells, beads, and later with metal buttons. The Leiden cap has two silver buttons and the remains of the two original eagle feathers. War caps were prized possessions and were thus carefully kept by their owners, who periodically preserved them by cleaning, repair, replacement of parts, and repainting with a layer of clay. Some Navajo informants said that specific types of caps were associated with specific clans in earlier times (Franciscan Fathers 1910: 460-463; Hill 1936: 9; Kluckhohn et al. 1971: 272-280; cf. Fane 1991: 76-77). The cap Ten Kate collected is one of the more modest and simple examples from a great many varieties.

A pouch with carrying strap, made from mountain lion skin and with a silver button on the front to secure the flap (RMV 361-61) is presently missing from the collection and must be considered lost.

Jewelry

Ten Kate noted that the Navajo turned their surplus income into silver jewelry. He observed that the Indians wore a variety of ear and fingerrings, bracelets, and leather belts with shiny oblong silver plates. In addition, silver buttons adorned their blouses, shirts, leggings, and moccasins. Even some of the headstalls of the horses were crafted from or covered with silver. For the manufacture of such finery they melted and hammered American silver dollars. Besides silver jewelry, the anthropologist observed Indians wearing yellow and red copper bracelets and necklaces of shell and turquoise discs. He regarded many of these fashion accessories as of high artistic value and testimony to the good taste of the Navajo, a quality he also saw in their weaving. The Indians also valued their jewelry highly and almost always refused the American jewelry Ten Kate had brought to exchange. They demanded cash, specifically silver dollars, and considerable sums for their finery and proved adept traders. Thus he was unable to obtain the traditional shell and turquoise necklaces and only acquired a few simple silver specimens.

The Navajo wore jewelry long before the arrival of the Spanish. Necklaces, bracelets, and earrings were made from strings of turquoise, shell, and coral, valued raw materials that were obtained in intertribal trade. In earlier times bracelets were also made from deer horn. This material became pliable when boiled and could be bent into the required shape. Turquoise was then applied with piñon gum.

Well before 1800 the Navajo wore items of iron, copper, brass, and silver jewelry obtained through exchanges with Plains and Mexican Indians and through trade with Spanish-Americans and Mexicans. Informants stated that copper and brass jewelry had preceded silver jewelry. These materials were referred to in the Navajo language as red, yellow, and white metal respectively, the latter known as *beshlah-k'ai*. Although historical documentation is lacking, it is quite probable that some Navajo men were involved in smithing during this early time. The first reference to a Navajo silversmith dates from about 1850 and mentions Atsidi Sani (Old Smith), who learned the craft from a Mexican *platero* ('silversmith'). In 1853 a Mexican silversmith started working at the Navajo Agency at Washington Pass. Silver belts and horse bridles became cherished items of status among Navajo men, and women prided themselves with brass bracelets. As parts of annual issues, the Navajo received copper and brass kettles as well as copper and brass wire. In addition, they obtained American and Mexican silver coins. All could be used as raw materials for making jewelry. During their captivity at Fort Sumner from 1864 to 1868, more Navajos probably learned to make copper, brass, and silver jewelry, and after the return of the people to their homeland, the production by tribal craftsmen increased rapidly, with silver soon eclipsing the use of less precious metals.

The use of turquoise in silverwork since approximately 1880 increased with the passage of time. Navajo artisans at first worked to satisfy tribal demand, and as the Indians began to transform their growing wealth into silver items, jewelry became of major importance in interethnic trade, as it could be pawned and redeemed. Gradually a trade in silver finery with neighboring Native peoples developed. From the Navajo, the craft of silversmithing spread to the Zuni (see chapter 10), Hopi, and Rio Grande Pueblos. With the completion of the transcontinental railroad through northern New Mexico and Arizona at the time Ten Kate was conducting his fieldwork in 1882–83, a new market opened up. Travelers and the first tourists began to pick up items of Navajo silver jewelry as souvenirs and as fashion accessories. Production soon increased and was facilitated by using a variety of stamps to decorate silver items, and White traders such as the Fred Harvey Company began to play an increasingly important part in supplying the tourist and eastern markets. Guided by their innate craftsmanship and tribal aesthetics, the Navajo incorporated new techniques, tools, shapes, forms, designs, and symbols, resulting in a extensive palette of silver and turquoise jewelry and exquisite utilitarian items that keeps captivating a contemporary audience (Matthews 1883; Franciscan Fathers 1910: 271–285; Woodward 1938; Adair 1944: 3–28, 36, 193–194; Mera 1960; Bedinger 1973: 1–22, 41–50, 105–118; Neumann 1977; Jernigan et al. 1981; Witherspoon 1981; Wheat 1982; Lincoln 1982; Roessel 1983a: 62–65; Frank and Holbrook 1990: 3–24; Cirillo: 1992: 67–82; Kline 2001; Tisdale 2006).

A necklace collected by Ten Kate (Fig. 231) features a variety of seed and trade beads, many of irregular shape. Necklaces were a common fashion accessory. Before silver jewelry and glass beads were introduced, necklaces were

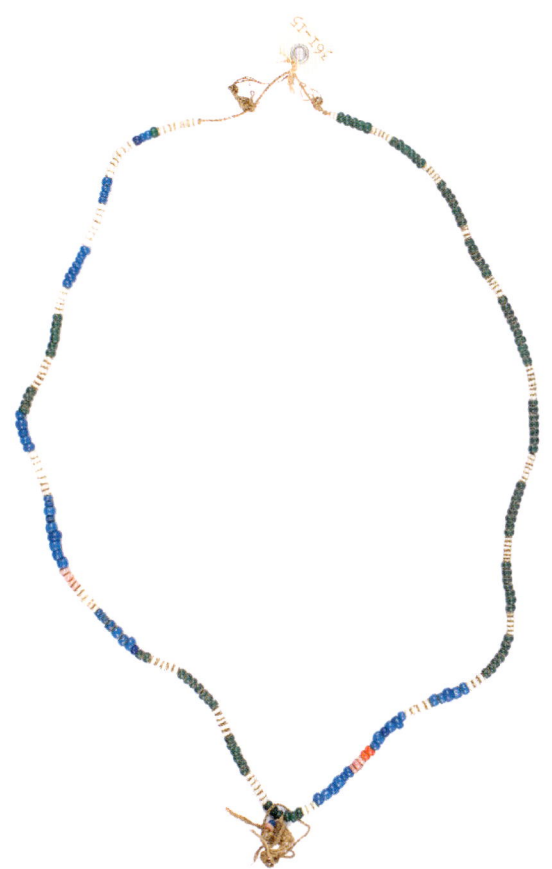

Fig. 231 Necklace; cotton, glass; l. (doubled over) 28 cm; ca. 1880 (RMV 361-15).

fashioned from a variety of seeds and beads. Among the former, dried juniper berries dominated. Traditionally beads were made from bone, turquoise, coral, and abalone and clam shell, but the Navajo obtained the beads from marine sources mostly as finished products from their Pueblo neighbors. In colonial times the Spanish imported coral to distribute as gifts. Prehistoric Anasazi sites also yielded beads from marine origins, and these were collected and threaded by the Navajo. Some necklaces, probably for ceremonial purposes, were made from the claws of lynxes and mountain lions. Amulets of scented grass were sometimes worn on necklaces. Necklaces of round, ovoid, and so-called squash-blossom (actually pomegranate) beads, made from silver, rapidly replaced the glass bead necklaces, and within a short time a wide variety of pendants were developed and added (Orchard 1929: 65–67; Woodward 1938: 31–33; Kluckhohn et al. 1971: 299–302; Bedinger 1973: 34–36, 79–85; Tanner 1978; cf. Frank and Holbrook 1990: 177; Tisdale 2006: 62–65, 98–101).

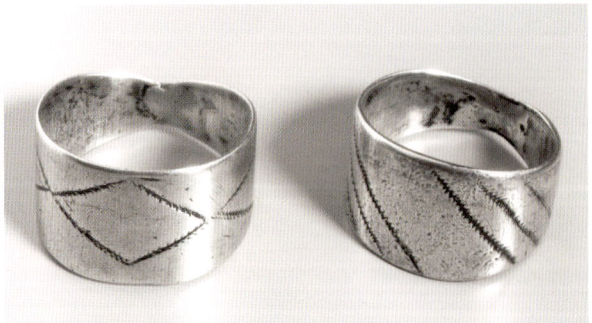

Fig. 232 Two finger rings; silver; d. 2 cm, w. 1.2 cm; ca. 1880 (RMV 361-26a, b).

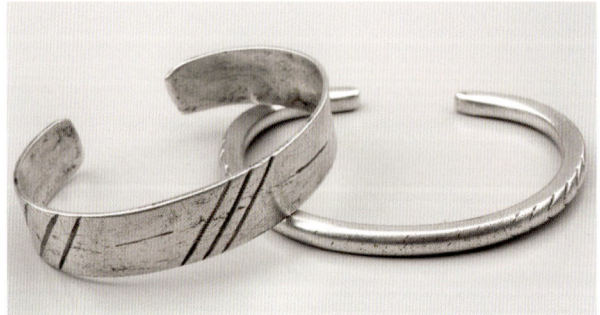

Fig. 234 Two bracelets; silver; RMV 361-27b: d. 4.5–6.2 cm, w. 1.8 cm; RMV 361-27a: d. 5.2–7 cm, w. 0.5 cm; both ca. 1880.

Finger rings, referred to as *yoscah*, were a new fashion accessory among Navajo women and became immensely popular in the last quarter of the nineteenth century. While men usually wore none or just a few, women often covered much of their fingers with silver rings. Early rings were roughly incised with an iron awl or stamped with a cold chisel, such as those Ten Kate collected, one showing a connecting band of chevrons, the other clusters of parallel diagonal lines (Fig. 232). Since 1880 semiprecious stones were being applied to rings (Woodward 1938: 28; Adair 1944: 49–50; Kluckhohn et al. 1971: 308–309; Bedinger 1973: 85–89, 105–112; Tisdale 2006: 104–105).

A third ring in the Ten Kate collection, collected in 1883, is exceptional because of its substantial size and lack of decoration (Fig. 233). Until 1880 the majority of Navajo silversmiths confined their production to relatively simple items of jewelry: rings, buttons, and bracelets. Only a few possessed the skill to make complex artifacts such as elaborate bridles, elegant powder chargers, tobacco cases

in the shape of small army canteens, and spherical beads. The earliest study of Navajo silversmithing was carried out by Fort Wingate army surgeon Washington Matthews, who had earlier combined his career with ethnographic studies while stationed in Dakota Territory. With Matthews, Ten Kate visited Navajo households and camps in early August 1883, where the Dutch anthropologist observed Indian silversmithing on several occasions. Several years earlier the military physician had hired two Navajo craftsmen to demonstrate their skills, documented their work meticulously, and completed his research by additional observations and interviews with Native craftsmen about their work (Matthews 1883).

Bracelets and rings were among the earliest types of jewelry manufactures by the Navajo themselves and became the most frequently worn jewelry items by both Navajo women and men. Early bracelets consisted of strings with seeds of juniper and piñon and beads of bone, stone, turquoise, horn, coral, and shell. RMV 361-27a, a bangle (Fig. 234 right), is probably made from a silver dollar or a thick and square silver rod that was rounded and incised with clusters of diagonal grooves around the edges of its surface. For the Navajo it was better to wear a series of silver bracelets worth one silver dollar each than a purse of coins that could easily be lost. RMV 361-27b (Fig. 234 left) is made from an ingot of silver and has diagonal lines across its upper surface, applied with a file or cold chisel. The wire bangles represent the earliest and simplest forms of Navajo bracelets, but soon the broad-band-type was added to the repertoire. Stamps with designs came into vogue in the early 1880s and were copied from stamps used by Mexican leather workers. Their use spread rapidly among Navajo silversmiths as they enabled more elaborate decoration in addition to saving time on producing such items. However, none of the specimens Ten Kate collected in 1883 have stamped decoration

Fig. 233 Ring; silver; d. 2.4 cm; ca. 1880 (WMR 17993).

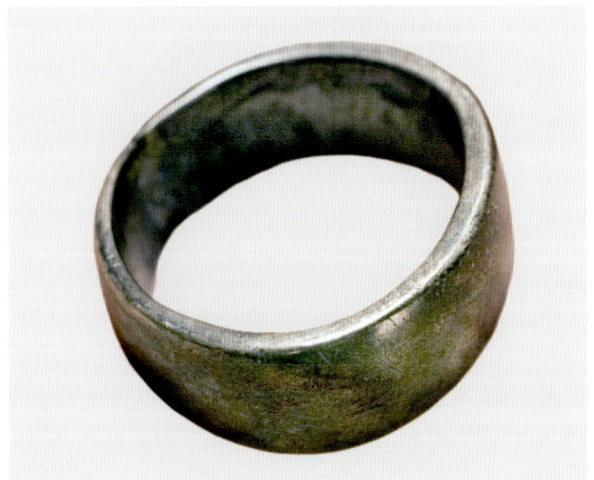

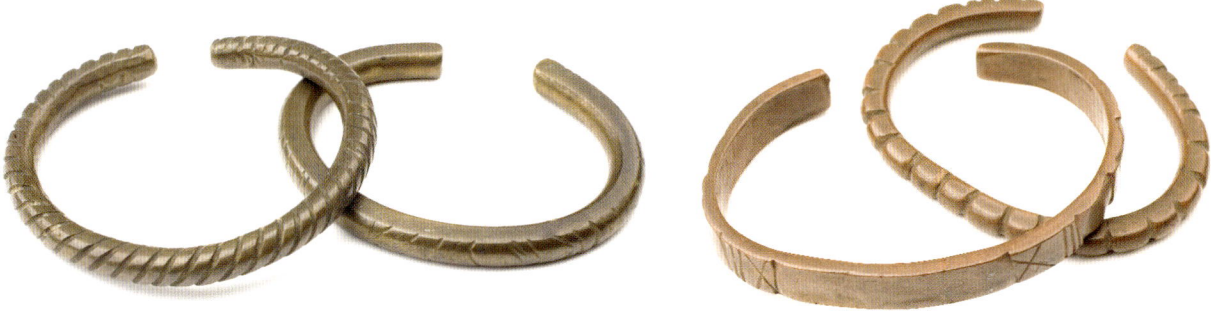

Figs. 235, 236   Four bracelets; brass; RMV 361-28a: d. 5–6.5 cm, w. 0.6 cm; RMV 361-28b: d. 5.5–6 cm, w. 0.6 cm; RMV 361-62a: d. 5–6.5 cm, w. 0.5 cm; RMV 361-62b: d. 5–7.2 cm, w. 0.8 cm; all ca. 1880.

(Woodward 1938: 22–28; Adair 1944: 20–22, 35–39; Bedinger 1973: 23, 33, 42–44, 89–99; cf. Jernigan et al. 1981: 14; Roessel 1983a: 126; 1983b: 517; Frank and Holbrook 1990: 37–39, 58–59, 114, 188–192; Tisdale 2006: 93–97).

Ten Kate also acquired a set of four bracelets (Figs. 235, 236) made from a brass wire or rod, the edges being rounded to a greater (cf. RMV 361-28a) or lesser (cf. RMV 361-28b) extent. The designs are incised and filed. Files were obtained in trade from Whites and were sometimes adapted as engraving tools, but Navajo artisans made their own chisels, while awls came from both sources (Matthews 1883: 174; cf. Mera 1960: pl. 1; Roessel 1983b: 517; Fane 1991: 78).

Pieces of turquoise, strings of beads, and iron rings preceded the wearing of silver earrings. Babies of both sexes had their ears pierced soon after birth. The oldest silver earring, hammered into a flat hoop, was excavated on the rim of Canyon de Chelly and was dated to the early 1860s. By the late nineteenth century women had temporarily almost abandoned wearing earrings.

This heavy type of silver earrings collected by Ten Kate (Fig. 237) was worn by men and was turned over the ear when riding a horse. Other earrings were elaborated with hinged pendants, a hollow silver ball, a squash-blossom bead, or a cone-shaped pendant. In the late nineteenth century the popularity of such earrings declined, and men preferred to wear traditional *jaclas*, strings of turquoise, in their ears instead (Woodward 1938: 28–32; Adair 1944: 48–49; Kluckhohn et al. 1971: 302–304; Bedinger 1973: 56–58; Tisdale 2006: 102–103; cf. Frank and Holbrook 1990: 42–43, 62; Bauver 2007: 5, 40, 43).

Buttons were made of copper, brass, or silver. They were applied to footwear to secure moccasins, to leggings, shirts and blouses, pouches and purses and their straps, belts, horse gear, and wrist guards. In many cases they were applied only for their ornamental effect. American and Mexican coins of various denominations provided the raw material, as these already had more or less the required shape and size and only needed a copper loop soldiered on. Silver buttons came in many shapes and varieties, from simple to complex. Buttons could be flat, convex, conical, or semispherical, and such shapes were obtained by hammering coins into an appropriately shaped hardwood or iron mold or by pounding the round disks over a curved die (Woodward 1938: 30–31; Adair 1944: 45–48; Kluckhohn et al. 1971: 309; Bedinger 1973: 28–31, 51–53; Tisdale 2006: 88).

Fig. 237   Pair of plain circular earrings; silver; d. 5 cm, w. 0.4 cm; ca. 1880 (RMV 361-29a, b).

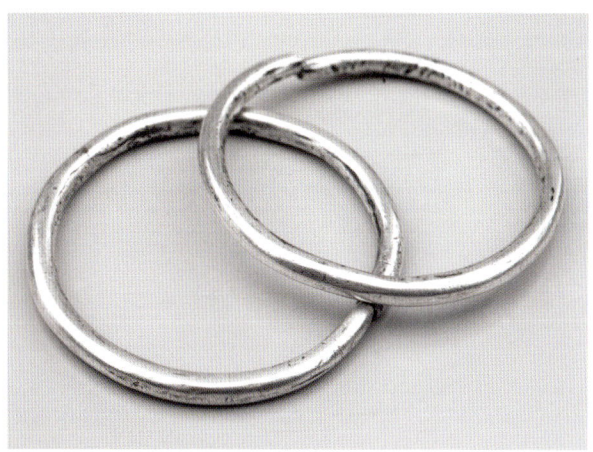

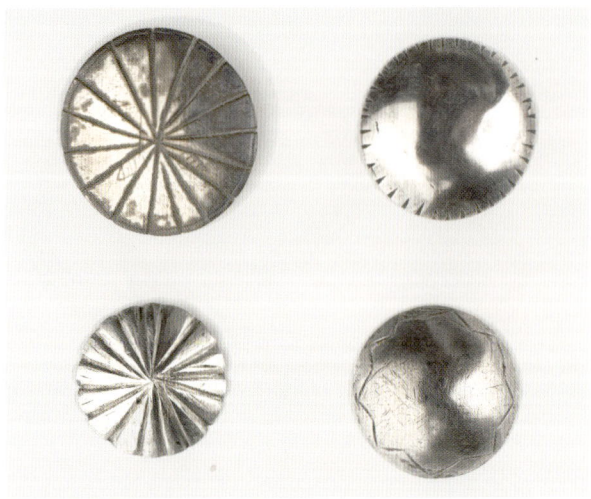

Fig. 238 Four buttons with incised designs; silver; d. 2.5–3.5 cm, h. 0.4–0.6 cm; ca. 1880 (RMV 361-30a, b, c, d).

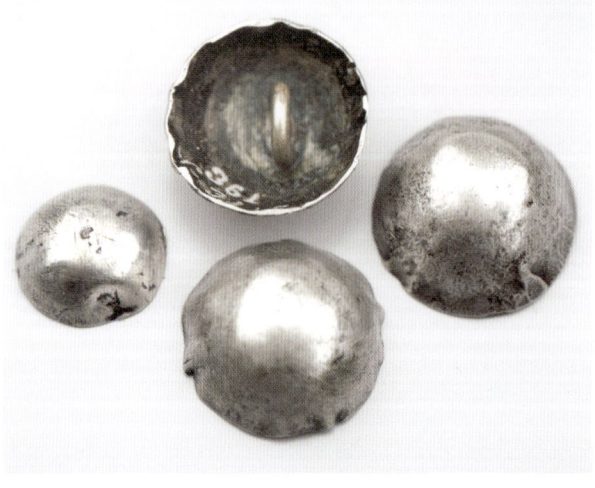

Fig. 239 Four semi-spherical buttons; silver; 1.2–2.5 cm, h. 0.8–1 cm; ca. 1880 (RMV 361-31a, b, c, d).

The four buttons of series RMV 361-30 (Fig. 238) show different types of incised designs. RMV 361-30a is slightly conical and has a pattern of straight lines radiating from the center, probably stamped with a cold chisel. The other three are slightly dome-shaped. RMV 361-30b shows an edge with incised parallel nicks, possibly the remains of the original coins serrated edge. RMV 361-30c is incised with a zigzag pattern around its perimeter. RMV 361-30d, the largest, shows the same radiating pattern as the first button in the series, but an additional feature is the engraving of several feather designs between these lines (cf. Frank and Holbrook 1990: 41, 39, 101, 107, 144, 168, 180-181, 195-196; Fane 1991: 81).

Fig. 240 Wrist guard; leather, brass; w. 8.2 cm, d. 7 cm; ca. 1870–1880. (RMV 361-63).

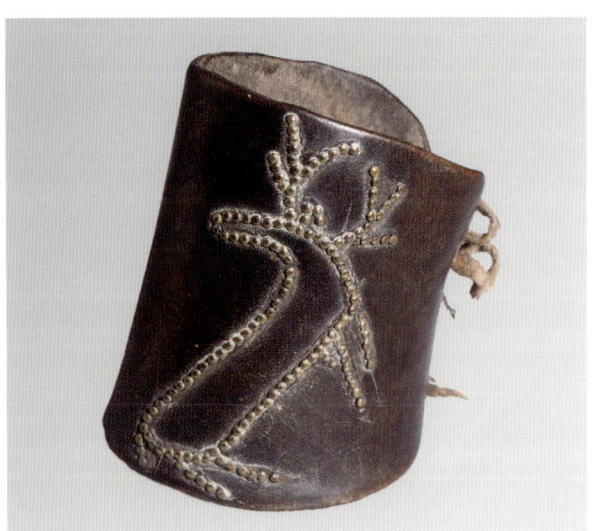

The production of semispherical buttons (Fig. 239) preceded the manufacture of spherical ones, as the latter required additional technical knowledge. An eyelet of copper wire was soldered to the back to fasten the buttons on leather or cloth. Silver items were traditionally polished with powdered sandstone or ashes, but this practice was gradually replaced by the increasing use of sandpaper and emery paper. Blanching took place by using aluminum sulphate, which was found in Navajo territory (Matthews 1883: 175; Kluckhohn et al. 1971: 309).

Leather wrist guards (*ketòhs*) were usually worn on the left to protect the wrist against the snapping string of the bow when arrows were released. Early specimens made from bark and hide might have been reinforced with stone or shell. When bows and arrows were replaced by firearms, wrist guards increasingly became a fashion accessory (Ostermann 1917: 9; Lincoln 1982: 141). Especially after 1880 they were decorated with panels of wrought and cast silver showing a variety of designs and metal buttons, sometimes brass, often silver. Turquoise was frequently added and sometimes other stones (Woodward 1938: 40-41; Adair 1944: 34-35; Mera 1960: 50-63; Kluckhohn et al. 1971: 51-53; Bedinger 1973: 53-56; Ellsberg 1977; Jernigan et al. 1981: 41-42; Tisdale 2006: 106-107).

The specimen collected by Ten Kate (Fig. 240) is made of harness leather and shows a design executed in tiny brass tacks, representing a male deer sinking through its hind legs after being shot. Whether this depiction is simply representational or was considered magical, empowering the hunter on his chase, is not known. In any case such a pictorial representation on an early wrist guard is extremely rare. A similar design of a deer is documented on an early tobacco case, made in the shape of an army canteen (Matthews 1883: pl. 16; cf. Frank and Holbrook 1990: 53, 60, 70–71, 89–90, 102, 126, 135, 153–155, 171–172; Fane 1991: 79).

Weaving and Textiles

During his visits to Navajo camps Ten Kate saw many women working on their looms. He recounts: "The loom with which the Navajos weave their blankets, is made entirely of wood and is very primitive in shape. It is operated by men as well as women. The blankets they weave are usually thick and heavy and made from the wool of their numerous herds of sheep and goats. They vary in price from two to 100 or 125 dollars, all depending on the quality. The most common ones are woolen and white in color with broad dark-blue and black transverse stripes. Those of better quality are less woolen and blue with individual black or red stripes, or white with black and red figures. The very best are smooth and multicolored with complicated patterns, like a Mexican serape. On the four corners of the blanket there are woolen tassels and straps to fasten them when they are being worn because seldom is a Navajo seen without his blanket. In addition, they make saddle blankets with just as much variety in color and quality as in the case of regular blankets. Usually two or three of these covers are folded up and placed under the saddle" (Ten Kate 2004: 241).

Army surgeon Washington Matthews, the first scientific fieldworker and expert on Navajo culture stressed: "It is in the art of weaving that the Navahoes excel all other Indians within the borders of the United States. In durability, fineness of finish, beauty of design and variety of pattern, the Navaho blanket has no equal. ... The whole art of weaving among the Navahoes is worthy of close study for many reasons, but not least for a psychological reason." He pointed out that the Navajo adopted the craft out of their own volition and developed it to such an extent that they became absolute masters in it. This exceptional cultural development required careful study and analysis, and he embarked on a series of publications that laid the foundation for Navajo textile studies (Matthews 1897: 20; 1900: 638; McGreevy 1997: 19–22).

According to Navajo oral tradition, they learned the art of weaving from Spider Man and Spider Woman. Previously they used twined bark fiber, grass, and shredded yucca sleeping mats. These were replaced by buffalo skins, buckskins, and sheepskins. They also wove blankets of rabbit skins on a vertical loom, using wool or buckskin for the warps, although rabbit skins were also sewn together to produce blankets. The latter also provided bedding, but most rabbit-skin blankets were used for dress or carrying a baby (Kluckhohn et al. 1971: 181–188). Remains of Navajo textiles found during archaeological excavations point to Pueblo antecedents for these weavings.

After the Spanish had introduced animal husbandry to the Southwest, the Navajo became successful sheepherders. The neighboring Pueblo peoples shared much of their ancient knowledge about the craft of loom weaving with the Najavo, especially after many of them took refuge with the Navajo after their revolt against the Spanish in 1680. Soon the Navajo were introducing textiles to their intertribal trading network, reaching beyond the Southwest and onto the Plains, and traded their valued manufactures with Spanish settlers. While early weavings were modeled after Pueblo textiles, the Navajo soon began to develop their own styles. Vegetal and mineral dyes were used to color the yarns. When the Santa Fe Trail opened in 1822, commercial yarns and new dyes became available in increasing quantity. Germantown yarns from Pennsylvania and other eastern states were readily adopted from the 1860s on, and with the inclination toward innovation, the diversity of textiles increased significantly. On the Santa Fe Trail and later with the completion of the transcontinental railroad machine-woven textiles from the east flooded the Southwest, and Indian weaving declined. However, new markets opened, both in eastern states as well as locally, for an emergent tourist class, and Indian traders soon became involved in a rejuvenation of Navajo weaving.

Navajo textile studies have a long history. Washington Matthews, U.S. army surgeon, stationed at Fort Wingate in the early 1880s, published the earliest studies of Navajo weaving (1884, 1897, 1900). Collector George Wharton James (1914) provided an early comprehensive description of Navajo Indian blankets and their weavers, and Charles Avery Amsden followed with a monograph in 1934, much relying on Matthews' earlier work. In the 1930s Gladys Reichard published extensively on contemporary Navajo weaving (1934, 1936a, 1936b, 1939). Harry P. Mera of the Laboratory of Anthropology introduced many corrections and refinements to earlier studies (1947). The 1972 and 1977 publications of Berlant and Kahlenberg promoted an awareness of the aesthetics of Navajo textiles in art circles, while Marian Rodee's (1977,

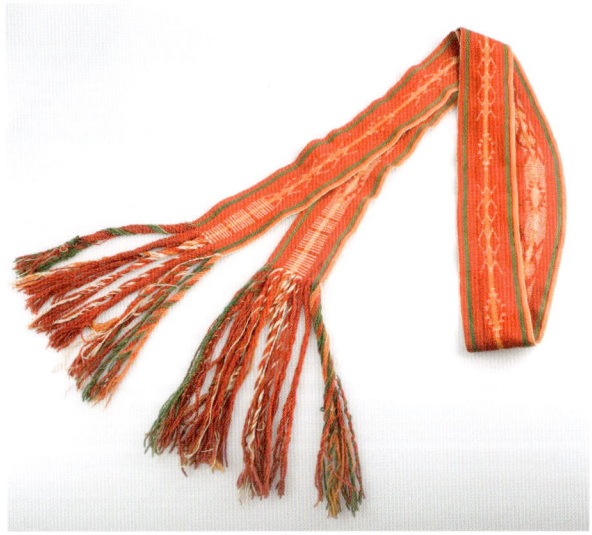

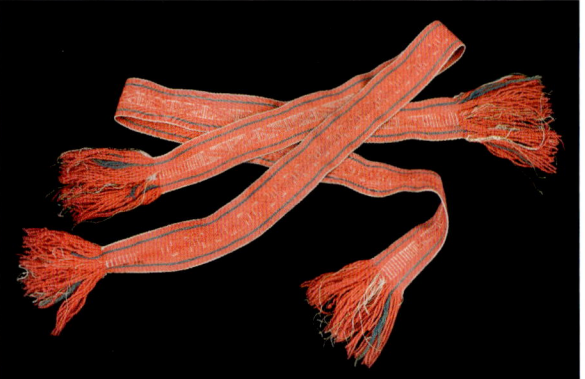

Fig. 242 Pair of woven garters/knee belts (*jad nézhi*); cotton, wool, dye; l. 82 cm (without fringe), w. 4.5 cm; ca. 1870–1880 (RMV 361-13, 14).

Fig 241 Woman's woven sash or belt (*sis* or *esdzán bizís*); cotton, wool, dye; l. 250 cm (without fringe), w. 8.8 cm; ca. 1870-1880 (RMV 361-12).

1981, 1987) publications, inspired by the collections at the Maxwell Museum of Anthropology in Albuquerque, New Mexico, educated a wide public. The publication by the Southwest Parks and Monuments Association on the history of Navajo trading posts and their role in Navajo weaving (H. James 1976) kindled interest in ethnohistorical studies in this field. Kate Peck Kent (1985) provided a comprehensive treatment of all aspects of Navajo weaving, the culmination of almost a lifetime of study (1961, 1983). The National Museum of the American Indian provided a Native point of view in the presentation of its own collection (Bonar 1996). Joe Ben Wheat's lifetime of research on Navajo and other Indian textiles was crowned with Ann Lane Hedlund's edition of his monumental *Blanket Weaving in the Southwest* (2003; cf. Wheat 1973, Hedlund 1990).

Belts, sashes, garters, and saddle cinches were woven on special narrow upright looms or backstrap looms, and there are indications that this was a specialized craft at which only some women were adept. Saddle cinches used the same weaving technique but were woven already attached to their iron rings (Taylor 2000). Wool and cotton were used, although the latter became more prevalent in the late nineteenth century. The front and back of belts and garters show patterns in reverse colors and their ends are fringed.

Belts tied the *bil*, the dark-colored women's dress consisting of two blankets sewn together, around the waist. Although this type of women's dress was abandoned around 1900, the belts retained certain popularity. In pre- and early reservation times such belts were suspended from

the beams of the hogan roof and used as a support during childbirth. Navajo men also wore these belts as sashes or as headbands to tie their hair, the latter being referred to as *ch'a*. These dress items were very valuable and in the late 1880s such finely woven specimens cost about twelve dollars (Shufeldt 1891; Ostermann 1917: 8-9; Kluckhohn et al. 1971: 240-244; Kent 1983: 85-89; Rodee 1987: 132-133; Fane 1991: 75; Wheat 2003: 94-96).

Ten Kate collected a sash of commercial cotton string in warp float weave (Fig. 241). Its red, orange, and green warps are two-ply Z-S spun split from a four-ply wool yarn and respun. These belts were originally woven of blue yarn, but later other colors came to be preferred, with red as a favorite (Franciscan Fathers 1910: 248-249). The edge stripes on this specimen are uneven and in combination with a very lovely pattern provide an unusual effect.

This narrow sash is woven on a different type of loom than the larger blankets and rugs. The loom is essentially a narrow backstrap loom similar to those of Central and South America, probably introduced to the Southwest around A.D. 1000 (Kent 1983: 125). Fragments of this style of belt have been found at prehistoric sites in the Southwest and are still woven today by both the Navajo and the Hopi, the latter referring to it as a "Navajo" or "squaw" belt, *tasápkwewa* (MacLeish 1940: 292, 304-308; Beardsley 1985: 32). In the reverse of the blanket loom, the warps are exposed and the wefts, usually of cotton, are passed back and forth. This technique is called "warp float" or "brocade." The top bar of the loom is suspended from a post or tree and the bottom bar is attached to a belt tied around the weaver's waist. By its very nature backstrap weaving can only produce textiles of limited width.

Although Ten Kate states that belt weaving had moved from the Navajo to the Rio Grande Pueblos, actually the reverse is probably true. While there is very little Pueblo weaving today, belt manufacture survives and many elaborate examples are woven for actual wear as well as the art market. Notable is the work of Navajo weaver Morris Musket, who has taken belt weaving to new artistic heights (Kent 1983: 88; Beardsley 1985; Doyle and Batkin 2004).

A pair of garters in the Ten Kate collection (Fig. 242) are made of commercial cotton string in executed in a warp float weave. The warps are two-ply Z-S spun red and green aniline dyed yarns, probably split from a four-ply yarn and respun. The wefts are of respun commercial cotton twine. Garters secured the hide leggings of men and women just below the knee. Like the belts and sashes, they were traditionally woven of dark colored yarn, but red later became the most prevalent. Ten Kate noted that these garters also became popular among the Rio Grande Pueblos and Zuni and were desirable trade items. Garters went out of fashion with the increased wearing of Western dress by the Navajo in the early twentieth century (Franciscan Fathers 1910: 249; Kluckhohn et al. 1971: 264-265). Ten Kate visited the Southwest at the time of many changes in materials, which were brought by the same railroad that made his trip possible. The new traders on the reservation sold things like balls of commercial twine and packets of new synthetic dyes and skeins of pre-dyed and spun yarns, which made a greater range of colors available to the Native weavers.

The weft of a saddle blanket acquired the Dutch anthropologist (Fig. 243) is made of white and indigo blue handspun wool; the red is raveled three-ply Z-S spun yarn; the pink is three-ply raveled and recarded Z-S spun yarn. The pink color is obtained by the blending of commercial red yarn with white handspun yarn; two edge cords of light blue are from two-ply Z-S handspun yarn. Both red yarns are probably cochineal dyed, obtained from the scales of an insect species in Mexico. The Old World variety of this dye, also obtained from insects, is called *lac*. The plant dye, indigo, is not grown in the Southwest, but was introduced by the Spanish along with sheep.

This is probably a Navajo blanket, although the simple stripe is common to Pueblo, Navajo, and Spanish American weavers. The loom, which is an upright rather than horizontal style, suggests Indian rather than Hispanic manufacture, and the absence of lazy lines suggest Hopi; however, the tassels at the four corners are tied tightly instead of loosely and indicate Navajo manufacture.

Stripes are common in weaving all over the world as the first step in ornamenting an otherwise plain fabric.

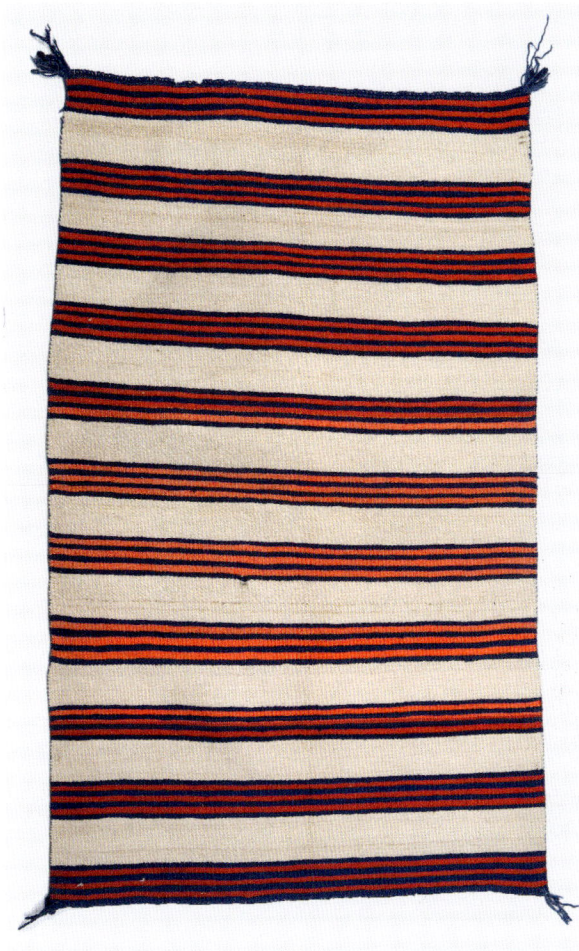

Fig. 243 Striped double saddle blanket, *akidah iinilii* (Kluckhohn et al. 1971: 83-86), or wearing blanket; wool, dye; 136 x 93 cm; ca. 1870-1880 (RMV 361-45).

The logical next step would be the addition of motifs superimposed on the stripes, but there is evidence that this was not the rule in the American Southwest. Although prehistoric textiles are extremely rare, those that have survived, usually sandals and basketry, which are essentially off-loom weaving, are patterned with angular zigzag, meander, and stepped frets. These designs are more familiar in prehistoric pottery (Kent 1983: 206-216).

All three major weaving traditions of the Southwest produced striped blankets, which usually can only be differentiated by examining details of manufacture. Perhaps the best description of this is as a general utility blanket—sometimes employed for a saddle, bedding, seating, door cover, or wrapped around the body as a kind of overcoat. Plain striped blankets were used in this way (as documented by photographs) until 1900-10, when they were finally totally replaced by commercially manufactured blankets from the Pendleton mills in Oregon.

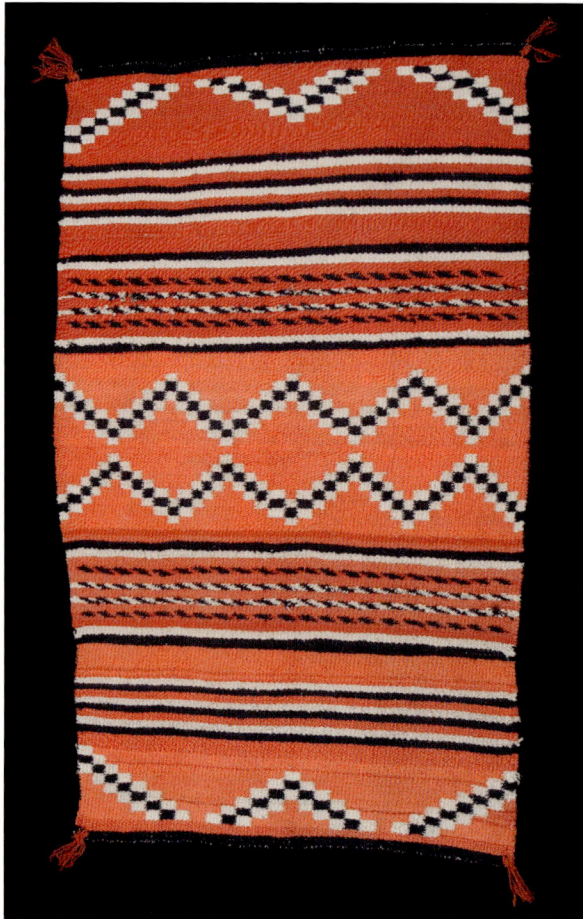

Fig. 244 Double saddle blanket; *akidah iinilii* (Kluckhohn et al. 1971: 83–86); wool; 128 x 79 cm; ca. 1870–1880 (RMV 361·46).

Striped blankets are deceptively difficult to make. It requires a surprising amount of control of the packing or beating of the wefts to produce even stripes. Counting of

Fig. 245 Single saddle blanket; wool; 77 x 62 cm; ca. 1875–1880 (RMV 361·47).

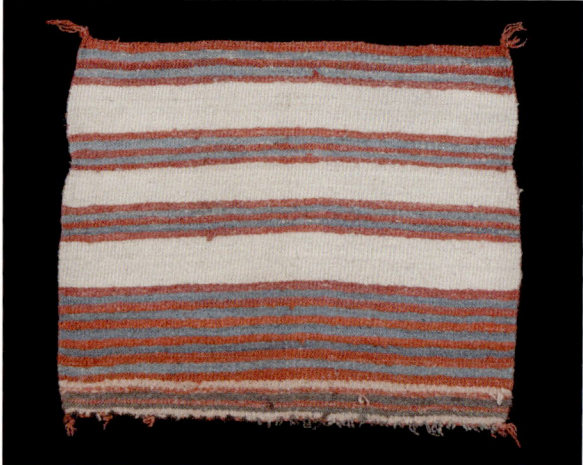

the number of wefts picks is also important in keeping the stripes of even width. To this day Navajo children first learn to weave by making a striped piece on a miniature loom, whereby they learn control of the basic techniques of weaving (Berlant and Kahlenberg 1977: 59–64; Rodee 1987: 177, fig. 422; 2002: 73–79; Wheat 2003: 383–386).

When the Navajo observed Spanish and Mexican riders, they began to copy the saddles they saw. The earliest consisted of two parallel leather tubes, stuffed with bark and animal hair, held together by three strips of hide, and with stirrups attached. Later they constructed saddles from wood, which required even more protection for the horse's back by a sheepskin or a blanket. The Navajo referred to the saddle blanket as *akidah iinilii*, meaning 'that which is put up on something' (Kluckhohn et al. 1971: 83–86; Rodee 1987: 130–132).

Another blanket collected by Ten Kate (Fig. 244) is woven from handspun natural white and aniline red wool. As with the previous blanket, this textile could be a general utility piece, although its smaller size places it more in the saddle blanket category. The all red background is more typically Navajo than the white preferred by Pueblo and Spanish American weavers. A blanket this size is folded in half and placed under the saddle with the folded edge in front and the ends with the ornamental tassels hanging from the rear. In some examples the tassels are quite long. Sometimes two blankets were used: one under the saddle and the other on top of it to make the rider more comfortable. The Navajo also rode bareback with only a textile of the roughly appropriate size. However, for blankets specifically woven to cushion saddles, techniques such as double weaves, twills, and two-faced were used, as were tufted angoras (Rodee 2002; McGreevy 2002: 52–60; Begay-Foss 2002).

A further blanket in the collection (Fig. 245) is likewise woven from handspun wool. Its warps are natural gray and brown, the wefts natural white, aniline red, and blue/gray. This blanket is made of softly spun wool, which is loosely woven and hence is well suited as a comfortable layer between horse and saddle. The general roughness of the surface suggests that it has been used. The warps are cut and knotted at one end, which could indicate an old repair or could mean that two textiles were woven on one set of warps and then cut apart.

The Navajo began weaving saddle blankets in quantity after being allowed to return to their homeland in 1868 after enforced deportation to and settlement at Bosque

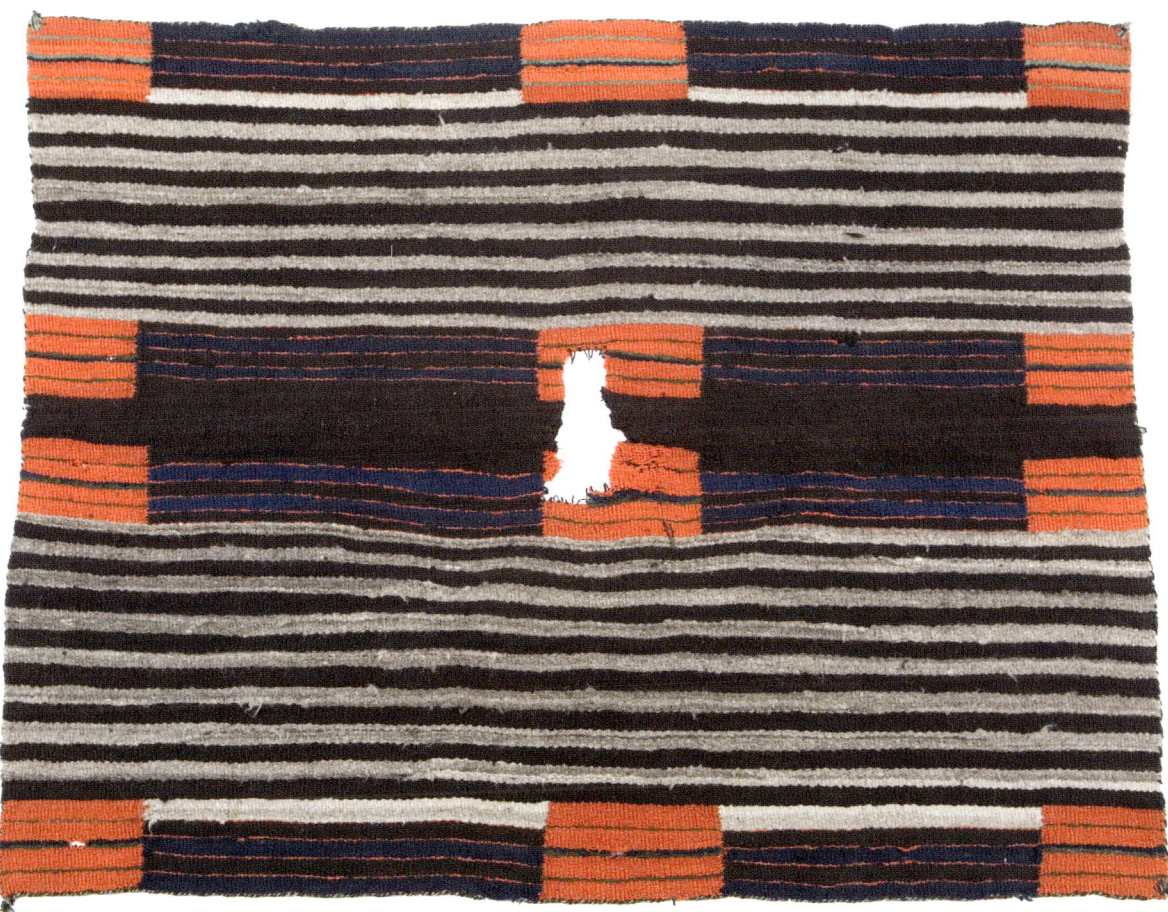

Fig. 246   Woman's wearing blanket; wool, dye; 128 x 95 cm; ca. 1875-1880 (RMV 2012-14).

Redondo for five years. They not only wove saddle blankets for their own use, but also traded these with their Native neighbors. The ranches of White settlers in the American West considerably increased the demand for such textiles, as they were appreciated because of their specific characteristics of being heavy, thick, sturdy, and absorbent. They were even exported to Mexico (Coulter 2002: 31–40; Price 2002).

The wefts of this wearing blanket (Fig. 246) are of handspun black, green, and indigo blue and handspun carded gray; the red yarn is three-ply S-Z spun, the green yarn is three-ply Z-S spun, probably aniline dyed; the recarded raveled red is two-ply Z-S spun; the edge cords are one blue and one green each and two-ply Z-S spun. The slit in the center of this textile may have been cut after wearing in order to use it as a poncho. Ponchos effectively leave the wearer's arms free and are well suited for horsemen.

This style was termed a woman's wearing blanket by early dealers. First produced in the 1860s and 1870s, the pattern is similar to the more famous chief's blanket, that is they are wider than they are long and have three horizontal bands with subordinate stripes, bars, or crosses (Whitaker 2002: 92). The major difference between the man's and woman's blanket is the color and width of the stripes between the three bands of design: black and white in the former and narrow gray and black in the latter. There is no evidence that this style was made or worn exclusively by women, although they are generally smaller in size than the chief's blanket. The chief's blanket was probably developed as a trade item for the Ute, who lived in the mountains north of the Navajo. They became a popular trade item throughout the Plains area, especially with the Cheyenne, and many early paintings show them on women rather than men (Wheat 1976; Berlant and Kahlenberg 1977: 64–66, 122–125; Bennett 1981; Whitaker 1981; Rodee 1987: 127–129; Whitaker 2002: 67, 92; Notarnicola 2005). Broad bands and alternating stripes were in harmony with Plains aesthetics.

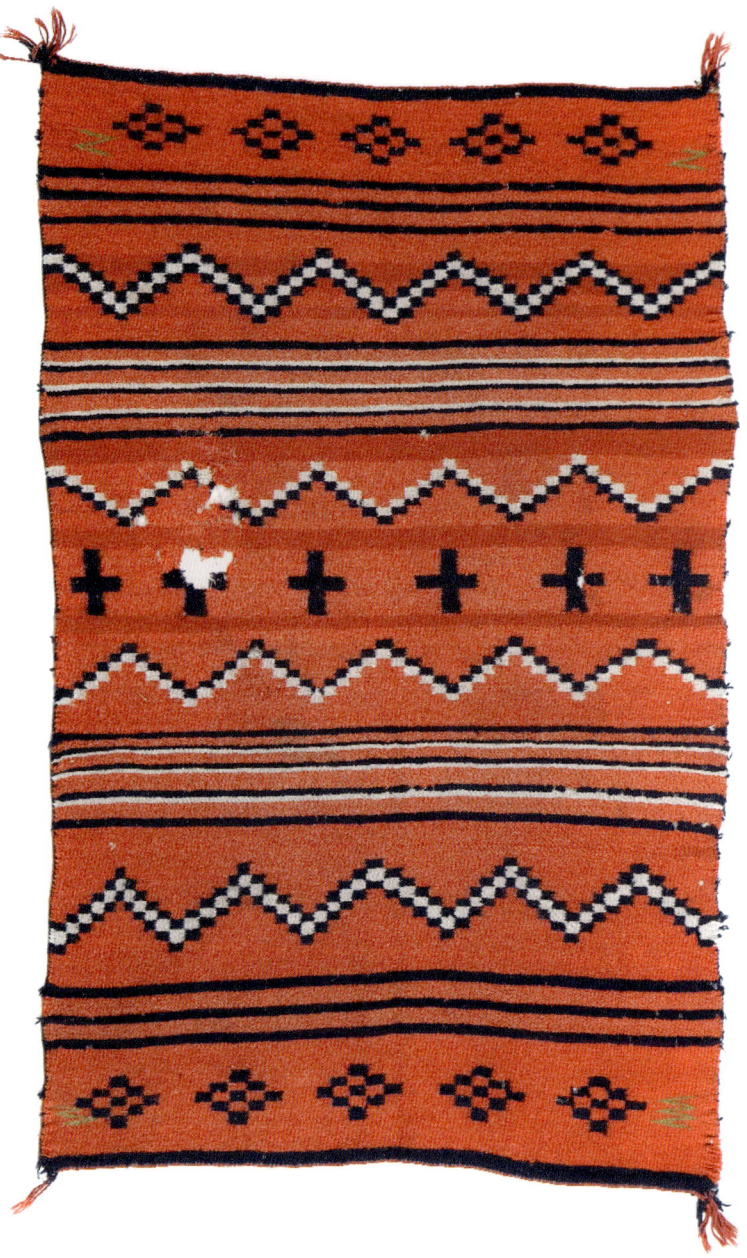

Fig. 247 Double saddle blanket, *akidah iinilii* (Kluckhohn et al. 1971: 83–86), or child's wearing blanket; wool, dye; 130 x 80 cm; ca. 1870–1880 (RMV 2012-15).

unlikely that many of these fine textiles would be given to children. Considering the handsome silvermounted tack that men provide for their prized horses, it seems more likely they are saddle blankets. Washington Matthews (1884: 387) described "small or half size blankets made for children's wear. Such articles are often used for saddle blankets (although the saddle cloth is usually of coarser material) and are in great demand among the Americans for rugs." Women wove small blankets especially for their husbands to take on trade expeditions to the Ute (Hill 1948: 392). Their smaller size meant they could be woven more quickly. The pattern of rows of stepped zigzags, open diamonds, and crosses reflect those on Navajo wedding baskets. This Late Classic blanket is the finest piece in the Leiden Ten Kate collection.

A final example in the collection is a blanket woven from natural white and brown wool and indigo blue wool, all Z-spun three-ply (Fig. 248). The narrow double blue lines run along the wide brown stripes. The selvage cord and warp are S-spun.

Army surgeon R. W. Shufeldt, who was stationed in northwestern New Mexico in the 1880s and was a keen ethnographer, observed the threat to traditional Navajo weaving and wrote: "As civilization advances westward and makes intrusion into the haunts of these simple people, the aboriginal industries of theirs must eventually die out rather than be stimulated and enhanced by contact. For with it civilization brings bright and cheap dyes of many shades; excellent Germantown wools that are not expensive; but more fatal than any of these, very good and durable blankets, of bright tints, that may be purchased by these Indians for a few dollars at the store of the trader, and thus obviate the tedious necessity of any further manufacture of their own in the future" (Shufeldt 1891: 393).

The warp of another saddle blanket (Fig. 247) consists of natural white wool with some green handspun. The wefts that create the red ground are three-ply Z-S; there are touches of three-ply Z-S raveled green in the corners, also of indigo blue and white handspun wool in the designs. The pattern in this blanket as well as the commercial yarns indicate a textile more valuable in its day than those that were entirely handspun. Blankets of this size and quality are frequently called "child's wearing blankets." It seems

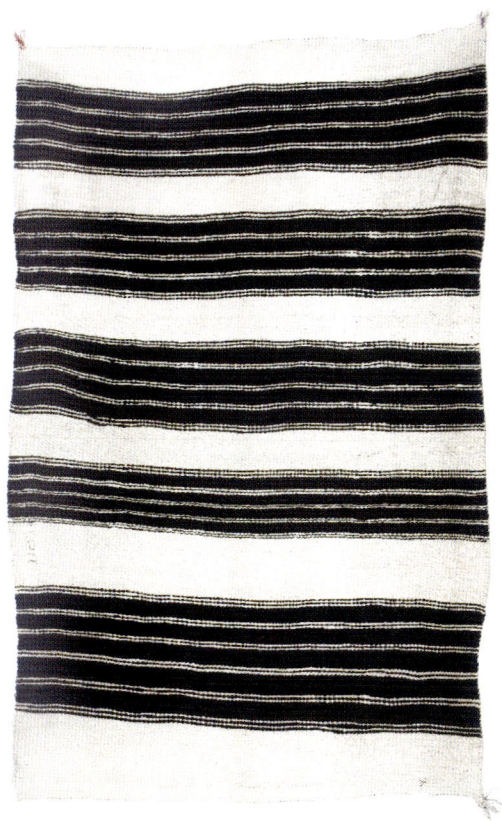

Fig. 248   Blanket; wool; 171 cm x 125 cm; 1870–1880 (WMR 17980).

Horse Gear and Weapons

The Navajo owned the best and finest horses of all the tribes Ten Kate visited in the Southwest. They were better fed, more robust, larger, and nobler in shape than any he had seen. Most horses were only half-tamed and rather skittish. Sorrels and brownish-yellow ones with black manes, tail, and legs and an eel-stripe were the most common. The horse gear and weapons of the Navajo matched those of the Apache to a certain extent. They had narrow wooden saddles covered with rawhide and wide stirrups of the same material, lassos or lariats of leather or horsehair, and headstalls for the horses, some richly ornamented with silver and with heavy Mexican bits. The traditional bows with iron-tipped arrows, held in quivers of mountain lion skin, were being displaced rapidly by Winchesters and Sharps.

A quirt of braided of harness leather (l. 82 cm, w. 3 cm; ca. 1880; RMV 361-52) is missing from the collection, but Arizona State Museum curator Wilma Kaemlein's 1964 notes and photograph show it to be elaborately braided, with braided knots spaced along its length. Both the

Navajo and Apache are known to have made this type. The Navajo braided the handle around a stick, which was then pulled out when the quirt was finished. Horse quirts were made in a variety of styles from simple to complex. A double strap of rawhide, knotted just below the bend with the knot as a grip, represented the economy type. Sometimes narrow rawhide strips were plaited around a stick that was removed when the plaiting and drying was finished. A leather thong was attached to noose around the wrist. Other quirts were made from several materials and required more craftsmanship. Several long and narrow strips of leather could be braided and inserted into the base of a wooden stick that was perforated at the other end, through which a leather wrist strap was threaded. The Navajo, who raced their horses, wove feathers into the leather braids to make their mounts fleet-footed. When harness leather became available through trade, it was increasingly used for braided quirts such as the Leiden example, which exhibits a series of braided knots along its length. Later some Navajos braided quirts from differently colored strands of horsehair, which they sold to Whites (Kluckhohn et al. 1971: 87).

A lasso or lariat collected by Ten Kate (Fig. 249) is braided from four strands of rawhide, made with a knot at one end and a loop at the other to form a running noose, to be used for catching livestock around the neck. It is well used. Where Ten Kate got this lasso is unknown, but he mentions Navajo lassos/lariats of rawhide and horsehair, and it is conceivable that he acquired it near Fort Defiance in August 1883. Ropes and lassos of rawhide, buckskin, wool, horsehair, and yucca, done in a variety of braiding techniques, are well documented for the Navajo (Kluckhohn et al. 1971: 92–97).

Fig. 249   Lasso or lariat; Navajo; rawhide; l. 12.1 m; ca. 1870–1880 (RMV 361-53).

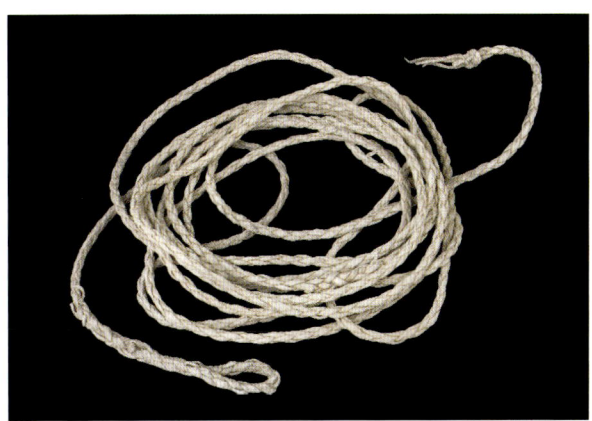

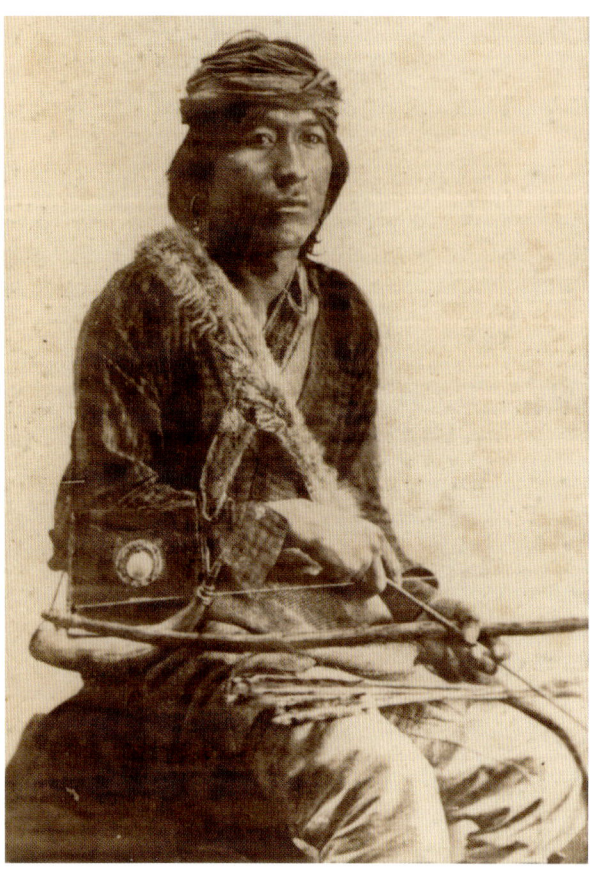

Fig. 250 Navajo man with bow, arrows, powder horn, and bag with silver ornament. Photograph by Alfredo Laurent, ca. 1882 (Ten Kate coll.; WMR 900588).

Simple sinew-backed bows and arrows with stone, later metal tips were used in hunting and warfare. Bows were preferably of oak, cedar, or sumac and sinew was harvested from bighorn sheep or deer. For arrows the twigs of wild currant, black greasewood, or other hard wood was harvested. Arrows were usually fletched with three split eagle feathers, fastened with sinew. At the point of the fletching a red and blue line is often applied around the shaft. Along its length, the arrows often exhibit an incised zigzag design, said to represent lighting. Eagle catching, which takes place from November to January, was a ritual affair because the birds were regarded to be holy human beings. The feathers were not only used for fletching and adorning men's caps, but also as medicine for shamans. Bows and arrows were carried in cases and quivers made from mountain lion skin (Franciscan Fathers 1910: 318–319; Hill 1938: 161–166; Kluckhohn et al. 1971: 33–43; Roessel 1983b: 509). Gunnerson (1959) has pointed out that the Navajo did little stone working and probably relied mostly on surface finds of prehistoric flint arrowheads to use on their arrows; in other cases they cut the

wooden shaft to a sharp point. She suggested that stone working and arrowheads became increasingly associated with ritual and taboo, as was basketry making, the reason why both crafts virtually became extinct (cf. Tschopik 1938). The Navajo readily adopted metal arrowheads and purchased baskets increasingly from the Southern Paiute and Southern Ute.

Although Ten Kate acquired a Navajo arrow (WMR 17998) in 1883, it remained in his possession until the summer of 1911, when he and his Japanese wife Kimi Fujii were in The Hague and donated this specimen and several Comanche arrows along with Japanese artifacts to the Museum of Anthropology, now the World Museum, in Rotterdam. It could not be located at the time of research for this catalogue.

References

Adair, John
    1944   *The Navajo and Pueblo Silversmiths*. Norman, OK: University of Oklahoma Press.
Amsden, Charles A.
    1934   *Navaho Weaving: Its Technic, and Its History*. Santa Ana, CA: Fine Arts Press.
Bauver, Robert
    2007   *Navajo and Pueblo Earrings, 1850–1945*. Los Ranchos de Albuquerque, NM: Rio Grande Books.
Beardsley, Grace
    1985   Design Development in Tarahumara and Pueblo Sashes. *American Indian Art Magazine* 10(4): 30–43, 71–73.
Bedinger, Margery
    1973   *Indian Silver: Navajo and Pueblo Jewelers*. Albuquerque, NM: University of New Mexico Press.
Begay-Foss, Joyce
    2002   Weaving Process and Techniques. In Coulter 2002: 119–133.
Bennett, Kathy
    1981   Navajo Chief Blanket: A Trade Item among Non-Navajo Groups. *American Indian Art Magazine* 7(1): 62–69.
Berlant, Anthony and Mary Hunt Kahlenberg
    1972   *The Navajo Blanket*. New York, NY–Los Angeles, CA: Praeger–Los Angeles County Museum.
    1977   *Walk in Beauty: The Navajo and Their Blankets*. Boston, MA: New York Graphic Society.
Bonar, Eulalie
    1996   (ed.) *Woven by the Grandmothers: Nineteenth-Century Navajo Textiles from the National Museum of the American Indian*. Washington, DC: Smithsonian Institution Press.
Cirillo, Dexter
    1992   *Southwestern Indian Jewelry*. New York, NY: Abbeville Press.

Conn, Richard C.

   1974   *Robes of White Shell and Sunshine: Personal Decorative Arts of the Native American.* Denver, CO: Denver Art Museum.

Coulter, Lane

   2002   (ed.) *Navajo Saddle Blankets: Textiles to Ride in the American West.* Santa Fe, NM: Museum of New Mexico Press.

Doyle-Falkenstein, Cheri and Jonathan Batkin

   2004   (eds.) *Warp to Weft: Weavings by Morris Musket.* Santa Fe, NM: Wheelwright Museum of the American Indian.

Ellsberg, Helen

   1977   Ketohs. *American Indian Art Magazine* 2(3): 66–71.

Fane, Diana

   1991   (ed.) *Objects of Myth and Memory: American Indian Art at the Brooklyn Museum.* New York, NY: The Brooklyn Museum.

Franciscan Fathers

   1910   *An Ethnologic Dictionary of the Navaho Language.* Saint Michael's, AZ: The Franciscan Fathers.

Frank, Larry and Mildred J. Holbrook

   1990   *Indian Silver Jewelry of the Southwest, 1868–1930.* West Chester, PA: Schiffer.

Gunnerson, Dolores

   1959   Tabu and Navajo Material Culture. *El Palacio* 66(1): 1–9.

Hedlund, Anne Lane

   1990   *Beyond the Loom: Keys to Understanding Early Southwestern Weaving.* Boulder, CO: Johnson Books.

Hill, Walter W.

   1936   *Navaho Warfare.* Yale University Publications in Anthropology 5. New Haven, CT.

   1938   *The Agricultural and Hunting Methods of the Navaho Indians.* Yale University Publications in Anthropology 18. New Haven, CT.

   1948   Navajo Trading and Trading Ritual: A Study of Cultural Dynamics. *Southwestern Journal of Anthropology* 4: 371–396.

James, George Wharton

   1914   *Indian Blankets and Their Makers.* Chicago, IL: McClurg.

James, H. L.

   1976   *Posts and Rugs: The History of Navajo Rugs and Their Homes.* Globe, AZ: Southwest Parks and Monuments Association.

Jernigan, E. W. et al.

   1981   *White Metal Universe: Navajo Silver from the Fred Harvey Collection.* Phoenix, AZ: The Heard Museum.

Kent, Kate Peck

   1961   *The Story of Navajo Weaving.* Cambridge, MA: Harvard University Press.

   1983   *Prehistoric Textiles of the Southwest.* Santa Fe, NM: School of American Research Press.

   1985   *Navajo Weaving: Three Centuries of Change.* Santa Fe, NM: School of American Research Press.

Kline, Cindra

   2001   *Navajo Spoons: Indian Artistry and the Souvenir Trade, 1880–1940.* Santa Fe, NM: Museum of New Mexico Press.

Kluckhohn, Clyde, Walter W. Hill, and Lucy Wales Kluckhohn

   1971   *Navajo Material Culture.* Cambridge, MA: Harvard University Press.

Lincoln, Louise

   1982   (ed.) *Southwest Indian Silver from the Doneghy Collection.* Minneapolis, MN: Minneapolis Institute of Arts.

McGreevy, Susan Brown

   1997   Matthews' Studies of Navajo Arts. In: K. Spencer Halpern and S. Brown McGreevy (eds.), *Washington Matthews: Studies of Navajo Culture, 1880–1894* (Albuquerque, NM: University of New Mexico Press), 16–27.

   2002   Looking Backward, Looking Forward: The Transitional Period Fulcrum, 1868–1910. In Coulter 2002: 41–62.

MacLeish, Kenneth

   1940   Notes on Hopi Belt-Weaving of Moenkopi. *American Anthropologist* 42: 291–310.

Matthews, Washington

   1883   Navajo Silversmiths. *Annual Report of the Bureau of American Ethnology* 2: 167–178.

   1884   Navajo Weavers. Washington: *Annual Report of the Bureau of American Ethnology* 3: 371–391.

   1897   *Navaho Legends.* Memoirs of the American Folklore Society 5. Boston, MA.

   1900   A Two-Faced Navaho Blanket. *American Anthropologist* 2: 638–642.

Mera, Harry P.

   1947   *Navaho Textile Arts.* Santa Fe, NM: School of American Research.

   1960   *Indian Silverwork of the Southwest.* Globe, AZ: Dale King Publications.

Neumann, David L.

   1977   Navajo Silver Bridles. *American Indian Art Magazine* 2(2): 70–77.

Notarnicola, Cathy

   2005   Navajo Chief's Blankets and the National Museum of the American Indian. *American Indian Art Magazine* 29(4): 64–71.

Orchard, William C.

   1929   *Beads and Beadwork of the American Indians.* Contributions from the Museum of the American Indian 11. New York, NY.

Ostermann, L.

   1917   Origin, Characteristics, and Costume of the Navajo Indians. *Franciscan Missions of the Southwest* 5: 1–11.

Price, B. Byron

   2002   The Cowboy Market for Navajo Saddle Blankets. In Coulter 2002: 103–118.

Reichard, Gladys A.

   1934   *Spider Woman: A Story of Navajo Weavers and Chanters.* New York, NY: McMillan.

   1936a   *Navajo Shepherd and Weaver.* New York, NY: J. J. Augustin.

   1936b   Color in Navaho Weaving. *Arizona Historical Review* 7(2): 19–30.

   1939   *Dezba: Woman of the Desert.* New York, NY: J. J. Augustin.

Rodee, Marian E.

   1977   *Southwestern Weaving.* Albuquerque, NM: University of New Mexico Press.

1981 *Old Navajo Rugs: Their Development from 1900 to 1940.* Albuquerque, NM: University of New Mexico Press.

1987 *Weaving of the Southwest from the Maxwell Museum of Anthropology.* West Chester, PA: Schiffer Press.

2002 Twentieth-Century Saddle Blankets. In Coulter 2002: 63–92.

Roessel, Robert A.

1983a Navajo Arts and Crafts. Rough Rock, AZ: Rough Rock Navajo Demonstration School Curriculum Center.

1983b Navajo History, 1850–1923. In: Alfonso Ortiz (ed.), *Southwest* (Handbook of North American Indians 10. William C. Sturtevant, gen. ed.; Washington, DC), 506–523.

Shufeldt, Robert W.

1891 The Navajo Belt-Weaver. *Proceedings of the U.S. National Museum* 14: 391–393.

Tanner, Clara Lee

1978 The Squash Blossom. *American Indian Art Magazine* 3(3): 36–43.

Taylor, Tobi

2000 Navajo Woven Saddle Cinches. *American Indian Art Magazine* 25(3): 70–77.

Ten Kate, Herman F. C.

1890 Zuni Fetishes. *Internationales Archiv für Ethnographie* 3: 118–119.

1885 *Reizen en Onderzoekingen in Noord Amerika.* Leiden: E. J. Brill.

2004 *Travels and Researches in Native North America, 1882–1883.* P. Hovens, L. A. Hieb, and W. J. Orr eds. Albuquerque, NM: University of New Mexico Press. [Translation of Ten Kate 1885.]

Tisdale, Shelby

2006 *Fine Indian Jewelry of the Southwest: The Millicent Rogers Museum Collection.* Santa Fe, NM: Museum of New Mexico Press.

Tschopik, Harry, Jr.

1938 Taboo as a Possible Factor Involved in the Obsolescence of Navaho Pottery and Basketry. *American Anthropologist* 40(2): 257–262.

Wheat, Joe Ben

1973 *Navajo Blankets from the Collection of Anthony Berlant.* Tucson, AZ: University of Arizona Press.

1976 The Navajo Chief Blanket. *American Indian Art Magazine* 1(3): 44–55.

1982 Early Southwest Metalwork. In Lincoln 1982: 13–22.

2003 *Blanket Weaving in the Southwest.* Tucson, AZ: University of Arizona Press.

Whitaker, Kathleen

1981 Navajo Chief Blanket: A Trade Item among Non-Navajo Groups. *American Indian Art Magazine* 7(1): 62–69.

2002 *Southwest Textiles: Weavings of the Navajo and Pueblo.* Seattle, WA: University of Washington Press.

Witherspoon, Gary

1981 Silver and Turquoise Jewelry in the Navajo World. In Jernigan et al. 1918: 47–52.

Woodward, Arthur

1938 *A Brief History of Navajo Silversmithing.* Museum of Northern Arizona Bulletin 14. Flagstaff, AZ.

The Zuni

10

The commander of Fort Wingate provided Ten Kate with transportation to Zuni in a military ambulance. By way of Nutrias, a small pueblo situated among fields tilled by the Indians, they approached Zuni. The valley was dominated by two huge mesas on the southern horizon. The pueblo was situated in the valley along the Zuni River floor, a compact village of stacked adobe houses around a plaza, the home of about 1,600 Indians living their lives very much in way they had for centuries. Presbyterian missionary Taylor F. Ealy and Indian trader Douglas D. Graham with their families were the only White residents of the pueblo in 1883, apart from the Cushing household.

Frank H. Cushing had come to Zuni in 1879 and stayed for several years, living amongst them as one of their own and establishing the method of participant observation. He was intent on documenting and analyzing a tribal culture in hitherto unknown detail, showing the complexity of their metaphysical ideas and way of life, which had developed over centuries in the semiarid desert. Palowahtiwa, the governor, provided the ethnologist with living space in his house, and when Mrs. Cushing joined him, their quarters were soon outfitted for comfortable living. Ten Kate was their guest during his stay in Zuni. Through his fieldwork, publications, and advocacy of Indian land rights, Cushing became legendary in his own lifetime and gained even more stature after his untimely death. After a week in Zuni, Ten Kate wrote in his notebook: "From the people he lives among I have been able to observe Cushing and know him through his work. Two things I have particularly gained from this acquaintance: a profound admiration for a man who has suffered for the sake of science alone, and the conviction that his method of studying the ethnology of a people is the only authentic one" (Ten Kate 2004: 278; cf. Hinsley 1981: 192-207; Hovens 1988; 1989: 119-126, 138-147).

Architecture and Subsistence

Ten Kate's description of Zuni is evocative: "In the main Zuni has the same character as all other pueblos; and the description, already provided, of the Hopi villages, of Tesuque and Laguna is generally applicable to Zuni as well. … For a description of the interior of Zuni dwellings I refer to that of the Hopis to avoid being repetitive; but the rooms are usually much larger and more spacious, while in many windows gypsum slabs (so-called Mary glass) serve as panes. Regular glass has already replaced gypsum slabs in not a few dwellings, however. … The ground plan of Zuni is longitudinal, and its axis runs roughly from East to West, while the tallest houses—consisting of four stories—are located in the southern center of the town. Only the color of the houses differs entirely from that of the aforementioned pueblos, and is purplish-reddish brown, just like the ground they rest upon. Here, too, hundreds of wooden ladders jut above the terraces, and numerous sheep corrals are found along the outskirts of the pueblo, filling the air with their penetrating stench. On the south side of the town flows the shallow, muddy Zuni River, a branch of the Rio Puerco. The only tree in the town is a small cottonwood. All around on the plain the eye perceives nothing but sand, sparse grass, and corn and melon fields" (Ten Kate 2004: 274-275).

Corn was the staple food of the Zuni and was planted in fields chosen strategically to obtain sufficient moisture. In Zuni philosophy corn belonged to the five vital elements for human existence, the sun, the earth, water, and fire being the other four. The major agricultural implements consisted of wooden plows and digging sticks. Mutton also figured prominently in the Zuni diet, and the Indians were proud of their flocks of sheep, which they took out to graze every morning. Only a small number of cows were owned, due to the lack of sufficient grasslands. Donkeys were the preferred means of transporting loads.

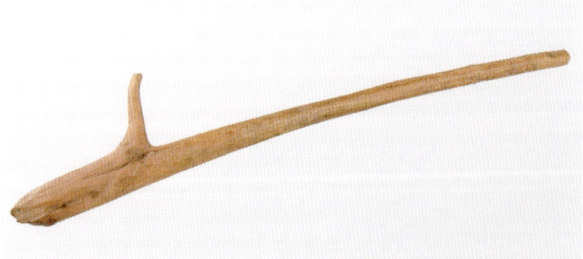

Fig. 251 Digging stick; *tazaquin, táhssahqueen* (TK), *ta-sa-quin-ne* (J. Stevenson 1883: 371); wood; l. 97 cm, d. 3.3 cm; ca. 1880 (RMV 362-154).

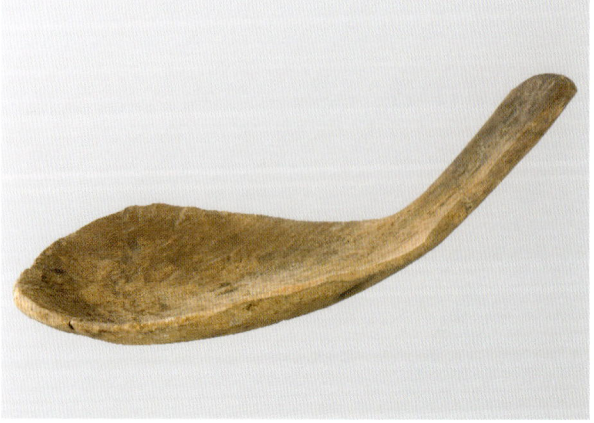

Fig. 252 Spoon; wood; l. 30.5 cm, w. 11.6 cm; ca. 1880 (RMV 362-156).

Game was scarce in the area right around the main village. Only ground doves (*Chamapelia*) appeared in large numbers in the sandy plain and among the cornfields, but were difficult to shoot. The forested mountains were the abode of deer and antelope, favorite prey for Zuni hunters. During the late summer and early autumn the Zuni staged communal hunts on horseback for rabbits and hares, affairs that also had religious significance. Ten Kate attended two of these in 1883 and 1888, participating in the latter one near Ojo Caliente.

Ten Kate (2004: 280) noted: "As for the Zunis' agricultural implements, these consist primarily of the crude wooden plow, ... and a wooden digging stick (*táhssahqueen*), which is approximately one meter in length. The broad flat point serves for making holes in the ground, which must hold the seed. The farmer rests his foot on a side blade, while the tool is otherwise handled as a spade." The Leiden specimen (Fig. 251) is made from heavy wood and its digging surface is broken off, indication heavy use. The Zuni also used flat wooden spades or shovels for removing bread from hot ovens and snow from their roofs (cf. J. Stevenson 1883: 371, figs. 495, 496).

Wooden household utensils such as spoons and ladles were quickly displaced by industrially produced metal varieties that were cheap and durable. Already in 1879 Colonel James Stevenson (1883: 370) noted that wooden utensils were becoming rare. Although most spoons and ladles were simple, the elongated shape of the spoon collected by Ten Kate (Fig. 252) is rather elegantly carved. Others were decorated with carvings, usually at the end of the handle (cf. Fane 1991: 102).

The Zuni, Hopi, and other Pueblo Indians used flat and slightly crooked wooden sticks, often compared to boomerangs because of their shape, for hunting small game, notably rabbits and hares. Sometimes they had painted geometric designs, symbolizing the prey. This specimen in the Ten Kate collection (Fig. 253) is undecorated.

Ten Kate participated in the 1888 Zuni hunt and provided a good description. Although the Indians used their traditional hunting sticks, he called these "javelins" in his narrative: "... took part in one of the big chase-hunts near Ojo Caliente, which are held every year after the gathering of the crops as a way of thanksgiving. This kind of hunt only takes place in the ... agricultural districts ... Hundreds of Indians on horseback, dressed festively and armed with javelins, took part in it. ... at the hunting-field ... the great father of the *Kôk'kô* or Holy Dance organisation, *A'wan tatchu Ko'yemshi*, with his assistant and a priest of the Huntingorder (*San'iakiakwe*) performed a simple but impressive ceremony that was attended in good earnest by everybody present. The great father said the prayers, while his assistant and the Hunting priest joined him every time with the word *athlu* (so be it). After that the great father and his assistant breathed on each other, after which the latter repeated the prayer of the father; they held hands when they did this. In this prayer, besides thanking for the crops of this year, they pray for a rich

Fig. 253 Rabbit hunting stick; *záyannuh, thleánnuk* (TK); wood; l. 55 cm; ca. 1880 (RMV 362-162).

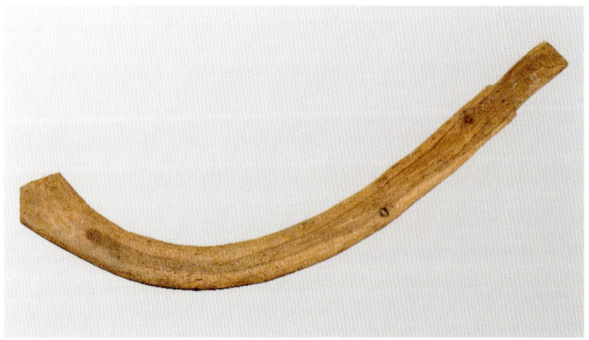

crop next season, for the well-being of the A'shiwi in general and for a joyful awakening in the Ko'thluwala'wa (residence of the Council of the Gods). Then all went to a little cedar tree, that had been set afire previously. Here the three again said prayers, this time for the dead, throwing héwé (wafer bread) into the fire as offerings. ... The hunters came to the great father in small groups, who gave them some héwé to offer into the fire. Finally the hunters quickly run there javelins through the flames, praying for good luck on their hunt, that could start only now. As I heard from Cushing, this prayer partly exists of archaic words."

"This kind of reckless and rash driving was new to me. The small, unsightly looking Indian horses, one of which I was riding, showed here what they were able to. The wild passion of the riders seemed to be shared by the horses. Divided in numerous small groups the men hunted the mainly flat, but rather woody plain at full gallop. Although this hunt was supposed to be a rabbit hunt, many hares, and even a prairie wolf as well, fell under the javelins which the Indians wielded dexterously. The motley flying troupe of riders, the dull droning of thousands of hoofs, the fearful game, the fierce sun, all constituted an unforgettable scene. Towards evening the riders and horses returned to Zuni covered with dust and sweat. Hundreds of rabbits and hares hung on the horses in bunches."

"The riders who bring booty have to perform another ceremony when they get home. The animal is carefully put on a blanket, with a corncob between their front paws and the head pointing towards the east. Every member of the family sprinkles some flour and prays for the ghosts of the dead game to return to their residence to send more rabbits and hares to the Zuni. Then the game is skinned and roasted according to fixed rules. Only then it may be eaten" (Ten Kate 1925: 139–141; Hovens 1995: 693–695).

Dress, Textiles, and Personal Adornment

According to Ten Kate, the dress of the Zuni was quite similar to that of the Hopi, with the exception of the Navajo-style headbands of the men. Western dress had replaced traditional skin clothing, and Ten Kate noted that trader Graham's store had been instrumental in that rapid change. Navajo blankets were also often seen as part of tribal costume. However, the Zuni also wove their own textiles, and Ten Kate was especially taken by the picturesque white blankets with black and green borders worn by women during dances. In addition, multicolored

sashes and garters with intricate designs were woven, as were dark-blue stockings. Girls and women wore their hair hanging loose, cut at the neck and parted on one side. Rabbit skins were sewn together and used as bedding, as among the Hopi. Babies were swaddled on cradleboards.

The prehistory and early history of Puebloan weaving is discussed in the textiles section of the Hopi chapter. The Zuni Pueblo is exceptional in that in historic times women rather than men sat at the loom, although the latter were not excluded from weaving. The major textile made at Zuni was the woman's blanket or shawl with embroidered borders, woven from native cotton. Men's dance kilts follow the same pattern. Wool was used for a great variety of daily, festive, and ceremonial dress items. Traditional dyes for yarn included a yellow from thistles (*Circium* sp.) or rabbitweed (*Bigelovia*), a brownish red from tickseed (*Coreopsis*) flowers, and black from the bark of sumac (*Rhus*). For mordant, alum was locally available.

Many black blankets were woven for men and worn while participating in and observing ceremonies. Used as shrouds for people to be buried in, they disappeared in the 1880s. Striped blankets, often with a white foundation, were the other main type. These tend to be less elongated and a bit more square that those of other Pueblos, as well as a bit more coarse, thick, and fuzzy (Douglas 1940). Zuni textiles are a subject deserving more scholarly attention.

For the manufacture of belts and sashes the Zuni could resort to the upright loom as well as the backstrap loom. In the latter case, weaving battens or weaving "knives" such as the one in the Ten Kate collection (Fig. 254) were used to tighten the weave. Although men were probably the weavers in preconquest times, women gradually took over the craft. However, for a long time the Zuni hosted a number of male Hopi weavers to supply their needs, especially for ceremonial garments (Spier 1924: 74–79).

Fig. 254 Weaving batten; *zéinüh* (TK); wood; l. 34.5 cm, w. 3.5 cm; ca. 1880 (RMV 362-155).

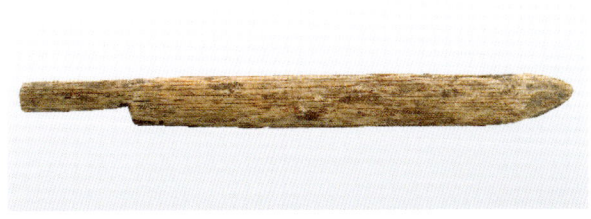

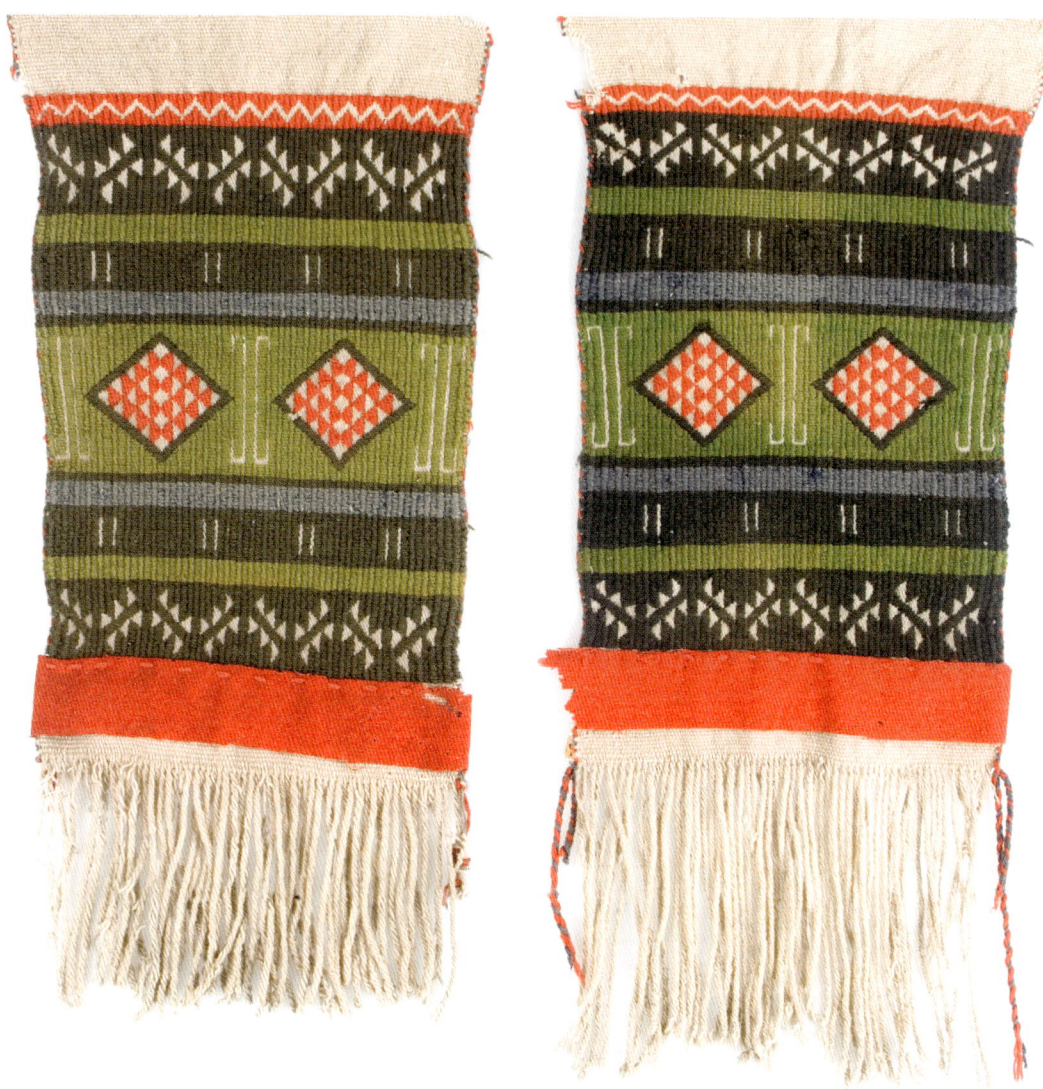

Fig. 255 Kachina dance sash (in two halves); *ta·kun·i·kwi·kya·tsi·napa* or *kâkâthléom* (TK); cotton, wool, pigments; l. 102 cm (without fringe), w. 26.5 cm; ca. 1880 (RMV 674·3, ·6).

The oldest known kachina dance sashes were collected among the Hopi in the 1870s by John Wesley Powell and Colonel James Stevenson (J. Stevenson 1883: fig. 501; Sayers 1981: 71; cf. Hedlund and Dittemore 2004: 61, fig. 2). Although the Hopi also traded these with their sedentary neighbors and even the Navajo as Ten Kate noted, very similar sashes were woven at Zuni and in many New Mexican Pueblo villages, as the fieldwork of Douglas has documented (Douglas 1938, 1939a, 1939b, 1940; Mera 1943; Kent 1983: 76-79). When Stevenson was collecting in Zuni for the Smithsonian Institution in 1879, he acquired a whole series of kachina dance sashes of either Hopi or Zuni manufacture (J. Stevenson 1883: 373-374, figs. 500-502). As parts of ritual attire, the kachina sashes were standardized to a great extent and show only few variations. Because virtually all kachina sashes that have been published are identified as Hopi, we heavily rely on fieldwork done in the Hopi villages for their interpretation.

The warp of the upright loom on which kachina dance sashes are woven, usually in two identical parts, varies from eight to twelve inches (MacLeish 1940: 310). The cotton used for these sashes was specially treated before spinning by whipping it with withes on a bed of sand, a procedure with symbolic connotations (Hough 1915: 85). Natural handspun white wool is used for the weft in a warp plain weave. The two halves are sewn together at the top, resulting in a long sash, the standard size being about ten inches wide and ninety inches long. In the 1880s cotton began to replace wool as the material from which the sashes were made.

The kachina sash collected by Ten Kate (Fig. 255) consists of two identical woolen panels, sewn together at the top, two thirds of which are plain, while the lower third is decorated with patterns of (now rather faded) four-ply Germantown yarns. The sash ends in a fringe and is trimmed with a strip of red trade cloth. The weaver has changed the weft to a cotton twine in the decorative lower parts of the sash, which are woven in a technique called "Hopi brocade," a relatively recent technique developed or acquired before 1880. The painting and embroidery of textiles was much older. Frederic H. Douglas (1938) has analyzed the technical aspects of brocading and stressed that it should not be confused with embroidery, as brocading involves the insertion of colored threads into the fabric while it is still being woven on the loom. Not standardized is the narrow band where the plain weave merges in the brocaded panel, and variations have been interpreted as individual "signatures" of weavers.

The interpretation of the design of these sashes has varied, but all interpretations were recorded among the Hopi. According to Alexander M. Stephen, the design shows *Wúyak-küita*, Broadface Kachina, with the diamond shapes representing his bulging eyes, the zigzag bands his bared teeth, and the hooked and striped elements the face painting of warriors. This interpretation corresponds with the role of Broadface as a guardian and protector of other kachinas (Stephen 1936: 35, 240), and he appears in this role during the Bean Dance (Powamu) on all three Hopi mesas, carrying a whip to underline his authority and protective role. The dancing Broadface Kachina also has a prominent row of teeth, executed in triangularly twisted light-colored cornhusks on a black facemask (Colton 1959: 26). The straight white double lines in the dark band are referred to as *Püükoñhoya*, the Twin Warrior Gods, and are symbolized by similar designs in facial painting. The lower end of the sashes is almost always finished with a band of red cloth sewn on, and finally the natural white woolen fringe, sometimes referred to as the beard of Broadface Kachina.

With the help of his informants, Hopi missionary H. R. Voth, who worked mainly at Oraibi around 1900, identified the zigzags as mountain lion teeth, the lozenges as melon blossoms or squashes, and the hooks as bean sprouts, an interpretation partially approximating the one solicited from Second and Third Mesa informants in 1968 (Wade

and Evans 1973; also cf. Sayers 1981: 71–73, 75). Wade and Evans (1973) suggest that the apparently diverse interpretations are interrelated and complementary and refer to rain and fertility, protective deities and spirits, natural and ceremonial cycles, and the maintenance of cosmic and social order, thus expressing the Hopi worldview in spatial, temporal, natural, spiritual, and mythic dimensions. The degree of consistency in Native explanations of designs generally decreases over time, and earlier interpretations therefore adhere more closely to traditional origins and meanings. However, any interpretation at any time provided by any weaver serious about his work fits into the fabric of Hopi metaphysics and life and as such should be regarded as authentic. The typical design of the dance sash has also been used on a Hopi man's shirt collected around 1900 at Oraibi and represents an adaptation of a traditional element to a new use (Whitaker 2002: 392–393; cf. Kent 1983: 81).

Ten Kate (RMV card file) described this sash as "dress for a mythical drama." The kachina sash was part of the ceremonial attire worn by male kachina dancers, wrapped around their waist, with the ends draped to the right side of their bodies, almost touching the ground, the brocaded panels facing outward. Less traditional is the wearing of these sashes as breechcloths, with the brocaded ends hanging at the front and back (James 1914: 166–167; Hough 1919: 258–260; Bartlett 1949: 2; Rodee 1977: 125–130; Fox 1978: 56–58; Sayers 1981; Kent 1983: 76–81; cf. Conn 1979: 186; Wright 1979: 35; Fane 1991: 149). In addition to the kachina sash, the Hopi braided a plain white cotton "rain" or "wedding" sash, ending in cornhusk balls with long fringes, symbolizing precipitation. It was presented to the Hopi bride on her marriage. A special weaving technique called "sprang" was used for such sashes (Fox 1978: 33–36, 58–59; Kent 1983: 82–84).

Traditionally the Zuni made blankets from the skins of rabbits and lynxes and from buffalo hides they obtained in trade from tribes further east. In prehistoric times the Hopi supplied their southern neighbors with cotton garments, although some cotton growing and weaving also took place at Zuni. Spanish and Mexican woolen blankets replaced these traditional specimens, and the Zuni began copying these textiles in a loose weave, producing a variety of plain and striped wearing blankets (Kent 1983: 44, 49; Fane 1991: 132–133). However, blanket weaving remained limited at Zuni, not the least because of the mushrooming Navajo supply. On his first expedition in 1879 Colonel James Stevenson (1883: 373–374) collected twenty-five

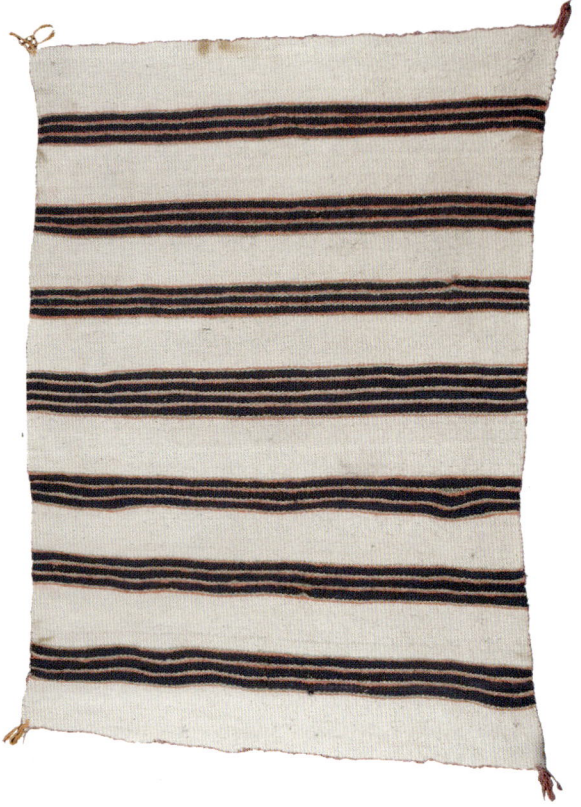

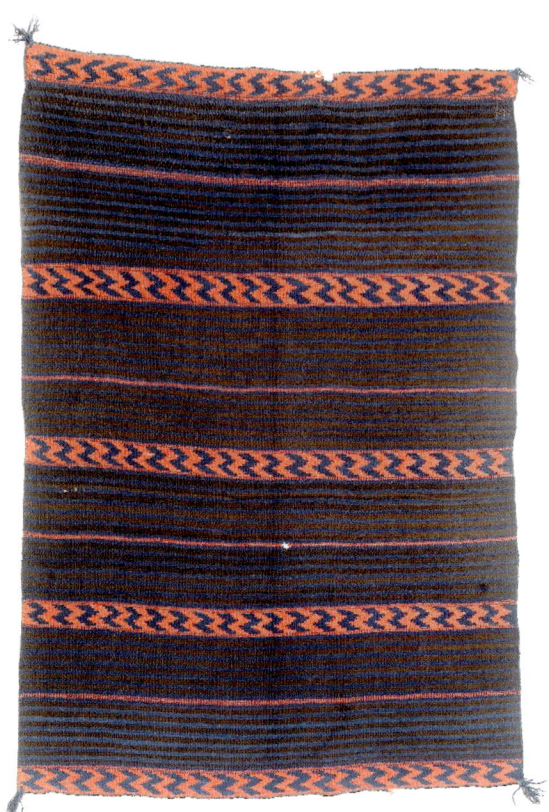

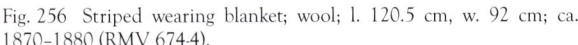

Fig. 256 Striped wearing blanket; wool; l. 120.5 cm, w. 92 cm; ca. 1870-1880 (RMV 674-4).

Fig. 257 Blanket; wool; l. 170.5 cm, w. 135 cm; ca. 1865-1875 (WMR 17981).

blankets in Zuni, almost all of Navajo manufacture. In 1881 he acquired not a single textile at Zuni, but several looms, loom parts, and weaving implements (J. Stevenson 1884: 580–581).

About the above specimen in the Ten Kate collection (Fig. 256) Marian Rodee (1992) noted: "Weft of handspun natural white, dark brown, indigo blue and indigo/rabbit-brush yellow green; red re-carded raveled single ply material; two edge cords of two-ply Z-S spun re-carded raveled red; edge tassels unusual in that two are orange and two purple red; a good example of the more loosely tied tassels used by Pueblo weavers; the stripes outlined with another color look more Zuni than Hopi; the young twigs and flowers of the rabbit brush which blooms in late summer and early fall produces a good dye and when over-dyed with blue it produces a good green."

Another Zuni wearing blanket obtained by Ten Kate (Fig. 257) is made of handspun white, dark brown, and indigo blue wool. The red is cochineal. The wool is loosely Z-spun, two-ply; only the selvage cord is three-ply, S-spun. The term for this style of blanket is "Moki," the old name

for the Hopi, because of the bands of narrow alternating dark blue and brown. Zuni as well as Navajo weavers also employ this pattern. The Zuni wove dress fabrics and blankets on the upright loom that was sometimes constructed using a roof beam and pegs in the floor as means of fixation. With wooden combs they tightened and evened out the weft threads. When the blanket reached its halfway point, it was reversed on the loom, after which the second half was woven from the bottom up (Spier 1924: 66–73; Fane 1991: 103). Ten Kate collected this specimen in 1888.

At the same time Ten Kate acquired a Zuni saddle blanket of all handspun wool in natural gray and black and with natural (red, yellow) and aniline (blue) dyed wool (Fig. 258). The threads are loosely Z-spun, two-ply, and the selvage cord is three-ply, Z-spun. During the 1880s weaving at Zuni declined rapidly due to the import of Western textiles and the ready acceptance of fine dress items for women from the Hopi and (saddle) blankets from the Navajo (Fane 1991: 129–130).

A fourth blanket in the collection (Fig. 259) shows signs of heavy wear. It is made of handspun wool, natural

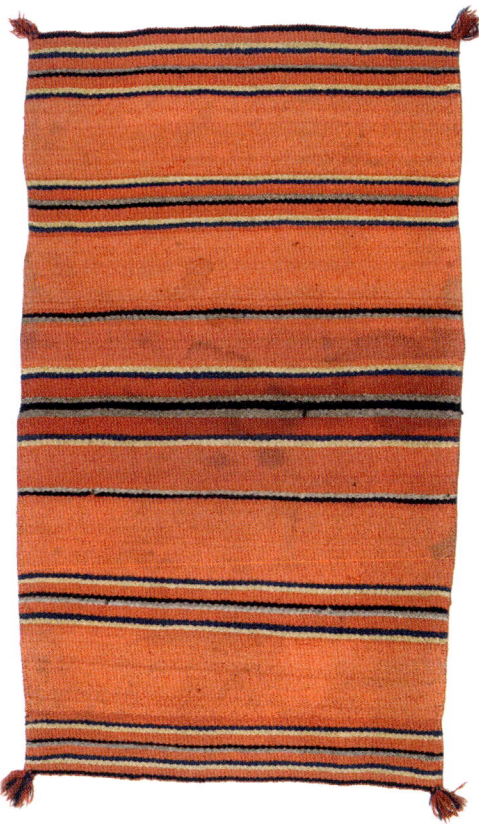

Fig. 258 Saddle blanket; wool; l. 122 cm, w. 78.5 cm; ca. 1880 (WMR 17982).

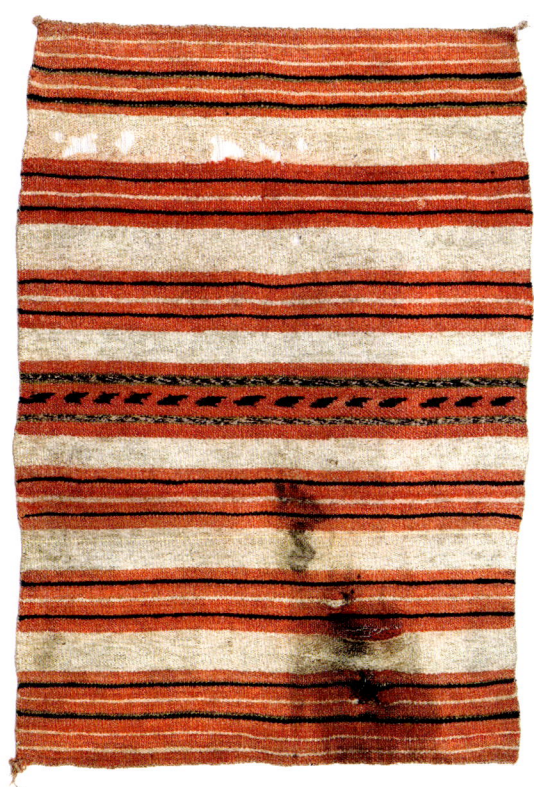

Fig. 259 Saddle blanket; wool; l. 91 cm, w. 67 cm; 1870-1880 (WMR 17983).

white, indigo, and blue. Red is probably cochineal and perhaps a yarn. The wool is loosely Z-spun, two-ply.

While working at Zuni in 1888 for the Hemenway Southwestern Archaeological Expedition, Ten Kate treated a number of Indians who were injured or ill. Among them was a ten-year old Indian girl with a serious wound in her thigh, stemming from a stray bullet. Able to prevent infection by lavish use of iodine and frequent renewal of bandages, the child eventually recovered. The parents were so grateful that they offered Ten Kate a horse, something he could not accept. Instead he was pleased to receive a piece of nicely painted pottery and a small (partly colored) saddle blanket (Ten Kate 1925: 143; Hovens 1995: 696), most probably this specimen.

Warp-faced belts were woven in two styles: the Navajo style with red and green wool warps and white cotton warps and wefts such as in this example collected by Ten Kate (Fig. 260), and the Hopi style with red, black, and green wool warps and black cotton wefts. The former were woven among the Navajo and Puebloans alike, while the manufacture of the latter was restricted to Pueblo weavers.

The patterns are made visible by floating the warps over the wefts. Zuni and other Pueblo women fastened their blankets or dresses with such belts around their waist, securing it on their left hip, with the long fringes hanging down, accentuating movement (Kent 1983: 85-89; Fane 1991: 130-131). Ten Kate called this specimen a man's belt.

Fig. 260 Woven belt; cotton, wool; *Enin-tsi-napa Ots'aiu* or *Cuiu-tsi-napa Ots'siu* (TK); l. 240 cm (with fringe 280 cm), w. 8 cm; ca. 1880 (RMV 674-5).

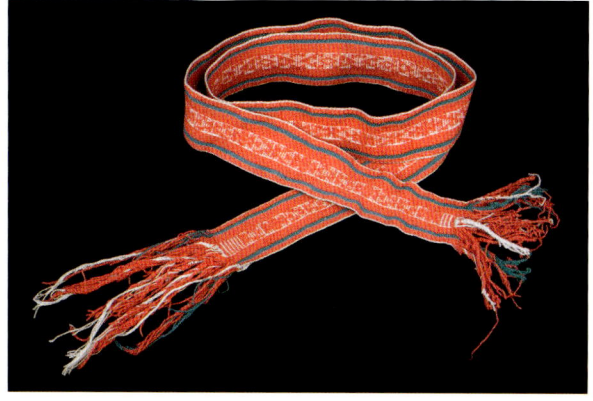

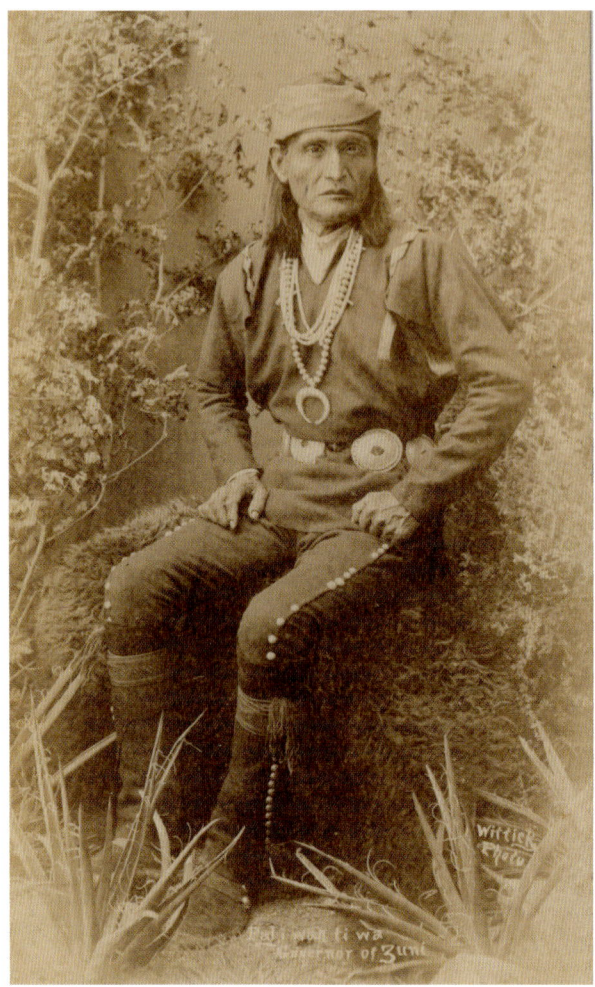

Fig. 261 Palowahtiwa, governor of Zuni; ca. 1882. Photograph by Ben Wittick (Ten Kate coll.; WMR 909049).

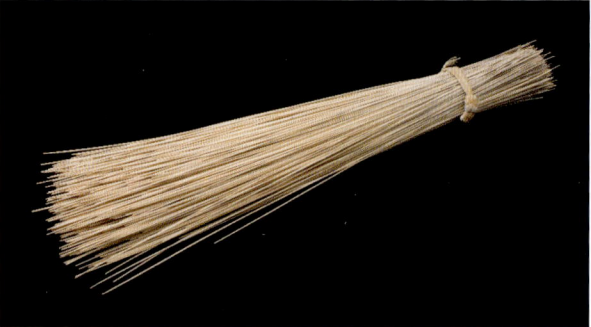

Fig. 264 Hair brush of bundled grass stems; *puhpáy, paypay* (TK), *i-pïsh-na-k'ia pé-pe* (J. Stevenson 1884: 583); grass, hide; l. 28.5 cm; ca. 1880 (RMV 362-160).

The moccasins are fastened with a silver button. Ten Kate noted that this pair was worn by a woman. A second pair of red-stained moccasins with crenate ankle flaps have two slits each and two silver buttons for fastening (Fig. 263).

Both women and men spent time on their appearance, and hairbrushes were a common part of personal grooming (Fig. 264). Ten Kate noted that similar hair brushes were in use among the Hopi, Pueblo peoples, and Navajo. James Stevenson (1884: 583, pl. 43) mentioned that the Indians used the butt end to comb their hair and the top end as a brush or broom to clean surfaces.

Jewelry

Ten Kate observed that some Zunis were engaged in silversmithing and erroneously concluded that the Navajo must have learned from them. One of the most expert smiths was Palawahtiwa, the governor of Zuni (Fig. 261). The rings, bracelets, buttons, and belt buckles he made expressed a mastery of technique and refined taste. He was equally adept in cutting and grinding turquoise, coral, and shell into flat round beads to produce monochrome

The Zuni dress items in the Ten Kate collection also include two pairs of moccasins. The soles of one pair (Fig. 262) are made from rawhide and have two separate uppers, the frontal upper of which is stained bright red, probably with hematite instead of mountain mahogany.

Figs. 262, 263   Moccasins; *mokwáwé* (TK); RMV 674-7: hide, sinew, pigment, silver; l. 26 cm, h. 11.5 cm; WMR 17984: hide, sinew, silver; l. 26 cm, w. 10 cm, h. 11 cm; both ca. 1880.

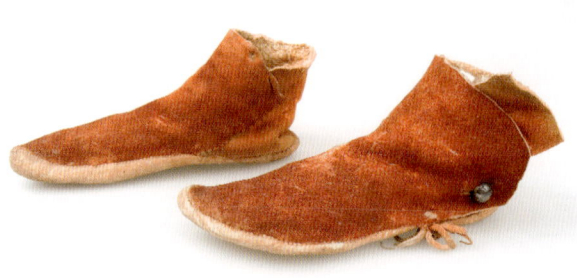

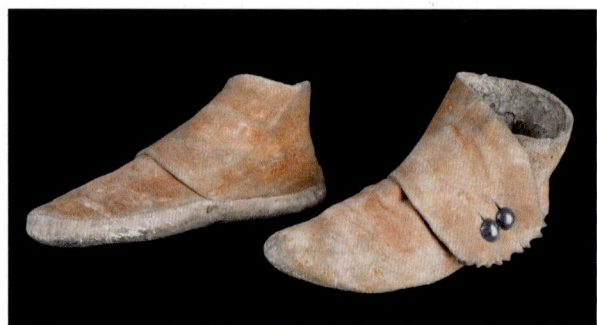

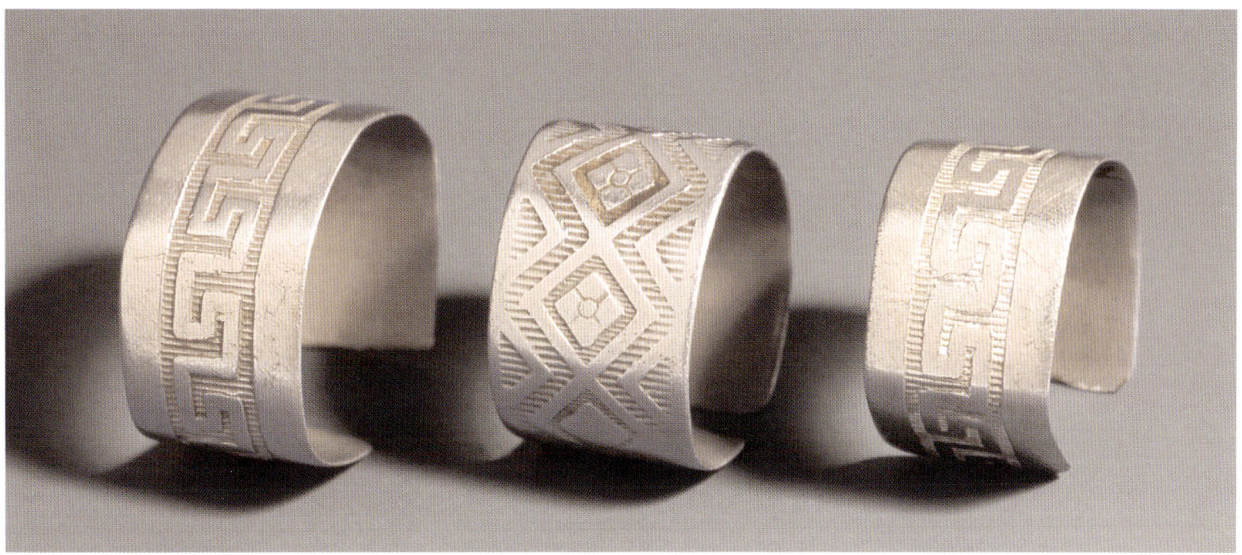

Fig. 265   Rings; silver; *Hé Koha·ne tsi Kya·Tsi'napa* or *Ne tsi Kya* (TK); d. 2–2.2 cm, w. ca. 1.4 cm; ca. 1880 (RMV 674·9a, b, 674·10).

as well as multicolored necklaces, which Ten Kate considered to be the best artistic industry could make. Coral and shell were obtained through trade from the shores of the Pacific and the Sea of Cortez and were considered most valuable. The Zuni also wore a ruby spinel which was found in their territory.

Of three silver fingerrings in the collection, two show a repeating fret design, while the third has a repeating diamond pattern (Fig. 265). The Anasazi ancestors of the Zuni had been expert craftsmen and produced a great variety of jewelry for personal adornment. Favored materials used and obtained through an extensive trading network stretching from the Pacific Coast to the Gulf of Mexico and northward into the Great Basin area included shell, coral, turquoise, and other precious stones. These materials were used raw or were expertly worked into beads used in necklaces, bracelets, or ear pendants. Native copper was also extracted and employed for ornaments (Cushing 1894, Fox 1989). Since about the 1830s the Zuni were producing their own metal jewelry in copper and brass, which they worked only with files and chisels. These materials were traded to them by Mexicans, who also were major clients for the finished work. The Zuni were quick to adopt Navajo silver jewelry as part of their dress. In 1879 John Hillers, who was with the Smithsonian's Stevenson Expedition, took photographs at Zuni which show people wearing silver necklaces, bracelets, and buttons. The Zuni learned the craft of silversmithing from Navajo artisan Atsidi Chon, popularly known as Ugly Smith, who stayed for a while at the

pueblo in 1872, making and selling jewelry and teaching his Zuni friend Lanyade the required skills for making tools and working silver into jewelry. Lanyadi taught his skills to Balawade, and both made the silver for Frank Cushing's attire. In 1879–80 Balawade taught other men, and the production of Zuni silver increased significantly. Cushing depicted one of the two Zuni silversmiths, probably Balawade, whom he befriended, in his "My Adventures in Zuni" and described his impressions of the craftsman: "... busy with his quaint forge and crude appliances, working Mexican coins over into bangles, girdles, earrings, buttons, and what not, for savage adornment. Though his tools were wonderfully rude, the work he turned out by dint of combined patience and ingenuity was remarkably beautiful" (Cushing 1882–1883; 1894; Adair 1944: 121–128; Bedinger 1973: 130–140; Frank and Holbrook 1990: 39; Ostler et al. 1996: 57-58).

The three silver rings Ten Kate collected at Zuni in the summer of 1882 were made of melted silver coins, which were hammered and stamped with dies (cf. Frank and Holbrook 1990: 71, fig. 76). These were the only items of silver jewelry Ten Kate acquired in Zuni. Because he stayed in the governor's house with Cushing and commented favorably about the jewelry making of Palowahtiwa, it is most probable that the rings were made by the Zuni headman. The rarity of Zuni silver jewelry at that early date and the value placed by the Indians on such items is illustrated by the fact that Colonel James Stevenson was unable to obtain silver jewelry during his 1879 and 1881 collecting expeditions.

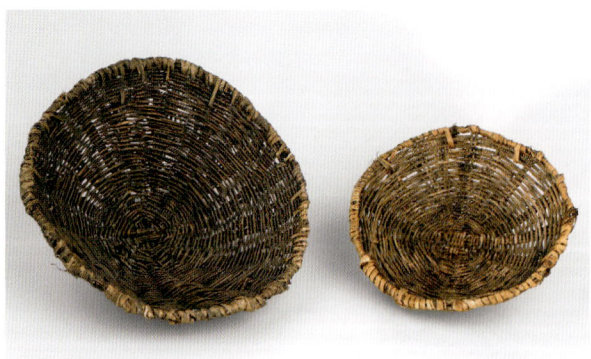

Fig. 266 Shallow wicker basketry trays; willow, yucca; RMV 362-152: d. 32.3 cm, h. 10.5 cm; RMV 362-151: d. 24.5 cm, h. 9 cm; both ca. 1880.

Basketry

According to Ten Kate, the Zuni did not excel in basketry and their containers were crudely woven and indistinct in shape. Ten Kate's negative judgement of the quality of Zuni basketry was shared by his contemporary Colonel James Stevenson (1883: 334), who collected 200 baskets at Zuni in 1879 and 1880 for the Smithsonian Institution. In a modern study, Andrew Hunter Whiteford (1988: 158–163) concurs, albeit noting some rare exceptions, such as coiled baskets in the shape of small ollas with a two-rod-and-bundle foundation. The shallow wicker peach baskets, in which decorative use is made of the light-colored rabbit-brush and red willow to create a checkered pattern, is also aesthetically pleasing (cf. Herold 2005: 93–94, 162).

The Zuni often purchased baskets from neighboring tribes to satisfy their demand for such containers, and thus they obtained different types from the Apache and Paiute, including pitch-coated water bottles from the for-

Fig. 267 Plaited basketry ring; *ha-kin-ne* (J. Stevenson 1883: 369); yucca; d. 11.4 cm, h. 2.7 cm; ca. 1880 (RMV 362-153).

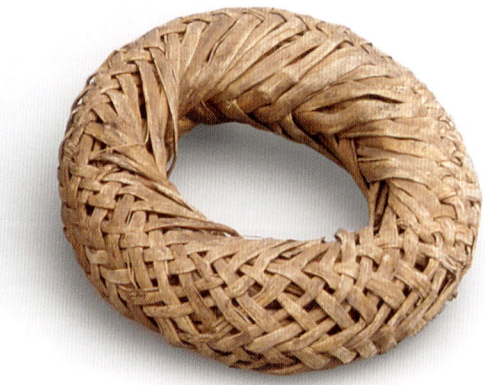

mer. However, they also produced a variety of baskets for different purposes themselves. Most common were wicker baskets of simple structure and weave and mostly lacking decoration (Fig. 266). Willow (*Salix*) was the preferred material for these containers, but dogwood (*Cornus*) and rabbitbrush (*Chrysothamnus*) were also used, often with the bark left on (J. Stevenson 1883: 368–370; Mason 1904: 500–503, pls. 28, 213; Tanner 1983: 75–78; Whiteford 1988: 158–167; Fane 1991: 139–141). The rims of both baskets collected by Ten Kate are wrapped with yucca strands.

Plaited rings of yucca (Fig. 267) were woven in small quantities. These were used by women to carry ollas to and from the river, to ease the weight of the vessels and stabilize them during transportation. In the home these rings were used as pot stands (J. Stevenson 1883: 369, fig. 486).

Pottery

In contrast to his opinion on Zuni basketry, Ten Kate expressed himself favorably about their pottery. He wrote: "... the Zunis surpass all other North American tribes in the making of pottery. The form is more delicate and austere, the ornamentation purer, and the color lovelier than I have seen anywhere. It consists of pots, pitchers, bowls, dishes, and cups of the most varied dimensions. One cannot enter any dwelling without one's eye alighting upon a number of these objects. Large ollas for holding water are particularly prominent. From the rim to the base the outline forms a wavy line which, the closer it gets to the bottom, practically turns into a straight line. Generally, the basic color of all the pottery is a more or less glossy white, while the ornamentation is black in color—in many places combined with reddish-brown. Except for those encountered among all peoples—decorations in the form of meanders, spirals, and wavy lines—decorations consist of figures which would be difficult to describe without detailed drawings because they are derived from Zuni mythology. The study of ornamentation alone should make a lengthy visit to Zuni quite worthwhile because in the images one encounters a vivid impression of the popular imagination, handed down and imitated from age to age, linking the hoary past with today. ... Pottery with animal shapes, mostly of birds, displays neither the clumsiness nor the monstrosity in that of the other Pueblo Indians. For the saucers and little bowls as well as the oblong pottery eating bowls—spoons if one will—light-brown is frequently the basic color."

"One of the most picturesque images that comes to mind was when, in the bright light of the early morning sun, a group of women and girls, with lovely water pitchers on their heads, came down along the small pathways between the cornfields surrounded with low adobe walls, to draw water from the sandy river. Merrily laughing and chatting, they passed each other along the pathway or lay kneeling down, to fill the ollas scoop by scoop with the muddy liquid. There was something oriental in that tableau with its fixed sky, overarching above the yellowish-reddish landscape, bounded in the distance by the bare perpendicular walls of the Tâ-ai-yállone or Thunder Mountain, which rose silently in isolation like a gigantic fortress in the background" (Ten Kate 2004: 279–280).

One of the Zuni potters was Wehwa, a male transvestite, about whom Ten Kate wrote: "Wéwha is the most mysterious amongst them. According to some people Wéwha is a man who has worn women's clothes ever since his early childhood and does women's work. Others say Wéwha is a woman, but most of them claim that Wéwha is a bisexual being. Wéhwas is unmarried, which is rare in Zuni. This he-she is what is called a personality, independent of character and very intelligent... And although Wéwha feels favorably disposed towards pale-faces, he-she adheres to the polytheistic belief of his ancestors with heart and soul. Wéhwa is one of the best-looking Zunis: sharp and regular features and tall and of strong built. In Wéwha's look there is something passionate and longing ..." (Ten Kate 1925: 137–138; Hovens 1995: 692–693; cf. Roscoe 1988).

Our firsthand knowledge of ceramic production at Zuni derives from the fieldwork carried out by anthropologists around the turn of the nineteenth century. Frank H. Cushing lived with the Zuni for several years and learned about their way of life through participant observation (Cushing 1886, 1920). Matilda Coxe Stevenson also studied pottery making, and although she published little on this aspect of her Zuni studies, she left valuable notes (M. Stevenson 1904). An important research project was carried out during the summers of 1924 and 1925, when Ruth Bunzel from Columbia University researched creativity in decorative style in the Pueblo ceramic tradition, concentrating her fieldwork on Zuni, Acoma, Hopi, and San Ildefonso. She not only observed and interviewed potters, but also learned to make pottery, being instructed by Zuni women and thus learning the intricacies of the craft and decorative style (Bunzel 1929). We owe it to Margaret Hardin of the Natural History Museum of Los Angeles

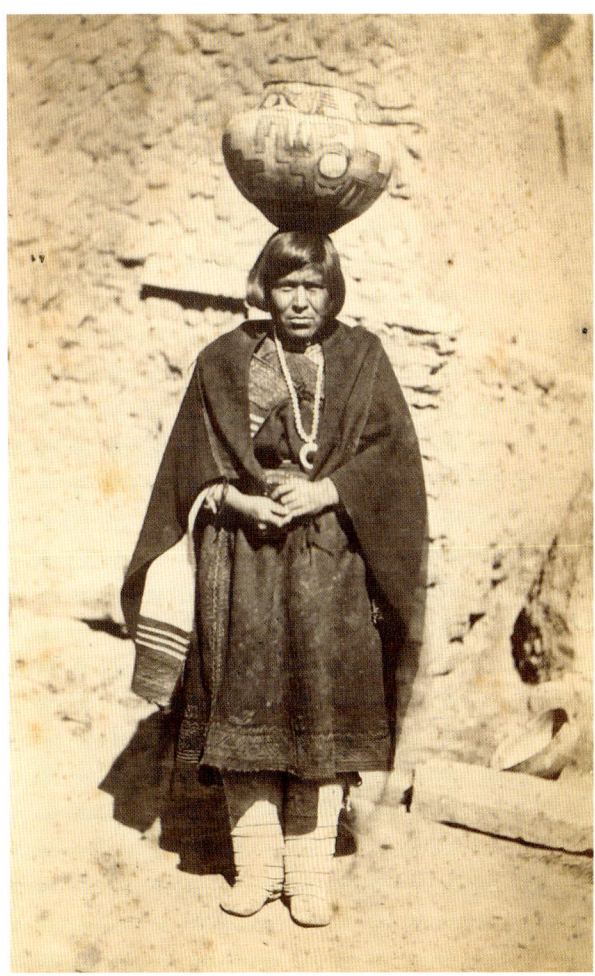

Fig. 268 Zuni woman in traditional dress, carrying olla; Zuni Pueblo, New Mexico, ca. 1880. Photograph by Henry Brown (Ten Kate coll.; RMV 414Kf2).

County that Matilda Coxe Stevenson's fieldwork notes on Zuni ceramics became more widely known. She must also be credited with the first major postwar study on the subject and the first large exhibition of Zuni ceramics, which was shown in Phoenix, Zuni, Taos, Las Cruces, and Washington, DC (Hardin 1983). At the Maxwell Museum of Anthropology on the campus of the University of New Mexico in Albuquerque, curator Marian Rodee and James Ostler of the Pueblo of Zuni Arts and Crafts Enterprise subsequently organized an exhibition and produced a catalogue on contemporary Zuni pottery and its makers (Rodee and Ostler 1986). We are fortunate that Milford Nahohai (1995), Ostler's colleague, has edited his conversations with Zuni potters, providing a contemporary Native point of view on an art and craft which has been undergoing a revival at Zuni.

Pottery is traditionally represented in many spheres of life at Zuni. Food was stored, cooked, and served in a large

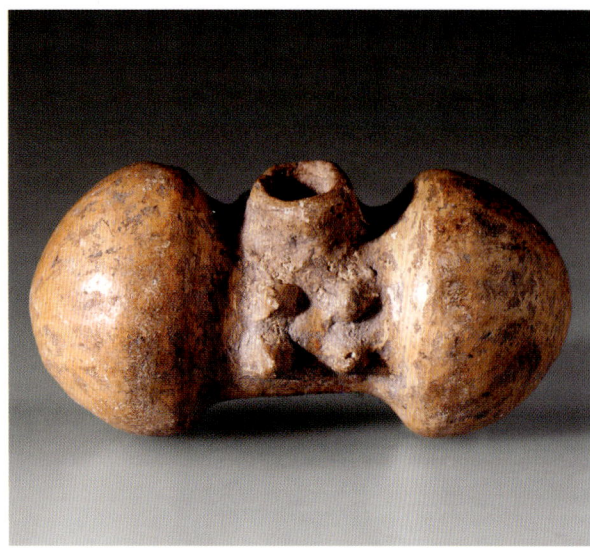

Fig. 269 Hunting canteen; *mewi:k'ilikdonne* (J. Stevenson 1883: 349); pottery; l. 8 cm, h. 4 cm, w. 3.5 cm; ca. 1880 (RMV 362-150).

variety of ceramic containers and dished up and eaten with pottery ladles and spoons. Water was drawn, transported, and kept in large vessels, commonly known as ollas. Piles of stacked vessels with their bottoms beaten out served as chimneys. Toys were made of pottery, and ceramics entered the religious sphere where a number of specialized containers were used to hold ceremonial media such as fetishes and sacred corn meal. Much traditional Zuni pottery is robust in appearance. The walls are thick and thus the vessels are heavy. Porosity of ollas is a necessary requirement, as this keeps the water cool through the slow process of natural evaporation.

The preferred clay for ceramics, dark gray shale, was located on top of Corn Mountain, but sometimes it was obtained from the mesas near the farming villages of Ojo Caliente and Pescado. Its procurement was physically challenging, as it required scaling a steep mountain along a narrow trail and descending it with a heavy load. This

Fig. 270 Ladles; *sa-sho-kon-ne* (J. Stevenson 1883: 360); pottery; RMV 362-157: l. 12.2 cm, w. 5.3 cm; RMV 362-158: l. 11.4 cm, w. 5 cm; RMV 362-159: l. 12.8 cm, w. 5.5 cm; all ca. 1880.

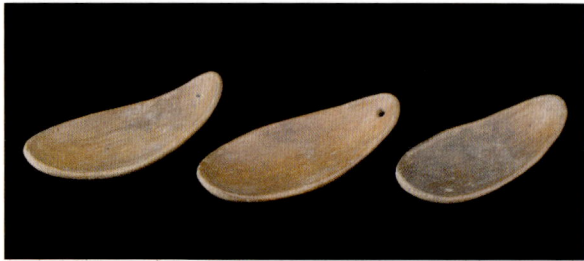

undertaking was associated with religious observances, as the Zuni regarded clay as the flesh of *He'teth o'kaya*, 'Clay Woman.' Notably the potters had to be "of pure heart," because otherwise Mother Earth would cease to supply them with their raw material. The digging and transportation was usually undertaken by "berdaches," men who dressed and lived as women. Men were forbidden to handle it and only women were potters, plastered the walls, and made building bricks (M. Stevenson 1904: 374–375).

After studying Zuni culture intermittently for over twenty years, Matilda Coxe Stevenson (1904: 373–374) concluded that even the older and wisest women were unable to enlighten the researcher about the meaning of specific designs on ancient pottery that came to light during excavations and that few women fully understood the meaning of the symbols they painted themselves on pottery. During her fieldwork on Pueblo pottery in 1924, Ruth Bunzel tried to ascertain the name and meaning of designs. She worked with a prominent Zuni woman, a potter who was the head of one of the priestly families and knowledgeable about religious beliefs and ritual practices. However, she was not able to complete her research at Zuni on this topic (Bunzel 1929). The names and meanings of naturalistic designs could be more easily determined than those of abstract designs and met with a degree of consensus (cf. Chapman 1928). Susan G. Kenagy (1977) has analyzed how the Zuni expressed their aesthetic sensibilities in decorating their pottery.

A special class of hunting canteen (Fig. 269) consists of two globular barrels, connected by a "tube" which contains the opening. Below the drinking hole, "nipples" protrude, which Cushing (1886: 514) explains as representations of animal mammaries, symbolizing the nourishment they provide animal offspring as well as the hunter through his prey.

Pottery spoons are of two types. One is shallow and elongated, slightly tapering at the one end at which it is held, all executed in flowing and continuous lines. The other type consists of two parts, a bowl with a handle attached to it, resembling a spoon, but larger in size. Both types are called *sa-sho-kon-ne*. They are made with a white slip with painted designs on the inner surface as well as undecorated in red (J. Stevenson 1883: 360), such as these three polished specimens in the Ten Kate collection, which all show signs of use (Fig. 270). Most Native terms in this section are derived from Stevenson's reports, and most were recorded by Cushing. Margaret Hardin (1983: 19) discusses the complicated Zuni ceramic nomenclature.

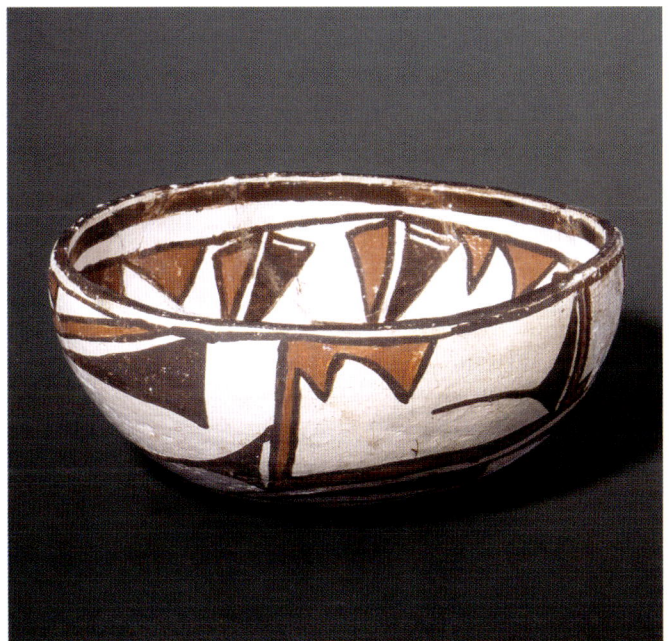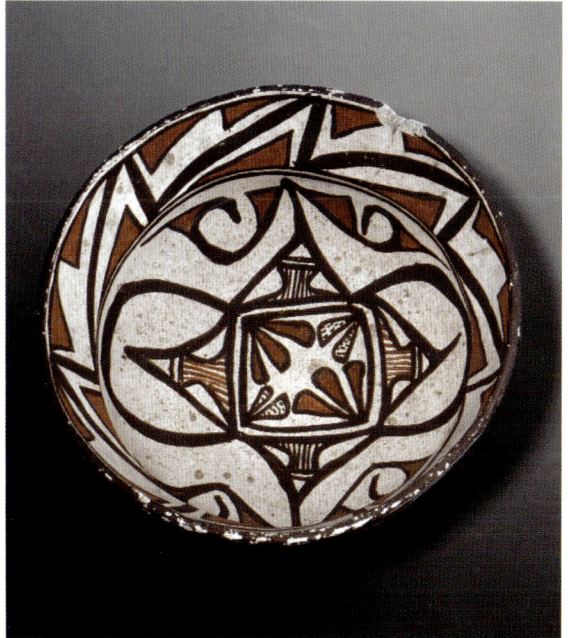

Figs. 271, 272   Bowls; pottery, pigments; RMV 674-31: d. 19.2 cm, h. 7.4 cm; RMV 674-32: d. 20 cm, h. 9.2 cm; both ca. 1880.

A deep polychrome pottery bowl in the Ten Kate collection (Fig. 271) has a flattened base and rounded sides. The base of the exterior is slipped red, while the interior has an overall design. The rim is black and there is no line-break. In Zuni pottery decorative lines, especially on the horizontal plane, tended to show "breaks," not only on the rim, but also on other parts of the vessels. This so-called line-break has been the source of much speculation and debate. Cushing noted that painted lines stopped at the mammary glands surrounding the drinking spout on the hunting canteens, and he concluded that paint was regarded as a barrier to the source of life. Vessels held various kinds of nourishment and thus acted as artificial sources of life. The Zuni ascribed a spiritual essence to all pieces of pottery, and their decoration tended to show such breaks to let the source of life flow freely and the spirit pass out of and into the vessel at will (Cushing 1886: 510–511, 514). When Bunzel asked the Zuni about its meaning, she was told that this line is called *onane*, meaning 'the road,' and symbolized the potter's life. Its closure was not practiced because it would mean that the potter finished her road, i.e., ended her life (Bunzel 1929: 69; cf. Kenagy 1977: 140–150). However, not all painted Zuni pottery displays these line-breaks (cf. Chapman and Ellis 1951).

The flat base of another bowl acquired by the Dutch anthropologist (Fig. 272) is slipped red. The upper part of its interior and exterior are slipped white and decorated with bands showing different designs, the inner one of which exhibits a line-break.

The base of a pitcher in the Ten Kate collection (Fig. 273) is polished red, while the interior is unpolished and shows a coating of dark green deposits. The white-slipped exterior is decorated with various painted designs.

Fig. 273   Pitcher; pottery, pigments; h. 12 cm, w. (incl. handle) 15.5 cm; ca. 1880 (RMV 674-33).

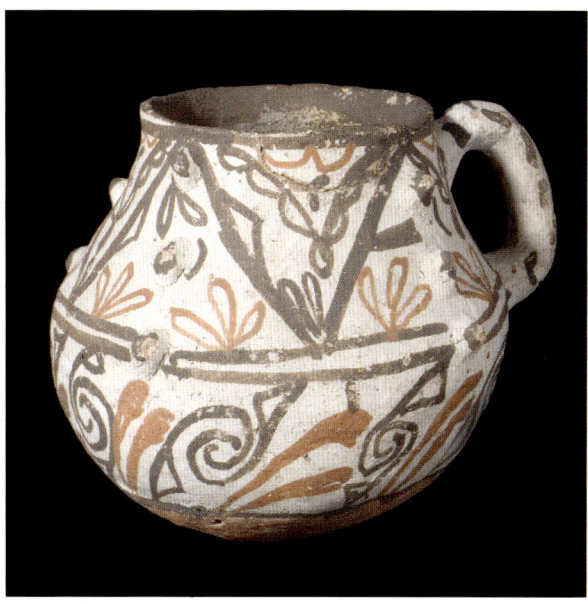

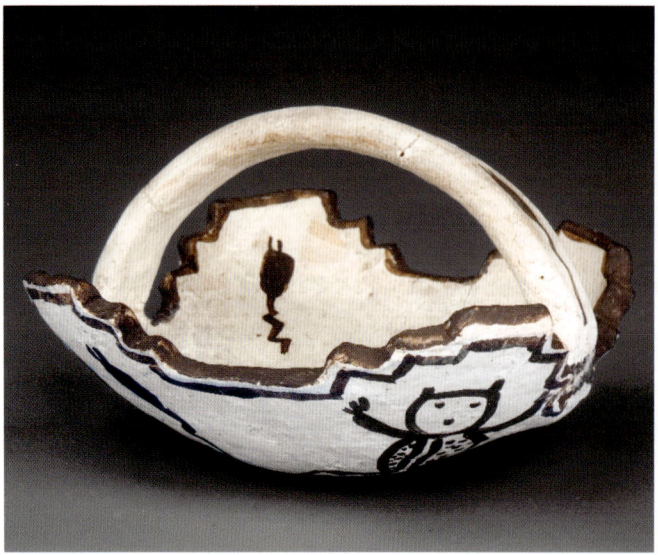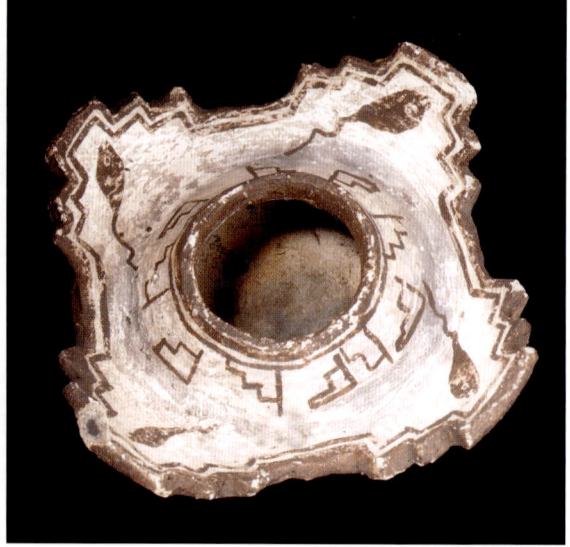

Figs. 274, 275   Corn meal bowls; *K'ia-wai-a wo-pu-k'ia á-wi-thlui-a-po-na sá-mu-te-a-pa* or *Ah-wehl-wi-ah-pä-sahl* (J. Stevenson 1883: 360); pottery, pigments; RMV 674-34: d. 16.7 cm, h. 10 cm; RMV 674-36: d. 12.5 cm, h. 5 cm; both ca. 1880.

Ten Kate noted that in Zuni ceremonies a type of bowl with terraced rim was used which held sacred corn meal—a blend of corn meal, turquoise, and shell, symbolizing earth, sky, and water respectively. He obtained two of these vessels, which in the literature are often referred to as "medicine bowls" (Fig. 274, 275). The sacred meal was kept in these bowls, and priests and women threw pinches to dancers and on religious objects during certain public ceremonies and distributed pinches in their houses to bless their homes. RMV 674-34 (Fig. 274) was broken in three pieces but restored. It shows no line-breaks. Ten Kate also denotes the dot-and-tail designs on the inside and outside of the bowl as tadpoles; on its underside two anthropomorphic frogs are painted (cf. J. Stevenson 1883: 360–361, figs. 442–453; Fane 1991: 116; Nichols et al. 2000: 70, 176–177).

The terraced rim is made when the clay is still soft and it is cut into the required stepped shape with a strand of horsehair. Sometimes the rim is not angular but scalloped. Many ceremonial corn meal bowls, though not all, have a loop-handle, and in some cases this is made from several strands of intertwined clay. The basic color is always white and the decoration black, including the rim's upper edge (J. Stevenson 1884: 546).

Cushing (1886: 518) has pointed out that the Zuni regarded the prayer meal bowl as an emblem of Mother Earth, who provides nourishment to the people. The round rim represents the horizons, and the terraced parts the rising mountains where the rain clouds originate. The handle represents the arching rainbow.

By far the most frequent design encountered on these ceremonial corn meal bowls is one that is usually identified as a tadpole: a dot with a wriggling tapering tail. This design is almost always applied on the inner side of the bowl, but frequently also on the outside. Only a few other figures of animals are sometimes painted on such ceramics, among them dragonflies, the horned toad (*Phrynosoma*), birds, and *kolowisi*, the feathered water snake. James Stevenson (1883: 360) has pointed out that "dot-and-tail" designs do not represent tadpoles but the crustaceous larvae of an insect commonly found at water pools and in streams. Cushing (1886: 518) adds that the "tadpole"-design is specifically associated with the rains and pools of the spring season, while other designs are associated with the rains and pools of the summer (dragonfly) or fall (frog). We suggest that the "tadpole" design refers to the American tadpole shrimp (*Triops longicaudatus*), which can be found in freshwater pools and ponds. During the summer and fall the shrimps are in their egg stadium, and when the pools and ponds fill up in the winter and spring, the larvae hatch. They develop a crustaceous body but propel themselves with their wriggly tail. The American tadpole shrimp is native to riparian habitats in the Zuni country and is also encountered in the numerous potholes dotting the El Malpais country.

Another example of Zuni pottery collected by Ten Kate is listed by him as "offering bowls." The reason for this identification is unclear, as the piece is typical of paint and condiment cups (Fig. 276). Both were much alike in form and decoration, but differed in size. James Stevenson (1883: 362–364; 1884: 569–573) noted that paint cups (*hel·i·po·ka·tehl·le* and *hel·i·po·ka·thel·tsan·na* for large and small cups) usually measured from one and a half to three inches in height, while condiment cups (*ma·pu·kia·tehl·le*) held from less than half a pint to a pint. He encountered both types of cups in singular, double, triple, and quadruple form. This quintuplet specimen in the Ten Kate collection is quite rare. The central vessel is raised and has four knobs applied on the outer surface.

The cups were usually in the shape of globular jars and aggregated in a variety of ways. Multiple cups could be joined on the bottom and sides, and sometimes a handle was added to a twin cup. Some cups were square in shape. White-slipped ware predominated and many vessels had decorations of painted rims and small designs, often the "tadpole," sometimes the horned toad or birds. Twin condiment sets often held pulverized rock salt from the shores of Zuni Lake and ground chili pepper. The Leiden specimen is unused and was probably new when Ten Kate purchased it.

A small bowl with scalloped rim (Fig. 277) is notable for its rather exceptional decoration: the effigy of *kolowisi*, the feathered water snake, undulating around the outer body of the vessel. It was possibly used during initiation ceremonies for boys, a ritual over which an effigy of the revered supernatural being presided. The exterior is unslipped and the base looks unslipped as well, although

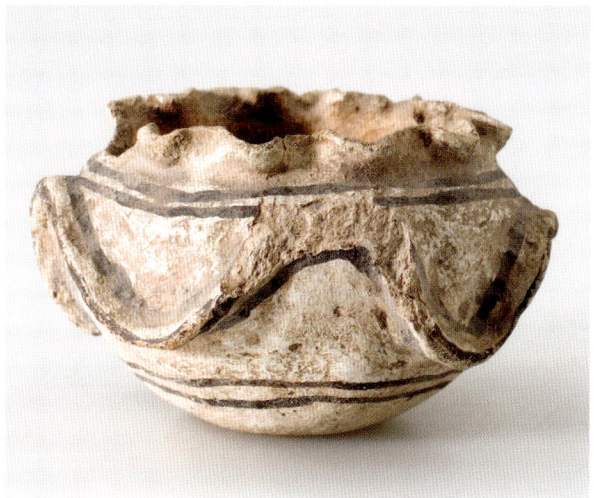

Fig. 277   Bowl; pottery, pigments; d. 11 cm, h. 7 cm; ca. 1880 (RMV 674·37).

this can be the result of use and wear. Some dried black organic matter is left inside. The painted lines around the upper and lower body show line-breaks.

A white-slipped cup in the collection has a handle and is roughly made (Fig. 278). The inside exhibits an abstract design in black and the outside is encircled with an orange-red vegetal design. This specimen resembling a tea cup was probably part of mass-produced ceramic items made for sale to tourists at the Gallup railway depot, where trains of the Atchison, Topeka & Santa Fe Railway stopped since 1882–83.

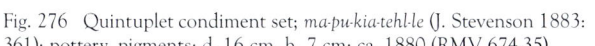

Fig. 276   Quintuplet condiment set; *ma·pu·kia·tehl·le* (J. Stevenson 1883: 361); pottery, pigments; d. 16 cm, h. 7 cm; ca. 1880 (RMV 674·35).

Fig. 278   Cup; pottery, pigments; d. 10 cm, h. 6.8 cm; 1882/83 (RMV 674·38).

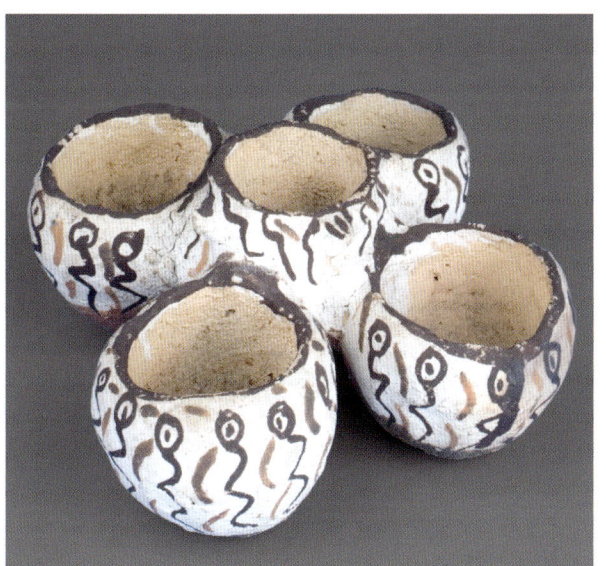

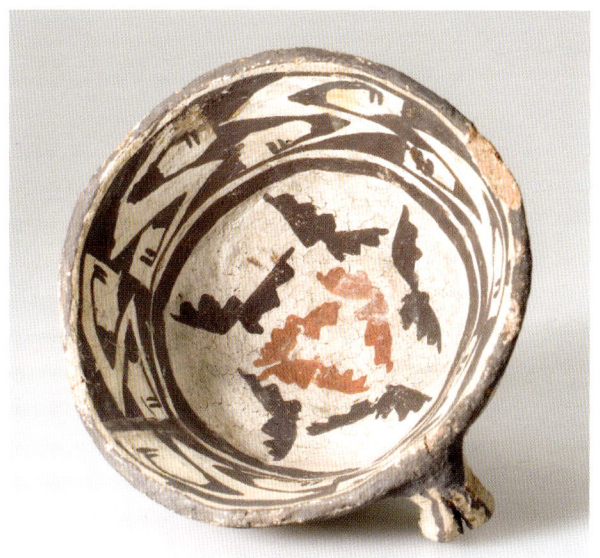

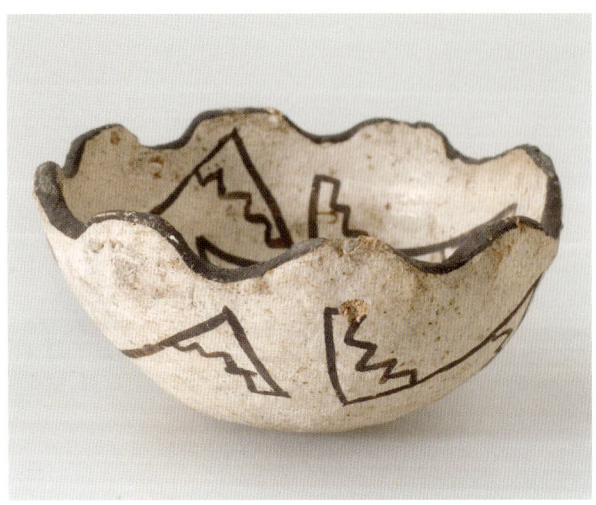

Fig. 279 Bowl; pottery, pigments; d. 10.2 cm, h. 5 cm; ca. 1880 (RMV 674-39).

This small white-slipped shallow bowl obtained by Ten Kate (Fig. 279) has a slightly undulating rim and displays pairs of raincloud designs on its interior and exterior surfaces. The clouds are associated with the kachina spirits who visited Zuni in the shape of clouds. As such, the Zuni regard cumuli as having distinct personalities. Altars were set up on paintings of white corn meal, representing kachina clouds.

Canteens were a practical necessity when living and working in the semiarid desert environment. The Zuni made a variety of these water containers. One side of the

Fig. 280 Canteen; pottery, pigments; w. 7.5-10.5 cm, th. 6.5 cm, h. 8.5 cm; ca. 1880 (RMV 674-40).

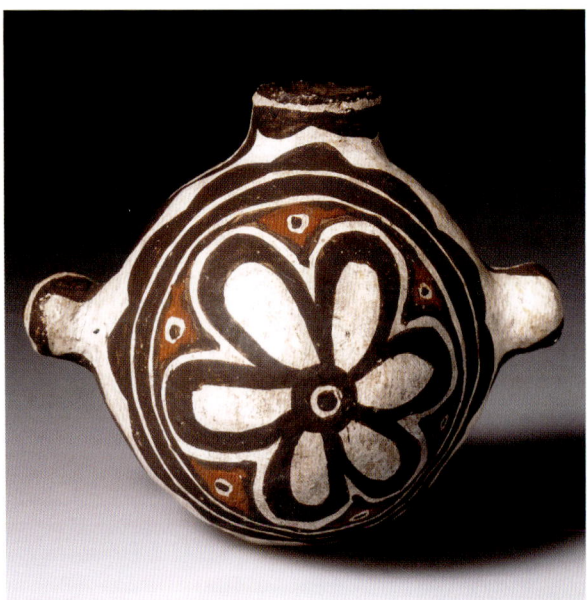

larger canteens is usually somewhat flattened and undecorated, as it is the side hanging against the body of the carrier, usually the back, while the bulging opposite side is often painted. Cushing has pointed to the similarity in shape between the one-side-flattened canteens and women's breasts. He explains this by the analogy in the Zuni mind between mothers' milk as nourishment for babies and water as the fluid of Mother Earth and as nourishment for the crops and adults, analyzing the similarity between the Zuni terms for a woman's breast, *mehana*, and the large, flat-sided canteen, *mehetonne*. He also points out that these canteens were coiled from the flat side up. When the women close the top, the analogy of the nipple, they look away because otherwise they believe to run the risk of becoming barren or that their young children will become blind or die. This is regarded as punishment for closing a source of life (Cushing 1886: 512–513).

Small redware and painted canteens were often carried by children. A larger type was generally used by the women when they went to work in the gardens and fields, and the largest type by the men when they left the village to hunt, to tend sheep, or to attend to religious duties in distant places. They could be redware or painted and were carried with leather thongs or fiber strings attached to loops or knobs protruding from the upper part of the canteen's surface. The larger canteens were usually carried on the back, with the strap running across the forehead. The smaller canteens could also be carried on the hip or at the side.

A design frequently encountered on Zuni ceramics is a motif which has been interpreted as a flower or a sun and has often been called a rosette. The rosette is usually enclosed by one or several circular bands, and the motif which is often painted freely floating on the outer center of a vessel, often water containers such as ollas and canteens, is therefore sometimes referred to as a medallion. It is also present on this canteen from the Ten Kate collection (Fig. 280). Zuni potters called this design *hepa'kinne*, meaning 'sunflower,' although its origin has also been attributed to the rosette symbol in Hispanic altar coverings (Bunzel 1929: 92–95). The petals are painted in black lines, with their centers open, taking the color of the white slip (cf. Fane 1991: 122–123). The Leiden specimen has a flattened back, which is slipped red and slightly polished.

Another flower design on Zuni ceramics is somewhat more naturalistic than the medallion or rosette motifs and can be found on the interior of bowls such as a this

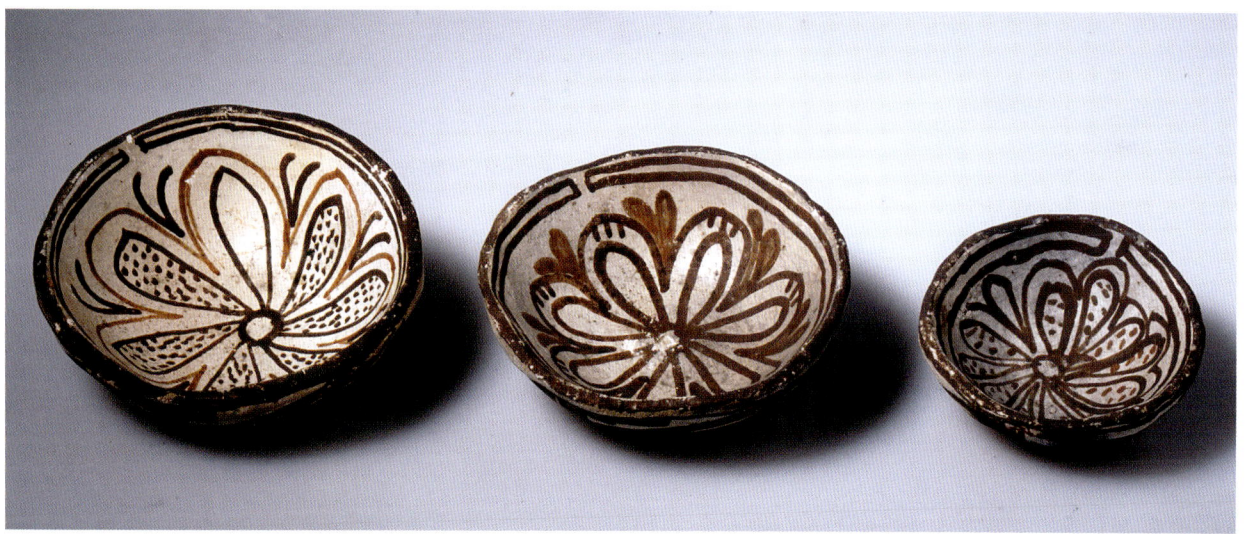

Fig. 281 Bowls with flower design; pottery, pigments; RMV 674-41: d. 9 cm, h. 3.6 cm; RMV 674-42: d. 8.3 cm, h. 3.2 cm; RMV 674-44: d. 7 cm, h. 3.2 cm; all ca. 1880.

trio acquired by Ten Kate (Fig. 281). The petals are painted in the same manner as in the rosettes, but frequently their centers are covered with black dots. They are surrounded by abstract or naturalistic leaves, executed in red. The exterior bases have a dull red slip. All three specimens show an interrupted double line around the inside edge.

A small shallow bowl (Fig. 282) with a creamy slip on the interior and exterior surfaces is painted with a design around the inner rim representing stepped rain clouds. The rim panel shows a line-break. The inside is decorated

with two designs, each depicted three times. Bunzel's Zuni informant termed the V-shaped motif *kiatowa t'sipopa, nitep'owa anpaltopa*, representing an arrowhead (Bunzel 1929: 98, 101). The polychrome bowl had a wire frame, indicating that Ten Kate had it hanging on a wall in his home for some time during the 1880s.

Of two small jars in the collection (Fig. 283), RMV 674-45 is notable for the horizontal handles at its sides. The interior is unslipped; the exterior has a white slip on which "tadpole" motifs (cf. Figs. 274, 275) are painted. There are no line-breaks. RMV 674-46 is a thimble-shaped miniature jar with a scalloped rim. The interior is unslipped but the base is blackened because of unknown use. The exterior has a white slip and a design in red and black of a cross, flanked with two hooked motifs, which extends onto the base.

Fig. 282 Bowl; pottery, pigments; d. 9 cm, h. 3 cm; ca. 1880 (RMV 674-43).

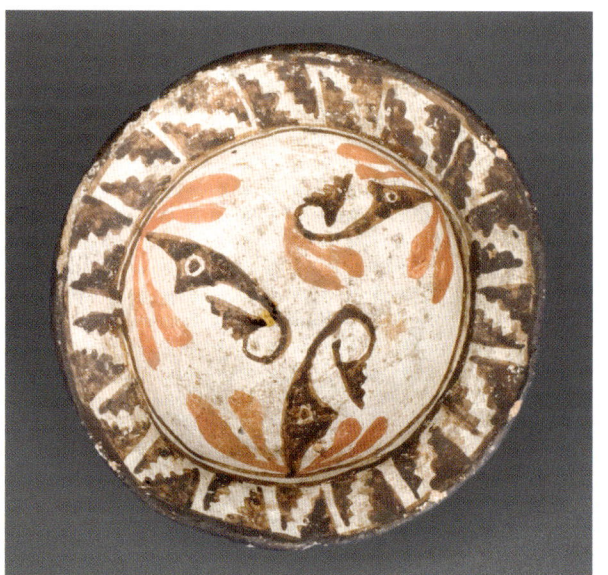

Fig. 283 Jars; pottery, pigments; RMV 674-46: d. 3 cm, h. 2.2 cm; RMV 674-45: d. 7 cm, h. 5 cm; both ca. 1880.

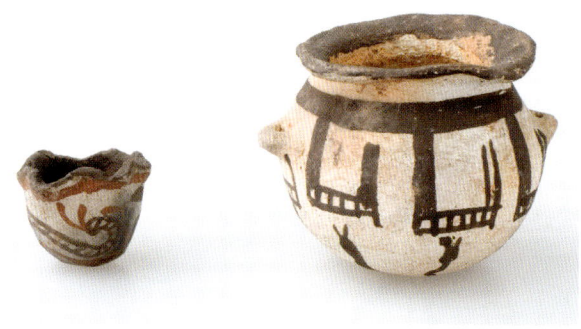

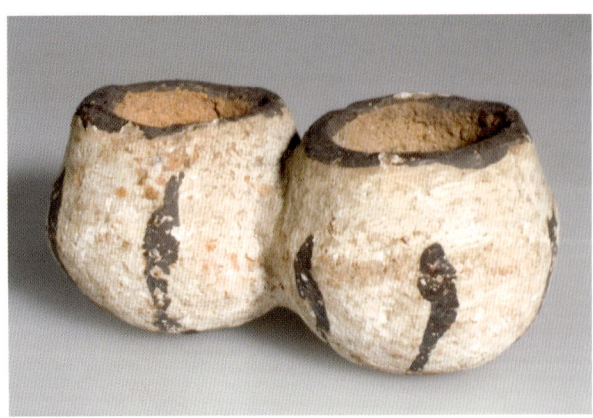

Fig. 284 Twin jar; pottery, pigments; l. 8 cm, w. 4.4 cm, h. 3.7 cm; ca. 1885 (RMV 674-47).

These double jars (Fig. 284) show signs of heavy wear. Their interior is unslipped; the white-slipped exterior exhibits "tadpole" designs (cf. Figs. 274, 275).

Zuni potters also produced effigy vessels and figurines. Among the figurines, owls were most numerous. Game animals were also encountered and sculpted in a naturalistic way, emphasizing their specific characteristics such as horns of antelope and mountain sheep, deer antlers, and duck bills. Ten Kate noted that the ceramic animal effigies of the Zuni were much more refined than those of the Rio Grande Pueblos. The Indians were well aware of the tourists passing by train through Gallup or staying in the area for a while since the completion of the

intercontinental railroad in 1883. They catered to the travelers' wish to take home souvenirs by making pottery animal effigies, of which owls became by far the most prevalent. However, they also produced images of other animals, such as horned toads and game animals, sculpted in a naturalistic way. Through tourism the repertoire of figurines gradually expanded and included a variety of animals introduced by the Whites like horses, cows, pigs, and chickens.

The historic origin of Zuni ceramic animal effigies reaches further back and is documented as early as 1851. The molding of the animal effigies was usually in two halves, put together, and finished with a hole in the bottom to prevent exploding in the firing process (J. Stevenson 1883: 364; Ladd 1979: 493; Batkin 1987: 174; Fane 1991: 125; Rodee and Ostler 1985: 26–27, 65). For the Zuni the owl represents wisdom. It can see what others cannot see, not only in the dark of night. Contrary to the prevalent owl imagery of ill omen or evil in much of Native America, for the Zuni it is a beneficient and sacred bird.

The larger of the two owl effigies in the Ten Kate collection (Fig. 285) has a small hole at the top, around which the slip is blackened. Ten Kate noted that it was used as an oil lamp. It is realistically made, with extended wings at the sides and a protruding crooked beak and flat tail. The smaller one is rather poorly made and also shows signs that it was used to provide light.

Fig. 285 Owl effigies; *muhukwi* (J. Stevenson 1883: 364); pottery, pigments; RMV 674-56: h. 4.8 cm; RMV 674-48: h. 7.5 cm; both ca. 1880.

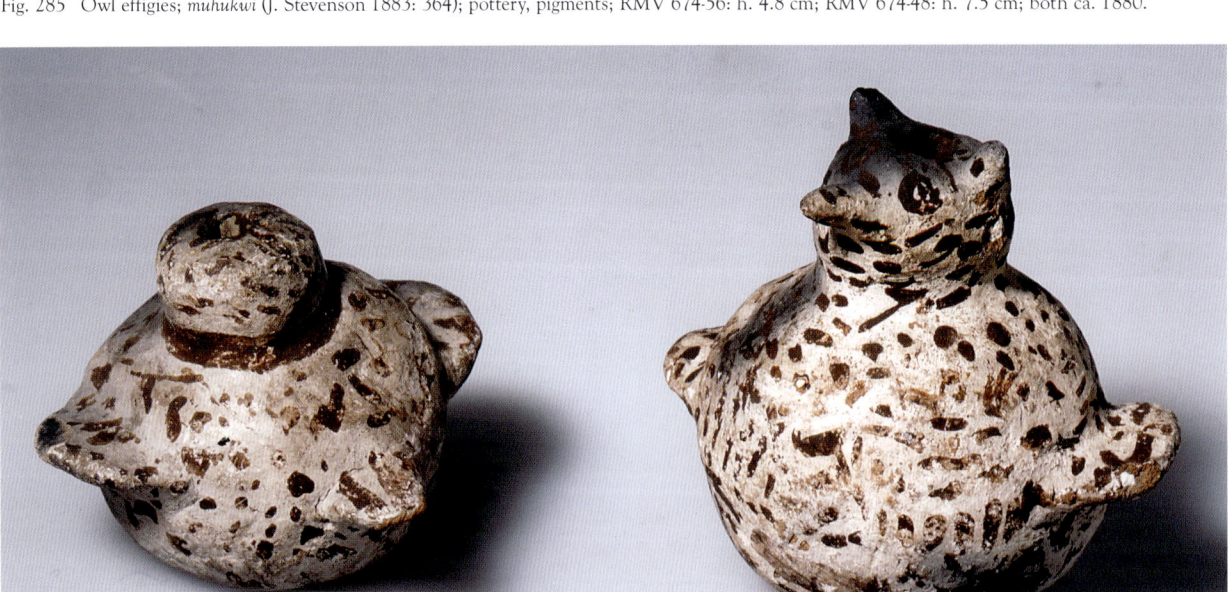

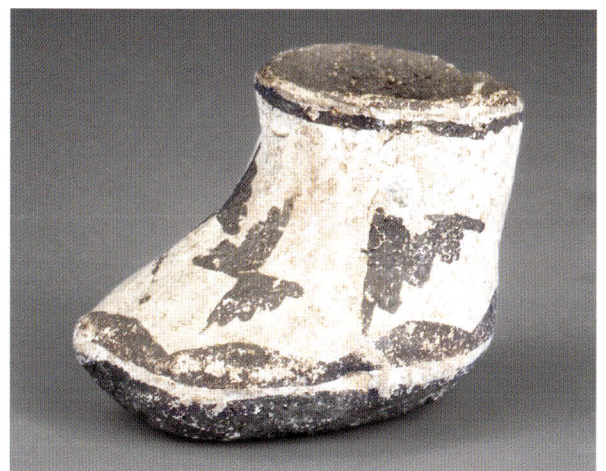

Fig. 286   Moccasin effigy jar; *mokk'wa:we* (J. Stevenson 1884: 544); pottery, pigments; l. 6 cm, h. 4.5 cm; ca. 1880 (RMV 674-49).

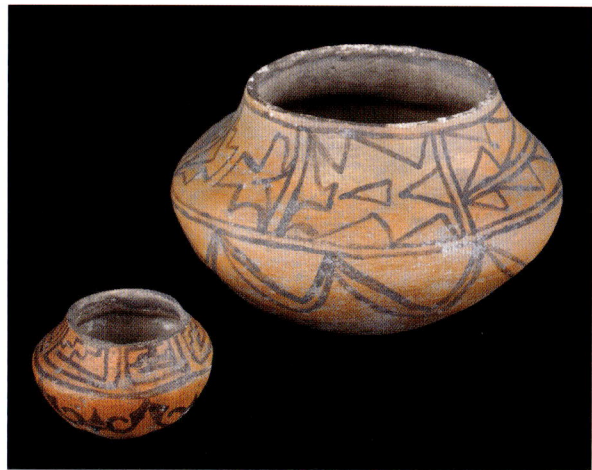

Fig. 287   Bowls; pottery, pigments; RMV 674-51: d. 8.4 cm, h. 5 cm; RMV 674-50: d. 20 cm, h. 12 cm; both ca. 1880.

Vessels in the shape of moccasins were a Zuni ceramic peculiarity (Fig. 286). To some of these a pottery handle was attached at the heel, and James Stevenson (1884: 544) referred to them as cream or milk pitchers. However, to function effectively in this capacity, the vessel had to be handled rather awkwardly.

Two jars in the collection have deeply concave bases and rough unslipped interiors, while the exteriors are finished with a bright orange polished slip (Fig. 287). A design band is applied above and below the shoulder of both specimens.

The Ten Kate collection also contains three small corrugated vessels (Figs. 288, 289). The larger one (RMV 674-52) is well made with a regular coiled surface, which is left with seemingly little treatment and is thus truly corrugated.

The coils on the outside of the other two vessels have been smoothed, but the surface has received treatment, apparently aimed at producing a corrugated effect. RMV 674-53 shows crescent-form indentations, possibly made with a thumb nail, and the irregular indentations on RMV 674-54 were probably made with the square end of a small stick. Almost contemporaneous with Ten Kate's collecting activities in Zuni was the visit to the village in 1885 by the military officer R. W. Shufeldt from Fort Wingate. He cooperated in scientific surveys and zoological collecting projects of the Smithsonian Institution and collected a number of small corrugated vessels during his visit to the Pueblo, although several were decorated both with corrugation and painted designs, a novelty (Shufeldt 1910).

Figs. 288, 289   Corrugated vessels; pottery; RMV 674-52 (jar): h. 10 cm, w. 8.5 cm; RMV 674-53 (jar): d. 5.8 cm, h. 5 cm; RMV 674-54 (pitcher): h. 6 cm, w. 5.6 cm; all ca. 1880.

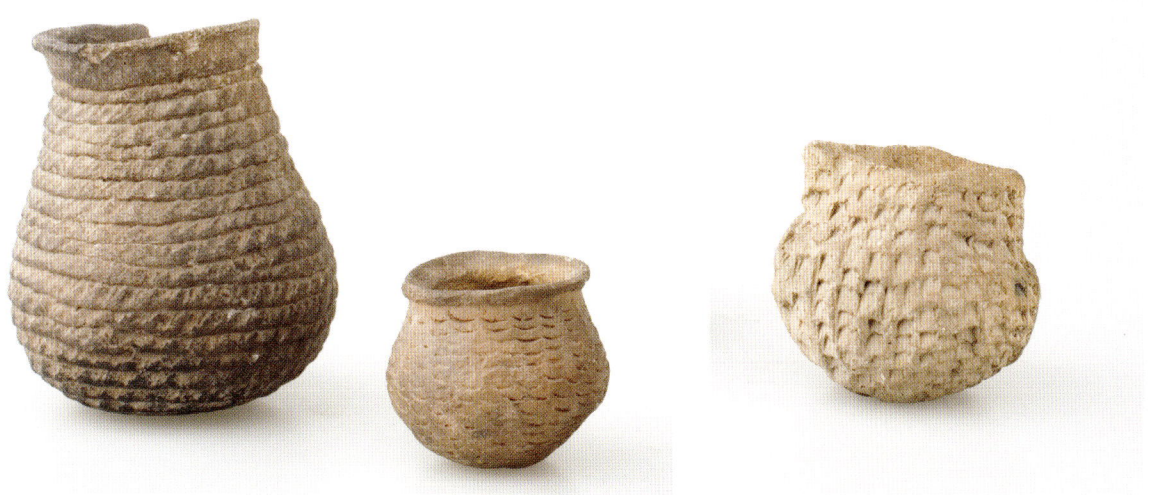

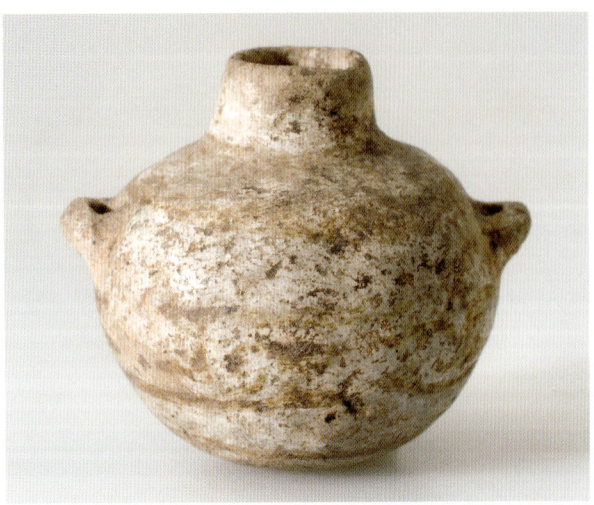

Fig. 290 Jar; pottery; h. 5.9 cm, w. 6.8 cm; 1880 (RMV 674-55).

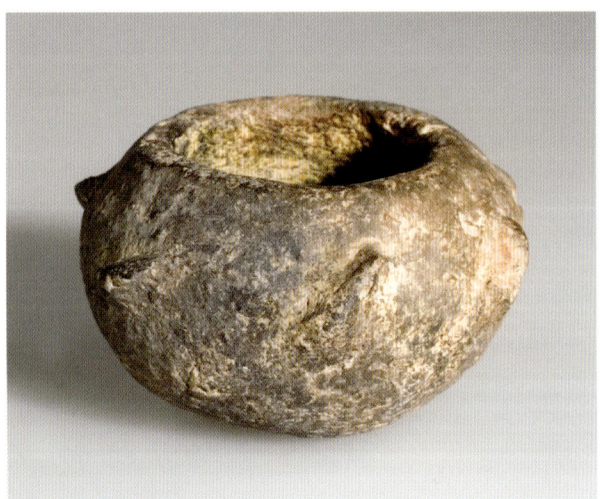

Fig. 291 Vessel; pottery; d. 5.4 cm, h. 3.5 cm; 1880 (RMV 674-57).

Corrugated wares are common in archaeological sites in the Southwest but consistently postdate plainwares. Cushing (1886: 489–493) also noted the prevalence of corrugated Zuni pottery and interpreted this class of prehistoric as well as historic ware as the outcome of imitation of basketry containers. The surface of these pottery containers indeed shows a striking similarity with the surfaces of basketry counterparts. Cooking pots, water bottles, and jars were the main types of Zuni corrugated ware in Cushing's time.

Corrugation of clay vessels has frequently been explained as the result of aesthetic sensibilities of the potters and their clients. However, more functional hypotheses have also been proposed such as reduced time and cost of production, ease of manipulation, improved heat transfer, increased durability, and demarcation of social boundaries.

All three types of "corrugation" represented in the sample of the Leiden collection have been noted by William Henry Holmes (1886: 271, 278–282, 299) as being present in prehistoric sites, and he correctly terms the two latter "intaglio." However, he also observed new and unused small vessels with intaglio surface decoration, usually rudely made as the two pieces in the Leiden collection, but underfired and therefore brittle, unlike the Leiden examples. He suspected that some Hopi potters tried their hands at making small replicas of prehistoric wares, but did not preclude the possibility of Navajo manufacture, motivated by the opportunities for cash income from unsuspecting collectors and tourists. One wonders why Holmes did not expect the Zuni to have catered to this

new market, as the Gallup railroad depot was only a short distance away. This latter interpretation is our hypothesis for the moment.

The Zuni pottery collection assembled by Ten Kate also includes a miniature water jar with globular body, side lugs, and small mouth, its white-slipped body exhibiting a faded design (Fig. 290), and a darkly colored miniature jar displaying six appliquéd diagonal bars on its body as decoration (Fig. 291).

"Tadpole" and leaf designs are painted on the interior of a small and shallow bowl (Fig. 292). The rim painting on the interior rim shows no line-break.

Fig. 292 Bowl; pottery, pigment; d. 13.8 cm, h. 3 cm; ca. 1880 (RMV 2012-1).

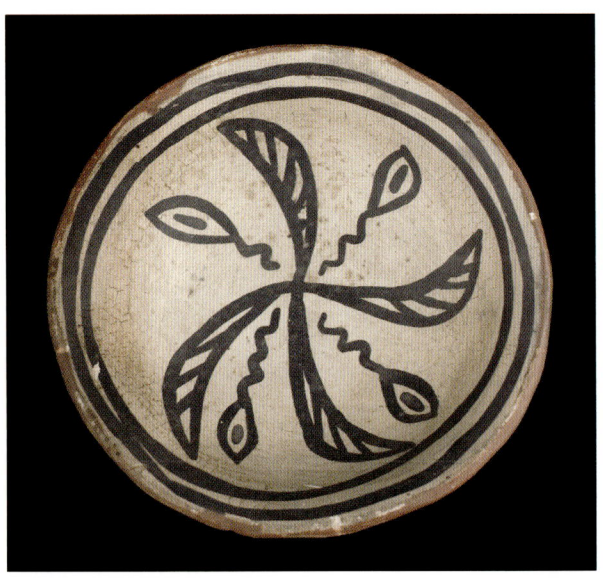

While working at Zuni in 1888, Ten Kate provided medical assistance to a number of Indians who were injured or ill, among them a ten-year old Zuni girl suffering from a serious bullet wound in her thigh. By the lavish application of iodine and frequent renewal of bandages, Ten Kate successfully prevented infection of the wound and the child eventually recovered. The grateful parents offered Ten Kate a horse, which the anthropologist could not accept, but he was pleased to receive a piece of beautifully painted pottery and a small (partly colored) saddle blanket (see Fig. 259, p. 193; Ten Kate 1925: 143; Hovens 1995: 696). This small bowl with a white slip and six butterfly designs in black probably represents this gift (Fig. 293). In Puebloan art the butterfly is a fertility symbol and signifies weather benefitting the crops. Its depiction on ceramics and basketry is like a prayer for rain. There are no line-breaks.

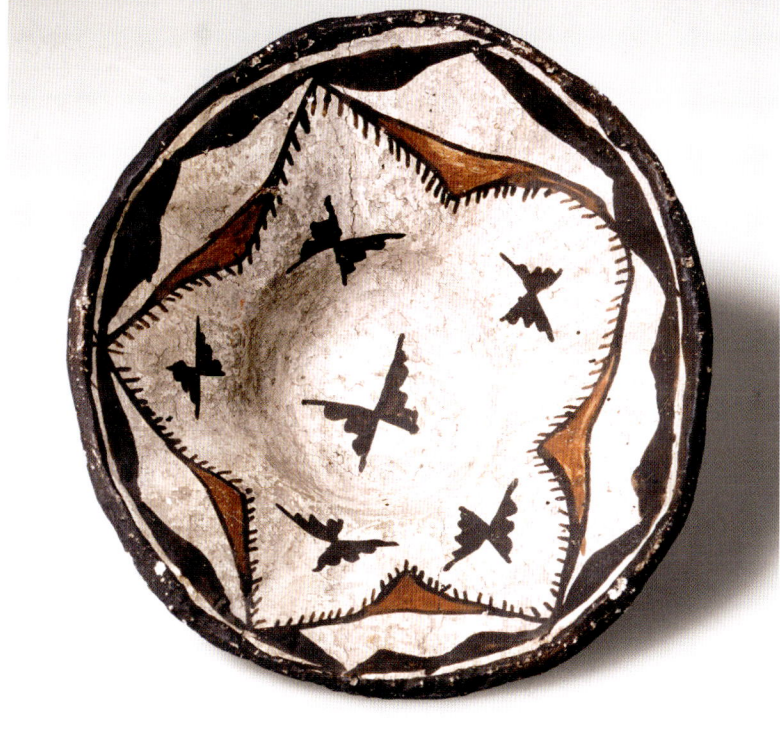

Fig. 293   Bowl; pottery, pigment; d. 11.7 cm, h. 4.9 cm; ca. 1880 (RMV 2012-3).

Another small Zuni bowl acquired by Ten Kate (Fig. 294) likewise shows a white slip and is decorated with painted designs in red and black.

A small jar in the Leiden collection (Fig. 295) has a white-slipped outer surface with black decorative motifs and exhibits line-breaks; the inside of the vessel is unslipped.

Fig. 294   Bowl; pottery, pigment; d. 8.4 cm, h. 3.7 cm; 1888 (RMV 2012-2).

Fig. 295   Jar; pottery, pigment; d. 9.5 cm, h. 8.1 cm; ca. 1880 (RMV 2012-4).

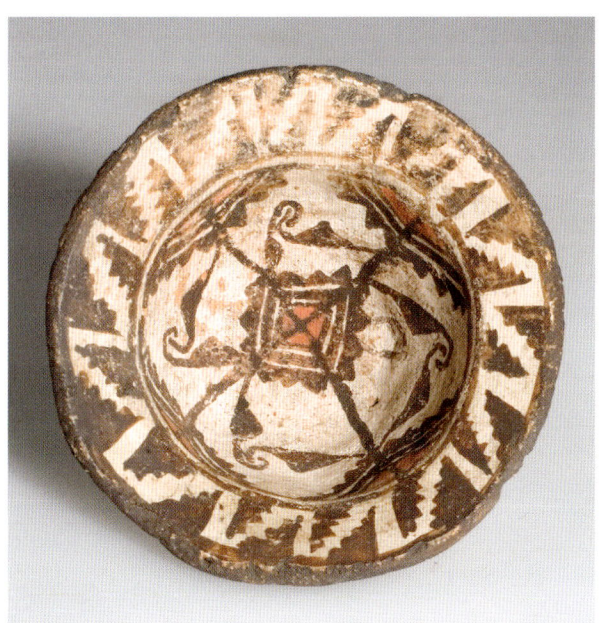

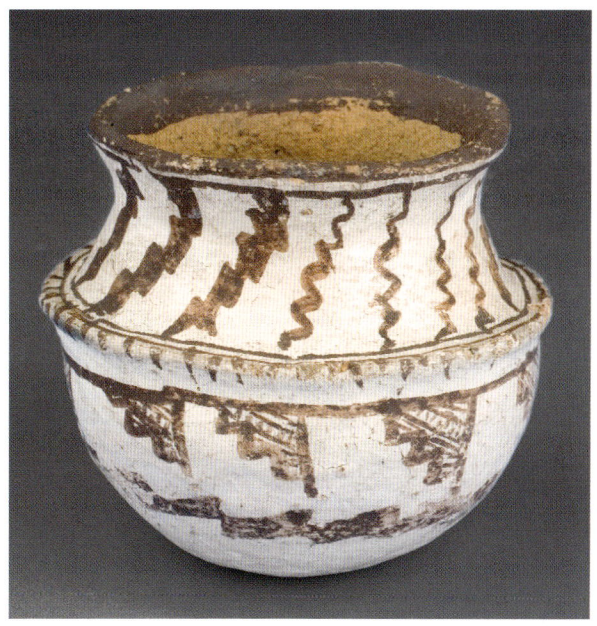

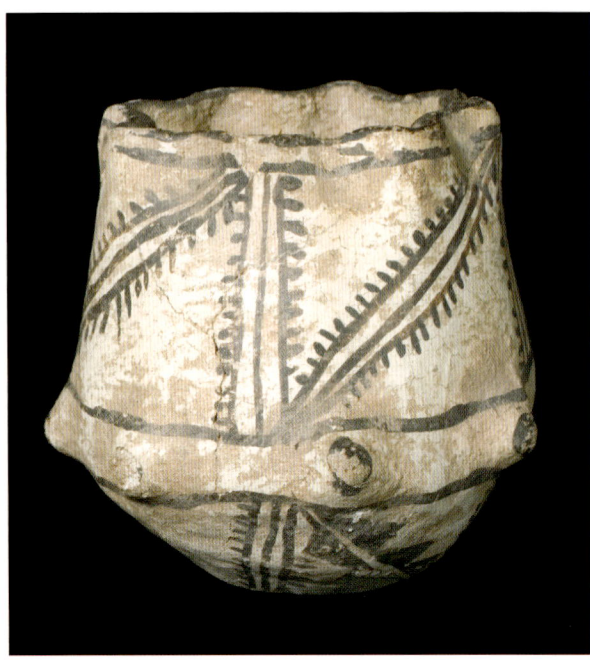

Fig. 296 Jar; pottery; h 7 cm, d. 8 cm; ca. 1870–1880 (WMR 17974).

Fig. 297 Model cradleboard; wood, hide; *wi-ha yä'thl-to-k'ia thlém-me* (J. Stevenson 1884: 583); l. 40 cm, w. 22.5 cm, h. of hood 13.5 cm; ca. 1880 (RMV 362-161).

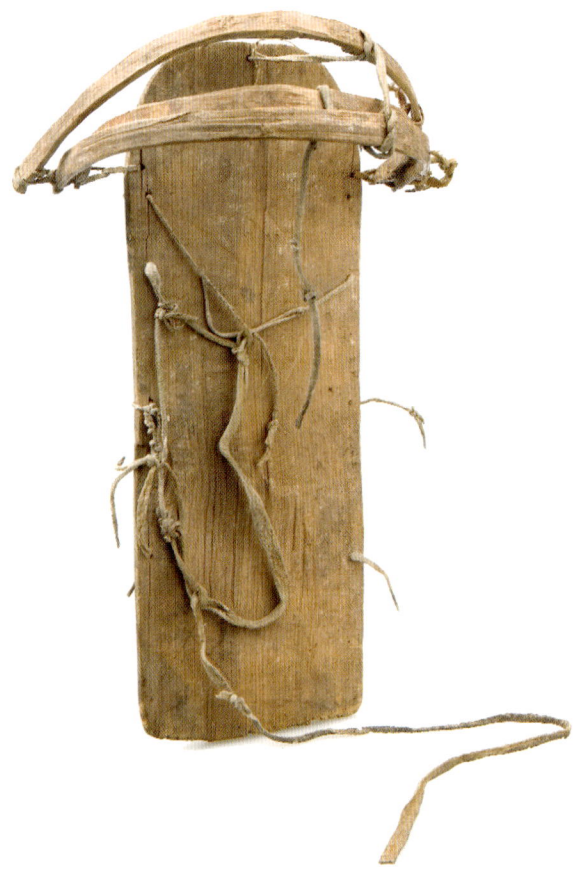

In 1929 Ten Kate donated a miniature black-on-white jar to the Museum of Anthropology (now the World Museum) in Rotterdam (Fig. 296). Cushing gave it to him in 1883 as a present and told his friend that it came from a Zuni grave. The gift must have been precious, as Ten Kate kept it virtually until the end of his life (he died in 1931). The jar has a white slip on its outer surface and exhibits painted designs. Its rim is crenellated and at its widest circumference has a number of small protruding knobs. It lacks a line-break.

Courtship and Marriage

Ten Kate noted that Zuni girls took the initiative to enter into marriage by announcing to their parents whom they wished to marry. He saw engaged couples on the rooftops at sunset, the girls lovingly combing the hair of their boy-friends. The latter were required to assemble a bundle for their bride, mostly consisting of fine garments, including a pair of hardsoled moccasins. On acceptance of the bundle, the marriage was officially recognized and the couple moved in with the woman's family. Ten Kate stressed that the position of married women in matrilineal societies such as that of the Zuni was quite strong. They owned property and were entitled to keep their children in the case of divorce, something that was uncommon. Misbe-having men could be sent away.

Zuni cradles consisted of a wooden board, usually of pine, with a collapsible faceguard of crescent hoops made from green cedar, secured with hide thongs, and covered with skin to protect the baby's face from the sun, sand, and insects. Zuni girls were given toy cradles and dolls to play with, and these miniature cradles (Fig. 297) are true to the full-size specimens (Mason 1887: 191–193; Dennis 1940: 110–111; cf. Fane 1991: 104). The small blanket ac-quired with the cradle is lost.

Fetishes

Ten Kate observed the custom of keeping fetishes among the Zuni priests and wrote: "Another artifact, a genuine fetish, demonstrating the animistic concepts of the Zunis, is a small stone image in the rough shape of a bird, which carries an arrowhead on its back. Whenever he travels in hostile country or is on the warpath, a priest of the Bow directs prayers to it, and he carries it with him in a little bag. This fetish represents an eagle, the god of the 'upper world.' According to their beliefs, this god possesses 'a spirit and a living heart.' The Zuni priest addresses his prayers to this spirit. He offers food to the heart (the arrow head). He asks for protection against the enemy and against ambushes, in particular. The arrowhead, the 'magic war medicine' (*sáwanikia*), represents the shield which must protect the warrior's vulnerable side (his rear); for no one has eyes and hands on his back. A warrior does not ask for protection on the side where he has arms and legs" (Ten Kate 2004: 284-285). In reality, the use of fetishes for protection was not restricted to priests, but was more widespread among the Zuni.

Predatory gods and their attendant predatory animals, both referred to as *Wé-ma-á-hâ-i* ('prey beings'), play a major role in Zuni cosmology. Their powers are encapsulated in "fetishes," amulets providing their owners with supernatural protection and support. According to Zuni tradition, Sun Father sent his two children to the newly created earth, where the people were being killed by predatory animals. Using lightning emanating from their shields, the children turned the animals into stone. They preserved the power of the animals within the stone, but turned it around to become beneficial for the people.

Also in mythological time, *Poshai-ankia*, the Father of the Medicine Societies, established order among the predatory animals, assigning them to guard the six cardinal directions. These guardians were called *Apithlan shiwani*, Bow priests, and they mediate between *Poshai-ankia* and the people. In addition to the main guardians, each of these have "younger brothers" in all other directions, who serve as protectors of the hunt.

The Zuni frequently found stones resembling an animal and assumed these to have the protective powers as related in mythology. Their shapes were often abstract, but increasingly such stones were carved to bring out the shape of the animal more clearly. Members of religious societies often left their fetishes collectively in charge of a keeper, who stored them in special containers of basketry or pottery. The fetishes were used individually as well as collectively, in the latter case during certain ceremonies, such as the Council of the Fetishes around the time of the winter solstice or the midwinter tribal hunts. In these rituals, prayer is directed toward the powers residing in the fetishes and blessings are requested, not the least success in the hunt. The keepers ritually fed the fetishes in their custody to ascertain their well-being.

In the 1940s, when Whites began showing an interest in acquiring fetishes in return for goods or cash, stone animal effigies were being carved from any stone, regardless

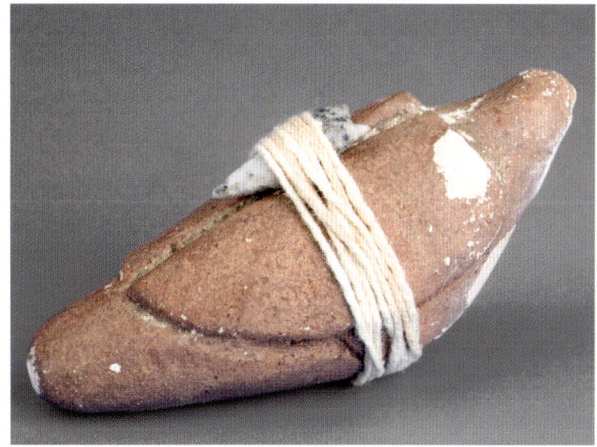

Fig. 298 Eagle fetish; white sandstone, pigment, chalcedony, cotton; l. 9.2 cm, w. 4 cm, h. 4 cm; ca. 1880 (RMV 362-148).

of shape. Both abstract and naturalistic types have been carved by Zuni craftsmen since then in increasing numbers, resulting in a major cottage industry (Cushing 1883; Kirk 1943; Ostler and Nahohai 1989; Rodee and Ostler 1986: 15-23).

Ten Kate discussed an eagle fetish obtained by him (Fig. 298) with Cushing and jotted down the following notes: "The fetish represents the god of the upper world, and therefore is shaped like an eagle. The Indians believe that it is alive, with a beating heart and an active consciousness. They direct prayers to its spirit, and they offer food to the heart. The prayers are pleas by the owner, a priest from the Order of the Bow, for protection against enemies, especially against being ambushed. That is why the arrowhead, the *sáwanikia* or magic medicine of war, tied to the back, to indicate that only the 'faulty or wanting' side (the back) of the warrior requires protection, 'because nobody has eyes or arms and hands on his back.' However, 'the warrior does not need to ask for protection for the side where he has his face and hands.' The arrowhead or stone knife, on the back of the fetish is meant to stop or deflect the enemies' arrows." Later Ten Kate partially published these notes in the *Revue d'Ethnographie* (1884: 163; 1890; cf. Cushing 1883).

It is likely that Ten Kate collected this fetish from a member of the Bow priesthood himself, as he met several members, but an acquisition through Cushing is also possible. Ten Kate's native nomenclature for the fetishes is mostly in accordance with Cushing's, although the Dutch anthropologist notes additional terminology in some cases. According to Cushing (1883), this red eagle of the southern skies is called *K'iä-k'iä-li-á-ho-na*.

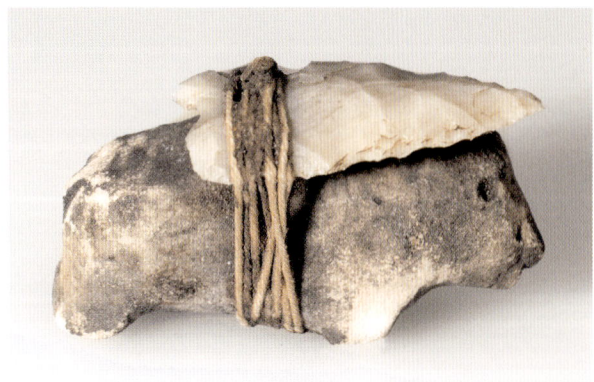

Fig. 299 Badger fetish; *TiKya awa Tonashi wéma* (TK); stone, sinew; l. 3.5 cm, h. 2 cm, w. 1.5 cm; ca. 1880 (RMV 674-11).

Zuni fetishes were carved from a variety of stones and often painted with the correct directional color. The arrowheads tied to these objects, in the case of Ten Kate's fetish made from chalcedony and tied with native cotton cord, can have several meanings: It can be a protective device to keep the fetish safe from physical harm and witchcraft, and it can be an expression of a gift of prayer to the fetish.

In the Zuni language the ending *wema* means 'prey' and refers to that category of animals. The badger, represented by this fetish collected by Ten Kate (Fig. 299),

belongs to this class. It carries an arrowhead on its back. *Poshai-ankia*, the Father of the Medicine Societies, deemed the badger courageous but not very determined and appointed him guardian of the south, as his den faces the direction where the winter sun stands. Red is associated with that direction. The series of fetishes Ten Kate collected in 1888 consisted of hunting fetishes rather than guardian fetishes, as the latter were still secretly kept and much revered, were few in number, and usually collectively owned, while the hunting fetishes were much more prevalent and individually owned. They were kept by their owners in small skin pouches, partially filled with sacred corn meal to feed them (Ten Kate 1884: 118).

The mountain lion can be identified by his long tail. *Poshai-ankia*, the Father of the Medicine Societies, judged the mountain lion to be courageous and determined. Therefore he made him the master of the gods of prey and appointed him guardian of the north. The color yellow is associated with the north, and these fetishes were preferably carved from yellow limestone (Figs. 304–307). The eyes of RMV 674-14 (Fig. 301) were formerly inlaid with green turquoise. RMV 674-16 (Fig. 302) carries a chalcedony arrowhead on its back. RMV 674-27 (Fig. 303) carries an obsidian arrowhead on its back, secured with vegetal fiber.

Figs. 300–303 Mountain lion fetishes; *A-pi-thla shi-wa-ni awa Hâtitäsh ana wéma* (TK); *Sania Kya Kwe awa Hâtitäsh ana wéma*; stone, sinew; RMV 674-13: stone, sinew; l. 3.5 cm, h. 2 cm, w. 1.5 cm; RMV 674-14: alabaster; l. 7.5 cm, h. 1.8 cm, w. 1.5 cm; RMV 674-16: stone, sinew; l. 3.8 cm, h. 1.7 cm; RMV 674-27: stone, fiber; l. 7.2 cm, h. 4 cm, w. 3.2 cm; all ca. 1880.

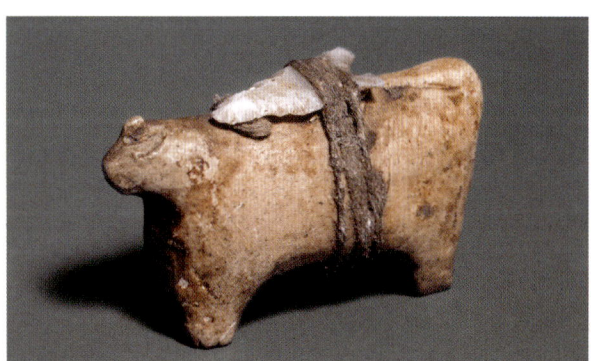
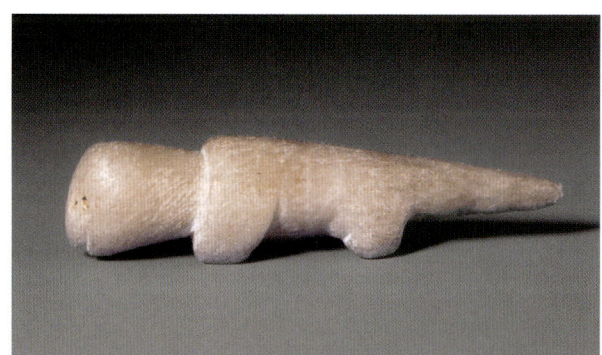
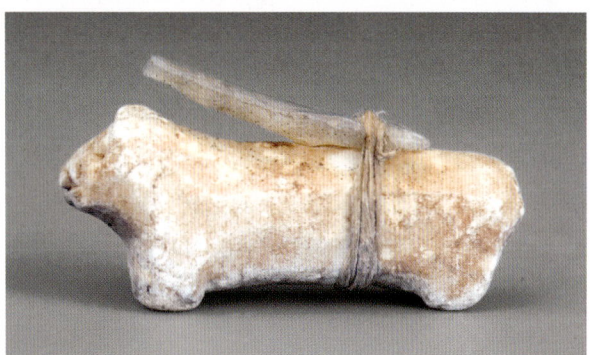
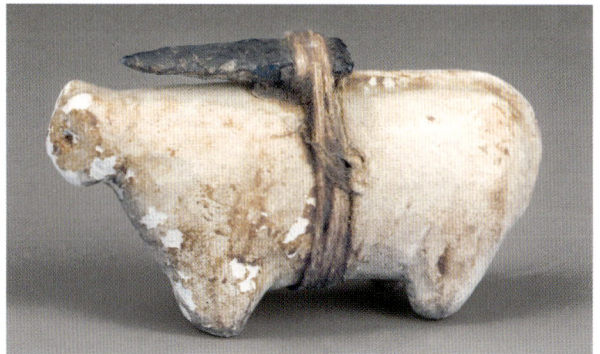

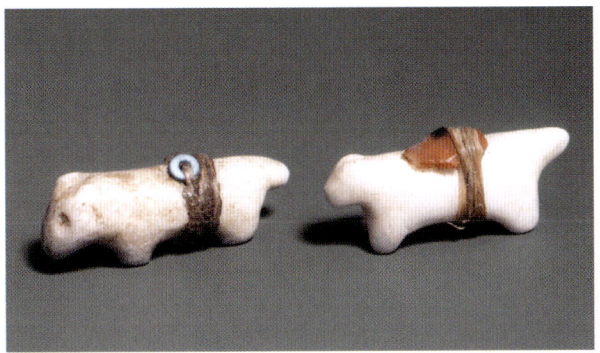

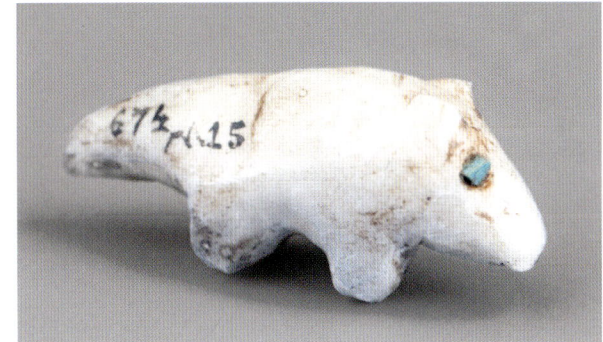

Figs. 304, 305   Three coyote fetishes; *Sania Kya Kwe awa Suski wéma*; RMV 674-12a: stone, sinew, chert; RMV 674-12 b: stone, sinew, turquoise; l. 2.5 cm, h. 1 cm; 674-15: l. 3.4 cm, h. 1.5 cm; all ca. 1880.

Coyote fetishes (Figs. 304, 305), according to Ten Kate, were common among the members of the hunting society. They were carried by men on the hunt, as the cunning and tireless coyote was esteemed as a hunter and represents the hunting god of the west (Cushing 1883: pl. 2, fig. 2; Ten Kate 1884).

The predatory shrew was appointed guardian of the underworld by *Poshai-ankia*, and black is the associated directional color. The shrew was regarded as a comparatively weak prey animal, and therefore such fetishes are extremely rare and unsophisticated in the execution of additional carving, if any, of the natural stone (Fig. 306; Cushing 1883: pl. IX, fig. 1; Ten Kate 1890: 119, pl. VIII, fig. 21).

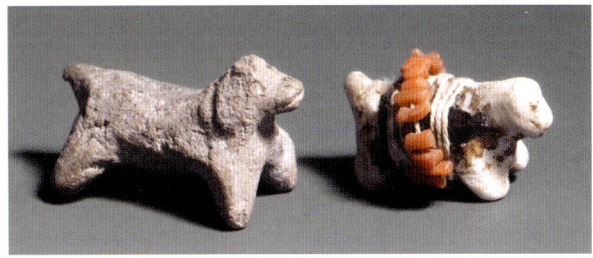

Fig. 307   Lynx fetishes; *Sania Kya Kwe awa We ma we*; RMV 674-18: stone; l. 3.4 cm, h. 2 cm; RMV 674-19: stone, obsidian, coral, cotton; l. 2.6 cm, h. 1.7 cm; ca. 1880.

The lynx (bobcat) is the hunting protector of the south. RMV 674-18 (Fig. 307 left) represents the yellow or red bobcat, *Tépi thlúp-tsi-na* or *Té-pi á-hona* (Ten Kate 1890: 119, pl. VIII, fig. 22). RMV 674-19 (Fig. 307 right) represents the white bobcat (*Té-pi k'ó-hana*, TK 1890: 119, pl. VII, fig. 19) and carries an obsidian arrowhead and red coral beads.

Poshai-ankia appointed the wolf guardian of the east, the direction with which the color white is associated. Ten Kate (1890: 119) recorded the name of the white wolf: *Jú-na-wi-ko k'ó-ha-na*. One of the three wolf fetishes obtained by him (Fig. 308) has turquoise eyes (one missing).

Fig. 306   Shrew (mole) fetish; *Ti-Kya-awa Kya-hi Tsi wéma*; *K'iä'-lu-tsi wéma* (TK); white sandstone, black pigment; l. 1.9 cm, h. 0.7 cm; ca. 1880 (RMV 674-17).

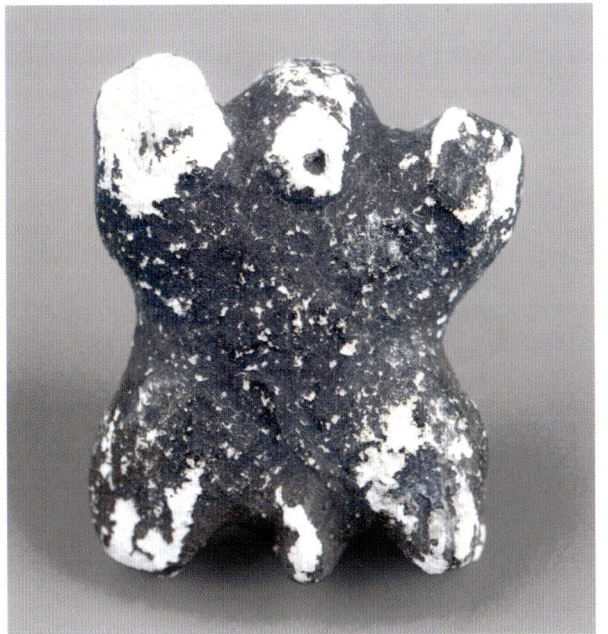

Fig. 308   Wolf fetish; *Sani-a Kya Kwe awa Yunawi Kóna wema*; *Tikya awa Yunawi Kóna wema*; stone, turquoise; l. 4 cm, w. 1.7 cm; ca. 1880 (RMV 674-20).

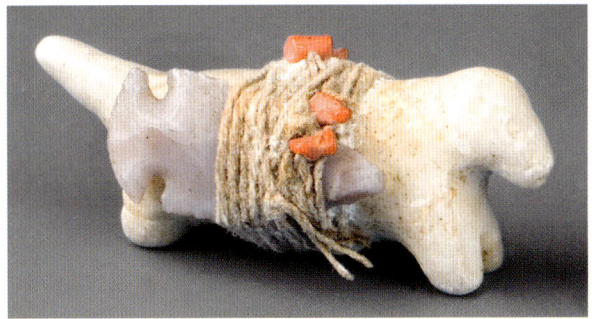

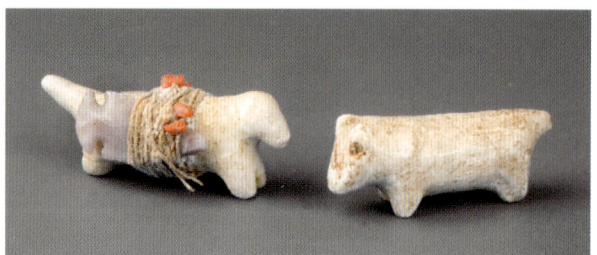

Fig. 309 Wolf fetishes; *Sani-a Kya Kwe awa Yunawi Kóna wema; Tikya awa Yunawi Kóna wema*; RMV 674-21: stone, coral, cotton; l. 4.5 cm, h. 2 cm, w. 1 cm; RMV 674-22: stone, turquoise, pitch, fiber, chert, abalone; l. 4 cm, h. 2.3 cm, w. 1.8 cm; both ca. 1880.

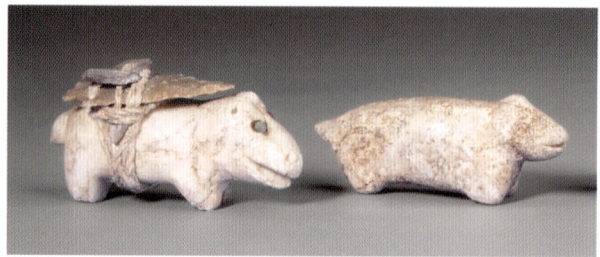

Fig. 310 White bear fetishes; *Ain-shi k'ó-ha-na wé-ma* (TK); *A pithla shi-wani awa* or *Motsi Kwah na tsija* or *Aingshi Kó'kama wéma*; RMV 674-23: stone, turquoise, abalone, fiber; l. 5 cm, h. 2.4 cm, w. 2 cm; 674-24: stone; l. 4.9 cm, h. 2 cm; both ca. 1880.

The other two specimens are more elaborately decorated. Attached to RMV 674-21 (Fig. 309 left) are a chalcedony arrowhead and a number of coral beads. RMV 674-22 (Fig. 309 right) has eyes of inset turquoise, and carries a chert arrowhead, abalone and other shell beads, attached with vegetal fiber string. One turquoise eye remains, while the other side shows the black pitch with which the turquoise eyes were glued in place.

White bear fetishes (Fig. 310) are also called scalping fetishes by members of the Bow priesthood, who regard the white bear as war chief. He represents the guardian of the upper world. *Poshai-ankia*, the Father of the Medicine Societies, regarded the bear as the younger brother of the mountain lion, because he was also courageous and determined. He made him the guardian of the west. Blue is the color associated with that direction. RMV 674-23 (Fig. 310 left) has inlaid turquoise eyes and carries a finely carved arrowhead and four pieces of abalone shell (Ten Kate 1890: pl. VIII, fig. 18).

Ten Kate noted (1890: 118) that the black bear fetish represents the peace god of the west. The specimen he collected (Fig. 311) is covered with a thick layer of dark brown pigment, possibly the remains of corn pollen that was used to feed the fetish or as prayer. The fetish is adorned with a necklace of red coral beads and has a roughly chipped arrowhead on its back, fastened with deer sinew that is covered with pitch (cf. Fane 1991: 98–99).

The eagle is the peace god of the upper world (Cushing 1883: 17, 29, pl. II, fig. 5, pl. VIII). The ancestry of Zuni bird fetishes goes back to at least early Pueblo II times, as such a specimen made of wood and very similar to Zuni eagle fetishes was unearthed during excavations by the Museum of Northern Arizona in ruins north of the San Francisco Mountains. From the Pueblo III period dates a similar type of hematite excavated at Pueblo Bonito in Chaco Canyon (Bartlett 1932). Although Zuni eagle fetishes come in different shapes, varying from realistic to abstract, this specimen from the Ten Kate collection (Fig. 312) is remarkably similar to the one from early Pueblo II times because of its elongated, flattened, and streamlined form. However, the anthropologist noted that the two protrusions from the head indicated that it probably was not an eagle but a ground owl fetish. Such bird fetishes were often suspended during ceremonies, which explain the piercing of this specimen (Ten Kate 1890: 119).

Fig. 311 Black bear fetish; *Ain-she wéma* (TK); *Ti Kya awa Ainshe wéma*; stone, coral, sinew; l. 4.5 cm, h. 2.5 cm, w. 3 cm; ca. 1880 (RMV 674-25).

Fig. 312 Eagle or ground owl fetish; *Tikya awa Kyoï Kyäli wéma*; stone; l. 2.7 cm, h. 0.8 cm; ca. 1880 (RMV 674-26).

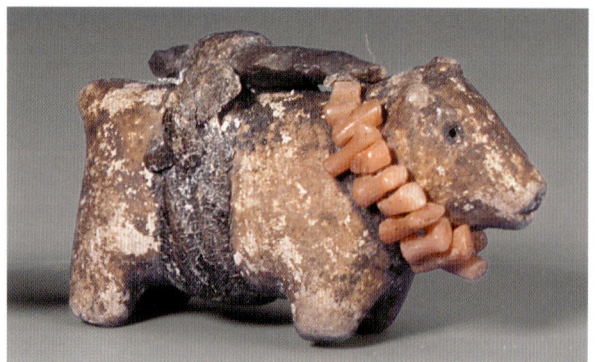

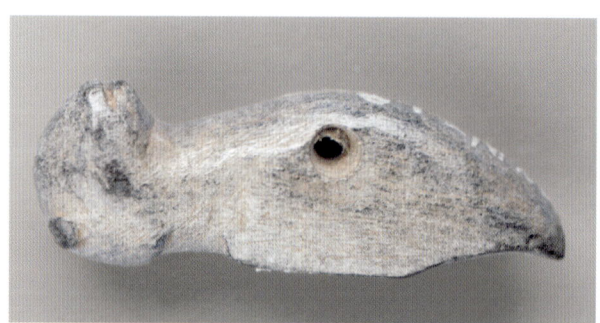

Ten Kate noted how daily life in Zuni was permeated with religion. Beliefs were associated with many recurring activities, requiring prayers and offerings. The anthropologist pointed out that although such behavior was regarded as based on superstition by Westerners, this only exemplified the common fallacy of presenting Indians as heathen savages and lacking morals.

Nai'uchi, the leading priest of the Order of the Bow (*A'pithlanshiwani*), was Ten Kate's main informant on Zuni religious beliefs. This priesthood of the warriors, the most important among several Zuni priesthoods, was responsible for the care of the twin war gods, *Ahaiiuta* and *Matsailema*, whose effigies were renewed each year and placed in a shrine, a ritual to ensure the protection of the tribe. They also offered monthly prayers by placing feathered prayer sticks on a small hill near the village. Two years after his settlement in Zuni, Cushing had become a member of the Bow priesthood after an initiation ceremony. This society was also responsible for law and order, justice, and the execution of sentences.

Soon after his arrival in the village, Ten Kate was able to witness the *Kakokshi* or 'Good dance.' He relates: "This is a type of worship and it supposedly represents the dance the soul of the departed attends as an observer at its consecration in the presence of the god-priests, and which, it is alleged, is later performed now and then in this life by the soul itself with the dancers. ... In the beginning I counted thirty-one dancers, all of them dressed in the same fashion, along with a dancer dressed as a woman— and a priest. The former were completely unclad, except for a blanket wrapped around the middle. The upper body and legs were smeared with white flour. Heavy necklaces of shells, beads, and turquoise hung from their necks down to their chests, with a glittering *haliotis* shell shining in the middle. Light-green masks with long black beards covered their faces. The long raven-black hair hung down loosely over their backs. On top of their heads were stuck yellow parrot feathers from Mexico. White feathers from a pelican were fluttering in back. The blankets, fastened around their hips and reaching almost down to their knees, consisted of finely woven white wool and were hemmed with dainty black and green borders, while the lovely hide of a gray fox was dangling from behind. Fastened below the right knee, but on the inside, there was a tortoise shell with rattling deer and antelope hooves, while the left one was enveloped by a dark band at the

same height. Their feet were clad in lovely leather moccasins, partially covered by spruce branches, which were fastened around their ankles. In the right hand they held a gourd shell rattle, and a broad silver bracelet adorned their wrists. Finally, they carried green spruce branches in their left hands."

"The dancer disguised as a woman was wrapped in a magnificent white blanket fringed with black hems, reaching down to his knees, and wore his hair in more or less the same style as the Moqui girls, while a similar green mask covered his face. The priest was the only one without a mask. A single white feather was stuck in his hair, which was bound together in back in a knot. His torso was clad in a dark cotton jacket. His legs were attired with broad white trousers and leather leggings. On his feet he wore soft footwear from the same material. In his left hand he held a small vase with sacred flour and a staff with eagle feathers."

"The ceremony begins at the south side of Zuni. Close behind one moment, then right next to each other, they stomp incessantly with their right feet, and then with their left, which do not budge from position, with the upper body slightly stooped. After an initial silence, a robust chant with a powerful cadence chimes in soon afterwards accompanied by the rattling of the tortoise shells and the shaking of the rattles. The priest and the woman dressed as a dancer stand at the head of the long, stomping row. Only during intermissions does the former strew the sacred flour over the ground with his right hand, always chanting, and with his gaze fixed on the dancers. The second one stands at the right side of the first dancer and executes the same motion as the former. After dancing for awhile, the row suddenly stands still and heads to the three or four various open spaces (plazas) inside the center of the pueblo. There they repeat in succession the same movements and the same chant and after a short while eventually vanish together in a kiva."

"In the intervening period some new personages appear wearing the most ludicrous attire. Their heads are completely covered with a gigantic round mask of dried clay with round holes for eyes and mouth, strongly recalling a deep sea diver's mask. They are completely unclad except for a loin cloth and are anointed from top to bottom with pinkish mud. These are the *keóyemoshi* or 'guardians of the sacred dance,' whose task it is to amuse the spectators during the dance intermissions. For the most part they engage in coarse jests, comic dialogues, and practical jokes, performing almost exactly the same role as

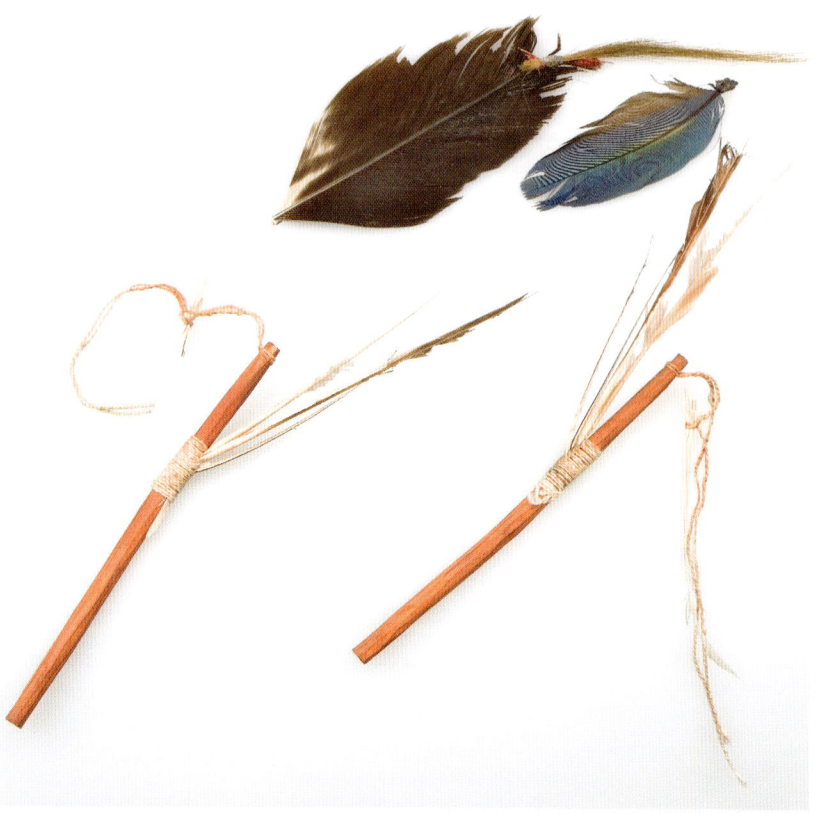

Fig. 313 Two prayer sticks; wood, pigment, feathers, cotton; sticks: l. 15 cm; ca. 1880 (RMV 362-149).

formed me, the words of this chant become a prayer for rain and an abundant harvest through the intercession of the spirits of their ancestors, especially whenever they are regarded as 'makers of the clouds.' ... The final scene of the dance consisted of a kind of pantomime ..." (Ten Kate 2004: 275–277).

Ten Kate could easily imagine the difficulty Cushing had to contend with in the beginning when he wanted to write down his observations and make sketches in the presence of the Indians. He noted the disapproving expression on the faces of bystanders when he was taking notes during the ceremony, but went on recording by writing intermittently.

Ten Kate made notes on the prayer sticks offered by the members of the Priesthood of the Bow, including Cushing (Fig. 313): "These sticks, which are wrapped in corn husks, have a length of roughly fifteen centimeters and a cross-section of nearly one-half centimeters and in the main resemble those of the Moquis. They are hewn from the wood of the mountain mahogany tree, the hardest wood the Zunis know and which at the same time is used to make their clubs. The hardness of this wood symbolizes the prayer for courage and strength against the enemy. The red color, with which the sticks are painted, is called *a'hokon* (depiction of war) and denotes blood. With one exception the feathers come from various birds of prey and are named *la'tsumaywuh* or 'powerful feathers.' They have a dual signification: destruction and spiritual fortitude. One prays to be in a condition to pursue the enemy just as relentlessly as the birds of prey their victims. The only feather that does not come from a bird of prey is the one from the wing of a wild duck, which is one of the Zuni water gods and thus the symbol of strength and swiftness on the warpath. The downy feathers are called *ha'showahn* (ear) and probably signify that the 'misty spirits of the gods' may hear the prayer." Later he added a note: "Mr. Cushing is not completely sure about this last statement." Ten Kate also published his notes on prayer sticks in the *Revue d'Ethnographie* (1884).

our clowns. The dignity of these *keóyemoshi* is sacred, and every year a number of them are selected from the priesthood. Making all kinds of jokes, they go inside various houses to ask for *héwé*, paper thin corn bread, for the dancers resting inside the kiva, who never tarry there for long and resume their dance with renewed ardor. Every time they come out the kiva after a round-dance, a new dancer disguised as a woman has been added to the others, so that by the end of the dance there are a half-dozen. Moreover, in the middle of the day they were joined by a dancer by a dancer who took his place in the middle of the row, clad for the most part like the other dancers, but without being anointed white, and with a gigantic mask on his head besides."

"As time passed by, the more numerous became the spectators who had taken up position in colorful, picturesque groups on the flat roofs of their houses, from where they could view the plaza. Here, the longer time went on, the more the row of bronzed figures with their rattles were passionately moving up and down, while droning out 'haha-hahajeha-haha!' ... As Cushing later in-

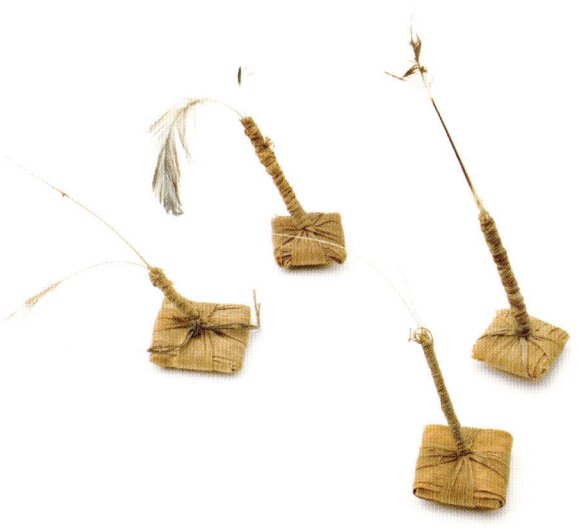

Fig. 314   Four shuttlecocks; *pokyánnoni* (TK), *pokinanane* (M. Stevenson 1904), *pokianawai* (Culin 1907: 720); cornhusk, wood, feathers, native cotton; average h. 13.5 cm, bases vary from 3.4 by 3.4 cm to 4.3 by 4.4 cm; ca. 1880 (RMV 674-8).

Games

Ten Kate acquired several artifacts used in games by the Zuni, among them four shuttlecocks (Fig. 314), which he identified as "children's toys." Their bases are woven from cornhusk. The sticks are wrapped with cornhusk and tied with native cotton thread of various colors. Small turkey feathers are tied to the tops. The game, involving the throwing of the cocks and lively betting, was played by boys and adults. The Zuni name for the game pieces derived from the fact that when the shuttlecocks were rubbed against the palm of the hand, they made the sound similar to that when a rabbit ran across frozen snow (M. Stevenson 1903; Culin 1907: 720–721; Fane 1991: 137).

Game sticks such as the one collected by Ten Kate (Fig. 315) were used during footraces of men, who had to kick them up and ahead each time as fast as they could.

Warfare and Weapons

Ten Kate noted that the Zuni were one of only a few tribes southwest of the Rocky Mountains who took scalps. It was one of the preconditions for being accepted into the Order of the Bow. Each member owned a bandoleer of braided hide, decorated with stone arrowheads, each of which indicated a scalp taken. Thus Cushing had a shoulder bag on which five arrowheads were attached, indicating he had killed and scalped five enemies. However, the anthropologist had obtained these scalps through White intermediaries who had such items in their personal collections of Indian artifacts.

The Navajo and Apache were the principle enemies of the Zuni, as they were prone to steal horses and sheep and plunder their harvests. However, the establishment of American rule and the placement of the Navajo and Apache on reservations substantially ameliorated the situation, especially with the soldiers at Fort Wingate ready to be deployed in case of tensions and hostilities.

As most important traditional weapons among the Zuni Ten Kate noted bows and arrows and wooden clubs. However, these were increasingly being replaced by firearms obtained in trade. The Indians formerly made round shields of rawhide that were decorated with paint. For hunting rabbits and hares, the Zuni like the Hopi, used a flat throwing stick, much like a boomerang, called *zjai-annùh* (cf. Fig. 253).

This war club (Fig. 316) was donated to the Leiden Museum by Frank H. Cushing (cf. J. Stevenson 1883: 371, fig. 491). War clubs were used in hand-to-hand combat, especially with the Apache and Navajo, the traditional enemies of the Zuni. Ten Kate recorded the names by which they referred to their enemies. The Tonto Apache

Fig. 316   War club; wood; l. 52 cm; ca. 1860–1870 (RMV 675-5).

Fig. 315   Game stick; *tiskwana kya thlám* (TK); wood; l. 13 cm; ca. 1880 (RMV 674-60).

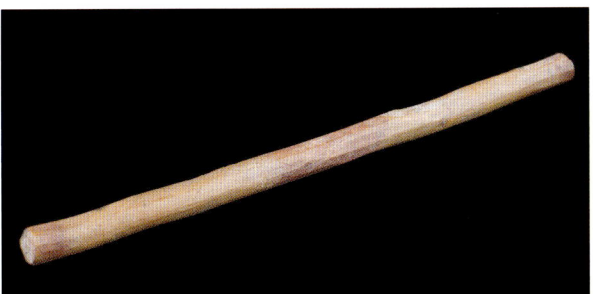

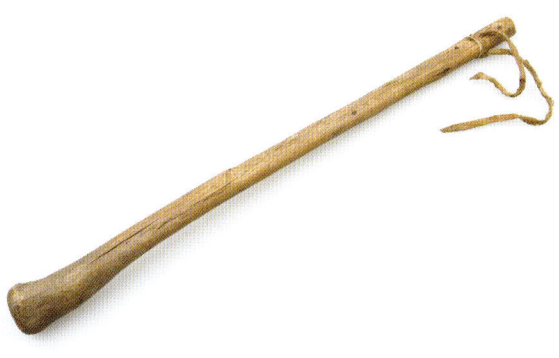

were called *Tsji'shekwe* ('plundering people'), the White Mountain Apache *Wilatsu'kwe* ('people with the lightning shell,' meaning: sudden attackers).

For eight days Ten Kate did fieldwork at Zuni, talking to informants, observing everyday life and the occasional ceremony in the pueblo, jotting down in his notebook everything he learned and witnessed. In addition, he aggregated a small collection of artifacts. He thoroughly felt at home in Zuni and was reluctant to leave. However, on 5 September 1883 he bade farewell to his Zuni hosts, and Cushing accompanied him on horseback to Nutrias, which they reached late in the afternoon. In the evening Cushing told Ten Kate about the ordeals of his life and work, the opposition he had to overcome to do fieldwork and defend Zuni land rights. Before going to sleep, he sang several Zuni songs, and this occasion cemented what would become a lifelong friendship between the two anthropologists. The next day the men rode to Fort Wingate and stayed with Dr. Washington Matthews. Ten Kate concluded his account of Zuni and Cushing as follows: "On the afternoon of the following day I said farewell to Ténatsali. With the last exchange of handshakes I gave him as a memento the best thing I could give: my revolver, my trusty companion on so many journeys, which he had praised for its accuracy over yonder in the valley of *Äshik'ia-mót-ella*. When I had gazed after Ténatsali as long as I could, and the clacking of his mustang's hoofs finally vanished, I felt that I had parted from a friend" (Ten Kate 2004: 291).

References

Adair, John
    1944   *The Navajo and Pueblo Silversmiths.* Norman, OK: University of Oklahoma Press.
Bartlett, Katharine
    1932   A Unique Pueblo II Bird Fetish. *American Anthropologist* 34: 315–319.
    1949   Hopi Indian Costume. *Plateau* 22: 1–10.
Batkin, Jonathan
    1987   *Pottery of the Pueblos of New Mexico, 1700–1940.* Colorado Springs, CO: Taylor Museum of Anthropology.
Bedinger, Margery
    1973   *Indian Silver: Navajo and Pueblo Jewelers.* Albuquerque, MN: University of New Mexico Press.
Bunzel, Ruth
    1929   *The Pueblo Potter: A Study of Creative Imagination in Primitive Art.* New York, NY: Columbia University Press.
    1932   An Introduction to Zuni Ceremonialism. *Annual Report of the Bureau of American Ethnology* 47: 467–544.

Chapman, Kenneth M.
    1928   Bird Forms in Zuni Pottery Decoration. *El Palacio* 24(1): 23–25.
Chapman, Kenneth M. and Bruce Ellis
    1951   The Line-Break: Problem Child of Pueblo Pottery. *El Palacio* 58(9): 251–289.
Colton, Harold S.
    1959   *Hopi Kachina Dolls.* Albuquerque, NM: University of New Mexico Press. [Revised edition.]
Conn, Richard
    1979   *Native American Art in the Denver Art Museum.* Denver, CO: Denver Art Museum.
Culin, Stewart
    1907   *Games of the North American Indians.* Annual Report of the Bureau of American Ethnology 24. Washington, DC.
Cushing, Frank H.
    1882–1883   My Adventures in Zuni. *The Century Magazine* 25: 191–207, 500–511; 26: 28–47.
    1883   Zuni Fetishes. *Annual Report of the Bureau of American Ethnology* 2: 3–45.
    1886   A Study of Pueblo Pottery as Illustrative of Zuni Culture Growth. *Annual Report of the Bureau of American Ethnology* 4: 467–521.
    1894   Primitive Copper Working: An Experimental Study. *American Anthropologist* 7: 93–117.
    1920   *Zuni Breadstuffs.* Indian Notes and Monographs 10. New York, NY: Museum of the American Indian.
Dennis, Wayne and Marsena G. Dennis
    1940   Cradles and Cradling Practices of the Pueblo Indians. *American Anthropologist* 42: 107–115.
Douglas, Frederic H.
    1938   Notes on Hopi Brocading. *Plateau/Museum Notes* 11: 35–38.
    1939a   *Weaving in the Tewa Pueblos.* Denver Art Museum Leaflets 90. Denver, CO.
    1939b   *Weaving of the Keres and Tiwa Pueblos and Jemez.* Denver Art Museum Leaflets 91. Denver, CO.
    1940   *Weaving at Zuni Pueblo.* Denver Art Museum Leaflets 96–97. Denver, CO.
Fane, Diana
    1991   (ed.) *Objects of Myth and Memory: American Indian Art at the Brooklyn Museum.* New York, NY: The Brooklyn Museum.
Fox, Nancy
    1978   *Pueblo Weaving and Textile Arts.* Santa Fe, NM: Museum of New Mexico Press.
    1989   Southwestern Indian Jewelry. In: Andrew H. Whiteford et al., *I am Here: Two Thousand Years of Southwest Indian Arts and Culture* (Santa Fe, NM: Museum of New Mexico Press), 61–88.
Frank, Larry and Millard J. Holbrook
    1990   *Indian Silver Jewelry of the Southwest, 1868–1930.* West Chester, PA: Schiffer.
Hardin, Margaret Ann
    1983   *Gifts of Mother Earth: Ceramics in the Zuni Tradition.* Phoenix, AZ: The Heard Museum.

1987   Zuni Pottery: The Roots of Revival. In: Lowell J. Bean (ed.), *Seasons of the Kachina* (Hayward, CA: Ballena Press), 133–163.

Hedlund, Ann Lane and Diana Dittemore

2004   Arizona State Museum's Textiles and the Southwest-Northwest Continuum. *American Indian Art Magazine* 30(1): 60–67.

Herold, Joyce

2005   Baskets of the Southwest and Great Basin. In: Jill R. Chancey (ed.), *By Native Hands. Woven Treasures from the Lauren Rogers Museum of Art* (Laurel, MS: Lauren Rogers Museum of Art), 76–107.

Hinsley, Curtis M.

1981   *Savages and Scientists: The Smithsonian Institution and the Development of American Anthropology, 1846–1910.* Washington, DC: Smithsonian Institution Press.

Holmes, William Henry

1886   Pottery of the Ancient Pueblos. *Annual Report of the Bureau of American Ethnology* 4: 246–360.

Hough, Walter

1915   *The Hopi Indians.* Cedar Rapids, IA: Torch Press.

1919   The Hopi Indian Collection in the United States National Museum. *Proceedings of the U.S. National Museum* 54: 235–266.

Hovens, Pieter

1988   The Anthropologist as Enigma: Frank Hamilton Cushing. *European Review of Native American Studies* 2(1): 1–5.

1989   *Herman F. C. ten Kate (1858–1931) en de antropologie der Noord Amerikaanse Indianen* (Herman F. C. ten Kate and the Anthropology of the North American Indians). Meppel: Krips. [Ph.D. thesis, University of Nijmegen.]

1995   Ten Kate's Hemenway Expedition Diary, 1887–1888. *Journal of the Southwest* 37(4): 635–700.

James, George Wharton

1914   *Indian Blankets and Their Makers.* Chicago, IL: A. C. McClurg and Company.

Kenagy, Susan G.

1977   Zuni Pottery Aesthetic, 1880–1930: A Social, Cultural and Psychological Study of Indigenous Aesthetic Appeal. M.A. thesis, California State University at Long Beach.

Kent, Kate Peck

1983   *Pueblo Indian Textiles: A Living Tradition.* Santa Fe, NM: School of American Research Press.

Kirk, Ruth F.

1943   Introduction to Zuni Fetishism. *El Palacio* 50: 117–129, 146–159, 183–198, 206–219, 235–245.

Ladd, Edmund J.

1979   Zuni Economy. In: Alfonso Ortiz (ed.), *Southwest* (Handbook of North American Indians 9. W. C. Sturtevant, gen. ed.; Washington, DC: Smithsonian Institution), 492–498.

MacLeish, Kenneth

1940   Notes on Hopi Beltweaving of Moenkopi. *American Anthropologist* 42: 291–310.

Mason, Otis T.

1887   Cradles of the American Aborigines. *Annual Report of the Smithsonian Institution for 1886:* 161–212.

1904   Aboriginal American Basketry: Studies in a Textile Art without Machinery. *Annual Report of the U.S. National Museum for 1902:* 171–548.

Mera, Harry P.

1943   *Pueblo Indian Embroidery.* Laboratory of Anthropology Memoir 4. Santa Fe, NM.

Nahohai, Milford and Elisa Phelps

1995   *Dialogues with Zuni Potters.* Zuni: Zuni Ashiwi Publishing.

Nichols, Linda Foss et al.

2000   *Voice of Mother Earth: Art of the Puebloan Peoples of the American Southwest.* Nagoya: Nagoya–Boston Museum of Fine Arts.

Ostler, James and Milford Nahohai

1989   *Zuni Fetishes.* Zuni: Pueblo of Zuni Arts and Crafts.

Ostler, James, Marian Rodee, and Milford Nahohai

1996   *Zuni: A Village of Silversmiths.* Zuni–Albuquerque, NM: Zuni A:Shiwi Publishing–University of New Mexico Press.

Rodee, Marian E.

1977   *Southwestern Weaving.* Albuquerque, NM: Museum of New Mexico Press.

1992   Leiden Textile Report. Leiden: Rijksmuseum voor Volkenkunde.

Rodee, Marian E. and James Ostler

1985   *Zuni Pottery.* West Chester, PA: Schiffer.

1986   *The Fetish Carvers of Zuni.* Albuquerque, NM–Zuni: Maxwell Museum of Anthropology–Pueblo of Zuni Arts and Crafts.

Roscoe, Will

1988   We'wha and Klah: The American Indian Berdache as Artist and Priest. *American Indian Quarterly* 12(2): 127–150.

Sayers, Robert

1981   Symbol and Meaning in Hopi Ritual Textile Design. *American Indian Art Magazine* 6(1): 70–77.

Shufeldt, R. W.

1910   Examples of Unusual Zuñian Pottery. *Records of the Past* 9: 208–212.

Spier, Leslie

1924   Zuñi Weaving Technique. *American Anthropologist n.s.* 26: 64–85.

Stephen, Alexander M.

1936   *Hopi Journal.* Elsie Clews Parsons ed. New York, NY: Columbia University Press.

Stevenson, James

1883   Illustrated Catalogue of the Collections Obtained from the Indians of New Mexico and Arizona in 1879. *Annual Report of the Bureau of American Ethnology* 2: 307–464.

1884   Illustrated Catalogue of the Collections Obtained from the Pueblos of Zuni, New Mexico, and Walpi, Arizona in 1881. *Annual Report of the Bureau of American Ethnology* 3: 511–594.

Stevenson, Matilda Coxe

1904   *The Zuni Indians.* Annual Report of the Bureau of American Ethnology 23. Washington, DC.

Tanner, Clara Lee

1983   *Indian Baskets of the Southwest.* Tucson, AZ: University of Arizona Press.

Ten Kate, Herman F. C.

1884   Notes sur l'ethnographie des Zunis. *Revue d'Ethnographie* 3: 161–163.

1885   *Reizen en Onderzoekingen in Noord Amerika.* Leiden: E. J. Brill.

1890   Zuni Fetishes. *Internationales Archiv für Ethnographie* 3: 118–119.

1925   *Over Land en Zee; Schetsen en Stemmingen van een Wereldreiziger.* Zutphen: W. J. Thieme.

2004   *Travels and Researches in Native North America, 1882–1883.* P. Hovens, L. A. Hieb, and W. J. Orr eds. Albuquerque, NM: University of New Mexico Press. [Translation of Ten Kate 1885.]

Wade, Edwin and David Evans

1973   The Kachina Sash: A Natural Model of the Hopi World. *Western Folklore* 32: 1–18.

Whitaker, Kathleen

2002   *Southwest Textiles: Weavings of the Navajo and Pueblo.* Seattle, WA: University of Washington Press.

Whiteford, Andrew Hunter

1988   *Southwestern Indian Baskets: Their History and Their Makers.* Santa Fe, NM: School of American Research Press.

Wright, Barton

1979   *Hopi Material Culture: Artifacts Gathered by H. R. Voth in the Fred Harvey Collection.* Flagstaff, AZ–Phoenix, AZ: Northland Press–Heard Museum.

11

Equestrian Warriors:
Indians of the Plains

In October 1883 Ten Kate set out on the last leg of his research journey. During the final weeks of his stay in the United States he wished to acquaint himself with the Indians of the Plains, the archetypal American Indian of dramatic newspaper stories and popular literature, the warriors on their mounts with fluttering feather head-dresses, attacking emigrant caravans, White settlements, and railroad trains on the frontier: a threat to progress and civilization. However, Ten Kate was keenly aware of the fate of the Native nations, who were fighting to retain their land and independence but gradually losing the battle and becoming exiles in their own country.

From Trinidad in south-central Colorado he traveled by train eastward onto the Kansas plains, gradually descending from an elevation of about 3500 feet. In Coolidge he stepped out onto the platform and enjoyed the fresh fragrance of the endless dew-covered rolling plains. During breakfast he heard that the train had been held up by outlaws a couple of days earlier, whereby the engineer and fireman were killed in a firefight. However, the robbers had eventually been chased away by the heavily armed personnel in the wagon of the Wells & Fargo Express Company.

He continued his train journey eastward by way of Dodge City, Newton, Wichita, and Wellington to Caldwell, a gateway to Indian Territory. The first stint of fieldwork was undertaken among the Cheyenne and Arapaho at the Darlington Agency. Subsequently, Ten Kate traveled to Anadarko, the agency of the Wichita, Kiowa, Comanche, and Apache. Finally, he spent time at Fort Sill, where he found "a medley of races," including nine different Native tribes. On several occasions he had to cross streams swollen by summer rains. He had to wait several hours until the water in the Cimarron River (Red Fork of the Arkansas) had subsided before he could cross the still foaming water, catching his breath and cargo on a sandbank in the middle of the stream and crawling out

covered in red mud on the other bank. At the rapidly flowing Canadian River an Indian showed him how to reach the other side by zigzaging across the stream. However, at the torrential Sugar Creek he was forced to stay for the night, which he spent with a Wichita family. Several Natives assisted him during the crossing the next morning.

At the Darlington Agency Ten Kate obtained the services of two young Cheyennes as interpreters, Bullbear, the son of the famous Northern Cheyenne chief, and Henry Roman Nose, who had formerly been a prisoner of war at Fort Marion in Florida. At Fort Sill the anthropologist worked with the military interpreter Horace P. Jones, who had lived more than twenty years among the Comanche, and the former scout Philip McCusker, who had married a Comanche woman and spoke Comanche and Kiowa fluently.

Subsistence, Hunting, and Horses

While traveling across southern Kansas and Oklahoma, Ten Kate noted that the Indians' livelihood, the immense herds of buffalo, had been exterminated by White hunters. The slaughter had reached its zenith between 1872 and 1874, when more than three million animals were killed, and Ten Kate saw thousands of bleached skulls and bones along the railroad tracks. Their subsistence base destroyed, the Plains Indians could do little but accept the terms of the treaties forced upon them and settle on reservations. Immediately White settlers took over most of their lands.

The herds of pronghorn antelope and deer had also been decimated by White hunters and settlers for their meat. The Plains Indians in Indian Territory still stalked these animals to feed their families, but their prey was much less bountiful than in earlier days. The Comanche and Kiowa still ate prairie dogs, and the Comanche supplemented their diet with catching small tortoises. They

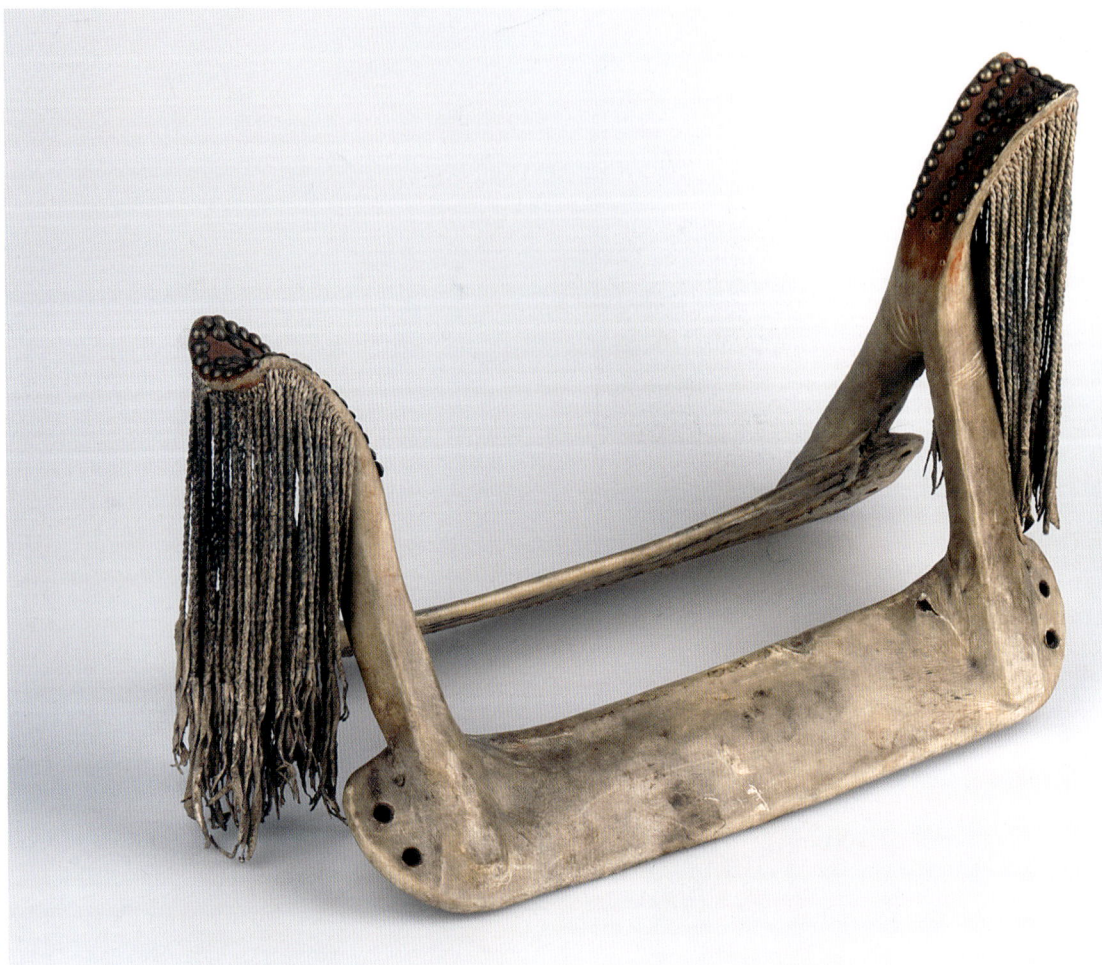

Fig. 317   Comanche woman's saddle; *nárinno* (TK); wood, hide, brass, pigment; l. 48.5 cm, w. 26 cm, h. 30 cm; ca. 1870 (RMV 362-13).

collected the fruits of the persimmon, from which a kind of cake was made, whose flavor very much resembled that of currant-rye bread.

Ten Kate noted that reservation lands were leased to White ranchers to pasture their cattle in return for a fee, which was distributed among the resident Indians. Many Natives were also engaged in ranching and at the Darlington Agency the Cheyenne and Arapaho were reported to own 3,000 heads of cattle and 6,000 horses. A small number were engaged in agriculture, and especially among the Comanche corn was planted and cultivated. However, Ten Kate realized that ownership of substantial numbers of cattle and horses did not necessarily mean that the Indians were engaged in viable business enterprises as ranchers. He noted that they were completely dependent on the government and its annual appropriations and that once independent and proud nations had been turned into beggars. He wrote: "Rendered powerless by lack of

game, they have been tamed for good. ... Thus nothing remains for the Indian but to keep silent, eat the bread of charity, or struggle and starve" (Ten Kate 2004: 343–344).

Most Kiowas and Comanches used Mexican saddles while riding horses, although a few rode bareback and a few traditional saddles consisting of wooden frames covered with animal hide were still in use.

Native Americans used frame and pad saddles, especially the former following Spanish examples. The wooden structure of this Kiowa frame saddle (Fig. 317) is characteristic of the general type. It consists of two parallel flat wooden panels and two forked bows at each end, serving as pommel and cantle. The frame is tightly covered with a layer of white buckskin, accomplished by applying the skin when wet and subsequently letting it dry and shrink, thus securing the construction. The inside of the high pommel and lower cantle are stained red and their perimeters decorated with a row of shiny brass tacks and twisted hide fringe. The holes in the base are for leather thongs with which the saddle is strapped to the back of the horse, often after inserting hide padding. A seat of hide is usually suspended between pommel and cantle. Many Comanche and Kiowa women and some men used such leather-covered wooden frame saddles (Merrill et al. 1997: 11).

Several variations of frame saddles can be distinguished, based on the shape of the parallel panels, pommels and cantles, and their distribution, although not unequivocally, suggests three geographical types from west to east. Ten Kate noted the similarity of the frame saddles of the Comanche and Southern Ute (Wissler 1915a: 6–14, 21, 24–25, 31–38; cf. Brasser 1976: 146; Coe 1976: 168–169; Hail 1980: 222–227; Walton et al. 1985: 210–213).

Dwellings, Interior Furnishings, and Cradles

The majority of the Cheyenne, Arapaho, Comanche, and Kiowa still lived in tipis, but Ten Kate observed that of the hundreds he saw, not a single one was covered with buffalo hides. Only among the Comanche a few old-style dwellings, called *káni* or *kánik*, were still in use. White canvas, obtained from the United States government, was in universal use. Ten Kate had seen tipis among the Southern Ute in the Colorado Rockies, but on the Plains he also observed screens of poles and brush surrounding the tents, serving as windbreaks and protection against drifting snows. He noted that the smoke flap at the top of each tipi was always turned away from the wind. Western household furnishings had partially replaced those of Native manufacture, and in several Cheyenne tipis Ten Kate saw wooden beds, imported from the east coast. Traditional were the square and rectangular rawhide parfleches, gaily painted with geometric designs and used to store personal belongings. Babies were swaddled on carrying boards or cradles, held tight by elaborately beaded covers. Ten Kate was particularly enamoured with their graceful constructions.

On the reservation of the Wichita Ten Kate saw a number of traditional grass houses. These consisted of pliant poles, approximately five to six meters long, bent at the top and attached to each other, with the thicker bottom end of these poles set in the ground, occupying a circle of four to five meters. Willow branches and long grass covered this frame, and Ten Kate compared this kind of abode to a cross between a gigantic beehive and a pointed haystack. A hole in the top and the low entryway were the only openings. He spent one night in one of these dwellings with an Indian family.

While Barbara Hail of the Haffenreffer Museum of Anthropology in Bristol, Rhode Island, was doing fieldwork on Southern Plains Indian cradles, her Kiowa-Delaware informant Linda Poolaw aptly defined their meaning as "a house for the beginning of life." They were "gifts of pride and love," as a descendant of a cradle maker called them.

Originally, cradles consisted of a board slightly longer and wider than the body of the infant, on which the baby was secured by hide bindings and swaddled in skins. Later wooden sides were added. The lattice or slat-frame cradle appeared after 1830 and became prevalent among the Comanche, Kiowa, Arapaho, Cheyenne, and Lakota. It consisted of two narrow pointed boards and two shorter cross sections that were made into a sturdy V-shaped frame, of which the long boards spread outward at the top. Such construction and the decoration of the frame were usually done by men. Rawhide was used for backing the frame and as protective strips for head and feet, and a hide cover in which the baby was swaddled was laced onto that construction. Their adoption facilitated transportation of babies on horseback by hanging cradles from pommels. Children usually spent most of the first two years of their lives swaddled and cradled. Swaddling was a widespread practice in Native North America, as it was believed that it physically protected infants, quieted them down, strengthened their muscles and character, and resulted in a strong bond with mothers (Mason 1887: 198–203; Orchard 1929: 168; Berlandier 1969: 87–88; Maurer 1977: 270; Hail 1980: 143–151; 2003: 17, 23–25, 31–34; Schneider 1983b; Hovens and Krosenbrink 1994; cf. Walton et al. 1985: 172–179 for northern Plains cradles).

Plains Indian women often used cradles as a medium to express their technical and aesthetic skills in quillwork and beadwork. The value attributed to particularly stunning baby carriers could equal the price of a horse. Among the Cheyenne and Arapaho the women were organized into sacred guilds of quill and bead workers, and initiates were allowed to use symbolic designs of religious significance (Marriott 1955; cf. Conn 1979: 126–127).

Ten Kate's collection included a Southern Cheyenne model cradle (RMV 362-14; wood, hide, glass; total l. 41 cm, l. of cradle bag 24 cm, w. 6 cm; ca. 1870–1880), which was stolen in 1964 during an exhibition. On this slat-frame cradle, the beaded designs on both sides of the baby's head, executed in lazy stitch, probably had a protective

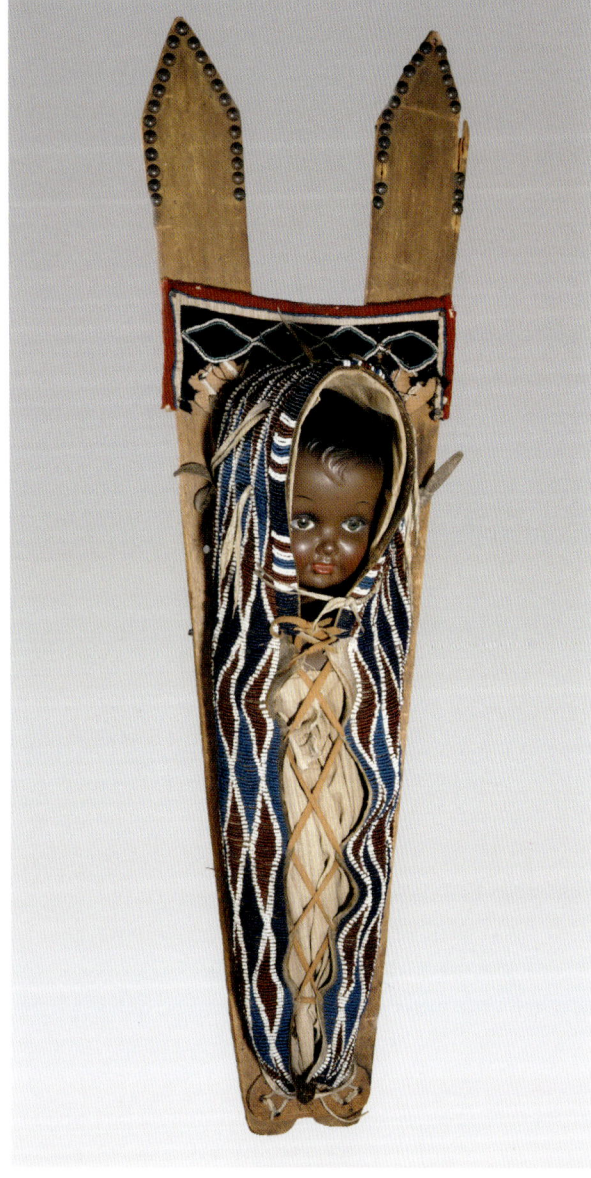

Fig. 318 Kiowa doll cradle; *pajop* (Merrill et al. 1997: 62), *paih'dodl* (Hail 2003: 23); wood, hide, cloth, glass, brass, papier maché; l. 74 cm, w. 24 cm, h. 16.5 cm; ca. 1870–1880 (RMV 710-13).

function. The design motif of stepped triangles is said to represent tipis, and their doors are shown in beaded rectangles of contrasting color (cf. Conn 1979: 151; Hail 1980: 147-149; Feder 1982: 81, 109).

The Kiowas made cradles in three sizes: model cradles for dolls to play with, a small-size cradle for newborn babies, and a slightly larger one for older infants. The rawhide bib, protecting the head of the infant, is typical for Kiowa cradles and is present in this model collected by Ten Kate (Fig. 318). The slat-frame of Osage orange (a.k.a. bois d'arc, *Maclura pomifera*) is partially covered with cloth. Canvas and cloth almost completely replaced hides

during the late nineteenth century. The curvilinear, abstract leaf-shape design of the beadwork is outlined in undulating vertical rows of white beads sewn in spot-stitch, the resulting panels filled in with red and blue beads in lazy stitch. The designs used were regarded as individual property, but bead workers occasionally allowed others to use their motifs. The emphasis by Kiowa bead workers on originality resulted in a great artistic variety of cradles (Conn 1979: 154; Merrill et al. 1979: 18- 19, 50, 53-54, 130-131; Hail 1980: 143-146; 2002: 26- 29; Schneider 1983a: 239; 1983b; Brasser 1998: 54-55; Levy 2001: 910).

Dress

Many Cheyennes, Arapahos, Comanches, Kiowas, and Wichitas still wore hide leggings and moccasins. Those of the women were made of beautiful soft tanned leather, tastefully decorated with colored beads, notably blue and white ones. Sturdy blue cloth was often used for men's leggings and cut with fluttering hems. Those of both sexes sometimes had discs of German silver sewn on. Most Indians wore robes made of two woolen blankets sewn together, replacing the older buffalo robes. Women increasingly donned calico blouses, skirts, and dresses, and many Wichita women wore broad leather belts with German silver discs around their waists. Ten Kate was impressed by the Kiowa's footwear, because it was especially beautiful with fiery red square flaps, decorated along the edges with beads, and hanging down to the side of the foot below the ankles. Observantly, the anthropologist noted that although many of the materials used for making Indian dress were of Western manufacture, their cut and style was unmistakably Native. The costume of women was generally less elaborate than that of the men who were more inclined toward dressing up and showing their finery. On special occasions like powwows and dances the Indians donned robes and headdresses elaborately painted and decorated with beadwork and feathers. The Cheyenne and Arapaho Indian police wore light blue uniforms when on duty and provided quite a contrast.

Most Indians wore their hair in traditional fashion. The women parted it in the middle and let it hang loose on their shoulders. The men generally had two long braids, hanging on the chest. The small braided scalplock on the crown of the head was worn to the left or back.

Plains women and men often carried several small beaded bags on their belts, serving a variety of purposes. Narrow pointed ones were used as awl or paint stick cases

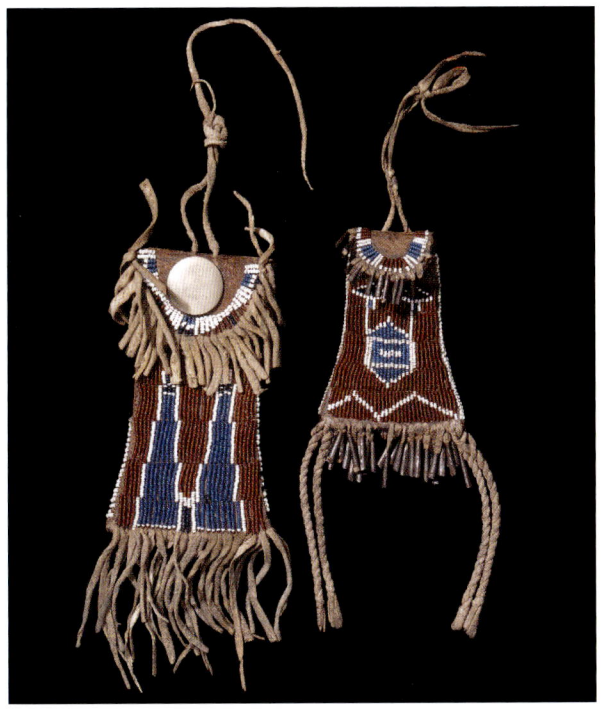

Fig. 319 Comanche belt bag; harness leather, glass, German silver; l. 47 cm, w. 8 cm; ca. 1880 (RMV 362-10). Kiowa paint bag; harness leather, glass, tin, pigment; l. 10–12 cm, w. 8 cm; ca. 1880 (RMV 710-20).

(Fig. 320). Wider ones, mostly hourglass-shaped, often contained materials necessary to start a fire, a piece of flint and a piece of steel, and they are often referred to as strike-a-light bags (Fig. 319). However, they could also hold other items such as whetstones, sewing materials, ration tickets, and occasionally pigments for painting. Women also kept dried scented plants in these bags, serving as perfume pouches. While both sexes carried such bags on their belts, men were known to have these attached to bow and quiver cases. Leather and beaded fringe, twisted rope, and tin cones are common decorative additions. The earliest type of strike-a-light bag is rectangular. Since 1860 such belt bags were increasingly made in a trapezoidal shape. The brownish-red beads were rather popular among the Kiowa and this color is sometimes referred to as "Kiowa-red." Typical of the Kiowa is the white-beaded outlining of design features. The beading of these belt bags could extend partially or wholly across the reverse side. A Kiowa origin of this type of belt bag has been suggested, but there is little data to distinguish between Kiowa and Comanche belt bags (Conn 1979: 153; 1982: 85, 138; Hail 1980: 200-202; Hassrick and Markoe 1986: 150, 152; Hail and Schwarz 1987: 54, 67-68; Wooley 1990a; Hanson 1994: 83-93; Merrill et al. 1997: 14, 117; Brasser 1998: 67-68; 2000: 112, 122, 125; Levy 2001: 909).

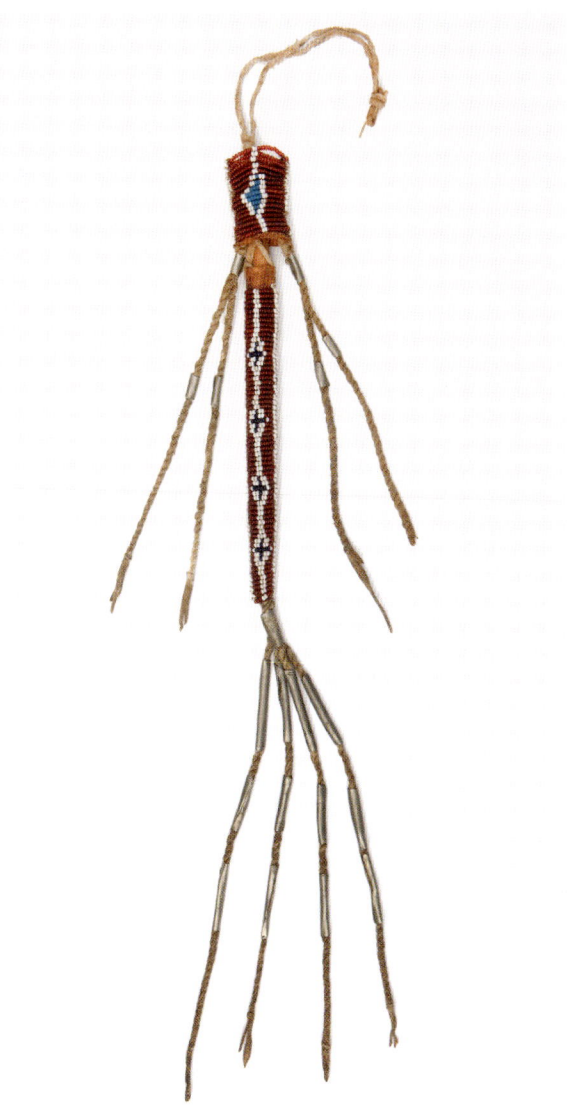

Fig. 320 Kiowa paint stick case; hide, glass, German silver, wood; l. (of case) 17 cm, with fringe 38 cm; ca. 1880 (RMV 362-17).

A small pouch collected by Ten Kate (Fig. 319 left) was used as a strike-a-light bag. It fits in well with the variety of Southern Plains belt bags from the collection of Forrest E. Fenn in Santa Fe, which is one of the most extensive and finest in the private domain (Hanson 1994: 83-93).

A typical trapezoidal bag in the collection (Fig. 319 right) still contains the remains of a bright red pigment, indicating its use. The lower part on the back has a beaded panel in similar colors as the front, but with slightly different designs.

The stacked diamond pattern displayed on a Kiowa specimen (Fig. 320) lends itself for application on such elongated and narrow beaded surfaces and can be found on paint stick and awl cases (Wooley 1990a: 53-54; cf. Maurer 1977: 201; Levy 2001: 909).

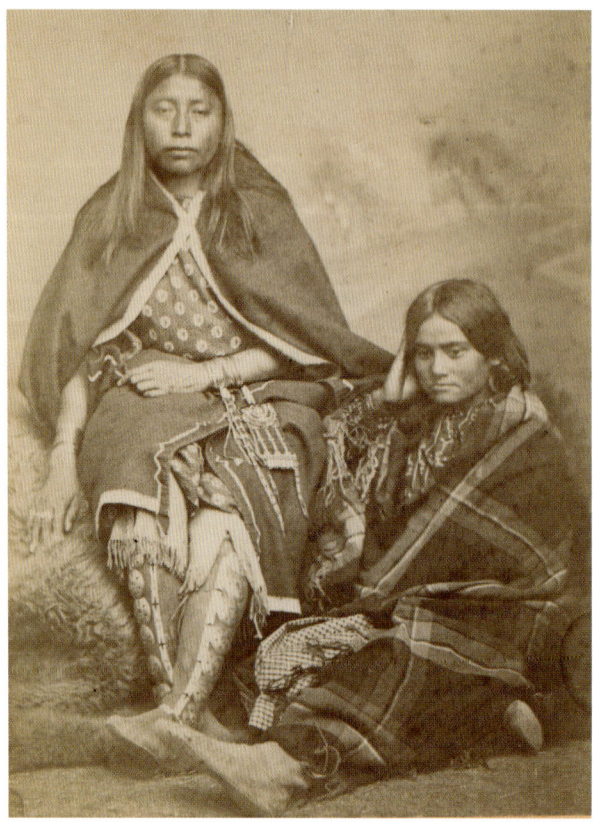

Fig. 321 Comanche women: Cha-wa-ke (Looking for Something Good; left) and unidentified individual. Photograph by Will Soule, Fort Sill, Oklahoma, ca. 1869–1874 (Ten Kate coll.; WMR 900572).

The Comanche collection of Jean Louis Berlandier (1969, Ewers 1969), dating from the period between 1826 and 1850 and now at the Smithsonian Institution, provides a seminal starting point for a thorough analysis of Southern Plains Indian attire. John C. Ewers (1980; cf. 1983: 107–109) laid the exemplary groundwork with an analysis of women's clothing, and a younger generation of scholars has followed up with studies of cradles (Schneider 1983a, Hail 2003) and belt bags (Wooley 1990a). The inventory of the Smithsonian's Kiowa collections has recently been completed and published and should facilitate and encourage further research (Merrill et al. 1997).

On the southern Plains, among the Comanche, Kiowa, and Apache, moccasins often have a V-shaped insert as a vamp. The seams are frequently covered with a leather fringe, as is the seam at the heel, and the insert is often painted red, yellow, or blue. In other cases the seams on the upper are covered with beadwork, resulting in a long and narrow V-shape extending to the toes, sometimes reaching a beaded border along the seams where sole and upper are sewn together. This pattern of decoration was adopted by tribes on the central and northern Plains, irrespective of the type of moccasin construction (Wissler 1916: 110; cf. Ewers 1969: 181, 184; Hail 1980: 113–114; Hanson 1994: 66–68; Brasser 1998: 53; Kavanagh 2001: 891).

Among the Southern Plains tribes a tradition of applied quill- and beadwork was lacking. Dress and accessories were decorated by painting and the addition of a variety of leather fringes, tin cones, and metal buttons of brass and German silver. When documentation is lacking, it is difficult or impossible to distinguish between Kiowa and Comanche dress items.

In this example of Comanche footwear in the Ten Kate collection (Fig. 322) a beaded border along the seam where upper and sole are sewn together is lacking, resulting in a simple beaded V-design in beadwork along the length of the vamp, executed in white, red, and blue. The hide is stained with a red pigment and the pair have a hard rawhide sole. This latter trait was probably introduced to

Fig. 322 Comanche moccasins; *naap* (TK); hide, glass; l. 25.5 cm; ca. 1880 (RMV 362-11).

Fig. 323 Southern Cheyenne moccasins; *wooághno* (TK); hide, glass; l. 28 cm; ca. 1880 (RMV 362-15).

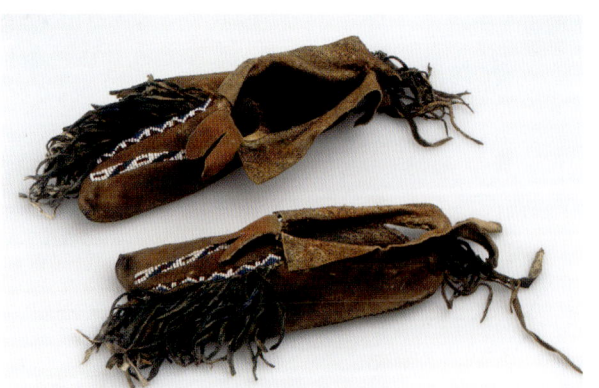

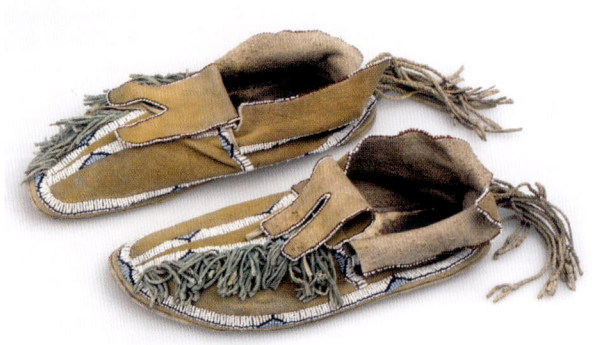

the southern plains by the Apache, from where it rapidly spread northward so that by 1850 all tribes made this variety. Comanches of high status had ermine trailers sewn at the heels of their footwear (Schneider 1967: 3, 6, 15).

The Southern Cheyenne moccasins (Fig. 323) have a hard rawhide sole, which became more prevalent on the Plains by the mid-nineteenth century, a process furthered by the observation of Euro-American footwear on the one hand and the use of stirrups on the other (Hatt 1916: 185–189; Webber 1989: 11). The uppers are painted yellow on the outside, and the applied leather fringe on the vamp is stained green. The fringe at the heel is braided. The V-shaped beaded design on this specimen is applied irrespective of the pattern of the moccasins, following southern Plains examples (cf. Fig. 322). The bilobed tongue and split cuffs are bordered with red and white beads. The triangular pattern along the seam is applied in an odd number, with one on the front, in typical Cheyenne manner (Hail 1980: 106–109; Moore et al. 2001: 869).

On the Southern Plains, Indian women sewed hard-soled moccasins and leggings together into boots and applied paint, beads, cloth, and brass and nickel-silver discs to them, the degree of decoration varying from simple to elaborate. A pair of rawhide-soled boots for a young girl acquired by Ten Kate is painted a light yellow on the outside (Fig. 324). Two bands of red cotton are applied vertically on the outside leg and two lozenge-shaped pieces of the same material above the heel. These are outlined with bands of glass beads.

Ten Kate purchased this pair from a Plains Apache family. However, it is quite possible that they were of Kiowa manufacture. Alternatively, the Plains Apache readily adopted the material culture of their neighbors in Indian Territory and produced similar footwear (cf. Hatt 1916: 198–200; Conn 1974: 104–107; 1982: 56, 96, 143; Hail 1980: 114–115; Hanson 1994: 72–73; Merrill et al. 1997: 109–110). Berlandier (1969: 51) was favorably impressed by the dress of Plains Apache women in 1830 and wrote: "Lipan women are the best turned out of all the nomadic women. Though they dress entirely in tanned deerskins, they are clean and elegant. Their faces are agreeable, their features interesting, and the simplicity of their dress makes them stand out among other native women."

Ten Kate purchased another pair of hard-soled moccasins among the Kiowa (Fig. 325), and Norman Feder confirmed their identity as such. The cuffs are covered in red cloth, their margins beaded. The back seam is covered by a hide fringe, an element sometimes explained as eras-

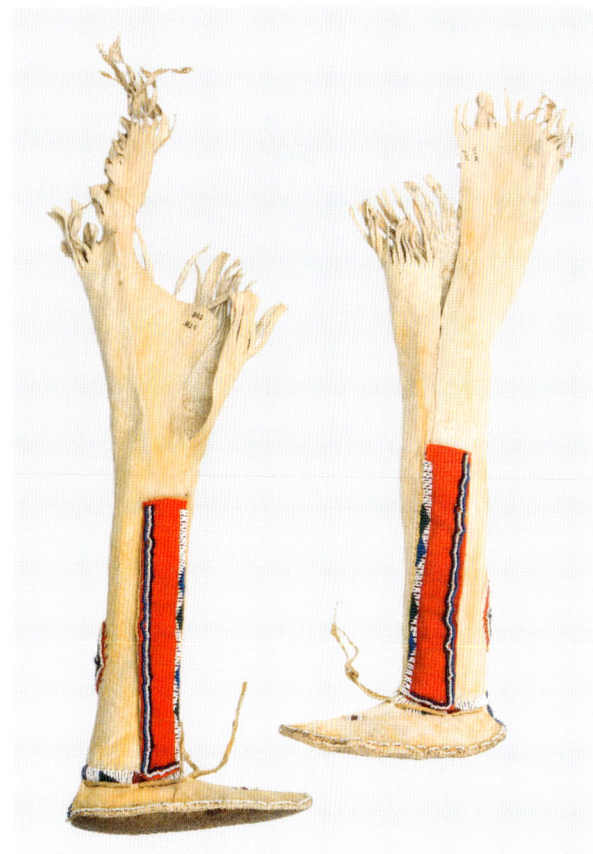

Fig. 324   Plains Apache or Kiowa girl's boots; hide, pigment, glass, cotton; h. 48 cm, l. of sole 18.5 cm, w. 7 cm; ca. 1880 (RMV 362-16).

ing moccasin tracks. Transverse alternating bars in white and red beads decorate most of the surface. The triangular tab at the front exhibits a triangular beadwork pattern in blue (cf. Merrill et al. 1997: 111–112).

Fig. 325   Kiowa moccasins; *johi* (Merrill et al. 1997: 63); hide, glass, cotton; l. 27.5 cm, w. 9.5 cm, h. 7.5 cm; ca. 1880 (RMV 710-3).

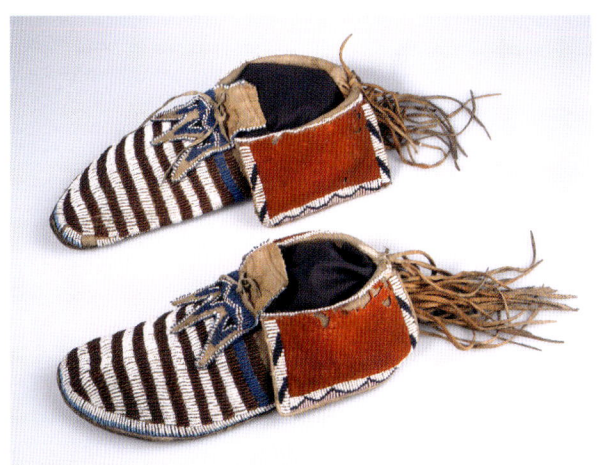

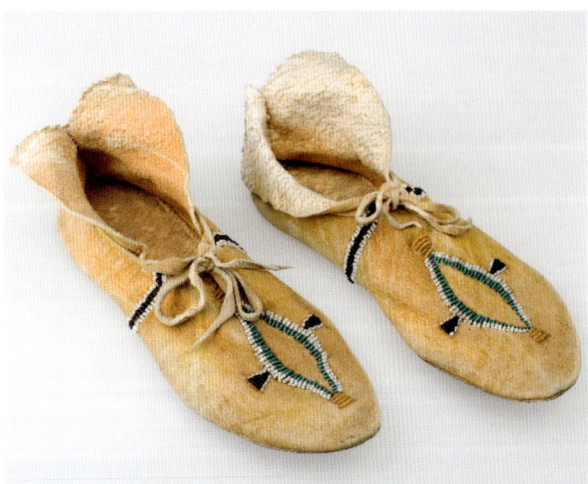

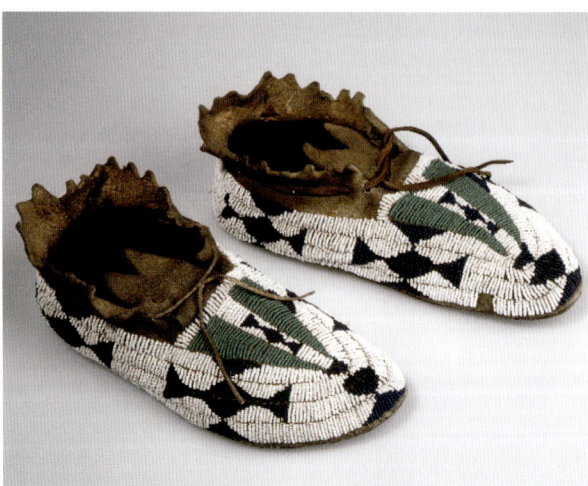

Fig. 326 Kiowa or Kiowa-Apache woman's moccasins; *johi* (Merrill et al. 1997: 63); deerhide, glass; l. 24 cm, w. 9.5 cm, h. 6.5 cm; ca. 1880 (RMV 710-12).

Fig. 327 Southern Cheyenne moccasins; hide, glass; l. 26 cm, w. 10 cm, h. 8.5 cm; ca. 1880 (RMV 710-25).

Typical for the Southern Plains style of footwear are the slanted cut of the cuffs sloping toward the heel, the split heel part of the cuff, the lack of tongue, the string going all around, and the yellow painted buckskin (Fig. 326). A single curvilinear band of beadwork on the front is typical for the Kiowa and Plains Apache. The narrow bands of black and white beads are typical for the latter, while the use of "greasy-yellow" beads is observed in Kiowa beadwork (cf. Brasser 1998: 53).

Although late-nineteenth-century Cheyenne moccasins differ little from other Central Plains footwear, several features make them characteristically Cheyenne: the very careful and precise beadwork, the design in the central front lane, a narrow strip of beadwork running up the back of the heel and covering the seam, and the cross made up of triangles. The double V-shaped triangles on the fronts are usually referred to as "buffalo tracks" by museum curators (Fig. 327).

Originally belts were made from deerskin or buffalo hide. Commercial harness leather became popular be-cause of its durability and sturdy basis for aesthetically displaying slightly convex German silver conchas and discs, standing out shining and hard against their dark and pliable background. Such shiny discs, made from brass or German silver, were also used as hair ornaments by Plains men. Their arrangement in rows was a Native idea (Fig. 328; cf. Hanson 1975: 93-97; 1994: 76-77; Conn 1979: 160-161; Hail 1980: 140-141; Lanford 1993).

German silver, also referred to as nickel silver, is an alloy consisting of sixty parts copper, twenty-five parts zinc, and fifteen parts nickel. The designation comes from its place or origin, Germany, more particularly the town of Hildburghausen. This metal became prevalent in the Plains Indian trade in the 1860s, and until 1880 its use was widespread and intensive. As the material glutted the market, its status underwent rapid devaluation (Davis et al. 1965: 21).

Ornaments of Spanish origin, an attractive combination of German silver and colored glass beads, were used to decorate items of dress, fashion accessories such as

Fig. 328 Wichita woman's belt; harness leather, iron, German silver; l. 87 cm, w. 8 cm; ca. 1880 (RMV 362-18).

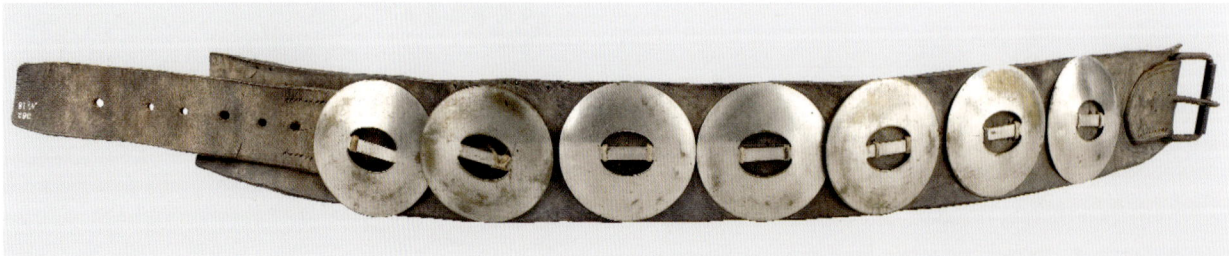

226

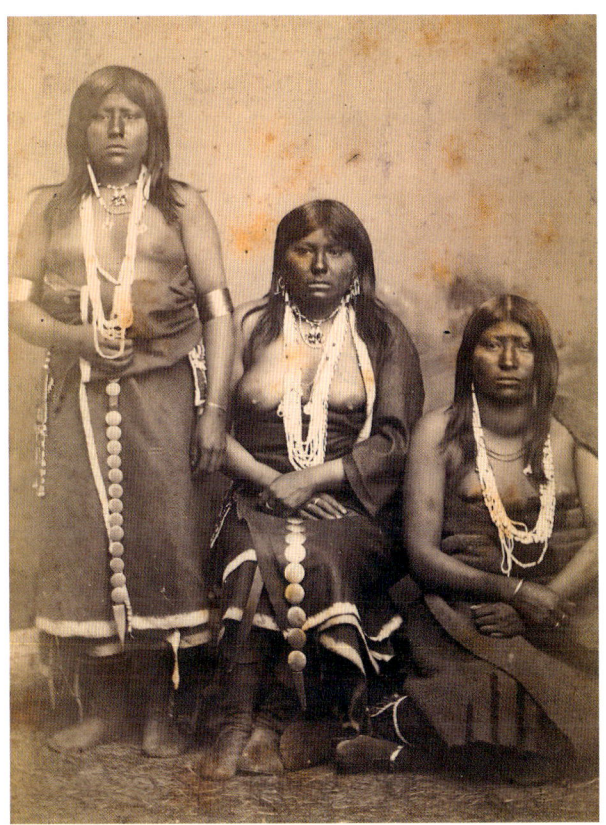

Fig. 329 Wichita women wearing bead, shell, and German silver jewelry; Indian Territory (Oklahoma), ca. 1880. Photographer unknown (Ten Kate coll.; RMV 414Cb30).

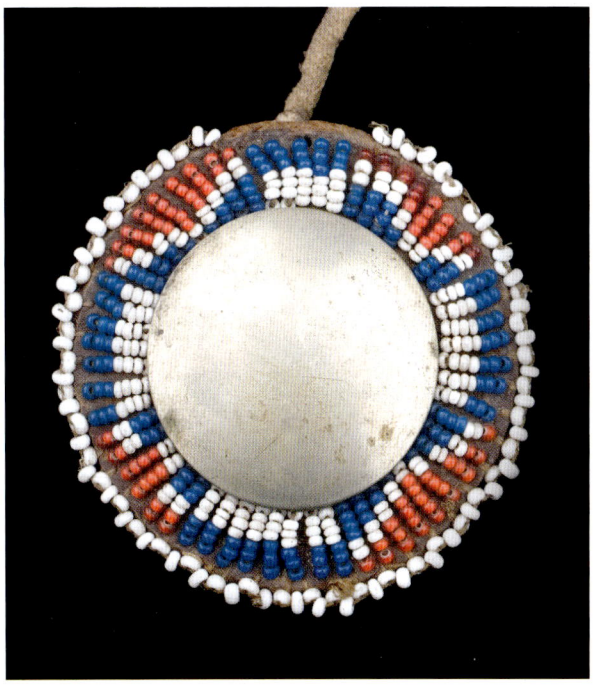

Fig. 330 Kiowa ornament; hide, glass, German silver; d. 5.5 cm; ca. 1880 (RMV 710-24).

Fig. 331 Kiowa fan; wood, eagle feathers, glass beads, cloth; l. 73 cm, w. 15.5 cm; ca. 1870–1880 (RMV 710-8).

belts, pouches, and hair pendants, and saddles (Fig. 330). The Kiowa referred to the latter ornaments as *taugauga* (Merrill et al. 1997: 27).

Feather fans were used for different purposes by Plains Indians, from the mundane to the sacred. Apart from their primary utilitarian use to whisk cooling air across the body, they were used during dances and ceremonies, including shamanic curing rituals. In these latter cases, fans could be elaborately decorated. In the syncretistic Peyote religion feather fans with netted beadwork form an integral part of the ceremonies of the Native American Church (cf. Maurer 1977: 201; Conn 1979: 157; Wooley 1990b: 100). Sioux Indian women made a variety of fans from eagle feathers that were used by men and women alike. Many were simple and even lacked a handle. Frequently a string of sweetgrass (*Hierochloe*) was attached, so that the fan scented the air when used.

The Leiden example (Fig. 331) is not documented as to where it was collected. It is a fine specimen with its decoration in cloth and beadwork. Because of the greasy-yellow beads it was probably obtained from the Kiowa (cf. Woodruff 1934: 636; Densmore 1948: 202, pl. xxiv b).

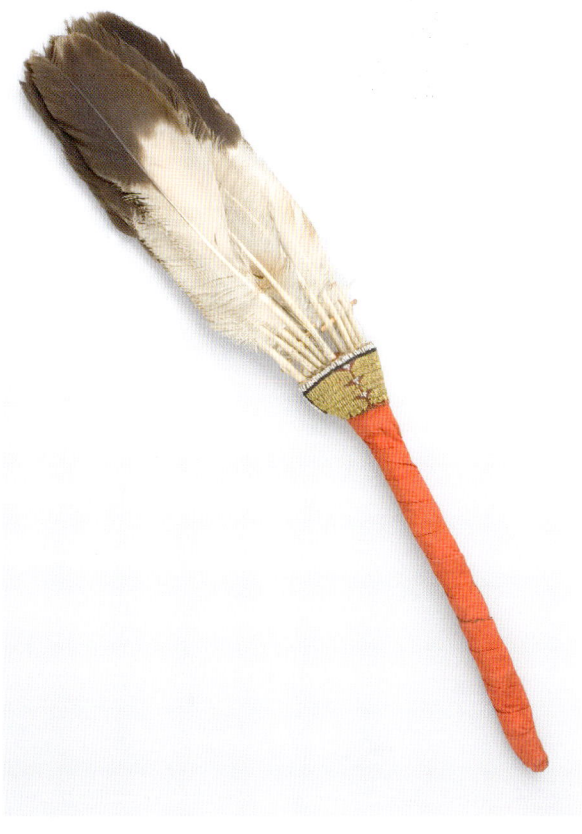

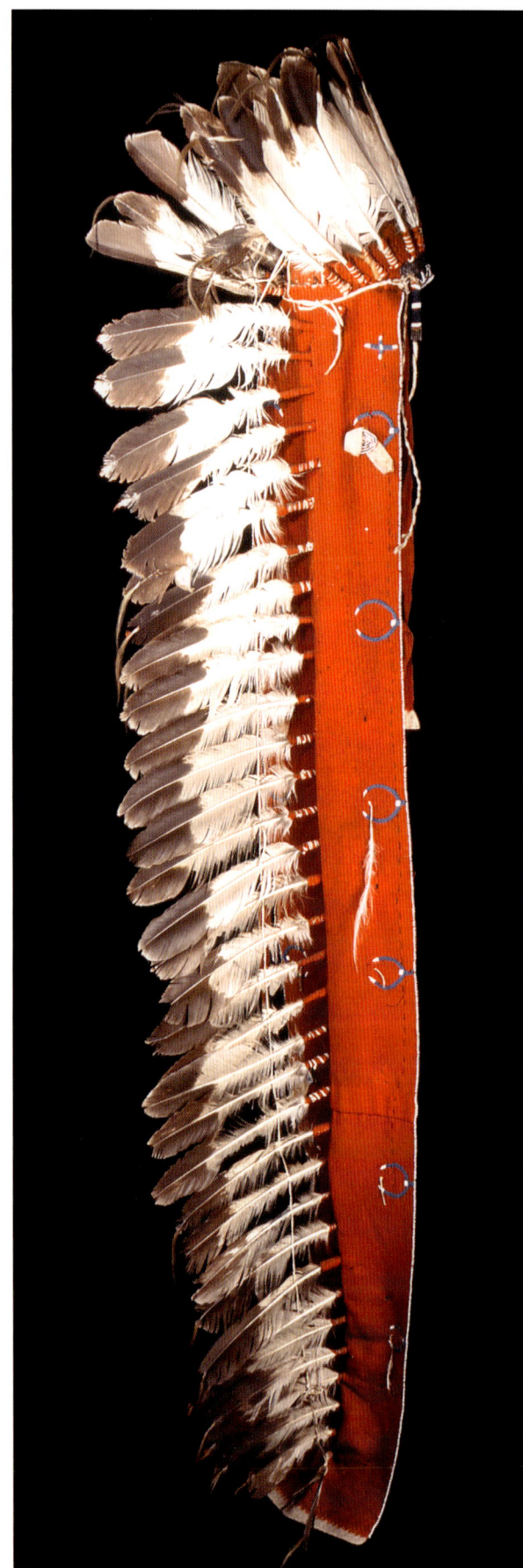

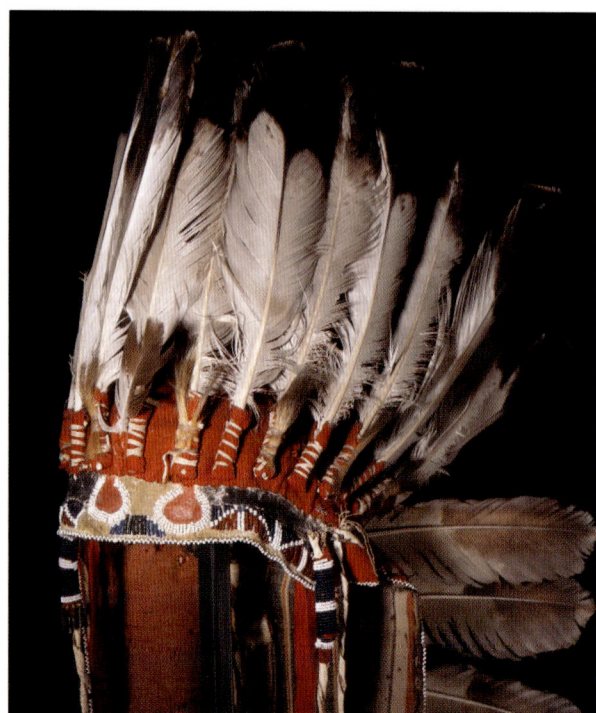

Figs. 332, 333 Comanche feather war bonnet with single trailer; hide, wool, eagle feathers, horsehair, glass; l. 208 cm, h. 45 cm; ca. 1870 (RMV 710-5).

Warfare and Weapons

All Plains tribes in Indian Territory owned firearms, often of the latest model. However, many still valued their traditional weapons: bows, arrows, tomahawks, shields, and lances. Among the Comanche Ten Kate met warriors still proud of their bow (*eth, hoomok*) and arrows (*páka*), kept in a quiver (*hóko*) of mountain lion skin, and their long lance (*tsjik*). The arrows all had iron points, which had replaced stone arrowheads as they were not damaged or broken so easily, and Ten Kate mentions the often repeated story that the Indians broke up the agricultural implements they were given by the government to make them into projectile points. The Comanche had abandoned their custom of dipping arrowheads in rattlesnake venom because of the fatalities that had occurred. To Ten Kate's surprise, the Comanche denied having had tomahawks. He noted they had war whistles (*hoke*), prepared from the brachium of an eagle, which were used during attacks on their enemies.

Ten Kate observed that there were considerably more women than men among the Cheyenne, Comanche, and Kiowa, one of the consequences of war, and after a long exposé on Indian-White relations on the Plains, the anthropologist remarked: "I apologize for this long digression, but

I found it difficult to remain silent about what should be fully publicized. The most recent history of this tribe again demonstrates the barbarity of our own race toward our natural compatriots, to whom we ascribe shortcomings we ourselves possess in no lesser degree" (Ten Kate 2004: 328).

Indians of the Plains used feathers from eagles, hawks, turkeys, pheasants, and grouse for their war bonnets. Plains feather war bonnets came in a variety of types. The Blackfeet wore a hide and cloth headband with eagle feathers standing straight up. Much more common and especially popular among the Sioux and the Upper Missouri village tribes (Mandan, Arikara, Hidatsa) was the crown war bonnet, consisting of a hide cap with a backward flaring crown of eagle feathers. The crown shape symbolized the Sun, the source of life. The third type, represented by the Leiden example (Figs. 332, 333), consisted of a crown feather bonnet with a single or double half or full trailer of cloth attached to the back, studded with eagle feathers. These were usually worn while mounted. Feather war bonnets used to mark the status of their wearers, but when the intertribal and interethnic wars on the Plains came to an end, such headgear was increasingly used by Indian men for festive occasions of a social nature (Douglas 1951; Howard 1954b; Schneider 1967: 15-16, 24; cf. Coe 1976: 160, 175; Conn 1979: 165; Hail 1980: 116-124; Walton et al. 1985: 103-110; Horse Capture 1992).

Berlandier (1969: 51, 115) described how the Comanche went to war in the 1820s: "... their clothing is quite varied. I have seen some of them elegantly attired, wearing bonnet and cloak of feathers cunningly fashioned, while others were hideously arrayed in the horns and scalp tufts of buffaloes, with their bodies covered with hideous painting. ... Their shields are decorated with feathers flowing from their borders. Their heads are covered with a bonnet of feathers, to which they add a sort of tail of feathers long enough to cover the shoulders, and which streams in the air when they ride fast." Berlandier (1969: pl. 3) is also the source of the earliest known illustration of Comanche warriors by lieutenant José María Sánchez y Tapia.

Most of the feathers on the Leiden bonnet are from the tails of young golden eagles, each bird providing about twelve feathers. There are thirty-two feathers cascading on the trailer and eighteen on the crown. Their shafts are wrapped in red stroud and the feathers are held in position by a hide lace. The headband is ornamented with painted and beaded tabs with circular and triangular designs and beaded appendages at the sides (cf. Ewers 1969: 177-180; Kavanagh 2001: 897).

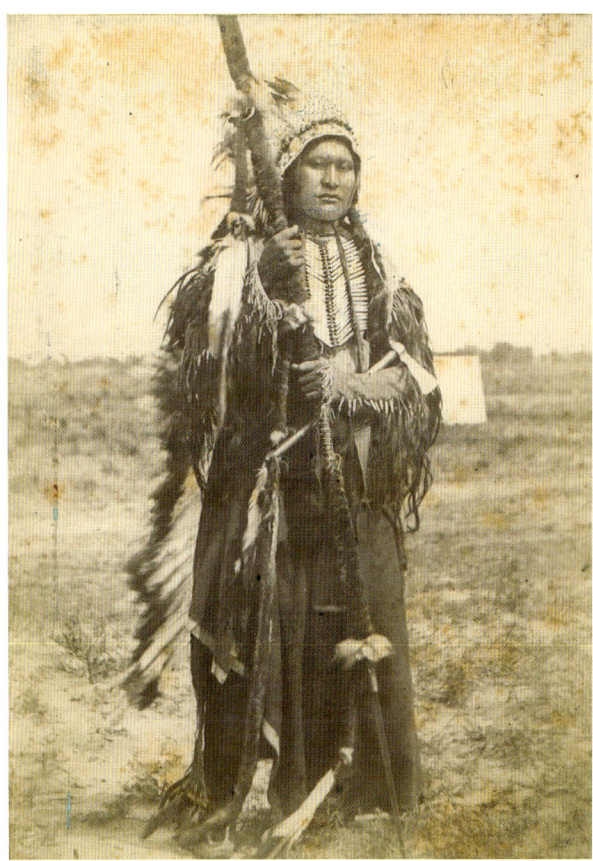

Fig. 334 Cheyenne chief Powder Face in full regalia, with trailer headdress and tomahawk; Indian Territory (Oklahoma), ca. 1880. Photographer unknown (Ten Kate coll.; RMV 414Cb23).

Little scientific study has been made of arrows of Native North American manufacture. Mason (1894: pl. xliii) illustrates a Comanche arrow with a shaft made from osier, banded with red and green paint, three feathers and down, with an iron blade and sinew wrapping (also cf. Laubin and Laubin 1980: 111-226; Hamilton 1982: 12-28). Although Ten Kate acquired these Comanche arrows (Fig. 335) in 1883, they remained in his possession until

Fig. 335 Two Comanche arrows; WMR 17996: wood, iron, sinew; l. 67.5 cm; WMR 17997: wood; l. 75.5 cm; both ca. 1870-1880.

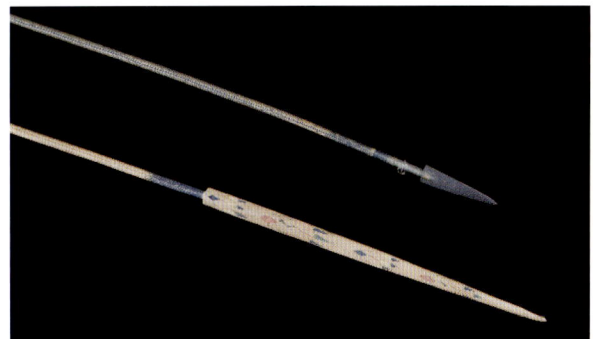

1911, when he and his Japanese wife Kimi Fujii donated them along with Japanese and other artifacts to the Museum of Anthropology, now the World Museum, in Rotterdam. The city's mayor and aldermen announced this and several other donations in the main local newspaper on 5 September 1911 and gratefully accepted the generous gifts.

Pipes and Smoking

Among the Cheyenne and Arapaho Ten Kate observed both the solemn ceremonial smoking of pipes as well as recreational smoking. The anthropologist was offered the pipe while visiting the tipi of the venerable Cheyenne Chief Bullbear. Those in attendance sat in a circle. The Indian headman pointed the stem (*heess*) to the four cardinal directions, said a prayer, and took a few draws from it, after which it was handed around in a circle until it came back to the chief, who also offered it to his wife. The bowl of the pipe was called (*heeoogk*) and was made from catlinite, a red sandstone quarried in southwestern Minnesota by Indians from several tribes, including the Cheyenne. However, since their settlement in Oklahoma they obtained the red rock or finished pipe bowls through the mail from a trader in Sioux City. Often these were not carved by Native people but by Whitemen. The Cheyenne also smoked American trade tobacco, but mixed this with finely cut sumac (*Rhus*; Cheyenne: *mahénnohánye*) leaves, producing a more mellow flavor.

Games

During his visits to camps in Indian Territory Ten Kate saw the Indians engaged in many different games. Cheyenne and Arapaho children often played a throwing stick game, in which long sticks with a buffalo horn on their tips (*sko, skaô*) were thrust forward and points could be scored by hitting the horned tip. Men played cards, engaged in dice games, and raced horses, not infrequently betting property and cash. Singing, dancing, and storytelling were also favorite pastimes, and Ten Kate witnessed reed flutes (*wónuh*).

Religion

Ten Kate noted that the religion of the Plains Indians was animistic, based on the belief that every natural phenomenon was infused with spiritual power. The sun was re-

garded as the Supreme Being and often addressed as the Great Father, the creator of life. The anthropologist listed and discussed a number of traditional dances. Dances during which hunting scenes were enacted were common among those tribes depending primarily on buffalo and deer for their livelihood. Most tribes engaged in the annual Sun dance during which self-mutilation took place.

Ten Kate wrote that religious traditions were waning on the Plains and the he assumed that the Indians had begun to loose faith in their gods, deities, and spirits, as they had not been able to protect the people against the onslaught of the Whiteman. Moreover, among the Cheyenne the old religious leaders of the medicine societies were dying and only a few of them trained young successors to take their place and assume ritual responsibilities.

Ten Kate discussed beliefs and customs surrounding death and the afterlife with Comanche Chief Mowway. The old man told him that when Comanches passed away, they went to *Apameen*, the Land of the Father, where they were joined by all the animals who died. Thus *Apameen* was the equivalent of the popularized idea of "happy hunting grounds," as the anthropologist pointed out, although that concept was foreign to the Comanche. When the sun was setting in a red glow, the Indians believed that this was caused by red dust clouds, driven up by thousands of Comanches dancing in the land of *Apameen*.

According to Ten Kate, the Southern Cheyenne interred their dead. However, their northern relatives placed the bodies of their deceased in trees. The Comanche buried their men with their horse and property. However, traditional customs were changing, as Ten Kate witnessed at a Comanche burial. The lamentations of women and the physical mutilation were still traditional, as was the attire and facial painting of the dead chief. But the body of the headman was transported on a wagon and interred without any grave goods, as requested by the Indian Agent who tried to prevent destruction of property and encouraged compliance with American customs.

The Northern Plains

During his 1882–83 journey of fieldwork, Ten Kate never visited the northern Plains. However, his collection contains twenty ethnographic artifacts from this region. The circumstances of their acquisition are described in a letter the anthropologist sent from St. Louis on 16 December 1882 (ARMV no. 273), when he was on his way from his visit to the Iroquois of upper New York State and the cities of the Northeast to the Southwest and northern Mexico. While in New York State, he had passed through Niagara Falls and in this city had met a dealer from whom he bought a collection of northern Plains Indian artifacts, which according to the dealer came from the Two Bears band of Yanktonai Sioux from Fort Rice, Dakota Territory.

Researches into the origin of this collection revealed that almost contemporaneously with Ten Kate's purchase of these artifacts, two shipments of Yanktonai materials came through New York State, on their way to the museum of the University of Vermont in Burlington, now the Robert Hull Fleming Museum. They were presented to the museum as a long-term loan by Captain Ogden Benedict Read, who was stationed with the Eleventh Infantry Regiment in Montana and Dakota Territories between 1876 and 1887, taking part in military action against the Sioux and other northern Plains tribes. Read had compiled a written inventory of the loan, but a number of artifacts on this list were never acquired by the museum. It has been suggested that some of these items became separated from the two shipments and might have ended up in Ten Kate's collection. The Burlington museum also listed some specimens from the Read inventory as "discarded" or "exchanged." However, incomplete and less than consistent administration and inexpert care of collections resulted in confusion about the identity of documented artifacts and specimens actually present when the Read collection was inventoried in 1984–85. It is possible that some of these items never arrived in Burlington or ended up elsewhere, possibly in Ten Kate's collection. However, it is not very probable that Read would have omitted well-documented items from his list. An alternative explanation for the origin of Ten Kate's northern Plains collection is the contemporary shipment of a smaller collection by another army officer stationed in Dakota Territory.

By the mid-nineteenth century the Nakota or central division of the Sioux ranged over eastern North and South Dakota, southwestern Minnesota, and northwestern Iowa. They were divided into the Yankton, who lived in the southern part of this region, and the Yanktonai, who were their northern neighbors. The latter were divided into the Upper Yanktonai with three bands and Lower Yanktonai with only one band, also known as Hunkpatina, meaning 'campers at the horn or end of the camping circle.' The Nakota always regarded themselves as the elite of the Sioux Nation in more sense than one. They used to state that their dress was plain but elegant; not ragged like that of the Santee to the east, nor overly flashy like that of the Teton (Lakota) to the west (Howard 1966: 17).

All Sioux groups shared a basic culture pattern based on a common origin, language, and territory. Trade and the exchange of marriage partners between bands as well as political and military alliances strengthened cultural homogeneity. However, some cultural differences existed between bands and changed over time. The Yankton and Yanktonai, who began moving from the woodlands of central Minnesota onto the tall grass prairies of the eastern Dakotas in the late seventeenth century became buffalo hunters and were substantially influenced by the way of life and customs of the semisedentary Mandan, Hidatsa, and Arikara, with whom they maintained intermittent friendly and hostile relations. Thus they sometimes lived in earth lodges, used bullboats, and made basketry and pottery vessels. Howard (1966: 11, 17) even goes so far as to state: "In their economy, housing, dress, and ceremonials, the Middle Dakota sometimes resembled the other Missouri River Valley tribes more closely than the Eastern of Western divisions of their own people." DeMallie (2001b: 788) agrees and adds that Yankton culture showed western Sioux traits because of their close association with the Teton, while the Yanktonai were receptive to cultural influences from their northern neighbors, the Ojibwa and Cree of the Plains. As to their material culture and art, Dennis Lessard (1990b: 42-43) has stated that the Yankton and Yanktonai style is less well defined than that of the Teton. They used a broader color palette and proved receptive to influences from the Mandan, Hidatsa, and Arikara.

From the 1850s through the 1870s the Hunkpatina were headed by Chief Matononpah or Two Bears. He was present at the signing of the Fort Pierre Treaty on 8 March 1856, regulating peaceful Indian-White relations, trade, law and order, and annuities between General William S. Harney and the Sioux Indians, 3,000 members being present at that occasion. Two Bears was head chief of the Lower Yanktonai and Bone Necklace, White Bear, Mad Bear, The Buck, Running Bear, Lousy, and Little Soldier were recognized as subchiefs. In 1863 Two Bears led his people in the Battle of White Stone Hill, but they were defeated by General Sully on 3 September. Two Bears and his band settled on the east side of the Missouri River in the area where Fort Rice, North Dakota, was built in 1864, one of the forts constructed between 1863 and 1866 to protect travel on and along the strategic river. The military installation was commanded by Colonel Charles

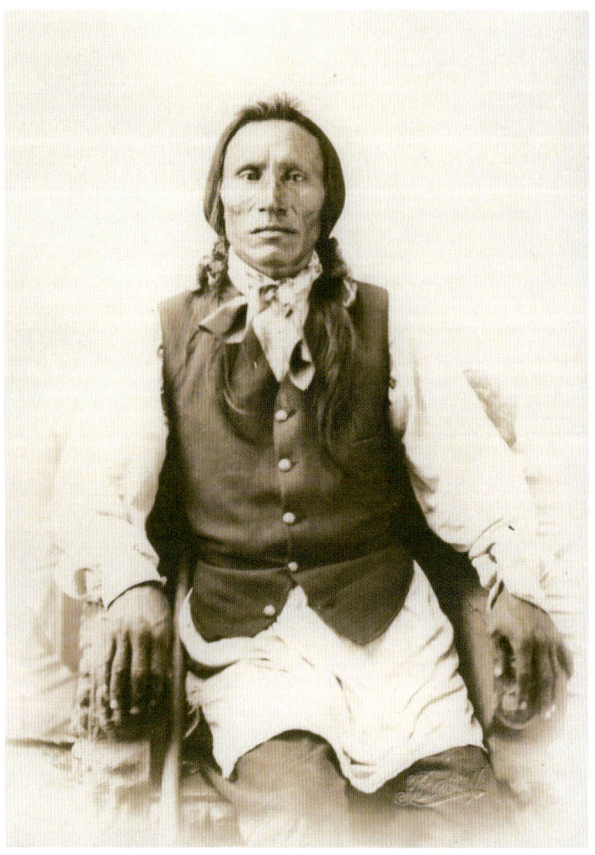

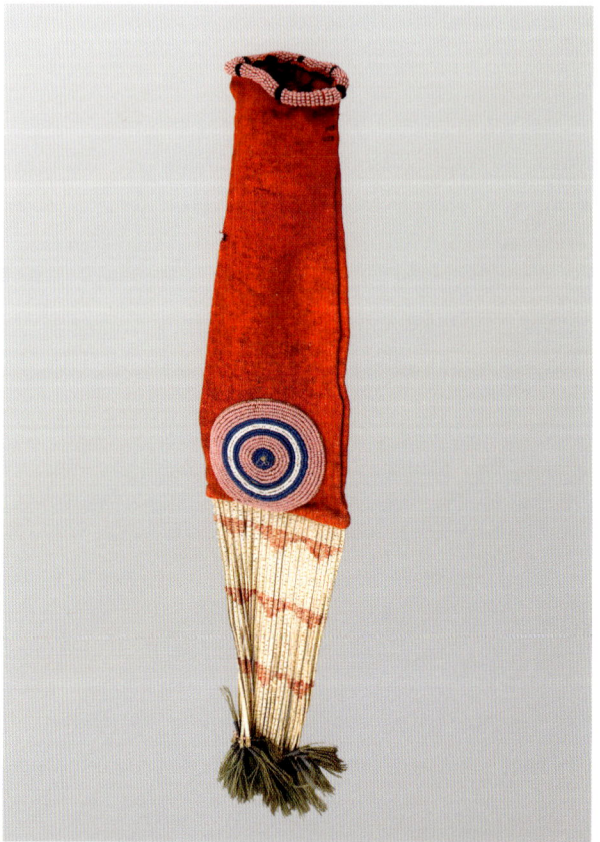

Fig. 336 Hunkpatina Yanktonai Chief Two Bears. Photograph by David F. Barry, ca. 1870 (State Historical Society of North Dakota, 022-H-0015).

Fig. 337 Yanktonai pipe bag; wool, glass, porcupine quills; l. 43.5–73 cm, w. 16.5–20.5 cm; ca. 1860–1870 (RMV 362-22).

Dimon, and the Indian headman was instrumental as a mediator between the military authorities and the chiefs of the Sioux bands wishing to give up their resistance against White colonization. The consequence was that his camp was repeatedly attacked by warriors from hostile bands. This motivated Two Bears to combine his 300 warriors with military forces of General Alfred Sully to go after Sioux enemies. With the establishment of Fort Yates, Fort Rice was discontinued in 1877 and the Two Bears band settled on the northern part of the Standing Rock Reservation, not far from the former fort. Five years earlier Two Bears had visited Washington, DC, and at that occasion was photographed (BAE neg. 3537). He died in the winter of 1878-79 (Fig. 336; Hassrick 1964: 3–31; Howard 1966: 11–19; Athearn 1967: 47, 176–180, 185; Jacobson 1980; DeMallie 1986; 2001b).

Early types of northeastern Plains tobacco bags consisted of the whole skin of small animals such as otter, mink, beaver, skunk, prairie dog, or duck, of which the legs and tails were decorated with quillwork (Ewers 1963: 46–47). This developed into the general Plains type of a

tubular soft skin bag containing tobacco, a stone pipe bowl (see Fig. 349, p. 239), a tamper, flint, and a piece of firesteel. Women also had such bags, albeit smaller in size. These tobacco or pipe bags were usually decorated with beadwork along seams and rims, beadwork panels, frequently showing different designs on the front and back, quillwork, and a variety of fringes: from a simple leather fringe to quill-wrapped fringes, partially strung with beads, with attached tin jinglers or added horsehair tufts. Since about 1850 pipe bags made from blue and red trade cloth called "stroud" became increasingly common among the Yankton and Yanktonai, while other Sioux groups continued to make such bags from buffalo hide, deerskin, and later from cowhide. The name for the woolen cloth is derived from the English city of Stroud, a production center for woolen textiles (cf. Wissler 1904: 238–239, 250; Lyford 1940: 26–27; Brasser 1976: 94–95, 115, 141, 152, 168; 1998: 64–66; Coe 1976: 187; 2003: 192–195; Maurer 1977: 148, 160, 163, 170–171, 184; Thompson 1977: 162, 178, 181–183; Hail 1980: 13, 188–195; Conn 1982: 83, 102, 112, 145; Feder 1982: 76–77; Walton et al. 1985:

239-240, 244-248; Hassrick and Markoe 1986: 143-147, 149; Maurer et al. 1992: 147, 238-239, 266; Penney 1992: 162-163, 182-185, 190, 192, 201; Brokenleg and Hoover 1993: 49; Hanson 1994: 120-123; Greene 2001: 1047; DeMallie 2001b: 787).

The bottom panel of this Yanktonai pipe bag in the Ten Kate collection (Fig. 337) consists of quill-wrapped rawhide slats and is exceptionally long. The middle panel is decorated with a sewn-on beaded disc.

A fringed and beaded men's shirt collected by Ten Kate (Fig. 338) is of the classic poncho type, the body and arm parts left open at the sides, which was worn by Indian men on the northern and central Plains. Essentially the shape of the animal skin determined the pattern for the shirt. It was made from two full hides, sewn together at the sides, and hence is referred to as binary in construction. The skin of the hind legs forms appendages hanging down. Similar shirts with pictographs of warriors or battle scenes and attached scalps were worn during raids by warriors of the soldier societies, while *Wicasa Yatapika* ('Shirt Wearers'), head chiefs, were clad in painted shirts, often with tufts of human hair representing the people they were responsible for. These are referred to as war shirts or scalp shirts (Schneider 1967: 5, 8-9, 15; cf. Wissler 1904: 260-261; 1910: 120-122; 1915b: 48-57, 85-90; 1916: 102-104; Orchard 1929: pl. 13; Woodruff 1934: 634; Lyford 1940: 19-22; Conn 1974: 59, 64-69; 1979: 145; 1982: 50, 111, 142, 148; Feder 1964: 23, 40-45; 1982: 87, 103; Brasser 1976: 20, 83, 119; 1998: 33-35; 2000: 130-131; Coe 1976: 171-172; Maurer 1977: 144, 147, 172, 178; Thompson 1977: 152, 155-158, 166, 175-176; Hail 1980: 10, 68-77; Walton et al. 1985: 113-127; Hassrick and Markoe 1986: 80-81, 88-89, 94; Hail and Schwarz 1987: 33, 74; F. D. Lessard 1990a; Maurer et al. 1992: 186-187, 236; Penney 1992: 146-151, 156-157, 186-187, 204-205; Brokenleg and Hoover 1993: 50; Horse Capture 2001: passim; Breen 2002: 1-3, 65-69, 240, 255; McLaughlin 2003: 160-170; Dempsey 2007: 39-40).

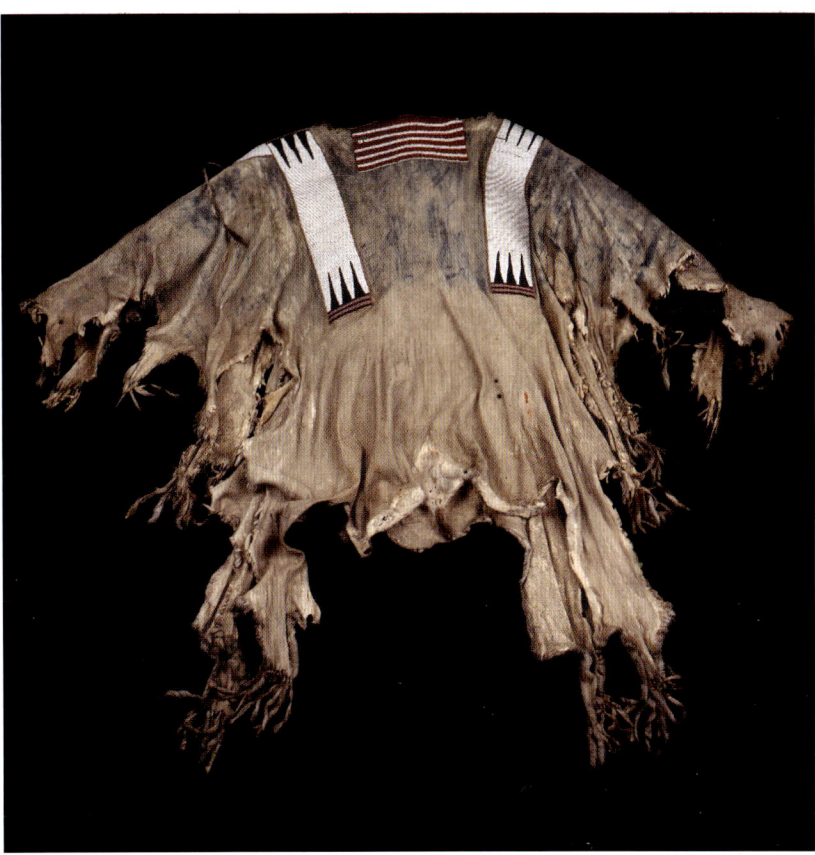

Fig. 338 Yanktonai man's shirt; antelope hide, sinew, glass, pigment; l. 52 cm, w. 97 cm; ca. 1860-1870 (RMV 710-1).

The upper front panel is painted in blue in the traditional streaked manner, the color associated with the sky. Although the lower part is unpainted, the yellowish color is associated with the earth. Such painting used to be a prerogative of the *Wicasas* ('Shirt Wearers'), a select group of tribal leaders organized in a separate society appointed to oversee the execution of policies determined by the council (Hassrick 1964: 26-9; F. D. Lessard 1990a: 27). The painting lost its political significance in the late nineteenth century. Further decoration is provided by two broad beaded strips along the upper sides of the sleeve and shoulders, two strips vertically over the upper breast, and a short strip across the throat. The "three finger" design, executed in black beads on a white background, is common in the region. The overlay or spot-stitch beadwork is typical for the Yanktonai, although they also used lazy stitch to some extent. Quilled and beaded strips were often applied to cover up the seams of the garment. Tabs and facings in various shapes at the front and back of the collar are typical of Plains shirts. The appendage beaded in red and white stripes of this shirt is said to represent the sun (Wissler 1904: 260; Taylor 1962; cf. Brasser 1998: 35).

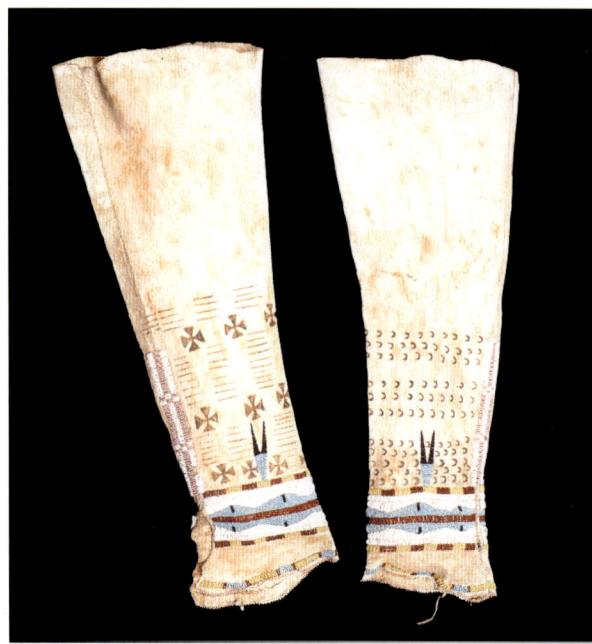

Fig. 339 Yankton or Yanktonai women's leggings; hide, pigment; l. 54 cm; ca. 1840-1870 (RMV 710-2).

Women's leggings extended upwards from the moccasins to just short of the knee and were secured with a hide thong. Usually only the lower third is decorated, as the dress covers the upper part of the leggings. A vertical strip of beadwork often covers up the seams. Schneider

Fig. 340 Northern Plains feather headdress; hide, cotton, feathers, horsehair; h. 47 cm, d. 34 cm; ca. 1860-1870 (RMV 710-4).

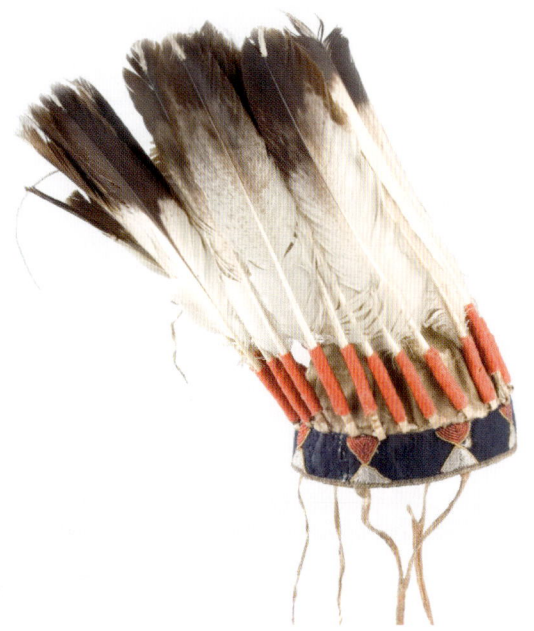

(1967: 6-7) distinguishes three types of women's leggings on the Plains: a type tapered at the ankle to fit into the moccasins; a more or less straight tubular type with a beaded panel, such as the Leiden specimen (Fig. 339), which is closed with a leather thong after putting on; and a similar type which is left open.

The imprinted dark-brown marks on this pair probably refer to the war record of the husband (stripes), captured horses or horses given away as presents (hoof marks), and participation in ceremonials (crosses). Similar markings can be seen on the leggings of Yankton warrior Wahktageli (Big Soldier) in the 1833 painting of Karl Bodmer. The inverted blue trapezium, topped with two sharp black triangles, suggests pronghorn antelope. Symbolic designs in beadwork on dress are also prevalent among the Arapaho (cf. Kroeber 1901; 1902; Lyford 1940: 25; Conn 1979: 152; Hail 1980: 96-100; Walton et al. 1985: 160-163; Hanson 1994: 74).

Plains feather headdresses came in several types (Fig. 340, cf. also Figs. 332, 333). In most cases they were associated with war honors, each black-tipped tail feather of the eagle representing a demonstration of exceptional bravery during an encounter with an enemy, and formally recognized by fellow warriors. Besides badges of honor, the eagle feathers were also often regarded as sources of supernatural power, required in raiding and warfare. The blood-red wrapping of the feathers' stems reinforces the association with warfare (Howard 1954b; Ewers 1957: 118; cf. Woodruff 1934: 634-635; Brasser 1976: 84; Coe 1976: 160, 175; Thompson 1977: 159, 175; Conn 1979: 165; 1982: 105, 146-147; Walton et al. 1985: 103-109; Hassrick and Markoe 1986: 82, 95; Penney 1992: 215-220; Brokenleg and Hoover 1993: 42, 44, 46, 61-62; Flood 1996: 62; Brasser 2000: 135, 151).

Yanktonai men caught mature golden and bald eagles from pits dug into the high bluffs overlooking the Missouri River. The holes were covered with a screen woven from willow branches, on which a stuffed rabbit skin and some red meat were fastened. The Indian trappers attracted the birds by poking the skin and meat with a stick and caught the legs of the eagle when it swooped down to catch the prey. Buckskin gloves protected their hands. It was generally a communal affair of a group of men, who prepared themselves ritually for the catch and followed prescribed rules for protecting themselves against the eagle's power (Howard 1954a; cf. Wilson 1928).

Belt pouches were primarily used by women and belts often held multiple pouches. One of these usually contained

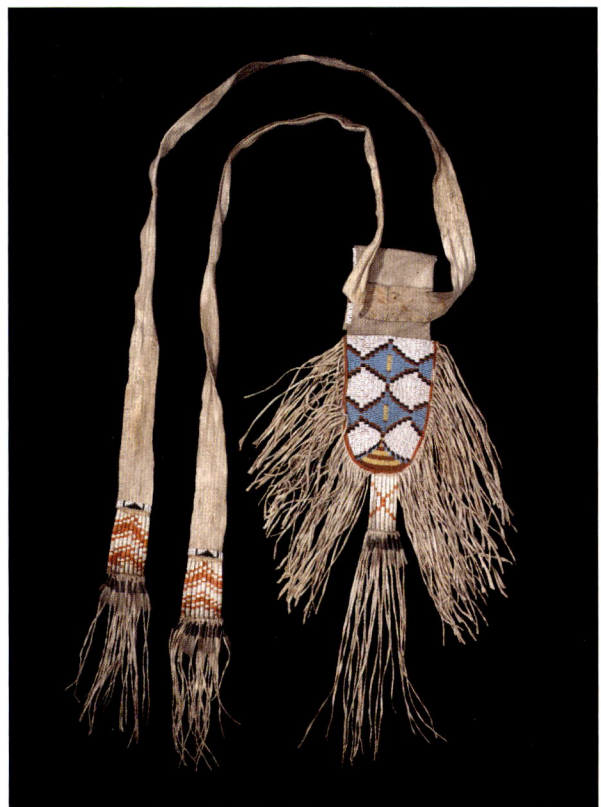

Fig. 341 Yanktonai woman's belt and strike-a-light pouch; hide, porcupine quills, glass beads, horsehair, tin cones; l. of belt 269 cm, h. of pouch 59 cm (with fringe), w. 20.5 cm; ca. 1870–1880 (RMV 710-6).

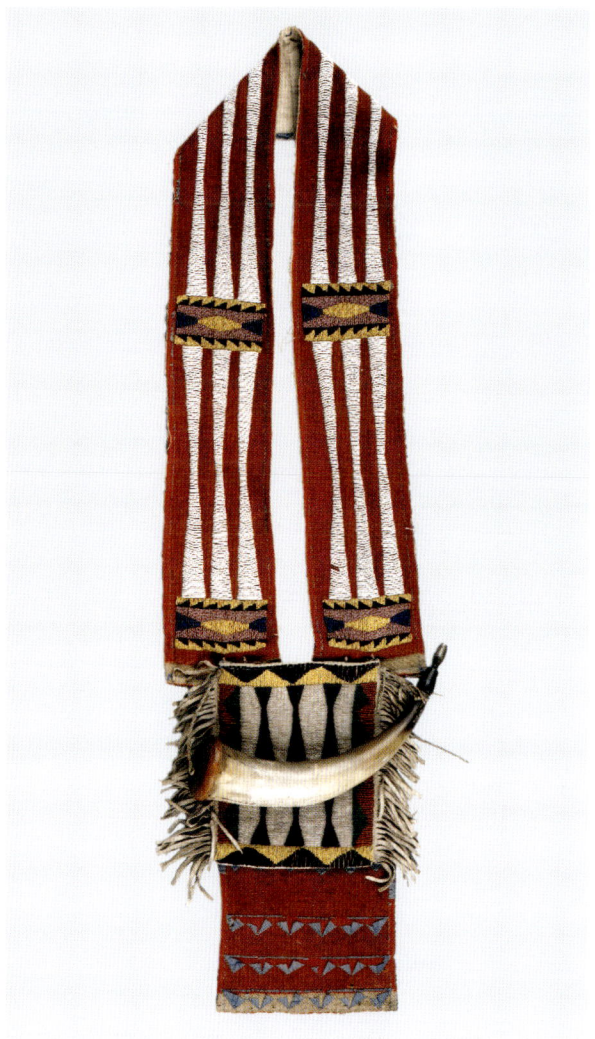

Fig. 342 Yanktonai powder bag; hide, wool, glass, cow horn, wood; bag: h. 20.5 cm, w. 18 cm; ca. 1850–1860 (RMV 710-7).

strike-a-light materials, such as flint and a piece of steel for making fire. Other pouches held sewing materials, painting sticks, ration tickets, and the like (Densmore 1948: 194–195). The fringed ends of this woman's belt (Fig. 341) are nicely quill-wrapped, as are the fringes on the bottom of the bag, resulting in a quilled panel with an X-design. In all cases tin jinglers are attached. The fineness of the fringe adds to the elegance of the belt and pouch.

The Sioux colored porcupine quills by cooking them with parts of various dye-producing plants. Buffalo berries (*Shepherdia*) and squaw berries (*Condalia spathulata*) produced red, while petals of wild sunflowers (*Ratibida columnifera*) and roots of curled dock (*Rumex crispus*) resulted in a yellow color. Black preferably came from wild grapes (*Vitis vulpina*), as hickory nuts (*Hicoria ovate*) or black walnuts (*Juglans nigra*) only produced a dark brown (Lyford 1940: 42–43; cf. Richards 1994: passim).

Bandolier bags became popular among the Indians of the Great Lakes region but soon spread to tribes further west because of their versatility. Originally they were used to carry gunpowder, shot, and equipment for guns. However, they also frequently contained personal belongings

during travel. Finally, they lent themselves as an item of personal apparel, showing off finery in cloth, bead-, and quillwork (Hassrick and Markoe 1986: 151, 155, 161).

This Yanktonai shoulder bag with powder horn for carrying bullets, wadding, and gun flints became popular among the Sioux in the 1850s (Fig. 342). In 1855 G. K. Warren collected a rather similar hunting pouch among the Brulé in Nebraska. The red and white design on the shoulder strap is encountered among the Sioux, Pawnee, Crow, Ute, and Nez Percé before the reservation period (Hanson 1996: 57–59, 81, 83; DeMallie 2001a: 721). It is also found on the Yanktonai gun case in the Ten Kate collection (see Fig. 354, p. 242). Such bags frequently occur on war records painted on buffalo robes, but their production ceased in the 1870s. The blue ribbonwork on the Leiden example is faded and partially worn off.

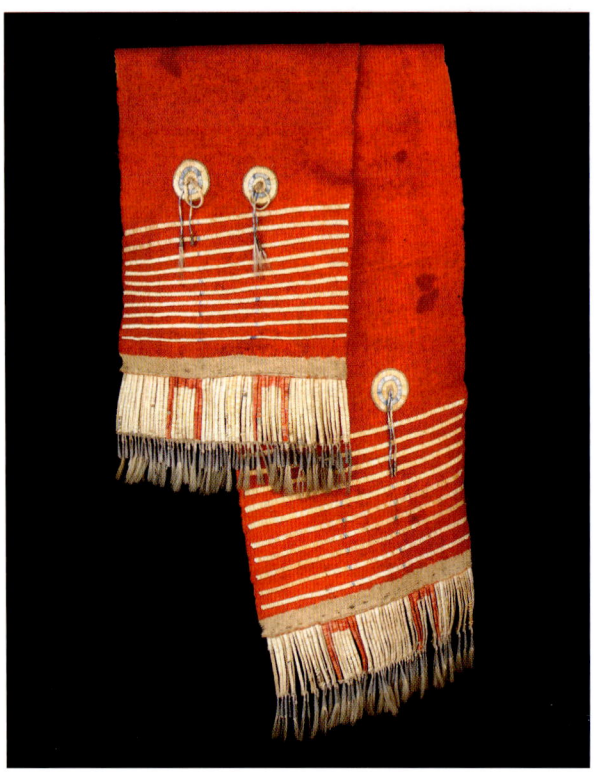

Fig. 343 Yanktonai breechcloth; wool, porcupine quills, metal, horse-hair; l. 117.5 cm, w. 28.5 cm; ca. 1870–1880 (RMV 710-9).

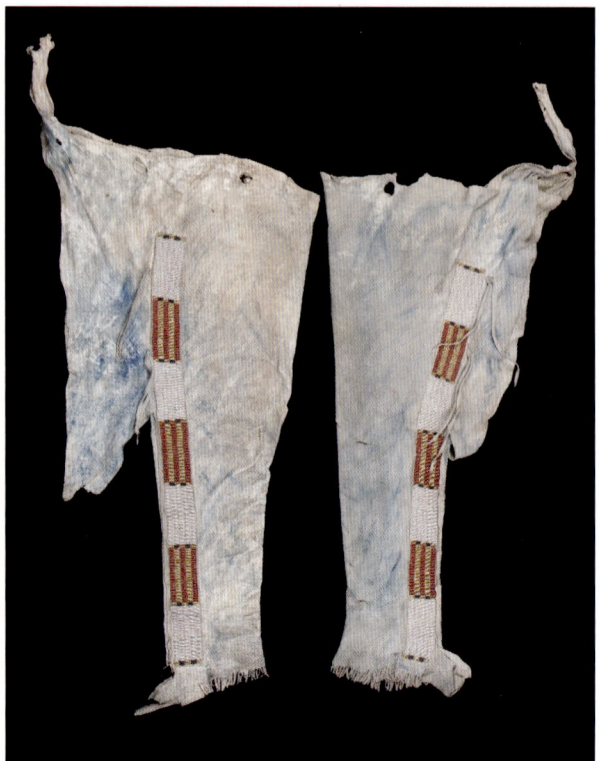

Fig. 344 Yantonai man's leggings; hide, glass; l. 84 cm, w. 40 cm; ca. 1860–1870 (RMV 710-11).

It is not known whether the breechcloth was a traditional item of dress on the Plains or was the result of contacts with Anglo-Americans. There is no conclusive evidence on this issue, but early trade journals from the northern Plains mention the absence of breechcloths for some remote groups (cf. Schneider 1967: 7–8, 17). Blackfeet elders stated that in early days young men made breechcloths from the top part of tipi covers where the smoke had mellowed and softened the skin (Walton et al. 1985: 146). In the course of the nineteenth century Indian men began wearing this item of dress made from blue or red stroud obtained in trade. The Yanktonai and Yankton wore their breechcloth "riverine style," which meant that it was looped over a hip belt with the cloth hanging a few inches over it at the back and about a foot in the front.

Although quillwork on cloth is relatively rare, quilled or beaded rosettes are typical decorations on such items of dress (Fig. 343; cf. Orchard 1916: pl. 15; Coe 1976: 174; Walton et al. 1985: 148–149). The quill-wrapped fringes show four horse track designs. The cone-shaped metal tinklers with tufts of dyed horsehair are frequently encountered on Sioux garments since the 1850s, increase in frequency in the period between 1870 and 1890, and then steadily decline (Gallagher and Powell 1953). A breechcloth

similar to the Leiden specimen, made by the wife of Two Bears, was in the Ogden B. Read collection of the Fleming Museum in Burlington, Vermont, but was discarded or exchanged (Markoe 1986: 171). The Leiden example is an exceptionally fine one and was probably only used for special occasions.

Traces of pigment suggest that the man's leggings in the Ten Kate collection were almost painted blue all over (Fig. 344). These leggings, with their vertical beaded strips along the sides, are characteristic of the northern Plains style for men. The beadwork design is a translation in beads of an ancient Sioux quillwork design observed on earlier shirts (cf. Feder 1964: 40–41, 44–45; Brasser 1976: 99; Thompson 1977: 151, 154; Hassrick and Markoe 1986: 87, 94; Penney 1992: 153, 207–208; Breen 2002: 3–5, 62–64, 241, 253–254). The small instep at the bottom is typical for the regional style. Many other Yanktonai man's leggings have beaded or quilled rosettes in the front at the bottom of the leg, a miniature reflection of the large rosettes encountered on men's shirts and those of various sizes on blanket strips. While living in Minnesota, the Yanktonai donned soft-soled moccasins, but on the Plains they changed to hard-soled footwear (Howard 1966: 14; Schneider 1967: 6; Feder 1980a, 1980b).

236

An earlier type of woman's dress was the sidefold dress, made by folding a skin horizontally a quarter from the top and then vertically in the center, the slit joined together with a leather thong. One arm was put through a slit in one side, while the dress was secured on the other side with a shoulder strap. This type went out of fashion in the early nineteenth century (Feder 1964: 21–23; 1984; Schneider 1967: 9, 12, 14; Breen 2002: 39–44). Another type was similar but had two shoulder straps, without or with cape-like detachable sleeves. The one-piece long dress, usually of binary construction, using two hides from elk, antelope, or deer was commonly worn by Plains Indian women after the introduction of the horse and guns, which made procurement of large numbers of skins from these fleet-footed animals easier. Capes and yokes with elk teeth, dentalium shells, and beadwork were added for festive occasions. In the case of this dress obtained by Ten Kate (Fig. 345) the yoke consists of a third piece of hide sewn on to the binary dress. Sioux women speak of blue yokes as "blue breast beading" if the beads used are blue or the beadwork is applied on a blue background that dominates the color of the yoke. It represents a body of water which reflects the sky. Because of the heavy beading, their weight could reach up to twenty pounds. Since the 1820s affluent women made Native-style dresses from trade cloth and by mid-century this type was prevalent (Wissler 1904: 239–240; 1915b: 65–89; Schneider 1967: 14–15, 19–23, 27–30, 32; Ewers 1980: 74–77). The tails of the deer hides are frequently retained as swinging pendants, often decorated with fringes (as in this case) and beads. The hem is decorated with domed beaded panels and a hide fringe (cf. Wissler 1910: 125–127; 1915b: 65–70, 87–88; 1916: 99–102; Farabee 1921; Woodruff 1934: 635–636; Lyford 1940: 23–24; Conn 1974: 59–65, 74–75; 1979: 149; Maurer 1977: 146, 153, 173, 180, 191; Hail 1980: 88–90, 96; Conn 1982: 52, 142–143; Feder 1982: 83; Walton et al. 1985: 154–160; Hassrick and Markoe 1986: 98, 105; Maurer et al. 1992: 223, 250; Penney 1992: 152–153, 178–179, 188–189; Brasser 1998: 36–37; Her Many Horses 2007).

Sioux women made cradles for their sisters' and brothers' infants and often more than one was presented to the parents of the new baby as an expression of love, respect, and solidarity (Hassrick 1964: 109, 312). Such soft cradle covers, made from either hide or cloth, were called *waupusta* among the Sioux (Fig. 346). Mothers carried their babies in their arms wrapped in such triangular hide or cloth hoods and covers. The upper parts or hoods were elaborately decorated with bead- and quillwork and were

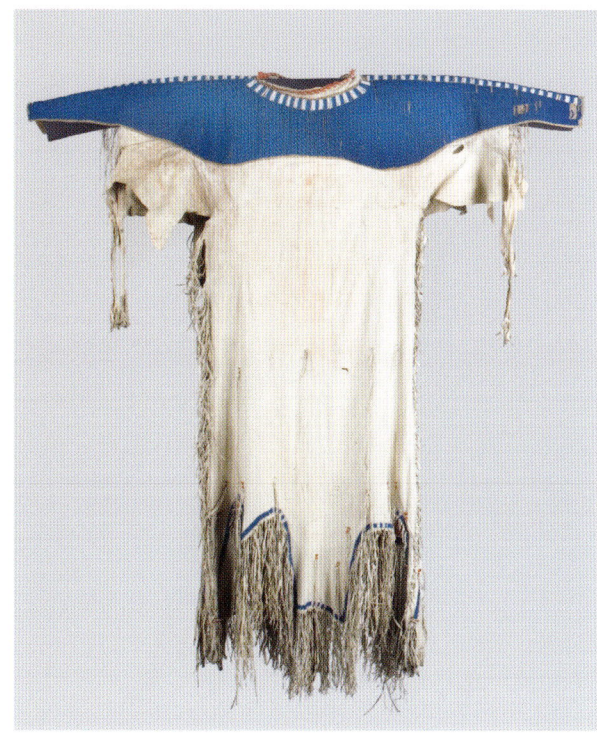

Fig. 345 Woman's dress; hide, glass; l. 135 cm, w. 40 cm; ca. 1870–1880 (RMV 710-10).

drawn around the infant's face, while the soft wrapping cushioned the baby's body. When carrying a baby on their back, the hood was fastened on a frame of wooden slats (Dorsey 1896: 275–276; Howard 1966: 15; Hail 1980: 144, 148; R. Lessard 1990; Greene 1992; Hovens and Krosenbrink 1994; cf. Feder 1978 for Pawnee cradles).

Fig. 346 Yanktonai soft cradle; wool, cotton, hide, glass, horsehair, metal; l. 95.5 cm, w. 46 cm; ca. 1860–1870 (RMV 710-14).

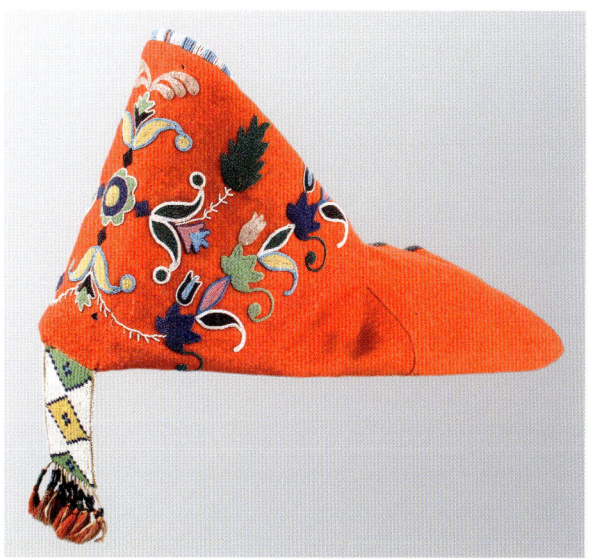

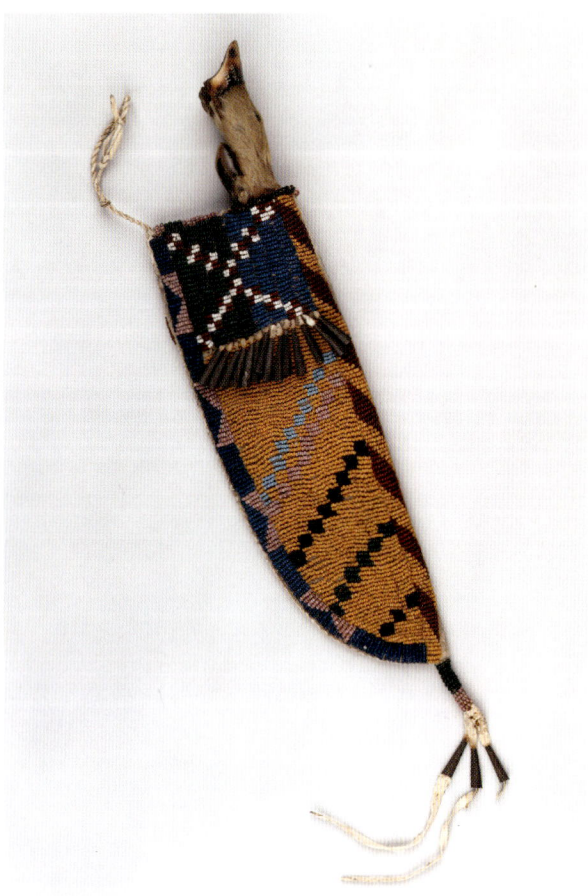

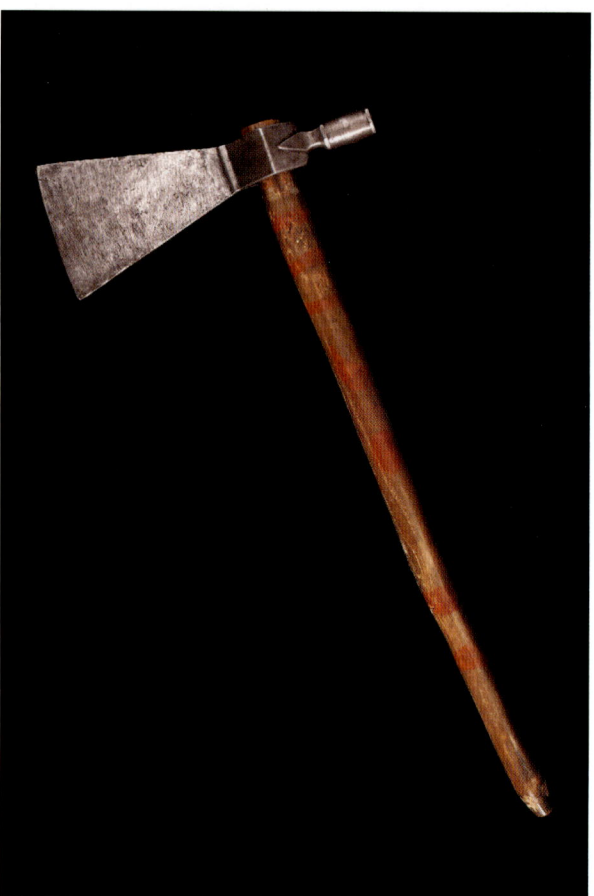

Fig. 347 Yanktonai knife sheath and single-edged hafted knife; hide, glass, metal, bone; l. 37 cm (with knife in sheath), w. 8 cm; ca. 1860-1870 (RMV 710-16).

Fig. 348 Sioux pipe tomahawk; wood, steel, pigment; l. 49 cm; ca. 1860-1870 (RMV 710-17).

This type of soft cradle could be found anywhere on the Plains. The floral beadwork patterns on the Leiden specimen are an excellent example of the style that developed among the Yanktonai and Yankton due to their assimilating many Red River Métis by intermarriage after the 1840s, the Sioux even referring to the Métis as "the flower beadwork people" (Thompson 1977: 169; Brasser 1985: 225-226; 1987: 129-130; Walton et al. 1985: 172-179; R. Lessard 1990: 44, 46; Penney 1992: 172-177). The red stroud is lined with blue cotton. Horsetail tassels in tin cones decorate the end of the beaded tab, creating a tingling sound while the baby is transported.

As soon as Europeans introduced knives, Indians put these hardy and efficient tools to good use. Men usually carried large knives for use during warfare, hunting, and butchering, while women used smaller ones such as this specimen in the Leiden collection (Fig. 347) for preparing hides and meat. The beadwork decoration on the wide cuff or cuff-like upper part of the sheath differs from that on the lower part and is inspired by earlier quill decora-

tion patterns. The back shows a typical Yanktonai floral beadwork pattern (cf. Wissler 1904: 250-251; Woodruff 1934: 639-640; Lyford 1940: 31; Feder 1964: 38, 53, 55-56; Hanson 1975: 49-54; 1994: 24-27; Maurer 1977: 146, 153, 188; Thompson 1977: 151, 185, 188-189; Walton et al. 1985: 231-233; Hassrick and Markoe 1986: 163-164, 167; Porsche 1987: 58; Penney 1992: 164-165, 202-203, 213; Brasser 1998: 59; Breen 2002: 152-164, 194-195, 267-268, 276; Coe 2003: 152).

Plains Indians used a variety of war clubs made from wood or wood and stone. Long-handled stone-headed war clubs were preferred while doing battle on horseback, and these and wooden clubs, variously decorated, were wielded for earning coups as war honors and as festive regalia (cf. Johnson 1967; Feder 1964: 36, 57-61; Conn 1979: 123; Hail 1980: 157-158, 162-163; Gilman 1982: 58, 91; Hassrick and Markoe 1986: 134-135; Brokenleg and Hoover 1993: 56, 64; Hanson 1994: 36-39; Breen 2002: 169-171, 269; Coe 2003: 144-145). Iron hatches of Western manufacture, termed tomahawks, were accepted as a combat weapon while on fighting on foot. When pipe bowls were added to the upper blade of the axe, probably by an enterprising White trader in the early eighteenth century with an insight into the Native worldview, pipe tomahawks of double functionality were the result and became referred to as "smoak tomahawks" by English traders (Fig. 348). Such artifacts represented war and peace and fitted into the Plains environment in a functional as well as spiritual sense. In the 1830s Indians paid a horse for such metal trade items, to which they added the wooden stem. Some stems of pipe tomahawks were elaborately decorated with carvings, paint, quill- and beadwork, brass tacks, wire, inlay, horsehair, and beads and became attributes of status for leading warriors and chiefs. Most were obtained through White traders, but Indians manufactured some of their own. Because of the profusion of pipe tomahawks over time, they increasingly became part of an Indian man's festive dress. The "tiger-stripe" pattern painted on the stem, such as in the Leiden specimen, or applied by carving or burning is characteristic of the decoration on many hafts of pipe tomahawks (West 1934, 1: 317–325, 2: 962–970; Peterson 1965: 33–43, pls. 91–101, 109–302; Hanson 1975: 38–43; Brasser 1976: 125–126; King 1977: 24–27; Thompson 1977: 164, 170; Ewers 1986: 19, 36–41, 44–45, 48–59; Hail 1980: 160–168; Gilman 1982: 63, 101; Hassrick and Markoe 1986: 131–134; Coe 2003: 147).

Among the Plains Indians smoking took place in social and ceremonial contexts, but even during social occasions certain strict procedures regarding etiquette were followed (cf. Deloria 1967: 23). Women also imbibed the fragrant weeds, using somewhat smaller pipes than their male counterparts. Many species of *Nicotinia* grew in North America, and several of these were used, often mixed with other dried herbs and bark. This Indian tobacco was often referred to in Algonquian as *kinnikinnick*.

The L-(elbow) or T-(inverted T)-shaped stone pipe bowls, either square or round, were the most prevalent basic types (Fig. 349). They could be decorated with incised and carved designs and since the early 1800s were inlaid with lead or pewter. Most pipe bowls were carved from the reddish-brown soft pipestone, quarried at a traditional site in southwestern Minnesota, since 1937 Pipestone National Monument and under Indian administration. Ewers (1986: 47) estimated that over fifty percent of Plains Indian stone pipes come from this source. Another important quarry was situated west of Lake Winnipeg and known as Roche Rouge. The red pipestone is usually referred to as "catlinite," because the artist George Catlin

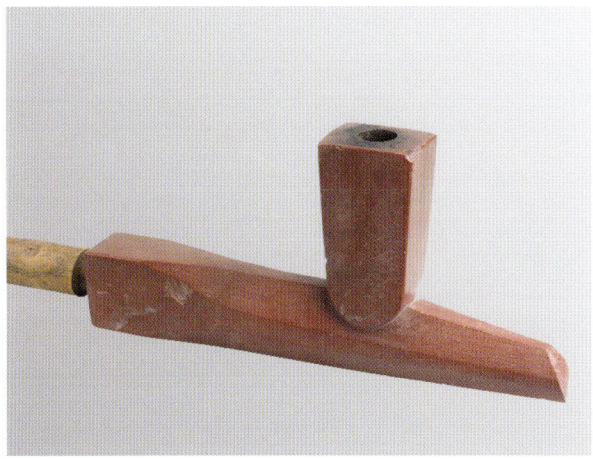

Fig. 349 Sioux pipe bowl; catlinite; l. 51 cm, h. 19 cm; ca. 1800–1850 (RMV 710-18).

first described and depicted the quarry, the pipes, and their use, based on his visit to the site in Minnesota in 1836. The soft stone allowed the carving of human and animal effigies as well as tin inlay in decorative patterns. When not in use, pipe bowls were stored in quilled and beaded pipe bags (see Fig. 337, p. 232).

The wooden pipe stems, frequently decorated with paint, feathers, quill- and beadwork, carvings, horsehair, and brass tacks, were mostly flat before 1850, but later were usually round. Ash was the preferred wood for stems, but hickory and oak were also used. The French called the pipes *calumet*, the French word for 'reed.'

Beyond the social context, pipes were used in the political arena as tokens of good faith and peace, while in a ceremonial context pipes played an important role in rituals to establish contact with the supernatural world, while among some tribes certain sacred pipes symbolized the cosmos and the people and were kept in sacred bundles that needed periodic renewal. The Sioux traded pipe bowl-sized blocks of catlinite as well as carved and finished pipe bowls with their neighbors (McGuire 1899: 571–584; West 1934: passim; Murray 1968; King 1977; Ewers 1963: 26–28; 1986: passim; cf. Woodruff 1934: 643–644; Densmore 1948: 200–201, pl. xvi; Feder 1964: 34–36, 54–67 passim; Brasser 1976: 140–142; Coe 1976: 185–186; 2003: 198–201; Thompson 1977: 149, 162–163, 171, 178–179, 186–188; Ewers 1963: 34–37; 1978; Conn 1979: 118–121; 1982: 103, 145; Hail 1980: 233–248; Gilman 1982: 18, 60, 93; Walton et al. 1985: 237–243; Hassrick and Markoe 1986: 148–50; Maurer et al. 1992: 122, 124, 135, 146, 152–153; Penney 1992: 267–272; Brokenleg and Hoover 1993: 52, 55, 63–64; Flood 1996:

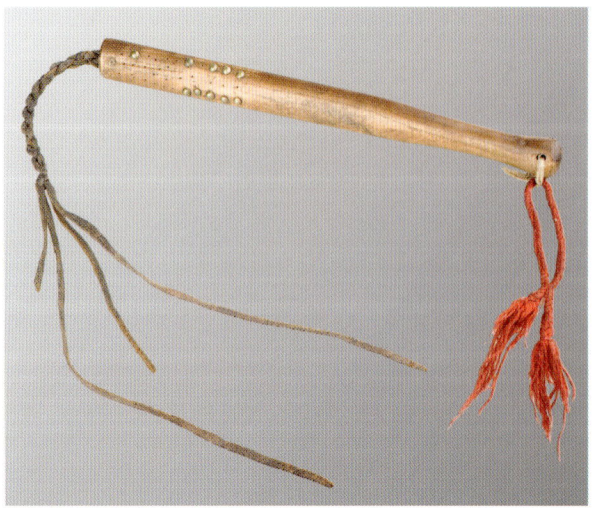

Fig. 350 Plains quirt; wood, hide, brass, wool, cotton; l. of handle 45.5 cm, w. 2.4 cm; ca. 1860–1870 (RMV 710-19).

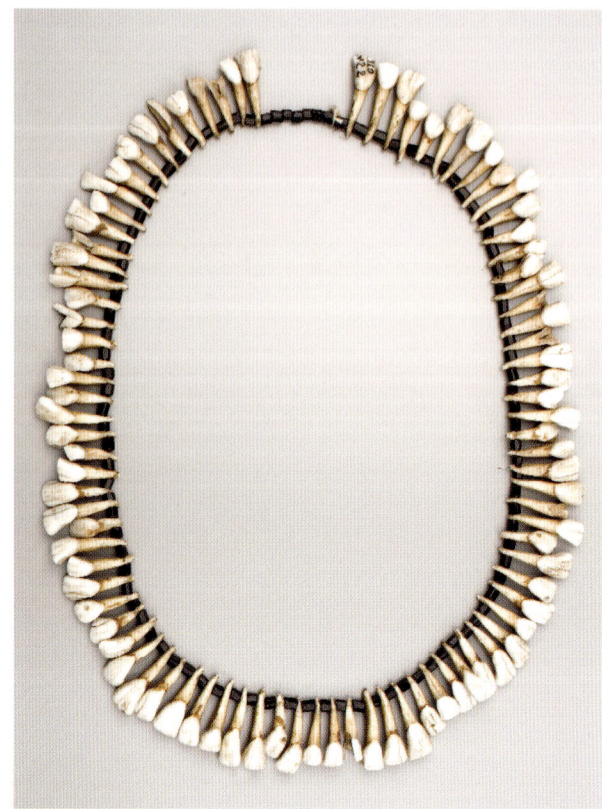

Fig. 351 Sioux elk tooth necklace; hide, tooth; l. 42 cm; ca. 1860–1870 (RMV 710-22).

78–79; Vanstone 1996: 18, 67; DeMallie 2001b: 787; Breen 2002: 178-186, 191-193, 272, 275; McLaughlin 2003: 201-249). The Leiden pipe bowl was damaged when acquired and the missing tip restored with plaster. With its rectangular shape, sleight anterior pointed projection, and tapering bowl the Leiden specimen is typical of early nineteenth-century Eastern Plains pipe bowls.

The horse spread northward and eastward across the Plains from the Spanish settlements in New Mexico and Texas and between 1750 and 1800 all Plains tribes became mounted. Equestrian nomadism enabled them to exploit the buffalo herds throughout the year. The acquisition of horses increasingly became an incentive for intertribal raiding. Much of the Spanish equine material culture accompanied the spread of the horse throughout the Southwest, Plains, and beyond.

Plains Indian horsemen used quirts and horse whips to spurn their mounts. They came in various types, from simple flat and round ones with partially braided hide lashes such as this example (Fig. 350) to complex and elaborate ones, with carved designs, painting, decorative patterns in brass tacks, beaded wrist straps, and feather and beaded pendants. Handles were made from wood or antler. Within tribes the different types were distinguished by different terms. A specific type of quirt is made from twisted horsehair, woven in a style called *soumak*, a much sought after article in intertribal trade, imported from South America or obtained from the few Southwestern Native craftspeople who might have learned this difficult technique (Dorsey 1896: 280; Wissler 1915a: 27-29; cf. Densmore 1948: 204; Brasser 1976: 78; Maurer 1977: 140,

179; Thompson 1977: 164; Coe 1976: 169; Hassrick and Markoe 1986: 139-140; Conn 1979: 117; 1992: 44, 141; Maurer et al. 1992: 112; Penney 1992: 264-266; Hanson 1994: 39; Pohrt 1978).

Through a hole in the end of the handle was looped a braided woolen strap, with a piece of cotton. Besides for spurning horses, quirts were used to count coup on enemies, and to punish transgressors (Pohrt 1978; Hanson 1996: 38).

A collar of thirteen bear claws, separated by broadbean-shaped beads, was originally part of the Ten Kate collection (RMV 710-21), but was stolen during an exhibition in 1963. Bear claw necklaces were especially worn by chiefs and shamans, indicating their status and power. However, hunters who had slain a grizzly or black bear were also allowed to display such ornaments as proof of their bravery. Often the wearing of bear claws indicated the existence of a spiritual bond between wearer and the animal. Hunters and warriors also wore necklaces of eagle claws, hoping to acquire the much valued properties of this bird of prey. Sometimes the claws were set in fur collars, and the Pawnees preferred an otter skin for this purpose (cf. Thompson 1977: 161; Conn 1979: 169; Hail

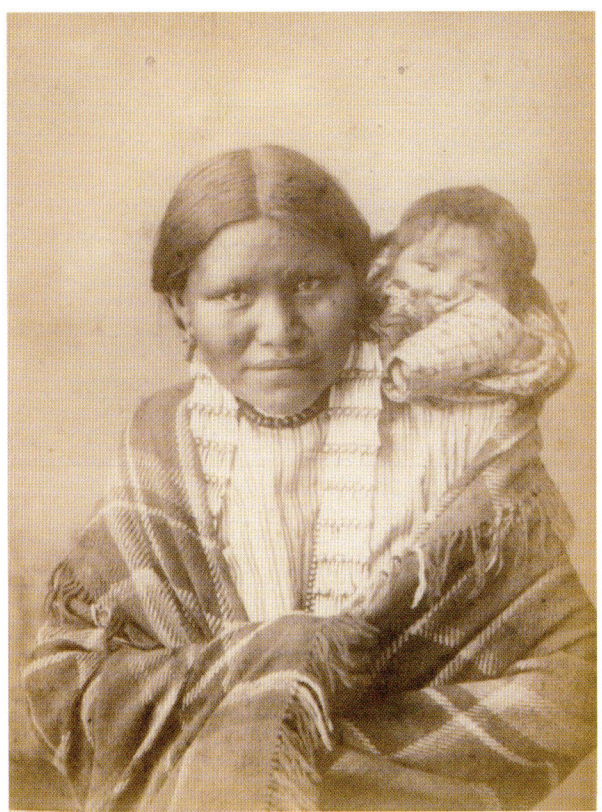

Fig. 352 Wife of Hunkpatina Yanktonai Chief Two Bears, wearing dentalium shell jewelry. Photograph by George W. Scott, ca. 1870 (State Historical Society of North Dakota, 0160-11).

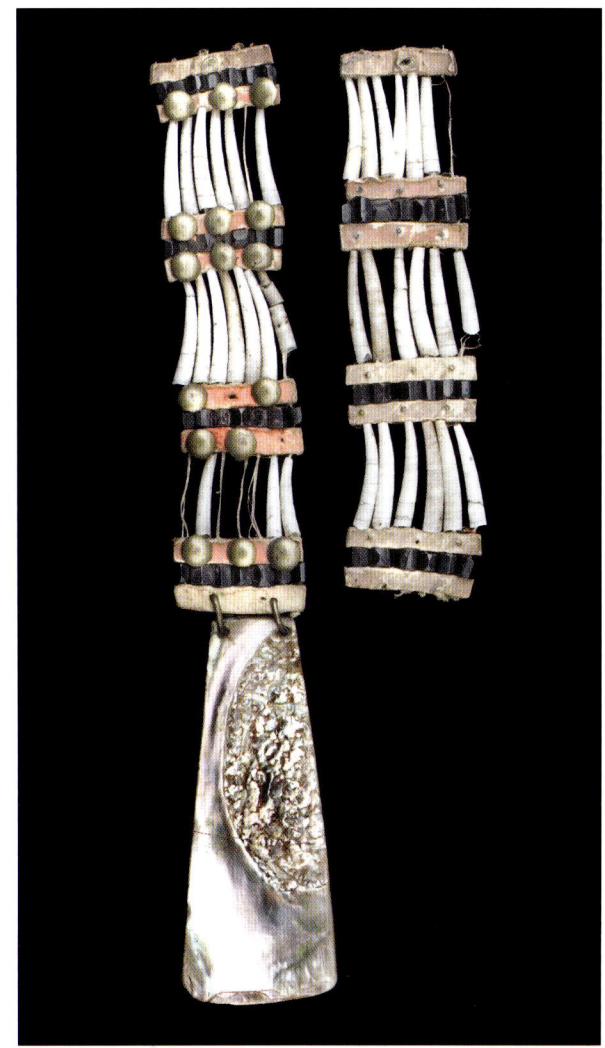

Fig. 353 Yanktonai ear ornaments; hide, abalone, dentalium shell, glass, brass; l. (with pendant) 26 cm, w. 4.5 cm; ca. 1860–1870 (RMV 710-23).

1980: 133; Penney 1992: 110–113; Hanson 1994: 106; McLaughlin 2003: 260–262). Howard (1966: pl. 66) illustrates a Stanley J. Morrow photograph of Mato-Wakan or Medicine Bear, a Yanktonai chief, wearing a similar bear claw necklace.

Elk tooth necklaces (Fig. 351) were typical attire of men, showing their hunting skills and attractiveness as marriage partners. When elk became depleted as the result of overhunting by Indians and White settlers, bovine teeth came in use as a substitute (cf. Hail 1980: 132).

Ear ornaments consisting of vertical panels of dentalium shells, interspaced with strips of hide or beads, and with abalone (*Haliotis cracherodii*) pendants, were worn by men and women. Of similar construction and materials were chokers, also worn by both sexes. The abalone and dentalium were obtained in trade from the Pacific coast (cf. Hail 1980: 134; Hassrick and Markoe 1986: 107–108; DeMallie 2001b: 790–791). The abalone pendant on one of the pair in the Leiden collection is lost (Fig. 353).

In aboriginal times the Yanktonai in central Minnesota used long bows, wooden ball-headed and gunstock war clubs, soft hide armor, and shields. When firearms were obtained in trade, they became increasingly coveted possessions. Having lost their primary function on the Plains, the wooden war clubs became part of dancing regalia (Howard 1966: 15).

The practice of making hide cases for weapons, notably lances and bows, was well established on the Plains, and when firearms came in use, it did not take long before gun cases were made. The earliest specimens seem to be associated with the introduction of the Northwest or Indian trade gun in the fur trade era on the northern Plains between 1780 and 1820. Their utilitarian value lay in preventing damage. By keeping the weapons dry, rust was prevented and powder and percussion caps remained dry, ready to use. In reservation days women carried their husband's elaborately decorated gun cases during festive occasions (cf. West and Johnson 1966; Brasser 1976: 148; Coe

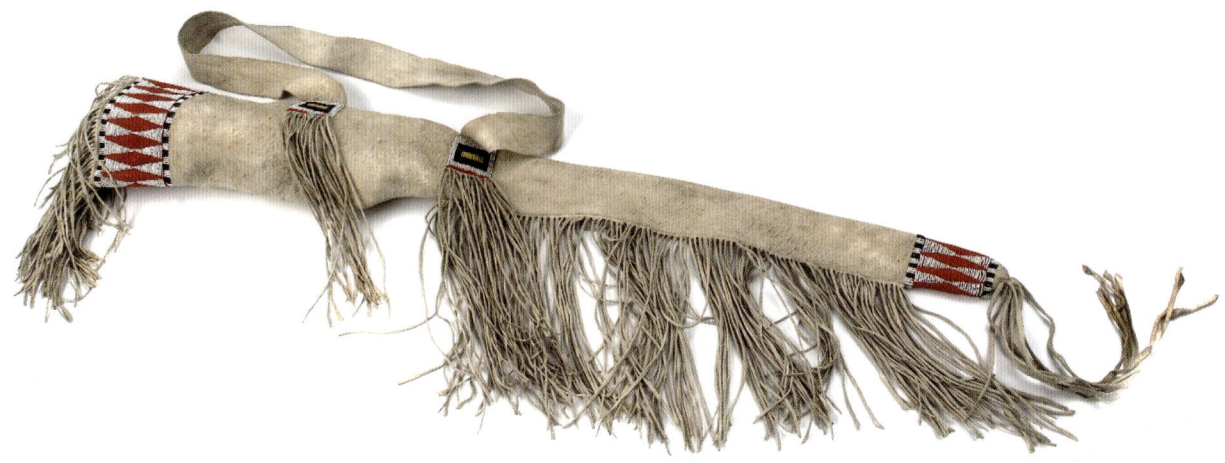

Fig. 354 Yanktonai gun case; hide, glass, cloth; l. 185 cm; ca. 1860-1870 (RMV 710-27).

1976: 185; Maurer 1977: 180; Conn 1982: 128–129, 148; Walton et al. 1985: 231–236; Hassrick and Markoe 1986: 132–133; Porsche 1987: 57; Penney 1992: 198, 211–212).

Long fringes decorate the butt, barrel, and muzzle parts of this gun case (Fig. 354), as well as the attachment points of the shoulder strap. Such a strap is only present in a minority of specimens in museum collections. The

white beadwork on the red cloth background is beautiful in its simplicity and is characteristically Sioux (cf. Fig. 342). This beaded and fringed artifact shows no signs of wear and was apparently acquired new and unused.

While living in central Minnesota, the Yanktonai used long bows for hunting deer in the extensive forests. However, when they moved onto the Plains to become buffalo

Fig. 355 Yanktonai bow case and quiver with bow and arrows; hide, glass, wood, sinew, snakeskin, iron, brass; bow: l. 93.5 cm, w. 3.2 cm; arrows: average l. 64 cm; bowcase: l. 129 cm; ca. 1870-1880 (RMV 710-28).

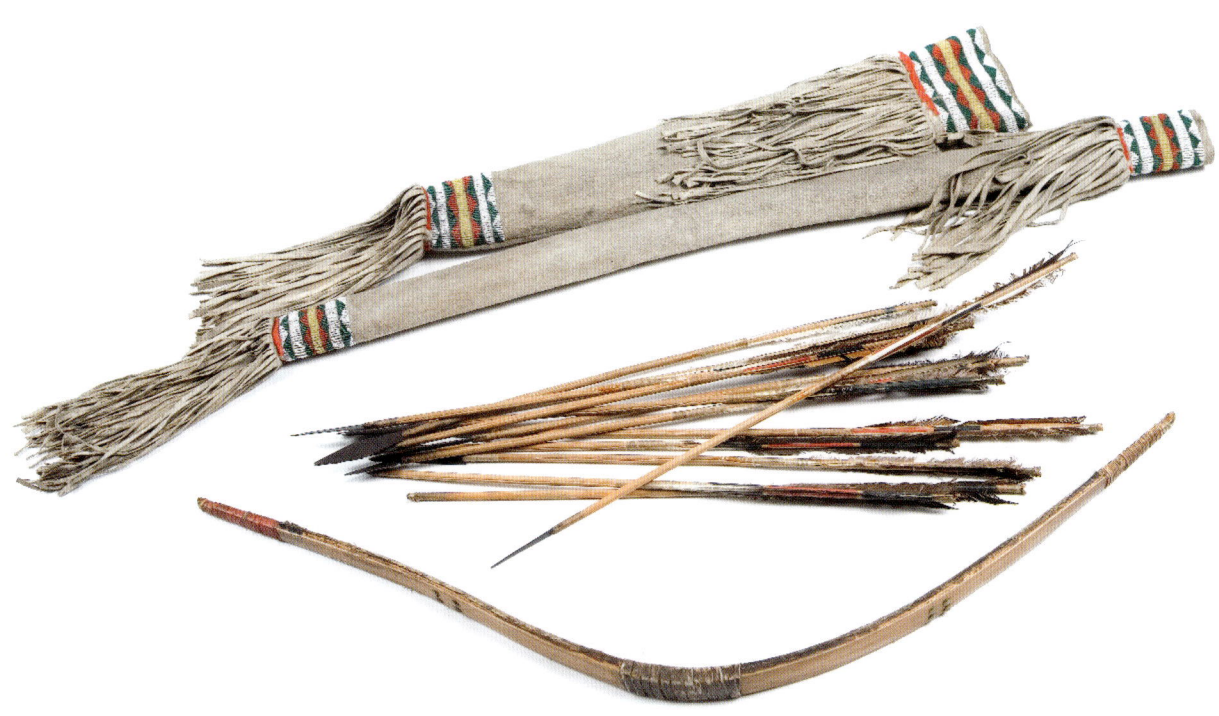

hunters, they employed the short bow that could be handled better on horseback. These bows were also used in warfare (Jacobson 1980: 13, 15).

This ensemble acquired by Ten Kate (Fig. 355) consists of separate compartments for the bow and the arrows. For bows a variety of woods were used, often ash or hickory, but also hardwood from wild fruit trees of apple, cherry, and plum. Bows were strung with sinew, but not left taut while not in use. The inside of the Leiden bow is covered with snakeskin, and two square panels of four brass tacks decorate the front. It has a hide grip and the ends are wrapped in sinew to prevent splitting. The preferred wood for making arrows was gooseberry (*Ribes* sp.), but cherry (*Prunus* sp.) and juneberry (*Amelanchier*) were also used with some frequency. Feathers from turkey buzzards and wild turkeys provided material for fletching, bound with sinew, and secured with glue made from buffalo hoofs. In this case each arrow has three feather fletches, while the shaft between the feathers is partially painted red and black, colors associated with war. Originally arrows had points made from flint, slate, or bone, also fastened to the shaft with sinew and glue. As soon as iron became available, metal arrowheads replaced the traditional ones. Although some were made commercially in American factories and by blacksmiths at trading posts and military forts, many were made by the Indians themselves. They used metal axes to cut roughly shaped arrowheads that were subsequently more finely shaped and sharpened by filing, such as in the case of the seventeen arrows in this set (Hassrick 1964: 228-230; Hanson 1975: 26-31; McLaughlin 2003: 255).

Many Plains bow cases lack decoration or are only summarily embellished with a strip of beadwork or some paint. However, some are exquisitely beaded and painted, such as this example with alternating transverse bands of white, green, red, and yellow beads, with parallel straight and triangular patterns. Other cases have beaded decoration lengthwise, such as one in the G. K. Warren collection, exhibiting a beadwork design similar to the powder bag (Fig. 342) and gun case (Fig. 354) in the Ten Kate collection. The quiver was stiffened by sewing a stick along its length (cf. Mason 1894: pls. lxxxiii-lxxxv; Wissler 1910: 155-162; Woodruff 1934: 642; Feder 1964: 36-38, 50, 52; Coe 1976: 179; Thompson 1977: 158, 166-167, 174, 180-181; Hail 1980: 169-172; Conn 1982: 82, 128, 147-148; Hassrick and Markoe 1986: 126-127, 133; Brokenleg and Hoover 1993: 57, 64; Hanson 1994: 41-47; 1996: 80-83; Brasser 1998: 60; Breen 2002: 127-136, 263-264; McLaughlin 2003: 252-259).

References

ARMV
  1882-1883 Letterbooks. Archives, Rijksmuseum voor Volkenkunde/National Museum of Ethnology, Leiden.
Athearn, Robert G.
  1967 *Forts of the Upper Missouri*. Lincoln, NE: University of Nebraska Press.
Berlandier, Jean Louis
  1969 *The Indians of Texas in 1830*. Washington, DC: Smithsonian Institution Press.
Brasser, Ted
  1976 *Bo'jou, Neejee! Profiles of Canadian Indian Art*. Ottawa, ON: National Museum of Man.
  1985 In Search of Métis Art. In: J. Peterson and J. S. H. Brown (eds.), *The New Peoples: Being and Becoming Métis* (Winnipeg, MT: University of Manitoba Press), 221-229.
  1987 By the Power of Their Dreams: Artistic Traditions of the Northern Plains. In: Julia Harrison et al. (eds.), *The Spirit Sings: Artistic Traditions of Canada's First Peoples* (Toronto, ON–Calgary, AL: McClelland and Stewart–Glenbow Museum), 93-131.
  1998 Blessed with Beauty: Quillwork and Beadwork of the Plains and Woodland Indians. In: Allen Wardwell (ed.), *Native Paths: American Indian Art from the Collection of Charles and Valerie Diker* (New York, NY: Metropolitan Museum of Art), 25-72.
  2000 Plains. In: G. T. Vincent, S. Brydon, and R. T. Coe (eds.), *Art of the North American Indians: The Thaw Collection* (Cooperstown, NY: Fenimore Art Museum), 103-186.
Breen, Lise
  2002 *The Nathan Sturges Jarvis Collection of Eastern Plains Art*. Brooklyn, NY: Brooklyn Museum of Art.
Brokenleg, Martin and Herbert T. Hoover
  1993 *Yanktonai Sioux Watercolors: Cultural Remembrances of John Saul*. Sioux Falls, SD: Augustana College, Center for Western Studies.
Coe, Ralph T.
  1976 *Sacred Circles*. Kansas City, KS: Nelson Atkins Gallery of Art.
  2003 *The Responsive Eye: Ralph T. Coe and the Collecting of American Indian Art*. New York, NY–New Haven, CT: Metropolitan Museum of Art–Yale University Press.
Conn, Richard
  1974 *Robes of White Shell and Sunrise*. Denver, CO: Denver Art Museum.
  1979 *Native American Art in the Denver Art Museum*. Denver, CO: Denver Art Museum.
  1982 *Circles of the World: Traditional Arts of the Plains Indians*. Denver, CO: Denver Art Museum.
Davis, M., J. Gallagher, and F. Schneider
  1965 German Silverwork in the Anadarko, Oklahoma, Area. *University of Oklahoma, Papers in Anthropology* 6: 22-39.
Deloria, Ella C.
  1967 Some Notes on the Yankton. *Museum News* 28(3-4): 1-30.

DeMallie, Raymond J.

1986 The Sioux in Dakota and Montana Territories: Cultural and Historical Background of the Ogden B. Read Collection. In Markoe 1986: 19–70.

2001a Sioux until 1850. In: Raymond J. DeMallie (ed.), *Plains* (Handbook of North American Indians 13. W. C. Sturtevant, gen. ed.; Washington, DC: Smithsonian Institution), 2: 718–760.

2001b Yankton and Yanktonai. In: Raymond J. DeMallie (ed.), *Plains* (Handbook of North American Indians 13. W. C. Sturtevant, gen. ed.; Washington, DC: Smithsonian Institution), 2: 777–793.

Dempsey, L. James

2007 *Blackfoot War Art: Pictographs of the Reservation Period, 1880–2000.* Norman, OK: University of Oklahoma Press.

Densmore, Frances

1948 A Collection of Specimens from the Teton Sioux. *Indian Notes and Monographs* 11(3): 163–204.

Dorsey, James Owen

1896 Omaha Dwellings, Furniture, and Implements. *Annual Report of the Bureau of American Ethnology* 13: 263–294.

Douglas, Frederic H.

1951 *War Bonnets.* Denver Art Museum Leaflets 110. Denver, CO.

Ewers, John C.

1957 *The Blackfeet: Raiders on the Northwestern Plains.* Norman, OK: University of Oklahoma Press.

1963 Blackfoot Indian Pipes and Pipemaking. *Bulletin of the Bureau of American Ethnology* 186: 29–60.

1969 Artifacts Collected by Jean Louis Berlandier Among the Indian Tribes of Texas. In Berlandier 1969: 167–189.

1976 *Indian Art in Pipestone: George Catlin's Portfolio.* London: British Museum Publications.

1978 Three Effigy Pipes by an Eastern Dakota Master Carver. *American Indian Art Magazine* 3(4): 51–55, 74.

1980 Climate, Acculturation, and Costume: A History of Women's Clothing among the Indians of the Southern Plains. *Plains Anthropologist* 25(87): 63–82.

1983 A Half Century of Change in the Study of Plains Indian Art and Material Culture. *Papers in Anthropology* 24(2): 97–112.

1986 *Plains Indian Sculpture: A Traditional Art from America's Heartland.* Washington, DC: Smithsonian Institution Press.

Farabee, W. C.

1921 Dress among the Plains Indian Women. *Museum Journal* 12(4): 239–251.

Feder, Norman

1964 *Art of the Eastern Plains Indian: The Nathan Jarvis Collection.* New York, NY: Brooklyn Museum.

1978 Pawnee Cradleboards. *American Indian Art Magazine* 3(4): 40–50.

1980a Plains Pictographic Painting and Quilled Rosettes: A Clue to Tribal Identification. *American Indian Art Magazine* 5(2): 54–62.

1980b Crow Blanket Strip Rosettes. *American Indian Art Magazine* 6(1): 40–45, 88.

1982 *American Indian Art.* New York, NY: Harry N. Abrams.

1984 The Side Folded Dress. *American Indian Art Magazine* 10(1): 48–55, 75–77.

Flood, Renee S.

1996 *Children of the Earth.* Chamberlain, SD: Akta Lakota Museum.

Gallagher, O. R. and L. H. Powell

1953 Time Perspective in Plains Indian Beaded Art. *American Anthropologist* 55: 609–613.

Gilman, Carolyn

1982 *Where Two Worlds Meet: The Great Lakes Fur Trade.* St. Paul, MN: Minnesota Historical Society.

Greene, Candace

1992 Soft Cradles of the Central Plains. *Plains Anthropologist* 37: 95–113.

2001 Art until 1900. In: Raymond J. DeMallie (ed.), *Plains* (Handbook of North American Indians 13. W. C. Sturtevant, gen. ed.; Washington, DC: Smithsonian Institution), 2: 1039–1054.

Hail, Barbara

1980 *Hau Kola! The Plains Indian Collection of the Haffenreffer Museum of Anthropology.* Providence, RI: Haffenreffer Museum of Anthropology.

2003 (ed.) *Gifts of Pride and Love: Kiowa and Comanche Cradles.* Norman, OK: University of Oklahoma Press.

Hail, Barbara and Gregory C. Schwarz

1987 *Patterns of Life, Patterns of Art: The Rahr Collection of Native American Art.* Hanover, NE: University Press of New England.

Hamilton, T. M.

1982 *Native American Bows.* Columbia, MS: Missouri Archaeological Society.

Hanson, James Austin

1975 *Metal Weapons, Tools and Ornaments of the Teton Dakota Indians.* Lincoln, NE: University of Nebraska Press.

1994 *Spirit in the Art: From the Plains and Southwest Indian Cultures.* Kansas City, KS: Lowell Press.

1996 *Little Chief's Gatherings: The Smithsonian Institution's G. K. Warren 1855–1856 Plains Indian Collection.* Crawford, NE: The Fur Press.

Hassrick, Royal B.

1964 *The Sioux: Life and Customs of a Warrior Society.* Norman, OK: University of Oklahoma Press.

Hassrick, Royal B. and Glenn E. Markoe

1986 The Read Collection: Catalogue. In Markoe 1986: 79–175.

Hatt, Gudmund

1916 Moccasins and their Relation to Arctic Footwear. *Memoirs of the American Anthropological Association* 3: 149–250.

Her Many Horses, Emil

2007 (ed.) *Identity by Design: Tradition, Change, and Celebration in Native Women's Dresses.* Washington, DC: National Museum of the American Indian.

Horse Capture, George P.

1992 The Warbonnet: a Symbol of Honor. In: Evan M. Maurer et al., *The Native American Heritage: A Survey of*

North American Indian Art (Chicago, IL: Art Institute of Chicago), 60-67.

Horse Capture, Joseph D. and George P. Horse Capture
2001 *Beauty, Honor, and Tradition: The Legacy of Plains Indian Shirts.* Washington, DC–Minneapolis, MN: National Museum of the American Indian–Minneapolis Institute of Arts.

Hovens, Pieter and Lilianne Krosenbrink
1994 Managing Papooses: The Anthropology of Cradling and Swaddling in Native North America. *Yumtzilob* 5(4): 283-314.

Howard, James A.
1954a Yanktonai Dakota Eagle Trapping. *Southwestern Journal of Anthropology* 10: 69-74.
1954b Plains Indian Feathered Bonnets. *Plains Anthropologist* 2: 23-26.
1966 *The Dakota or Sioux Indians: A Study in Human Ecology.* University of South Dakota Anthropological Papers 2. Vermillion, SD.

Jacobson, Claire
1980 A History of the Yanktonai and Hunkpatina Sioux. *North Dakota History* 47(1): 4-24.

Johnson, Michael G.
1967 Stone Clubs. *Powwow Trails* 3(9-10): 12-16.

Kavanagh, Thomas W.
2001 Comanche. In: Raymond J. DeMallie (ed.), *Plains* (Handbook of North American Indians 13. W. C. Sturtevant, gen. ed.; Washington, DC: Smithsonian Institution), 2: 886-906.

King, Jonathan C. H.
1977 *Smoking Pipes of the North American Indian.* London: British Museum.

Kroeber, Alfred Louis
1901 Decorative Symbolism of the Arapaho. *American Anthropologist* 3: 308-336.
1902 The Arapaho II: Decorative Art and Symbolism. *Bulletin of the American Museum of Natural History* 1: 36-150.

Lanford, Benson L.
1993 Historic Plains Indian Jewelry. *American Indian Art Magazine* 18(4): 64-72, 99.

Laubin, Reginald and Gladys Laubin
1980 *American Indian Archery.* Norman, OK: University of Oklahoma Press.

Lessard, F. Dennis
1990a A Wicasas Shirt in the Derby Collection. In Wooley 1990b: 27-29.
1990b Defining the Central Plains Art Area. *American Indian Art Magazine* 16(1): 36-43.

Lessard, Rosemary
1990 Lakota Cradles. *American Indian Art Magazine* 16(1): 45-53, 105.

Levy, Jerrold E.
2001 Kiowa. In: Raymond J. DeMallie (ed.), *Plains* (Handbook of North American Indians 13. W. C. Sturtevant, gen. ed.; Washington, DC: Smithsonian Institution), 2: 907-925.

Lyford, Carrie A.
1940 *Quill and Beadwork of the Western Sioux.* Haskell, KS: Indian Arts and Crafts Board.

McLaughlin, Castle
2003 *Arts of Diplomacy: Lewis & Clark's Indian Collection.* Cambridge, MA: Peabody Museum of Archaeology and Ethnology.

McGuire, Joseph D.
1899 Pipes and Smoking Customs of the American Aborigines. *Annual Report of the Board of Regents of the Smithsonian Institution for 1897*: 251-646.

Markoe, Glenn E.
1986 (ed.) *Vestiges of a Proud Nation.* Burlington, VT: Robert Hull Fleming Museum.

Marriott, Alice
1955 Trade Guild of the Southern Cheyenne Women. *Oklahoma Anthropological Society Bulletin* 4: 19-27.

Mason, Otis T.
1887 Cradles of the American Aborigines. *Annual Report of the Smithsonian Institution for 1886*: 161-212.
1894 North American Bows, Arrows, and Quivers. *Annual Report of the Smithsonian Institution for 1893*: 631-679.

Maurer, Evan M.
1977 *The Native American Heritage: A Survey of North American Indian Art.* Chicago, IL: Art Institute of Chicago.

Maurer, Evan M. et al.
1992 *Visions of the People: A Pictorial History of Plains Indian Life.* Minneapolis, MN: Minneapolis Institute of Arts.

Merrill, William L., Marian K. Hanssen, Candace S. Greene, and Frederick J. Reuss
1997 *A Guide to the Kiowa Collections at the Smithsonian Institution.* Smithsonian Contributions to Anthropology 40. Washington, DC.

Moore, John H., Margot P. Liberty, and A. Terry Straus
2001 Cheyenne. In: Raymond J. DeMallie (ed.), *Plains* (Handbook of North American Indians 13. W. C. Sturtevant, gen. ed.; Washington, DC: Smithsonian Institution), 2: 863-885.

Murray, Robert A.
1968 *Pipes of the Plains.* Washington, DC: National Park Service.

Orchard, William C.
1916 *The Technique of Porcupine Quill Decoration among the North American Indians.* Contributions of the Museum of the American Indian 4(1). New York, NY.
1929 *Beads and Beadwork of the American Indians.* New Contributions from the Museum of the American Indian, Heye Foundation 11. York, NY.

Penney, David W.
1992 *Art of the American Indian Frontier: The Chandler-Pohrt Collection.* Seattle, WA–Detroit, MI: University of Washington Press–Detroit Institute of Arts.

Peterson, Harold L.
1965 *American Indian Tomahawks.* Contributions of the Museum of the American Indian 19. New York, NY.

Pohrt, Richard A.
1978 Plains Indian Riding Quirts with Elk Antler Handles. *American Indian Art Magazine* 3(4): 62-67.

Porsche, Audrey

1987   *Yuto'Keca: Transitions: The Burdick Collection.* Bismarck, ND: State Historical Center.

Richards, Lynne

1994   Folk Dyeing with Natural Materials in Oklahoma's Indian Territory. *Material Culture* 26(2): 29–47.

Schneider, Mary Jane

1967   Plains Indian Clothing: Stylistic Persistence and Change. *Bulletin of the Oklahoma Anthropological Society* 17: 1–55.

1983a   The Production of Indian-Use and Souvenir Beadwork by Contemporary Indian Women. *Plains Anthropologist* 28(101): 235–245.

1983b   Kiowa and Comanche Baby Carriers. *Plains Anthropologist* 28(102-1): 305–314.

Taylor, Colin

1962   Early Plains Indian Quill Techniques in European Museum Collections. *Plains Anthropologist* 7(15): 58–69.

Ten Kate, Herman F. C.

1885   *Reizen en Onderzoekingen in Noord Amerika.* Leiden: E. J. Brill.

2004   *Travels and Researches in Native North America, 1882–1883.* P. Hovens, L. A. Hieb, and W. J. Orr eds. Albuquerque, NM: University of New Mexico Press. [Translation of Ten Kate 1885.]

Thompson, Judy

1977   *The North American Indian Collection: A Catalogue.* Berne: Berne Historical Museum

Vanstone, James W.

1996   *Ethnographic Collections from the Assiniboine and Yanktonai Sioux in the Field Museum of Natural History.* Fieldiana, n.s. 26. Chicago, IL: Field Museum of Natural History.

Walton, Ann, John C. Ewers, and Royal B. Hassrick

1985   *After the Buffalo Were Gone: The Louis Warren Hill Sr. Collection of Indian Art.* St. Paul, MN: Northwest Area Foundation.

Webber, Alika Podolinsky

1989   *North American Indian and Eskimo Footwear.* Toronto, ON: Bata Shoe Museum.

West, George A.

1934   *Tobacco, Pipes and Smoking Customs of the American Indians.* 2 vols. Bulletin of the Public Museum of the City of Milwaukee 17. Milwaukee, WI.

West, Ian M. and Mike Johnson

1966   Northern Plains Guncases. *Powwow Trails* 2: 8–9.

Wilson, Gilbert L.

1928   Hidatsa Eagle Trapping. *Anthropological Papers of the American Museum of Natural History* 30: 99–245.

Wissler, Clark

1904   Decorative Art of the Sioux Indians. *Bulletin of the American Museum of Natural History* 18: 231–277.

1910   Material Culture of the Blackfoot Indians. *Anthropological Papers of the American Museum of Natural History* 5: 1–175.

1915a   Riding Gear of the North American Indians. *Anthropological Papers of the American Museum of Natural History* 17(1): 1–38.

1915b   Costumes of the Plains Indians. *Anthropological Papers of the American Museum of Natural History* 17: 39–91.

1916   Structural Basis to the Decoration of Costumes among the Plains Indians. *Anthropological Papers of the American Museum of Natural History* 17: 93–114.

Woodruff, K. Brent

1934   Material Culture of the Teton Sioux. *South Dakota Historical Collections* 17: 605–647.

Wooley, David

1990a   Kiowa Belt Pouches in the Derby Collection. In Wooley 1990b: 51–56.

1990b   (ed.) *Eye of the Angel: Selections from the Derby Collection.* Northampton, MA: White Star Press.

12

Indian Territory:
Civilized and Wild Tribes

In the 1830s President Andrew Jackson sanctioned a policy of forced removal of eastern Indians tribes to areas across the Mississippi, thus opening up lands for White settlers. This had a major effect on many tribes in the eastern states and whole nations were escorted by the army on a westward trek, most ending up in "Indian Territory," which was set aside for these Native peoples. Soon the borders of this territory were transgressed by the vanguard of a new wave of colonists, and the government responded by forcing the Indians to accept land cessions until Indian Territory had decreased to about the limits of the present state of Oklahoma.

In an effort to evade forced removal, some Indian tribes in the Southeast tried to accommodate to the new conditions by abolishing Native traditions and adopting a Western lifestyle. Intermarriage with Whites and Christian missionization had already played a major role in the process of cultural change. The Southeastern Indians had become farmers and adopted Western crops. A major adaptation several tribes were prepared to make was the adoption of a Western-style democratic political system of self-government, with democratically elected leaders, a constitution, law books, and an executive branch responsible for education, welfare, and public safety. Known as the "Five Civilized Tribes," the Cherokee, Chickasaw, Choctaw, Creek, and Seminole had thus hoped that they would be acknowledged as "civilized" Indians with the same rights and privileges as White settlers. Although these hopes were dashed when the removal policy was executed, these tribes held on to that strategic course as they realized that adaptation to the dominant standards of life was their only way of survival. Thus they continued along this course in Indian Territory, where Ten Kate visited them in the fall of 1883.

While doing fieldwork among the Plains Indians in Indian Territory, Ten Kate's funds ran low and he resolved to go to Dallas to arrange a transfer of money from the Netherlands to the United States. By covered wagon he went south to Henrietta, a little on edge as the mail wagon on that route had been violently robbed two weeks earlier, despite the accompaniment of a number of soldiers. However, he arrived safe and sound in the frontier town and continued his journey south by rail. Dallas was the largest city he visited in the American West, and it offered urban facilities such as comfortable hotels, good restaurants, and local branches of national banks. However, it proved to be more difficult than he had thought to have money transferred from the Netherlands. To cover his hotel costs and prevent eviction by the landlord, he even had to sell his pocket watch. After nine days the financial transaction came through, enabling him to begin the last part of his journey on 9 November 1883.

The Choctaw and Chickasaw

From Dallas Ten Kate traveled north by train to Caddo, in the region where the Choctaw had settled after their forced removal from their Mississippi homeland. The anthropologist was especially interested to learn how the Indians had fared after this forced exodus. One of the first things he noticed was the high degree of miscegenation that had taken place with Blacks and Whites, creating a mixed-blood population with few people able to claim full-blood status. Ten Kate learned that a group of Choctaws had succeeded in evading removal and remained behind in Mississippi, while a small community still existed in southern Louisiana, near New Orleans. When he passed through the United States in 1888 on one of his many subsequent journeys, he encountered several full-blood Choctaw women in that city on the Gulf coast, selling medicinal plants and spices and still showing some peculiarity of dress and hairstyle (Ten Kate 1889b).

The Choctaws he encountered in Indian Territory lived in log cabins and clapboard houses, just like their

White neighbors, and they wore Western dress. The only distinctive elements of their attire were the colorful scarves and the red-painted ostrich feathers the men stuck on their broad-rimmed felt hats. A long history of Christianization had virtually obliterated the aboriginal religious beliefs and associated ceremonies, and only among the older generation there were probably people still retaining some original metaphysical ideas and practicing some traditional customs shielded from Western eyes. Among the Chickasaw, formerly part of the Choctaw, the *peshofa*, a traditional medicine-making ceremony persisted. Ten Kate concluded that the Choctaw, even more than the Creek and Cherokee, had lost their original character.

At Old Boggy Depot, twenty miles north of Caddo, Ten Kate paid a visit to Allan Wright, a Presbyterian minister and former governor of the Choctaw Nation. Both men discussed Wright's Choctaw lexicon, which had been published in 1880. The anthropologist found in Wright a full-blood Choctaw, but one who was living a completely Western lifestyle. Wright was an avid assimilationist and advocated the transformation of American Indians into American citizens through education and Christianization. However, he was proud of his Native heritage, an attitude Ten Kate encountered in many places in Indian Territory. Wright had a White wife, and the only vestiges of his Indian background were some of the dishes served during dinner: *tafula*, the national dish of the Choctaw, consisting of corn mush or hominy, and *banáha* and *paskahawvshko*, two types of Indian bread, the latter of soft spongy dough.

The Choctaw still held their lands communally as they did in aboriginal times. Their government was modeled after Western examples but retained traditional elements. At the head stood the *chito mingo* or *miko*, the supreme chief, and three district chiefs, all of them elected officials and periodically faced with a vote of the people. The location of their council meetings was recently changed from Doaksville to Tushkahoma. Ten Kate would have liked to attend a session of the Choctaw council, but time constraints necessitated him to travel on. Before leaving Caddo, he encountered several Chickasaws who lived on a reservation west of the town. They left him with the impression that they had retained more of their traditional customs that the Choctaw.

From the Chickasaw Ten Kate obtained this fringed bag of raccoon skin (Fig. 356), which has an inner lining of cloth, as has the inner side of the carrying strap, although much of the latter has disappeared. Such hunting bags were used to carry shot, wadding, and a hunting knife. White-tailed deer (*Odocoileus virginianus*) was a favorite prey and contributed significantly to the daily diet. It was hunted intensively in the fall and winter season during the rut and communal feeding on acorns. Communal hunting guaranteed a winter's supply of meat (Hudson 1976: 274–279; Brightman and Wallace 2004: 482). However, when the Chickasaw were removed to Indian Territory, where there was much competition for wild food resources and deer less plentiful, individual hunting became prevalent.

Another artifact Ten Kate presumably acquired from the Chickasaw is a powder horn carried on a buckskin strap (Fig. 357). The wide end of the horn is capped with a wooden disk. The tip of the powder horn has been removed and replaced with a brass rifle shell to pour the powder. Originally it had a wooden peg as a stopper, but this is now lost. Images of animals (two turtles, a large fish, a horse, and two unidentified quadrupeds), a hunter with a rifle, and plants are carved into the horn's surface, as is the name "Joe Mant."

The origin of this type of powder horn has been somewhat contentious, as both Indians and White settlers made

Fig. 356 Chickasaw hunting bag; raccoon skin, cotton; bag: l. 22 cm, w. 24 cm; ca. 1870–1880 (RMV 362-24).

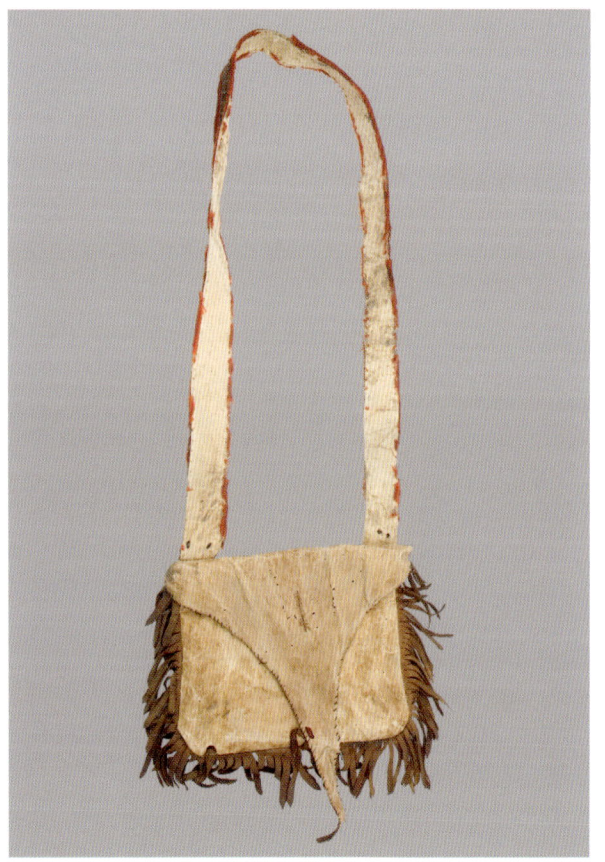

13

Mexico

In January 1883 Ten Kate traveled south from Tucson to Mexico, crossing the international border at Nogales. In Sonora he stepped from the train in Hermosillo, where he saw a number of Yaquis and Mayos who worked as laborers and servants for Mexican businesses and families. He was disappointed not to encounter a representative of the legendary Seri tribe, the Native warriors who had gained a reputation for their ferocious opposition to Spanish and Mexican domination. Sometimes these Indians came from their stronghold on Tiburon Island and brought pelican skins and pottery to town to trade. These skins were prepared in an attractive way, but Ten Kate was unable to obtain a specimen for his collection. The Dutchman continued on by train to Guaymas, a small town on the coast of the Gulf of California and in the former territory of the then already extinct Guaymas Indians. Here part of his luggage was stolen, but the anthropologist resigned to his fate when the local judge threatened to throw him in jail if he kept insisting on filing a complaint.

On 16 January Ten Kate crossed the Gulf of California on the steamboat "Mexico" and landed at La Paz near the southern tip of the peninsula. He was keen to join Lyman Belding, who was on his third stint of ornithological fieldwork in that region. They hoped to work together, each scientist assisting the other. Ten Kate was disappointed to find that the Indians who had originally populated central and southern Baja California were extinct, due to the introduction of European diseases. Only small groups of Cochimis and Cocopas had survived in the remote north. Thus the anthropologist had to limit his fieldwork to searching for the cultural remains of the original inhabitants, traversing the lower peninsula and visiting islands in the Gulf of California, exploring caves and burial sites, village sites and kitchen middens, and rock art (see chapter 14, "Archaeology"). However, he was able to make observations on the Yaqui, who inhabited the mainland but also used the resources of the islands in the Gulf of California.

The Yaqui

When exploring the island of Espiritu Santo, Ten Kate encountered traces of the Yaqui. He observed many piles of stones and brush where the Native fishermen spent the night around a fire to protect themselves against the mosquitoes. At Whale Bay the anthropologist saw stone dams which the Indians had constructed in order to trap fish and crustaceans during the high tide. He also found large shells of the massive leatherback sea turtles, a favorite prey of the Yaqui. On Carmen Island he stumbled upon a maze pattern of large stones, several meters in size, and learned that it served to play the game of "la casa de Montezuma," the Yaqui equivalent of the Pima "House of Tcuhu" and of a prehistoric Hohokam game (Ten Kate 1908).

After his exploits on Baja California and the islands in the gulf, Ten Kate returned to Guaymas on the coast of the mainland. He wished to carry on his research among the Yaqui, but had to adjust his plans when informed that the Indians living inland were hostile. Several people who had tried to go to Belém on the Rio Muerto, the chief town of the Yaqui, never came back and were presumed to have been killed. However, on the northwest side of the bay and adjoining the poorest part of Guaymas was a Yaqui settlement, for the most part consisting of squalid huts of straw, reeds, and branches. It was where the townspeople disposed of their garbage, a resource exploited by the Indians for anything of value. However, many Natives perished from diseases incurred in such surroundings. During the summer after Ten Kate's visit an epidemic resulted in many casualties. The Yaqui were a valuable source of labor and also worked as carriers of freight in the harbor and around town, as day laborers, and as servants.

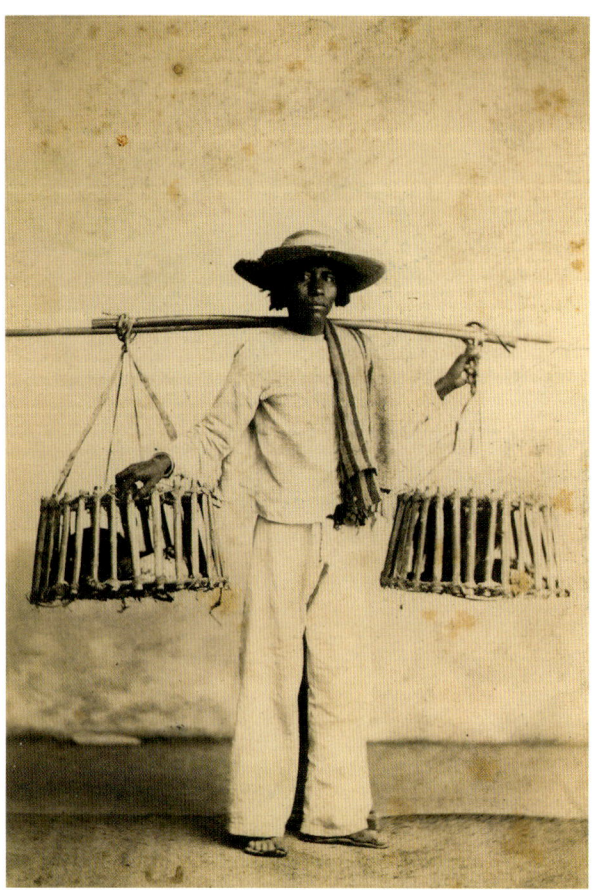

Fig. 361 Yaqui man; Guaymas, Sonora, Mexico, ca. 1882. Photograph by Alfredo Laurent (Ten Kate coll.; RMV 414Cb32b).

Most were dressed in loose, white cotton clothing, and wore large straw hats (Fig. 361).

Ten Kate visited the Yaqui settlement, where Easter festivities took place. The *pascola* was performed on a daily basis and the anthropologist recorded his observations: "The Yaquis are having a merry time … Song and dance are the order of the day, with the *pascóla* particularly popular. The *pascóla* is danced by a single man to the music of a violin and a flute. The dancer is unclad, apart from the hips which are covered by a cloth. His face is covered with a wooden mask, which is colored black and is decorated with white figures, including a cross. In his right hand the dancer holds a *sonagay*, a kind of tambourine-type drum, with which he strikes on the palm of his left hand now and then. The *taynuhboi* is wrapped around his ankles, making a gentle rattling-rustling sound as he moves his feet—not unlike the sound of a rattlesnake. The taynuhboi consists of a string of tightly interwoven, silky, silver-white chrysalises of a *Saturnia*, into which some small stones have been placed. The dancer hardly budges from his spot though he moves the extremities of the body vigorously,

and the steps he carries out automatically bring the American minstrels to mind. The melody as well is probably largely of Spanish origin, as is already evident from the violin" (Ten Kate 2004: 124-125).

Ten Kate would have liked to photograph the Yaqui, but the Indians protested, stating that they feared to die soon if they allowed the White man to capture their image. However, with the assistance of Alfredo Laurent, a photographer from Guaymas, and an amount of cash he was able to persuade several Natives to sit before the camera. They were greatly amazed when soon after their image gradually appeared on the glass plates.

The Hispanicized Indian term *pascola* is derived from the Cahitan *pahko o ola*, meaning 'old man of the fiesta' (Spicer 1940: 174), and the term refers as well to the character as to the dance he performs. Masked ritual clowns have been a part of Yaqui ceremonials for many centuries and later developed into the pascolas. They perform a variety of roles at different ceremonial occasions: as clowns, ceremonial hosts, and dancers at different occasions, including Easter festivities, and are central to Yaqui ethnic identity (e.g., Spicer 1940: 182-189; 1954: 76-77, 183-184; Barker 1957). The dance is syncretistic, combining traditional Indian and Christian elements. Ten Kate's description of a Yaqui pascola performance, although rather short, is one of the earliest anthropological accounts of this dance, which is performed annually during the season of Lent, shortly before Easter. The pascolas and their performances have drawn widespread interest as a multitude of publications testify, including several scientific studies from different perspectives (e.g., Bogan 1925; Spicer 1940: 173-203; Painter 1986; Griffith and Molina 1980). Bronislaw Malinowski, who was in Tucson in 1939 to consider a position with the University of Arizona's Anthropology Department, wrote a functionalist analysis of the Yaqui Easter Fiesta and the pascolas he saw performed at Old Pasqua Village (Troy 1998: 178-180). In the 1930s an interdisciplinary group of researchers from Texas and Harvard Universities did fieldwork among the Sonora Yaqui and gathered a contemporary collection of artifacts for the Texas Technological College in Lubbock (now: Texas Tech University) and the Peabody Museum in Boston (Holden et al. 1936: 11).

Among the objects collected by Ten Kate at the time was an unpainted tambourine-type flat drum, of a similar make as RMV 362-58 (Fig. 364), which is listed in the original inventory but lost today (RMV 362-12; wood, hide; *luhágay* [TK[; no measurements known; ca. 1880).

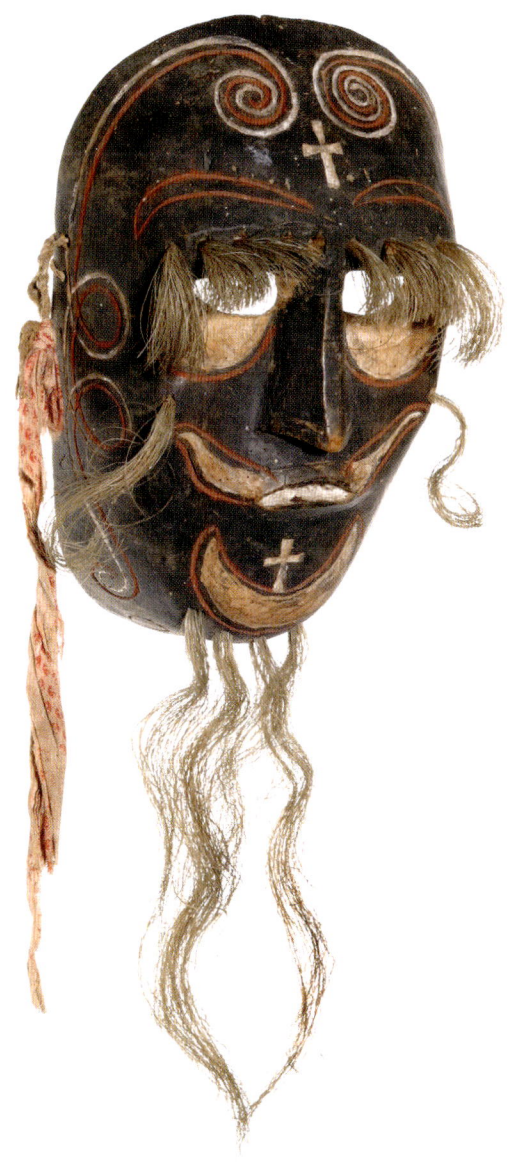

Fig. 362 Pascola mask; *pahko'la mahka* (Painter 1986: 244); wood, pigments, horsehair, cotton; h. of mask 20 cm, with beard 35 cm, w. 10–14 cm; ca. 1883 (RMV 362-56).

In his account of the pascola performance near Guaymas, Ten Kate does not mention the use of another rhythmic instrument, the *sena'asom*, a rattle consisting of a stick with metal disks like on a tambourine and often reported as used in pascola dances. Kurath (1960: 62) suggests that this instrument could have been developed from Spanish examples, but might also be aboriginal as a derivation of the Aztec stick rattle, *chicahuaztli*, used in agricultural ceremonies.

Ten Kate collected this mask (Fig. 362) in March 1883 among the Yaqui, who lived on the outskirts of the town of La Paz on the Californian Peninsula. The mask is rigged

for wear by cotton cords and calico ribbons through three holes on each side and there is little sign of use. Ten Kate probably purchased it soon after its manufacture, possibly after the dance he witnessed.

Horsehair for the beard and eyebrows are set in holes and secured by wooden pegs. The mask shows many tiny holes made by wood borers. The outside surface is covered in a matte black base paint. Carved in low relief are eyebrows, moustache, scroll patterns, a cross (the so-called splayed cross or *croix patée*), several elements of which are also painted white and red, a technique called paint-cloisonné. The mouth and eyes are carved through the surface to allow the wearer maximum comfort.

Pascola masks are usually carved from cottonwood, but sometimes other soft wood was used, such as willow, pine, and cedar (*Bursera inopinnata*). They are painted black, after which designs are applied in several colors, usually white, red, and pink. Sometimes designs are carved and painted or inlaid with abalone shell. Frequently occurring designs include crosses, circles, triangles, dots, stars, moons, and facial features such as eyelashes, moustaches, wrinkles, and tears. The cross, usually painted, carved, or carved and painted on the forehead of the human face mask and sometimes also on the chin, is most often interpreted as a protective emblem against evil, but also as a reference to the four cardinal directions and as a symbol of Christianity. The Yaqui regard this type of cross as a protective device. In addition, animal figures occur, such as insects (butterflies) and reptiles (lizards, snakes), but also goats, pigs, and monkeys. Pascola masks come in human and animal varieties. Among the latter are effigies of coyotes (dogs), goats, and monkeys. Animal hair is often used to apply a head of hair, eyebrows, and beards. *Ixtle* (maguey agave fiber) serves the same purpose. The mask is fitted with cotton string or leather thongs to strap it securely to the face of the dancer.

The pascola masks of the Cahitan-speaking Yaqui and Mayo are unique. The pascola belongs to a series of beliefs and ceremonies referred to by the Indians as the "religion of the woods," possibly a hunting ritual complex that merged with Christian beliefs and rituals. Yaqui oral tradition also associates the pascolas with the devil. Among the Yaqui an individual pascola often acted as host for many ceremonies. The Yaqui pascola's status is that of a clown, with his ambiguous position and morality, hovering between revered elder and demonic figure. The black color of the mask surface is associated with death and sorrow,

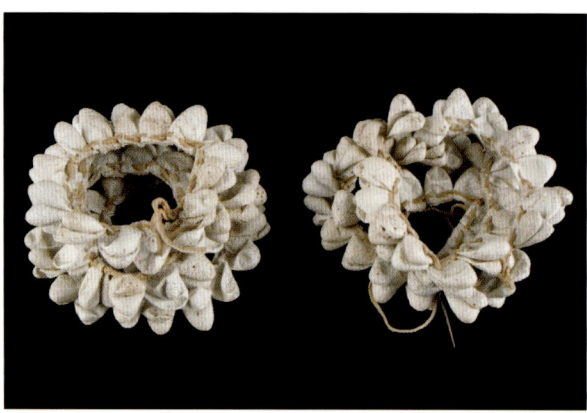

Fig. 363 Cocoon ankle rattles (set of two); *taynùhboy* (TK), *teneboim* (Spicer 1980: 110); cocoon, hide, stone; l. 125 cm; ca. 1880 (RMV 362-57).

while red refers to demons as well as mirth and joy. White is associated with purity and fertility and usually used for the cross and stylized flower designs on the surface of the mask (Spicer 1980: 102-110; 1983: 258-259, 262; Lutes 1983; Painter 1950: 17-18; 1986: 244; Griffith and Molina 1980: 22-24; Kolaz 1985; Griffith 1989).

A strong continuity in Yaqui pascola masks throughout time between the 1880s and 1980s and among the Yaqui across the Greater Southwest in Arizona and Sonora has been noted by Griffith and Molina (1980: 22;

Fig. 364 Pascola drum; *sonagay* (TK); wood, vegetal fiber; d. 38-44 cm, h. 10 cm; ca. 1880 (RMV 362-58).

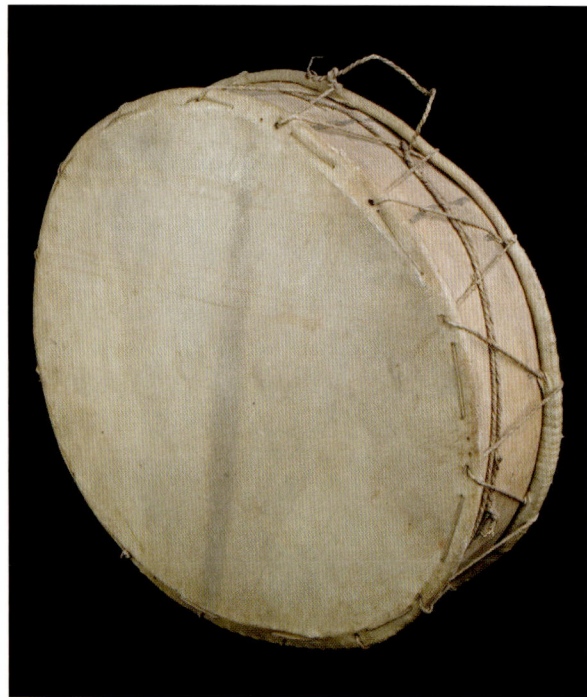

Kolaz 1985: 39). The pascola mask collected by Herman Ten Kate is probably the oldest documented and preserved mask of this type and remains in almost pristine condition. It already bears many of the primary characteristics of Yaqui pascola masks that were carved much later and further reinforces the conclusion about a strong temporal continuity (Tom Kolaz, pers. com.; cf. Fabila 1940: 219, 226).

According to Ten Kate, the cocoon ankle rattles he obtained (Fig. 363) were from the giant silk moth and were taken from the silky, silver-white chrysalises of *Saturnia*. Cut in half and cured, the two compartments were filled with small pebbles and sewn onto a buckskin thong that was wound around the ankle by dancers (cf. Densmore 1932: pl. 29; Fabila 1940: 218-219; Spicer 1940: 180; 1980: 110; 1983: 258; Kolaz 1985: 40; Painter 1986: 245-246; Choate 1997: 98).

Oval two-headed tambourine-type drums such as the one acquired by Ten Kate (Fig. 364) were played by the *tampaleo* ('drummer') using one stick. The side is made from a thin board which is bent, with the overlapping ends sewn with vegetal fiber. The lashing consists of braided vegetal fiber. The sides are perforated with two round holes on opposite sides to "let the sound out," and tuning is done by heating the drum over a fire (cf. Densmore 1932: pl. 26; Fabila 1940: 227; Spicer 1980: 108; 1983: 259; Choate 1997: 39, fig. 49, 45, fig. 62, 54, fig. 84). In relation to this drum Ten Kate noted the name of Luis Pangasi, probably the man who made it or the *tampaleo* from whom he obtained it.

This club (Fig. 365) is appropriately made from the heavy ironwood, making it an effective weapon in close combat. It is octagonal-shaped in cross section with a thinner round handle, typical for Yaqui war clubs, as the one collected in 1887 in Sonora by Edward Palmer (Spicer 1983: 252). The handle is perforated and has a loop of narrow strands of braided hide to create a wrist strap.

Fig. 365 Yaqui warclub; *garóte* (TK); ironwood; l. 45.5 cm, w. 3.5 cm; ca. 1880 (RMV 362-60).

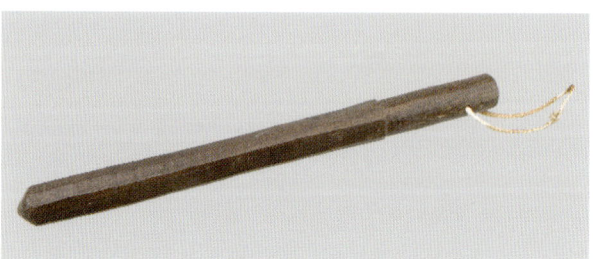

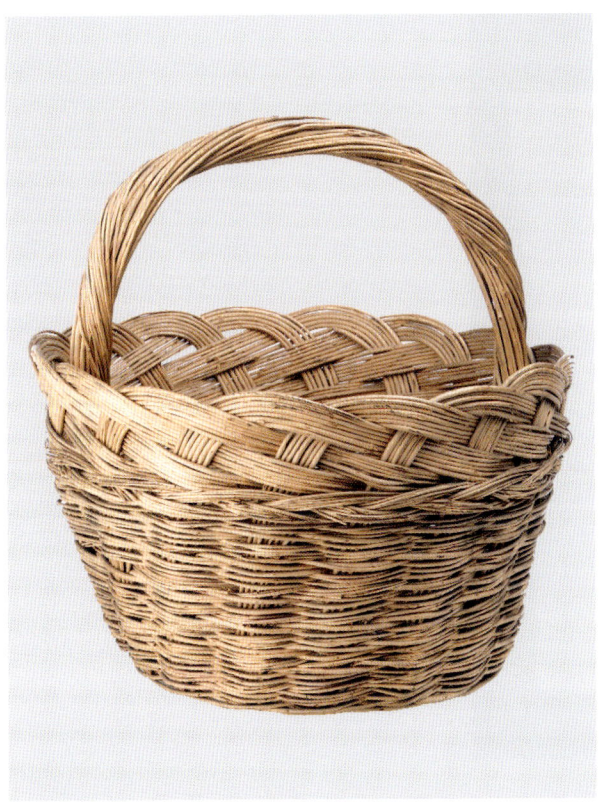

Fig. 366 Yaqui wicker basket; willow, pigment; d. 35.5 cm, h. (without handle) 22 cm; ca. 1880 (RMV 362-61).

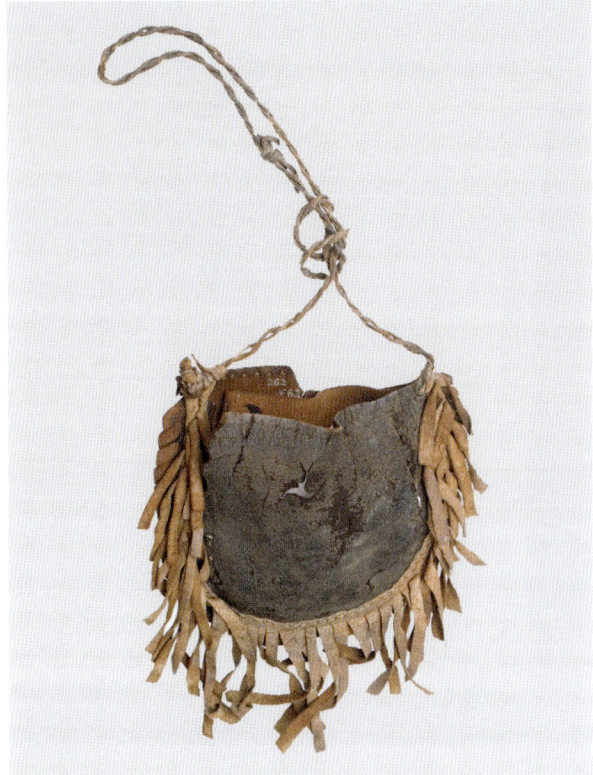

Fig. 367 Yaqui fringed pouch; hide, sinew; h. (without fringe) 13 cm (with fringe 50.5 cm); w. 13.2 cm; ca. 1880 (RMV 362-62).

Fig. 368 Pair of Yaqui women's earrings; silver; l. 5 cm, w. 2.2 cm; ca. 1880 (RMV 362-63).

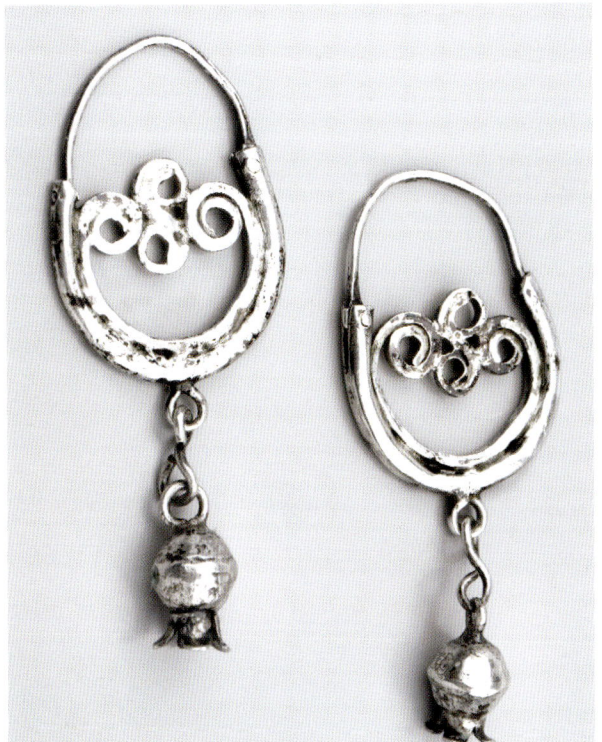

The Yaqui made lidded baskets in twilled weave from palm leaves, larger ones for secular purposes and elongated smaller ones for holding sacred objects. In addition, they engaged in trading woven mats and porch screens in Guaymas. Wicker baskets such as this example (Fig. 366) with its scalloped rim and handle are rarer (Mason 1904: 526–527, pls. 236–237). The Leiden basket shows bands of reddish purple pigment around the interior base.

According to Ten Kate, pouches such as the one he obtained for his collection (Fig. 367) were carried by Yaqui men and used for keeping tobacco or small items of personal property. The skin has been artificially blackened. The interior is divided in two by a hide partition.

The basic horseshoe-pattern of these earrings (Fig. 368) frames a four-scroll pattern of silver wire, and a squash blossom-type appendage on a chain is an added embellishment.

Central and Southern Mexico

In 1888 Ten Kate returned to Mexico, although in quite different circumstances. At that time he was a staff member of the interdisciplinary Hemenway Southwestern

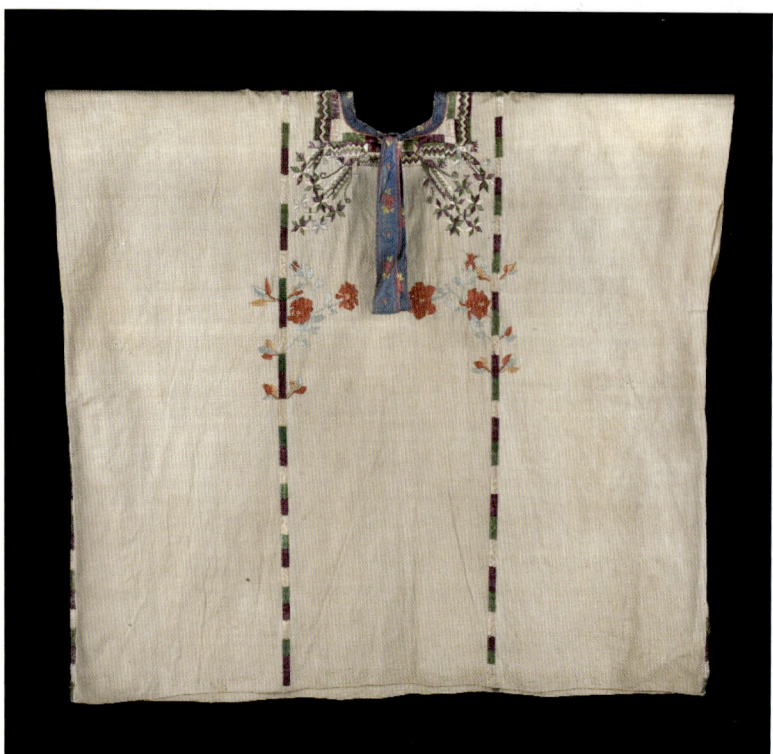

Fig. 369 Nahua woman's shirt; *Zitlatlamayo-huipilé* (TK), *huipil*; cotton, silk; l. 95 cm, w. 107 cm; ca. 1888 (RMV 682-1).

Archaeological Expedition (see chapter 14, "Archaeology"). This work sparked an interest in Mesoamerican influences on prehistoric Southwestern Indian cultures, and the anthropologist wished to do some research on this matter in the lake district of Michoacan and Jalisco, among the Tarascans and the tribes of the Sierra de Nayarit. First he studied collections in the museum in Mexico City, visited the sites of Cholula and Teotihuacan, and paid a visit to the Amateco of Amatlán village near Córdoba in the state of Veracruz. During this trip he acquired a number of dress items. The anthropologist noted that the Amateco retained much of their traditional dress, in contrast to the Native population in other regions (Ten Kate 1889a, 1889b).

Ten Kate described the village of Amatlán as one of the most interesting places he visited in Mexico. The traditional clothing traditions of the Amateco (i.e., Huastec inhabitants of Amatlán) drew his attention and he reported on the long, often beautiful white blouses with extensive decorations of embroidered flowers, which he called *huipilé*, and on the sashes and *soyates*, which he termed *itlpicátl*, which were woven of colorful cotton and palm leaves (Ten Kate 1889b).

The anthropologist collected at least three *huipiles*, through which he was able to document some of the gar-

ments that were to be found in the Amatlán area. However, on his trip he did not so much acquire the traditional Amatec garments, but, as he himself wrote in his fieldnotes, obtained garments that were imported to Amatlán from different surrounding (Mixtec, Zapotec, and Chinantec) areas. This is a very interesting phenomenon that is well known to have existed in different towns in Mexico, but which has not been documented extensively for this area in this specific period. About the town where Ten Kate aggregated his small collection of indigenous Mexican dress, Cordry and Cordry (1968: 222) write: "In a charming tropical setting (...) lies the town of Amatlán—which formerly enjoyed considerable wealth from vanilla and pineapples. In those days women made and wore beautiful *huipiles*, and also—which is most unusual—they liked to enlarge their wardrobes by buying *huipiles* from other Indian regions. They were fond of the red *huipiles* from the Chinantla (so different from their own) and of the hand-woven, figured white ones which they possibly purchased in Igualapa, Guerrero."

In general, Amatec women wore folkloric garments that were inspired by or derived from Mixtec and Zapotec dress. During their yearly visits to the Otatitlán Sanctuary, the Amateco acquired fabrics and ideas for embroideries from the Mixtec and Zapotec pilgrims who visited the town and sold their traditional garments at the fair. Otatitlán is famous for its church, home to El Cristo Negro, one of three black Christ images that exist in Mexico. The traditional Amatec suit consists of a white *enagua* or wraparound skirt that reaches the ankles and a loose *huipil* of rectangular cut and laterally embroidered with diverse flowers in multicolored thread. Five or six necklaces of shining beads were usually added. The hair was done in two braids, adorned with silk ribbons that matched the colors of the embroideries of the garments.

It is important to note that this small Ten Kate collection of Mexican dress from the 1880s is of specific interest and is of a unique quality because of its very early date. Relatively few indigenous textiles from before the 1950s have been preserved in museums. Archaeologically hardly any material survived, and from colonial times very little remained. Some sixteenth- and seventeenth-century garments were conserved and are curated at the National Museum of Anthropology in Mexico City (cf. Avila 1996, 1997). The Ten Kate collection of early Mexican textiles is the earliest material of its kind in the Netherlands, and worldwide very few textile examples have been collected and preserved from the late nineteenth and early twentieth centuries. This was partly due to the disdain with which traditional indigenous costume was looked upon by collectors. In addition to Ten Kate's specimens, the Leiden museum curates an exceptionally well documented collection of mid- to late-twentieth-century Mexican and Guatemalan textiles collected by Irmgard Johnson Weitlaner, Bodil Christensen, and Prof. Dozy (e.g., Johnson Weitlaner 1976; cf. also Van Broekhoven 2005).

The *huipil* forms part of the traditional indigenous female costume of Mesoamerica. *Huipiles* are and were used in different parts of Mexico, Belize, Guatemala, and El Salvador. It is a kind of sleeveless blouse or tunic for which no good English equivalent exists. In general, the *huipil* is made out of a rectangular piece of cloth woven in three parts. The three parts are sewn together with an opening for the head in the middle. The cloth is woven on a backstrap loom. Generally cotton, wool, or silk is used, nowadays sometimes replaced by commercially woven cloth, but in the late 1800s when Ten Kate was collecting, the cloth was hand-woven.

The word *huipil* comes from the Nahuatl word *huipilli*. In Mixtec the word for *huipil* is *shiku lestu*, which in sixteenth-century Mixtec is *dzico*, a word that also means 'virtuous' or 'proper,' which implies the wearing of a *huipil* was seen as the proper attire for a woman (Jansen, pers. com. in Van Broekhoven 2005). Different types of *huipiles* exist for different occasions such as marriage, festivals, daily use, and burial. Both children and adults wear *huipiles*. Certain symbols that are embroidered on the blouses remain reserved for single or married women or for girls who have passed the age of fifteen.

One of the *huipiles* purchased by Ten Kate in Amatlán village, Veracruz, is woven from coarse linen (Fig. 369). It is embroidered with flowers and other figures in different

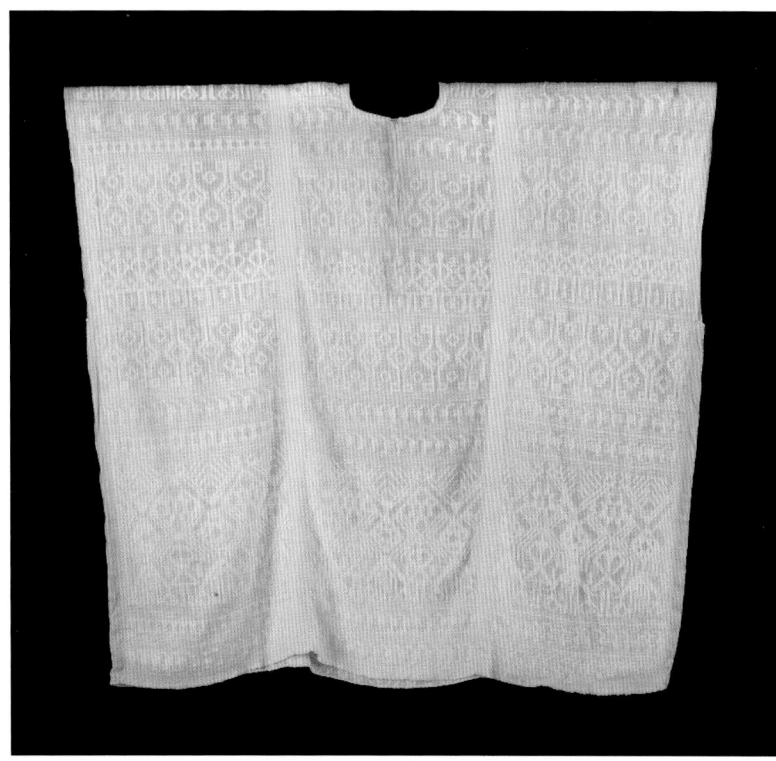

Fig. 370   Zapotec woman's shirt; *Lamisteco-huipilé* (TK), *huipil*; cotton, silk; Choapan, Oaxaca; l. 99 cm, w. 108 cm; ca. 1888 (RMV 682-2).

kinds of colored silk thread; the collar is finished with an embroidered blue edge of red and blue flowers. The remarks on Ten Kate's inventory card read: "huipilé from Zitlatlamayo," adding "jacket for women interlaced with coloured silk." Although Ten Kate bought the piece from the Amateco in Amatlán, according to his own description it is a Nahua *huipil*.

A second *huipil*, likewise purchased in Amatlán village, Veracruz, is made from fine hand-woven cotton and silk and consists of three parts (Fig. 370). The whole blouse is decorated with gauze-weave anthropomorphic and geometric designs. Although Ten Kate bought this specimen among the Amateco, it was probably imported from Choapan, Oaxaca, either by merchants from Amatlán that went to buy them in Oaxaca or had bought them somewhere en route from merchants from the Zapotec area who came to sell them in Amatlán. The *huipiles* from Choapan are known for their high quality and exceptional texture. They are considered among the highest quality in the whole of Mexico, and it is exceptional to find such an early example. Ten Kate recorded the indigenous term *Lamisteco-huipilé*. This seems to imply that it was sold to him by a Mixtec vendor or by someone who bought it in the Mixteca.

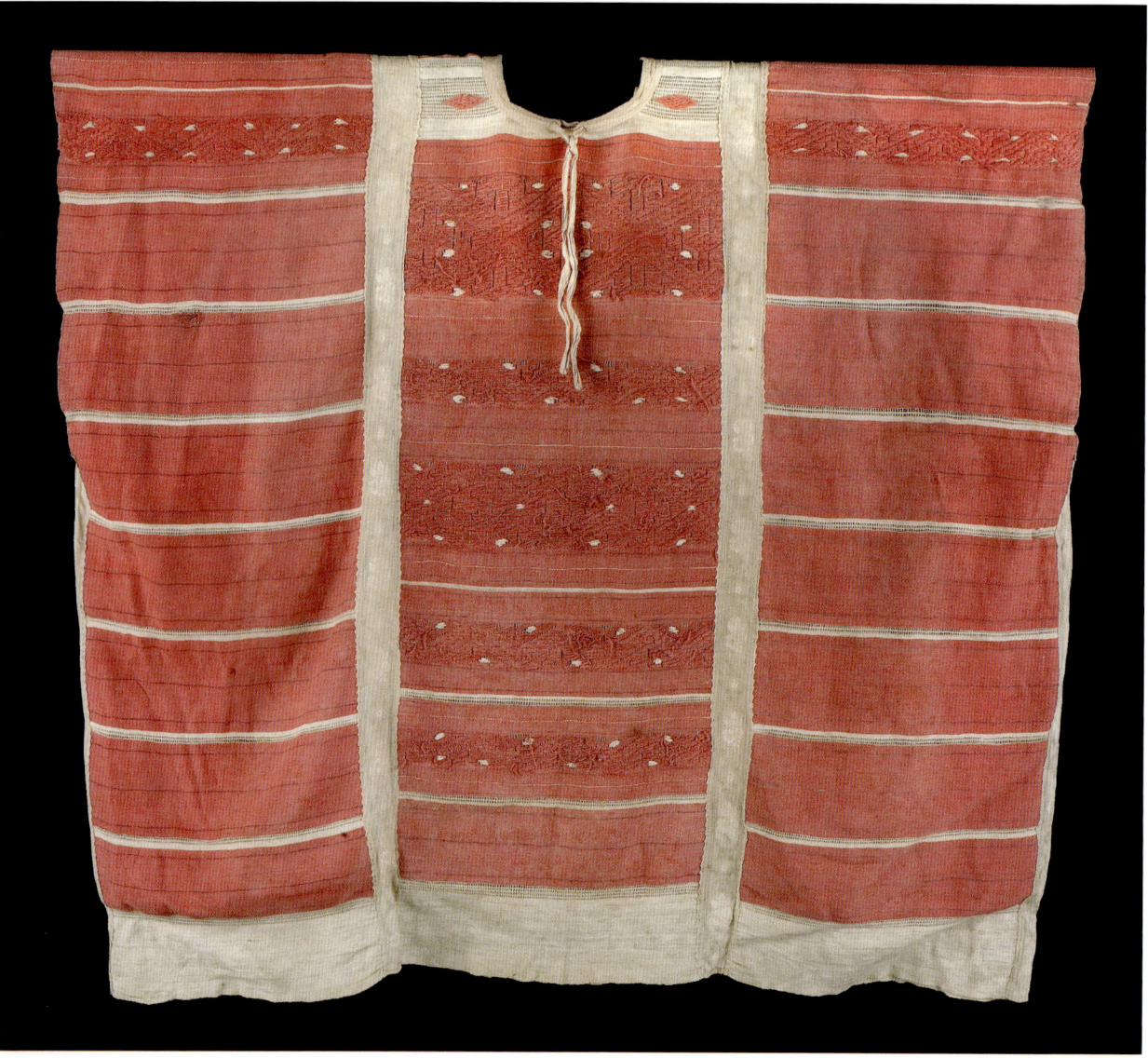

Fig. 371   Chinanteca woman's shirt; *Lamisteco-huipilé* (TK), *huipil*; cotton, silk; l. 93 cm, w. 106 cm; ca. 1888 (RMV 682-3).

The third dress item collected by Ten Kate in Amatlán is a Chinantec *huipil* made of hand-woven cotton and silk, dyed with natural cochineal dye (Fig. 371). Since precolonial time natural fibers such as cotton, wool, and *ixtle* (maguey agave fiber) have been colored by use of natural dyes in Mesoamerica. The methods of dyeing have hardly changed in the course of time, although nowadays synthetically manufactured dyes are beginning to replace natural ones. The most well-known natural dyes are *cochinilla* (or cochineal), *añil* (or indigo), and the *caracol púrpura* (or purple snail). Cochineal, made from a small parasite bug that lives on the *nopal*-cactus, is used for red dyes; indigo is used for blue dyes, and the *caracol púrpura pansa* is used for purple dyes. Yellow was made from the *armientos del*

zacatlaxcalli (Turok 1996: 67) and black from charcoal. Different shades of red, yellow, and other colors were made by mixing different hues or by adding charcoal or chalk.

This *huipil* is made up of three panels that are sewn together by using two white silk ribbons. Nine horizontal divisions make up the left and right part of the *huipil*, while the central part is divided in four horizontal divisions, of which the upper one is much larger than the lower three. Again Ten Kate records this specimen as *Lamisteco-huipilé*. This seems to imply that it was sold to him by a Mixtec vendor or by a person who bought it from someone from the Mixtec area who was either trading in Veracruz or in the Chinantec region, a known phenomenon until the present day in Mexico.

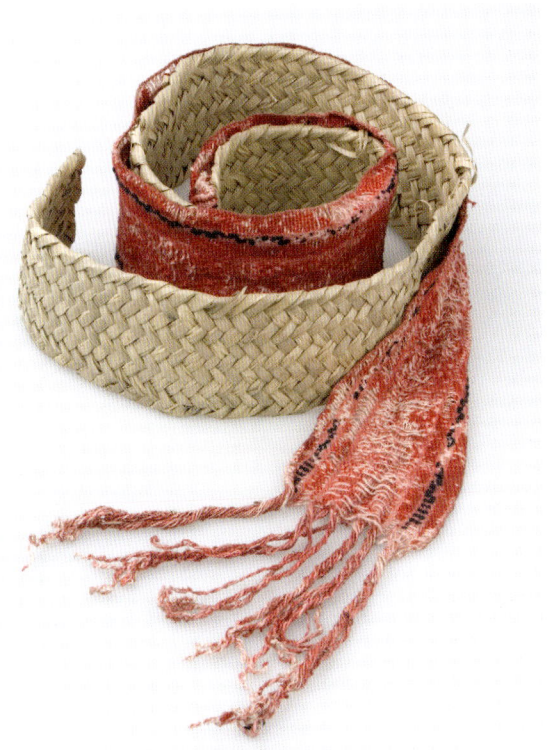

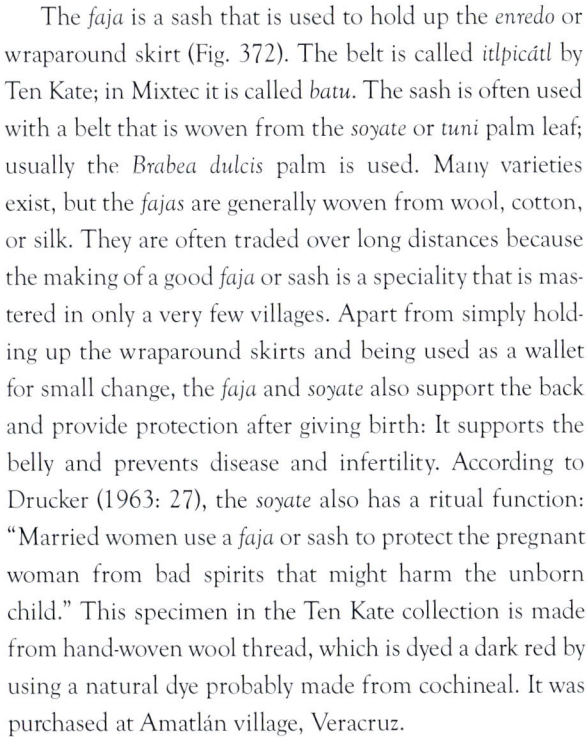

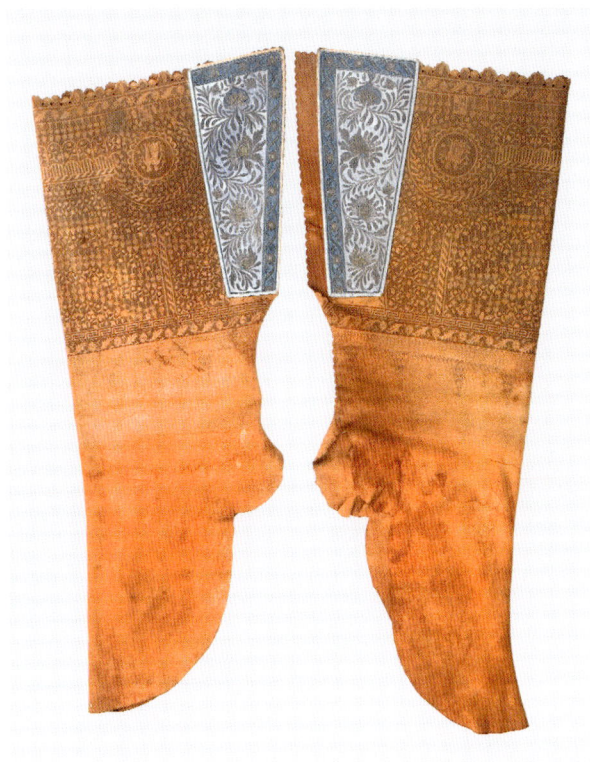

Fig. 372   Nahua woven *faja* or sash and accompanying belt; belt: *itlpicátl* (TK); palm leaf, wool; l. 154 cm, w. 11.5 cm; ca. 1888 (RMV 682-4).

Fig. 373   Leggings; Oaxaca; hide, cotton, silk; l. 88.5 cm, w. 38.5 cm; ca. 1888 (RMV 682-5).

The *faja* is a sash that is used to hold up the *enredo* or wraparound skirt (Fig. 372). The belt is called *itlpicátl* by Ten Kate; in Mixtec it is called *batu*. The sash is often used with a belt that is woven from the *soyate* or *tuni* palm leaf; usually the *Brabea dulcis* palm is used. Many varieties exist, but the *fajas* are generally woven from wool, cotton, or silk. They are often traded over long distances because the making of a good *faja* or sash is a speciality that is mastered in only a very few villages. Apart from simply holding up the wraparound skirts and being used as a wallet for small change, the *faja* and *soyate* also support the back and provide protection after giving birth: It supports the belly and prevents disease and infertility. According to Drucker (1963: 27), the *soyate* also has a ritual function: "Married women use a *faja* or sash to protect the pregnant woman from bad spirits that might harm the unborn child." This specimen in the Ten Kate collection is made from hand-woven wool thread, which is dyed a dark red by using a natural dye probably made from cochineal. It was purchased at Amatlán village, Veracruz.

Leggings or chaps were used to protect the bare skin when riding horses or mules. The pant legs are not connected to each other and there is one separate legging for each leg. When worn, the leggings are tied to a belt that secures them with thongs attached at the hip. Short leggings were simply gartered at the knee and never attached to a belt.

This pair of leggings was collected by Ten Kate around 1888 in Oaxaca (Fig. 373). It is an extremely fine set and elaborately decorated. The top part of the main leggings are stamped with a broad band consisting of geometric and naturalistic motifs, including frets and flowers, and possibly water symbols and heraldic shields, surrounding a central panel showing two human figures, a man and a woman, ornately dressed in European style. Below them a building has been symbolically indicated. Probably they were meant to represent a hacienda owner and his wife. For additional decoration each legging has a separate sewn-on hide panel, covered with blue cloth, which in turn is covered with ornate silk embroidered with floral and vegetal patterns in relief. This ornate pair of leggings was probably owned by a rich haciendero.

References

Avila Bolaños, Alejandro de
1996   Tejidos que cuidan el alma. In: Ruth D. Lechuga (ed.), *Textiles de Oaxaca* (Artes de México 35).

1997   Threads of Diversity: Oaxacan Textiles in Context. In: Kathryn Klein (ed.), *The Unbroken Thread: Conserving the Textile Tradition of Oaxaca* (Los Angeles, CA: The Getty Conservation Institute).

Barker, G. C.
1957   The Yaqui Easter Ceremony at Hermosillo. *Western Folklore* 16(3): 256–262.

Bogan, Phebe M.
1925   *Yaqui Indian Dances*. Tucson, AZ: The Archaeological Society.

Choate, Harris S.
1997   *The Yaquis: A Celebration*. San Francisco, CA: Whitewing Press.

Cordry, Donald and Dorothy Cordry
1968   *Mexican Indian Costumes*. Austin, TX: University of Texas Press.

Densmore, Frances
1932   *Yuman and Yaqui Music*. Bulletin of the Bureau of American Ethnology 60. Washington, DC.

Drucker, Susan
1963   *Cambio de Indumentaria: La Estructura Social y el Abandono de la Vestimente Indigena en la Villa de Santiago Jamiltepec, Mexico*. Mexico, D.F.: El Colegio de México.

Fabila, Alfonso
1940   *Las Tribus Yaquis de Sonora*. Mexico City: Instituto Nacional Indigenista.

Griffith, James S.
1989   Cahitan Pascola Masks. In: Ross Coates (ed.), *Gods among Us: American Indian Masks* (San Diego, CA: San Diego State University Publications in American Indian Studies), 73–86.

Griffith, James S. and Felipe S. Molina
1980   *Old Men of the Fiesta: An Introduction to the Pascola Arts*. Phoenix, AZ: The Heard Museum.

Holden, W. C. et al.
1936   Studies of the Yaqui Indians of Sonora. *Texas Technological College Bulletin* 12(1): 1–142.

Johnson Weitlaner, Irmgard
1976   *Design Motives on Mexican Indian Textiles*. 2 vols. Graz: Akademische Druck- und Verlagsanstalt.

Kolaz, Thomas
1985   Yaqui Pascola Masks from the Tucson Area. *American Indian Art Magazine* 11(1): 38–45.

Kurath, Gertrud Prokosh
1960   The Sena'asom Rattle of the Yaqui Indian Pascolas. *Ethnomusicology* 4(2): 60–63.

Lutes, Steven V.
1983   The Mask and Magic of the Yaqui Pascola Clown. In: N. Ross Crumrine and Marjorie Halpin (eds.), *The Power of Symbols: Masks and Masquerade in the Americas* (Vancouver, BC: University of British Columbia Press), 80–91.

Mason, Otis T.
1904   Aboriginal American Basketry: Studies in a Textile Art without Machinery. *Annual Report of the U.S. National Museum for 1902*: 171–548.

Painter, Muriel Thayer
1950   *The Yaqui Easter Ceremony at Pascua*. Tucson, AZ: Tucson Chamber of Commerce.
1986   *With Good Heart: Yaqui Beliefs and Ceremonies in Pascua Village*. Tucson, AZ: University of Arizona Press.

Parsons, Elsie Clew and Ralph L. Beals
1933   The Sacred Clowns of the Pueblo and Mayo-Yaqui Indians. *American Anthropologist* 36: 491–514.

Spicer, Edward H.
1940   *Pascua: A Yaqui Village in Arizona*. Chicago, IL: University of Chicago Press.
1954   *Potam: A Yaqui Village in Sonora*. Memoirs of the American Anthropological Association 77. Menasha, WI.
1980   *The Yaquis: A Cultural History*. Tucson, AZ: University of Arizona Press.
1983   Yaqui. In: Alfonso Ortiz (ed.), *Southwest* (Handbook of North American Indians 10. W. C. Sturetvant, gen. ed; Washington, DC: Smithsonian Institution), 250–263.

Ten Kate, Herman F. C.
1885   *Reizen en Onderzoekingen in Noord Amerika*. Leiden: E. J. Brill.
1889a   Schrijven van Dr. H. F. C. ten Kate aan de Redactie. *Tijdschrift van het Koninklijk Nederlands Aardrijkskundig Genootschap* 6(1–3): 105–106.
1889b   Ethnographische und anthropologische Mittheilungen aus dem amerikanischen Südwesten und aus Mexiko. *Zeitschrift für Ethnologie* 21: 664–668.
1908   The House of Tcuhu. *American Anthropologist* 10: 174–175.
2004   *Travels and Researches in Native North America, 1882–1883*. P. Hovens, L. A. Hieb, and W. J. Orr eds. Albuquerque, NM: University of New Mexico Press. [Translation of Ten Kate 1885.]

Troy, Timothy
1998   Professor Bronislaw Malinowski's Visit to Tucson. *Journal of the Southwest* 40(2): 129–186.

Turok, Marta
1996   Trama Natural: De Fibras, Gusanos y Caracoles. In: *Textiles de Oaxaca* (Artes de Mexico 35).

Van Broekhoven, Laura
2005   *Weefsels van het Volk van de Regen*. Leiden: Rijksmuseum voor Volkenkunde. Digital publication: http://www.rmv.nl/publicaties/22Mixteeks_textiel/n/pub_top.asp.

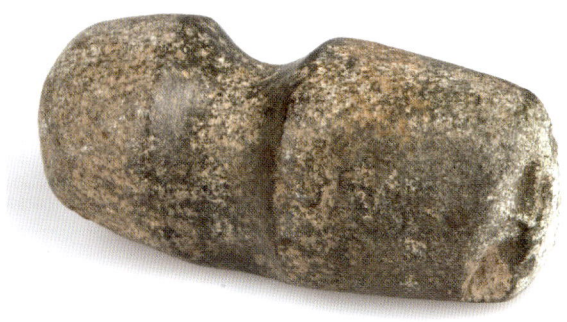

Fig. 375 Hohokam 3/4 axe; stone; l. 15.3 cm, d. 5.6–6.1 cm; Casa Grande ruins, Arizona; A.D. 1150–1450 (RMV 362-198).

ungrooved base. Two types are distinguished: axes with ridges flanking the grooves and those without ridges. Cutting mesquite or ironwood, they sometimes broke and often were recycled as hammers or mauls, such as the one in the Ten Kate collection (Fig. 375). The peak of production of stone axes occurred during the Classic Period, and their higher frequency at Classic platform mounds suggests a possible relation to status. The Pima searched for Hohokam stone axes in ruins and used these to sharpen *metates* (Russell 1908: 110; Haury 1976: 291–292; Neitzel 1991: 187).

On the site of the Casa Grande ruins Ten Kate collected a sample of fourteen Hohokam potsherds (Fig. 376): two Gila Plain rimsherds (micaceous, one wide-mouth jar and one bowl); two Gila Plain body sherds; one Gila Red (?) handle fragment; one Gila Red smudged body sherd; one Sacaton Red-on-buff bowl rim (pointed); one Casa Grande Red-on-buff jar rim; three Sacaton Red-on-buff body sherds (one bowl, two jars); one Casa Grande Red-on-buff body sherd (jar); and two Gila Polychrome bowl rimsherds.

With the exception of utilitarian plainware, Red-on-buff pottery is the most common at Hohokam sites. Because of the spatial patterning of finds, it has been hypothesized that this type of pottery may have been produced at only a few locations and distributed from there over

Hohokam territory. However, more research is required for more definitive answers. Gila Polychrome was a second type of pottery unearthed in Hohokam sites, but in much smaller quantities and was possibly a Salado introduction (Haury 1976: 191–254; Neitzel 1991: 184–186; also cf. Abbott 2000).

Micaceous schist was used to temper pottery along the Middle Gila. The presence of Gila Polychrome indicates a Civano phase occupation of the site where Ten Kate collected these sherds. The Civano phase marks the cultural florescence of the Hohokam culture during its "Classic" period and is thought to date to A.D. 1300 to 1450.

Ten Kate (1889a: 220) remarked that Hohokam pottery for utilitarian as well as ceremonial use testified to the artistic sensibilities and good taste of these prehistoric Indians. Gila and Salt Red are a particularly handsome utilitarian pottery to modern taste, especially when the interior of bowls was polished and smudged, producing a glossy finish. Gila Polychrome with its striking black-on-white interior designs and dull red exteriors intriguingly contrasts with the earlier Red-on-buff pottery, whose design repertoires changed from arrays of small zoomorphic and other elements to curvilinear, then interlocking (weaving) designs, and finally to rectanguloid geometric ones (cf. Haury 1976: 191–254).

Another group of Hohokam potsherds and shell fragments were collected by Ten Kate from ruins near Tempe, Arizona. The assemblage is from the Santa Cruz phase, from which period many Hohokam sites in the Phoenix-

Fig. 376 Hohokam potsherds; pottery; Casa Grande ruins, Arizona; A.D. 1300–1450 (RMV 362-208a).

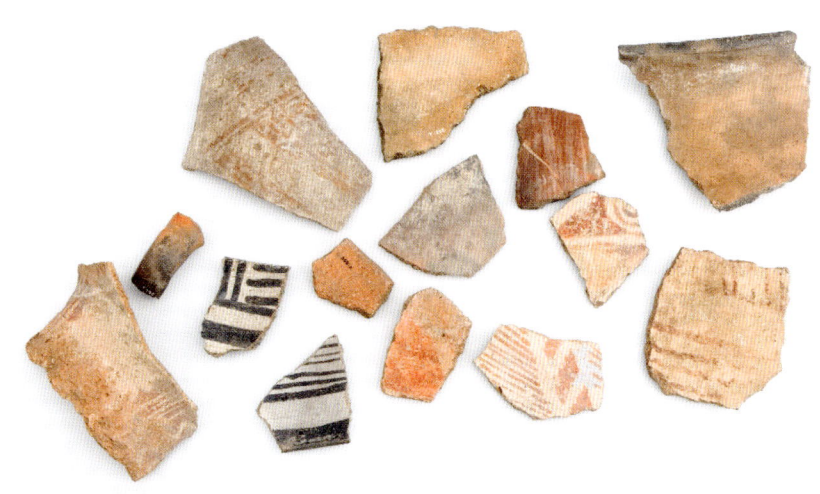

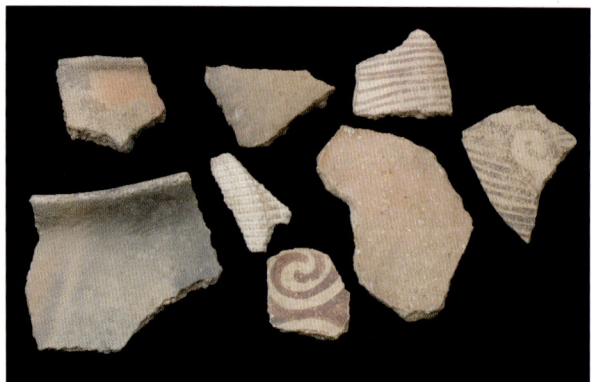

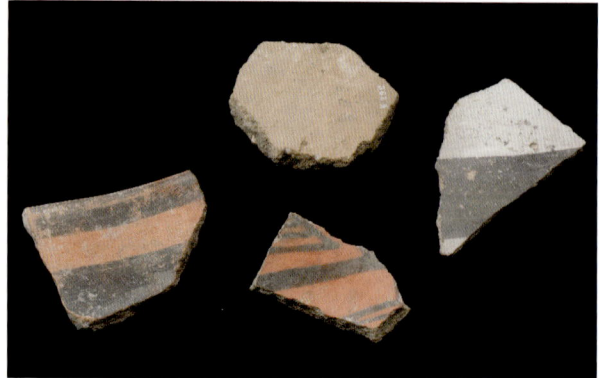

Fig. 377 Hohokam potsherds and shell fragments; pottery, shell; from ruins near Tempe, probably Pueblo Grande and La Cuidad, Arizona; A.D. 850–1000 (RMV 362-208e).

Fig. 378 Mogollon potsherds; pottery; A.D. 1100–1200 (RMV 362-208b).

Tempe area date (Wilcox 1987, 1993). Non-micaceous sands, sometimes with phyllite, were used to temper the pottery of the Salt River Valley. The set (Fig. 377) includes one Gila Plain bowl rim; two wide-mouth jar Gila Plain rims; four Gila Plain jar body sherds (sand temper), one Santa Cruz Red-on-buff rim sherd; three Santa Cruz Red-on-buff body sherds (two jars, one bowl); and two Cardium shell fragments (unworked).

Many shell ornaments were found in Hohokam sites, as well as large amounts of shell debris, testifying to the work spent on the manufacture of such precious jewelry. The Indians made shell into beads of various shapes and sizes, necklaces, and pendants, the latter by using whole shells or pieces of flat shell cut in various geomorphic, zoomorphic, and anthropomorphic shapes, bracelets, rings, tinklers, miniature trumpets, etc. The source of most shell found in Hohokam sites was the Gulf of California, several hundred miles to the southwest. Species favored included *Olivella* (for beads), *Glycimeris* (for bracelets), *Pecten*, *Conus*, *Laevicardium*, and *Spondylus*. Burials contain a high frequency of exotic materials, especially shell, and marine shell is associated with status differentiation during the Classic Period. The elite probably controlled access by organizing special expeditions to the Gulf of California and enlisting specialized craftspeople for the production of shell artifacts, although alternative interpretations are being considered. Artistic production peaked in the Sedentary Period, while the Classic Period produced the largest quantity (Haury 1976: 305–324; Vokes 1984; McGuire 1985, 1992; McGuire and Howard 1987; Wilcox 1987: 139; Neitzel 1991: 187–189; Stone 2003: 144–147). Ten Kate (1889: 49) wrote about the Hohokam: "Art in shell was very much developed among these ancient people. Seashells were the favorite material of the manufacture

of personal ornaments, and much of the shellwork shows traces of having been used as a base for inlaying. The backs of the shells were coated with a kind of black cement, manufactured from the gum deposited upon the twigs of the *hedondilla*, or greasewood, by a certain insect. In this gum were embedded little mosaic fragments of turquoise and of red shells, and then rubbed down smooth." Relatively little unworked shell was found in Hohokam sites. Those pieces that remained intact were raw material or pieces used as scoops and paint containers (Haury 1976: 309).

During his sojourn among the Apache on the San Carlos Reservation in southeastern Arizona, Ten Kate spent a short time among the prehistoric ruins in that area. At San Carlos, on the edge of the mesa, huge stones set in a pattern indicated a large prehistoric building. About five and a half miles north of the Indian Agency, he surveyed several ruins that were virtually level with the ground. Here the anthropologist observed and collected potsherds similar to those found in the Phoenix area and on the Pima Reservation. He was aware of the fact that Adolph Bandelier had examined this site extensively a bit earlier.

The Mogollon potsherds collected by Ten Kate (Fig. 378) include one orange-colored (unidentified) Black-on-red rimsherd (bowl, round rim, wide band to rim, with blocky black element below band); one St. John's Black-on-red bowl sherd; one (unidentified) Black-on-white (Cibola White Ware: a large black blocky trianguloid design element); one smudged redware jar sherd (Salt Red? this specimen is lost); and one plainware jar sherd (with rounded, fine quartz sand temper). This is probably a Bylas phase (1175/1200–1300) assemblage. As defined by Johnson and Wasley (1966), the Bylas phase was a time in the Gila Valley from the gorge east of Safford to San Carlos when the farming population lived in surface rooms built using adobe reinforced with rocks arranged around a courtyard in areas above the river convenient for farming. Identifying indigenous ceramics include plain and corrugated utilitarian ware and Casa Grande Red-on-buff (Safford Variety) and San Carlos Red-on-brown ware.

From San Carlos Ten Kate traveled to Fort Apache to carry on fieldwork among the Coyoteros. On the northern wall of the canyon at Fort Apache, in the immediate vicinity of the fort, high above a stream on a nearly inaccessible place, he observed a series of deeply incised petroglyphs. He was able to identify animals, human hands and feet, curved lines, and stars and was inclined to believe that the Apache had made these. Continuing his journey to Laguna Pueblo, Ten Kate had to spend a whole day in Show Low, waiting for transportation. He used this opportunity to explore the region's ruins and to collect sherds.

The potsherds assembled at the time (Fig. 379) consist of one Pinedale Black-on-white jar sherd; one Fourmile Polychrome bowl rim; one bowl sherd similar to Fourmile Polychrome (exterior) with white lines on thick red slip interior; one bowl sherd similar to Fourmile Polychrome (exterior), with black-on-red interior; two Brown corrugated sherds (one bowl rim, one bowl body sherd): fine corrugations.

This was possibly Whipple Ruin, also seen by Bandelier (1892), the site where charcoal would be found in 1929 whose tree-rings would bridge the gap between the late prehistoric period and an until then "floating" chronology based on wood found in Chaco Canyon sites (Haury and Hargrave 1931). Fourmile Polychrome was a White Mountain Red Ware made north of the Mogollon Rim in the fourteenth century. Bowls and jars were common, but also several animal effigy jars have been excavated. The focus of decoration is on the interior center, and asymmetric treatment is quite common. Designs include stylized macaws and other birds, butterflies, flowers, and masked faces, and an association with a Southwestern regional cult focused on weather control and fertility has been suggested. The large-diameter bowls are thought today to have been used in supra-household feasting, their bold exterior designs communicating information about identity to the participants. Fourmile Polychrome is the climax of technostylistic development of White Mountain Redware (Carlson 1970: 65–73, 116; 1982: 218–221; Crown 1994; Mills 2007).

In August 1883 Ten Kate traveled with a small party of Whites from Fort Defiance on the Navajo Reservation by way of Keam's Canyon to the Hopi mesas to witness the

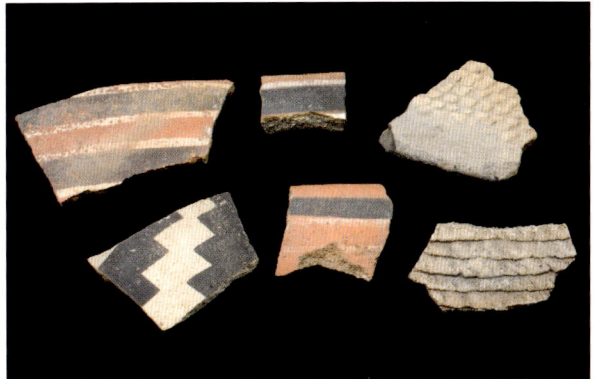

Fig. 379 Mogollon potsherds; pottery and pigments; A.D. 1325–1400 (RMV 362-208d).

snake dance. About half a mile from Keam's store on the northern wall of the canyon he saw petroglyphs, among which the swastika or whirlwind design stood out. Others included a human hand, a horned head, a horse with several riders on its back. While passing through a canyon, he saw a cliffhouse built in a niche high in the wall, but was sorry not to be able to explore the site as it proved to be inaccessible. Soon after they discovered two others, but similarly positioned. Ten Kate had to continue his journey musing about the mysterious who had built and occupied these homes and were called Anasazi according to his Navajo guide. When he returned from the Hopi villages, he spent time at Keam's trading post, where Keam let him examine the impressive collection of Anasazi and Hopi pottery assembled by Alexander Stephen, who had been studying the way of life of the Hopi since about 1880. Stephen was away prospecting for precious metals and at that time also engaged in cataloguing his collection, which he offered for sale to the U.S. National Museum in 1884. The Smithsonian Institution declined and in 1892 Jesse Walter Fewkes purchased it on behalf of Mrs. Hemenway (Wade and McChesney 1981). It is now at the Peabody Museum, Harvard University.

Ten Kate noted that the Hopi freely interpreted the designs on the prehistoric pottery and spoke of the Anasazi as their forefathers. On the basis of available craniological evidence, Ten Kate thought it highly probable that the Hopi, Zuni, and Pueblos were descendants of the Anasazi. He assumed that the prehistoric settlements were abandoned because of periods of prolonged drought. Today the Pueblo people prefer the term "Ancestral Pueblos" to the Navajo word Anasazi, which means "enemy ancestors."

While doing ethnographic fieldwork in Zuni Pueblo, Ten Kate picked up several prehistoric artifacts in the

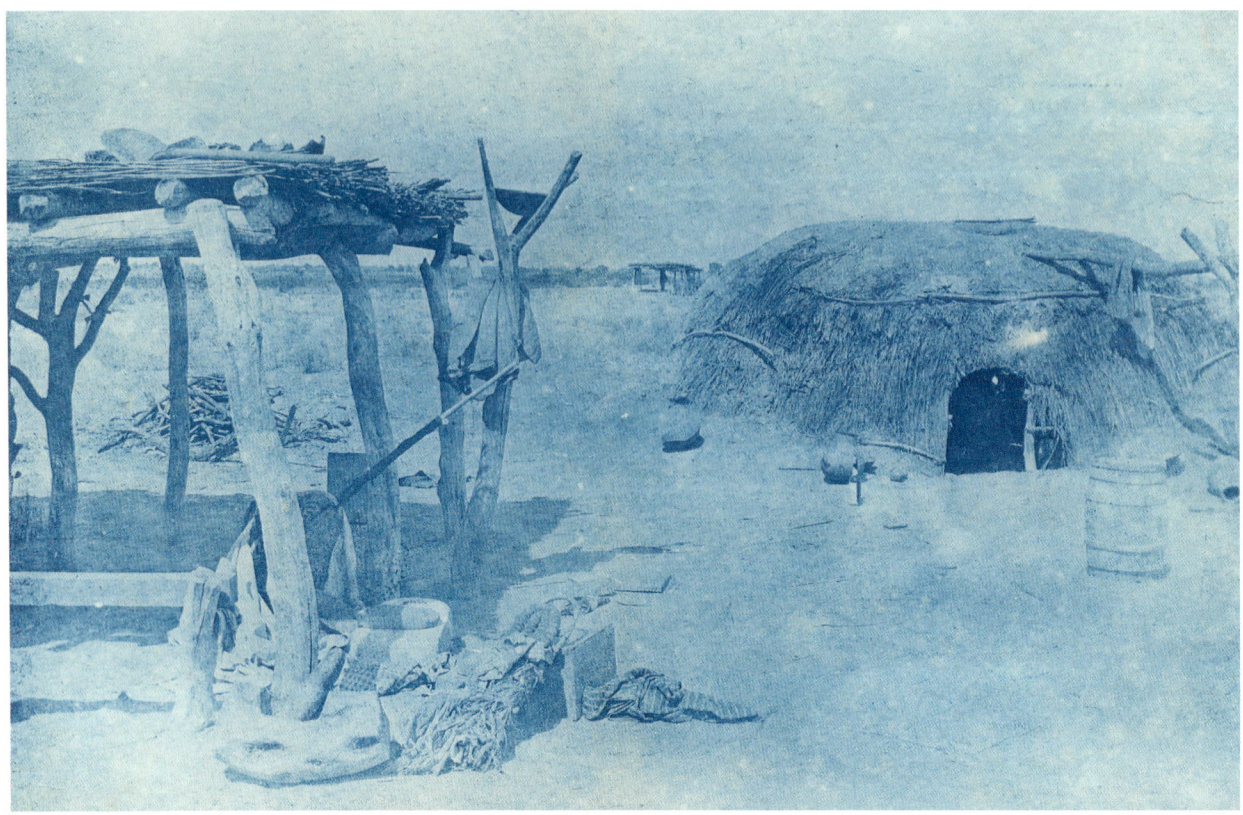

Fig. 380 Pima camp at Sacaton Switch; Arizona Territory, March 1888; blue cynotype. Photograph probably by Frank H. Cushing (Ten Kate coll.; RMV 414Kd5).

vicinity, probably from ruins contemporary with Halonawan, where he would later engage in excavations. A grooved stone axe, found at a ruin near Zuni, is today part of the Paris Ten Kate collection (MQB 71.1885.82.1; stone; l. 20.9 cm, w. 9 cm; A.D. 1250-1350). Stone axes were used for cutting wood. The stone blades were either three-quarters or fully grooved, to facilitate being hafted securely to a wooden handle. Such axes were valued tools and archaeologists have found these tools as burial goods in graves of males, females, and children (Smith et al. 1966: 242; see Fig. 382, p. 272). Also housed at the Musée du quai Branly is a square mortar collected by Ten Kate near Zuni (MQB 71.1885.82.2; stone: volcanic rock; l. 7.5 cm, w. 19.5 cm; A.D. 1250-1350).

The Hemenway Southwestern Archaeological Expedition, 1887-1888

Frank H. Cushing's early anthropological studies were partially sponsored by Mary Hemenway, a philanthropist from Boston. During the summer of 1886, on his way back home from fieldwork in Surinam and the Caribbean, Ten Kate visited Cushing, who was working on his publi-

cation on Zuni folktales at her North Shore home. Mrs. Hemenway was impressed with Ten Kate's fieldwork in the Southwest and on the southern Plains and offered him material support for further fieldwork. However, personal circumstances stood in the way of accepting this generous offer. However, when Cushing embarked on an interdisciplinary archaeological expedition, aimed at researching cultural patterning and the relationships between the prehistoric remains of settlements in the Southwest and the contemporary Native tribes, a venture funded by Mrs. Hemenway, Ten Kate was invited to join the undertaking as physical anthropologist.

In the fall of 1887 the Dutch anthropologist arrived in the Phoenix area at the camp of the Hemenway Southwestern Archaeological Expedition. Because Cushing was in California seeking medical treatment, Ten Kate soon began supervising excavations at the Hohokam sites, conserving human remains, studying the skeletal material, and preparing these for shipment to the Army Medical Museum in the capital. After Cushing's return he also did additional anthropometric research among the Pima, Papago, and Maricopa. In June of 1888 the expedition packed up to move to Zuni for excavations at Halonawan, one of the ancestral villages. There he continued his archaeological and somatological work and did ethnographic research on Zuni ideas and practices on health, illness, and healing. In the fall he went for a short visit to Mexico, before hurriedly returning to the Netherlands, where his father lay critically ill (Ten Kate 1925: 86-146; Hovens 1989: 123-124; 1995: 688-698).

The Leiden Hemenway Collection

The artifact collections of the Hemenway Southwestern Archaeological Expedition where shipped to Salem, Massachusetts, where Mrs. Hemenway planned to build a Pueblo Museum. While working for the Hemenway Expedition in 1887-88, Ten Kate obtained a small personal collection of Indian artifacts in Arizona and New Mexico. It consisted of sixty-five numbers and was donated to the National Museum of Ethnology (Rijksmuseum voor Volkenkunde) in Leiden when he returned to Europe. Most objects are ethnographic, mainly Zuni pottery, fetishes, and prayersticks (series 674 and 682; see chapter 10, "The Zuni"). A few pieces of pottery in the collection might be prehistoric or historic replicas, but are included in the Zuni chapter. Inventory number RMV 674-62 is a series of forty prehistoric stone projectile points from the Zuni area, probably surface finds.

Before Ten Kate left the expedition, Cushing gave him four prehistoric and one contemporary artifacts for the Leiden museum: a stone axe, two bone awls, two flat, worked long-bone fragments from Halonawan, and a Zuni wooden club (series 675).

In 1911 Hemenway material was exchanged by Charles Peabody with director J. H. Holwerda of the National Museum of Antiquities (Rijksmuseum voor Oudheden) in Leiden: seven artifacts, most from the Civano phase of the Hohokam Classic period found at Los Muertos and originally from the Thomas V. Keam collection. In exchange, Peabody received artifacts from Indonesia and the Pacific. Trader Keam was a middleman in the acquisition of many archaeological and ethnographic collections from Arizona by American museums (e.g., Wade and McChesney 1981). One of his collections was purchased for Mrs. Mary Hemenway in the 1890s by Jesse Walter Fewkes, who had succeeded Cushing as director of the Hemenway Expedition. In 1912 Holwerda transferred this material to the National Museum of Ethnology (series 1830).

Ten Kate collected this figurine among the Pima (Fig. 381). It cannot be ruled out completely that a Pima made

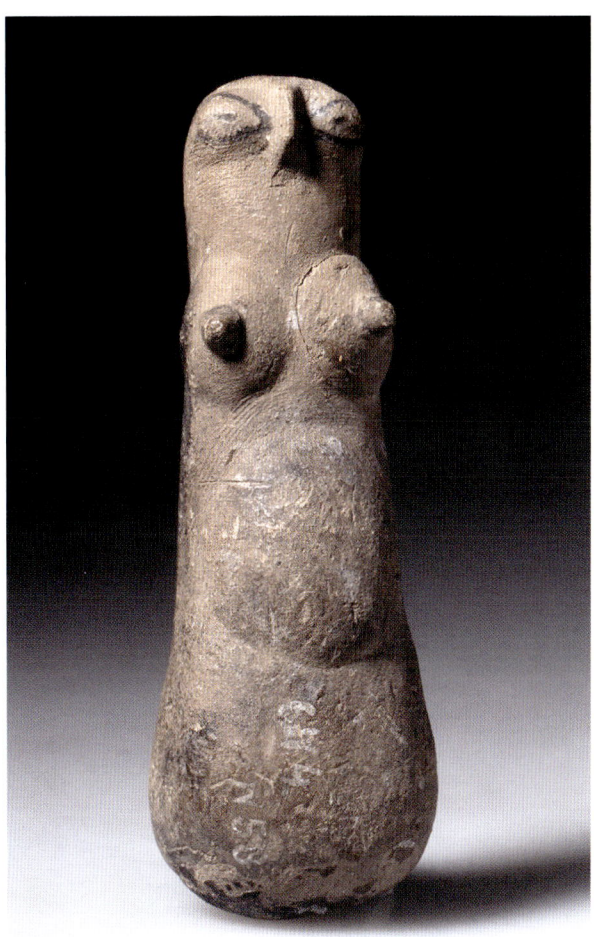

Fig. 381 Hohokam fertility figurine; pottery; h. 8.2 cm; ca. 1150-1450 A.D. (RMV 674-58).

the clay effigy, copying Hohokam figurines they frequently found in their territory. However, an original Hohokam origin is more likely. Clay figurines were common in early Hohokam sites and changed stylistically through time. Although the cylindrical base of the Leiden figurine is exceptional, it is not unique (e.g., Schwabe 1989: 172–173). During his survey of the Pima Reservation in March 1888 Ten Kate noted that the Indians were not adverse to picking up Hohokam artifacts for their own use. Thus Pima medicine men used Hohokam medicine slates in their rituals (Hovens 1995: 666). This figurine was probably used as an amulet by the Pima.

Haury (1976: 255-267) made the original study of Hohokam human figurines, noting their high frequency and presence in all phases of development, association with funeral rites in the Colonial and Sedentary periods, and disappearance at the beginning of the Classic Period. Further he hypothesizes an association with house-blessing and fertility rites. In contrast, none of the figurines

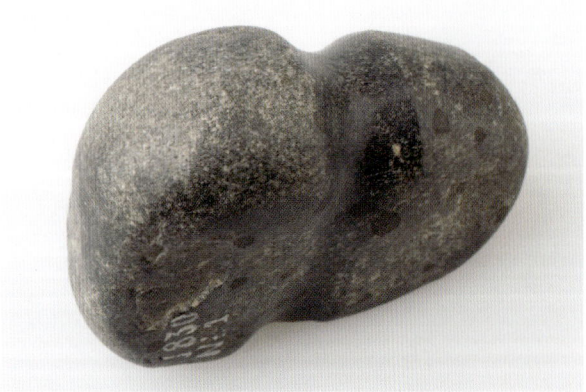

Fig. 382   Hammerstone; stone: pebble; Hopi area; l. 8.7 cm, n.d. (RMV 1830-1).

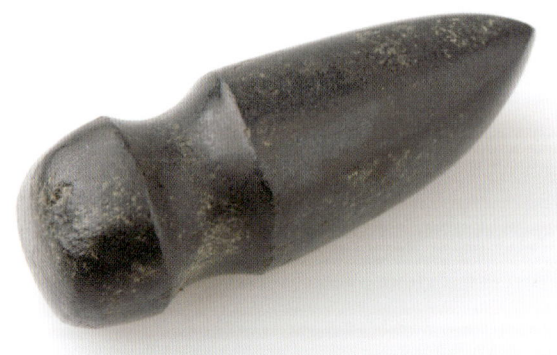

Fig. 383   Axe; stone: black diorite; Los Muertos Compound XX, Civano phase, Hohokam Classic period; l. 13.3 cm; A.D. 1300–1450 (RMV 1830-2).

excavated from Salt-Gila Aqueduct Project Sites were associated with burials, and they were excavated in Civano contexts, postdating the Classic Period (Crown 1983: 317–318; also see Schwabe 1989).

Hohokam Lithic Technology

The inventory of Hohokam lithic tools is characterized by relatively modest technological sophistication, internal diversity, and temporal change (e.g., Bernard-Shaw 1983: 440–442). However, the quality of the stones available for various tools was valued, and they were quarried in distant areas, reaching Hohokam settlements either through expeditions or trade (Stone 2003: 133–134).

RMV 1830-1 (Fig. 382) is a fully grooved hammerstone made from black pebble. The original Keam collection codes of this and the following specimens are given in parentheses. This is "Keam Coll. 3094."

Fig. 384   Hammerstone; stone: pebble; Los Muertos Ruin I, Civano phase, Hohokam Classic period; d. 7.7 cm; A.D. 1300–1450 (RMV 1830-3).

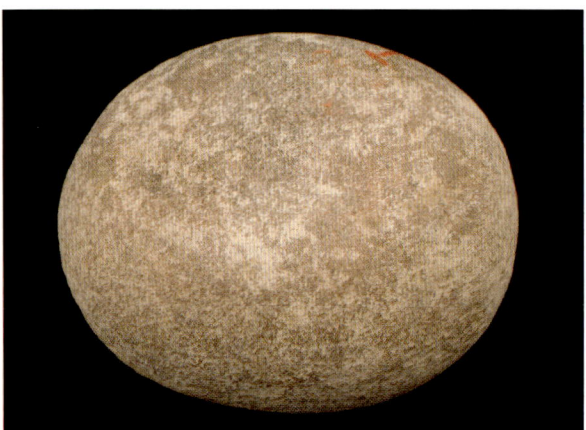

RMV 1830-2 (Fig. 383) is a three-quarters grooved stone axe ("XX 1314 [?]"; cf. also Fig. 375). The Hohokam cultural sequence in southern Arizona began with the adoption of pottery, now thought to have occurred about A.D. 200. Four main periods are recognized: the Pioneer, Colonial, Sedentary, and Classic periods, each of which is divided temporally into phases. The Civano phase of the Classic period, to which this axe is dated, was the moment of Hohokam cultural florescence. It was then that Casa Grande was built, large platform mounds reached their ultimate expression as ritual-civic centers, and perhaps as many as 24,000 people occupied the Salt and Gila River valleys of what today is called the Phoenix Basin (Wilcox 1979, 1991).

Hammerstones such as RMV 1830-3 (Fig. 384; "I [# obliterated])" were derived from diorite or andesite pebbles found in the nearby Salt River, chosen for their shape, weight, or hardness. They were not modified before use and are identified by wear patterns. Pitted surfaces are common on hammerstones used for battering action, while those used for grinding exhibit polished and abrasively crushed surfaces (Haury 1976: 279–280; Bernard-Shaw 1983: 394–395).

The material deriving from the Keams collection further includes two tabular stone knives, RMV 1830-4 (Fig. 385; "XX [# in red obliterated]") and RMV 1830-9 (Fig. 386; "XXV 1823c" [in red], "1823c" [in black on top]). A sharp blow to a fine-grained pebble produced a flat (tabular), but fairly heavy flake whose sharp surface could be used to cut through the tough leaves of agave in a sawing action parallel to the longtitudinal axis. Production of agave for food and textiles began in Preclassic times, and the desert plant became an incipient cultivar, much emphasized during the Hohokam Classic period when the heart

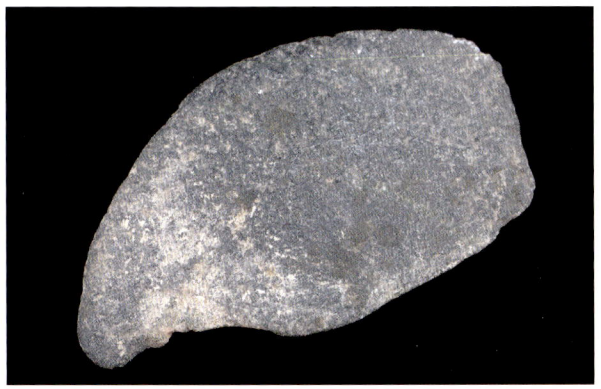
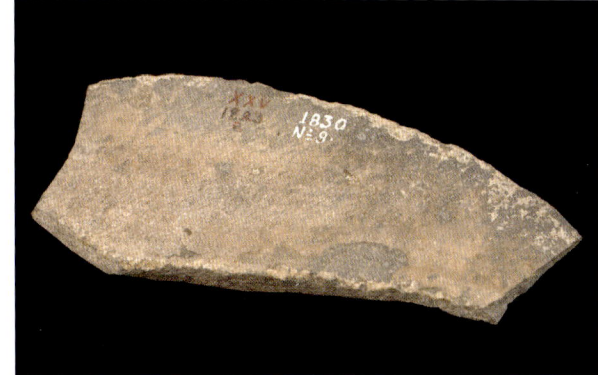

Figs. 385, 386 Tabular knives; stone: pebble; RMV 1830-4: Los Muertos Compound XX, Civano phase, Hohokam Classic period.; l. 11.5 cm; RMV 1830-9: Los Muertos Compound XXV, Civano phase, Hohokam Classic period; l. 20 cm; A.D. 1300–1450.

of the plant was roasted and the fibers were used for sandals, cordage, and the like. As an anomaly, Bernard-Shaw (1983: 395–396, 442–443) noted the lack of association of tabular knives and agave roasting pits in the Salt-Gila area. Tabular knives were probably manufactured by specialist craftsmen (Neitzel 1991: 186–187).

Pebbles of hard andesite, jasper, and quartzite from streams were used for polishing purposes, notably the surfaces of pottery. Abrading stones, such as RMV 1830-5 (Fig. 387) were larger and had a coarser surface, suited for smoothing wood, shell, and rock (Haury 1976: 283–284).

This knife (Fig. 388) is made of a coarse-grained metamorphic rock, probably schist (cf. Bernard-Shaw (1983: 395).

RMV 1830-7 (Fig. 389; "XII 1347 [?]") may possibly be a palette. Rectangular stone palettes, sometimes elaborately carved, were used in the cremation death ritual. Most had a lead oxide residue on their inner surface, suggesting that a change of color from white to red was desired in rit-

ual. Palettes are usually made from schist or phyllite. Schist can be easily split into tabular pieces and can be shaped into rectangular blanks. Early types are unworked flat stones of various shapes, but soon rims or borders were added to rectangular palettes. During the Colonial Period

Fig. 388 Knife; stone; l. 14.7 cm, w. 9.5 cm, th. 1.8 cm; n.d. (RMV 1830-6).

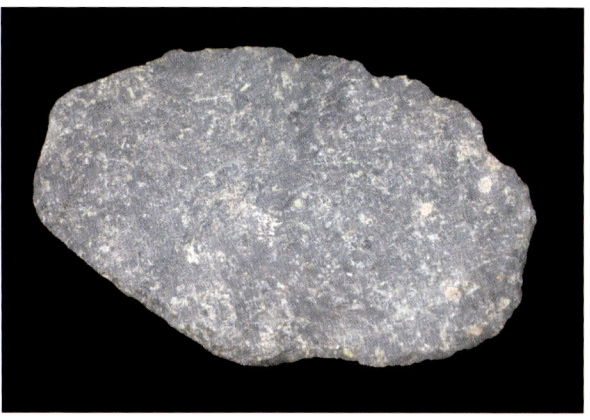

Fig. 389 Worked stone, possibly a palette; micaceous schist; Los Muertos or Las Acequias Ruin XIII, Hohokam Classic period; l. 10 cm; A.D. 1150–1450 (RMV 1830-7).

Fig. 387 Abrading stone; l. 18.5 cm, w. 9 cm, th. 4 cm; n.d. (RMV 1830-5).

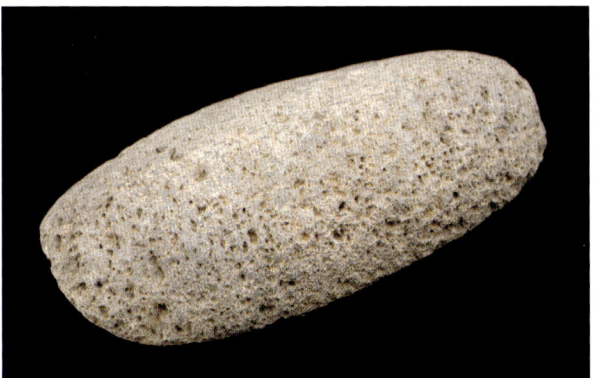

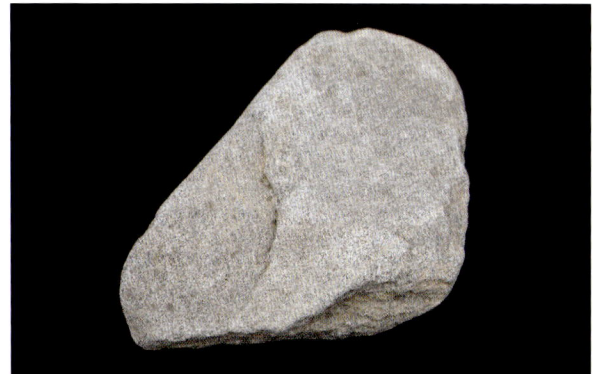

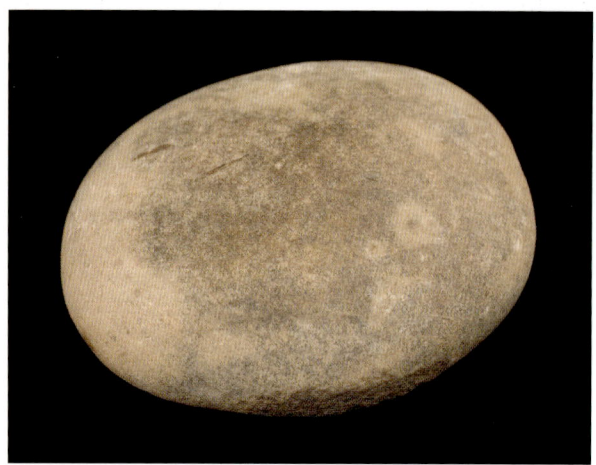

Fig. 390 Discoidal stone; Los Muertos Compound XXII, Civano phase, Hohokam Classic period; l. 10.7 cm; A.D. 1150-1450 (RMV 1830-8).

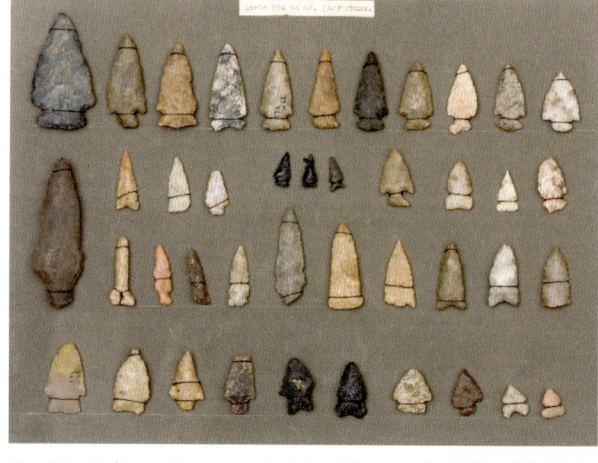

Fig. 391 Lithic artifacts; stone; l. 1.8 to 8.8 cm; A.D. 1250-1350 (RMV 674-62).

human and animal effigies were added as edge decoration on the slate-like schist, and the production and distribution of palettes is concentrated in the Hohokam core area. In the Sedentary Period production also takes place outside the core, resulting in distinct decorative patterns. The breaking of palettes and other artifacts is a custom associated with funerary ritual (Haury 1976: 286–289: Krueger 1993; White 2004).

According to Alan Ferg of the Arizona State Museum, the discoidal stone with worked edge and polished base (Fig. 390; "VVII 1694b" [in red], "1775b" [in black on top]) is probably a one-handed *mano*-made-of-a-pebble, for use on a slab-*metate*. Bernard-Shaw (1983: 399–400) has pointed out the variability in shape and use of *manos* found in Hohokam sites (cf. Haury 1976: 281–282). Studies of food grinding stones from the prehistoric and historic Southwest and the Middle East have shown that tool morphology is less associated with differences in wild and domesticated plant species that were processed. Instead, such variability is more closely related to differing processing strategies, such as the grinding of dried seeds and kernels into flour, fresh soaked kernels into *masa*, and oily seeds into paste (Adams 1993, 1999).

The Hemenway Expedition started excavations at the ancestral Zuni site of Halonawan (Red Ant place) in the summer of 1888 and later also dug at the site of Heshotauthla. The Indians did not object to the disturbance of the graves of their *Oiotékwe* (the Old Ones), and Ten Kate credited Cushing with allaying fears and overcoming any opposition (Ten Kate 1925: 134; Hovens 1995: 690–691). Unfortunately, little was published about the research findings on the Hemenway Expedition's work in the Zuni

area. The following artifacts came from Halonawan, where Ten Kate was involved with excavations in July and August 1888.

Halonawan Material Culture

In the decades preceding A.D. 1300 many small settlements in the wider Zuni area were abandoned and large pueblos emerged in the Ramah-El Morro region, east of present-day Zuni Pueblo. In the fourteenth century a shift in location took place and new towns emerged on a short stretch on the Zuni River and Ojo Caliente Wash, most of these still occupied in historic times. These included Halonawan North, on the present site of Zuni Pueblo and now virtually completely covered by the modern village, and Halonawan South, just south of the pueblo, across the Zuni River. Cushing's house at Zuni was built directly on top of the site. Grayware was the most prevalent pottery type excavated at Halonawan South, accounting for almost fifty percent, followed by St. Johns redwares (seventeen percent) and Tularosa black-on-white (eight percent). The main occupation of this site is dated as from A.D. 1275 to 1325 (Kintigh 1985, Anyon 1992, Huntley and Kintigh 2004, Kintigh et al. 2004).

An assemblage of forty-two lithic artifacts collected by Ten Kate at Halonawan, applied in four rows on a fiber board (Fig. 391) includes forty chipped-stone arrow and dart points, one drill, and a knife. The projectile points, drills, and knife are predominantly made from chert of various colors, but some points are of chalcedony and obsidian. Chert was widely available and used to make projectile points, although obsidian (a volcanic glass) was sharper.

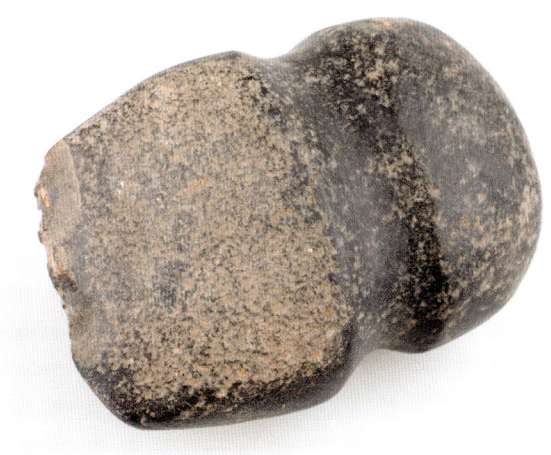

Fig. 392 Axe; stone; l. 17.8 cm, w. 5.3 cm, th. 3 cm; A.D. 1250–1350 (RMV 675-1).

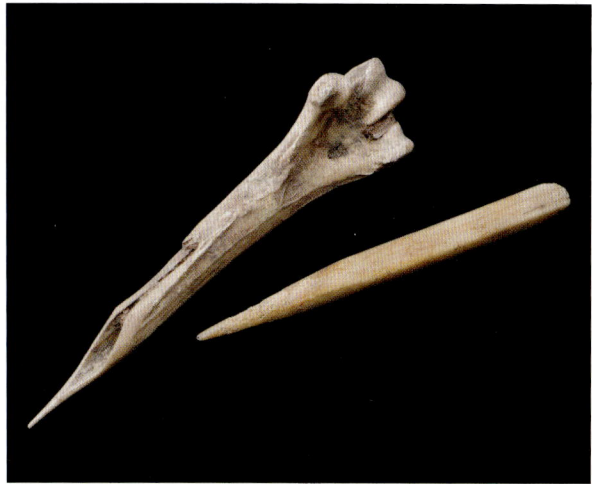

Fig. 393 Two awls; bird bone; l. 4 and 3.5 cm; A.D. 1250–1350 (RMV 675-2, -3).

Small and simple projectile points were used with a bow-and-arrow; they were smaller than dart points, which were hafted on heavier shafts and propelled with a hooked stick called an "atlatl." In addition to utilitarian arrowheads, elongated points of chalcedony and chert with barbed or serrated edges were made, probably by skilled specialists, and their ritual importance has been suggested because of their strong association with burials (Wasley and Johnson 1965; Crabtree 1973; Neitzel 1991: 190–191).

Like with Hohokam axes, a stick the width of the groove was bound around this axe and then tied snugly to the axe at the base (Fig. 392; cf. MQB 71.1885.82.1). This is a full grooved type.

Ten Kate recorded the Zuni names for the two bird bone awls he collected (Fig. 393) as *Í pi to kya si mi ne* (RMV 675-2) and *Í pik thla k* (RMV 675-3). Bone work was especially plentiful in Halonawan, Hawikuh, and other Zuni ancestral sites, and Frederick Webb Hodge published a topical study on the subject. The inventory of bone artifacts from Hawikuh included awls, needles, pins, weaving tools, spindle whorls, chisels, knives, polishers, tubes, flutes, whistles, bird-calls, beads, hooks, gaming pieces, effigies, rings, pendants, etc. Three types of bone awls, made from the bones of small mammals and birds, mostly turkeys, are distinguished: unworked splinters, partial bird or animal bones with unmodified butt, and bones with carefully modified tips and butts. In the latter case, the butts are carved in a zoomorphic shape. In historic times such effigy awls were used to pierce the septum of the nose of members of priesthoods, through which an feather was stuck during ceremonies. Other awls were set in a

bone or wood handle. Awl sizes varied from one and a half to nine inches. There is no particular association of bone awls as grave gifts with gender or age (Hodge 1920; Smith et al. 1966: 244–246, 258–259).

The articular end of RMV 675-2 remains more or less intact and is used as a handle. The point is skillfully crafted. If it blunted through use, it could be resharpened and reused. RMV 675-3 shows that almost the entire surface of the bone was worked, and Hodge regarded this type as the most attractive in appearance. This specimen with its differently shaped ends, one pointed like an awl, the other flattened like a spatula, was apparently for multiple uses and referred to as awl-spatulas. They might have been used in weaving baskets (Hodge 1920: 86, 98–102).

The collection also contains two flat, worked long-bone fragments, whose use is undetermined (Fig. 394). Ten Kate recorded the Zuni name for these specimens. A plethora of bone fragments were excavated at Hawikuh and contemporary sites in the Zuni area (Hodge 1920).

Finally, the group of Halonawan artifacts collected by Ten Kate contains another stone axe. At the back of the point, a flake has broken off (Fig. 395; cf. MQB 17.1885.

Fig. 394 Two bone fragments; *ti-musunak'ya* (TK); l. 18.3 cm, w. 2.0–2.2 cm, th. 0.5 cm; A.D. 1250–1350 (RMV 675-4).

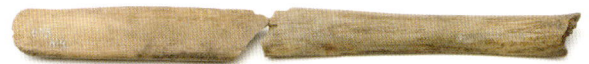

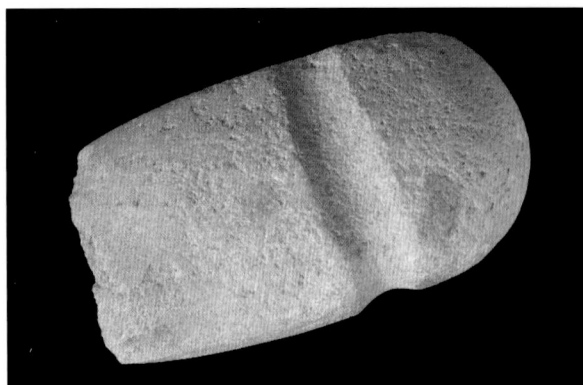

Fig. 395 Axe; stone; l. 15 cm, w. 10 cm, d. 6 cm; A.D. 1250-1350 (WMR 17975).

82.1 and Fig. 392). Ten Kate received this artifact from Dan Dubois, a local settler, married to an Indian woman, who had found it when excavations were going on at the site of Halonawan.

References

Abbott, David R.
2000 *Ceramics and Community Organization among the Hoho-kam.* Tucson, AZ: University of Arizona Press.

Adams, Jenny L.
1993 Toward Understanding the Technological Develop-ment of Manos and Metates. *Kiva* 58(3): 331-344.
1999 Refocusing the Role of Food-Grinding Tools as Cor-relates for Subsistence Strategies in the U.S. Southwest. *American Antiquity* 64(3): 475-498.

Anyon, Roger
1992 The Late Prehistoric and Early Historic Periods in the Zuni-Cibola Area, A.D. 1400-1680. In: B. J. Vierra (ed.), *Current Research on the Late Prehistory and Early History of New Mexico* (New Mexico Archaeological Council, Special Publication 1. Albuquerque, NM), 75-84.

Bandelier, Adolph F.
1892 *Final Report of Investigations among the Indians of the Southwestern United States.* Papers of the Archaeological In-stitute of America, American Series 4. Cambridge, MA: Peabody Museum of American Archaeology and Ethnology.

Bernard-Shaw, Mary
1983 The Stone Tool Assemblage of the Salt-Gila Aqueduct Project Sites. In: L. S. Teague and P. L. Crown (eds.), *Hoho-kam Archaeology along the Salt-Gila Aqueduct, Central Arizona Project* (Tucson, AZ: Arizona State Museum), 373-444.

Carlson, Roy L.
1970 *White Mountain Redware: A Pottery Tradition of East-Central Arizona and Western New Mexico.* Tucson, AZ: University of Arizona Press.
1982 The Polychrome Complexes. In: A. H. Schroeder (ed.), *Southwestern Ceramics: A Comparative Review.* Arizona Archaeologist 15 (Special Issue), 210-234.

Carpenter, J. P., G. Sánchez, and M. E. Villalpando
2005 The Late Archaic/Early Agricultural Period in Sonora, Mexico. In: Bradley J. Vierra (ed.), *The Late Archaic Across the Borderlands* (Austin, TX: University of Texas Press), 13-40.

Crabtree, D. E.
1973 Experiments in Replicating Hohokam Points. *Tebiwa* 16(1): 10-45.

Crown, Patricia L.
1983 Worked Sherds, Whole Vessels, and Figurines Re-covered from Salt-Gila Aqueduct Project Sites. In: L. S. Teague and P. Crown (eds.), *Hohokam Archaeology along the Salt-Gila Aqueduct, Central Arizona Project. Vol. 9: Material Culture* (Tucson, AZ: Arizona State Museum), 311-332.
1991 The Hohokam: Current Views of Prehistory and the Regional Systems. In: P. L. Crown and W. J. Judge (eds.), *Chaco and Hohokam: Prehistoric Regional Systems in the American Southwest* (Santa Fe, NM: School of American Research Press), 135-158.
1994 *Ceramics and Ideology: Salado Polychrome Pottery.* Albu-querque, NM: University of New Mexico Press.

Haury, Emil W.
1976 *The Hohokam: Desert Farmers and Craftsmen.* Tucson, AZ: University of Arizona Press.

Haury, Emil W. and Lyndon L. Hargrave
1931 *Recently Dated Pueblo Ruins in Arizona.* Smithsonian Miscellaneous Collections 82(11). Washington, DC.

Hodge, Frederick Webb
1920 Hawikuh Bonework. *Indian Notes and Monographs* 3(3): 65-151.

Hovens, Pieter
1989 *Herman F. C. ten Kate (1858-1931) en de antropologie der Noord Amerikaanse Indianen* (Herman F. C. ten Kate and the Anthropology of the North American Indians). Meppel: Krips. [Ph.D. thesis, University of Nijmegen.]
1991 The Origins of Anthropology in Baja California: The Fieldwork and Excavations of Herman F. C. ten Kate in 1883. *Pacific Coast Archaeological Society Quarterly* 27(4): 15-22.
1995 Ten Kate's Hemenway Expedition Diary, 1887-1888. *Journal of the Southwest* 37(4): 635-700.

Hovens, Pieter and Louis A. Hieb
2004 The Science of the Indians: Herman ten Kate, Anthropology, and Native American Studies. In: Herman ten Kate, *Travels and Researches in Native North America, 1882-1883* (P. Hovens, L. A. Hieb, and W. J. Orr eds. Albu-querque, NM: University of New Mexico Press), 15- 41.

Huntley, Deborah L. and Keith W. Kintigh
2004 Archaeological Patterning and Organizational Scale of Late Prehistoric Settlement Clusters in the Zuni Region of New Mexico. In: E. C. Adams and A. I. Duff (eds.), *The Protohistoric Pueblo World, A.D. 1275-1600* (Tucson, AZ: University of Arizona Press), 62-74.

Kintigh, Keith W.
1985 *Settlement, Subsistence, and Society in Late Zuni Prehis-tory.* Anthropological Papers of the University of Arizona 44. Tucson, AZ.

Kintigh, K., D. M. Glowacki, and D. L. Hunteley
2004 Long-Term Settlement History and the Emergence of Towns in the Zuni Area. *American Antiquity* 69(3): 432–456.

Krueger, Kari Ann
1993 A Definitive Analysis of Hohokam Stone Palettes. M.A. thesis, Northern Illinois University, De Kalb, IL.

McGuire, Randall H.
1985 The Role of Shell Exchange in the Explanation of Hohokam Prehistory. In: D. E. Dove (ed.), *Proceedings of the 1983 Hohokam Conference II* (Arizona Archaeological Society Occasional Paper), 471–479.
1992 *Death, Society, and Ideology in a Hohokam Community.* Boulder, CO: Westview Press.

McGuire, R. H. and A. V. Howard
1987 The Structure and Organization of Hohokam Shell Exchange. *Kiva* 52(2): 113–146.

Matthews, W., J. Wortman, and J. S. Billings
1893 *Human Bones in the Hemenway Collection in the U.S. Army Medical Museum.* Memoirs of the National Academy of Sciences 6. Washington, DC.

Merbs, Charles F.
2002 Washington Matthews and the Hemenway Expedition. *Journal of the Southwest* 44: 303–335.

Mills, Barbara J.
2007 Performing the Feast: Visual Display and Suprahousehold Comensualism in the Pueblo Southwest. *American Antiquity* 72(2): 210–239.

Neitzel, Jill
1991 Hohokam Material Culture and Behavior: the Dimensions of Organizational Change. In: G. J. Gumerman (ed.), *Exploring the Hohokam: Prehistoric Desert Peoples of the American Southwest* (Dragoon, AZ–Albuquerque, NM: Amerind Foundation–University of New Mexico Press), 177–230.

Noguera, Eduardo
1958 *Reconocimiento Arqueológico en Sonora.* Dirección de Monumentos Prehispánicos, Informe 10. Mexico City.

Russell, Frank
1908 *The Pima Indians.* Bulletin of the Bureau of American Ethnology 26. Washington, DC.

Schwabe, Johannes
1989 *Die Tonfiguren der Hohokam und ihr zeremonieller Kontext.* Stuttgart–Wiesbaden: Franz Steiner Verlag.

Smith, W., R. B. Woodbury, and N. F. S.
1966 *The Excavation of Hawikuh by Frederick Webb Hodge: Report of the Hendrick-Hodge Expedition, 1917–1923.* New York, NY: Museum of the American Indian.

Stone, Tammy
2003 Hohokam Exchange in Social Context. In: D. R. Abbott (ed.), *Centuries of Decline during the Hohokam Classic Period at Pueblo Grande* (Tucson, AZ: University of Arizona Press), 128–147.

Ten Kate, Herman F. C.
1883 Quelques Observations Ethnographiques Recueillis dans la Presqu'Île Californienne et en Sonora. *Revue d'Ethnographie* 2: 321–326.

1885 *Reizen en Onderzoekingen in Noord Amerika.* Leiden: E. J. Brill.
1887 Sur Quelques Objets Indiens Trouvés près de Guaymas. *Revue d'Ethnographie* 6: 234–238.
1889 The Hemenway Southwestern Archaeological Expedition. *Internationales Archiv für Ethnographie* 2: 48–49.
1889a Eenige mededeelingen omtrent de Hemenway-expeditie. *Internationales Archiv für Ethnographie* 6(4–5): 216–224.
1925 *Over Land en Zee; Schetsen en Stemmingen van een Wereldreiziger.* Zutphen: W. J. Thieme.
2004 *Travels and Researches in Native North America, 1882–1883.* P. Hovens, L. A. Hieb, and W. J. Orr eds. Albuquerque, NM: University of New Mexico Press. [Translation of Ten Kate 1885.]

Turney, Omar
1929 *Prehistoric Irrigation in Arizona.* Phoenix, AZ: Arizona Historian.

Villalpando, María Elisa
2000 The Archaeological Traditions of Sonora. In: M. S. Foster and S. Gorenstein (eds.), *Greater Mesoamerica: the Archaeology of West and Northwest Mexico* (Salt Lake City, UT: University of Utah Press), 241–254.

Vokes, Arthur
1984 The Shell Assemblage of the Salt-Gila Aqueduct Project Sites. In: L .S. Teague and P. L. Crown (eds.), *Hohokam Archaeology along the Salt-Gila Aqueduct, Central Arizona Project* (Tucson, AZ: Arizona State Museum), 465–574.

Wade, Edwin L. and Lea S. McChesney
1981 *Historic Hopi Ceramics: The Thomas V. Keam Collection.* Cambridge, MA: Peabody Museum Press.

Wasley, William W. and Alfred E. Johnson
1966 *Salvage Archaeology in the Painted Rocks Reservoir, Western Arizona.* Anthropological Papers of the University of Arizona 9. Tucson, AZ.

Wells, E. Christian
2006 *From Hohokam to O'odam: the Protohistoric Occupation of the Middle Gila River Valley, Central Arizona.* Sacaton, AZ: Gila River Indian Community, Cultural Resource Management Program.

White, Devin Alan
2004 *Hohokam Palettes.* Tucson, AZ: Arizona State Museum.

Wilcox, David R.
1979 The Hohokam Regional System. In: G. Rice et al. (eds.), *An Archaeological Test of Sites in the Gila Butte-Santan Region* (Arizona State University Anthropological Research Papers 18. Tempe, AZ), 77–116.
1987 *Frank Midvale's Excavations at La Ciudad.* Arizona State University Archaeological Field Studies 19. Tempe, AZ.
1993 Pueblo Grande in the Nineteenth Century. In: C. E. Downum and T. W. Bostwick (eds.), *Archaeology of the Pueblo Grande Platform Mound and Surrounding Features* (Pueblo Grande Museum Anthropological Papers 1. Phoenix, AZ), 43–72.
1991 Hohokam Social Complexity. In: P. L. Crown and W. J. Judge (eds.), *Chaco & Hohokam* (Santa Fe, NM: School of American Research Press), 253–276.

Index